THE AMERICAN CIRCUS

AN ILLUSTRATED HISTORY

THE AMERICAN CIRCUS

AN ILLUSTRATED HISTORY

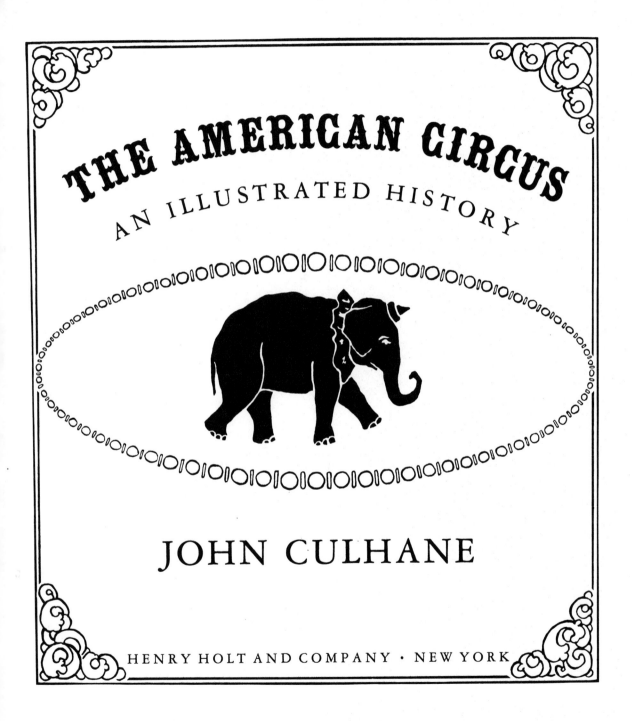

JOHN CULHANE

HENRY HOLT AND COMPANY · NEW YORK

Published by Henry Holt and Company, Inc.,
115 West 18th Street, New York, New York 10011.
Published in Canada by Fitzhenry & Whiteside Limited,
195 Allstate Parkway, Markham, Ontario L3R 4T8.

Library of Congress Cataloging-in-Publication Data
Culhane, John.
The American circus : an illustrated history / John Culhane. —
1st ed.
p.   cm.
Bibliography: p.
Includes index.
ISBN 0-8050-0424-6
1. Circus—United States—History.   I. Title.
GV1803.C85   1989
791.3'0973—dc20   89-2182
                                                              CIP

Henry Holt books are available at special discounts
for bulk purchases for sales promotions, premiums,
fund-raising, or educational use. Special editions
or book excerpts can also be created to specification.
For details contact:
Special Sales Director
Henry Holt and Company, Inc.
115 West 18th Street
New York, New York 10011

First Edition

Book design by Claire M. Naylon
Printed in the United States of America
1 3 5 7 9 10 8 6 4 2

To my three-ring family circus:
Hind, Michael, and T. H. Culhane

Friday I tasted life.
It was a vast morsel.
A circus passed the house.

—EMILY DICKINSON

BEING A HISTORY OF THE CIRCUS,
THIS BOOK TAKES THE FORM OF A CIRCUS PROGRAM,
WHICH HAS BEEN CALLED SINCE BEFORE BUFFALO BILL:

PROGRAM OF DISPLAYS

ix

ACKNOWLEDGMENTS

My first thanks go to my father and mother, Jack and Isabel Fissinger Culhane, and to my grandfather, Dr. T. H. Culhane, a family doctor in our hometown of Rockford, Illinois, from 1890 to his death in 1942. They started me on this history by taking me, as a two-year-old, to the 1936 edition of Ringling Bros. and Barnum & Bailey Circus, where I promptly fell in love with the clown I later learned was Lou Jacobs. The following year, they took me to the street parade and performance of the Cole Bros. Circus with Clyde Beatty, where I was recruited for a ring gag by two clowns I later learned were Otto Griebling and Emmett Kelly. In 1938, they took me to both the Tom Mix Circus, with that genuine cowboy and his great horse, Tony; and to the Al G. Barnes and Sells-Floto Combined Circus, augmented that year by the stars of the striking Ringling show. At the age of four, I first saw Gargantua; Terrell Jacobs the Lion Tamer; Mabel Stark, the tiger queen; the Cristiani troupe of equestrians; Frank ("Bring 'Em Back Alive") Buck; the Flying Concellos; the Great Wallendas—and Lou Jacobs again. So I can say, with the Yale professor and weaver of words William Lyon Phelps, "Heaven lay about me in my infancy, and it had a circular shape."

My grandfather T. H. was a fellow townsman and personal friend of the first two twentieth-century authors to write histories of the circus in America; and, strange to say, those authors, like me, were born in Rockford, Illinois. Earl Chapin May was the son of a circusman who trouped with the Orton and Older Circus from 1856 to 1861, then settled in Rockford, and, later, nearby Rochelle. In 1932, May published *The Circus from Rome to Ringling*, the first comprehensive history of the circus in America written in this century. I kept it next to my copy of the Arabian Nights when I was a boy, and read over and over about Freddy Ledgett, the "skinny Rockford kid" who learned to ride in the ring barn of Rockford's own W. B. Reynolds's circus opposite the Winnebago County courthouse. My introduction to tragedy was reading that Ledgett's riding career was ended by the worst train wreck in circus history: the ramming by an empty World War I troop train of the Hagenbeck-Wallace Circus train near

Gary, Indiana, in 1918. Sixty-eight persons were killed; Ledgett and 126 others were seriously injured.

The second circus historian from Rockford was George Leonard Chindahl, who was born there in 1877 and attended Rockford public schools and Rockford Business College before moving to Chicago in 1898 to study and then practice law. When he died in 1957, he left the manuscript of his lifelong study of the circus, which the Caxton Printers of Caldwell, Idaho, published in 1959 as *A History of the Circus in America.*

My grandfather, father, and mother were all amateur circus historians, and walking encyclopedias of circus visits to Rockford from Grandpa's account of Ringling's first visit, in 1891, to the day in 1953 when Dad got Emmett Kelly, Sr., to tell us about the terrible Ringling fire in Hartford in 1944. Grandpa was a close friend of Fred Sterling, the editor of the *Rockford Register* who became lieutenant governor of Illinois; and Sterling was a close friend of John Ringling and spent his vacations for many years traveling with The Greatest Show on Earth in Ringling's private railroad car, the "Jomar." My cousin Marian Dooley married Sterling's grandson Bill, and from their unpublished Ringling lore my mother has written an account of Sterling's relationship with the Ringling brothers for Rockford's *North End News.* Thanks to all of them.

The third history of the American circus in this century is *The Circus in America* (1969), written by my own friend and mentor Charles Philip "Chappie" Fox, former director of the circus museum in Baraboo, Wisconsin, with Tom Parkinson, former circus editor of *Billboard.* In 1975, my research took a great leap forward when Chappie gave me his personal copy of his book *A Ticket to the Circus: A Pictorial History of the Incredible Ringlings* inscribed to "my good friend John Culhane, a red-hot circus fan."

I began my history of the American circus with an article in the *Rockford Register-Republic* for August 7, 1956, headlined "Only Big Top Died—Circus Coming Back," an interview with an old-time circus press agent named William B. Naylor. I thank my editors at the *Rockford Register-Republic,* Jack Winning, Fred Senters, and the late Tom Reay, Bob Monohan, and Rex Karney, for assigning me all those circus stories. And I thank two librarians at the Rockford Public Library, Louise Johnson, reference librarian, and Florence Bailey, of the fine arts room, for helping me begin my research.

My partner in all my proceedings is my wife, Hind Rassam Culhane, who has participated in the creation of all my books from beginning to end. When I was courting Hind, she was a foreign student from Baghdad at Rockford College, and I invited her to performances of the Clyde Bros. and Polack Bros. circuses at which I was, respectively, guest clown and assistant elephant tender. Hind quickly understood and accepted the situation: the circus was going to weave its way as a main theme through our life together. Indeed, she and I have spent many research "vacations" at places where circus history is to be found. At each of these places, we have found kind people who have helped us to understand that marvelous institution better. Polack Bros.' Jack Joyce once let her lead a camel he had trained for a liberty act against all expectations for camels.

At the Ringling Bros. and Barnum & Bailey Circus, my heartiest thanks go to Kenneth Feld, owner, president, and producer of The Greatest Show on Earth, who approaches the circus not only as a business but as an American cultural institution.

Irvin Feld, Kenneth's father, whom the *New York Times* in an editorial at his death called "The Man Who Saved the Circus," said in 1974, when I told him that I was writing this book, "If there's anything you need, just ask."

Irvin died in 1984, so it was Kenneth I asked. I thank him for encouragement as well as help.

I also thank Ringling Bros. and Barnum & Bailey Combined Shows, Inc., for permission to reproduce material involving circus names it owns, among them Ringling Bros. and Barnum & Bailey Circus, Barnum & Bailey Greatest Show on Earth, Ringling Bros. World's Greatest Shows, Sells-Floto Circus, Hagenbeck-Wallace Circus, Sparks Circus, John Robinson Circus, Al G. Barnes Circus, and Forepaugh-Sells Bros. Circus.

At the Greatest Show on Earth, I also thank Shirley Feld; Bonnie Feld; Allen J. Bloom, senior vice president; Jerome S. Sowalsky, vice president and general counsel; Susannah G. Smith; Charles F. Smith; Rodney Huey; William Pruyn; Patty Britt Johnson; Mel Cabral; Debbie Linde; and the late Don Foote.

At every circus, I found help and kindness, and I thank you all. At the Big Apple Circus, Paul Binder, founder and artistic director, and his wife, the Danish equestrienne from a great European circus family, Katja Schumann; Alan B. Slifka, chairman of the board; Jim and Tisha Tinsman. At Clyde Beatty–Cole Bros. Circus, the late Frank McClosky, president; at Carson & Barnes, D. R. Miller, president and director; at Hubert Castle International Circus, Hubert Castle; at Clyde Bros. Circus, William Jack, manager in 1974; at Gatti-Charles Continental Circus, Matthew Gatti, manager, and Toby Ballantine, boss clown (1976); at Cristiani Circus, Ernesto Cristiani, in 1956 the papa of the famous equestrian clan; at Hamid-Morton Circus, George A. Hamid, Jr., owner; at Hanneford Circus, Tommy Hanneford, president; at Polack Bros. Circus, William B. Naylor, press agent (1956); at Wallenda-Leontini Circus, the late Karl Wallenda, manager; at Circus Vargas, the late Clifford Vargas, owner and president; at Cirque du Soleil, Guy Laliberté, cofounder, general manager, and fire-eater.

At the John and Mable Ringling Museum of Art in Sarasota, Florida: John Lentz, acting director in 1983, and his wife, Evi Kelly Lentz, widow of John's longtime friend Emmett Kelly, Sr.

At the Circus World Museum, Baraboo, Wisconsin: Greg Parkinson, executive director, and his father, Robert L. Parkinson, chief librarian and historian of the museum; and William L. Schultz, former executive director.

Thanks to Elizabeth Taylor, director of the Hammond Museum, for loaning me the rare first edition (1870) of The Public Life of W. F. Wallett, the Queen's Jester and for inviting me to speak on Westchester and Putnam counties as the birthplace of the American circus.

Thanks to the late Larry Earl Bone, director of the Mercy College Libraries, for arranging the long-term loan of all their circus materials, including The Memoir of John Durang, American Actor 1785–1816, an equestrian with John Bill Ricketts's circus; and to W. Bruce Fulton, acting director; Marieta Tobey, head of reference services; and reference librarians Jeanne Reid and Julio Rosario, for helping me with all the fact checking.

Thanks to Bettie Diver, director, Dobbs Ferry Library, for the long-term loan of all its circus material, including the invaluable Pictorial History of the American Circus by John and Alice Durant.

Thanks to Daniel J. Boorstin, former Librarian of Congress, for making available many extremely rare circus volumes, and to Dan and his wife, Ruth Frankel Boorstin, for a memorable conversation on the circus in American history.

Thanks to Trish O'Leary and Sydney Callahan of the American Antiquarian Society in Worcester, Massachusetts, for use of its unparalleled facilities for research in early American newspapers and for giving me a copy of R. W. G. Vail's "Random Notes on the History of the American Circus" reprinted from the proceedings of the society for April 1933.

Thanks to Florence Oliver, Somers, New York, town historian, and Mabel Addis, former president of the Somers Historical Society. Much of the research for this book was done in the Somers Historical Society library in its second-floor offices in the Elephant Hotel in Somers, built by Hackaliah Bailey with the profits from showing the elephant Old Bet early in the nineteenth century, which was as close as I could get to the birthplace of the institution I was chronicling.

Thanks to Olympia and Ciro Cosentino for giving me the copy they found in Maine of P. T. Barnum's *Struggles and Triumphs* that one Benj. H. B. Alden bought at "Barnum's circus, Rockland, Maine, June 10th, 1878."

Thanks to Amal Rassam and Ghassan Rassam for their unfailing help; to Leonard Kamzler, a fine professional photographer, who gave me for this book his rare, historic photo of two generations of trapeze greats, Tito and Chela Gaona with Antoinette Concello; and to my sister and brother-in-law, Lisebeth and Joseph W. Keating, for finding me the out-of-print biography of the Ringling brothers by Alvin F. Harlow.

Thanks to Kenneth O. Gilmore, editor-in-chief of *Reader's Digest*, and his wife, Janet; and to my editor at the *Digest*, Clell Bryant, and his wife, Jill Tucker Bryant, on whom I first tried out my chapter on Westchester and Putnam counties as the birthplace of the circus. Thanks to Edward T. Thompson, the editor for whom I wrote "The Comeback of the Circus in America," which appeared in the March 1976 *Reader's Digest*—my first article for that magazine; and to Susan Jacobson Thompson for assigning me to write "Unforgettable Emmett Kelly."

Thanks to my editors at *The New York Times Magazine*, Glenn Collins, Joan Bundy, Harvey Shapiro, Gerald Walker, and William H. Honan, and to Arthur Ochs Sulzberger, Barbara and Arthur Gelb, Ed Klein, Jack Rosenthal, and Max Frankel, for help and encouragement on the circus articles I have written for the *New York Times*.

Thanks to Ted Slate, *Newsweek* librarian; and to *Newsweek* colleagues who helped in my circus research: Don Holt, Hal Bruno, Rod Gander, Larry Martz, Dick Boeth, George and Daryl Alexander, and Janet and Arthur Zich.

Similarly, at the old Chicago *Daily News*, thanks to Mike Royko, Bob Herguth, Lois Wille, and Bob Schultz.

And at *Geo*, William Albert Allard and the late Rick Frederickson.

Special thanks to those performers who conducted for me short courses in their specialties with patience, wit, and insight.

For any kind of animal: Gunther Gebel-Williams, animal master; his wife, Sigrid Gebel; and their daughter, Tina, and son, Mark Oliver. They could certainly make a great circus all by themselves.

On the business of getting the show on the road: Tim Holst, associate producer of The Greatest Show on Earth, and former Ringling Red Unit performance director, ringmaster, clown, and student at the Clown College; Charly Baumann, executive performance director; Bob Dover and Jack Joyce, former performance directors; and Peggy Williams, former assistant performance director, Blue Unit.

For the flying acts, to Antoinette Concello; Victor, Tito, Armando, Chela, and Richie Gaona; and Miguel, Juan, and Patricia Vazquez.

For the clowns, Lou Jacobs, Otto Griebling, Emmett Kelly, Sr., Glen "Frosty" Little, Mark Anthony, Ron Severini, Prince Paul Alpert, Duane Thorpe, Jim Tinsman, Peggy Williams, Bill Ballantine, Eddie Arvida, and Jack LaPearl.

For elephants, Bill "Buckles" Woodcock, Barbara Woodcock, and their offspring, Dalilah Woodcock and Shannon Woodcock.

For horses, the late Kay Frances Hanneford.

For tigers, Charly Baumann.

For lions, Wolfgang Holzmair and Dave Hoover.

For athletes, Helen Wallenda, Dolly Jacobs, and Pedro Carrillo.

For horses, the late Kay Frances Hanneford.

For costumes, the late Don Foote, and Mel Cabral and Arthur Boccia.

For staging, choreography, and scenic design, Bill Bradley, Jerry Fries, Crandall Diehl, and Reid Carlson.

For circus music, Bill Pruyn and Jim Ille.

For circus talent scouting, Trolle Rhodin.

The following people provided me with anecdotes, theories, introductions, references, and other passports to the world of the circus: Richard Schickel; Richard Culhane; Noel and the late Sophie Bakhazy Rassam; Shameem Rassam and the late Ibrahim Abdul Gelil; Glenn and Sarah Collins; David and Mary Ella Stone; Mark and Cher Culhane; Charles F. and Sue Thomas; Charles and Adele Gregory; Leonard Maltin; Richard Fraenkel; Jeannette Rassam; Michael and Cornelia Smollin; Byron and Maria Janis; Shamus and Juana Culhane; Arthur and Carol Kornhaber; Gene and Judy Wolkoff; Howard and Janet Berntsen; Kenneth L. and Betty Woodward; John and Ann Nevin; Lawrence D. Carlson; Norman Bargren; Angela and the late Ruben Gilanian; Kay and the late John J. King; Bill and Margaret Fissinger; Alfred and Bernadette Fissinger; Ella Shephard; Leona Carlson; Kurt Vonnegut and Jill Krementz; Gil and Pat Miret; Arnold I. Bramow; Steve Lisles; James Conner; Ken, Mary, and Kara Fredrickson; Hector and Paula Correa; Milos and Rita Nemec; Francois and Adma d'Huerle; Frances Mahoney; Ann Grow; Brian Lea; Jack and Mavis Gill; Serge Vinogradov; Sophia Vinogradov; Ray and Carol Favata; Walter Cronkite; Joan Tramontano; Tom Crangle and the late Nini Finkelstein Crangle; John and Josie May; Robin, Marsha, Zachary, and Zelda Williams; Richard Williams; John and Tracy Avildsen; Frank Capra and Frank Capra, Jr.; Charles Maryan; Maury and Meg Breslow; and Virgil and Anne Burnett.

My agent, Carl Brandt, and Rob Cowley, an editor with a vast knowledge of American history and early circus history, started this book on its way. Tracy Bernstein, circus-loving editor at Henry Holt and Company with an up-to-date knowledge of the institution, finished the job and shepherded the book to press. Also at Holt, thanks to Kim Lewis, Francesca Marx, and designer Claire M. Naylon.

As I write this, my mother has just sent me with her weekly letter a clipping from the *Rockford Register-Star*, announcing that the first six inductees into the Clown Hall of Fame at Delavan, Wisconsin, included Otto Griebling and Emmett Kelly, Sr., the two clowns who put me in a ring gag in Rockford when I was three, along with movie clown Red Skelton, Felix Adler, and two clowns that I often clowned with in Madison Square Garden, New York, as an adult: Mark Anthony and Lou Jacobs. One of the greatest happinesses of my life is that I have grown up to guest-clown frequently with various circuses, and not only with my beloved Lou Jacobs but with my sons, Michael and T. H. Culhane, the youngest graduates of the Ringling Bros. and Barnum & Bailey Clown College and the youngest professional clowns in the 120-year history of The Greatest Show on Earth. They gave me valuable insights into the way that grand old institution works on a day-to-day basis.

The saga of the circus in America goes on. My wife, Hind, and I encourage our sons, twenty years hence, to bring this history back up to date.

PREFACE

America's love affair with the circus, live and in person, has lasted now for over two hundred years; mine, for over fifty. The circus has survived the minstrel show, the medicine show, and vaudeville, and it has learned to use film and television as moving circus posters in a colorful return of Barnumesque ballyhoo. And yet there has heretofore been no book to tell the whole story—from Thomas Pool in New York in 1786, drinking a glass of wine as he stands on the back of a horse "in full speed," to Gunther Gebel-Williams in New York in 1989, controlling a herd of twenty elephants and twelve horses spanning three rings with a single spoken command. There has been no full chronicle of America's circus clowns, either, from John Durang, on tour in Canada with John Bill Ricketts's circus in 1797, burlesquing equestrians like Pool and Ricketts by

doing their tricks while pretending to be drunk, to Denis Lacombe, caricaturing a symphony conductor embroiled in "The 1812 Overture" on the 1988 U.S. tour of Canada's Cirque du Soleil. "What's really special about the Cirque," Lacombe told *Life* magazine for October 1988, "is that we went back to the roots of the circus two hundred years ago and brought it into the 1980s." That is also what is special about this book.

It's the saga of the good days and the bad. The most recent bad days for the circus began about the same time as television. Things hit bottom on July 16, 1956, in Pittsburgh, when John Ringling North, the owner of Ringling Bros. and Barnum & Bailey Circus, announced tersely: "The tented circus as it exists today is, in my opinion, a thing of the past." With that, The Greatest Show on Earth ended its tour in

EXPECT THE UNEXPECTED. My father and I saw this poster in the window of Nihan & Martin's Drug Store on Main Street in our hometown one day in 1948. "Imagine!" said Dad. "A rhino in Rockford!" In the more than forty years since then, I've heard no other words that so succinctly sum up the incomparable wonder of the circus. (Circus World Museum, Baraboo, Wisconsin)

midseason and returned to winter quarters. The Big Top, North said, was the victim of television competition, labor troubles, terrible weather for canvas tents, traffic problems for audiences trying to get to the circus, and increased freight rates for railroads trying to bring it to them.

A lot of circus lovers feared that not just the tented circus but the circus itself was dying. Already that year, the Clyde Beatty Circus and the King Bros. & Cole Bros. Circus had closed down. The Kelly-Miller Circus managed to keep going by advertising itself as the "last of the tented circuses—see it now or miss it forever." *Life* magazine lamented, "A magical era has passed."

The decline continued throughout the 1960s. The surviving circuses were small and, worst of all, had few superstars who could perform crowd-pleasing superfeats.

But as Mark Twain would have enjoyed saying (he once remarked that he would rather have been a circus clown than a writer), reports of the death of the circus were greatly exaggerated. For today, over thirty-three years later, the American circus in America is alive and well and soaring.

Ringling Bros. and Barnum & Bailey Circus has had a dramatic rebirth, starting with its purchase in 1967 by the late show-business entrepreneur Irvin Feld, who died in 1984, and continuing under his son, Kenneth Feld. At the end of North's reign, Ringling Bros. was playing to about two million people a year. In 1986, Ringling's two national companies played to 11,800,000. Income has risen accordingly—up from an $8-million gross the final year that North ran the show to more than three times that twenty years later. How the Felds did it is a saga within a saga—the story of how a father started it after the Big Top folded by returning the circus to the indoor arenas in which it began, by bringing to America the circus performer acknowledged to be the greatest of his time, and by founding a clown college to ensure a fresh supply of circus clowns, and how the son continued the return of old-time circus by bringing back the Barnumesque ballyhoo that accompanied its golden age.

Most important, the comeback of The Greatest Show on Earth seems to have revitalized the whole American circus. There were, in the late 1980s, about thirty circuses showing in the United States, including such veterans as Clyde Beatty–Cole Bros., the second largest U.S. circus and the largest still under canvas; Al G. Kelly and Miller Bros. Three-Ring Circus; Bentley Bros. Circus; and Allan C. Hill's Great American Circus. Circus Vargas is still pitching its tent in Los Angeles; and in Hugo, Oklahoma, D. R. Miller celebrated his fiftieth anniversary as proprietor of Carson & Barnes Circus in 1986—and kept right on going. Moreover, the success of numerous indoor shows has made the circus a year-round attraction instead of just a summertime treat.

"To audiences everywhere," said Robert Lewis Parkinson, head of Circus World Museum's Library and Research Center in Baraboo, Wisconsin, "a circus means performing horses and riders, elephants, clowns, jungle cats, rare and exotic animals and people, thrilling demonstrations of the skills of acrobats and aerialists, and daredevils. Experience has proved that when these basic acts aren't done in a way that captures the imagination of the public, the public is disappointed."

The experience of the seventies and eighties has shown that when these essential acts *are* done charismatically, the circus revives as if by magic.

The circus worldwide is a subject so vast that there has never been a complete history. And the saga of the circus in America—a huge subject by itself—begs to be told. There have been four fine attempts, by Earl Chapin May in 1932, John and Alice Durant in 1957, George L. Chindahl in 1959, and Charles Philip Fox and Tom Parkinson in 1969. But all of these books are out of print and out of date. This means that they don't chronicle some of the greatest chapters in circus history, like the career of Gunther Gebel-Williams, one of the greatest wild animal trainers in the world history of the circus, or the Ringling Bros. and Barnum & Bailey Circus Clown College, which probably saved the art of the American circus clown from being lost forever. They could not tell of the violent death of Karl Wallenda, called the greatest circus daredevil of all time, or the spectacular high-wire career of Philippe Petit, who came to the circus after walking a wire between the twin towers of the world's tallest building, the World Trade Center in New York City. And there is no account of the quest for the quadruple somersault from the flying trapeze, as vital a matter for circus fans of the last half of the twentieth century as the triple was in the first half—or the attempt in the late nineteenth century to turn a triple somersault from a springboard.

And too, since 1977, there has been the delightful development of the one-ring Big Apple Circus, which plays in a heated tent in New York City's Lincoln Center every Christmas season and tours New England in the summer. Here, the very new and the very old come together, for when you see Bill "Buckles" Woodcock in that one Big Apple ring, making his elephants do amazing things, you are seeing a direct descendant of the Orton family, who were showing camels in their American circus just after the Civil War, a family that liked to say, "We were circus when the Ringlings were still wearing wooden shoes."

I wanted to read a book with all that in it, so I wrote this one. It's an attempt to tell the whole story, from the one ring of Thomas Pool in Philadelphia that began the saga in 1785 to the one ring of the Big Apple Circus under the royal blue tent in New York City in 1989, and from the first three-ring circus in 1881, taken from town to town on a railroad train by P. T. Barnum and James A. Bailey, to the three-ring circus of Ringling Bros. and Barnum & Bailey, being presented all over the United States in the 120th consecutive season of America's longest-running entertainment institution.

And then there was the matter of pictures. The circus book I wanted to see as well as read would be illustrated with the paradigmatic images that mean the circus in America to us Children of All Ages: circus trains unloading at dawn, roustabouts putting up tents, elephants being watered, the circus parade beginning, the bandwagon, and the calliope trailing clouds of steam and crowds of small boys.

There are many rare pictures here, never before seen in a book. Sometimes they are combined with pictures you might have seen, to give you a three-dimensional view of circus life: not just Clyde Beatty braving forty lions with his pistol and his whip and his chair, but Beatty in the back lot, playing with his dog; not only the Wallendas on the high wire and the Zacchinis being shot from a cannon, but the Wallenda-Zacchini family orchestra, whiling away the hours between shows.

Looking at these pictures and seeing where they fit into the saga of the circus in America, you see the whole grand pageant of American history marching before your eyes. Here is General George Washington on Jack, the white horse he rode in the American Revolution and later gave, sold, or traded (accounts differ) to John Bill Ricketts to become the first sideshow attraction in the history of the American circus.

Here are pictures showing circus greats performing and pictures showing circus greats being ordinary human beings.

Here are two centuries of clowns, from Durang to Dan Rice to Slivers Oakley to Lou Jacobs, Otto Griebling, and Emmett Kelly—and many pratfalls in between.

Elephants? Here is the statue of Old Bet in front of the Elephant Hotel, in Somers, New York, "birthplace of the American circus," where I did much of the research for this book; and photographs of Jumbo, dead and alive; and of Buckles Woodcock's incredible Anna May.

Our daredevils run the gamut from Blondin, who crossed Niagara Falls on a wire, to the seven-person high-wire pyramid of the Great Wallendas (seen also in a never before published photograph from Karl's widow, Helene, as they looked when they first came to America), to perhaps the most beautiful spangled lady ever to perform in the circus: Princess Victoria, the wire walker. In private life, she was Victoria Codona Adolph, sister of the ill-fated aerialist Alfredo Codona. She died in 1983, at the age of ninety-four, and how I wish she could have lived a century and received from me this book and seen herself on its jacket, back on her wire again!

And here is Miguel Vazquez completing the first-ever quadruple somersault from the flying trapeze to the hands of the catcher—taken by a clown on July 10, 1982, as Ringling Bros. and Barnum & Bailey Circus played Tucson, Arizona.

All their stories are told in this book. The research has taken thirty-three years; the writing, seven. And the reason I wanted to tell their stories goes back in my memory to the year I was two years old, and in the traditions of my family a long way before that.

What I most want to do is to give a sense not only of what the circuses in America have been, and who ran them, and who was in them, but of who went to see them, and where, and what they felt about what they saw, and how it all helped shape the American consciousness.

Ernest Hemingway, a lifelong circus lover whose first complete sentence was about the circus ("I don't know Buffalo Bill," he said at eighteen months, having just been taken to the rival Pawnee Bill show), tried to explain its appeal in an article in the 1953 program for Ringling Bros. and Barnum & Bailey Circus: "The circus is the only ageless delight that you can buy for money," wrote Hemingway. "Everything else is supposed to be bad for you. But the circus is good for you. It is the only spectacle I know that, while you watch it, gives the quality of a truly happy dream."

But Hemingway didn't explain *why* the circus is good for you, or what it is about the circus that makes the truly happy dream, except to give two broad hints: the fliers, as the trapeze artists are called, "catch each other the way you are caught in good dreams," and the clowns "bring the true comic that makes the dreams we wake from laughing."

We can miss the heart of the circus because its skin is so appealing. We see the glitter of the spangles, smell the fresh sawdust that blends so well with the ancient smell of excited animals and humans, hear the calliope (which circus folk pronounce "cally-ope"), taste the peanuts and popcorn and—oh, so refreshing on a hot summer day—the ice-cold pink lemonade (I'll tell you about the origin of pink lemonade); we buy a flashing light for a child, and sit her on our lap, and think, "This is the circus!" But these are the things that change, like the chameleons my father used to buy me from the tall boards on which they were displayed, creatures that were green on his Kelly green suit and red on my mother's red dress but that aren't sold anymore because our ideas about cruelty to living things have changed.

Much about the circus has changed in the last half century, but the essential circus hasn't changed at all.

I saw my first circus when I was two years

old—and I fell in love first with a clown. He had a big smile, big as a mud puddle. He had a huge red nose and hair that stuck out from the sides of his head like sunset-colored cotton candy. His eyebrows went up and up and up, and he had a little hat that sat on top of his bald pate.

During the circus, the clown I loved walked right by me carrying a huge hot dog. The bun was as big as a rolled-up rug. The wiener was a real, live dachshund. I laughed, and as I laughed, I fell in love with the circus for life.

My father, who loved the circus as whole-heartedly as his father before him, and couldn't wait to introduce me to its calculated combination of goofiness and glory, told me with satisfaction that I talked all year long about that clown as I waited for the circus to come back again to Rockford, Illinois, the town where I marked my growing up by the annual reappearance of the circus.

Our family memory of the circus in America goes back for over a century. Dr. T. H. Culhane, my grandfather, saw Ringling Bros. Circus the first time it came to Rockford, in 1891, the show's second year on rails; and he and my grandmother saw Buffalo Bill on their honeymoon at the Chicago World's Fair in 1893. My father and I saw Tom Mix, who had been a real U.S. marshall before he became a movie and circus cowboy, but that wasn't a patch on seeing William F. "Buffalo Bill" Cody, genuine nineteenth-century Pony Express rider, buffalo hunter, and U.S. Army scout. My grandparents saw him dash into the arena on his water-smooth silver stallion, pull his mount to its haunches, remove his big cowboy hat, and make a sweeping gesture of salute, while his shoulder-length white hair waved in the breeze and the band played "The Stars and Stripes Forever." And when I heard my grandfather tell about it, I felt as if I had seen him, too.

Grandpa took my father to see Leitzel and Codona, the tragic lovers of the circus world; May Wirth, the bareback rider; Bird Millman, the high-wire walker; Mabel Stark, who wrestled a tiger; the giraffe-neck women; they even saw cone-headed Zip, the same Zip that Barnum himself showed to Charles Dickens. (Dickens said, "What is it?"; Barnum answered, "That's what it is, a 'What Is It?'" and from then on, he billed the attraction as "Zip, the What-is-it?"—for who could better name an unforgettable character than the creator of Scrooge, Uriah Heep, and Oliver Twist?)

We were all sorry we missed seeing Jumbo.

So I grew up hearing the legends of these stars of my father's and grandfather's time before me. And I grew up seeing the circus legends of my lifetime. The clown with the mud puddle smile, I eventually learned, was Lou Jacobs. And, from Lou, I learned how the heart of the circus doesn't change.

In the spring of 1985, I took my wife and sons and a two-year-old friend to see the 115th edition of Ringling Bros. and Barnum & Bailey Circus in Madison Square Garden. At that circus I got the same old feeling watching Gunther Gebel-Williams make many tigers roll over together, command elephants by the power of his voice alone, and ride two horses standing up, while another representative of the same human race, Lou, the Clown Hunter, is played for a fool by a little dog dressed as a bunny rabbit. It was the same Lou Jacobs, in his sixtieth year with The Greatest Show on Earth, charming my wife and sons and our two-year-old friend just the way, half a century before, he had charmed two-year-old me.

From the beginning, it was the contrast between the achievements of the human beings and trained animals in the acts and the foibles and failures of the clowns that made the circus for me. And all the circuses I have seen since have not altered that fundamental perception.

From the circus—in, around, and above the

ring that has always symbolized for man his ultimate wholeness—we learn to reconcile the basic conflicts in human nature, between what we are and what we aspire to be. This is the heart of the circus: successful acts of human skill and daring harmonized by the counterpoint of clownish failure.

———————

I expect the day will come when the American circus will travel to stations in space. Acrobats and aerialists will do astonishing things in a weightless environment. But you may be certain that the clowns will be as inept at tasks in space as they are at tasks on earth. And you may be certain that we'll laugh, because—well, what other reaction can you have to the human nature that we share with the superstar and the buffoon? We're all in this together, the acrobat and the clown. For every enterprise that succeeds grandly, dozens go awry; for every complete success, we have dozens of Lou's "hunting" expeditions. But the failures of human beings do have this qualification: we keep trying—and the circus celebrates that fact in its hundreds of thousands of glittering tries.

That's the main point: the circus is a celebration of human survival. For over two hundred years in this country, it has mirrored the American dream of boundless aspiration while burlesquing the idea of constant success. But we clowns do have a history of overcoming our conceits and self-delusions just in time to catch each other before we fall.

And that is why the circus is a truly happy dream, and its history a valuable comment on the human comedy.

THE AMERICAN CIRCUS

AN ILLUSTRATED HISTORY

DISPLAY·1

The First Lords
of the Ring

In the beginning was the ring.

The circus was founded by a horseman who aspired to ride standing up on the back of his horse. He discovered that if he trained his horse to canter in a circle at a constant speed, while both he and his horse were leaning slightly inward, centrifugal force would help him keep his balance. He also discovered that a horse cantering in a circle of a certain size would provide just the right amount of centrifugal force for achieving the most graceful balance.

His name was Philip Astley, and he invented the circus ring in England in 1768. Its diameter would eventually be standardized at thirteen meters, or approximately forty-two feet, the size that is still preferred to this day. But a horse and rider performing in a ring does not, by itself, make a circus. It was his next step that created a circus: he had his equestrian feats interrupted by equestrian clownery called "Billy Buttons, or the Taylor Riding to Brentford," depicting the disastrous attempts of a tailor to mount a steed and gallop off to a waiting customer.

Astley's new form of entertainment was such a success that he added other riders, other acts, and a professional clown. The majority of the acts, such as trick riding, tumbling, juggling, ropedancing, and trained animal performances, dated from antiquity, but the idea of interspersing the physical feats with the antics of clowns was new—and defined what was not yet called the circus.

PRESIDENTS AND CIRCUSES. *George Washington visited the circus of John Bill Ricketts on April 22, 1793, and January 24, 1797, and sold Ricketts this horse for $150. Later that year, President John Adams visited Ricketts's New York circus. The fondness of American presidents for the circus extends from Washington and Adams to Abraham Lincoln's friendship for Dan Rice to Ronald Reagan appearing in Ring Two of The Greatest Show on Earth in 1985 to introduce the Ringling Brothers and Barnum & Bailey Circus's Safe Kids Program. (General Washington on a White Charger; American; National Gallery of Art, Washington; gift of Edgar William and Bernice Chrysler Garbisch)*

Astley always referred to his establishment as a riding school or, later, amphitheatre. In 1772, he took the show to France and performed before Louis XVI and his court; ten years later, he returned to open an amphitheatre in Paris. That same year, he traveled as far as Belgrade, visiting Brussels and Vienna on the way; during his life he built nineteen permanent circuses. When Britain and France went to war, Astley leased his Paris circus to Antonio Franconi, and the Franconi family became the founders of the French circus. It was they who, perhaps in a finer adjustment to centrifugal force, are reputed to have standardized the circus ring at forty-two feet.

It was one of Astley's riders, Charles Hughes, who first called the circus a circus. Aspiring to a success like Astley's, he set up a similar show in 1782, a few hundred yards south of London's Westminster Bridge, and called it The Royal Circus, using the Latin word for ring. He introduced the circus to Russia in 1793, when he added a company of trick riders to the stud of horses he had been commissioned to deliver to Catherine the Great. He was rewarded with a private circus in the royal palace in St. Petersburg. The Russian circus was later developed by a Frenchman named Jacques Tourniaire (1772–1829).

The circus came to America in August 1785. That summer, a native-born American named Thomas Pool put on a public entertainment in Philadelphia that he referred to as "equestrian feats." For his show, he erected a small building where, among other tricks, he balanced a glass of wine while the horse he stood on ran around the ring.

The announcement for Pool's first performance on Saturday, August 20, appears in the *Pennsylvania Packet* of August 15, and demonstrates how much the show owed to Astley.

BY PERMISSION

Mr. Pool,

The first American that ever exhibited the following

EQUESTRIAN FEATS

OF HORSEMANSHIP,

ON THE CONTINENT.

Intends performing To-morrow, the 24th instant, near the Centre House, where he has erected a MENAGE, at a very considerable expense, with Seats convenient for those Ladies and Gentlemen who may please to honor him with their company.

1. Mounts a single horse in full speed, standing on the saddle, throws up an orange and catches it on the point of a fork.

2. Mounts a single horse in half speed, dismounting and mounting many times, and will on that stretch, vault over the horse, back again, and mount on the near side.

3. Mounts a single horse in full speed, with his right foot in the near stirrup, and his left leg extended at a considerable distance from the horse, and in that position leaps a bar.

4. Mounts two horses in full speed, with a foot in the stirrup of each saddle, and in that position leaps a bar, and from that to the top of the saddles at the same speed.

5. Mounts a single horse in full speed and fires a pistol, and falls backward, with his head to the ground, hanging by his right leg, and while hanging, fires another pistol under the horse's belly, and rises again to his seat on the saddle; and—

Lastly will be exhibited "The Taylor humourously riding to New York" . . .

At the conclusion of the performances Mr. Pool will introduce three horses, who will lay themselves down as if dead. One will groan apparently through extreme sickness and pain, afterwards rise and make his Manners to the Ladies and Gentlemen. Another, having laid down for a considerable time, will rise and sit up like a Lady's lap-dog.

Every time of performance there will be new feats. Mr. Pool flatters himself the Ladies and Gentlemen who may be pleased to honor him with their company, will have no reason to go away dissatisfied; he even hopes to merit their approbation.

The Performance will begin at 5 o'clock in the Afternoon precisely.

TICKETS, for the First Seats, at Five Shillings, and for the Second Three Shillings & Nine Pence each, may be had at the two Coffee Houses, at Major Nichol's at the Conestoga Wagon, Mr. Thomson's, at the Old Indian Queen, and at the place of performances.

No tickets to be given out at the doors.

***Mr. Pool beseeches the Ladies and Gentlemen who honor him with their presence to bring no Dogs with them to the place of performance.

The Exhibition, in future, to be held on Wednesday and Saturday.

———

It wasn't yet a circus. It had a riding ring, in and around which human beings and animals performed feats of physical skill and daring, but these acts were not yet interspersed with the antics of a clown or clowns.

But then the announcement of the exhibition to be given the following week, on Saturday, August 27, 1785, contained the

conclusive addition: "Between the different parts a Clown to amuse the spectators."

By making good on the promise contained in those ten words, Thomas Pool presented the first circus, as opposed to simple "feats of horsemanship," on this continent.

Pool never became famous as our first circus impresario, probably because his time in the sun was so short. At the close of August, when he had performed no more than three or four times, notice appeared that:

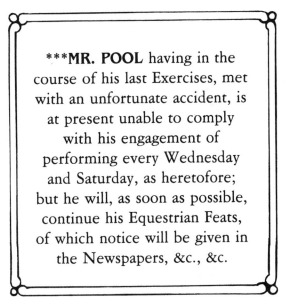

***MR. POOL having in the course of his last Exercises, met with an unfortunate accident, is at present unable to comply with his engagement of performing every Wednesday and Saturday, as heretofore; but he will, as soon as possible, continue his Equestrian Feats, of which notice will be given in the Newspapers, &c., &c.

In 1786, Pool appeared in Boston during July and August and in New York in September. He had changed the name of the humorous portion back to the name that Astley gave it, "The Taylor Riding to Brentford." Pool also opened a riding school in Boston in the middle of July 1786; perhaps that was how he earned his living after that. In any case, the name of Thomas Pool, the American-born founder of the circus in America, is seen no more in the annals of America's circuses.

The second man to start a circus in the

United States was a Scotsman, a pupil of Astley's greatest rival, Charles Hughes. His name was John Bill Ricketts. On April 3, 1793, in a ring in a building on the southwest corner of Twelfth and Market streets in Philadelphia, Ricketts added an acrobat and a ropewalker to the equestrian feats and the clowning. Philadelphia was the capital of the United States, its largest city, and the home of the first president, George Washington. What apparently established Ricketts's circus—the first one in America to be billed by that name—was a visit by Washington. It gave the new entertainment the presidential seal of approval.

Washington happened to be a superb rider. Thomas Jefferson called him "the best horseman of his age, and the most graceful figure that could be seen on horseback." And as a horse lover, Washington enjoyed the company of the Scottish riding master. They used to ride together, discussing such matters as the relative gaits of the sensational Narragansett pacer, developed in Rhode Island, and the natural pacer of Washington's Virginia.

Circus tradition has it that Ricketts told Washington's adopted son, G. W. P. Custis, "I delight to see the General ride, and make it a point to fall in with him when I hear he is abroad on horseback. His seat is so firm, his management so easy and graceful that I, who am a professor of horsemanship, would go to him and learn to ride." Custis relayed Ricketts's compliment to Washington. It came at a tense time in international relations. France and Great Britain were at war, and both wanted an alliance with the United States. American ship owners were developing a profitable carrying trade with both countries, but France had helped America win its freedom from Great Britain. Ricketts could see that the tension was telling on Washington, and invited him to relax by seeing a new kind of entertainment built around horseback riding. "I've got a rider coming over who can stand with one foot on the saddle and one foot in his mouth while his horse gallops around the ring at twelve miles an hour," Ricketts told Washington on one of their rides. "Come to my show when you feel like resting."

On April 22, 1793, Washington issued a proclamation of neutrality that permitted American sailing ships to carry tonnage for either warring nation. And that night, the President of the United States relaxed from his labors by attending Ricketts's circus.

What did Washington see? Ricketts, standing on the saddle of his moving horse, then leaping a ribbon stretched in his path and coming down again on the saddle. Ricketts hanging from the horse by one leg, brushing his hat on the earth. Ricketts throwing an orange into the air while circling the ring and catching it upon the tip of his sword. Ricketts leaping from moving horse to earth and back again; riding with one foot on each of two running horses; standing on his head in the saddle.

He saw the "Flying Mercury" act, which would become a circus standard: a boy standing on Ricketts's shoulders as Ricketts stood on the saddle. In addition to trick riding, there were other acts that originated in the tradition of the acrobatic street performer. There were Francis Ricketts, acrobat and brother of the proprietor, and "Seignior" Spinacuta, who did ropedancing. There was the first woman performer in the history of the American circus, Mrs. Spinacuta, who rode two horses at full gallop. And there was Mr. McDonald, the clown, who did "comic feats on horseback."

The circus clown was related to the court fool, the commedia dell'arte buffoon, and the Shakespearean jester, but already, by the 1770s, he was adapting his comic effects to the circus ring. One important target for the clown's humor was to be found in the other circus acts. Thus "the clown to the horse," who burlesqued equestrians, and "the clown to the rope," who burlesqued ropedancers, became standard features of the circus. A second prototype for clowning grew out of the verbal duels between "the clown to the ring" and the stately "lord of the grooms," or riding master.

Ricketts prospered, and he built a new white amphitheater, which he called the Pantheon, for his ring, with tall, slender columns in front. On top of the conical roof he placed a weathervane depicting the model for his "Flying Mercury" act, a figure standing on a horse in the attitude of the Roman god Mercury, patron of travelers, such as was often posted in Roman days where two or more roads met. In the autumn of 1794, Ricketts took his show on a wagon tour, traveling as far north as Boston and as far south as Baltimore. He opened a second amphitheater on October 19, 1795, this one on Broadway in New York. Despite having to close his new building during the worst days of the yellow fever epidemic the next year, he all but dominated the New York entertainment scene during the 1795–96 season.

Moreover, he finally got John Durang, the first known native American clown, to work for him. Durang left his Lancaster, Pennsylvania, home at the age of fifteen to tour with a traveling showman. He learned to dance and clown on a rope, and Ricketts was so impressed that he offered Durang a job. Durang declined because he didn't feel that he rode well enough. Circus clowning was becoming more and more a matter of the "stupid" clown burlesquing the straight acts—and a clown could get hurt fooling around on a horse. However, in 1795, when Ricketts, flushed with success, repeated the offer, Durang started practicing trick riding.

From 1795 to 1799, Ricketts offered equestrian programs and pantomimes in his Philadelphia ring. By 1796, the program consisted of riding, tightrope dancing, ground and lofty tumbling, clowning, and the pantomime—a dramatic and patriotic entertainment based on Washington's suppression of the Whiskey rebellion of 1794. This was the first circus Spectacle, or "Spec"—which would evolve into the traditional parade pageant of the circus within the Big Top or arena, embroidering some historical or imaginative theme with most of the performers and animals in the circus participating.

When Ricketts opened a second amphitheater in New York, this notice appeared in the *New York Gazette* for March 16, 1797:

The famous American horse
CORNPLANTER,
will at the word of command ungirth his saddle, and take it off his back—he will also pick up a handkerchief (and) gloves . . . The horse was purchased in New York three years ago, and only cost one hundred dollars. Mr. Ricketts is conscious of his being the best trained horse in America.

A little over one month later came one of those moments when the history of America and that of the circus rode in the same ring. The *Gazette* for April 29 reported: "The celebrated Horse Jack, who was in the American war with General Washington, and presented to Mr. Ricketts, will make his first appearance in the CIRCUS this Evening."

We can still see these two veterans of the

American Revolution, General Washington and his prancing white charger Jack, in the painting by an unknown nineteenth-century artist that hangs in the National Gallery in Washington, D.C. But Washington's contemporaries could see their great hero's famous steed, then twenty-eight years old, in the flesh at Ricketts's circus—the first sideshow attraction of the circus in America.

In the summer of 1797, Ricketts led his troupe on a tour into Canada, with John Durang as a key member. When Durang died in 1822, he left the only extensive memoir of the first thirty years of American circus life, and it is from him that we know what America's first traveling circus was like. One of the featured acts was a three-high pyramid on two horses. Master Hutchins, a nine-year-old, was on Ricketts's shoulders, and Ricketts was on Durang's. "We were the first equestrians that ever was in Canada," wrote Durang, "therefore the Canadiaen inhabitents where ignorent of the science and thought the whole thing a conjuration." Much easier to understand were the clowns who showed how *not* to ride a horse. Ricketts, like Astley and Pool, featured a variation of "The Taylor Riding to Brentford," in which Durang played the tailor. In fact, Durang did a lot of things in Ricketts's circus:

My business was the Clown on foot and horseback, and obliged to furnish all the jokes for the ring, and to ride the Tailor to Brentford, with the dialogue which I was obliged to speak in French, German, and English (the principle inhabitants are French, a great many Germans, a few merchants, and British soldiers). I rode the foxhunter, leaping over the bar with the mounting and dismounting while in full speed, taking a flying leap on horseback through a paper sun, in character of a drunken man on horseback, tied in a sack standing on two horses while I changed to

woman's clothes; rode in full speed standing on two horses, Mr. Ricketts at the same time standing on my shoulders, with master Hutchins at the same time standing in the attitude of Mercury on Mr. Rickett's shoulders forming a pyramid. I performed the drunken soldier on horseback, still vaulted, I danced on the stage, I was the Harlequin in the pantomimes, occasionally I sung a comic song. I tumbled on the slack rope and performed on the slack wire. I introduced mechanical exhibitions of fireworks. In short, I was performer, machinist, painter, designer, music compiler, the bill maker, and treasurer.

Durang gives us the first description we have of the American circus in actual performance. Today's arena shows have reduced the fear of bad weather, but the specter of injury is still as great, as is the determination to give a good performance against all odds:

I ventured thro' the storm as I knew my presence was necessary to be at the Circus. I arrived late in the afternoon and we performed that night. The roof of the circus leaked, and was very wet. In riding the Tailor, the horse's legs slipt from under him and he fell flat on his side with my leg under him. I escaped the misfortune of breaking it, but my knee swelled very much, after which I danced a hornpipe to show the people I was not hurt—yet the next day I was layed up and for three days. An old French doctor cured me—she also cured a woman of cancer in the breast by applying a live toad to the part affected.

By 1797, Ricketts's success had spawned a competitor. Lailson and Jaymond, a circus from France, opened its own circus building in Philadelphia with a performance on April 8, 1797. It stood at the corner of Fifth and Prune streets and had a great brick dome. Like Ricketts,

RICKETTS'S CIRCUS. *After George Washington, who Thomas Jefferson said was the best rider in America, John Bill Ricketts was probably next. As these 1793 newspaper clippings testify, Ricketts was prepared to ride "with his knees on the saddle, the horse in full speed; and from this position leap over a ribbon extended 12 feet high." Or he could juggle four oranges while riding a speeding horse. He could even ride a horse in "full speed" standing with one leg on the saddle while his "pupil" rode standing on one foot on Ricketts's shoulder. Ricketts's circus also included "many Surprizing Feats on the Tight Rope" by Seignior Spiracuta. And, because this was a true circus— a spectacle in which feats of skill and daring performed in, over, and around a ring are burlesqued by a clown— Ricketts also announced that "Mr. McDonald will perform several COMIC FEATS (Being his First Appearance in America)." (Circus World Museum, Baraboo, Wisconsin)*

RICKETTS'S "PANTHEON." Ricketts's circus appeared at this second "Pantheon" from 1795 to December 17, 1799, when the building burned to the ground. For almost seven years, from the opening of his first circus, in 1793, Ricketts was successful and lucky. In both Philadelphia and New York, he built larger amphitheaters for his shows. In 1795, he also had a circus in "Ricketts' New Amphitheatre," Boston, according to a photostat of a handbill at the American Antiquarian Society. In August 1795, the Connecticut Courant *announced his showing at Hartford on August 16–20. His luck turned when both his New York and Philadelphia circuses burned the same year. In 1800, Ricketts tried to return to England to make a fresh start but was lost at sea. (Circus World Museum, Baraboo, Wisconsin)*

Philip Lailson was his own principal rider. Jaymond was a rider and actor who filled the program with dramatic pieces. There were also two clowns, Mr. McDonald and William Sully, and a bandleader, Mr. Collet. And there was an important historical first. Lailson's company paraded daily through the main commercial streets in an attempt to advertise the show. According to Stuart Thayer, "This is the first record of any kind of street display by a circus in America." Lailson's success in Philadelphia was immediate, and by the end of the year he had followed Ricketts to New York, where he advertised a performer, Miss Venice, as the first woman rider in the country—who would "ride standing on a single horse, with all the gracefulness of her sex"—despite the fact that Mrs. Spinacuta had ridden in Ricketts's circus four years before.

Lailson and Jaymond did not flourish, however. The great brick dome of their Philadelphia building collapsed in 1798, but their programs were also too heavy—with dramatic pieces. Their circus was advertised for sale in 1798 and 1799, when the company, according to the acrobat George Stone, "embarked for the West Indies and was never heard of afterwards."

Ricketts realized, he told Durang, that an equestrian performance blended with dramatic offerings was ultimately doomed to fail. He dropped the actors from his troupe unless, like Durang, they could also ride and do acrobatics. Drama survives in the circus today as the Spec, which often includes pantomimes with few or no words, such as an American astronaut planting a flag on the moon; but the hybrid of circus acts and dramatic pieces eventually died out.

Ricketts's popularity, on the other hand, increased. He was more than just a great equestrian. As an impresario, he was the man who made people see the circus as, in the contemporary judgment of the *Quebec Gazette*, "this

new field of innocent and agreeable amusement, which is so well adapted to improve youth in a useful and elegant art, as well as to please the aged and most serious class of spectators." And, of course, the clowns reassured the spectators that there were plenty of people who couldn't ride a horse to save their souls.

Washington, "the best horseman of his age," ended his second term as president of the United States in March 1797, and retired to his home in Mount Vernon—but not before Philadelphia merchants tendered him a farewell dinner, choosing Ricketts's amphitheater, the Pantheon, as the scene of the festivities. A tableau depicting the president waving goodbye brought tears to the eyes of many of the spectators.

On December 26, 1798, Ricketts opened his winter season at the Pantheon. He appeared in Canadian winter dress to draw attention to his Canadian tour. He did an Indian scalp dance. He leaped his horse over the heads of twenty soldiers—probably in five ranks of four. Then he did another patriotic pantomime, this time on the traitor Benedict Arnold. Washington had put Arnold in command of Philadelphia during the Revolution, only to see him shift his allegiance to the British. Once again, the circus aided in the mythologizing of American history, the way film and television do today.

From the beginning, fire has been the deadliest enemy of the circus, and fire was the beginning of the end of John Bill Ricketts. In 1799, his circus in New York burned down. He returned to Philadelphia, where on December 17, during a circus pantomime called "Don Juan" in which the old sinner goes to hell, a drunken stagehand carrying a lighted candle entered the loft over the stage where scenery was stored. Five hundred people were watching the circus below when the candle ignited paint and canvas. All escaped, but Ricketts's second and last circus building was destroyed, along with the hotel next door, where he lived.

John Bill Ricketts was now bankrupt and homeless. But he wasn't through yet. Though the dome of Lailson's circus at 42 South Fifth Street had collapsed, the structure, now open to the sky, was still sound. Ricketts leased it and advertised that he would show in daylight, "after the manner of the old Amphitheatres of Rome, Madrid, etc."

He started his season on April 3, 1800. William Sully was his clown, who led the others in ground and lofty tumbling. John Durang was featured both as a rider and as a tightwire walker. Ricketts and ten-year-old Master Hutchins, who rode two ponies at once, did the "Flying Mercury." The child's father, Mr. Hutchins, Sr., was also in the company. Ricketts's horse, Cornplanter, was featured. On April 10, they began doing "The Taylor Riding to Brentford," but by now the role of Billy Buttons, the tailor, had become the province of the clown, and Sully was playing it.

After three weeks, the show closed. Durang said that the cost of leasing the building plus the size of the company payroll made operating expenses too high for the engagement to be profitable.

Ricketts decided that his circus might make a profit in the West Indies. He outfitted a ship with stalls for the horses and set sail. Durang, who stayed behind, reports that pirates seized the ship and ran it into Guadeloupe. They claimed as prizes of the sea the circus horses and the lumber needed to construct a circus building, and put them up for sale.

Ricketts did have one last piece of luck. A merchant bought the horses and lumber and made a deal with Ricketts to use them to put on a circus. Ricketts earned back all he had lost in a few days.

But then Master Hutchins, the two-pony rider, became ill and died; and Francis, Ricketts's son, was imprisoned for reasons unknown. (He would later appear in America as a featured performer for several years, though he never owned a circus of his own.)

Understandably discouraged, John Bill Ricketts set sail for England late in 1800. The talented rider and tenacious entrepreneur had every reason to believe that he could recoup his fortunes in that circus-loving land. But the ship was lost at sea with all on board.

———◆———

After Ricketts was lost, interest in the circus declined in America. Robertson and Franklin appeared in the new arena at New York's Vauxhall Garden in 1802, and in 1803 they gave the only circus performance in the United States of which a record can be found. Pepin and Breschard's Circus, which had already made a name for itself in Europe, arrived in Plymouth, Massachusetts, in late 1807. It was Victor Pepin, a dashing rider born in America but raised and trained as a cavalry officer in France, who slowly revived America's interest in the new entertainment form. In 1808, Pepin and Breschard's Circus was the first to visit Boston, and on September 26, 1809, they put on in Charlestown, Massachusetts, "the Battle and Death of General Malbrook," a spectacular pantomime, "performed on foot and horseback," with a cast including Mr. Pepin, Mr. and Mrs. Breschard, Mr. Cayetano, Mr. Codet, Mr. Menial, and Mr. Grain.

Business was so good that this circus split in two, and the unit known as Cayetano, Codet, Menial & Redon put on a show in Newburyport, Massachusetts, in 1810, which a young patron named Sarah Anna Emery could still describe vividly when she wrote her memoirs sixty-nine years later:

The third of May, the first circus that ever visited Newburyport came into town: an Italian troupe, Messrs. Cayetano & Co. A board pavilion was erected in an unoccupied lot . . . this was furnished with seats in the pit, which surrounded the ring; above was a gallery, with boxes comprising the dress-circle. There was a stand for musicians. . . . Tickets to the boxes were one dollar; to the pit, fifty cents; children under ten years of age half price. This was a most respectable and fine looking company, their horses were splendid animals, all the appurtenances in the best style. The performance commenced by the "Grand Military Manaeuvres by Eight Riders."

. . . This was prior to the formation of brass bands. The music consisted of some half dozen performers on the bugle, clari-onet, bass-viol and violin. . . . As the moment arrived for the performance to commence, at a bugle-call in dashed the eight horsemen, in a showy uniform, in single file; they rushed around the ring; then followed a series of splendid feats of horsemanship and military tactics. . . . The military exercises over, Master Tatnal performed several gymnastic feats. He was followed by Master Duffee, a Negro lad, who drew down the house by feats of agility, leaping over a whip and hoop. Mr. Codet signalized himself in feats of horsemanship. Mr. Menial, the clown, amused the audience by buffoonery and horsemanship. Mr. Cayetano executed on two horses the laughable farce of the "Fish woman, or the Metamorphosis." With a foot on each horse, he rode forward habited as an immensely fat fish-woman, in a huge bonnet and uncouth garments. Riding rapidly round the ring, he divested himself of this and several other suits, ending in making his final bow as an elegant cavalier.

The young African next performed feats of horsemanship and vaulting, danced a horn-pipe, and other figures, ending by dashing round the ring, standing on the tips of his toes. The horse, Ocelot, posted himself in various attitudes, danced and took a colla-tion with the clown. Mr. Cayetano per-formed "The Candian [Canadian] Peasant," and feats of horsemanship with hoops, hat and glove, terminating by the leap of the four ribbons separated and together. Mr. Cayetano performed the pyramid, young Duffee on his shoulders as "Flying Mer-cury." Then came the Trampoleon exercises by Messrs. Menial, Codet and the young Af-rican; somersets over men's heads and a leap over six horses. The next scene was the Ped-estal, the horse of knowledge posted in different attitudes. The performances con-cluded with the Taylor riding to Waterford upon the unequaled horse Zebra, by Mr. Menial, the clown. This was a most laughable farce, Zebra being a Jack trained to the part. This elicited a storm of applause, and the play ended with cheer after cheer.

This was a real circus, and Sarah Anna Emery mentions all the elements that made it a good one: the ring, performing horses and riders, clowns, thrilling demonstrations of the skills of acrobats, and the band playing. The circus did not as yet have jungle acts, rare and exotic animals and people, aerialists, or daredevils— unless you count "somersets over men's heads and a leap over six horses" as daredevil feats. And it did not have an elephant. But it would have an elephant, in New York, two years later.

The saga of the circus in America was under way.

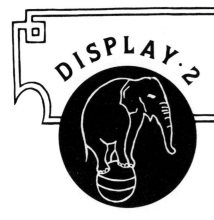

DISPLAY·2

The Wild Animal Exhibitors' Ball

"Clowns and elephants," P. T. Barnum often said, "are the pegs upon which the circus is hung"; and the very first circus was certainly hung upon a clown. The elephant didn't get into the circus until the nineteenth century.

Why does the circus need an elephant? As good an answer as any was provided by a Ringling Bros. and Barnum & Bailey Circus press agent named F. Beverly Kelley, who used to say, "The Elephant is the largest animal you'll ever see this side of delirium tremens." As the largest mammal to be found on land, the elephant just naturally seems to belong to the circus, which developed at least partly out of the human desire to marvel at superlatives, and yet to see human beings undaunted by them. At the circus we get to see people and animals that can be rated the largest, the smallest, the fastest, the fattest, the most ferocious—or any other superlative—and then to let the clowns make us laugh at them; and at ourselves, for being so impressed.

After John Bill Ricketts was lost at sea, the circus in America almost disappeared. No superstars or superfeats caught the fancy of the public as had Ricketts and the greatest riding America had ever seen. However, another idea was catching on: that of the traveling menagerie. And when that was combined with the idea of the circus, the institution would undergo another substantial change.

The first elephant on the North American continent was the three-year-old female that arrived in New York Harbor on April 13, 1796, on a ship owned by the Salem shipmaster Capt. Jacob Crowninshield. Crowninshield had paid $450 for the animal in Bengal and soon sold her to a Philadelphian named Owen for $10,000, an enormous sum at the time.

Crowninshield's elephant—recorded his-

ISAAC A. VAN AMBURGH. By 1835, he was entering, according to a poster for the Zoological Institute of New York, "To the lion, lioness, leopard & leopardess, all in one cage. To the black maned cape lion, lioness and royal tigress, in the same cage. To royal tiger & tigress. And to the lion, leopard, and panther in the same cage." Gradually, he began to train these animals. Circuses continued using his potent name as a title until 1922. (Circus World Museum, Baraboo, Wisconsin)

tory gives the creature no other name—was a sensation. She went on the road, touring the eastern seaboard and leaving a trail of handbills and newspaper notices that we can follow from South Carolina to upstate New York. On September 19, 1797, for instance, she was in Newburyport, where a handbill informed the public that "the Elephant, according to the account of the celebrated Buffon [French naturalist Comte Georges Louis Leclerc de Buffon, 1707–1788], is the most respectable Animal in the world." Mistaking the elephant's sex, the handbill goes on: "In size he surpasses all other terrestrial creatures, and by his intelligence makes as near an approach to man, as matter can approach spirit." The elephant's nearness to man may also have been suggested by her fondness for the bottle: "He . . . drinks all kinds of spirituous liquors; some days he has drank [sic] 30 bottles of porter, drawing the corks with his trunk."

The elephant came to Philadelphia, and a handbill announced: "A respectable and convenient place is fitted up adjoining the Store of Mr. Bartlet, Market-Street, for the reception of those ladies and gentlemen who may be pleased to view the greatest natural curiosity ever presented to the curious, which is to be seen from sunrise till sundown, every day in the week." Admission for adults cost "one quarter of a dollar"; for children, "one eighth of a dollar."

Crowninshield's elephant made the vital linkup with the circus in 1812, when she was exhibited in New York City with the circus of Cayetano, Codet, Menial & Redon. However, it was the second elephant to come to these shores, though she may never actually have been exhibited with a circus, who convinced circus owners that the circus and the elephant were made for each other.

Hackaliah Bailey, a farmer of Stephentown, later known as Somers, New York, had a brother who was a sea captain, and it was this brother who brought the second elephant to America on his ship. The captain had bought a female African elephant at auction in London for $20, and he sold it to Hackaliah for $1,000; he made a profit of 5,000 percent, and yet, as it turned out, he did not cheat his brother.

The captain put the elephant on board a sloop bound up the Hudson River for Sing Sing, the nearest river town to Hackaliah's home. Hackaliah walked the animal from Sing Sing to Somers, a crossroads village in upper Westchester County, fifty-six miles away. Natural businessman that he was, Hackaliah walked the elephant only by night so that the public would not glimpse the beast along the route "for nothing." During the day, the elephant was exhibited for a small fee, and good profits were immediately forthcoming. Bailey called the elephant Old Bet.

In the history of the American circus, there are many events and dates that are all but impossible to verify, and the arrival of Old Bet is one. Gil Robinson, son of John Robinson (1802–1888), circus proprietor to three generations of Americans, claimed that the arrival of Old Bet in America "occurred in 1805, three years after the birth of my father." It was at least before August of 1808, when Bailey signed "articles of agreement" by which Andrew Brown and Benjamin Lent took over the showing of Old Bet for a year and split the profits with him.

Bailey's example had given a lot of men in the Somers area the idea that there was money to be made by investing in unusual animals for exhibition. Several of Bailey's neighbors went into the touring menagerie business. Among them were not only Brown and Lent, but John J. June, Lewis B. Titus, Caleb S. Angevine, Aaron Turner, and the Howes and Crane families, all of whom lived within a day's buggy ride of each other in the Somers area.

Brown and Lent agreed to pay Bailey "twelve hundred dollars each for the equal two thirds of the use of the Elephant for one year from the first day of this month. Bailey on his part furnishes one third of the expenses and Brown and Lent the other two thirds."

The deals now came thick and fast. On December 9, 1809, Cyrus A. Cady and John E. Russell sold "Nero, the Royal Tiger, and Cage, for $1,000 to Benjamin Lent." Four days later, Hackaliah Bailey traded "one quarter of the earnings of an elephant for the purchase of one quarter of Lent's tiger."

Finally, in 1816, Bailey took on a teenage partner named Nathan Howes. He sent Old Bet on the road with the tiny Nathan Howes Menagerie, with the agreement that they would split the profits fifty-fifty. Bailey waited for his share for many weeks, but not a penny came back to him, nor did any answers to the inquiries he sent. Finally, Bailey went after young Howes and caught up with him in New Bedford, Massachusetts.

In person, Hackaliah Bailey demanded his share of the profits. Adroitly avoiding being trampled by the big crowds who had come to see Old Bet, Nate Howes blandly replied that there were no profits.

Understandably suspicious, Bailey said, "You shall not travel any longer in charge of this elephant as long as I own any interest in him."

"I would like to see you prevent it," replied young Nate. "Our written contract stipulates that I am to have charge of the elephant, and next fall we are to settle up."

"But it also stipulates that you are to remit to me one half of the profits as fast as they accrue," said Bailey.

When Howes insisted that they had yet to make money on Bet, Bailey offered to buy him out. Howes declined. Bailey then said he would like to sell Howes his share. Howes de-clined. Bailey warned Howes not to travel with Old Bet one more mile.

At dawn the following day, Howes went out to the barn to get Old Bet for the journey to the next village. Beside the elephant he found Bailey, waiting for him with a loaded musket in his hands. It was not, however, his intention to shoot Howes. As the young man approached, Bailey lifted the musket to his shoulder and aimed it at the elephant.

"Hey! That's half my elephant!" Howes shouted.

"I'm only aiming at my half," answered Bailey.

The story spread like wildfire, even appearing in the newspapers. Indeed, a cartoon appeared burlesquing this Yankee variation on Solomon's dilemma, with Bailey preparing to shoot "his half." But like Solomon's solution, this one worked, too: Howes promptly handed over Bailey's half of the money, and the tour continued.

Then, about halfway through 1816, Old Bet was shot to death.

At The Elephant Hotel, which Bailey built in Somers with his profits from exhibiting Old Bet, you can see today the item from the *New York Post* for April 16, 1817, reporting that "The skeleton of that unfortunate Elephant that was shot the 26th of July last in District of Maine, so well-known to the public, is got up for inspection and may be seen at number 301 Broadway from Monday, the 7th until Wednesday, the 30th instant, every day in the week, Sunday excepted, from nine in the morning until sunset. The weight of the elephant, when it was shot, was upwards of 70 hundred pounds. Admittance 25 cents."

Further information on Bet's murder appeared in the *Evening Post* for Christmas Eve, 1821: "This elephant was wantonly shot in the town of Berwick in 1816, as she with her keeper was passing from Boston to the District of Maine. This animal was known by the name of Bet . . . she was considered one of the most docile and tractable of her race, but she fell by the hand of a ruffian. She is now put up in as good style as it is possible to expect, considering her immense size."

Ironically, Old Bet's ability to turn a profit was apparently the cause of her murder. A Rev. Dr. William Bentley of Salem, Massachusetts, noted in his diary that "the poor Elephant was destroyed in Maine, because he took money from those who could not afford to spend it."

In fact, the first elephant killed in the United States was probably the victim of a volcanic eruption in Indonesia. In those years, in the best of times, New England towns like Berwick, Maine, had so little hard cash that it would take a rare beast indeed to induce its citizens to part with their money. But 1816 was known as the year in which there was no summer. The eruption of the volcano Tambora in 1815 caused severe weather conditions in North America and Europe the next year. Snow fell in June and July. The second of four cold waves, which began July 9, caused water in Maine to freeze as thick as window glass and killed the corn crop. It is easy to imagine that someone in these bizarre circumstances might kill the elephant to prevent it from taking money out of the community, and he may even have looked upon Old Bet as an instrument of the Devil.

Whatever its motive, the murder established the elephant as an American moneymaker. Astley had hung the world's first circus, in England, on the clown and the horse, and Pool and Ricketts did the same thing in America, but Old Bet had shown that, as an attraction, nothing could beat the elephant.

Bailey buried Old Bet in Somers, near his Elephant Hotel, the hotel that Bet built, that fine, red brick Georgian building that was known as the best hostelry between New York and Albany in stagecoach days. In front of the hotel entrance Bailey erected a tall granite pillar crowned by a gold-lacquered wooden statue of the elephant.

The hotel is now the Somers Town Hall, and the statue still commands the fork in the road.

———

After Bet's death, Hackaliah Bailey toured with several traveling menageries and operated steamboats on the Hudson River. But he loved best to tell stories of the elephant that was the foundation of his fortune. And soon others followed in the giant footsteps of his martyred pachyderm.

In 1818 an elephant named Columbus was shown in New York City, along with a pair of camels and a pair of antelope. In 1819, New York saw an elephant named Horatio. Gradually, the elephant was surrounded by a show with riders, acrobats, and other performers, and exhibitions in larger towns brought substantial profits.

A tiny traveling menagerie called the Zoological Institute didn't have an elephant when it went on the road in 1820, but it did have that high-toned, educational-sounding name. It was for the name even more than the animals that June, Titus, and Angevine bought it. These were still puritanical times, when amusement was frowned on but education was valued. "Levity" was constantly attacked from the pulpit, but how could even the most pious object to an organization with a name like that? Seeing strange beasts wasn't frivolous, it was a scientific education.

It was the Somers crowd that went in for exhibiting animals, including elephants, in a big way. This was the old story in economics: somebody makes a killing at something, and all his neighbors try the same thing. The competition that resulted from this sudden increase in the number of menageries inspired the leader in the field, June, Titus, Angevine & Co., to bring about a merger with its most important competitors: Raymond & Ogden; Lewis, Bailey & Co.; Purdy, Welch & Macomber; J. R. and W. Howe Jr. & Co.; Kelley, Raymond & Co.; Mead, Miller & Co.; Kelly, Berry and Waring; and Ganung & Strang & Co. The merger was arranged through a trust agreement executed on January 14, 1835, at Somers. The management of all the property of the associated firms, the allocation of animals to the various menageries, and the designation of nonconflicting routes was entrusted to a board of five directors. The first five were James Raymond, Hiram Waring, Caleb S. Angevine, Lewis B. Titus, and William Howe, Jr. Their capital totaled $329,325, which was the appraised value of the animals, equipment, and real estate used by the merged firms, and they called their association, or joint stock company, by that educational-sounding name, The Zoological Institute.

Those outside the syndicate called them "The Flatfoots."

The derisive name was first used when another circus tried to put on a show in New York state, the territory that the syndicate considered its exclusive domain.

Syndicate members John J. June, Lewis B. Titus, Caleb S. Angevine, and Jerry Crane responded, as with one voice: "We put our foot down flat, and shall play New York," by which they meant *exclusively.*

The Flatfoots all but monopolized the business in their area, but by now the circus was in its "westering" phase, and a dozen impresarios were spreading the love of the new entertainment form through America. As mud roads were slowly replaced by metalled turnpikes, heavier wagon loads were possible, and soon these roads were being traveled by circuses with such names as Robertson and Franklin; Pepin and Breschard; Cayetano & Company; Thomas West; James West; William Blanchard and his family troupe; Buckley and Wicks; and Rufus Welch.

Everywhere they went, they converted Americans to the circus. In 1825, General Andrew Jackson, military hero of the War of 1812 and soon to be the seventh president of the United States, visited Louisville, Kentucky, and on March 31 was invited by Victor Pepin to attend his circus. Old Hickory's entrance into the building was heartily cheered by an audience of about seven hundred people. Pepin had been giving riding lessons in Louisville over the winter of 1824–25, and by February had had enough money to put up a circus building. His ring horses had been in training only for a few weeks, but they performed well enough to be called "brilliant" in the *Louisville Public Advertiser.*

———

In the early 1820s there were thirty or more traveling menageries touring the eastern United States from Maine to Alabama and west to the Appalachians. And there were a number of circuses. But it wasn't until the late 1830s that the promoters could figure out a way to combine the menagerie with a circus, allow the two to roll together, and make both seem "educational."

The way was paved by Isaac A. Van Amburgh, who developed from a caretaker of animals in a menagerie into a "lion tamer" in the circus. Van Amburgh blurred the distinctions by presenting his jungle acts as living illustrations of the Holy Bible. After that, menageries started engaging equestrians and clowns to present performances in circus rings, and the distinction between circus and menagerie gradually faded.

They called Van Amburgh "The Lion King."

OLD BET AND THE ELEPHANT HOTEL (*left*). *Old Bet was the second elephant to come to America but the most important animal in circus history. Circus tradition says that Old Bet arrived in New York harbor in 1805 and was bought by Hackaliah Bailey of Somers, New York, from his sea captain brother for $1,000. Bailey made a small fortune exhibiting Old Bet and leasing her to others, such as Nathan B. Howes of nearby Brewster. In 1816, while Howes was exhibiting Old Bet in Maine, she was shot to death by an angry farmer. In 1827, Bailey erected a wooden image of Old Bet on a tall stone pedestal in front of his inn in Somers, New York. Over 150 years later, the statue still stands in front of that building, which now houses the Somers Village Hall and Historical Society. Nathan Howes went on to found, with his partner Aaron Turner, the show that gave P. T. Barnum his start in the circus business. Because of such pioneering, this section of the country is called the Cradle of the American Circus. (Circus World Museum, Baraboo, Wisconsin)*

LEWIS JUNE (*opposite, top right*). *He got his start in the circus world by driving a cage wagon of animals across strange country with Sands & Nathans during the tenting season of 1831. The four June brothers, James, John, Stebbins, and Lewis, born into a North Salem, New York, family of twelve children, organized, promoted, and worked for early circus and menagerie companies in the 1830s. James M. June (1809–1862) was a senior partner with Lewis B. Titus and Caleb Sutton Angevine in June, Titus and Angevine Co., which owned the famous menagerie called the Zoological Institute. Lew June, wrote historian Earl Chapin May, "developed into such an efficient general agent that he was able to route four circuses simultaneously and to keep track of the various partners' holdings which may explain why, in appearance, he was such a hard-bitten gentleman with a very firm mouth over a firmer stubbled chin." (Circus World Museum, Baraboo, Wisconsin)*

LEVI NORTH & SON (*opposite, top left*). *The Flatfoots interested another neighbor, Isaac Quick, in forming the Quick & Mead circus using their animals and a rider named Levi J. North, the first great American-born equestrian. (Circus World Museum, Baraboo, Wisconsin)*

LEWIS B. LENT (right). *The Flatfoots made one of their smartest moves when they admitted Lewis B. Lent of Somers, who helped them realize all the great advantages of centralization and control. Lew Lent owned the circus that went by the name of the Equescurriculum, and was manager for many years of the Winter Circus on Fourteenth Street, New York City. No other American town was large enough to support a permanent circus the way New York, London, and Paris could, so the Flatfoot syndicate sold stock in their enterprise and sent traveling companies into the various states. In August 1872, P. T. Barnum purchased the buildings on Fourteenth Street that had housed the Lent Circus; in November he opened there a "Museum, Menagerie, Hippodrome, and Circus," but just before Christmas the buildings burned to the ground, destroying the whole collection. Undaunted as always, P. T. Barnum had other circuses up his sleeve. (Circus World Museum, Baraboo, Wisconsin)*

He was born on the banks of the Hudson in Fishkill, New York, in July 1811. His grandfather was an American Indian who had adopted the name Worboys Van Amburgh. As a nineteen-year-old living in Peekskill, New York, Isaac Van Amburgh went looking for a job to nearby North Salem, where June, Titus, and Angevine had just purchased the Zoological Institute. Like Clyde Beatty after him, he started as a so-called cage boy, cleaning the cages of wild animals. But Isaac had a way with wild animals, and he soon developed the first trained wild animal act—at least in modern times. As a wild animal dealer, Titus appreciated this novelty, and he knew, before Barnum, though not so well as Barnum, that novelty plus publicity meant money.

June, Titus, and Angevine had a menagerie that traveled in sixty wagons. They dressed Van Amburgh in a Roman toga in tribute to the combination of lions and gladiators in the Circus Maximus in ancient Rome, and they distributed thousands of posters. The next year, 1821, the Van Amburgh Menagerie took New York City by storm. In the winter, Van Amburgh would train lions, tigers, bears, and elephants in barns throughout New York's upper Westchester and lower Putnam counties.

Van Amburgh first entered a cageful of wild animals on the stage of the Richmond Hill Theatre, New York, in 1833, and astounded the country. O. J. Ferguson, his biographer, described what happened: "The effect of his power was instantaneous. The Lion halted and stood transfixed. The Tiger crouched. The Panther with a suppressed growl of rage sprang back, while the Leopard receded gradually from its master. The spectators were overwhelmed with wonder. . . . Then came the most effective tableaux of all. Van Amburgh with his strong will bade them come to him while he reclined in the back of the cage—the proud King of animal creation."

When Van Amburgh entered that cage of man-eating cats, he was also facing attacks from humans. Congress had long since repealed its Revolutionary War law against theatrical shows, and presidents Washington and Adams had attended circuses; nevertheless, circuses were regularly attacked in the press and the pulpit as "traveling death" and "moral ruin." A Staten Island newspaper pointed out that a single visit of the Great Eastern Circus took from the community "enough money to sustain three missionaries among the heathen for a year." Things were less stringent out in the Territory, but as far west as Cincinnati, men were still fined or jailed for playing cards or billiards or for riding a horse on Sunday.

So Isaac Van Amburgh countered religious prejudice by quoting the Bible to justify his touring menagerie. Didn't God say in Genesis 26 that He had made man in His own image and given him dominion over all the animals? Why, then, it was a religious act for trained animals to kneel at his feet. And when Van Amburgh made a lion lie down with a lamb and then brought a child into the den, he was "completing the picture of the triumph of faith over the savage beast." In fact, you were practically offending God *not* to see a menagerie. Didn't the Book of Job have the Lord telling Job to "Behold now behemoth, which I made with thee: he eateth grass as an ox." Biblical scholars identified the behemoth as a hippopotamus. Well, where could you see a hippo but in a menagerie, or a menagerie at the circus?

Van Amburgh earned up to $400 a week going into lions' dens here and abroad. By appearing as a feature of the Flatfoot shows, he saved enough money to start his own menagerie and circus.

Nathaniel Hawthorne, in his *American Notebooks*, describes the menagerie he saw on September 4, 1838, near North Adams, Massachusetts:

This day an exhibition of animals in the vicinity of the village, under a pavilion of sailcloth,—the floor being the natural grass. . . . In an inner pavilion an exhibition of anacondas,—four,—which the showman took, one by one, from a large box, under some blankets, and hung round his shoulders. They seemed almost torpid when first taken out, but gradually began to assume life, to stretch, to contract, twine and writhe about his neck and person, thrusting out their tongues and erecting their heads. Their weight was as much as he could bear, and they hung down almost to the ground when not contorted,—as big round as a man's thigh, almost,—spotted and richly variegated. Then he put them into the box again, their heads emerging and writhing forth, which the showman thrust back again. He gave a descriptive and historical account of them, and a fanciful and poetical one also. A man put his arm and head into the lion's mouth,—all the spectators looking on so attentively that a breath could not be heard. That was impressive,—its effect on a thousand persons,—more so than the thing itself.

Hawthorne had probably seen Isaac A. Van Amburgh, who was one of the only performers of the day to put his head into a lion's mouth—providing cartoonists with one of their all-time favorite circus themes. Hawthorne continued:

The country boors were continually getting within the barriers, and venturing too near the cages. The great lion lay with his fore paws extended, and a calm, majestic, but awful countenance. He looked on the people as if he had seen many such concourses. The hyena was the most ugly and dangerous looking beast, full of spite, and on ill terms with all nature, looking a good deal like a hog with the devil in him, the ridge of hair along his back bristling. He was in the cage with a leopard and a panther, and the latter seemed continually on the point

of laying his paw on the hyena, who snarled, and showed his teeth. It is strange, though, to see how these wild beasts acknowledge and practice a degree of mutual forbearance, and of obedience to man, with their wild nature yet in them.

In the show Hawthorne describes, we see the circus and the menagerie coming together. The menagerie and the equestrian circus had been developing side by side as separate types of entertainment, each independent of the other. But a circus owner might introduce a monkey or a trained dog into the equestrian circus for variety's sake. Then another circus owner would compete by exhibiting a cage or two of wild animals as an added attraction. The menageries, meanwhile, would add acts like the ones that Hawthorne saw, a snake handler and a lion tamer. Others would add a clown or an equestrian act. And the success of these combinations gradually effected a merger of circuses and menageries.

When the weather in the East and Midwest turned too cold for tented exhibitions, traveling menageries and circuses would head for Florida, entering the state from Dothan, Alabama, and leaving through Thomasville, Georgia, to go back home. Tallahassee lay directly in their line of travel, and on February 14, 1832, the Tallahassee paper carried an ad for "A Grand Menagerie of Living Animals" to be exhibited for three days beginning February 16, including "Tippo Sultan, the great hunting elephant, the tiger of Brazil, the camel of Arabia imported in 1830, the cougar of South America, two panthers of North America, a prairie wolf, an ichneumon of Egypt, together with a great variety of the monkey tribe; also Dandy Jack, the celebrated equestrian, who will perform many interesting and diverting feats on his much admired Shetland pony. Good music during the performance."

It was almost a circus, but it didn't have a clown.

Nearly three years later, on December 27, 1834, the same newspaper announced that French, Hobby and Company's Baltimore Circus and Menagerie would show in Tallahassee beginning January 12, 1835, again with Dandy Jack and his pony—but this time, it was a complete circus: "Elephant, camel, lion, leopard, tiger, hyena, kangaroo, panther, black bear, armadillo, emew, swan, catamunda, ichneumon, large number of apes, monkeys and baboons. Dandy Jack and his pony. Animals exhibited one hour, then equestrian performance. Band." And as a final touch: "Comic song by clown."

————————◆————————

These were the so-called mud shows. Moving at night in wagon trains over country roads that were often a foot deep in mud, such "caravansaries" covered only two or three miles an hour. A good jump between towns in the days of horse-drawn wagons was ten or fifteen miles. A hostler rode ahead of the wagon train to find the shortest route and to "rail" every fork and crossroad. This meant taking a rail from a farmer's fence and placing it across the road that was not to be taken so that the wagons would avoid making a wrong turn.

The shows were usually ballyhooed by an advance agent and a clown. The agent would arrive on horseback about one week ahead of the show. He would ring a bell or beat a drum or blow a bugle to get folks' attention, then talk up the show while persuading tavern owners and storekeepers to let him tack up his bills, usually in return for free passes to the performance.

On circus day, the clown would come into

town a couple of hours before the circus to draw a crowd to Main Street or the courthouse square or, in New England, the village green, where he would beguile them with acrobatics, clowning, and snappy jokes. Then the wagons would arrive with their few head of stock, and show in canvas enclosures or roofed-over pavilions, if they had them. The regular members of the troupe split the profits, and every member was expected to perform several jobs. Regular salaries were seldom paid.

The ring was always the heart of the circus, but the early rings, usually made by piling up a circular mound of dirt, were housed in buildings built for the purpose. When the circuses first took to the roads, they played in enclosures made by surrounding the ring with sailcloth sidewalls stretched around posts and trees. No one had thought of a tent yet—or a pavilion, as tents were called in those days. If it rained, the show could not go on.

Then, in 1825, Joshua Purdy Brown, another native of Somers, put up the first circus tent in Wilmington, Delaware. This simple idea of a canvas tent that was easily portable yet kept both rain and blazing sun off performers and spectators alike proved the perfect innovation to permit the circus to serve a nation on the move.

Brown was probably born in 1802, so he was only about twenty-three years old when he went into partnership with a man identified as J. Bailey and put a notice in the Delaware *Gazette* advertising that their circus would appear in Wilmington on November 22, 1825. He called it "Pavilion Circus," which would have meant to his readers a sailcloth tent, especially a large one, that rose to a peak above. (In the 1850s "pavilion" began to designate wooden-walled structures with canvas roofs.) In that tent, he would give "Equestrian Exhibitions." Of course, late November wasn't the ideal time for a circus in an unheated tent, so he added:

"If the weather should prove favorable there will be a performance tomorrow evening; otherwise, this performance will be the last."

In 1826, the year after J. Purdy Brown put up the first Big Top, Aaron Turner and Nathan Howes, now partners, pitched a round tent, ninety feet in diameter, over their ring. On a windy day, the tent sounded like a windjammer under full sail. But circuses no longer needed to cancel their shows when it rained. J. Purdy Brown died in Mobile, Alabama, in 1834, when he was only a few years over thirty. Howes, who lived on into the golden age of the circus in the 1870s, long got the credit, with Turner, for the origin of the circus Big Top.

Portable tents provided the mobility that first distinguished the American circus from the amphitheater circuses of the Old World. And when European circuses did begin to show under canvas, their tents were designed with the four center poles forming a square to maintain the one-ring design while expanding the area for the audience. But the American Big Top put up its tent poles in a single-file line as the American circus expanded to two, and then three, rings, enlarging the area for performers as well as the audience.

Pat Valdo, a clown in 1910, became John Ringling's performance director. (Ringling Museum)

———

European and American circuses have both thrived on superstars performing superfeats. In the late 1820s, more than a quarter of a century after the death of John Bill Ricketts, the circus in America finally got two of the kind of stars who have given it needed boosts throughout its long history. Isaac A. Van Amburgh, "The Lion King," was the first of them. The second was the equestrian called "The North Star."

Like most great riders, Levi J. North was small, only five feet six, but so proportioned that he looked his best on the back of a horse. Born in 1814 in Newton, Long Island, he began as an apprentice to Isaac Quick, but quickly became a rider. Just twelve years old, he made his debut in 1826, appearing at the Military Garden in Brooklyn with the Washington Circus, a partnership of Quick, Jeremiah P. Fogg, and Abraham H. Mead, all (not surprisingly) of Westchester County, New York. Before long, North's dark-skinned, light-haired good looks and consummate grace on horseback had made him the leading principal rider in the United States, and the circus had its first superstar rider since Ricketts.

In fact, using the word *star* to mean a person distinguished in his field may have originated with North. "The North Star brightens the ring," one newspaper put it, and so it was for forty years, either in his own circus or those of others. When, in 1866, at the age of fifty-two, North rode through his farewell season with Lent's New York Circus, he was still a star. But it was in 1839 that he had found his superfeat. In that year, he turned a full feet-to-feet somersault on the back of a running horse—the first time the feat had ever been performed. "The North Star" was now a superstar.

As for Van Amburgh, his biographer, Ferguson, wrote with fine nineteenth-century effusion that his "fame spread through civilization and is now contemporaneous and extensive with the Universe itself." Van Amburgh made his London debut at Astley's on August 27, 1838, and was said to have earned £300 a week, a fortune in those days. Queen Victoria went to see him six times when he performed at Drury Lane; he had his portrait painted by Landseer; and the portrait was exhibited in the Royal Academy—all extraordinary honors at that time.

As the 1830s came to a close, others tried to emulate Van Amburgh—but not always successfully. The editor of the *Age* for August 26, 1838, noted that "there have already been several cases in which lions have snapped off the heads of persons persisting in this sort of foolish experiment."

But Isaac A. Van Amburgh was one of the few early lion tamers to die in bed. When he suffered a fatal heart attack in Philadelphia on November 29, 1865, at the age of sixty-four, he was a wealthy man, and his fame survived him. Hyatt Frost, a leading showman who began managing Van Amburgh's show in 1846, continued to use the Van Amburgh name. And Van Amburgh himself lived to hear his superfeat celebrated in a popular song called "The Menagerie":

> *He sticks his head in the lion's mouth*
> *And holds it there a while;*
> *And when he takes it out again,*
> *He greets you with a smile.*

The status that the circus had attained by the end of the 1840s is evident in a New York newspaper's report from a rural correspondent on the Grand Showman's Ball of 1849. It was the third annual affair held at the Elephant Hotel to celebrate the anniversary of the birth of George Washington, first in war, first in peace, and first among American circus fans.

Somers, N.Y., Feb. 23rd, 1849
The Grand Showman's Ball—Brilliant Fete at the Elephant Hotel—Grand Assemblage of the Westchester Upper Crust—Wealthy Bachelors—Rustic Beauties—Three Hundred Couples at the Ball—A Twelve Hour Banquet: Five Millions Represented in a Country Dance—The Rival Belles—Magnificent Carousal Below Stairs.

Westchester, which may be truly styled the empire county, has been agitated to its very centre for more than a fortnight past, in consequence of the stupendous arrangements for the annual celebration of Washington's Natal day, at the Elephant Tavern. . . .

The principal masculine personages who figured at the ball were the proprietors of menageries and circus companies with their immediate dependents and associates, most of whom (and I say it more in sorrow than in anger) are hopeless bachelors of the deplorable age of forty-five and upwards who although rich as grand Turks set more value upon a trained horse or elephant than the attractions of lovely women.

It may convey to you some idea of the wealth of this County when I state to you, as a fact within my own knowledge, that in a country dance at one time on the floor there were individuals engaged whose aggregate wealth amounted to upwards of five millions of dollars and the foundations of whose fortunes were laid in the exhibition of wild animals through the U.S. . . .

The Grand Showman's Ball was the high tide of the Flatfoots. Among those whose fortunes were thus laid was stately, plump Lewis B. Lent, who was taking a year's leave in California in that year of the Gold Rush but had left instructions that he was to be listed as a host at the syndicate's annual demonstration of its strength and security. During 1846, 1847, and 1848, "Lew" Lent had assisted the syndicate in simultaneously managing Lent & Co.'s American Circus and June, Titus & Angevine's Menagerie and Circus. Levi J. North would end his career riding for Lent. Isaac A. Van Amburgh, who had first appeared as a feature of Flatfoot shows, would have his own circus and menagerie from 1846, but it would be managed by Hyatt Frost of the Flatfoots. From the 1830s until the early 1850s, the Flatfoots firmly controlled the circus scene in the eastern United States and could make or break other circuses.

What happened to the Flatfoots in the end? Hackaliah Bailey, whose promotion of Old Bet had inspired their activities in the first place, had a nephew, George F. Bailey, who married the daughter of Aaron Turner and who became identified with a hippopotamus the way his uncle had been famous for his elephant. As a young man, Bailey convinced his father-in-law that there was more profit in buying his own menagerie animals than in renting them from the Flatfoots. Bailey was right, and when he inherited the profitable Aaron Turner Circus in the 1850s, he changed the name to the George F. Bailey Circus and kept it independent of the Flatfoots for about ten years; then he became a Flatfoot himself. The Flatfoots and everybody else were impressed with George Bailey, who designed and built the circus's first hippo wagon—in effect, a traveling water tank.

The George F. Bailey Circus was the final operation of the Flatfoots. After 1863, the syndicate members concentrated all their efforts on it and operated the show under Bailey's name until they acquired the P. T. Barnum show in 1875. Barnum's earlier circus associates had left him, and he was making a mess out of trying to run the show alone. With the Flatfoots managing it, the Barnum show quickly became a moneymaker again; then they sold it, in 1880, to James Hutchinson and James Bailey (the Bailey in Barnum & Bailey). The sale ended the spectacular career of the syndicate of upper Westchester circus owners. George F. Bailey, the last of the Flatfoots, died in 1903 at the age of eighty-five.

will be introduced by their keeper, and go through many sagacious performances.

The following are some of the Animals in this collection :

African Lion and Lioness,	Grizzly Bear,	Alpacca Kangaroo,
Numidian Lion,	One White Polar Bear,	Rocky Mountain Bear,
Asiatic Lioness,	Spotted Hyena,	Jackall from South Africa,
Brazilian Tiger,	One California Lioness,	Kangaroo from N. Holland,
Hunting Leopard,	Poonah Bear,	A Colony of Apes, Monkeys,

Babboons, Parrots, Cranes, Owls, &c., forming what is termed a **HAPPY FAMILY**.

During the Exhibition, the visitor will have an opportunity of beholding the Real, Genuine, Original, GENERAL

Gen. Tom Thumb

The celebrated and world-renowned Man in Miniature, who is 22 years of age, weighs only 15 Pounds, and is but 28 Inches high.

EQUESTRIAN ENTERTAINMENT

Separate and Distinct from the Zoological & Tom Thumb Exhibitions.

Are the following Brilliant CIRCUS PERFORMANCES, to which the visitors of the two former, all those who choose, may attend without additional charge. The Circus Troupe, it will be seen, contains some of the most prominent Riders, Vaulters, Gymnastic and Comic Talent in the country, and the entertainments are NOVEL, DIVERSIFIED AND BRILLIANT, a   Magnificent Band of Music.

DISPLAY·3

Barnum!

And now, ladies and gentlemen, we direct your attention to the smallest human being ever born, General Tom Thumb. All other midgets are veritable giants beside him. A mature and perfect man in all respects save that of size. Weighing but half a dozen pounds, a high hat entirely covers him. In very truth, Nature's weakest effort. Hands no bigger than shilling pieces; fingers no longer than interrogation points; arms as small as cigarettes; legs the thickness of lead pencils; feet the size of postage stamps; head smaller than an orange. An animated human toy—the great and only—General Tom Thumb.

That was the spiel that P. T. Barnum personally wrote for the barker who introduced Tom Thumb. "Uncle Bob" Sherwood, one of Barnum's clowns, has pointed out that Barnum usually allowed his barkers to make up their own ballyhoo. But Tom Thumb, in all respects, was a separate case.

Sherwood said of Phineas Taylor Barnum that "He was a wonder at knowing what would appeal to the people and how to get their attention," and it was this genius that made the circus in America what Barnum called it: "The Greatest Show on Earth."

That superlative meant to Barnum not only the best of everything the circus had exhibited before him—horses and clowns and menageries—but also the exhibition of people and animals who were mysterious deviations from nature's usual course. It has been said that Barnum introduced the freak show to the circus, and that is true; but what interested Barnum about freaks was not that they were deformed but that they were unique. His first

TOM THUMB. *This advertisement from the* New York Herald *for August 15, 1855, shows Barnum's famous midget appearing before Queen Victoria and her son, the Prince of Wales, in 1844. Undoubtedly the most popular of all the rare and exotic people who have appeared with any circus, his real name was Charles S. Stratton, and he made his debut at Barnum's American Museum when he was five years old and twenty-five inches tall. (Circus World Museum, Baraboo, Wisconsin)*

reaction to Tom Thumb was that he was "perfectly formed" though uniquely small. Barnum visited Jumbo, the largest elephant in the world, many times in the London Zoological Gardens, observing the fascination he held for multitudes, and once he rode high up in a howdah on Jumbo's broad back. Jumbo filled him with wonder, so Barnum had to have him. He worked for the sense of wonder that is innate in human beings—which is why, in the end, he summed up the appeal of the circus by saying, "As long as there's babies there'll be circuses."

Some of his most famous attractions—Joice Heth, billed as "George Washington's nurse," and "The Feejee Mermaid," for instance—were humbugs; yet many more were the real thing. Not knowing whether Barnum was going to astonish or humbug you was part of his attraction. And most people seemed to enjoy being humbugged occasionally; perhaps because they sensed the good-humored acquisitiveness and simplicity of heart with which he established himself as the most celebrated showman in the history of the world. Barnum invented the American version of the circus: the *three-ring circus*, to which you wanted to return again and again because it always gave you more than you could take in. This is, when you think of it, the principle behind Walt Disney's theme parks. And if some things in Barnum's circuses and Disney's parks were real, and others were not, and the line was not sharply drawn, well, wasn't that actually like real life, in which appearances are sometimes deceiving—but not always?

Pool and Ricketts had given America a circus that combined performing horses and riders with clowns; Crowninshield and Hackaliah Bailey had added the elephant; the Flatfoots had realized how much all people wanted to see rare and exotic animals; and Isaac A. Van Amburgh had brought jungle animals into the

acts. But P. T. Barnum knew how much people wanted to see the rare and exotic in their own species as well as others, and on that observation he built his circuses.

In recent years, articles in newspapers, magazines, and encyclopedias have fostered the misconception that Barnum did not become a circus showman until he was past sixty; in fact, he was connected with the circus, in one capacity or another, most of his life.

Phineas Taylor Barnum was born July 5, 1810, in Bethel, Connecticut, not twenty miles from the part of New York state that was becoming famous as the cradle of the circus, and at the very time when Hackaliah Bailey and his associates were showing Old Bet in that area and beyond. His grandfather, Ephraim Barnum, had been a captain in the Revolutionary War; his father, Philo Barnum, was "a tailor, a farmer, and sometimes a tavern keeper, but didn't do very well at any of them." As a child, Barnum said later, "I was very acquisitive . . . a small peddler of molasses candy (of home make), ginger-bread, cookies and cherry rum, and I generally found myself a dollar or two richer at the end of a holiday than I was at the beginning." However, when Barnum's father saw that his son had money of his own, he "kindly permitted me to purchase my own clothing, which somewhat reduced my little store."

But Barnum had already seen the value of cookies and candy in a meat-and-potatoes world. "This is a trading world," he wrote, "and men, women and children who cannot live on gravity alone, need something to satisfy their gayer, lighter moods and hours, and he who ministers to this want is in a business established by the Author of our nature."

When Barnum was fifteen his father died, and the support of his mother and four younger brothers and sisters fell largely on his shoulders. Phineas had to buy on credit the shoes he wore to his father's funeral, but he was soon making money as a clerk in a store in Grassy Plain, a mile northwest of Bethel. The store sold or bartered groceries, hardware, and dry goods, and his bosses soon sized him up as a natural Yankee trader. And it was in Bethel, when he was sixteen, that Barnum saw what he wanted in the way of a wife: an eighteen-year-old "tailoress" named Charity Hallett.

In the fall of 1826, Barnum went to Brooklyn to clerk in a store. His maternal grandfather, Phineas Taylor, missed him, and wrote to offer half of his carriage house on Main Street rent free if his young namesake would come back from New York and establish some kind of business in Bethel. In February 1828, Barnum returned to open a retail fruit and confectionery store, which also sold oysters and ale.

Oysters and ale appealed to the kind of man who liked to hang around the shops on America's Main streets. Among these was none other than Hackaliah Bailey, and Barnum listened with great interest to his tales of Old Bet and their travels. For Barnum, Bailey was the showman as hero. "Hack," as Barnum called him, had started out with an elephant and ended up with the Elephant Hotel, a small fortune, and a locally famous name. "My store had much to do in giving shape to my future character as well as career . . ." wrote Barnum.

During the five years that Barnum was a storekeeper in Bethel, the countryside rang with talk of the circus doings of the Somers crowd just across the state line. In 1829, when he was nineteen and she was twenty-one, Barnum married "Chairy" Hallett. He wrote years later, "if I had waited twenty years longer I could not have found another woman so well suited to my disposition and so admirable and valuable in every character as a wife, a mother, and a friend."

By the time he was twenty-one, he was pub-lisher of a Danbury, Connecticut, weekly newspaper, *Herald of Freedom*. As publisher, he was arrested three times for libel and found out that he rather enjoyed notoriety. In the third case, a criminal prosecution was brought against him for writing that a Bethel man, prominent in the church, had "been guilty of taking usury of an orphan boy." Barnum meant *extortion*; the mistake cost him a fine of one hundred dollars and sixty days in the Danbury jail. He continued to edit his paper from his cell.

When he got out of jail, there was a parade, and reading the account of it in the *Herald of Freedom* for December 12, 1832, one sees that it was the forerunner of Barnum's famous circus parades: "P. T. Barnum and the band of musicians took their seats in a coach drawn by six horses, which had been prepared for the occasion. The coach was preceded by forty horsemen, and a marshal, bearing the national

Chester, a Nile hippo in the Ringling Bros. and Barnum & Bailey Menagerie, in 1948. (Ringling Museum)

standard. Immediately in the rear of the coach [were] . . . the Committee of Arrangements and sixty carriages of citizens, which joined in escorting the editor to his house in Bethel."

Cannon roared when the parade commenced its march, there were cheering crowds along the route, and the band played all the three miles to his house. Their last selection was "Home, Sweet Home."

Two years later, the circus of June, Titus, and Angevine, out of nearby Somers, New York, spoke proudly of having a circus parade with "an omnibus for the sole purpose of carrying the band and pulled by four beautiful bay horses"—but Barnum had done better than that just getting out of jail.

By 1834, Barnum had decided that "ordinary trade was too slow for me." He sold his newspaper to his brother-in-law and his general store to two friends, and took his wife and their infant daughter, Caroline, to New York "to seek my fortune." For another year he floundered, going from venture to venture; and then he found his vocation. He successfully presented Joice Heth, a wizened black woman, as the 161-year-old nurse to America's greatest hero, General George Washington. The press reported nearly everything she said and did, and the public read it all with vast amusement. Caught smoking a pipe by *Evening Star* reporter Grant Thorburn, she was asked how long she had had the habit. "One hundred and twenty years," she replied. Immediately, an editorial praised her candor; most women, it pointed out, are "unwilling to tell their age." So many people wanted to see someone who had been close to Washington and/or was the oldest person on earth that Joice Heth grossed $1,500 a month. Barnum took her on tour to Providence, and then to Concert Hall in Boston. And he rashly promised a famous surgeon, Dr. David L. Rogers, that he could perform an autopsy on her when she died. Less than two years later, in February of 1836, Joice Heth

was dead, and Barnum was about to learn the lesson of his life.

Barnum attended the autopsy; so did Richard Adams Locke, a writer admired by Edgar Allan Poe, who had been assigned to the story by the *New York Sun.*

The next day, the *Sun* carried an editorial by Locke: "DISSECTION OF JOICE HETH—PREVIOUS HUMBUG EXPOSED." It contained a detailed account of the postmortem, and reported Dr. Rogers's conviction that Joice Heth could not have been more than seventy-five or eighty years old.

In the next few weeks, Barnum got an education in the ways of press and public. Much indignation was directed at him, but it served only to make him more famous. Then the *New York Herald* confused the public when it tried to top the *Sun* by reporting: "ANOTHER HOAX! *Joice Heth is not dead."*

By the time the controversy died down, the public was sure of only one thing: Barnum had amused them. Barnum would insist to the end of his life that *he* had been humbugged, too, by the man who had sold him, for $1,000, Joice Heth and a document with which Washington's father allegedly bought a slave nurse for his son for "thirty-three pounds lawful money of Virginia." And in the controversy, Barnum found his true vocation: "to cater to that insatiate want of human nature—the love of amusement."

The Age of Showmanship had begun.

Joice Heth's death left Barnum with one other client, an Italian named Signor Vivalla who juggled, balanced crockery, and walked on stilts. He quickly got Vivalla and himself jobs with the circus. "In April, 1836, I connected myself with Aaron Turner's travelling circus company as ticket-seller, secretary and treasurer, at thirty dollars a month and one-fifth of the entire profits, while Vivalla was to receive a salary of fifty dollars," Barnum wrote. "As I was already paying him eighty dollars a month, our joint salaries reimbursed me and left me the chance of twenty per cent of the net receipts."

Turner, an uneducated English immigrant who had been a shoemaker in Danbury, Connecticut, responded to the circus craze of the 1820s by getting up a small show with trained horses, acrobats, and a clown. In 1827, in partnership with Nathan Howes, he had toured with the second Big Top in history. Now he was going to be associated with P. T. Barnum in Barnum's first tour as a circus showman.

"We began our performances at West Springfield, April 28th," Barnum wrote, "and as our expected band of music had not arrived from Providence, I made a prefatory speech announcing our disappointment, and our intention to please our patrons, nevertheless. The two Turner boys [Napoleon B. and Timothy V. Turner], sons of the proprietor, rode finely. Joe Pentland, one of the wittiest, best, and most original of clowns, with Vivalla's tricks and other performances in the ring, more than made up for the lack of music. In a day or two our band arrived and our 'houses' improved."

Like Van Amburgh before him, Barnum regularly suffered puritanical criticism. Always a churchgoer, he attended services at Lenox, Massachusetts, only to hear the preacher denounce "our circus and all connected with it as immoral." After the closing hymn, Barnum walked up the pulpit stairs and handed the preacher a written request that he be allowed to reply to the charge of immorality. He signed it "P. T. Barnum connected with the circus, June 5, 1836." When the minister ignored the note, Barnum, a good orator with a powerful voice, waited until after the benediction and then simply gave his own sermon defending the circus. "The affair created considerable excitement," Barnum later reported, "and some of the members of the church apologized to me for their clergyman's ill-behavior." En-

couraged by his success, Barnum gave his alternative sermon at least once more on the tour, at a church in Port Deposit, on the lower Susquehanna.

Throughout his most successful years, Barnum was a great believer in notoriety for fun and profit. The street parade that accompanied his release from jail had demonstrated that notoriety could be fun. Aaron Turner taught him how profitable it could be—though the experience was no fun for Barnum.

On a Sunday morning in Annapolis, Maryland, Turner was having refreshments in the crowded hotel barroom when Barnum, dressed in his Sabbath best, passed through on his way outside. Suddenly, Turner pointed to him and said to the hotel loungers: "I think it's very singular that you permit that rascal to march your streets in open day. It wouldn't be allowed in Rhode Island, and I suppose that is the reason the black-coated scoundrel has come down this way."

"Why, who is he?" asked half a dozen men.

"Don't you know?" said Turner. "Why, that is the Rev. E. K. Avery, the murderer of Miss Cornell!"

The Avery case was the newspaper scandal of the day. Three years earlier, Sarah Cornell, a thirty-year-old factory worker, had been found hanging in a farmyard near Tiverton, Rhode Island, apparently murdered. In her belongings investigators found a note that cast suspicion on the Reverend Avery, a Methodist minister who lived nearby. In May 1833, Avery was put on trial for murder before the Supreme Judicial Court, the first trial of a clergyman for murder in the United States. He was acquitted by the court, but was so condemned by public opinion that he disappeared from Rhode Island. He would later turn up as a farmer in Ohio, but that didn't help Barnum now.

Barnum kept on walking, but out on the street, he soon found himself followed by a mob of about one hundred people.

"Let's tar and feather him!" one said; and others brought up a rail for him to straddle as they ran him out of town. Then someone else cried, "We'll show him how to *hang* poor factory girls."

Barnum pleaded for his life: "Gentlemen, I am not Avery; I despise that villain as much as you . . . my name is Barnum; I belong to the circus which has arrived here last night. . . . Old Turner, my partner, has hoaxed you with that ridiculous story."

To check Barnum's alibi, the lynch mob dragged him back to Turner, half tearing his coat from his back.

"The fact is," Turner told them, "my friend Barnum has a new suit of black clothes on and he looks so much like a priest that I thought he must be Avery."

Some of the crowd apologized to Barnum; some thought that they should lynch Turner or, at least, that Barnum should "get even with him."

Spluttering with rage, Barnum asked Turner what could have made him play such a dangerous trick on him.

"My dear Barnum, it was all for our good. Remember, all we need to ensure success is notoriety. You will see that this will be noised about town as a trick played by one of the circus managers upon the other, and our pavilion will be crammed to-morrow night."

Barnum never forgot the lesson. He later conceded that they had fine audiences while they remained at Annapolis, but he added, "it was a long time before I forgave Turner for his rascally 'joke.'" By October of 1836, Barnum had taken $1,200 as his share of the profits, left Turner, and organized his own traveling show. This consisted of Vivalla, musicians, and a black singer and dancer, all traveling by horse and wagon and performing in "a small canvas tent." Difficulties dogged him. At Camden, South Carolina, one of his musicians was jailed for six months for advising the black barber who was shaving him to run away to the Free States or to Canada.

By December, Aaron Turner had decided to disband his circus. Barnum met him in Columbia, South Carolina, hired Joe Pentland, the clown, acrobat, and magician, bought four horses and two wagons from Turner, and marched off to Georgia with a show he called "Barnum's Grand Scientific and Musical Theatre."

After performing in Alabama, Kentucky, and Tennessee, Barnum disbanded his circus at Nashville in May 1837. Vivalla left him to perform "on his own account for a while" before retiring to Cuba. Barnum went back to New York to spend a few weeks with his family, then returned west in July with a new show. "We were not successful," wrote Barnum. "One of our small company was incompetent; another was intemperate—both were dismissed; and our negro-singer was drowned in the river at Frankfort."

Perhaps the problem was that he didn't have a clown. After less than two months, he reengaged Joe Pentland, buying his horses and wagons.

Barnum was back in New York on April 23, 1841, after a not very profitable absence of eight months. "I resolved once more," he said later, "that I would never again be an itinerant showman."

"Show business," wrote Barnum about his first forays into circus life, "has as many grades of dignity as trade, which ranges all the way from the mammoth wholesale establishment down to the corner stand. The itinerant amusement business is at the bottom of the ladder. I had begun there, but I had no wish to stay there; in fact, I was thoroughly disgusted with the trade of a travelling showman, and although I felt that I could succeed in that line, yet I always regarded it, not as an end, but as a means to something better."

Barnum was writing advertisements for the

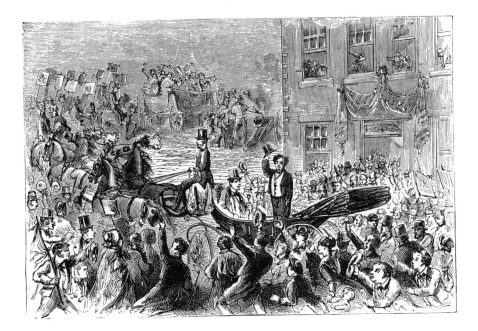

BARNUM'S DELIVERANCE FROM PRISON, *which could well have resulted in his lifelong love of parades:* "P. T. Barnum and the band of musicians took their seats in a coach drawn by six horses," *reported the* Herald of Freedom, *". . . preceded by forty horsemen, and a marshal bearing the national standard." In 1871, the first year of P. T. Barnum's Circus, Barnum would advertise "*THE GREAT STREET PAGEANT *with its Royal Golden Chariots, Made in London, Forty Feet High, Surmounted with Revolving Tableaux of Golden Elephants, Lions, and Tigers, Mingling with a gorgeously caparisoned retinue of living Elephants, Camels, Gnoos, and Zebras." In short, Barnum believed in traveling in style. (From Barnum's* Struggles and Triumphs, *1877 edition*)

BARNUM WATCHES JENNY LIND GET ACQUAINTED WITH HIS JUGGLER'S DOG. *While on tour in Albany, Barnum was so impressed by a juggling act that he engaged the Italian juggler, "Signor Antonio," for a one-year contract at $12 a week plus expenses.* "I did not know exactly where I should use my protégé, but I was certain that there was money in him." *The first thing Barnum did was to change Antonio's name to Vivalla, which sounded more exotic. He did the same thing again and again, as when he sold Hiram and Barney Davis of Long Island as "The Wild Men of Borneo." As "Zip, the What-is-it?" (William Jackson) said on his death bed:* "Well, we fooled 'em for a long time, didn't we?" (From Barnum's *Struggles and* Triumphs, *1877 edition*)

Bowery Theater at $4 a week when he "casually learned . . . that the collection of curiosities comprising Scudder's American Museum, at the corner of Broadway and Ann Street, was for sale"—for $15,000.

It was probably the word *curiosities* that held the magic for the man who understood the power of curiosity. Suddenly, Barnum's enormous energies were focused. At the age of thirty-one, he made up his mind to buy a museum.

"*You* buy the American Museum!" said a friend who knew the state of his finances. "What do you intend buying it with?"

"Brass," replied Barnum, "for silver and gold have I none."

Seemingly, Barnum made a sucker's deal. He went to Francis Olmstead, a retired merchant who owned the building that housed the museum. He asked Olmstead to purchase the collection in his own name, but "to give me a writing securing it to me provided I made the payments punctually, including the rent of the building; to allow me twelve dollars and a half a week on which to support my family; and if at any time I failed to meet the instalment due, I would vacate the premises and forfeit all that might have been paid to that date."

"Who are your references?" asked Olmstead.

"Any man in my line," said Barnum, and the eight names he gave showed what he thought his line was. He named two theater owners, a journalist, and a list that sounded like the history of the circus in America up to 1841: "Messrs. Welch, June, Titus, Turner, Angevine, or other circus or menagerie proprietors. . . ."

The financial difficulties that followed would have driven a lesser man to give up in despair; but Barnum knew what he was doing. He had studied the business maneuvers of the Zoological Institute and was determined to avoid what he saw as the syndicate's mistakes. "The American Museum," he was later to write, "was the ladder by which I rose to fortune."

Barnum opened his American Museum on the morning of New Year's Day, 1842. He had watched the circus develop from what was essentially a horse show with a clown into a show that combined equestrian and clown acts, elephants and other exotic animals, and thrilling demonstrations of the skills of acrobats. Now Barnum was going to popularize an element that he would eventually add to the scope of the circus: rare and exotic people, unkindly called freaks.

Consider what America was like in the 1840s. Human beings here probably had as much curiosity about the mysteries and wonders of the wide world as anyone anywhere, but there wasn't much to satisfy that curiosity. For the common people in the cities there were some theaters, but there was no zoo, no aquarium, no museum of natural history. Mrs. Frances Trollope, the mother of novelist Anthony Trollope and herself a prolific author, was living in Cincinnati at this time and lamented: "I never saw a people who appeared to live so much without amusement as the Cincinnatians." Card games and billiards were against the law. Dances were rare; dinner parties or concerts almost unheard of. The lone theater in Cincinnati drew a few men. "Ladies," wrote Mrs. Trollope, "are rarely seen there, and by far the larger proportion of females deem it an offence against religion to witness the presentation of a play."

Barnum realized that he could fill his museum with live freaks, dramatic theatricals, flower shows, beauty competitions, and other sensational attractions and still have it regarded as an educational, and therefore perfectly moral, institution, because it was, after all, a museum. "It was only necessary to properly present the museum's merits to the public, to make it the most attractive and popular place of resort and entertainment in the United States," he wrote. And he was right. The museum's combination of information, amusement, self-improvement, titillation, and respectability perfectly suited the times. What one saw there were the kinds of attractions people would be seeing in the circus before Barnum was through.

Barnum's first successful exhibit was the "Feejee Mermaid," which had a seemingly human head topping the finned body of a fish. Like Joice Heth, the Feejee Mermaid was a fake: the embalmed head of a monkey joined with a fish tail. "To awaken curiosity to see and examine the specimen," said Barnum, "I envoked the potent power of printer's ink." He was the first master of the media, and excused his misuse of that power in the service of a hoax by saying, "I used it mainly to advertize the regular business of the Museum, and this effective indirect advertising is the only feature I can commend, in a special show of which, I confess, I am not proud."

He should, in fact, have been deeply ashamed, for he was introducing an element into the circus that would do it great harm. Barnum was presenting illusion as reality, thus beginning the evolution from reality to image that would accelerate as the world became more technological. "We risk being the first people in history," wrote the social historian Daniel J. Boorstin in 1962, "to have made their illusions so vivid, so persuasive, so realistic, that they can live in them." Yet today, there is much more reality in the circus, which is live and in person, than in television, films, and radio, where a false image can so much more easily be manufactured.

Among the other attractions at the museum was "The Great Model of Niagara Falls, With Real Water!" Many honeymooners who couldn't afford a trip to the real falls came to Barnum's museum. However, Barnum's Niagara was a miniature model only eighteen inches high, as the honeymooners were usually dismayed to discover. But, said Barnum, "they had the whole Museum to fall back upon for 25 cents, and no fault was found."

To his credit, Barnum preferred exhibits that were not fakes or disappointments, and he soon found some famous ones. Among the genuine curiosities were Chang and Eng, Siamese twins who were connected by a ligament below their breastbones; they sometimes quarreled and went for long periods without speaking to each other. Later there was Colonel Routh Goshen, advertised as an Arab giant born in Jerusalem, who was eight feet two inches in height and weighed five hundred and ninety pounds. W. C. Coup, later Barnum's partner, claims in his memoirs that Goshen "was not an Arabian, but a negro picked up by 'Yank Robinson' in Kentucky." Whatever his origins, he *was* big. This wasn't the movies: you didn't stand him on a box like Alan Ladd and make him seem as tall as Gary Cooper.

Barnum was attracted to the most and least of anything, and he was particularly attracted to giants and midgets—and contrasts. Next to Colonel Goshen he displayed a Belgian giant, only seven feet eight but as slender as the Colonel was stocky. Barnum recounted that the two were bitter rivals who decided one day to settle their animosity with club and sword. A dozen employees kept them from attacking each other until Barnum could be summoned from his downstairs office.

"Look here!" he shouted up at them. "This is all right; if you want to fight each other, maiming and perhaps killing one another, that is your affair; but my interest lies here—you are both under engagement to me, and if this duel is to come off, I and the public have a right to participate. It must be duly advertised and take place on the stage."

Goshen and the Belgian, Bihin, reacted to Barnum's singleminded devotion to showmanship as people usually reacted to his various humbugs: they were amused. The two giants started to laugh. Barnum said it was the beginning of their friendship.

At Barnum's museum you could have a good time all day long, for only a quarter. The doors opened at sunrise for country boys, such as Barnum had been, who were used to getting up before dawn, and a continuous program lasted until ten o'clock at night. For years it was New York's most popular tourist attraction. Many families brought their lunches and spent the whole day. On St. Patrick's Day, 1843, so many Irish families visited that the museum was filled by noon and the sale of tickets had to be stopped. The line of those waiting outside for someone to leave got longer and longer, but no one left. "Sure, an I'm not going out at all, at all," a typical satisfied customer told Barnum, "nor the children aither, for we've brought our dinners and we are going to stay all day."

Barnum's solution is now legendary. He had a sign painter take a piece of canvas four feet square and letter on it: TO THE EGRESS.

"The Aigress," said many an Irishman. "Sure that's an animal we haven't seen."

Thus did many that day enrich their vocabularies by learning that *egress* means "exit." And thus did Barnum begin again to accommodate those who had long been waiting with their money at the Broadway entrance.

The egress story has been told again and again. But it is seldom reported that when Barnum originally told it in his autobiography, it was as a joke on the ignorant Irish immigrants. As a descendant of two of those refugees from the potato famine, I don't mind Barnum's joke. As Barnum always said, "people like to be humbugged."

"I confess that I liked the Museum mainly for the opportunities it afforded for rapidly making money," Barnum was to write. But that doesn't quite say it all. Barnum was motivated by money, to be sure; he had very much the merchant mentality, even if his merchandise was amusement. But he was also satisfying his own sense of wonder and his own desire to know and understand, and it was these cravings that made first his museum, and then his circus, great.

Barnum's museum was where many immigrants first saw American Indians reenact the ceremonies of their cultures; saw puppet and marionette theater in all its diversity, from English Punch and Judy to Italian *fantoccini*; saw miniature models of Paris, Jerusalem, and Dublin that gave them a vision of what great cities could be; saw, at close range, rare and exotic living creatures such as the anaconda, the orangutan, the alligator; saw a waxworks (which Barnum, a lifelong teetotaler, devoted to the evils of drink); developed their national identity at an art gallery featuring paintings of famous Americans; enjoyed exhibitions of glassblowing, singing, dancing, and instrumental music. It contained, in fact, many of the things we see at Disneyland, Walt Disney World, and EPCOT today.

Like Disney, who made his attractions look like castles, forts, and mountains, Barnum used the museum building itself as an advertisement. He started by draping it with bright banners; then he lit it up at night, which was unheard of in New York at that time; eventually he had huge representations of exotic creatures painted on the outside.

What we now call media events were probably originated by Barnum at his museum. He held baby shows and gave prizes to customers whose babies were the most anything: the prettiest, the tallest, the fattest. Barnum realized, as many promoters and businessmen did not, that newspapers catering to mass audiences needed to entertain as well as inform, and he was not surprised when the media responded to these events with free publicity. He followed up with contests for superlative kinds of flowers, birds, dogs, even poultry. From all this would spring, in 1881, his circus rival Adam Forepaugh's contribution to American culture: the beauty contest.

Barnum's greatest contributions to the human capacity for delight and wonder were two attractions in the superlative degree: Tom Thumb, the smallest man, and Jumbo, the largest elephant.

The Tom Thumb saga began because Barnum was infinitely adaptable. The Hudson River was iced over and river traffic was suspended one day in November 1842. Barnum had intended to take a riverboat back to New York City from a business trip to Albany, but instead he caught the old Housatonic Railroad for the first leg of his journey, and stopped off in Bridgeport to see his half brother, Philo.

Phineas T., whose memory for prodigies was prodigious, recalled that someone had once told him "of a remarkably small child in Bridgeport," and asked his brother if he knew who that might be. Practically anybody in Bridgeport would have known: a poor man named Sherwood Stratton had a five-year-old son who weighed no more than his little pet dog.

The next day Philo Barnum brought the boy to his brother. The child was twenty-five inches tall and weighed fifteen pounds; his foot was only three inches long. "The smallest child I ever saw that could walk alone," wrote Barnum afterward, "but he was a perfectly formed, bright-eyed little fellow, with light hair and ruddy cheeks and he enoyed the best of health." The little boy was bashful at first, but many have spoken of Barnum's cheery voice, kindly smile, and wonderfully magnetic personality, and soon the child was chirping that he was the son of Sherwood E. Stratton, and that his own name was Charles S. Stratton.

As a connoisseur of human curiosity, Barnum instantly felt the attraction of such a diminutive fellow human being. "After seeing him and talking to him," Barnum wrote, "I at once determined to secure his services from his parents and to exhibit him in public." Nevertheless, Barnum was initially cautious. The deal was for four weeks only, at three dollars per week, with Barnum paying all traveling and boarding charges for the boy and his mother.

Barnum referred to Charles privately as "my dwarf." This was an error, for Charles was a midget: a perfectly proportioned miniature human being. Not until 1886, three years after Stratton's death at the age of forty-five, and five years before Barnum's death at eighty, was the pituitary gland, located at the base of the skull, discovered to be responsible for "freaks of nature" such as Charles Stratton. A defective pituitary withheld growth hormones, and the result was a stunted individual. A dwarf, on the other hand, has a normal upper body, but his lower limbs are misshapen because of a malfunctioning thyroid.

Barnum's creation of Tom Thumb from the tiny clay of Charles Stratton is one of the earliest and still most outstanding examples of the image maker's art. One hundred and thirty-one years later, when Irvin Feld, president of Ringling Bros. and Barnum & Bailey, the continuation of Barnum's Greatest Show on Earth, sought to publicize the Hungarian midget, Michu, he simply said: "Seven inches shorter than Barnum's Tom Thumb"—and the image still leaped instantly into the public mind. (It should be noted, however, that Feld was using a little Barnumesque humbug. At thirty-three inches tall, Michu is indeed seven inches shorter than Tom Thumb—but Tom Thumb at the end of his life, when he'd grown fifteen inches beyond the twenty-five inches he was when Barnum started exhibiting him.)

The image that Barnum created for five-year-old Charles Stratton began with a new name. When Mrs. Stratton brought her little boy to New York on December 8, 1842, she was surprised to learn from handbills and posters that she was the mother of "General Tom Thumb, a dwarf of eleven years of age, just arrived from England."

Barnum changed Charles's nationality because "I had observed (and sometimes, as in the case of Vivalla, had taken advantage of) the American fancy for European exotics. . . ." He changed Charles's age because the public might wonder if a five-year-old would eventually grow to normal height, whereas an eleven-year-old only twenty-five inches tall was probably not destined to grow much. (By the age of twenty-three, Tom Thumb was ten inches taller. When he died, at forty-five, he was not only forty inches tall but he had blown up, on a diet of rich food and fine wines, to a portly seventy pounds. The name derived from the legend of King Arthur; Sir Tom Thumb was supposed to have been one of King Arthur's knights. A well-loved English poem described

> *His stature but an inch in height,*
> *Or quarter of a span;*
> *Then think you not this little knight*
> *Was prov'd a valiant man?*

According to nursery lore, Thumb dwelt in a tiny golden palace with a door one inch wide, rode in a coach drawn by six white mice, and was killed in a duel with a bumblebee. Sir Tom Thumb was the stuff of legend; so, hoped Barnum, would be General Tom Thumb. As a last touch, the contrast of the exalted military rank with the tiny child was deliciously droll, and not to be resisted.

None of it *was* resisted. Carefully coached by Barnum, Tom Thumb learned to perform a variety of roles that fit his image. In the uniform of a Revolutionary War soldier, waving a ten-inch sword and singing "Yankee Doodle Dandy" in his tiny voice, Tom Thumb performed a military drill. In flesh-colored tights, holding a bow and carrying a quiver of arrows, he was Cupid. As Little David from the Bible he staged a mock battle with *two* Goliaths, the giants of Barnum's American Museum, Colonel Goshen and Monsieur Bihin. Tom Thumb even played Napoleon—a pocket-sized portrayal of the Little Corporal that would soon make him the talk of London and Paris.

Even at that early date, Barnum had a proper appreciation of the power of the press, and he had the "General" perform for New York editors. At one editor's house, Thumb leaped up onto the dinner table, danced among the plates and goblets, and jumped over the roast. The editors returned the favor by serving up loads of free publicity. Tom Thumb was soon a favorite of the public. At the end of his four weeks' trial, the child received a one-year contract at $7 a week, plus a $50 bonus at the end of the engagement. Long before the year was up, Barnum had voluntarily raised his salary to $25 a week. His profits from the American Museum, once Tom Thumb became its star, were grand enough for Barnum to own the museum free and clear and to buy out his only rival within the first two years.

In 1844, Tom Thumb signed a third contract with P. T. Barnum, giving the midget $50 a week and expenses, and Barnum the right to exhibit him in Europe. It was while they were in England that the world was able to see what a masterpiece of image making Barnum had wrought. The British were accustomed to midgets, giants, and dwarfs as attractions, and when Barnum arrived he was offered $10 a week to exhibit Tom Thumb by the proprietor of a small waxworks show, who knew the going rate for such talent. Since Barnum was now paying the General $50 a week, he was understandably appalled. The next evening, Barnum asked an intelligent, wealthy, and respectable English couple who saw and were impressed by Tom

Thumb what *they* would advise him to charge for admission. The wife said tuppence; the husband said that a single penny was "the usual price for seeing giants and dwarfs in England."

"Never shall the price be less than one shilling sterling," answered Barnum bravely, "and some of the nobility and gentry of England will yet pay gold to see General Tom Thumb."

The great service that Queen Victoria did the circus in America has never, I think, been sufficiently recognized. Van Amburgh, "The Lion King," was one of America's most celebrated figures even before he made his English debut in 1838. But after 1839, when the young Queen paid no less than six visits to Drury Lane in one month's time for the express purpose of seeing him, even staying after the performance one evening to watch him feed the lions, Van Amburgh became a figure that even the American upper crust could admit to appreciating.

Barnum knew this, and he intended to use his letter of recommendation to the American ambassador from Horace Greeley, the prestigious editor of the *New York Herald Tribune*, to see if he could show Tom Thumb at Buckingham Palace. Unfortunately, he was told, the royal family was in mourning for the death of Prince Albert's father "and would not permit the approach of any entertainments."

So Barnum relied on contrived scarcity to make people curious about the midget he had brought from America. He successfully exhibited the General at a first-rate London theater for just three nights—then declined to continue the engagement. Instead, he rented a mansion previously occupied by a lord, hired liveried servants, and sent out invitations to nobility and editors, to call on his "ward." "Most of them called, and were highly grati-

fied," said Barnum; but a surer sign that his master plan was working came when "the word of approval was indeed so passed around in high circles, that uninvited parties drove to my door in crested carriages, and were not admitted."

However, Barnum was "always particular to send an invitation immediately to such as had not been admitted"—and they were not too proud to come back.

After a few nights of this, the Baroness Rothschild, wife of the richest banker in the world, sent her carriage for Barnum and Thumb, and he knew they had arrived. He made sure that the press knew it too.

Now it was time to put Tom Thumb on public display at the Egyptian Hall in Piccadilly, and soon there was a command from Her Majesty Queen Victoria to appear at Buckingham Palace. Queen Victoria also requested that the six-year-old General "appear before her, as he would appear anywhere else, without any training in the use of the titles of royalty," as she desired "to see him act naturally and without restraint."

Barnum, too, acted naturally. He hung a sign on the door of the Egyptian Hall:

CLOSED THIS EVENING, GENERAL TOM THUMB BEING AT BUCKINGHAM PALACE BY COMMAND OF HER MAJESTY

Queen Victoria was amused—and completely charmed—by General Tom Thumb. He sang, danced, did his imitations for her, and boldly told her that he wanted to see the Prince of Wales. The Queen told him that the three-year-old prince was taking his nap, but she promised that they would meet on some future occasion. And so it was, the next time Her Majesty asked to see Tom Thumb.

"General," said the Queen, "this is the Prince of Wales."

BARNUM TRAINING TOM THUMB. *In 1842, Barnum hired Charles S. Stratton for four weeks only. The midget and his mother arrived at Barnum's house on Thanksgiving Day. Barnum spent the next three weeks teaching the child jokes and make-believe roles day and night. Barnum said that little Stratton learned quickly because of his love for the ludicrous. When he was ready to make his debut, Barnum took him on a tour of the newspaper offices, and asserted that the boy had "just arrived from England" (Barnum always maintained that Americans had a "disgraceful preference for foreigners"). When he invaded the home of James Gordon Bennett, editor of the* New York Herald, *who happened to be eating dinner, Tom hopped over the roast and danced between the knives and forks like a Scot doing a sword dance. (From Barnum's* Struggles and Triumphs, *1877 edition)*

THE GREAT DUKE AND THE LITTLE GENERAL. *Of the many roles played by Tom Thumb during his four-year tour of England, France, Spain, and Belgium, he was most popular as Napoleon. Pacing the floor as the French emperor in England, he was asked by the real Duke of Wellington what he was thinking about. Answered Tom Thumb, without smiling, "The loss of Waterloo." (From Barnum's* Struggles and Triumphs, *1877 edition)*

"How are you, Prince?" said the General, shaking him by the hand; and then, standing beside the future Edward VII, he said, "The Prince is taller than I am, but I feel as big as anybody," and strutted up and down the room proud as a peacock, while everybody present shouted with laughter.

Queen Victoria enjoyed the General, and the British public enjoyed reading about her enjoyment, and soon a Tom Thumb craze was sweeping England. Children played with Tom Thumb dolls and Tom Thumb cutouts and danced the Tom Thumb Polka. *Punch* called him "Pet of the Palace," and people loved to tell Tom Thumb stories. Barnum made sure that the press could supply them with plenty of stories to tell. Tom Thumb had fought off the Queen's pet poodle with a cane. Tom Thumb had done his Napoleon impersonation for a crowd that included the Duke of Wellington. Afterward, went the story, Tom Thumb was in a meditative mood, and Wellington asked what he was thinking about.

"I was thinking of the loss of the Battle of Waterloo," said the quick-witted six-year-old impersonator of Bonaparte to the general who had defeated him. The story spread through England and into France. Frenchmen wanted to see this General Tom Thumb that everyone was talking about, and Barnum was quick to oblige them.

Barnum's success in Paris was even greater than his success in London. "The French are exceedingly impressible," wrote Barnum, "and what in London is only excitement, in Paris becomes furor." His two shows a day at the Salle Musard were sold out two months in advance. "I was compelled," said Barnum, "to take a cab to carry my bag of silver home at night."

"Tom Pouce," as they called him, had no fewer than four audiences with the King and Queen of France. In his first visits, there was

one impersonation he tactfully left out. Commented the editor of the official *Journal des Débats*: "We will not mention a celebrated uniform which he wore in London, and which was amazingly successful with our oversea neighbors. The General Tom Thumb had too much good taste to take this costume to the Tuileries."

But Barnum said later that King Louis Philippe, quite aware of the "celebrated uniform," asked to see him in it and was rewarded with a secret performance of Tom Thumb impersonating the King's predecessor. In return for this favor, King Louis Philippe granted Barnum's request that Tom Thumb's blue-and-white carriage, eleven inches wide and twenty inches high, be permitted in the group reserved for royalty in the Longchamps Day parade.

———————

The crowds that welcomed General Tom Thumb home to America in February 1847 were larger than Barnum's museum had ever before accommodated; so in April, Barnum and Tom Thumb's parents toured all the large cities of the East and many New England towns with their tiny celebrity. In Washington, they were received at the White House by President and Mrs. Polk.

There was hardly an American now who didn't want to see Tom Thumb and Barnum, but Barnum wanted only to see his wife and children. In May of 1848, in Pittsburgh, Tom Thumb's father and Barnum agreed that Barnum should go home, where he had spent little enough time with his family for the past thirteen years.

So Barnum set about building, for himself and his family, the famous Iranistan, a palace combining Byzantine, Moorish, and Turkish architecture, whose spires and minarets appealed to his taste for the spectacular. He copied it mainly from the Brighton Pavilion, a fantastic building that was one of the homes of Queen Victoria's spendthrift uncle, George IV. Iranistan lasted from its housewarming on November 14, 1848, until a workman's pipe accidentally burned it to the ground on December 17, 1857; its architecture excited the wonder of such visitors as General George A. Custer and Mark Twain. But the importance of Iranistan to circus history is mainly this: it confirmed Barnum's impression, gained first from Hackaliah Bailey, that people are mighty curious about elephants, for Iranistan is remembered largely for the elephant that plowed its fields.

The circus, meanwhile, had finally become Barnum's instrument for making sure that the greatest number of people got to see his greatest attraction. In 1849, says Barnum, he "projected a great travelling museum and menagerie, and, as I had neither time nor inclination to manage such a concern, I induced Mr. Seth B. Howes, justly celebrated as a 'showman,' to join me, and take the sole charge. Mr. Sherwood E. Stratton, father of General Tom Thumb, was also admitted to partnership, the interest being in thirds."

Seth B. Howes, of course, was the younger brother of Nathan Howes, who toured with Old Bet in partnership with Hack Bailey, and he had been Aaron Turner's partner in a circus before Turner and Barnum became partners in 1836.

There is no doubt that Barnum was pressed for time. In 1849, he was managing not only his American Museum but a concert tour for Jenny Lind, "the Swedish Nightingale," the project that first made popular and very profitable the concert tour in America.

The first step of Barnum, Stratton, and Howes was to outfit an expedition to Ceylon for elephants. They sent one of the June family from North Salem, and in 1851, after a year's

time and many adventures, June and his associates came back with thirteen pachyderms, including a female and her calf, only six months old.

Jenny Lind was making her second visit to New York at the time and was staying in Irving House on Broadway. Barnum had ten of the elephants harnessed in pairs to a chariot and paraded up Broadway past the Swedish Nightingale's hotel. As Barnum had hoped, the elephants not only created a sensation on the streets but also drew further attention to his Nightingale.

Barnum's circus was advertised as taking place "with the presence and under the 'patronage' of general Tom Thumb." Added to Tom Thumb, the elephants, and a native who could handle them, the managers provided "a caravan of wild animals and many museum curiosities," and Barnum put the cost of the entire outfit, including horses, vans, carriages, tent, etc., at $109,000. The tent was typical Barnum: 110 feet long, a canvas mammoth compared to the typical little round top of the time. The outfit also preserved another Barnum trademark: its title did not contain the names of Howes or Stratton, only Barnum. It wasn't called a circus, either, as we see from the bill announcing its first appearance in Hartford, Connecticut, on June 1, 1851:

Grand Entrance of P. T. Barnum's Asiatic Caravan, Museum and Menagerie

The Cortege Comprises 110 Horses, 80 Men. A Young Calf Elephant Will Carry Upon His Back The Lilliputian General, Tom Thumb.

Six Beautiful Lionesses
Fresh from the Jungles

A BURMESE BULL FROM THE ISLAND OF JAVA!

General Tom Thumb Will Sing and Dance

Mr. Nellis, the Man Without Arms, Will Load and Fire a Pistol, and Do Other Feats With His Toes.

A Fine Military Band Will Perform Popular Airs As The Procession Enters the Town.

. . .

ADMISSION TWENTY-FIVE CENTS

In 1851, it was the circus that made it possible for people to see Tom Thumb, and the circus would ever after be the place to go to see strange and exotic people. This Barnum circus toured for four profitable years. Then Barnum sold his interest in the caravan except for one elephant, which he settled on a six-acre farm near Iranistan. Its keeper was dressed in Oriental attire, given a timetable for the New York and New Haven railroad, and instructed to go to work plowing Barnum's fields whenever that part of the countryside could be seen from the windows of a train.

Barnum stirred interest in elephants as had nobody since Hackaliah Bailey. "Hundreds of people came many miles to witness the novel spectacle" of an elephant pulling a plow, wrote Barnum. "Letters poured in upon me from the secretaries of hundreds of State and County agricultural societies throughout the Union. . . ."

Most of their questions were the same:

1. Is the elephant a profitable agricultural animal?
2. How much can an elephant plow in a day?
3. How much can he draw?
4. How much does he eat?
5. Will elephants make themselves generally useful on a farm?

"I suppose," said Barnum, "some of my inquirers thought the elephant would pick up chips, or even pins as they have been taught to do, and would rock the baby and do all the chores, including the occasional carrying of a trunk, other than his own, to the depot."

Barnum answered all the letters with a form letter always marked "Strictly Confidential." His answer was that elephants would prove very unprofitable to farmers because, in the first place, they cost from $3,000 to $10,000; in cold weather, they will not work at all; in any weather they would not earn even half their living, because they would eat up the value of their own head, trunk, and body every year; and he begged his correspondents not to do so foolish a thing as to undertake "elephantine agriculture."

Barnum added, as a "confidential" afterthought, "to me the elephant is a valuable agricultural animal, because he is an excellent advertisement to my Museum." It was a non sequitur that, in Barnum's case, made perfect sense.

When he judged that he had gotten as much mileage out of the elephant as he could (his six acres having been completely plowed over sixty times or more), Barnum sold the animal to Van Amburgh's Menagerie.

When P. T. Barnum's name would again be coupled with an elephant, it would be—naturally—with the biggest elephant in the world.

ROYAL HONORS TO TOM THUMB. *On his European tour, Tom Thumb traveled in style—in a miniature carriage drawn by matched ponies with two small children on the box dressed in sky-blue livery and cocked hats. "The General left America a diffident, uncultivated little boy," wrote Barnum in his autobiography. "He came back an educated, accomplished little man. . . . He went abroad poor, and he came home rich." (John Culhane Collection)*

ELEPHANTINE AGRICULTURE. *The first herd of elephants in the United States, of which this "plow elephant" is one, was collected for Barnum's Great Asiatic Caravan, Museum, and Menagerie in 1851. Barnum had the American genius for large-scale organization. Chartering a ship, he and his partners imported ten elephants that marched up Broadway pulling a chariot while Jenny Lind, at Barnum's request, reviewed the procession. The troupe, featuring Tom Thumb (his father, Sherwood Stratton, was a heavy investor), toured for several years with its lions, elephants, clowns, and curiosities, and according to Barnum made a good deal of money. But in 1854 the show was disbanded and the managers, who included Seth B. Howes, the leading circus producer before Barnum, went on to other things. Barnum, however, retained an elephant as a souvenir and "a capital advertisement for the American Museum." He used the beast for work on his Bridgeport farm, a portion of which lay conveniently near the railroad tracks. "The keeper was furnished with a time-table of the road," Barnum remembered, "with special instructions to be busily engaged in his work whenever passenger trains from either way were passing through." (John Culhane Collection)*

A child's awe and delight at seeing an elephant, the biggest animal in the world, is often the early memory on which the love of the circus is built. Duane Thorpe, Ringling Bros. and Barnum & Bailey's "Uncle Soapy," a clown in the 1990s who began in the circus in the 1940s as assistant to performance director Pat Valdo, looks back over a big chunk of American circus history and says, "As long as there is a child, an elephant and a clown on earth, there'll be a circus." (Ringling Museum)

Dan Rice:
Democracy's Jester

Two men associated with the circus in America in the nineteenth century attained the status of folk heroes: P. T. Barnum and Dan Rice. Van Amburgh and Levi North and Tom Thumb were superstars, but even fame and fortune aren't enough to make most people want to be a midget or to court death cavorting in a lion cage or tumbling on the bare back of a horse. Many, however, wanted to emulate Barnum and Rice, who were awarded gold and headlines for capturing the spirit of a people. Barnum was the American showman as hero; Rice, the hero as American clown.

Tall, lanky, bearded, dressed in red-and-white stripes like an American flag, calling himself Uncle Sam, singing songs that burlesqued the nascent American way, Rice was a genius at revealing Americans to themselves. To this day, Rice's Uncle Sam is a world-famous symbol of the United States.

But before Dan Rice was a symbol, he was a superb entertainer. He became a star as a wisecracking circus clown in 1845, when he was twenty-two, joking and singing in a clear, strong, magnetic voice that charmed nearly everyone who heard it; and he stayed a star until the 1880s, when he was in his sixties and alcohol was eroding his attractive personality. In midcentury, he was the highest paid person in the United States; his $1,000 a week was very much more than the salary earned by his friend President Abraham Lincoln. His career tells a lot about the American people in the years just before, during, and immediately after the Civil War.

The effect that Dan Rice had on audiences was captured by Mark Twain in *Huckleberry Finn*, although many don't know that the clown Huck sees at the circus is almost certainly Rice. Published in 1885, *Huckleberry Finn* takes

DAN RICE, one of the most highly acclaimed entertainers in the history of the circus and one of America's most beloved figures in the nineteenth century. Rice was famous for a highly individual act that included singing, dancing, exchanging jokes with the audience, performing feats of strength, reciting poetry and parodies of Shakespeare, trick riding, and exhibitions of animals such as his blind horse Excelsior. (Circus World Museum, Baraboo, Wisconsin)

place "forty to fifty years ago," or between 1845 and 1855, when Rice was doing the "Pete Jenkins from Mud Corners" routine that Twain describes in the book. This was Rice's variation on Joe Pentland's variation on "The Taylor Riding to Brentford."

The way Astley invented the gag, a tailor who supposedly doesn't know how to ride convulses audiences by doing everything wrong before revealing that he is as good a rider as the best. Pool and Ricketts brought this first circus clown routine to the American circus in the eighteenth century, and Joe Pentland, the equestrian clown who toured with Barnum in the 1830s, changed the rider from a tailor into a sailor.

It was clever of Dan Rice to change Pentland's drunken sailor into a drunken backwoodsman, because, by 1848, the nation was moving rapidly westward, and the man of the frontier—drunk or sober—was a more popular comic stereotype than the man of the sea. "A drunken man tried to get into the ring," reports Huck Finn:

Said he wanted to ride; said he could ride as well as anybody that ever was. They argued and tried to keep him out, but he wouldn't listen, and the whole show come to a standstill. Then the people begun to holler at him and make fun of him, and that made him mad, and he begun to rip and tear; so that stirred up the people, and a lot of men begun to pile down off of the benches and swarm toward the ring, saying, "Knock him down! throw him out!" and one or two women begun to scream. So, then, the ringmaster he made a little speech, and said he hoped there wouldn't be no disturbance, and if the man would promise he wouldn't make no more trouble he would let him ride if he thought he could stay on the horse. So everybody laughed and said all right, and the man got on. The minute he was on, the horse begun to rip and tear and jump and cavort around, with two circus men hanging on to his bridle trying to hold him, and the drunken man hanging on to his neck, and his feet flying in the air every jump, and the whole crowd of people standing up shouting and laughing till tears rolled down. And at last, sure enough, all the circus men could do, the horse broke loose, and away he went like the very nation, round and round the ring, with that sot laying down on him and hanging to his neck, with first one leg hanging most to the ground on one side, and then t'other one on t'other side, and the people just crazy. It warn't funny to me, though; I was all of a tremble to see his danger. But pretty soon he struggled up astraddle and grabbed the bridle, a-reeling this way and that; and the next minute he sprung up and dropped the bridle and stood! and the horse a-going like a house afire, too. He just stood up there, a-sailing around as easy and comfortable as if he warn't ever drunk in his life—and then he began to pull off his clothes and sling them. He shed them so thick they kind of clogged up the air, and altogether he shed seventeen suits. And then, there he was, slim and handsome, and dressed the gaudiest and prettiest you ever saw, and he lit into that horse with his whip and made him fairly hum—and finally skipped off, and made his bow and danced off to the dressing-room, and everybody just a-howling with pleasure and astonishment.

That should be enough to make us understand Dan Rice's great popularity. He made audiences *howl* with astonishment and pleasure. About eighty years before, Philip Astley made a dirt ring so that he could stand up on a horse that was "a-going like a house afire," then added a clown to burlesque his abilities—and found that he had invented the circus; now, Dan Rice wove the equestrian feat *and* the clowning into a whole comedy routine about a drunk on the American frontier, and became the most popular person performing in the most popular entertainment medium in America. Think of Will Rogers spinning his lariat on the stage of the Ziegfeld Follies in the 1920s, chewing gum and making wisecracks on anything and everything in American life, wisecracks that were printed in newspapers and repeated all over the United States; or Bob Hope, kidding every species of American from politician to football coach over radio and television for more than half a century after Will Rogers's death: both followed the pattern set by democracy's first jester, Dan Rice.

He was born Dan McLaren on Mulberry Street in New York City, on January 25, 1823. He was the son of a Daniel McLaren whom the *Dictionary of American Biography* describes as "a grocer and henchman to Aaron Burr," and McLaren's wife, Elizabeth Crum, daughter of a Methodist minister. Their marriage was subsequently annulled, and Dan ran away while still a boy, making his way to Pittsburgh. There, according to "Uncle Bob" Sherwood, the Barnum clown who boasted that he served his apprenticeship under Rice, young Dan McLaren worked as a stable boy for "a celebrated horse trainer named McCoun, who put the boy to riding horses. He soon rounded into a winning jockey, and also became a wonderful trainer of balky animals." It was then, in adolescence, the usual time of identity seeking, that he traded his father's name, McLaren, for the name of his maternal grandfather, Rice.

Rice had a personality that people found easy to love. "He had the happy attribute of making hundreds of friends wherever he went," said Sherwood. And he went all over. As a jockey, he traveled the racing circuit until he was seventeen. By that time, he had gained too much weight for horse racing, so he became a riverboat gambler instead.

America's great rivers were her superhighways then, and the palatial steamboats that plied the rivers seemed to promise that the main chance lay within, in a cloud of fragrant smoke from fine cigars. But luck was not with him. After fighting a knife duel with a famous gambler in a dispute over a card game, says Sherwood, Rice found it wise to drop off the steam packet, and out of the professional card-sharp's life, at Pittsburgh.

He may have saved some of his winnings, because at seventeen, he also had a third interest in a Pittsburgh livery stable—next door to which the small Sam H. Nichols Circus was playing. The circus people let the strong, athletic young Rice practice with them. A Monsieur Guillot taught him the rudiments of weight lifting and cannonball tossing. Soon Rice was proficient in gymnastic and strongman routines, and he seemed a natural clown. He made his own clown costume of red-and-white breeches with blue ruffles, a blue jockey blouse and matching cap, and full-length striped hose. Wearing this outfit and calling himself "Yankee Dan," he made his debut in the circus ring as an unpaid guest clown in the fall of 1840.

While animal trainers such as Van Amburgh were all the rage then, so clowns would send them up by performing with dogs, mules, and even pigs. Dan Rice bought a half interest in Lord Byron, a purebred American razorback that quickly became the most popular pig in the United States and started Rice on his way to becoming the most popular performer.

"Who's the greatest rascal in the world?" Rice would ask, and the pig would walk all over the tent, seemingly considering the people in first one section of the audience and then another, before returning to the ring and rubbing Dan Rice's leg with his snout.

Rice came along when the dominant American attitude was the go-getter spirit of "Work Hard or Go Under," and Rice reflected that attitude—but kidded its excesses, too—with a song he wrote called "Root, Hog, or Die!" Many Americans, including Abe Lincoln, loved the story of the farmer who planted an immense field of potatoes to feed his hogs. As Lincoln would tell it, a neighbor says to the farmer, "Your hogs are doing very well just now, but you know out here in Illinois the frost comes early, and the ground freezes a foot deep. Then what are they going to do?" And Lincoln had the farmer replying: "Well, it will be a leetle hard on their snouts, I reckon; but them shoats will have to root, hog, or die." When Dan Rice and his pig did their duo, this story-in-song was always the finale. Rice had taught Lord Byron to answer questions by grunting at the right time and to spell words by nudging the correct letter cards with his snout. (The trick—the secret of "learned pigs"—lay in training them to respond to the almost inaudible click of the trainer's fingernail when they came to the right letter.) Audiences loved to see Rice and Lord Byron walk around the ring, with the pig weaving a figure eight in and out around his master's legs. They loved to see the two seesaw together. And they went wild when Rice would sing "Root, Hog, or Die!" and Lord Byron would walk over to a box of flags of many nations, pick out the Stars and Stripes, and wave it in his jaws.

Then the pig died, and Rice was reduced to working as a strongman in Nathan Howes's winter circus in Philadelphia, in P. T. Barnum's American Museum, and on a European tour. Rice's experience with Barnum ended in a burst of derisive laughter. Barnum advertised him as "The Young American Hercules" and boasted that Rice could support a pipe filled with 126 gallons of water while two men stood on his chest. However, the huge puncheon contained only six gallons, as the audience discovered on the fifth night of Rice's appearance, when it fell to the floor and broke open. Such impostures make good clown gags but are frowned upon in straight strongman acts. Rice's engagement came to an end.

For a few months Rice worked for Joseph Smith, the Mormon prophet, as some sort of agent. Then he joined a circus and made his first paid appearance as a clown in Galena, Illinois, in 1844. He was twenty-one years old.

In the one-ring circus, the entire audience could see, hear, and focus on a single buffoon. Rice, more than any other clown anywhere, was suited to be that performer. Singing, dancing, delivering speeches, exhibiting animals he had trained, bantering with the ringmaster, bantering with the audience, playing the audience against the ringmaster, performing all the feats of the strongman and the equestrian, burlesquing all the feats of the strongman and the equestrian, Dan Rice delighted audiences. A talent scout for the innovative and experimental circus impresario Doc Spalding saw Rice and told Doc about him. Spalding engaged the young clown.

Unlike most clowns of the day, Rice did not wear clown white, regarding himself as a jester in the Shakespearean sense rather than a buffoon. "A successful clown," he said later, "must possess more intellect, ability, and originality than a comedian. He must be a crack mimic, an elocutionist, a satirist, and so ready witted that he, to the ringmaster, is a stupid fool, a buffoon; to the audience a wise man whose every remark is impregnated with philosophy as well as humor. This is the dual character of the true clown." There were precedents for what Rice was doing: Joe Blackburn of Kentucky, considered by Rice to be the greatest clown of the 1830s, billed himself as "the gentleman jester"; Joe Cook had recited Shakespeare while wearing a dress suit; and two of Rice's contemporaries, Joe Pentland and Pete Conklin, used Shakespearean quotations in their acts. But Rice was so good at thinking on his feet that, in taking questions from the audience, he could answer as easily with wittily apt Shakespearean quotations as with comic ad-libs.

One of the costumes that Rice wore was based on the American flag. It consisted of tights, a blouse and pantaloons that were red-and-white striped like the flag, and a tall hat. He wore his own chin whiskers, a cape over his shoulders, and boots on his feet. When the great editorial cartoonist Thomas Nast began drawing his Uncle Sam character as a symbol of the United States, he based Uncle Sam's appearance—the goatee, the flag suit, the tall hat—on Rice in costume.

A man like Spalding, always alive to opportunities, was quick to see the value of Rice. Gilbert R. "Doc" Spalding, a distinguished-looking man in a Van Dyke beard, had been working as a druggist (hence the nickname) near Albany, New York, when he decided that he wasn't going to get the money he was owed by the Nichols Circus for paint he had sold it and loans he had made it. So he took over its management and operated it for five years as Spalding's American Circus. By that time, he was hooked on what was then called "the show business."

Spalding was an inventor and an innovator. He invented the quarter poles that circus tents use to take up the slack between the center and side poles. This intermediate circle of poles gave tents more size and capacity, preparing the way for the massive Big Tops of the circus's golden age. He perfected portable bleachers by inventing the stringer-and-jack type of eleven-tier seats. He used oil for illumination instead of the customary cluster of candles. And it was probably with Doc's encouragement that his brother-in-law, Van Ordern, began experimenting in 1853 with the moving of circus wagons by rail.

Seth B. Howes of the Somers area crowd lured Rice away from Spalding and made him a heavily advertised member of the Mabie Brothers Circus company. Rufus Welch took Rice away from Howes and the Mabie Brothers. The public didn't care who was presenting Rice: they just wanted to see, hear, and laugh at him.

With land transport so difficult in the days before the Civil War, many circuses had taken to the water. A circus boat had floated down the Ohio River as early as 1815, and in 1825, a circus took a canal boat on the Erie Canal to the Great Lakes. In 1848, when Rice was only twenty-five, Doc set the clown up with his own show, which traveled up the Mississippi on the steamboat *Allegheny Mail*. They opened at St. Louis, and it is likely that it was on this trip that they played Hannibal, Missouri, and were seen by young Sam Clemens, who never forgot that "all through the circus they done the most astonishing things; and all the time that clown carried on so it most killed the people." He sounds like Rice, for Mark Twain has Huck recall that "the ringmaster couldn't ever say a word to him but he was back at him quick as a wink with the funniest things a body ever said; and how he ever could think of so many of them, and so sudden and so pat, was what I couldn't no way understand. Why, I couldn't 'a' thought of them in a year."

The *Allegheny Mail* continued up to St. Paul, came back downriver, switched to the Ohio to play Cincinnati and Pittsburgh and points between, then returned to the Mississippi and headed toward New Orleans. Rice got yellow fever there, but recovered—and during his convalescence met an important fan: General Zachary Taylor, hero of the Mexican War of 1846–48. After Taylor won the Whig nomination for president at the party's 1848 convention, Dan Rice made speeches on his behalf at each and every circus performance. Being Dan Rice, he did more than simply campaign for Taylor. He suggested that it would be good publicity for Taylor if he and his party got up on Rice's circus bandwagon and paraded with him. Bandwagons had high decks so that musicians seated on them could be seen as well as heard by the crowds at street parades. When Rice's bandwagon arrived at the center of town, Dan Rice stopped his parade, stood up on his seat, and gave an emotional speech on Taylor's behalf.

"Look," shouted someone in the crowd, "Dan Rice is on Zachary Taylor's bandwagon."

The story made the rounds and, from then on, whenever anybody announced his support of a presidential candidate, he was said to have joined that candidate's "bandwagon." The circus, which has given so many words and expressions to American speech, had added another.

When "Old Rough and Ready" won the presidency, he named Dan Rice an aide with the honorary rank of colonel. Nothing like that had ever happened to a circus performer.

In 1849, Dan Rice left Spalding and started his own circus. Doc would never forgive him. The bitterness of their competition was reflected in one of the circus's nastiest episodes: the war of the "rat sheets."

For four years, the two circuses battled it out. Billposters covered up each other's advertisements, or defaced them. In handbills called "rat sheets," each accused the other of being guilty of whatever crimes they thought audiences would find convincing. The employees of each damaged the private property of the other and tried to damage their reputations.

In 1850, Doc Spalding had Rice thrown into jail for slander. It was a major miscalculation; Rice was developing a Barnum-like genius for publicity. Rice was inside this Rochester, New York, hoosegow for only two weeks, but it was more than long enough to write a ballad entitled "Blue Eagle Jail."

Rice became an instant martyr. The courts decided against him. He lost his farm and other real estate as a result of a legal foreclosure. But the public had decided for Rice. In April 1850 Congress adjourned to go to a benefit to help Dan Rice out of his financial difficulties. Members of both houses of Congress, the heads of departments, the president and cabinet, and the movers and shakers in Washington society had received satin invitations that they understood to be "comps" to the performance. Rice was going to be doing jokes about the political mighty, and nobody wanted to miss the show.

Henry Clay, the senator from Kentucky who was one of the most influential political leaders in the decades before the Civil War, arrived with a party of ladies and presented his satin invitations as passes of admission.

"How many in the party?" asked the doorkeeper.

"Twelve," answered Clay.

"Twelve dollars," said the doorkeeper.

Dan Rice was peeking through a peephole in the canvas, relishing Clay's agitation as he fumbled in his pockets and could not come up with the money. Rice knew that Clay wasn't the kind to carry much money with him; the clown had arranged for a well-known Washington tradesman to be standing by with a pocketful of silver dollars to help the Great Pacificator out of his embarrassment.

As Clay's party passed into the tent, Clay said, "I'll bet this is one of Dan's tricks."

President Zachary Taylor came, less than three months before he died in office. Daniel Webster was there, and so were John C. Calhoun and Stephen A. Douglas. And Rice, who often sneaked into even little towns beforehand to learn about their local celebrities so that he could lampoon them with his verses, now rattled off fifty original verses, satirizing everybody from the congressional pages to "Colonel" Rice's friend, President Taylor.

By borrowing money on his wife's jewelry, Rice started over again with his famous One-Horse Show.

The worth of a circus in those days could usually be gauged by the number of ring horses it carried, just as people would later gauge it by the number of elephants it boasted. Starting over, Dan had only one ring horse, named Aroostook. Most of his performers had deserted him, figuring that a show with one ring horse wouldn't bring many customers into the tent. Rice was left with only three musicians, an apprentice equestrian, and a tattooed man.

Early in 1851, Rice opened his little circus in New Orleans on a lot in the French Quarter adjoining the big circus of Doc Spalding. He began his show by telling the audience about his troubles but promising to entertain them anyway. He was leading Aroostook into the ring when a distinguished-looking man in a Van Dyke beard suddenly appeared before him and made an announcement: "Ladies and gentlemen, introducing Dan Rice—Dan Rice and his One-Horse Show!"

The man meant to make Rice a laughing-stock. But Rice bowed deeply to the intruder and made his rejoinder: "After all, Doctor Spalding, the taking of Troy was strictly a One-Horse Show!"

The audience rocked with laughter and applause. Spalding slipped away.

Once again, all America was talking about Dan Rice. He had turned an epithet on its head. City slickers might scoff at "one-horse towns" for their limited resources or capacity; Oliver Wendell Holmes might deride "a country clergyman, with a one-story intellect and a one-horse capacity"; but Dan Rice was there to show that less can mean more, and small can be better. Every craftsman who took pride that his personal best didn't need propping up by a lot of helpers started comparing himself to Dan Rice's One-Horse Show. There was

"the one-horse bootmaker," "the one-horse printer," "the one-horse baker"—and on June 23, 1855, an advertisement in the Baraboo, Wisconsin, *Republic* read: "HO, FELLOW CITIZENS! GIVE ATTENTION TO THE ONE HORSE HARNESS SHOP!"

The harness maker who used the Dan Rice phrase that had become a national catchword was a German immigrant named August Rungeling. He had only two sons in 1855, but he would have five more, plus a daughter; and five of his sons would become famous in circus history, once they had Americanized their surname as the Ringling brothers.

Dan Rice, meanwhile, had turned his liability into an asset. In 1852 he toured by steamer on the Mississippi and Ohio rivers, using the title "Dan Rice's One-Horse Show." He wrote a popular song called "The One-Horse Show." He kept rubbing it in. He concluded each evening's performance by reminding the audience that "quality is never measured by numerical standards." He would kiss Aroostook's head and add, "As Shakespeare wrote in *King Richard III*, 'A horse, a horse, my kingdom for a horse!'"

It hardly mattered that Spalding never showed up in person again. Rice got a fellow performer to play Spalding, and the two of them reenacted the incident every night. Then Rice and the show's groom developed a novel patter to open the show:

RICE: We will now have the showing of the steeds. Are the horses ready for the act?

GROOM: That they are, sir.

RICE: They are all properly harnessed, plumed and caparisoned?

GROOM: That's right, sir; they are all ready.

RICE: You're sure you got them all? You counted them?

LINCOLN'S FRIEND. *Carl Sandburg wrote: "The comic element of Lincoln may have drawn to him those who truly valued laughter." Dan Rice was drawn to Lincoln, and Lincoln to Rice. Rice was recognized everywhere by his distinctive chin whiskers, top hat, and his suit decorated with the stars and stripes, and cartoonist Thomas Nast caricatured him when he drew "Uncle Sam," the symbol of the United States. Sandburg, in his biography of Lincoln, asked if Lincoln, too, didn't have "something of the cartooned figure of Uncle Sam, benign, sagacious, practical, simple, at times not quite beyond taking a real laugh for himself and his country." (Circus World Museum, Baraboo, Wisconsin)*

YANKEE ROBINSON. *He started his first circus in 1854, and had two units in 1858 (the second was probably the first circus to feed and house all personnel on the show grounds rather than in hotels). He met Al Ringling in 1883. Wrote Alf T. Ringling, "While the boys were traveling with various circuses, Al Ringling had traveled with the then famous showman, and he earnestly urged the advisability of leasing Old Yankee's name. Yankee Robinson, about this time a victim of misfortune, had been forced to retire from business with nothing but his name, which to the circus-going public was a great one. The boys wanted this name as soon as they should organize their show, to recommend it to the public. The old showman, who had taken a liking to Al Ringling, readily consented to any kind of partnership the boys desired. Perhaps he was in that stage of desperation where men grasp at straws; or it may be that he saw with prophetic eye the bright future awaiting the pluck and energy of the Ringling boys." (Circus World Museum, Baraboo, Wisconsin)*

GROOM: Yes, sir. I counted them. They are all here and all ready.

RICE: How many are there, may I ask?

GROOM: One, sir!

RICE: That's right! Lead the animal forth and let the act commence.

The feud kept escalating, and Spalding again tried to top Rice. He hired the foremost English clown of the day, William Wallett (1808–1892), and took him down to New Orleans, scene of his humiliation by Rice two years before, where the One-Horse Show was again playing.

Wallett had been engaged by Van Amburgh's Circus when that American company played England in 1844, and Wallett had performed with Van Amburgh before Queen Victoria and Prince Albert. He ever after capitalized on the publicity to proclaim himself "The Queen's Jester," even to dressing like a medieval jester in motley, cap, and bells. He helped establish the Shakespearean jester as part of the circus when he supplanted Tom Barry as clown to the ring at Astley's in 1848. The original clown to the ring continually interrupted the circus activities with his antics, but they tended to be physical rather than verbal: riding, tumbling, leaping, dancing. Wallett was a competent equestrian and contortionist, but he engaged mainly in repartee, and when he was criticized for the new interpretation of the role he replied, "Others said that the speechifying was not in character, that a clown should have heels but no tongue; ignoring altogether Shakespeare's description of Yorick, his 'flashes of merriment that were wont to set the table on a roar.' He was remembered for his tongue and not for his heels."

Wallett's tongue was indeed memorable. When a heckler who wanted more physical clowning yelled "Variety!" Wallett told the audience: "He has left a wife and children at home, without the common necessaries of life, and he comes here tonight with two of the commonest women of the town; and that's what he calls variety." It was a tradition among Cambridge undergraduates to go to the circus and pay some unsuspecting underclassman to hiss Wallett—then sit back and enjoy the spectacle of Wallett making mincemeat of their classmate with his tongue.

Wallett came to America in 1849 and performed in various circuses before Doc Spalding snapped him up to work on his new enterprise, the *Floating Palace*. Wallett wrote:

> I shall never forget my astonishment upon first viewing her (or it). It was a regular circus, equal in size to the largest that are erected in England, built on an enormous flat-bottomed vessel. A really splendid amphitheatre, with boxes, pit, and gallery, capable of seating nearly three thousand persons. There were stabling for thirty horses, and sleeping apartments for the artists, crew, and servants. She was towed along from town to town by an enormous high pressure steamship, visiting all the chief places on the Upper and Lower Mississippi, the Illinois, the Missouri, and their numerous branches.

The decade of the 1850s was the golden age of the river, the era when river travel in general and showboats in particular were at their height. In 1851, Rice traveled with his own circus by canal boat and steamer, but he came ashore to put on the show. Spalding had a better idea. Inspired by the showboat owners who put on shows aboard their vessels, he and his new partner, an equestrian named Charles J. Rogers (1817–1895), built the *Floating Palace* at a cost of $42,000. It was an all-year-round attraction, touring the Ohio and Mississippi rivers in the spring, summer, and fall, and making a long stand in New Orleans during the winter (though they came ashore to put on their circus when the weather turned bad). The advertising agent preceded the *Floating Palace* by about two weeks in a small steamer called the *Humming Bird*, arranging at each landing place for fuel, fodder, and food for the troupe, and posting bills announcing the coming of the circus.

The *Floating Palace* would arrive, accompanied by two side-wheel towboats, the *Banjo* and the *James Raymond*. The two-story wooden structure housed an auditorium large enough to hold a stage, tiers of seats, and a regulation forty-two-foot circus ring; the windows were hung with red velvet draperies, and the ornate carvings on the walls and ceiling were illuminated by two hundred gas jets. In chilly weather, its patrons were warmed by steam pipes. Wallett exaggerated when he said that the *Floating Palace* was capable of seating nearly 3,000; but it could accommodate 2,300—800 people in its dress circle and "family boxes," 1,000 in the gallery, and another 500 who could pay a dollar apiece to stand on deck and look through the windows (the showboat equivalent of Standing Room Only at the Metropolitan Opera). Originally, chimes on the roof heralded the approach of the boat, until the perfect sound to announce a circus was discovered. On October 9, 1855, J. C. Stoddard, of Worcester, Massachusetts, was granted U.S. Patent No. 13,668 for his invention of a "New Musical Instrument to be Played by the Agency of Steam or Highly Compressed Air."

In short, it was a steam calliope. In 1857, Nixon & Kemp's Circus put the calliope on wheels and used it in a circus parade, and a new delight began moving across the land.

As a foreigner, Wallett reached New Orleans for the winter stand of 1852–53 without understanding the depth of the bitterness involved in the Spalding-Rice Rivalry. "We here came into opposition with Dan Rice, the great American clown, who treated me very kindly, notwithstanding he was at the head of the rival establishment," the English clown was later ingenuously to write. "Our two circuses were close together, and I was on such friendly terms with the other company, that I one night ran out in my dress into the ring where Rice was performing. There we fraternized, and he introduced me to his patrons. From this moment I became a great favourite with the frequenters of both circuses. For Dan was a sort of martyr in the eyes of the New Orleans people; and it was believed that our proprietors, who were rich and powerful, had come on purpose to crush his company.... But though I made a lasting friend of Dan, and got into the good graces of the people, I incurred the displeasure of my employers."

The Goliath that was Spalding & Rogers lost the custom of New Orleans as the word got around that Spalding was again picking on Dan Rice, the little David of the Blue Eagle Jail; so Spalding & Rogers moved their circus to Mobile—where they fired Wallett for fraternizing with the enemy.

That was a mistake. Rice had already told Wallett that he could at any time join him on the same terms Wallett then had with Spalding. A telegram from Wallett in Mobile brought a quick reply from Rice: "Come immediately; we have announced you."

Now began one of the high times in circus clowning. "He played ring-master to me as clown in one act, and then we exchanged characters, and I was master of the ring to him," said Wallett. And in Maria Ward Brown's *Life of Dan Rice*, Rice gave his impression of the difference between America's favorite and the Queen's jester:

> Wallett, when occasion permitted, quoted Shakespeare in an eloquent, impassioned manner that commanded admiration for his

VIEW OF THE FLOATING PALACE IN THE GULF OF MEXICO,
IN HER PASSAGE FROM MOBILE TO THE SALINE.
IN THE MEMORABLE STORM OF THE 28TH JANUARY 1853, IN WHICH THE GUARDS OF HER CONSORT THE NORTH RIVER, WHICH HAD HER IN TOW, WERE CUT AWAY TO ESCAPE SHIPWRECK.

SPALDING & ROGERS'S FLOATING PALACE. The decade immediately preceding the Civil War was the golden age of the boat circus. Gilbert R. Spalding and star rider Charles J. Rogers conceived the idea from showboat owners who presented dramas. The Floating Palace, inaugurated in March 1852, was towed from river city to river city by one or two steamers. This lithograph pictures a storm in the Gulf of Mexico on January 28, 1853, in which the guards of the steamer, The North River, which had her in tow, were cut away to escape shipwreck. In 1862, anticipating that the Civil War would make the lower Mississippi and its tributaries dangerous, Spalding and Rogers tied up their gorgeous riverboat at New Albany, Indiana, and took a circus to South America. In the early spring of 1865, the Floating Palace was destroyed by fire; the Spalding and Rogers partnership survived only a few months more. (Circus World Museum, Baraboo, Wisconsin)

THE BOSS OF ALL RIDERS. Gil Robinson, son of the founder of the John Robinson Circus, named "five great riders" of the nineteenth-century circus, and called his adoptive brother James (above) "the boss of all riders." In 1856, James turned twenty-three backward and forward somersaults over banners four feet wide without missing once. The other four greats named by Gil Robinson were Charles W. Fish, whom James defeated in a championship match ("he was remarkably graceful on a horse, but lacked Robinson's attractive physique and personality"), Robert Stickney, Frank Melville, and John A. Robinson, "a daring hurdle rider," killed at Crittenden, Kentucky, in 1865, by "bad men from the mountains." (Circus World Museum, Baraboo, Wisconsin)

ability and scholarly training; I followed him with a paraphrase. For instance, once Wallett quoted from *Macbeth* the familiar "Is this a dagger I see before me," etc. When I came on with a great flourish I paraphrased it thus:

> *Is that a beefsteak I see before me*
> *With the Burnt side toward my hand?*
> *Let me clutch thee! I have thee not,*
> *And yet I see thee still in form as palpable*
> *As that I ate for breakfast this morning.*

After four weeks, Wallett decided that he wanted to return to his wife and children at Vine Cottage, the house he had built at Frankfort, near Philadelphia.

But though Wallett lived until 1892, when he was eighty-five, this would be the only opportunity for circus lovers to see the greatest clowns of England and the United States in the same ring.

The 1850s were great years for the circus, and not just in clowning. There were about thirty circuses in America in 1852, and by that time, most of them had menageries.

However, the greatest circus achievements in that decade were really in athletic events. Before the Olympics were revived in 1896, the circus was the best place to see world-class athletic feats and contests, particularly equestrian sports and gymnastics. In those days most men rode horseback and occasionally, if not frequently, harnessed and drove horses, so a beautiful, well-trained horse and a skillful rider were judged with a critical eye. In 1853 the racecourse, or "Hippodrome Track," was introduced, and modern circuses began to hold chariot races in imitation of the Circus Maximus of ancient Rome. The greatest sports heroes, however, were the bareback riders. In the nineteenth century, circus riders and acrobats were lionized the way Olympic medalists are

today. They were great athletes, and none were better than the two great international personalities of the equestrian world, James Robinson and Charles W. Fish, who could both do the backward-back somersault.

From the very first circuses, from Astley in England and Pool in the United States, circus equestrianism had consisted of such feats as standing or sitting or jumping on and off a fast-moving horse, somersaulting or juggling or leaping over banners, boards, and through hoops—sometimes flaming hoops—held up by grooms and clowns. But what Hemingway called "the sequence of fact and motion which made the emotion" seems to have been most poignant with James Robinson. That was why he was called, simply, "The Man Who Rides."

In bareback riding the backward somersault is the natural somersault, because the rider both takes off and lands facing forward and thus can see where he is landing before his feet return to the horse's back. The rider's trick is to allow for the horse's movement by throwing himself forward—so that he comes down a foot or two in advance of where he was when he left the horse's back. That way, the horse will still be under him when he comes down.

A forward-forward somersault is more difficult. Once again, the rider somersaults in the same direction that his horse is running, but because his head follows his feet, he can't see where he is going to land.

The backward-back somersault is the most difficult of all. The rider faces his horse's tail and from that position turns a backward somersault. This gives him two handicaps. First, he can't see where the horse is going and, second, since the horse is running from, instead of with, the direction in which the rider has thrown his body, the rider is apt to be thrown backward toward the horse's head.

The horse's contribution to all this was to be "bomb-proof," as the expression went; for unless the back of the ring horse is as steady as a theater stage, disaster will inevitably result. In the circus drawings of Toulouse-Lautrec, the horses that his equestriennes ride are thickset, solid, stolid animals. They must never shy or change legs, nor can they "hump" when the rider alights, for that will throw him off balance. Their pace—a controlled canter—must be unvarying, with short, even strides. Ring horses—also called *voltige* horses or rosinbacks—are trained in noisy sessions, sometimes with garbage can lids being banged together or firecrackers being set off, to get them used to distractions. Even so, performers fear accidents such as when a dog yapped at the legs of the ring horse of the great May Wirth. The horse tried to avoid the dog, and May Wirth missed her landing and hit the ring.

James Robinson's horse, Bull, was as imperturbable as a slowly moving mountain, with a smooth, unvarying gait, thoroughly schooled against any faltering. When Bull's rump rose in his rhythmic course around the ring, Robinson would use the rise of the rump to launch himself even higher. When Robinson did the backward-back, he would stand well back, facing Bull's tail, then turn so swiftly that the cantering horse's back was still beneath him as he alighted. He never missed.

More than any other rider, James Robinson was responsible for the acrobatic school of bareback riding. In the 1850s, when he started his career, most of his competitors were still riding "pad"—in other words, with the aid of a pad covering the horse's back.

Robinson never rode pad, always bareback. The superfeats of this flash of pink tights and spangled trunks on the uncovered back of his steel gray horse soon put the pad riders out of the running. Now the horses used for equestrian gymnastics began to be called rosinbacks, after the resin placed on their backs to prevent the riders feet from slipping upon landing.

James Robison's physique was perfect for his art: he never grew above five feet five, and he had very small feet; he was also extremely strong and nimble.

The feat that he considered his greatest was achieved in 1856, when he was just twenty-one and riding for Spalding & Rogers: he turned twenty-three consecutive backward and forward somersaults, over banners four feet wide, without missing once.

Robinson was born James Michael Fitzgerald in Boston in 1835. He was adopted by John Robinson, the circus owner, who gave the boy his name and taught him to ride.

Buffalo Bill's publicist, Dexter Fellows, put James Robinson on the small, select list of those who have "that something which distinguishes circus genius from circus ability. All the great figures in arenic history had it," wrote Fellows. "James Robinson, greatest bareback rider of all time, had it. In the opinion of many old-timers, Charles W. Fish was a greater rider than Robinson, with a routine of more difficult stunts, but he lacked the color and showmanship of Robinson, to say nothing of the appeal to the eye. Robinson had the figure of an Apollo, while Fish, when pulled into tights, looked like the break-up of a hard winter."

Fish was also not the champion, even though he did, on several occasions, complete eighteen somersaults and finish by landing on one foot.

The Civil War would mean that horse-loving Southerners would miss the ongoing competition between Robinson and Fish, who stayed north of the Mason-Dixon line after 1861. But when the war was over, both would still be going strong—and would carry on their famous "$10,000 Championship Riding Contest" in most important cities in America and Europe for many years. (The purse was another example of circus humbug, Fish later confessed, for they competed "in reality, only for the championship.") Fish was Robinson's only real competitor, but Robinson retired in 1889 still what the circus posters proclaimed him: "CHAMPION BAREBACK RIDER OF ALL THE

EARTH. CROWNED EMPEROR OF THE ARENA. WEARER OF THE JEWEL-STUDDED DIAMOND BELT." He lived on amid his trophies and his memories until 1917.

———————

The circus was often the scene of the events most talked about in the 1850s. In 1858, both Abraham Lincoln and Stephen A. Douglas made campaign speeches (on separate days) in the circus tent—and to the circus crowd—of Spalding & Rogers. Douglas, of course, beat Lincoln and won reelection for a third term, and the war clouds continued to gather.

Coup, a veteran circus man who many years later would become associated with Barnum, spoke feelingly of the constant menace to circus men and women when traveling in the slave states, because it was widely believed that they were all Yankees. "Although the people were all anxious to see our show they had not a friendly word for us," said Coup, ". . . because of the extreme bitterness which then prevailed toward all Northerners." In this regard, the Southerners were correct about circus owner Fayette Lodawick Robinson (1818–1884), known to circusgoers—and history—as "Yankee" Robinson. In 1859, "Yankee" had to flee from a mob in Charleston, South Carolina, because of the hatred his abolitionist sympathies inspired, and that event underscored how close America now was to civil war.

In the summer of 1846, Yankee Robinson had met June & Turner's Circus at Galena, Illinois, and toured with it for two years, learning circus ways. In 1848, he was married, and he and his wife joined Lennox's Floating Circus at Evansville, Indiana. In 1854, he founded his own circus, and by 1857, he had saved enough money to "build a canvass." He gave his first tent show that year in Quincy, Illinois. In 1858,

he had two units, and the second was probably the first to feed and house all personnel on the show grounds rather than in hotels. One of these units began, in the last years of the decade, giving a circus in the afternoons and a performance of *Uncle Tom's Cabin* in the evenings, thus becoming the first of hundreds of tent shows to present Harriet Beecher Stowe's story about the horrors of slavery.

Robinson's other unit went down south to

Equestrienne Claude Valoise. (Ringling Museum)

Charleston. Earlier that year, John Brown, the militant abolitionist, made his famous raid on the federal arsenal at Harper's Ferry, Virginia, for which Brown was hanged.

"The John Brown excitement made things so hot that I had to run away and leave a show outfit which cost me $40,000," Yankee Robinson told the Baraboo *Republic* for May 14, 1884. "It was, in fact, the finest that had ever been seen up to that time. That broke me all up. . . ."

———————

Not surprisingly, at a time when the fate of the nation hung in the balance, the greatest popular hero was a man who walked across Niagara Falls on a tightrope. He called himself Blondin, and he performed one of the greatest acrobatic feats in history on June 30, 1859.

Blondin, who was described as having "no nerves to speak of," was born Jean-François Gravelet on February 28, 1824, in Saint-Omer, France, the son of a man who had fought under Napoleon. When he was five years old he was sent to the Ecole de Gymnase at Lyons, and after six months' training as an acrobat, he made his first public appearance as "the Little Wonder." When he made his first attempt to cross Niagara Falls on a rope, Blondin was thirty-five and already had a reputation as a circus tightrope walker. He had carried a young man named Harry Colcord across ropes in various circuses and also in opera houses. But now he took his circus act into the open air, for the most spectacular tightrope feat of all time.

The single hempen cable he would walk was 1,100 feet long and stretched from shore to shore. Its elevation above the water was 160 feet at one side; at the other, 270.

Blondin started his walk in the United States of America. If he finished, he would be in the Dominion of Canada. If he fell, either the fall would kill him or he would drown.

He picked up his balance pole—itself a thirty-eight-foot-long burden—and placed his foot upon the rope. He had trained himself not to look down. He looked straight ahead as he walked into clouds of damp vapor that rose from the swiftly boiling cataract below. And when he reached the center of the cable, he sat down.

Now Blondin began to do tricks. He got up, strolled forward a bit, then sat down again. He stretched himself full length upon the rope, lying upon his back, his balance pole laid horizontally across his chest.

Then he turned a back somersault.

He came upright, then walked rapidly the rest of the way to his landing stage in the British province of Upper Canada. Above the cataract's roar could be heard the crowd's cheers, and a Canadian band playing "La Marseillaise."

There was more. After an intermission of about twenty minutes, Blondin reappeared at the Canadian end of the rope with a camera and tripod on his back. This time he walked about two hundred feet of the cable before lashing his balance pole to the rope, unstrapping his camera and tripod, and taking a picture of his public on the shore. Then he shouldered the camera, unlashed his balance pole, and went back to Canada—only to reappear shortly with a chair. This time he covered about a third of the rope before placing his chair upon it, seating himself, and crossing his legs.

Now he gazed around himself with unforgettable insouciance.

Coming closer to the American end of the rope, he readjusted his chair and stood up on it.

It is said that people began to faint when they saw him do this. Yet circus daredevils will tell you that they don't fear the calculated risk as much as the spontaneous gamble with death; so to Blondin, the walk across Niagara Falls probably didn't seem as dangerous as his voyage from Europe to America, when he had leaped overboard to rescue a drowning man.

In the months that followed, Blondin crossed Niagara Falls a number of times, always with a new and theatrical twist. He did it blindfolded, wearing a sack on his head, trundling a wheelbarrow, on stilts, and sitting down midway to make and eat an omelette.

The public seemed most intrigued with his offer of a large sum of money to any man who would volunteer to cross Niagara on his back. A few volunteered—until they reconnoitered what one writer called "the swaying rope across the rushing flood."

No amateur would dare it. So Blondin's old employee, Colcord, agreed to let Blondin carry him to triumph or tragedy. In fact, Blondin carried Colcord across the falls several times in the autumn of 1859 and again in 1860, this time in the presence of the Prince of Wales, who was visiting Canada.

For the Prince of Wales, the rope was moved downriver so that it spanned the famous whirlpool. Unscrupulous papers reported, "The Prince of Wales Faints."

Edward did not faint, but he was nervous enough to say to Blondin before the crossing, "For heaven's sake, don't do anything extraordinary because I am here." Blondin replied, " 'Your Royal Highness, I'll carry yourself across, if you wish.' "

That same afternoon, Blondin—without anyone on his shoulders—walked the cable on stilts.

"Thank God it is all over!" said the future Edward VII of England when Blondin stepped safely ashore.

In 1861, Blondin appeared in London at the Crystal Palace, turning somersaults on stilts on a rope stretched across the central transept, 170 feet above the ground. He gave his final performance in Belfast in 1896, and he died in London on February 19, 1897. His like would not be seen again until the day in 1974 when Philippe Petit walked between the twin towers of the World Trade Center, the tallest building in the world.

The symbolism of Blondin's feats was not lost on Americans. A cartoon captioned "SHAKY" appeared in the *Vanity Fair* issue for June 9, 1860, just after Abraham Lincoln had been nominated for president. It showed "Mr. Abraham Blondin De Lave Lincoln" trying to cross a chasm on a wooden rail with a carpetbag hanging from his balancing pole. The Railsplitter's crossing rail is breaking, and in the carpetbag is a black slave. A man on the near side of the chasm calls out "Don't drop the carpet bag" to Lincoln, who is dressed like Blondin but looks uncertain—as Blondin never did.

The America Wagon, one of the four continent wagons built for the Barnum & Bailey parade of 1903. Soprano Marian Anderson has written that Circus Day was one of the great holidays of her childhood. "Our big outing each year was a trip to the Barnum and Bailey Circus. To us it was like a great journey away from home. We prepared for the day long in advance; it was the next biggest day to Christmas. Father would buy us something new to wear. A basket or two was prepared, and off we went, taking a trolley car for what seemed like an endless ride. We had wonderful lunches and afternoon snacks. Our eyes were big with delight, trying to follow all the acts going on at the same time under the big tent." (Circus World Museum, Baraboo, Wisconsin)

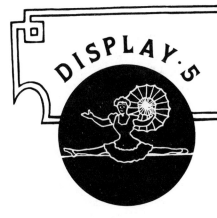

DISPLAY·5

The Circus During the Civil War

"Well, General," said President Lincoln to General Tom Thumb, "what is your opinion of the war as a military man?"

On their honeymoon in February of 1863, Barnum's famous midget and his wife had come to a dinner and reception at the White House that President and Mrs. Lincoln gave in their honor. Union morale was at the lowest point yet in America's twenty-two-month-old Civil War. At Fredericksburg in December, Lincoln's full-size General Burnside had lost 12,653 men, compared to Robert E. Lee's 5,309. Burnside was replaced by Hooker, but now both armies were in winter quarters near Fredericksburg, and plunging morale was reflected in an increasing number of desertions.

"My opinion," said Tom Thumb, then twenty-five years old and thirty-two inches tall, "is that my friend Barnum would settle the whole affair in a month!"

Daniel Boorstin and Brooks Mather Kelley, in their 1981 history of the United States, remind us that the Civil War was the bloodiest war in all American history—and the bloodiest war in the whole world during the nineteenth century. When it was over, 600,000 people would be dead. Of every ten men who fought, four became casualties, dead or wounded. "No other nation paid so high a price to hold itself together," Boorstin wrote. Those who fought the battle, and their wives and widows, and their children and orphans, desperately needed

TOM THUMB AND HIS BRIDE ON THEIR WEDDING DAY. The public announcement of the wedding of General Tom Thumb and Lavinia Warren made receipts at Barnum's American Museum shoot up to $3,000 a day. More people wanted a glimpse of the world's most famous small people than Barnum could accommodate. Tom Thumb's fiancée sold $300 worth of photographs of herself every day. Finally, Barnum offered the little General $15,000 if he would postpone the wedding for one month while continuing the joint appearance. "No, sir, not for fifty thousand dollars!" replied the groom-to-be. "Good for you, Charlie," said Lavinia, "only you should have said one hundred thousand." And so, at Grace Church, Manhattan, on Tuesday, February 10, 1863, when the man born Charles S. Stratton was twenty-five and his bride twenty-two, they became Mr. and Mrs. Tom Thumb. President Lincoln and his wife sent the couple a "gorgeous set of Chinese fire screens." (Circus World Museum, Baraboo, Wisconsin) diversion. Contemporary accounts suggest that the circus has seldom been so delightfully diverting.

The summer before the war began, however, there was a comic exhibition of a kind that would soon be gone with the winds of war. It was like something in a Grimms' fairy tale. Before every performance of Spalding & Rogers Circus in that summer of 1860, a man named Tom Watson took a ride down the Mississippi in a washtub pulled by four geese.

How did he do it? Life on the Mississippi was far enough away from life on the Thames that Americans didn't know the trick had already been exposed in England. More than sixteen years before, a clown named Dicky Usher, known for his original gags, used to sail along the Thames in a bathtub drawn by his four trained geese, Gibble, Gabble, Gobble, and Garble. The gag was taken up by Tom Barry in 1844, and then by two other clowns, before it was discovered that the tub was linked underwater by weighted ropes to a rowboat far ahead of it.

The days in which the Mississippi could be the scene of such innocent fun ended on April 12, 1861, with the fall of Fort Sumter. Rivers henceforth would be prizes of war.

In such circumstances, Spalding & Rogers decided to have the *Floating Palace* sit out the war tied to a wharf on the Ohio River in New Albany, Indiana, an important steamboat-building center.

As the war began, America had eleven big traveling shows: Robinson & Lake's Circus and Menagerie; Dan Rice's Circus; Spalding & Rogers Circus; Sands & Nathan's Circus; Geo. F. Bailey's Circus and Menagerie; Alexander Robinson's Southwestern Circus; Mabie's Menagerie; Van Amburgh's Menagerie; Stone & Murray's Circus; Howe & Cushing's Circus; and Nixon & Kemp's Circus.

Most of the circuses had their winter quarters north of the Mason–Dixon Line, although

a few wintered in and around New Orleans. Suddenly, the South was inaccessible to the northern-based shows, or their northern sympathies made them unwelcome there; so the circus was largely denied to the Confederate states. In the North and the West, it was mostly circus as usual.

For the northern circuses that were tenting in the South when the war started, the return trip posed problems. The circus band of Dan Castello's Great Show, a boat show, prudently played "Dixie" when it docked at Rebel ports as it moved upriver, and "Yankee Doodle" when it finally reached the Union lines.

The 1861 season of Robinson & Lake's Circus was booked to begin at Lexington, Kentucky, starring that greatest of all bareback riders, James Robinson. The circus put up its tents and raised the American flag to the top of its center pole. But the citizens of Lexington lowered the Stars & Stripes and ordered the circus to move north of the Ohio River.

In the 1862 season, Spalding & Rogers avoided the war entirely by sending their circus to South America under Rogers's management.

Dan Rice, who had dear friends on both sides of the Mason–Dixon Line (Lincoln; Jefferson Davis, president of the Confederate States of America; and Robert E. Lee, commander-in-chief of the Confederate armies, to name three), was on a southern tour when the war began. He returned to the North and opened the 1861 season in Washington, D.C., then went to Pittsburgh and began a tour of Ohio River towns. In some places in the North, his loyalty was questioned. The *New York Clipper* for May 15, 1861, said that "Many reports are in circulation concerning Dan Rice, some asserting that he talks 'secesh' in the South and Union in the North." In Cincinnati, reported the *Clipper*, Rice's circus flotilla had been menaced by a mob demanding that Rice hoist the Union flag instead of the Dan Rice Circus flag he customarily flew. Rice was reported to have pointed a howitzer charged with slugs at the mob and told them that he would not be coerced, then steamed on his boat to the Kentucky shore, "where he is now safely moored. . . . If true," concluded the *Clipper*, "then Dan Rice's occupation as a showman is gone in the Northern and Western sections of the country." On another occasion, Rice was greeted in a Philadelphia winter circus by hisses, catcalls, and demands that he be shot as "a Johnny Reb secessionist." Rice stood alone in the ring until the crowd, impressed by his fearlessness, let him speak. He told them that he had pretended to be sympathetic to secession so that he might escape to the North.

No public opinion poll was taken as to whether Rice was believed, but the next year, his circus was sold for debt. Once again, Dan Rice started over. With one horse and two Burmese cattle, he began touring again. He operated in the North every year of the war, meeting with friendliness in some places and hostility in others.

"I have never met a more nervy man; he was without equal in trying emergencies," wrote W. C. Coup many years later. "He would face a mob at any time and under any circumstances. Besides being a natural fighter he was a natural orator. He had a sonorous, penetrating voice, his enunciation was clear and distinct, and he knew the secret of flattering and delighting his auditors."

Coup was an eyewitness to an incident at Elkhart, Indiana, on "a very stormy day during the war." Again, the issue was the flags that flew from the tent. This time, the weather was too windy to permit the flying of any flags at all, and

> One pompous young fellow, inflated with conceit, appointed himself a committee and visited Dan, demanding that the flags be hoisted. He charged that Dan had made

secession speeches in the South. With an ugly mob at his heels the fellow declared that if the flags were not hoisted he would burn the whole outfit. Dan truthfully told the crowd that he had already erected, at Girard, Pa., a monument to the Union soldiers; that he owned more flags than the whole city of Elkhart, and that he would show them if they desired; but he absolutely refused to hoist a stitch of bunting upon such a demand. Threats and arguments were alike powerless to move him from his stand.

Coup himself thought Rice was being "rather foolish, in those exciting times, and there appeared to me great danger in the action." But Rice knew people and their psychology.

> He publicly announced that at the night show he would give a full history of the leader of the mob, and did so with a vengeance. He had learned by careful inquiries something of the character of this fellow, who was a cashier in a bank, and at the evening performance, and in the actual presence of the man and his associates, Dan mounted a stool and gave his enemy such a verbal castigation as few persons have ever received. As he progressed in his speech he waxed eloquent, and in a marvelously deep, clear and penetrating voice pictured the vices and foibles of this "patriotic" cashier, until the audience was ready to mob the man. Suddenly a rush was made to where he had been sitting. But he was gone and the eloquent showman was the complete victor.

Rice seems to have been something like a verbal gunfighter who must have a showdown with the fastest tongue in every town.

It was a hard time for Rice in many respects. He separated from his wife, and there were reports that he was drinking heavily. He missed performances. It became known that he had let Charles W. Noyes take over the training of his animals. This testified to Rice's troubled life, for he was acknowledged to be a great animal trainer. He had taught tricks to a giraffe, a buffalo, and even a rhinoceros; and four pair of mules that he trained he then sold for $5,000 a pair. Worse, the clown who appeared under Rice's name was sometimes really J. L. Thayer. Thayer left Rice and went out on his own; Noyes joined him in 1863 to form the Thayer & Noyes Circus. But Rice went on—though it now became necessary to advertise that "THE REAL DAN RICE WILL DEFINITELY APPEAR."

In the end, his allegiance to the Union was recognized, despite his friendship with many southerners. Indeed, Carl Sandburg, in *Abraham Lincoln: The War Years*, says that busts of Dan Rice and Abraham Lincoln stood side by side at the Sanitary Fair in Chicago in 1864. The one label for the two busts, reported *Leslie's Weekly*, was THE TWO AMERICAN HUMORISTS.

When Rice brought his show to Washington, D.C., for a week's engagement in June 1864, he was surprised and honored to find President and Mrs. Lincoln sitting on one of his trunks, waiting for him. Lincoln needed to get away from the strains of the Civil War for a few hours. What better place than the circus? And what better person than Dan Rice, with whom Lincoln had first swapped yarns years before, in Springfield, Illinois, when Lincoln was a young lawyer and Rice had come to town with a circus. Rice was always ready, as Sandburg said of Lincoln, "for participation in the witty, the grotesque, the foolish, the flippant, lighter-minded phases of life during a war drenched with grief and draped with sorrow."

In this, as in so many things, Rice and Lincoln were typical of the American people, who had the same need for levity to divert them from the war's incessant sorrow. And perhaps the greatest such occasion of the war years was provided by the wedding that P. T. Barnum oversaw, between two midgets who, for all the ballyhoo that surrounded them, were genuinely in love—General Tom Thumb and Lavinia Warren.

They decided to get married at one of the worst times in the four bitter years of the war. Lincoln had optimistically issued the Emancipation Proclamation on January 1, 1863, but everyone knew that no slave would be free until Union forces were finally victorious, and the terrible defeat at Fredericksburg the previous December made it look to be a long conflict.

Maybe that was why, in the words of one recent writer, "The war of giants was pushed off the front page by a wedding of midgets." The public had found Tom Thumb diverting for twenty years: it had watched him grow in public from a child to a young man, and now it watched him fall in love.

Tom Thumb was on vacation at his home in Bridgeport when Barnum hired Lavinia Warren for his museum in 1862. Born on October 31, 1841, she was twenty years old, Tom Thumb's height at exactly thirty-two inches tall, and weighed twenty-nine pounds. She had been a schoolteacher, and had no trouble maintaining discipline in a room full of third-graders who were already taller than she was. To see the West, she had toured with a cousin who had a Mississippi riverboat show. On tour, she met Ulysses S. Grant and Stephen A. Douglas. Douglas tried to kiss her, but she demurred.

When Lavinia Warren went on display at Barnum's museum, the only male midget at work was George Washington Morrison McNutt, the son of a New Hampshire farmer. McNutt was eighteen years old and twenty-nine inches tall, weighed twenty-four pounds, and was clean shaven—at a time when Tom Thumb had swelled to fifty-two pounds and grown a mustache. Barnum signed Morrison to a three-year contract for $30,000, renamed him Commodore Nutt, and put him into a Navy uniform.

Commodore Nutt was an immediate hit with

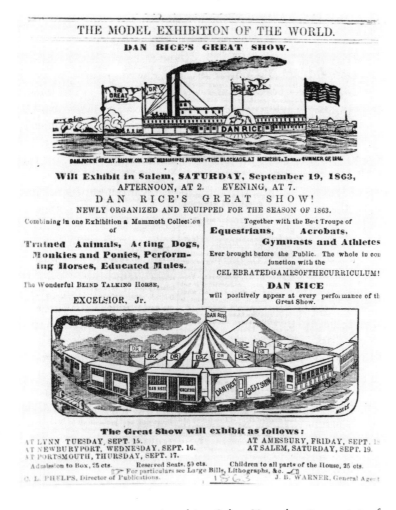

RUNNING THE BLOCKADE. An ad in a Salem, Massachusetts, newspaper for "DAN RICE'S GREAT SHOW," which "Will Exhibit in Salem, SATURDAY, September 19, 1863," reminds its Civil War readers that Rice ran the southern blockade on the Mississippi at Memphis in the summer of 1861. This was necessary because Rice had been accused of having secessionist sympathies. Citing war needs, General Frémont had seized one of the steamers on which Rice showed his circus. Rice petitioned the government for compensation and was awarded $32,000. Rice then requested that this money be spent on caring for wounded soldiers and their wives. After the war, Rice erected a $35,000 monument to the Civil War dead in his home town of Girard, Pennsylvania. (Circus World Museum, Baraboo, Wisconsin)

THE CIRCUS "SPEC," from "spectacle," is the traditional parade pageant of the circus within the Big Top or arena that includes most of the personnel and animals acting out an imaginative or historical theme. The first Spec was John Bill Ricketts's reenactment of his friend President Washington's triumph over the Whiskey Rebellion; the Bicentenniel Spec of Ringling Bros. and Barnum & Bailey featured a tribute to the astronauts who first landed on the moon. But here, during the American Civil War, the Spec was called "The Traitor's Doom," and dramatized a northern victory over the Confederacy. (Circus World Museum, Baraboo, Wisconsin)

the public, and in 1861 Lincoln invited Barnum to bring him to the White House. As Barnum and his new midget were leaving, Lincoln said: "Commodore, permit me to give you a parting word of advice. When you are in command of your fleet, if you find yourself in danger of being taken prisoner, I advise you to wade ashore." Everyone laughed except Nutt, who looked slowly up Lincoln's long legs. "I guess, Mr. President, you could do better than I could," he replied, and everyone laughed even harder.

The arrival of Lavinia at the American Museum created what Irving Wallace has described as "a Lilliputian triangle." Commodore Nutt became enamored of her. Then Tom Thumb grew tired of his miniature billiard table and his yacht, paid a visit to New York, and met Lavinia. The General went straight from his first chat with her to Barnum's private office, where, Barnum revealed in his autobiography, he asked his old friend and mentor for detailed information about Miss Warren and her family.

"Mr. Barnum, that is the most charming little lady I ever saw, and I believe she was created on purpose to be my wife."

"I will not oppose you in your suit," replied Barnum, "but you must do your own courting."

When he finally "popped the question," Miss Warren answered that she loved him, but she had to have her mother's consent and "you know that my mother objects to your mustache."

"I will cut that off and my ears also if that will induce her to give an affirmative to my question," he replied.

Commodore Nutt grew morose over his rejection, did some womanizing, and grew alarmingly thin. Gradually, however, he got hold of himself, agreed to serve as Thumb's best man, and was a friend of the couple until he died in 1881 at the age of thirty-seven, still a bachelor.

The wedding of General Tom Thumb and Lavinia Warren took place at Grace Church, New York City, Tuesday, February 10, 1863. Tom Thumb was twenty-five years old—and clean shaven; his bride was twenty-two. The guest list included 2,000 representatives of what the *New York Times* called "the elite, the *creme de la creme*, the upper ten, the bon ton, the select few, the very FF's of the City—nay of the Country." This meant members of Congress, the governors of several states, the Astors, Vanderbilts, and Belmonts. The Army of the Potomac was represented by Major General Ambrose E. Burnside. About 15,000 people had tried to get an invitation, some offering up to $75 for one card. But Barnum put a notice in the papers: "Money will not purchase wedding cards." Some of the uninvited tried to make their friends believe that they had to be out of town "on the advice of the doctor."

Broadway had been blocked from Ninth to Twelfth streets, and the police set up barricades and formed human chains to contain the immense crowd that waited from before dawn for a glimpse of the bride and groom. The wedding was scheduled to take place at high noon.

When Lavinia's wedding carriage arrived, right on time, the people jamming the streets, and every window, door, and balcony in the vicinity, sent up a great cheer.

The wedding itself didn't start until 12:30, when the great Barnum made his way up the aisle. Thousands of tulips were banked along the aisles, where an honor guard of New York City policemen stood at attention, and at the altar. In front of the altar a platform three feet high had been erected and covered with Brussels carpet so that the bride and groom could see and be seen.

Miss Minnie Warren, Lavinia's two-foot-one-inch sister, was maid of honor. The *Times* reported that the wedding was "done decently and in order. After Dr. Taylor gave the benediction, the General kissed his wife and, in the presence of the entire audience, bestowed upon her the 'killing' glance with which he has, in days gone by, captivated so many millions of equally susceptible damsels."

After the service, the crowds chased the carriage all the way to the Metropolitan Hotel. At the hotel, at three o'clock in the afternoon, the wedding presents were placed on exhibition in the bride's quarters, guarded by a stout policeman, and in other hotel parlors two thousand boxes of wedding cake were distributed. President and Mrs. Lincoln were unable to attend but sent, said the press, a set of Chinese fire screens, "richly inlaid with gold, silver, and pearl." Edwin Booth, the actor, gave a pair of tiny slippers. Mrs. Astor gave a coral leaf brooch and earrings with a diamond center; Mrs. Cornelius Vanderbilt, "magnificent pearls"; August Belmont, a miniature set of charms; and Mrs. Belmont, a necklace of Tuscan gold. Tiffany gave the couple a silver horse and chariot encrusted with rubies.

Barnum's wedding gift was a basket of polished tortoiseshell. When a spring was touched, a hidden bird clad in natural feathers rose up and sang sweet songs. The magical basket was said to have cost $1,000.

Later that evening, the couple was serenaded outside the Metropolitan Hotel by the New York Excelsior Band, which played "The Land of the Free, the Home of the Brave." So many thousands jammed the streets for a glimpse of the bridal couple that the little general finally appeared on the balcony. "But ladies and gentlemen," he said, after thanking everyone for their interest, "the little woman in the adjoining apartment is very anxious to see me. I must therefore make this speech, like myself, *short*."

The next day they set out on their honeymoon, which included their visit to the White House. The Lincolns gave a dinner and reception for them, at which the tiny couple stood with composure and dignity in the reception room of the Executive Mansion. They met five

cabinet members as well as several senators and congressmen and their children, right down to the smallest.

A guest named Grace Greenwood remembered the way Tom Thumb took the arm of his bride and led her almost to the feet of the President—who, of course, was six feet four, seventy-six inches to their thirty-two. "With profound respect they looked up, up, to his kindly face. It was pleasant to see their tall host bend, and bend, to take their little hands in his great palm, holding Madame's with special chariness, as though it were a robin's egg, and he were afraid of breaking it."

Lincoln was reportedly quite taken with Lavinia because her face resembled a miniature of the face of his wife. During the course of the evening, "while the bride and groom were taking a quiet promenade by themselves up and down the big drawing-room," recalled Miss Greenwood, "I noticed the President gazing after them with a smile of quaint humor; but, in his sorrow-shadowed eyes, there was something more than amusement—a gentle sympathy in the apparent happiness and good-fellowship of this curious wedded pair—come to him out of fairyland."

Lincoln's son Tad, who was then nine years old, also thought Mrs. Thumb looked like his mother. When refreshments came, Tad personally served General and Mrs. Thumb, placing wine and ices on a chair within their reach. Later, Lincoln overheard his son say to someone: "Isn't it funny that Father is so tall and Mr. and Mrs. Thumb are so little?" Said Lincoln to his son: "My boy, God likes to do funny things. Here you have the long and short of it."

———

Among those fighting in the Union army was Archie Campbell, who had graduated with the highest honors from the College of William and Mary in 1853. The following year he joined the John Robinson Circus as a talking clown, and was soon known for his pithy sallies. When he went to war, it seemed to him that nearly every place he fought was a place where he had once performed. In September of 1863, says Gil Robinson, Union and Confederate cavalry clashed at the town of Zollisoffer, Tennessee, and Campbell, then a sergeant commanding a section of artillery, was ordered to open fire from a position that was ready-made to place a battery. It was, he found, the dirt-banked circus ring where he had clowned three years to the day before this battle.

His reaction at the time, he later told Gil Robinson, was the reaction of a killer, not a clown. Giving the order to fire, he said, "Now by my halidom, will this people find pith in my remarks. Shrapnel shell, six-second fuse."

In 1864, Archie Campbell was captured by Confederate forces and sent to their notorious Andersonville military prison in Georgia, where starvation and poor sanitation led to the death of nearly 13,000 prisoners and the postwar trial and hanging of its commander. At Andersonville, however, Campbell reverted to the ways of a clown, and became such a favorite with the officers running the camp that they tried not to treat him as their prisoner. He even succeeded in obtaining better living conditions for other members of his regiment, the Fourteenth Illinois Cavalry.

Later he was released in an exchange of prisoners and returned to the circus ring.

———

To bring diversion and laughter to the soldiers, circuses performed at Union army posts and, by 1864, even in the war zones. Horace Norton and Frank J. Howes, who had organized a company in Chicago and brought it by rail to Nashville, Tennessee, set up their tents in the heart of the city, which was occupied by the Union, but found that they came under fire from southern guns.

"It was a common occurrence during our stay of six weeks there," recalled John H. Glenroy, a member of the troupe, "for shells to keep dropping and bursting four or five times a day within a distance of twenty yards from our canvas."

Worse than the shell fire, from a circus man's point of view, was the fact that, shortly after the arrival of the show, the Union commander, General George H. Thomas, commandeered all of their trained horses but one. The circus appealed to President Lincoln, who ordered the circus horses returned on the condition that it provide substitutes.

———

Sparing circus horses was a gesture that would seem quaint by the fall of 1864, when the Civil War became total war. Union General William Tecumseh Sherman, entering Atlanta on September 2, told the mayor, "War is cruelty and you cannot refine it." To break the spirit of the civilian South, Sherman and General Philip Sheridan began burning mills and barns and whatever their men could not carry. Sheridan told his soldiers to leave the people "with nothing but their eyes to weep with." In retaliation, Confederate President Jefferson Davis planned terror tactics of his own, designed to scare the North into ending the war and to show the South that it could strike into the heart of the Union's largest city. To execute his plan, Davis chose Jacob Thompson, a wealthy lawyer, Congressman, and Secretary of the Interior under President Buchanan. From headquarters in Toronto, Canada, Thompson fielded "a corps to burn New York City," an eight-man task force.

The terrorist plot called for the nearly simultaneous firing of New York hotels and places of amusement as a signal for a rising of the "Sons of Liberty," a secret society that supported the right of secession by any state at any time. There were said to be 20,000 such "Copperheads," as southern sympathizers in the North were known, in New York City alone. They would take over City Hall and police headquarters, and then blow up Fort Lafayette, the federal fort in New York harbor. As it turned out, one of the prime targets was that preeminent place of New York amusement, Barnum's American Museum.

Originally, the plot was to go into action on Election Day, November 8, 1864. But early that morning, General Benjamin Butler marched into New York City, announced that he knew something of the plot, and stated that he was there to arrest the conspirators.

The Sons of Liberty did not rise up. The Confederate captain who had drawn up the list of hotels to be burned and had arranged for the manufacture of the incendiary devices to burn them now decided against taking part. On the day the Confederacy was to have terrorized New York, Abraham Lincoln defeated General George B. McClellan by 400,000 votes.

The rebels might have returned to Canada if they hadn't read in the newspapers on that and succeeding days that Sherman had set fire to Atlanta, burning most of the city, and was now leading his 60,000 men on what turned out to be a march of devastation "from Atlanta to the sea."

Colonel Robert Maxwell Martin, twenty-six years old and the leader of the eight-man task force, decided to terrorize the North in return. Six of the eight terrorists agreed to stay in New York and reduce it to ashes. Their resolve was strengthened by the headlines concerning Sherman's march in the New York papers for Thanksgiving Day, November 25, 1864. A "rebel report" of Sherman's progress from Macon, Georgia, dated November 18, said that the Yankee army "are supposed to be still in the neighborhood of Griffin, burning everything in their rear."

That evening, Martin and the others divided among themselves sixty four-ounce bottles of "incendiary Greek fire"—the Molotov cocktail of the American Civil War. They registered under false names in nineteen Manhattan hotels and put the plot in motion.

While Colonel Martin set fire to the Hoffman House and the Fifth Avenue Hotel, Lieutenant Headley set fire to the Astor House, City Hotel, Everett House, and the United States Hotel. By nine o'clock, all nineteen hotels had been set afire. But in each case, quick-witted hotel workers put out the flames before they could do much damage.

Lieutenant John T. Ashbrook set fire to the LaFarge Hotel on Broadway, next door to the Winter Garden Theater, where 3,000 people were watching a performance of *Julius Caesar* starring the three Booth brothers—Edwin Booth as Brutus, Junius Brutus Booth as Cassius, and John Wilkes Booth as Marc Antony. The LaFarge fire was quickly put out, but "When the alarm was given at the LaFarge the excitement became very intense among the closely-packed mass of human beings in Winter Garden Theatre," reported the *Times*, ". . . and but for the presence of mind of Mr. Booth, who addressed them from the stage of the theatre, telling them there was no danger, it is fearful to think what would have been the result." The *Times* does not specify which Mr. Booth averted the panic—Edwin, Junius Brutus, or the man who, less than five months later, as an actor in another Confederate plot, would assassinate Abraham Lincoln.

Captain Robert C. Kennedy had already set three hotel fires and reinforced his courage with whiskey when he found himself in front of Barnum's brightly lighted American Mu-

MRS. DAN RICE, *who pawned her jewels so that her husband could come back from his darkest hour. When "Dr." Gilbert Spalding, the circus owner who went from being Rice's employer to being his rival and enemy, had Rice arrested for slander, hauled into a Rochester court, and thrown in the Blue Eagle Jail, Rice retaliated by composing a song, portraying himself as a martyr, with the same poetic name as his place of incarceration. Rice emerged from imprisonment more popular than ever, with the public taking his side against the thin-skinned Spalding. Rice's popularity did not protect him from the slander judgment, however, and the jester lost his farm and other real estate by foreclosure. The loyalty of his wife enabled him to start again, with his famous One-Horse Show. (Circus World Museum, Baraboo, Wisconsin)*

SINGING CLOWN. *In* Old Wagon Show Days, *Gil Robinson lists Nat Austin among "Five Great Clowns" of the nineteenth-century American circus. Austin was a singing clown, for before the advent of vaudeville, the phonograph, movies, radio, and television, it was the circus clown who introduced America's popular music. Such tunes as "Turkey in the Straw," "Down in a Coal Mine," and "The Man on the Flying Trapeze" were sold in the circus tent. Indeed, vaudeville was founded by a former singing clown, Tony Pastor. One of the last of the singing clowns was William Burke (1845–1906), a headliner with Barnum and Bailey in the 1880s, whose daughter Billie played Glinda the Good Witch in* The Wizard of Oz. *Singing clowns often led the crowd in a singalong. Gil Robinson's other four greats were George L. Fox, "Greatest in Pantomime"; Chas. Abbott, "Shakespearean jester"; John Lowlow, another singing clown; and Dan Rice, nicknamed "The Boss" long before Bruce Springsteen. (Circus World Museum, Baraboo, Wisconsin)*

seum, where extra performances were being given in celebration of Thanksgiving Day. The bill was topped by the kind of freak show that Barnum would soon bring to the circus:

THE TALLEST, SHORTEST AND FATTEST

Specimens of Humanity Ever Seen.

THREE MAMMOTH FAT GIRLS, Weighing ONE TON! 2,000 POUNDS! ONE TON!

THREE GIANTS 24 FEET HIGH

COL. GOSHEN, MONS. JOSEPH

AND ANNA SWAN

IN LIVING CONTRAST MAY BE SEEN.

In addition to the freak show, there were "kangaroos, [a] learned seal, and a menagerie of 50 other living animals not to be seen in any other collection."

Kennedy paid the thirty cents admission and carried his black valise, now half filled with the bottles of Greek fire, into the museum.

Mingling with the customers, he examined several exhibits. Suddenly, after descending the main staircase, he halted, opened the valise, took out a bottle of Greek fire, and threw it at the steps behind him. The crowd saw a sudden sheet of flame. Barnum's museum was ablaze. Captain Kennedy stepped out into the street and disappeared.

In the lecture room, 2,500 patrons were seeing *Waiting for the Verdict*, one of Barnum's morality plays. Assistant Manager John Greenwood, Jr., burst in with the terrifying word that the place was on fire. In calming a crowd, he was no Booth. Instantly the audience became a mob fighting to get out. There were injuries, but no one was killed.

By now, smoke was pouring out of the museum's entrance onto Broadway. The curious street crowd fell back as the red-shirted firemen arrived. Choking and hysterical, Anna Swan, the seven-foot, eleven-inch giantess from Nova Scotia, stumbled through the smoke at the entrance. When Greenwood and three firemen tried to help her, she sent them sprawling. It took six men to subdue her and a doctor to sedate her.

Other firemen put a ladder to a second-floor window and helped bring the wild animals out of the museum. On Broadway, amid the throngs, such prized creatures had to be guarded carefully.

When the sun rose on the day after Thanksgiving, every fire in the plot to burn New York City had been put out. Damage to the St. Nicholas Hotel, probably the worst damaged, was estimated at $3,000; Barnum estimated his losses at $1,000; otherwise, the damage had been light.

"Had all these hotels, hay barges, theatres, etc., been set on fire at the same moment, and each fire well kindled," reported the *New York Times* on November 27, "the Fire Department would not have able to extinguish them all, and during the confusion the fire would probably have gained so great a headway that before assistance could have been obtained the best portion of the city would have been laid in ashes. But, fortunately, thanks to the Police, Fire Department, and the bungling manner in which the plan was executed by the conspirators, it proved a complete and miserable failure."

Barnum, understandably anxious to minimize the danger to his establishment from fire, wrote a letter that the *Times* ran alongside its front-page story on the plot. According to Barnum, "every day, from sunrise until ten o'clock P.M. I have eleven persons continually on the different floors of the Museum, looking to the comfort of visitors, and ready at a moment's warning to extinguish any fire that might appear. From 10 o'clock at night until sunrise, I have from six to twelve persons in the Museum engaged as watchmen, sweepers, painters, &c.

"I always have a large number of buckets filled with water on and under the stage, and a large fire hose always screwed on to be used at a second's notice. I never allow an uncovered light in the Museum, and I heat by steam from a furnace in the cellar."

And he added: "My own sense of security is proved by the fact that I never insure for one-third the value of the Museum property."

Barnum would have cause to regret this policy less than eight months later.

———

In the spring of 1865, five days after the Confederacy surrendered, Abraham Lincoln was assassinated. Dan Rice, abruptly canceling his engagements, traveled home to Girard, Pennsylvania, and went into mourning for his old friend. That same spring, the *Floating Palace*, symbol of the circus's antebellum free river passage between North and South, which had remained tied to that wharf in Indiana throughout the war, burned to the waterline.

The glamour of the bareback rider, like the one above, attracted many American girls, including Jacqueline Onassis, herself an accomplished horsewoman by the age of twelve. Her cousin, Edie Beale, said, "One day she announced her intention to run away from home to become Queen of the Circus." At fourteen, Jackie made the tongue-in-cheek prediction that she would be the circus queen who, though admired "by the world's greatest men," married "the man on the flying trapeze."

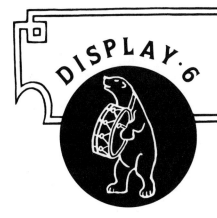

DISPLAY·6

The Wild Frontier

They struggled through mud, they forded streams (or dropped into them when bridges collapsed under their weight), they fled from prairie fires and faced down gunfighters, and one way or another, overcoming the thousand natural shocks circus folk are heir to, circuses got through—and were probably seen by more frontier Americans than any other form of professional entertainment. What Frederick Merk of Harvard University calls the "greatest migration of people in recorded history" was attended almost from the beginning by circuses that followed in its wake, first by wagon, then by riverboat, and finally by railroad train.

At first, all circuses traveled by wagon. That is the way the pioneer troupe of Thomas Pool traveled from Philadelphia to New York in the 1780s, and that is the way a circus owned by Nathan Howes and the two Crane brothers crossed the Alleghenies in 1831 on its way to Mobile, Alabama. Before 1836, circuses had reached Chicago. Thereafter, as the frontier retreated, circuses advanced. Every year between 1838 and the Civil War—with the possible exceptions of 1839 and 1844—circuses appeared in the frontier state of Missouri; in 1856, ten different circuses traveled to Missourians beyond St. Louis.

The Seeley Circus of 1840 is the first wagon show definitely known to have exhibited west of St. Louis. The *Boon's Lick Times* of Fayette, Missouri, for July 11, 1840, tells of its appearance that year in the villages of Fayette and Glasgow. The following year, the Johnson, Fogg, Stickney Circus brought to Fayette a trick horse named Champion, sixteen equestrians, a juggler, and a clown who played the

GRIZZLY ADAMS and P. T. Barnum formed a partnership in 1860 to exhibit Grizzly's animals in a tent at the corner of Broadway and Thirteenth Street in New York City. On the opening day a brass band preceded the animals down Broadway and up the Bowery. It was Barnum's first street parade as a showman. Adams rode on a float, mounted on his favorite bear, General Frémont. (John Culhane Collection)

banjo and "sang Negro songs." This troupe journeyed up the north bank of the Missouri River, reportedly as far west as the Platte country, returning on the opposite side of the river. This was scarcely four years after the U.S. Senate ratified the Platte Purchase treaty, whereby the Indians agreed to vacate their reservation northwest of the Missouri state line and move to new territory farther west, in return for $7,500, one hundred cows and calves for each tribe, five bulls, one hundred hogs, a mill, farm advisers, a blacksmith, a schoolmaster, several houses, and agricultural implements for a period of five years.

Emigrant traffic west over the Oregon Trail started about 1840. In the spring of 1842, a total of 112 persons left Independence, and by 1845 the number was about 3,000. The discovery of gold in California changed all that. Thousands of Americans decided to head for the gold fields, and it soon became apparent that St. Joseph, Missouri, was the best situated place for outfitting such a journey and for "jumping off." One observer reported that "the city was packed so full of people that tents were pitched about the city and along the opposite bank of the river in such numbers that we seemed to be besieged by an army. . . . Play and drink was the order of the day."

It didn't take the circus long to find them. So it is perhaps no surprise that three years later, in 1851, the St. Joseph city fathers passed City Ordinance No. 84, charging $50, the highest fee in Missouri, for each day a circus played there. Columbia charged $25, a typical fee for the time; Liberty and Springfield charged $10 and $5 respectively. St. Joseph was in the catbird seat. With its large influx of population, circuses would come there no matter what. Other cities had to keep the tax low if they didn't want to discourage circuses from making the trip.

In 1856, the Orton Badger Circus gave the first theatrical performance of any kind in Kansas City, Missouri. (Seventy-one seasons later, Orton Bros. Circus played out the 1927 season as a wagon circus.) Wagon travel was arduous. Bridges, if they existed, sometimes splintered under the weight or collapsed altogether. Spring rains created muddy roads that caused exhaustion. Nevertheless, some circuses traveled nearly 3,000 miles a year on the wild frontier.

As early as the 1850s, a number of wagon circuses, while making most of their moves by road, tried some special jumps on the recently built railroad tracks. By 1869, just after the hammering of the golden spike, the Dan Castello Circus was able to make the first train trip to the West Coast. In fact, the circus had reached California twenty years before Dan Castello made it by train. In 1849, a small company of troupers headed by Joseph A. Rowe, an equestrian, traveled by sailing "round the horn"; they played in a theater on Kearney Street in San Francisco on October 29 of that year. Then forty years old, Rowe had run off with one of the first circuses to play the southern United States, trouped the West Indies and South America, and was playing Lima, Peru, with his own show when gold was discovered in California. Rowe decided to get in on the Gold Rush, and after braving the long voyage to California, he charged a staggering $3 for a single seat and $5 for a box. (Typical circus prices throughout the pre–Civil War period were fifty cents for adults, half price for children and servants.) Nevertheless, 1,500 people greeted the performance with "thunders of applause" on opening night, according to the newspaper *Alta California*, which predicted that "Mr. Rowe's circus entertainments will relieve the tedium of many a long winter evening." The show consisted of trick rider Rowe and his trained horse, Adonis; Mrs. Rowe, an equestrienne; two ropedancers; and a riding clown named Folley who eventually quit the show because, he complained, he couldn't live on his $1,200-a-month salary. Nevertheless, Rowe played San Francisco for a year, then toured Australia. He was said to have cleared $100,000.

In 1857, Rowe and Co.'s Pioneer Circus of California toured the mining districts in the interior. The clown W. F. Wallett was with the company, and his autobiography described this taste of the frontier at its wildest. Indeed, at Nevada, California, Wallett and a friend had a narrow escape from death:

One night after the conclusion of the performance, we strolled out and looked in at a large saloon. This was divided into three departments. In one was a fandango party, comprised of Chilian, Mexican, and Spanish women, with a motley crew of men of all colours, languages, and nationalities. The second was devoted to refreshment, drinking, and card playing. The third to a game called "kino." There were ten or fifteen miners round the table, on which were piled immense quantities of gold for which they were playing. Some desperate ruffians entered, and I immediately suspected mischief. . . .

[Wallett and his companion, a man named Burnell, were] unfortunately unarmed. The place was brilliantly illuminated with camphine lamps. At the report of a pistol every lamp was instantly extinguished. I darted under the table like a shot, and pulled Burnell by the leg down beside me. Never shall I forget the horror of this moment. I could hear the heavy thud of bludgeons, and knew knives were doing their deadly work.

When the lamps were relighted, of course, there was no more gold on the table, "and the miners we had just seen in lusty enjoyment, lay around butchered and mangled in the most terrible manner . . . we resolved never to travel or go out at night without being well armed."

Moreover, despite the gold on that table, the boom was about over. Admission sank to fifty cents, which didn't save the season from being a disaster. Rowe went back to the South Seas the following year. He eventually came back to the Pacific coast, but his show folded in San Francisco in 1860. Thereafter, he was with other men's circuses as rider, ringmaster, and advance agent before dying in obscurity in 1887.

If murder was always a likely possiblity on the wild frontier, so was rough frontier justice. The Mabie brothers were setting up for a date in Texas when a sheriff came to them and announced that he had a triple hanging scheduled for circus day. If there was anything that could compete with the circus for the attention of Texans, it was a hanging. It would surely cut into circus receipts considerably. On the other hand, said the sheriff, if the Mabies would provide himself and his prisoners with complimentary passes to their show, the hanging would be postponed until after the performance.

Near the close of the performance, Pete Conklin, the clown, announced what by then was a circus custom: a "concert," or aftershow, for which tickets would be sold by agents passing among the audience. Then, by instruction of the Mabies, he announced a special, added attraction: "Ladies and gentlemen, immediately after our concert, the hanging will take place at the first big tree to the right as you pass out of our tent."

The wild frontier produced at least one star who was popular back east. James C. "Grizzly" Adams was renowned as a hunter and trapper of the Sierra Nevada and Rocky Mountains. In 1860, P. T. Barnum took him into a partnership to exhibit Grizzly's animals in New York City. Adams's skull had recently been smashed in by his bear General Frémont, in a moment of playfulness. The wound had nearly healed, Adams told Barnum, though the bear "did his business so thoroughly, I'm a used-up man. But I reckon I may live six months or a year yet." Adams brought twenty grizzly bears, several wolves, and buffaloes, California lions, tigers, and elk, but he proved to be as great an attraction as his animals. He wore a wolf's head trimmed with tails for a cap and had long, stiff, bushy gray hair and a long white beard. Adams performed with his animals in the tent for six weeks; then a doctor said he had not much more than that to live and insisted he take a rest. Instead, Adams sold his animals to Barnum but remained employed as their trainer and went on a tour of Connecticut and Massachusetts. He asked Barnum for a $500 bonus if he could tour ten weeks, explaining that he had neglected his wife long enough and wanted to be able to provide for her after he was gone. Barnum agreed. Adams toured for exactly ten weeks, collected his bonus, traveled home to Massachusetts, and died five days later. His animals were added to Barnum's museum collection but soon were sold to a menagerie, except the "Sea-Lion of the Pacific." The sea lion remained a popular attraction at the museum, where his tank was supplied with fresh seawater daily by the deckhands of steamboats.

———◆———

Nature could be as unpredictable—and occasionally as lethal—as man or beast. "No other human being can realize like the showman the volume of dread hardship and disaster held by those two small words, 'bad roads,'" wrote W. C. Coup. Coup began his circus career in the 1860s, running the sideshow of the E. F. & J. Mabie Circus, a wagon show that had to pass through the Southwest "over such wretchedly constructed highways that the slightest fall of rain was sufficient to convert them into rivers of mud. The heavy wagons would sink to their hubs in the mire and the whole [wagon] train would be stopped."

By the light of flaring torches a dozen big draft horses would be hitched to the wagons stuck in the mud. Teamsters would shout, curse, and sometimes beat the horses, and the animals would strain until their muscles stood out like knotted ropes. But often even a battalion of six teams could not move a wagon out of the mire.

Elephants were usually the answer: the shout would go down the line for Romeo. "In a few minutes," Coup remembered, "the wise old elephant would come splashing through the mud with an air that seemed to say, 'I thought you'd have to call on me!' He knew his place and would instantly take his stand behind the mired wagon. After he had carefully adjusted his huge frontal against the rear end of the vehicle the driver would give the command, 'Mile up!' Gently, but with a tremendous power, Romeo would push forward, the wagon would start, and lo! the pasty mud would close in behind the wheels like the Red Sea."

Shows that didn't own an elephant would sometimes see their wagons pulled apart and their horses fall sprawling into the deep, heavy mud, even up to their necks.

But mud was not so feared as prairie fire. Looking back, Coup called his escape from that danger "one of the most terrible and impressive experiences of my entire career."

One morning in the 1860s the circus had started north from a small town in Missouri. Their caravan stretched out across the prairie for a mile, and Coup reveled in its beauty. "The elaborate and gilded chariots," he wrote, "the piebald Arabian horses, the drove of shambling camels and the huge swaying elephants gave a touch of genuine oriental picturesqueness to the scene, strangely out of keeping with the wild Western landscape and surroundings." On all sides, the prairie was a profusion of wild-flowers of great variety. Coup stretched out on the top of a lumbering chariot, drank in their fragrance, and went to sleep.

He woke up suddenly "with a sense of un-accountable alarm." The first thing he noticed was the strange behavior of a jackrabbit about ten yards away from the trail. Instead of bound-ing off at the approach of the caravan, the jack-rabbit "sat there with his ears cocked straight up, his nose working nervously, and his heart pounding so heavily that its pulsations shook his gray sides." Then Coup saw a rattlesnake that seemed to be fleeing.

The captive animals in their cages now began to show unusual signs of restlessness. The lions and tigers commenced a strange moaning that wasn't like their usual roars and growls. "From the monkey cages came plaintive, half-human cries. These sounds were taken up by all the animals, big and little. Walking in the proces-sion, the elephants trumpeted and the camels screamed; every animal took part in a weird chorus. Then the air seemed to take on a hazy appearance, particularly in the direction from which we had come."

Finally, Coup realized what was happen-ing. He strained his eyes and saw a cloud of smoke far in the rear of the caravan. At that moment, he caught sight of a man on horse-back, on the crest of a rise in the prairie, who was riding toward them at top speed. As he galloped past them, he shouted the words that confirmed Coup's worst fear: "Whip up, man! The prairie's on fire! Move for the river straight ahead!"

The circus boss rode up to the lead chariot, drawn by "six splendid horses white as milk," and shouted to them to set the fastest possible pace.

"It was a genuine chariot race," said Coup, "in which the stake was life and the fine, death by flames."

At first they worried that the elephants and camels would slow them down, "but the way in which they swung themselves over the ground was a revelation."

"Where is the river?" the circus people screamed at one another. "Can we make the water?"

Suddenly, Coup saw the boss spur his horse, gallop ahead of the six whites, leap from the saddle, strike a match to the grass, remount, and ride away a short distance. As each team approached, he barked: "Wait till the flames spread a little and then break through the line of the backfire I've started and form a circle."

The grass that the boss set on fire was much shorter than the general prairie growth, and the fire he made in it would not acquire "the volume, intensity and sweep of that hurricane of flame" they were fleeing. At his command, each of his teamsters urged their teams on— and though they might rear up with fear before plunging through, each found refuge "inside a charred, blackened cicle fringed with flame."

"No sound I have ever heard," Coup said long afterward, "approached in abject terror the awful symphony of roars, growls, screams, wails and screeches that went up from the mad-dened beasts in that caravan as the great sky-reaching cylinder of flame and smoke rolled down upon us and was met barely forty rods [220 yards] away by the rapidly spreading line of our own backfire."

The six white chariot horses couldn't stand it. Crazed with fear, they pulled the chariot toward the oncoming fire storm. The frantic driver tugged on the reins, trying to stop his suicidal team, until the boss cried, "Jump!"

He jumped just in time, "for an instant later the white charioteers had disappeared under the great red and black barrel that was rolling upon us."

As the circus folk stood and prayed, unsure whether their next breath would be flame or air, "the tornado of fire . . . swept around our little oasis of burned ground and passed on towards the river."

They couldn't look for their horses until the ground cooled. When it did, they didn't have far to go before they came upon some wheels and other ironwork that was all that was left of the lead chariot, and a little beyond, the burnt and blackened flesh of the six splendid horses.

But it wasn't all blood, mud, fire, and twisted necks on the wild frontier. Out of these rough-and-ready conditions came—so circus legend has it—one of its most refreshing traditions: the semiofficial circus drink, pink lemonade.

Pete Conklin was doing tumbling and general acrobatics with the Ed and Jerry Mabie Circus as it trouped about Texas in the 1850s when, without warning, Tony Pastor, their only clown, jumped the show. The Mabies made Pete Conklin a clown to save it, and he did, but they gave him no raise for his efforts. So Conklin told Jerry Mabie that if he didn't get more money, he would jump the show too.

Mabie doubted it. As Earl Chapin May wisely observed, "Texas in 1857 was no place for a lone, broke Yankee circus man." Conklin's brother George, an early wild animal trainer, said that the Mabies were astonished when Pete packed his bags and went. But Pete had a plan: he had saved some money, and he used it to buy two mules and a covered wagon, sugar, tartaric acid, and some lemons—which were very scarce in Texas in 1857. He trailed the Mabie circus, sleeping with his precious lemons by night and selling lemonade to the circusgoers by day. And he cleaned up.

"The Mabies regarded him sourly but did not interfere," said May. Wherever the circus played, Conklin found water and set up a lemonade stand near the lot. He had been a singing clown, so he now became a singing lemonade seller, and his song went:

> Here's your ice-cold lemonade
> Made in the shade,
> Stick your finger in the glass:
> It'll freeze fast.

Pete Conklin was as successful a lemonade seller as he had been a clown—until the very hot day when he found no water but lots of customers in the vicinity of the circus lot. Rushing around in desperation among his former coworkers, he came upon a tub of water in which Fannie Jamieson, the beautiful bareback rider, had just been soaking her red tights. To the tub of pink water, Pete added the usual ingredients, then ballyhooed the results as the champagne of circus drinks: pink lemonade. Earl Chapin May and Pete's brother George insist that this is the origin of the tradition of pink lemonade at the circus, and if it isn't, it should be.

———◆———

It was circus women as well as circus men who saw to it that the circus in America survived—and even thrived—in the frontier period. Mollie Bailey and Agnes Lake owned circuses that were models of how to take advantage of a nation's growing pains.

In 1844, Mollie Bailey was born Mary Arline Kirkland on the Kirkland plantation near Mobile, Alabama. She was educated at a "ladies' academy" in Tuscaloosa, Alabama, where her report card said: "Excellent in dramatics and tableau work." She was already noted for her beauty and her musical ability when, in 1858, the Bailey Family Circus—no kin to the other Baileys of the American circus—came to Mobile. Among the Bailey family members was a rusty-haired, teenaged bandmaster named James Augustus Bailey. Mary Arline decided that "Excellent in dramatics and tableau work" meant that she had a future in show business, and that her lifetime partner should be young "Gus" Bailey. When her parents objected, she eloped with Gus on the night of March 21, 1858, which she ever after remembered as moonlit. Combining their musical talents, they started a little concert company and toured Arkansas doing songs and dances and comedy pieces. Mary now called herself Mollie Bailey.

Then came the Civil War. Mollie Bailey's husband joined Hood's Fifth Texas Brigade, and Mollie became a nurse in the Confederate army. She had a little girl by then, so she boarded the baby in Richmond, Virginia, and spent her days at the military hospital.

The Baileys also salved war wounds with music. In a lull in the fighting, James Bailey composed the song "The Old Gray Mare (She Ain't What She Used to Be)." As a marching song, it was once as familiar to Texans as "The Eyes of Texas." (It would become the official song of the National Democratic Convention in Houston in 1928.) When Mollie wasn't nursing the wounded, she sang to them, and she often gave performances in camps and hospitals.

But the favorite story about Mollie Bailey told how she smuggled through enemy lines, wrapped in paper packages tucked in her hair and sewed in the hem of her skirts, quinine badly needed by the Third Texas Brigade; and how during this adventure she came into the possession of information that aided Rebel blockade runners. This legend would benefit her immeasurably as a circus proprietor in southern states after the war.

At first, Reconstruction was hard for the Bai-

leys. Their family grew to eight children, but Gus Bailey's health never really recovered from the effects of the malnutrition and cold he had suffered during the war. Gus and Mollie worked together on a Mississippi River showboat, he as the bandleader, she as an actress and singer, until his strength gave out.

Mollie was always strong. About 1875, they started a circus that trouped Arkansas in horse-drawn wagons. When Gus could no longer run it, she took over its management. In 1885, she took their show to Texas, and there she found that she was regarded as the embodiment of the brave women of the Confederacy. Texans called her "Aunt Mollie," and she began calling her show "A Texas Show for Texas People." On the three center poles of her Big Top, she flew the flags of the Union, the Confederacy, and the Lone Star state of Texas. Civil War veterans were always admitted free, Union and Confederate alike, and the Confederate veterans spread word about what she had done during the war. They began arranging their reunions to coincide with the scheduled appearance of her circus. Texas county fairs vied to have "Aunt Mollie's" show on their fairgrounds.

She got into the habit of buying a parcel of land in each of the many towns that she played in, and eventually she owned land in 150 Texas towns. "By 1890," wrote Esse Forrester O'Brien, Texas and circus historian, "more than half the time she showed on her own lots, thus saving occupation taxes—a new idea in the show business." She also took a personal interest in the communities where she showed, often giving benefit performances for local charities or for flood or drought relief.

In 1898 her husband died, but Mollie Bailey went on. She was now a Texas institution. "Aunt Mollie's Coming" was all her publicity had to say to fill her tent with Lone Star circus fans. In 1905, she made her circus a railroad show by buying a Pullman and two boxcars, and in many a town that she visited, "Open House" aboard her Pullman on a siding became a great social occasion.

Gradually her children began participating, as performers (Birdie and George); bandmaster (William); in advance advertising (James); and overseeing the circus lot (Brad). Mollie Bailey retired in 1914 to her home in Houston, and her sons took over the management of her circus. In 1918 she died, and the following year her sons decided to convert the Mollie Bailey Circus from a railroad show to trucks. Her circus did not long survive "Aunt Mollie," though. She was the one with the knack of bringing a small family show over miserable roads to entertain out-of-the-way communities that otherwise would have gone without.

But perhaps the quintessential circus owner of the wild frontier was another woman: Agnes Lake, owner and proprietor of Lake's Hippo-Olympiad & Mammoth Circus. In the 1870s, her circus was a top attraction in many of the towns that were sprouting on the wild and frequently lawless frontier like whiskers on a cowboy.

Agnes Mersman was an Alsatian, born in 1827 and brought to America by her parents when she was three years old. In 1842, when she was fifteen, the tents for Robinson & Eldred's Circus were pitched a few blocks from her home in Cincinnati, Ohio. The star clown of the show was William "Bill" Lake. Passing her home one day, Bill Lake saw Agnes Mersman swinging in her yard. He bantered with her, gradually revealed himself as the star of the show, and gave her free tickets for herself and her family.

Before the circus left Cincinnati, the two had decided that they wanted to get married immediately. When Agnes's parents opposed the match, the couple decided to elope to St. Louis. Obeying the social mores of the time, Agnes

would not go on the same boat with Bill. But a week after the show left town, she booked passage on the *White Cloud*, an Ohio River steamboat, and made the trip. In St. Louis, no clergyman or justice of the peace would marry a man to a girl who looked even less than fifteen, so Bill and Agnes took another steamboat to New Orleans. It was the same story, but at least there a judge told them that if they would ride to Lafayette, Louisiana, ten miles away, a Judge Raynell would marry them.

Late that fall, Bill Lake got another job clowning, with Rich's Circus, for the winter season in Mexico. But he had to leave his wife behind in New Orleans. "This was in the perilous period culminating in the war with Mexico," wrote Gil Robinson, "and Americans were exceedingly unpopular in the cities south of the Rio Grande." Mexican authorities confiscated Rich's Circus. Bill Lake, hidden in a cellar by a friendly priest, barely escaped with his life.

When Bill Lake finally got back to Agnes, he had nothing but the clothes on his back. His failure to get another circus job in the South sent them back to Cincinnati. There they found Agnes's parents still displeased over the elopement, wrote Agnes's son-in-law, "but the combined arguments of the young couple finally overcame their objections and the family became reconciled."

Circus job prospects weren't immediately better in the Midwest. Lake had to leave his wife with her parents while he took a job as a clown in the Sam Stickney Circus.

The following year, however, both Lake and his wife joined the reorganized Rich Circus. Agnes was a good rider when Bill Lake met her; she had used the time since their marriage to become an excellent wire walker. For two seasons with the Rich Circus, Agnes did her wire walking act and Lake clowned with a troupe of performing dogs.

FAMILY CIRCUSES. *The circus in both Europe and America is very much a matter of families. From one generation to another, members are trained from earliest childhood in the skills and discipline necessary to participate in this special form of entertainment. The Cooke family, which moved from Scotland to New York City in the early 1800s, was an equestrian group that intermarried with the Coles and the Ortons, two other well-known circus families. Orton's Badger Circus ran from 1858 to 1861; Orton & Older, 1858 to 1861; Orton Bros., 1862 to 1869; Miles Orton, 1881 to 1884, 1888 to 1890, 1898 to 1906; R. Z. Orton, or Orton Bros., 1890 to 1932. The Ortons are represented today by Bill "Buckles" Woodcock, son of Sarah Orton and Bill Woodcock, one of the greatest elephant trainers of his generation, as Buckles is of his. Buckles's wife, Barbara, formerly married to elephant trainer Rex Williams, is the mother of elephant man Ben Williams. Buckles and Barbara and their children Dalilah and Shannon were a family act with the Big Apple Circus in the 1980s—more than 130 years after the first Orton circus. (Circus World Museum, Baraboo, Wisconsin)*

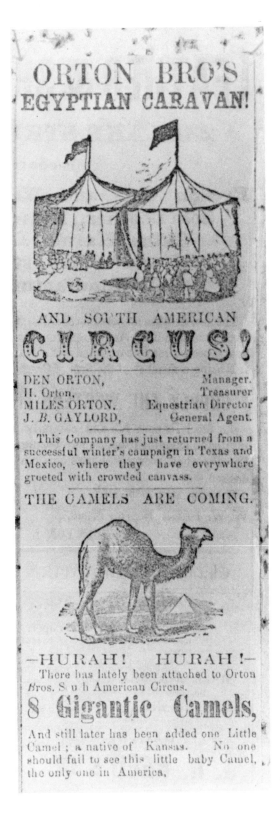

WILLIAM LAKE. *The lawlessness of the wild frontier took the life of William Lake, who began as star clown of the Robinson & Eldred Circus in the 1820s. The William Lake Circus, organized in 1863 with Lake's wife, Agnes, as star equestrienne, became one of the most popular tent shows in America; but Lake was shot and killed in Granby, Missouri, in 1869, by a local gunslinger to whom he had refused admission to the circus. (Circus World Museum, Baraboo, Wisconsin)*

EMMA LAKE. *Gil Robinson recalled, "Col. Cody {Buffalo Bill} considered my wife, Emma Lake, one of the most remarkable horsewomen he had ever met, and he showed his appreciation by presenting her with a very unique bridle of horse hair, made by the Indians. The bit and buckles were made from silver nuggets, presented to Col. Cody from time to time. The tassels were made from scalps of Indians— trophies of his prowess as an Indian fighter." Not only was Emma's father murdered, but her stepfather, "Wild Bill" Hickok, was shot in the back while playing cards in a Deadwood saloon in 1875. A friend, Leander Richardson, cut off twenty inches of Wild Bill's light brown hair and saved it for his widow. Human hair had enormous personal significance on the frontier. The Indian scalps could have come from several of the sixteen recorded Indian fights in which Cody engaged, including the much publicized scalping, on July 17, 1876, of the Cheyenne warrior Yellow Hair (erroneously translated as "Yellow Hand"). "In after years," wrote Robinson, "Col. Cody asked for the return of the bridle, but as my wife had passed away and it was one of my valued souvenirs of her career, I could not part with it. I still retain it with a pressed bunch of roses given to my wife by Queen Victoria, of England, and the silken tresses of 'Wild Bill' Hickok." (Circus World Museum, Baraboo, Wisconsin)*

JOHN ROBINSON. *When he died in 1886, eighty-four years old and only five years retired, the circus he had founded was in its sixty-second year. In 1924, his son Gil, "representing the last of the old Robinson family," attended the opening of the hundredth anniversary season. That December, Gil received a letter from William Howard Taft, former president of the United States and tenth chief justice of the U.S. Supreme Court, who wrote: "I am interested to know that you are writing a book of early circus days about your father. . . . When I was a boy in Cincinnati, and until after I came to the Bar, your father was a very noted figure in that community. His was the great circus of that section and he had a rugged individuality and a picturesque method of expression and a force of character and enterprise that impressed themselves on all the people. He had traveled all over the country when the country was rough and new, and he had met and overcome obstacles that seemed insuperable." (Circus World Museum, Baraboo, Wisconsin)*

PITT'S TOMBSTONE *would put her birthdate at 1841. She would thus have been with the John Robinson Circus when it was the first to show in Florida, in 1847, and in Texas ten years later. Robinson passed the management to his son, John F., in 1872, who passed it to his son, John G., and it continued to flourish in the 1890s, boasting "three generations of circus kings" and calling itself the "Greatest of All American Shows." (The Ringling Museum)*

The Lakes were featured performers when the *Floating Palace* opened at Pittsburgh, Pennsylvania, in March of 1852. For all nine years of that showboat's career, the Lakes were aboard. "On the Palace Agnes gained her reputation as a great wire walker," wrote Van Matre, circus historian and editor and publisher of *Circus Banner Line* magazine. "Her finale was pushing a wheelbarrow up a cable stretched between the ground and a 40-foot vertical pole. She also developed an animal act and was one of the first women to enter a cage with wild animals. Her acts were so startling and she was so versatile that in the latter part of her career with Spalding & Rogers Circus she appeared in the ring 6 times a day." In 1855, the Lakes had a daughter, Emma. In 1861, after the *Palace* went out of business for the duration of the war, Bill Lake formed a partnership with John Robinson that lasted for two seasons. For the Robinson & Lake Circus, Madam Lake, as she was then known, played the lead role in a "hippodrama" entitled "Mazeppa and the Wild Horse of Tartary."

"Hippodramas," combining horsemanship with a dramatic presentation, have been tried as long as there has been a modern circus. "Mazeppa" is perhaps the most popular. It was first performed in London on April 4, 1831, to inaugurate the new circus season at Astley's. Loosely based on a poem by Lord Byron, "Mazeppa" is the story of a youth who dares love above his station, and is condemned by his sweetheart's father, the Chief of the Tartars, to be lashed naked to the back of a wild horse, which is then to be whipped into a gallop over the Polish countryside. A peerless equestrian, Mazeppa survives, returns with an army to rescue his beloved from the detested suitor her father has chosen for her, defeats the army of the Chief of the Tartars, and has himself proclaimed chief. Playing Mazeppa, Agnes Lake easily mastered being tied to a galloping horse; shortly afterward, the American actress Adah

Isaacs Menken would shock her contemporaries on both sides of the Atlantic by mastering the illusion of being tied to a horse naked. Menken created the illusion by augmenting her trunks and scalloped top with a flesh-colored body stocking, but there were many who insisted to the day they died that her limbs and chest were bare.

Madam Lake's presentation was more modest. In the winter of 1862–63, she toured Europe as Mazeppa, and gave a special performance for the King of Prussia, afterward the German Kaiser. But she was back home in the spring in time to open with her husband's own circus, the William Lake Circus, which he founded in 1863.

The next seven years were happy ones for Bill and Agnes and their daughter, Emma. Then one day in August 1869, at Granby, Missouri, William Lake was standing in his customary spot at the front entrance of his show when a one-eyed man named Jake Killian with a reputation as the local bully insisted on staying for the after-show concert without buying another ticket. Lake tried to throw him out.

Killian reportedly spat a wad of tobacco at Lake's feet and snarled, "If I want to stay for your stinking concert, I'll stay!"

"You can walk out," Lake replied, "or be carried out."

Killian went away at that point, and Lake returned to the front entrance to chat with some friends.

Suddenly, Killian reached with a pistol over the shoulder of one of Lake's friends and put a bullet through Lake's heart.

When William Lake was buried next day, Killian had still not been apprehended. After the funeral, Agnes Lake told the assistant manager to gather all of the employees in front of the Big Top. When they were assembled, she climbed up onto the driver's seat of the bandwagon.

"Although Mr. Lake is dead," she told them, "I intend to carry on his circus just as though he were here with us. If any of you think I am incapable, all I ask is that you will give me two weeks' notice and I will endeavor to fill your places. I am determined to keep the show on the road—and I shall succeed."

When nobody gave notice, Agnes Lake broke down and cried.

When Agnes Lake had finished out her first season to good business, she confidently changed the title to Lake's Hippo-Olympiad & Mammoth Circus, and chose Kansas and the territories to its west for her tour. She chartered a special train for her tour of 1871. In the summer of that year she met James Butler Hickok in Abilene, Kansas. And here the history of the circus and the legend of the Old West become one.

In his *Treasury of American Folklore*, B. A. Botkin pointed out that "Wild Bill" Hickok, peace officer and "prince of pistoleers . . . touched the frontier at almost every point as woodsman and Indian fighter, Civil War spy and sharpshooter, frontier scout and marshal," and the "fastest and surest man with a six-shooter that the West ever knew."

He also touched the circus on the wild frontier through his romance with Agnes Lake.

The editors of the Kansas newspapers were giving her big write-ups in the summer of 1871. Before every matinee, she featured a free street parade and a hot-air balloon ascension. On July 31, the circus was doing a one-day stand in Abilene and was scheduled to appear in Topeka the following day. Abilene was then the main market for Texas cattle, and July was the height of the cattle-shipping season. Thus, Marshal Hickok and his deputies were busy keeping the Texas trail drivers orderly.

The first impression that Agnes Lake made on Wild Bill is suggested by the fact that the very next day, the marshal found he had official business in Topeka—but business that still left him time enough to visit the circus lot there as well.

When her circus moved out of the area, Agnes began to write him letters. Charles Gross, a worker at Abilene's train depot, later claimed that Hickok's first reaction was to ask Gross to write the widow Lake and tell her that Wild Bill was a married man and to leave him alone. A factor in Hickok's initial reluctance may have been their respective ages: at forty-four, Agnes was eleven years older than Wild Bill.

At the end of the 1872 tour, Agnes decided to give up her show and retire. At a private sale in 1873, she sold her circus. She was now a woman with a considerable fortune. Wild Bill, meanwhile, had been dismissed as marshal; Abilene no longer needed him. He now went into show business himself, joining Buffalo Bill Cody's stage troupe in the summer of

"Aerial Butterflies" have adorned the circus since at least the 1890s. (Ringling Museum)

1873. Buffalo Bill had not yet come up with the idea for a Wild West show; this was a stage show in which Hickok played a character called "Wild Bill."

Bill and Agnes met again when Cody's stage show, *Scouts of the Prairie*, played Rochester, New York, in March of 1874. "As soon as he learned of her presence, he arranged to see her in his dressing room," wrote Hickok's biographer, Joseph G. Rosa.

Soon after, Hickok quit the show apparently because he was unhappy playing a small supporting role to Cody's Buffalo Bill. He was next reported to be in New York City, where he allegedly wrecked the set of *Scouts of the Prairie* when he found that Buffalo Bill had hired somebody else to play "Wild Bill." For this outburst, he was fined three dollars. Once again he headed west, ending up in Cheyenne, Wyoming.

In 1874, Agnes's daughter, Emma, now nineteen years old and a fine bareback rider in her own right, talked her mother into joining the John Robinson Circus with her. They were back again in 1875, and at the end of that season, like her mother before her, Emma eloped with a circus man. He was Gil Robinson, son of Bill Lake's old partner, the owner of the show.

Alone now, Agnes decided to travel. Restlessly she moved from Chicago to San Francisco, then started back east. In February of 1876, she stopped off at Cheyenne. During the visit, Agnes Lake had a visitor. Hickok, no longer "Wild Bill," had been told that she was in town. On March 4, they took out a marriage license. The next day, they were married in a Methodist ceremony before twenty invited guests.

After the wedding, Hickok and his bride took the night train to St. Louis. A few days later, they arrived in Cincinnati, where they stayed at the home of Emma and her husband.

Two weeks after their marraige, Wild Bill went west again alone, on a train for Cheyenne, leaving Agnes with her daughter and son-in-law and promising that he would be back as soon as he had made a "strike" in the gold fields of Dakota. In 1874, gold had been discovered in the Black Hills by General Custer's expedition. To the lawless, hell-raising town called Deadwood that immediately sprang up there came many famous frontiersmen for one more try at fortune: California Joe, Colorado Charlie, Wild Bill, and later, Doc Holliday and Wyatt Earp.

For Hickok, it was a last try. He was nearly forty, pretty much a failure as most men saw it, and now his eyes were failing him. But with one good strike, he could retire. Or did he and Agnes, and Emma and Gil Robinson, dream a greater dream, of the kind of circus a fortune in gold could buy, with Emma Lake as star equestrienne? If Wild Bill dreamed that dream, it was not so wild: within eight years, it would be done—only it would be Buffalo Bill who would do it.

Hickok spent most of his twenty days in Dakota prospecting in the hills. He wrote Agnes twice. On July 17, he wrote her that he only lived to love her, and that "we will have a home yet." The second letter, on August 1, reveals his depression:

DEAD WOOD BLACK HILLS DAKOTA
August 1st, 1876
AGNES DARLING,
  If such should be we never meet again, while firing my last shot, I will gently breathe the name of my wife—Agnes—and with wishes even for my enemies I will make the plunge and try to swim to the other shore.
  J. B. HICKOK

While playing cards at the Number Ten Saloon on August 2, he was shot in the back by

Jack McCall, a gunfighter looking for a reputation. Aces and eights, the cards that spilled from his hand as he fell, have entered legend as "the Dead Man's Hand."

McCall was hanged for the murder. It was the middle of August before the news reached Cincinnati. Agnes Hickok wanted to go to Deadwood to claim the body and bring it home, but her friends talked her out of it. She visited her second husband's grave in 1877 and decided to leave it undisturbed.

In 1878, Agnes Lake Hickok returned to the circus, dividing her time between training horses and touring with her daughter. They went with the John Robinson Circus that year and with the Great Eastern Circus in 1879. Then, in 1880, they were with the Barnum Show when it played in Cheyenne on August 3. There was a big story about Agnes and her daughter on the front page of the *Cheyenne Daily Leader*, for they were well remembered in the West. Miss Emma Lake, the daring equestrienne with Barnum's Circus, "is the daughter of Wild Bill's widow," the reporter wrote. "Mrs. Agnes Lake Hickok accompanies her daughter everywhere and is her constant companion. She has herself had 36 years of experience with circuses, and what she don't know about them is not worth thinking about."

Agnes Hickok's last year on the road was with the John Robinson Circus in 1882. At the end of the season, she retired to Jersey City, New Jersey, to live with her son-in-law, Gil Robinson. Her daughter went on to be a great circus bareback rider. By this time, the comparatively small frontier wagon circuses of Agnes Lake's day were no more.

Agnes Hickok died on August 21, 1908, a few days before her eighty-first birthday. For twenty-four years, she had seen her late husband's old friend Buffalo Bill turn the frontier days they shared into Buffalo Bill's Wild West. That same year, 1908, a circus man joined forces with some Oklahoma ranchers and formed The Miller Bros. 101 Ranch Wild West Show. In Agnes Lake's day, the greatest heroes and villains of the real Wild West, people like Wild Bill, had deserted their ranches and cow towns one afternoon each year to see the circus. Now the Wild West *was* circus.

DISPLAY·7

The Circus—and P. T. Barnum—Take the Train

On May 10, 1869, the Union Pacific Railroad, going west, and the Central Pacific, going east, were connected at Promontory Point, Utah, by the driving of a golden spike. The continent was at last spanned by railroad tracks. The United States—and the circus—would never be the same again.

Dan Castello's Circus was already on its way west when the golden spike was driven. Castello, an ex-clown with a sharp eye for the main chance, was quick to take advantage of the new technology. His advance men rode the first through train to the West Coast, and Castello determined it was feasible to load a wagon show onto rails. So when Dan Castello's wagon circus, a mud show until then, reached Omaha, it boarded a train on the new Union Pacific.

Castello's circus was still technically a wagon show. It continued to carry enough horses for overland moves, and it made them. It took a detour from its first railroad journey to play Denver, about 110 miles south of the nearest railroad line; then its wagons struggled up mountain roads to Central City, followed by Golden, Georgetown, and Boulder, before returning to the railroad tracks at Cheyenne, Wyoming, to continue west.

Castello was seeing the future, and it was working. He carried an elephant by rail. His menagerie animals made the trip inside ten cage wagons aboard the train. Show gear was transported not in boxcars but on baggage wagons that rode flatcars.

The universal appeal of circusing had been joined to the young romance of railroading. When circuses included the word *railroad* in

PHINEAS TAYLOR (P. T.) BARNUM. On his death, the Times *of London eulogized: "He created the metier of showman on a grandiose scale, worthy to be professed by a man of genius. . . . To live on, by, and before the public was his ideal. . . . His name is a proverb already, and a proverb it will continue." The* Times *was prophetic: there has been a movie about Barnum, a television drama, and a Broadway musical. But his ongoing monument is the circus he founded, still going strong. (Circus World Museum, Baraboo, Wisconsin)*

the title, as in "Ringling Brothers' United Monster Railroad Shows of 1890," they catered to two passionate interests. Even as late as the 1930s, the magic was still potent: the posters of both the Al G. Barnes and Hagenbeck-Wallace circuses for 1933 and 1934 proclaimed "giant trains of steel thundering through the dawn / bringing to you all that is great in the amusement world."

It took a visionary named W. C. Coup to see the implications of the merger in all its manifold glory. First of all, because circus trains could carry many more people and animals and more equipment, circuses could be much bigger. This paved the way for America's distinctive three-ring circuses. Second, circuses could now choose which towns to play. Up to now, a show was limited by how far its baggage stock horses could walk overnight, about twenty miles over rough roads. Many times this meant having to stop in towns that gave only limited patronage. Now trains carried circuses to towns hundreds of miles away, while troupers got a good night's sleep—and rested troupers meant better performances.

"Under the old regime," a publicist for the Spalding & Rogers Railroad Circus wrote in 1856:

the Company are always fatigued and querulous; the Ring Horses leg-weary, and anything but the flashy animals they are pictured on the bills; the Clown loses his mother wit, if he ever had any, and is too sleepy to nourish any he may have acquired; the performers wade through a dull and vapid performance with the least possible labor; the musicians scarcely open their eyes until they give the long wished for blast for the afterpiece; the ticket seller gruffly makes the change for the ticket, in receiving which the door-keeper rudely thrusts you aside in his dreamy listlessness; the ushers follow you at a snail's pace while you hunt up a seat for

yourself; the landlord works all night to wake up the company to breakfast at three in the morning, and for his pains often has his bill disputed for a few pennies by the worn-out manager.

Before long, Castello's early experiments with a railroad show would pave the way for W. C. Coup, P. T. Barnum, and The Greatest Show on Earth.

———

When the Civil War ended in 1865, P. T. Barnum was the biggest promoter of individual attractions the world had ever known, but he was primarily an exhibitor of curiosities, human and otherwise, not a circus man. His showmanship brought into the halls of the American Museum 82,000,000 visitors, among them the Prince of Wales; Charles Dickens; and novelist Henry James and his Harvard professor brother, William (what did the author of *Psychology* make of Barnum?).

On Dickens's first trip to America, a five-month vacation in 1842, the great novelist found Americans "by nature frank, brave, cordial, hospitable, and affectionate," and the women in love with color. ("What various parasols! what rainbow silks and satins! what pinking of thin stockings, and pinching of thin shoes, and fluttering of ribbons and silk tassels, and display of rich cloaks with gaudy hoods and linings!") Nevertheless, he did not find Americans "a humorous people, and their temperament always impressed me as being of a dull and gloomy character." This disturbed him, and he thought he found a cause in the quality of American life. As he commented in his *American Notes*, "How quiet the streets are! Are there no itinerant bands; no wind or stringed instruments? No, not one. By day, are there no Punches, Fantoccini, Dancing-dogs,

Jugglers, Conjurers, Orchestrinas, or even Barrel-Organs? No, not one. Are there no amusements?"

By the time Dickens came back to America in 1867–68, to give readings from his novels (to which Barnum often made reference), every lack he had noted in the quiet streets of 1842 had been an attraction at Barnum's museum, and many more besides. Barnum himself—"the man who was trying to teach fun to Americans," as Irving Wallace correctly called him—gave Dickens a tour of his museum, during which Dickens bestowed the title "What-is-it?" on Zip the original Conehead.

Whatever reputation America had in 1868 as a place of fun probably owed as much to Barnum's American Museum as a hundred and twenty years later is owed to the creations of a similar genius, Walt Disney. And now there was to be an efficient and effective way of taking Barnum's fun all over America—the railroad circus.

It came about because his museum burned down.

On the bitterly cold night of March 2–3, 1868, Barnum's second American Museum, on the west side of Broadway between Spring and Prince streets in New York City, was destroyed by a terrible blaze. The water from the firemen's hoses froze into icicles that festooned the façade, giving the sad scene the beauty of a snow castle setting for a Hans Christian Andersen fairy tale.

Most of the famous places associated with Barnum were destroyed by fire. His showplace home, Iranistan, burned to the ground in 1857. His first museum, on Broadway at Ann Street, had been set afire by Confederate agents on Thanksgiving Day, 1864, as part of the abortive plot to burn New York. Then on July 13, 1865, a second and far more serious blaze at the American Museum broke out accidentally in the engine room.

By nightfall the famous building and a large part of its 600,000 exhibits were a mound of charred ruins. The whale tank was broken in an effort to put out the flames on the floors below, and the whales themselves were burned alive. Barnum lamented the loss of exhibits, including his priceless Revolutionary War relics, "which a half million of dollars could not restore, and a quarter of a century could not collect." His insurance was worth only $40,000. Still, Barnum benefited from the heroic efforts of such firemen as John Denham, of Hose Company No. Fifteen, who dashed into the burning building again and again to rescue his freaks. It took a derrick to rescue the giantess Anna Swan, who lost her entire savings of $1,200 in gold and her wardrobe in the fire. Denham had to kill—with a single blow of his axe—a Bengal tiger that leaped from a second-story window to the street below. A bear that didn't make it out the window burned to death, and volunteer fireman George Collyer had to put a thirty-foot python out of its misery. A sociable orangutan survived by fleeing to the nearby newspaper office of James Gordon Bennett.

Despite the horrors of the 1865 fire, the 1868 blaze is the one that is crucial to circus history, for it put Barnum out of the museum business.

For the new museum on Broadway, Barnum had joined with Isaac A. Van Amburgh, the lion-taming owner of Van Amburgh's Menagerie, to form a large combined show of Barnum's curiosities and Van Amburgh's animals, which would exhibit at the museum in the winter and tour the United States in the summer. Van Amburgh's lions and tigers died painfully in the fire, and the Barnum curiosities that had survived the fires of 1864 and 1865, valued at $288,000, were suddenly gone forever. The insurance paid $160,000.

Barnum was almost fifty-eight. Although no

longer wealthy, he did have enough potential income from the real estate the museum had stood on, plus other investments, to retire.

He did retire—for two years. "I have done work enough, and shall play the rest of my life," he said. He was so sure he wouldn't change his mind that he accepted an offer from George Wood, proprietor of Wood's Museum and his greatest rival, of 3 percent of Wood's receipts in exchange for the right to call Wood's Museum the successor to Barnum's. But perhaps the words of his close friend Horace Greeley, published the day after the first American Museum burned, were still in his mind.

In an editorial in the *New York Tribune*, Greeley showed that he knew better than Barnum what, for Barnum, was play. The editor mourned the loss of a museum that had been "a fountain of delight," a wonder "as implicitly believed in as the Arabian Nights' Entertainment," a site that "amused, instructed, and astonished." But he noted a powerful consolation: "Barnum's Museum is gone, but Barnum himself, happily, did not share the fate of his rattlesnakes. . . . There are fishes in the seas and beasts in the forests; birds still fly in the air and strange creatures still roam in the deserts; giants and pygmies still wander up and down the earth; the oldest man, the fattest woman, and the smallest baby are still living, and Barnum will find them."

And so he did—for the circus.

To P. T. Barnum, as to most geniuses at self-promotion, ideas that work inevitably seem to be their own; the ones that don't are usually suggested by somebody else. Thus it was that Barnum explained the idea of going on the road with a circus: "In the autumn of 1870 I began to prepare a great show enterprise requiring five hundred men and horses to transport and conduct it through the country. Selecting as manager of this gigantic enterprise Mr. William C. Coup who I had favorably

known for some years as a capital showman and man of good judgment, integrity and excellent executive ability, we spent several weeks in blocking out our plans."

But in fact this time the idea was not Barnum's; it was Coup's. In 1870, while Barnum was still devoting himself to what he called "serious reflections on the ends and aims of human existence," two callers came to visit him in Bridgeport: Coup and Dan Castello.

Natty, bearded William Cameron Coup was born in Mount Pleasant, Indiana, in 1837, the son of a tavern keeper. Like so many other bored but ambitious young people from small towns, he decided, upon seeing an overland circus when he was sixteen, that a mud show was not only the way out but the route to fortune and a famous name. That circus was owned by Seth B. Howes and Lewis B. Lent of Somers, New York, and Sherwood Stratton, the father of Barnum's Tom Thumb. Howes had rented Barnum's name for his circus, though Barnum had nothing to do with its operation; still, it was with P. T. Barnum's Colossal Museum & Menagerie that Coup learned show business.

In 1861 and throughout the Civil War, Coup was running the sideshow of the E. F. & J. Mabie Circus, another mud show, one that toured what was then the frontier territory of Illinois, Iowa, and Missouri. In 1866, at the age of twenty-nine, he quit Mabie to run the sideshow of the Yankee Robinson Circus, and eventually he became assitant manager of Robinson's big wagon circus. His wife talked him into leaving Yankee to take up livestock breeding on a Wisconsin farm. Unfortunately for her aspirations, the farm was near Delavan, Wisconsin, winter quarters of the Mabies, a seductive circus town where sawdust and spangles were seldom out of the conversation. Coup's old friend Dan Castello, back in the Midwest after taking his circus to California by

BARNUM'S AMERICAN MUSEUM. *Phineas T. Barnum opened his American Museum in an imposing five-story marble-fronted structure on lower Broadway at the corner of Ann Street, New York City, on the morning of New Year's Day, 1842. For two decades, it was one of America's most popular tourist attractions, the Disneyland of its day. Barnum had bought the American Museum established at that location in 1830 by John Scudder and transformed its lackluster collection of historical and scientific curiosities into an exhibition hall that was curiosity-provoking, entertaining, and, occasion-*

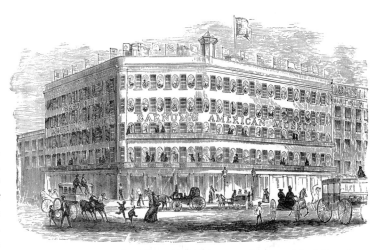

ally, educational. When it burned down in June 1865, Barnum leased an old building on the west side of Broadway between Spring and Prince streets, and the new American Museum was open for business on November 13, 1865. (John Culhane Collection)

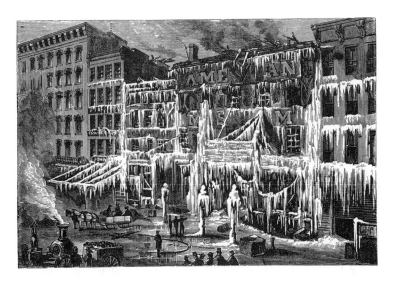

OUT OF THE ASHES. *On the morning of March 3, 1868, Barnum was reading the newspaper at Waldemere, his estate outside Bridgeport, Connecticut, when he suddenly exclaimed to his wife, "Hallo! Barnum's Museum is burned." On a night so cold that water from the fire hoses froze as it splattered against the granite walls, the new American Museum became a charred hulk covered with icicles. Most of the valuable animals were dead, and Barnum's collection of curiosities was gone. He announced his retirement a few weeks later. But when he came out of retirement in 1871, he would combine new rare and exotic humans and animals with equestrians, clowns, and acrobats into the circus that would become known as The Greatest Show on Earth. (John Culhane Collection)*

rail, now lured Coup into joining him in chartering a Great Lakes steamer called the *Benton* to play booming lumber camps along the shores of Lake Michigan.

When winter came, Coup and Castello were talking pie in the sky, as people always do in front of hot stoves, and Coup ventured that if the legendary P. T. Barnum would combine his name, money, and genius for hiring attractions with their organizational and managerial skills as circus men, they could create the greatest circus ever known.

They were bold enough to go see Barnum, and apparently they arrived at the right place at the right time. Barnum had recently returned from taking a long trip to show America to an English friend and his young daughter. On that trip, a German named Gabriel Kahn had asked Barnum to exhibit his son, Leopold, a nine-year-old midget who was even smaller than Tom Thumb had been at his age. Barnum christened the young midget, who was fluent in German as well as English, Admiral Dot, presented him for three weeks in San Francisco, then took him east as "The El Dorado Elf." At the same time, Barnum became a silent partner in an English tour for those famous survivors of his museum fires, the Siamese twins Chang and Eng, and giantess Anna Swan; and in a world tour for Lavinia and Tom Thumb. On October 8, 1870, Barnum wrote Coup from Bridgeport about his proposition:

MY DEAR COUP:

Yours received. I will join you in a show for next spring and will probably have Admiral Dot well trained this winter and have him . . . in the show. Wood will sell all his animals outright, and will furnish several tip-top museum curiosities. You need to spend several months in New York arranging for curiosities, cuts, [engraved plates for printing illustrations], cages, bills, etc. All things got from Wood I will settle for with him and give the concern credit. We can make a stun-

ning museum department. If you want to call it my museum and use my name it may be used by allowing me the same very small percentage that Wood allows for calling himself my successor (3 percent on receipts). You can have a Cardiff Giant that won't crack, also a moving figure, Sleeping Beauty, or Dying Zouave—a big Gymnastic figure like that in Wood's museum, and lots of other good things, only you need time to look them up and prepare wagons, etc., etc.

Yours truly,
P. T. BARNUM

I will spare time to cook up the show in New York when you come. I think Siamese Twins would pay.

At Delavan, home of so many early circuses, Coup and Castello assembled ten carloads of trained animals and circus paraphernalia and shipped them to New York.

On April 10, 1871, the "great show enterprise" of Barnum, Coup, and Castello opened in Brooklyn beneath three acres of canvas tent—the greatest spread ever used by a circus. Barnum was the new circus's financial backer and adviser; Coup and Castello its organizers; and the show boasted that it employed more people, horses, and other animals than any previously organized in America or Europe. Ten thousand people came to see—and they saw, all right: 600 horses, and some of Barnum's best wonders, including two mechanical figures, the Sleeping Beauty and the Dying Zouave—she appearing to breathe evenly, he to gasp realistically for breath—and such human attractions as Colonel Goshen, the "Palestine" giant, who was contrasted, in true Barnum fashion, with Admiral Dot, who sometimes used Goshen's hand as if it were the seat of a chair. (Dot eventually deserted show business to open a saloon in White Plains, New York, which was frequented by the hard-drinking heavyweight boxing champion John L. "I

Can Lick Any Man in the House" Sullivan.) In addition to the giant and the midget, there was Esau, the Bearded Boy; and Anna Leake, the armless woman; not to mention the thing that Barnum had called, in his letter to Coup, "a Cardiff Giant that won't crack."

The Cardiff Giant was Barnum at his humbugging worst. It was a fake of a fake—and he knew it. The original fake was a ten-foot-four-and-a-half-inch stone man unearthed October 16, 1869, on the farm of "Stub" Newell at Cardiff, a village near Syracuse, New York. Two Yale University professors, one a paleontologist, the other a chemist, pronounced the giant a true fossil; while the director of the New York State Museum announced equally authoritatively that the giant was a statue, though an ancient one, and "the most remarkable yet brought to light in this country." The president of Cornell University, however, said that the giant was made of gypsum, and detected the marks of a sculptor's chisel. While the experts argued, Stub, who buried "the petrified man" in the first place, pitched a tent over the Giant and sold tickets, first for a nickel, then for fifty cents, then for a dollar.

It takes a humbug to know a humbug. Barnum came to see it and sneered, "And they call *me* a humbug!" But he also noted the crowds arriving by special trains from Syracuse and offered Stub $60,000 for a three-month lease on the object. The offer convinced Stub that there must be more than $60,000 worth of sightseers' dollars in the giant, and he steadfastly refused. Barnum did the next best thing. He had an exact copy of the giant made and exhibited it in New York as the original.

But the Barnum circus of 1871 had many other attractions that were the real thing, notably a giraffe. "Other managers," Barnum explained, "gave up trying to import giraffes several years ago, owing to the great cost and care of attending them. No giraffe has ever lived two years in America. These very im-

pediments, however, incited me to always have a living giraffe on hand, at whatever cost—for, of course, their scarcity enhances their attraction and value as curiosities." And, he might have added, the giraffe's long neck is a wonderful image for advertising a circus.

Such attractions, as well as a family of Fiji "cannibals," were there to satisfy the public's wide-ranging curiosity. And so was Barnum, that first season. He was as big an attraction as a giraffe: all over America people knew about—even if they had not seen—the man who exhibited the wonders of the world at the American Museum in New York. He was thought of as a kind of magician who conjured up General Tom Thumb; an American Santa Claus for all seasons.

Barnum, his freaks, and his giraffe all had big drawing power. But the factor that most contributed to the show's success was Coup's advance publicity and advertising and his transportation arrangements. He knew how to let people know that there was a show, he knew how to get the show to them, and he knew how to get them to the show. Other circus promoters were used to thinking about drawing patrons from the town where they played and its immediate vicinity. Coup ordered his advertisers to post their bills as far as fifty, even seventy-five miles away. It is said that Coup's billposters hung as much paper in a week as other circus promoters had posted in an entire season. To make sure all the people who saw his posters could get to his circus, Coup arranged for railroads in New England and New York to run special excursion trains at reduced fares to the places where the Barnum show pitched its tents. Proof of the value of his efforts was the fact that attendance was often two or three times the population of the cities played.

Then Coup had another great idea, one that Barnum, as usual, took credit for: the specially designed circus train.

JO' JO'
THE RUSSIAN DOG FACED BOY.

THE ORIGINALS. *Chang and Eng were born, joined at the breastbone, near Bangkok, Siam (now Thailand) in 1811, arrived in America in 1829, married sisters in a double wedding, and reared twenty-two children between them. Barnum exhibited them in 1860. They died in 1874 at sixty-three. "Eng was sleepy and wanted to go to bed, but Chang complained that it hurt his chest to lie down. They argued about it while Eng smoked a pipe, then went to bed and Eng fell into a deep sleep. Eng waked up and asked his son, 'How is your Uncle Chang?' The boy said, 'Uncle Chang is cold. Uncle Chang is dead.' . . . Eng commenced crying, saying to his wife whom they called in, 'My last hour has come.' As he turned in alarm to the lifeless form by his side he was seized with violent nervous paroxysms. In two hours he was dead, although he had been in perfect health when they went to bed." The autopsy showed that any attempt to separate the twins would have been fatal, and that Chang died of a cerebral clot. No cause could be found for Eng's death. Tradition says he died of fright. (Circus World Museum, Baraboo, Wisconsin)*

JO JO THE DOG-FACED BOY, *born Theodore Peteroff in Russia. Carl Sandburg describes the side show "spieler" who declaimed, "La-deez and gen-tul-men, beneath yon canvas we have the curi-aw-si-ties and mon-straw-si-ties— the Wild Man of Borneo, the smallest dwarf ever seen of mindkind and the tallest giant that ever came into existence. . . . And I would call your particular attention to Jo Jo the dog-faced boy, born forty miles from land and forty miles from sea." R. W. G. Vail says that the first so-called freak exhibited in America may have been "a Maiden Dwarf, who is fifty-three years old, and of but twenty-two inches in stature" who could be seen in Boston "at the house of the widow Bignall, the next door to the King's Head Tavern, a little above Mr. Hancock's wharf" in 1771. The Massachusetts Spy for August 22 and 29 that year said that "she is willing to exhibit herself as a shew to such Gentlemen and Ladies as are desirous to gratify their curiosity, for one shilling lawful money for each person." Irvin Feld closed the freak show, saying, "I can't make money out of human misery." (Circus World Museum, Baraboo, Wisconsin)*

"Perceiving that my great combination was assuming such proportions that it would be impossible to move it by horse power," wrote Barnum, "I negotiated with all the railroad companies between New York and Omaha, Nebraska, for the transportation by rail, of my whole show, requiring sixty to seventy freight cars, six passenger cars, and three engines."

Not only was the circus train Coup's idea, but Barnum was even opposed to it at first, on the grounds that it would never work fast enough to justify its expense. But Coup made the decision to give up wagon travel for rail because "the receipts in the larger towns were frequently twice and three times as much as in the smaller ones. I became convinced that we could at least double our receipts if we could ignore the small places and travel only from one big town to another. . . . This was my reason for determining to move the show by rail the following season."

That would be the circus season of 1872, and it is a landmark in this saga: the first year that trains carried a circus completely designed to be moved by rail.

At New Brunswick, New Jersey, on April 18, 1872, using cars supplied by the Pennsylvania Railroad, Coup converted the Barnum circus to a railroad operation. That first day, work began at 8:00 A.M. and was finished twelve hours later; they were on schedule for their next stop, Trenton, New Jersey, where Coup rented sleepers for the performers and musicians, and coaches for the roustabouts. The only mishap occurred when a camel fell off a ramp at New Brunswick and was killed.

As the tour went on, loading time diminished. At New Brunswick, Coup hit on the idea of end-loading his circus trains. Cars were bridged with crossover plates, then wagons were pulled up a ramp onto the rear flatcar and pushed the length of the train. They would be chocked into place on their assigned flats with wedges to hold them steady even when the train was moving. Until then, roustabouts had to manhandle the wagons over the side of each freight car, a difficult and time-consuming procedure.

Coup ran into opposition, notably from Barnum. When the operation took twelve hours that first day in New Brunswick, Barnum didn't see how it could ever be streamlined. The railroads hadn't yet settled upon a uniform height and width for cars. Moreover, brake wheels were mounted at the end of each flatcar, and had to be removed before the wagons could roll from car to car. The yardmaster at Washington refused to remove them and ordered Coup to load the train one car at a time. That night, Coup took the yardmaster to dinner while his men removed the brake wheels. But Coup knew that the real solution was to build railroad cars designed for the needs of circuses that had to be continually, speedily, and safely on the move. He ordered sixty-five such cars built to his specifications.

When the circus pulled into Columbus, Ohio, on June 28, wrote Tom Parkinson and Chappie Fox in *The Circus Moves by Rail*:

> the crew found waiting for it a new and brightly painted train with uniform platform cars for wagons, chariots, cages, and carriages; a Wagner sleeping car for the artists; plainer sleeping cars for the laborers; boxcars for the extra items; and Palace cars for the horses and other large animals. . . . Now the show could travel 100 miles a night and still have time to put up tents and seats, give a street parade, and present two, even three, performances per day. It could skip undesirable towns and villages and instead play only the sizable cities, running Coup-styled excursions from the feeder towns.

Coup's coup, the railroad show, not only is still in use by the Ringling Bros. and Barnum

& Bailey Circus (by 1941, the Greatest Show on Earth was transported on four trains comprised of as many as 107 seventy-foot railroad cars), but it led to the development of the modern "piggyback" system of rail-truck freight handling, establishing Coup as one of America's great transportation innovators. The fact that Barnum later claimed the idea as his own shows how enthusiastic he became when he saw what could be done with circus trains. They could and did keep up with an ever-expanding country.

There was one more portentous circus development in 1872. Coup and Barnum added a second ring under their tent. The reason for the first two-ring circus was that Coup and Barnum were after larger audiences; they could put more people around two rings than around one.

Circus performers generally deplored this innovation from an artistic point of view. Intimacy was being sacrificed for spectacle. When a circus is larger than a single ring, you can't always see the fine points of the acrobats' performance, and you can't always hear the clowns or see their smaller gestures and expressions. To be sure, a circus of two (and later, three) rings has more room for elephants and horses—and spectacle in general—but other acts were suddenly distracting the audience's attention from anything smaller than a pyramid of pachyderms. M. R. Werner wrote in his biography of Barnum that "clowns and acrobats have considered that their decline in individual popularity was due to the increase in the magnitude of circus presentation, for it was impossible to do stirring or excruciating things in the air, in animal cages, or on the sawdust when two other groups were occupied in distracting the attention of the audience at the same time." And it is also true that, even in its three-ring

heyday in the 1920s, when Ringling Bros. and Barnum & Bailey got a superstar of the magnitude of Lillian Leitzel they presented her without competition from the other rings.

Nevertheless, the multiring circus was the wave of the future. Audiences loved it, perhaps because they liked to feel that they were getting more than their money's worth. The whole ambience of the giant circus, not the feats of the individual performer, was what they came to see. And, if they missed something, they could always come back.

The ever-growing size of Barnum's circus started people saying that it was "The Greatest Show on Earth"—and Barnum would eventually make that title the copyrighted name of his show.

Barnum later claimed that he had long wanted to build a permanent circus structure in New York City, to be called the Great Roman Hippodrome. While he was in Europe in 1873 to look for new attractions, he heard from Coup back home that the perfect site, an entire square block on Twenty-seventh Street, between Fourth and Madison avenues, was available. Barnum says he cabled Coup to lease it and build a huge indoor coliseum, 200 feet wide and 426 feet long. Again, Coup has a different version, namely that when he proposed the purchase Barnum flatly rejected the extravagance. Coup says he threatened to build the permanent circus structure with other backers, whereupon Barnum changed his mind.

However it happened, the permanent structure, called, not surprisingly, "P. T. Barnum's Great Roman Hippodrome," opened to the public in April 1874. Coup was general manager; Castello was director of amusements. In an arena that size, they could have chariot races—a spectacle tailor-made for a circus in which several rings created an outer oval. Six years later, when former Civil War general Lew Wallace published *Ben-Hur*, his novel of Rome in the time of Christ, many readers knew what the climactic chariot race looked like because they'd already seen one at the circus. The Great Roman Hippodrome had 10,000 seats, and a chariot race was a suitably scaled entertainment for an audience that vast; all 10,000 seats were filled for the opening.

Coup was on a roll. Attendance was so good at the larger, railroad-borne circus that he made ticket selling itself an attraction, giving equal billing to Ben Lusbie, "the quickest dispenser of show tickets in the world." The tiny, edgy Lusbie once sold 6,000 tickets in one hour. Later, working for Adam Forepaugh, Lusbie broke his own record, selling 6,153 tickets in an hour and three minutes. For this feat, the *National Police Gazette* proclaimed him the champion ticket seller of the world. Forepaugh had a poster drawn showing a mass of humanity waiting to be serviced by the lone man with the mustache in "4 Paw's Ticket Wagon: BEN LUSBIE / LIGHTNING TICKET SELLER AND CHAMPION OF THE WORLD."

———————

Barnum's Hippodrome show soon went on the road. Coup, who had worked himself almost to exhaustion on the project, continued to drive himself to make sure the road show was a success. But he found to his anger and disgust that he was competing against another Barnum show. Barnum had been egotistical enough to want his famous name on two shows, so he had leased its use to a man he may simply have thought of as a fellow teetotaler. To the rest of the circus world, however, Barnum's new partner was known as the prince of grifters, the biggest crook in the circus world, John "Pogey" O'Brien. To be sure, O'Brien *didn't* drink—the better to cheat honest men in their cups.

Rival circuses crowed in print: "Barnum Show Divided!" Coup was repelled to think that Barnum had lessened the value of his own name. Castello had already sold out his interest to Barnum; now Coup did, too.

Two years later, Coup went into partnership with a German named Charles Reiche to build the $500,000 New York Aquarium on Broadway. They had a falling out when Reiche wanted to open the aquarium on Sundays. Coup argued that "such a step would be an offense to the belief of the majority of our patrons; that it would bring into the place an undesirable element, from which it had been entirely free, and that the enterprise was enjoying a steady prosperity with which it would be wise to remain content."

Since they couldn't agree, and since they also jointly owned four giraffes and five small elephants, Coup proposed a real risk-taker's gamble.

"I'll stump you to flip a penny," he said, "to see which one of us shall take those giraffes and elephants as his portion and walk out of this place next Saturday night, leaving the other in full possession of all the Aquarium property."

They flipped. Coup lost the aquarium, which included a storage and supply aquarium on two acres of land at Coney Island. He took his animals; added to them a white whale (probably kept alive by the Barnum Museum method of a tank partially filled with salt water and seaweed, plus an attendant who continually moistened the whale's mouth and spout with a sponge dipped in salt water); added genuine Zulus and a Zouave drill team; and did what many circuses were doing now that Coup had shown them how: he took to the rails. In 1879, his New United Monster Shows was the largest consolidated circus in the United States, and yet another tribute to his organizational ability. Well publicized during the 1882 season was "a $20,000 Feature, A Series of Grand National [wax] Tableaux Presenting the Assassination of President Garfield by Charles Jule Guiteau,

Showing Every Incident From the Conception of the Crime to the Sentence of Death. Designs Executed by Wilson MacDonald Esq., America's Greatest Sculptor." Wax tableaux transported by railroad were the latest representational wonder, and the public took advantage of "Excursion trains on all railroads to these great shows."

Of all things, a severe railroad wreck forced the father of the railroad circus to close his show. He tried to come back by running a one-car circus, but unlike Dan Rice's One-Horse Show, it didn't bring Coup back to the big time. So he went home to the farm at Delavan, where he and Castello had cooked up that idea of going to Barnum to back the biggest circus ever. His fortune lost, he died forgotten in Florida, on March 4, 1895.

———————

Barnum got along without Coup very well. Old P. T.'s sixty-five-year-old wife, Charity, long an invalid, died in 1873. Barnum remarried the next year, at the age of sixty-four; his new wife, Nancy Fish, was twenty-four. She had been the English teenager touring the country with her father the year Barnum engaged Admiral Dot. Barnum stopped hesitating about the circus business and stopped being conservative. His seventeen years with a woman forty years his junior were among the happiest of Barnum's life and the best for Barnum as circus impresario.

In 1875, he offered all his show property at auction. This included the Hippodrome and his "World's Fair," consisting of museum, menagerie, and circus property. His idea was to focus on one traveling show, which would be "as good as money and experience could make it."

"Now I am properly prepared for our Centennial year," he wrote.

The year 1876 was the 100th anniversary of the Declaration of Independence. Barnum and his circus presided over America's birthday celebration as if it were his personal anniversary—which, in a sense, it was. Once, meeting the retired president Ulysses S. Grant, Barnum said, "General, since your journey around the world you are the best-known man on the globe." Grant replied in his blunt manner: "No, sir, your name is familiar to multitudes who never heard of me. Wherever I went, among the most distant nations, the fact that I was an American led to constant inquiries whether I knew Barnum." To millions all over the world, America seemed like Barnum, a nation that had invented itself as Barnum had invented himself; a country that was like his traveling spectacle, a three-ring circus of human aspiration; a society that was, like his shows, full of the sense that anything was possible.

For his United States Centennial circus, Barnum promised "patriotic features that will give the people a Fourth of July celebration every day."

He succeeded, and a great fireworks display at each and every performance was the least of it.

> My establishment travels in three trains of railway cars. We take along a battery of cannon, and every morning we fire a salute of thirteen guns. We introduce groups of persons costumed in the style of our Continental troops, and supplemented with the Goddess of Liberty . . . and some first-class singers who, with a chorus of several hundred voices, will sing the "Star Spangled Banner" and other patriotic songs, accompanied with bands of music and also with cannon placed outside our tents, and fired by means of electricity. We close our patriotic demonstration by singing "America" ("My Country 'Tis of Thee"), the entire audience rising and joining in the chorus. At

BARNUM'S GREAT SHOW AND THE GOLDEN AGE. Circuses reached their peak in number and popularity during the last quarter of the nineteenth and first decade of the twentieth centuries. With expanded railroad networks and better roads, there were at least forty large circuses touring the United States. As the larger circuses began to bypass the more isolated towns and villages, smaller traveling shows took their place. The special appeal of the circus for rural audiences was caught by American novelist Hamlin Garland in Boy Life on the Prairie *(1907) about Iowa in the 1870s: "No one but a country boy can rightly measure the majesty and allurement of a circus. To go from the lonely prairie or the dusty corn-field and come face to face with the 'amazing aggregation of world-wide wonders' was like enduring the visions of the Apocalypse." (Circus World Museum, Baraboo, Wisconsin)*

night we terminate our performances with fire-works, in which thrilling revolutionary scenes are brilliantly depicted. Our grand street procession will be a gorgeous and novel feature. It will begin to move when the salute is being fired, and I depend upon the patriotism of each town we visit to add to the effects of our National Jubilee by ringing of bells at the same time.

There was, of course, a performer dressed as that pioneer circus fan, the Father of His Country, George Washington. And the cen-

tennial menagerie included "a Gigantic Live American Eagle" trained to "hover overhead."

The printed program for his Centennial circus contained this pledge:

> And the Star Spangled Banner
> In triumph shall wave
> O'er the grandest of shows
> Even Barnum e'er gave.

For the rest of his life, Barnum would never be without a circus.

DISPLAY·8 Buffalo Bill's Wild West

"I have seen your Wild West two days in succession, and enjoyed it thoroughly," Mark Twain wrote Buffalo Bill. "It brought back to me the breezy, wild life of the Rocky Mountains, and stirred me like a war song."

Instant nostalgia is what the Wild West shows were about. Nostalgia for the American frontier as it was already passing from American life, and nostalgia after it had officially closed in 1890. Buffalo Bill's Wild West—throughout its thirty-year history, it was never advertised as a circus or a show—recalled the part of the American history even then romantically referred to as "the winning of the West"; and until movies and TV westerns overshadowed them, Wild West shows, or Wild West "concerts" or "aftershows" with circuses, were the chief supports of this tradition.

Buffalo Bill's Wild West wasn't really a circus, because it had no clowns. But it did have the other two essential ingredients of the circus: a combination of acts of skill and daring by human beings and animals, at least in some instances performed in and around a ring. Nevertheless, Buffalo Bill's Wild West belongs in the history of the circus in America because the Wild West show, which he originated, was eventually incorporated into the circus and was, for several decades, one of the most popular features.

In the 1920s, circuses began staging Wild West concerts or aftershows. Patrons could see these performances by sharpshooters, rough riders, cowboys, and Indians by remaining in the main tent after the main show and paying a small additional charge. Tom Mix had per-

BUFFALO BILL. This photograph was taken in the early 1900s by Fred W. Glasier, who spent his whole life recording contemporary circus life and the Indian life that was even then vanishing. He was hired by such circuses as Forepaugh-Sells, Barnum & Bailey, the Miller & Arlington 101 Ranch Wild West, and Buffalo Bill's Wild West show, and he took advantage of the opportunities to photograph the Indians in and around these shows. (Ringling Museum)

formed in several Wild West shows before going into the movies, and in 1934, he bought an interest in the Sam B. Dill Circus & Tom Mix Wild West. In 1935, he owned the show and renamed it the Tom Mix Circus. At the same time, Ringling Bros. and Barnum & Bailey Circus had a rip-roaring aftershow with Western star Tim McCoy. In the 1950s, when the needs of the new medium of television gave a rebirth to old cowboy movies and, hence, old cowboy stars, William "Hopalong Cassidy" Boyd joined the Cole Bros. Circus. By that time, the Wild West show and the circus were one.

They were also a long way from Buffalo Bill's Wild West. To people like Mark Twain, who had witnessed the winning of the West, Buffalo Bill Cody was the genuine article. To those in America and Europe who knew that chapter of history only from books and hearsay, Cody was larger than life—a D'Artagnan of the plains.

William Frederick Cody was born in Scott County, Iowa, on February 26, 1846. His antislavery father was a small farmer and sawmill operator. When he was six, Bill Cody saw his older brother Samuel killed when the big mare he was riding reared without warning and flung herself on her back, crushing him to death. Bill made up his mind to be the kind of quick-thinking rider to whom accidents would not happen.

His father died in 1857, and eleven-year-old Bill immediately went to work to support his mother and sisters, riding as a messenger between wagon trains that the firm of Russell, Majors and Waddell was sending across the western plains. When that firm started the Pony Express in 1860, fourteen-year-old Cody became a rider. At fifteen he joined the Union army, and served with the Ninth Kansas Cavalry as a dispatch rider. After the war, he worked for the U.S. Army as a civilian scout and dispatch bearer out of Fort Ellsworth, in

Kansas, then hunted buffalo to feed the construction crews of a division of the Union Pacific Railroad. He claimed to have slaughtered 4,280 head of buffalo in eight months, and was soon famous as "Buffalo Bill" Cody.

In the years when the United States was putting down Indian resistance to its intrusion onto the lands west of the Mississippi River, Cody was in demand as a scout and guide, mostly for the U.S. Fifth Cavalry. Commanders prized his almost total recall of all the vast western terrain he had traversed since 1857, a genius he combined with good marksmanship, endurance, and knowledge of Indian ways. In 1872, Cody was awarded the Medal of Honor (though the award was revoked in 1916 on the grounds that the medal was a military decoration, while Cody was neither an officer nor an enlisted man when he received it).

For most Americans, Buffalo Bill was a Western folk hero. Newspaper reporters and dime novelists vied to turn his exploits into articles and books. There has since been a lot of debunking of his legend, but he was, in fact, the real McCoy: accomplished horse wrangler, hunter, plainsman, and Indian fighter by the end of his teens; veteran of sixteen Indian fights, including the killing and scalping of the Cheyenne warrior Yellow Hair (the dime novels mistranslated his name to Yellow Hand) in Sioux County, Nebraska, on July 17, 1876. He was a civilian employed to scout and to carry dispatches, not to fight in battles; but on several occasions, he proved to be an effective fighter. When challenged by Yellow Hair, for example, he first engaged in a duel on horseback. Both their horses went down: Cody said afterward that he shot Yellow Hair's horse and that his own horse tripped in a gopher hole. On foot, "not more than twenty paces apart," they again "fired at each other simultaneously . . . his bullet missed me while mine struck him in the breast." Cody leaped on the Indian, drove his knife into Yellow Hair's heart, and then, "jerking his war-bonnet off I scientifically scalped him in about five seconds."

To understand the enormous impact of this deed on the public imagination, one must remember that only three weeks before, Indians had killed General Custer and his entire force of more than 250 soldiers at the Battle of the Little Bighorn River in Montana. It was reported that Cody had taken the first scalp in revenge for Custer's massacre.

Even before his killing of Yellow Hair, however, Cody had discovered a way to turn such exploits into fun and profit. In 1872, he went on the stage, starring in *The Scouts of the Prairie*, a drama by Ned Buntline, one of the dime novelists who had spread his name and fame. Audiences found him a superb showman, who knew just how to spice his re-created heroics with a good-natured strain of self-mockery. Between seasons, he frequently escorted hunting parties of rich Easterners and European nobility to his beloved West.

After the Yellow Hair sensation, a promoter named Nathan Salsbury came up with an even better idea for turning Cody into a celebrity. Salsbury, one of the most successful actors and managers of his day, sold Buffalo Bill on the idea as they sat in a restaurant in Brooklyn, New York, in 1882. Nearby, construction teams were readying the Brooklyn Bridge for its opening the next year.

Dexter Fellows, who spent years with Cody publicizing Buffalo Bill's Wild West, later gave an account of the moment of the birth of the show.

"Nobody's ever done it before," Fellows quoted Salsbury as telling Buffalo Bill—which was true.

"It's the greatest show idea yet. We'll tell the story of the West with cowboys, Indians, buffalo, and bucking horses, not on the stage of a theater, but in the outdoors. It will be like a circus yet not a circus. It will be lifelike

and true in every detail. Here's a show that will not only sweep the larger cities of America but will also take the capitals of Europe by storm.

"I've seen riders all over the world, but none of them can surpass the American and Mexican cowboy in horsemanship. We'll make them the nucleus of this show and reconstruct life on the frontier. It will have more thrills than any circus ever had under a tent. Circuses have put on Western riding acts, but they never got over because the riders were synthetic cowboys."

"It's a great idea," said Cody. "I need something new. There isn't much more left for me on the stage."

"That's just it. You typify the West. You're wasting your talents with these dime-novel thrillers you've been doing. There's a million dollars in this idea if you head the bill and organize the show while I manage it."

Cody and Salsbury agreed to wait a year, until they would have sufficient capital to launch the venture, and then to split the profits fifty-fifty.

Two months later, Cody returned to his hometown of North Platte, Nebraska, for a visit, and was incensed to learn that the town had no plans for celebrating the Fourth of July. The town fathers dumped the problem in his lap by appointing him grand marshal of whatever celebration there would be. Responding, as people usually did, to the magic name of Buffalo Bill, local riders supplied the riding and local ranchers supplied the stock, and Cody put together "The Old Glory Blow Out," in which more than a thousand cowboys competed in exhibitions of riding, roping, and shooting. It also featured the old Deadwood stagecoach, connected by legend with some of the wildest of Western history. This coach was the same Concord stage, said Cody, he had ridden on his return from his scouting expedition with General Crook in 1876; when he learned that it had been abandoned on the plains, he had organized a party to reclaim it for history and himself.

When the dust cleared, Cody realized that he had already put on the kind of Wild West show that he and Salsbury had daydreamed about in that restaurant in Brooklyn.

But when Cody launched what he called The Wild West, Rocky Mountain and Prairie Exhibition on May 17, 1883, at the fairgrounds in Omaha, it was without Nathan Salsbury. While Salsbury was in Europe with another show, Cody had fallen in with a Dr. W. F. Carver, a former dentist who boasted that he had killed 5,700 buffalo in a single winter and now considered himself an exhibition marksman. He and Cody formed a partnership to put on the Wild West show using Carver's money, and when Cody invited Salsbury to join a Cody-Carver partnership, Salsbury wired that Carver was "a faker in the show business" and refused to have anything to do with them.

Cody's show was a spectacular. It featured fancy shooting, a simulated buffalo hunt and a Pony Express ride, cowboys, and the same Indian war cries that had curdled the blood of white men only a short time before. Starred with Cody and Dr. Carver were Buck Taylor, "King of the Cowboys," and Captain A. H. Bogardus, billed as the world's champion pigeon shot. Two other frontiersmen, a former trapper and interpreter in the Indian territory named Gordon W. "Pawnee Bill" Lillie and another old scout, Major Frank North, "White Chief of the Pawnees," joined the show at its second stand.

They did not perform under a tent, and for good reason: canvas overhead would have been riddled with bullets at every performance.

The highlight of the show was the closing number, an attack on the Deadwood coach and its rescue by scouts led by Dr. Carver and Buffalo Bill. By now, Cody had had a program printed that told the history of the famous stage, and that stage typified the appeal of Buffalo Bill's Wild West: built in 1863 at Concord, New Hampshire, it was brought to California on the clipper ship *General Grant* around Cape Horn. It ran on the line from Northwood into Oregon until the Central Pacific Railroad was built across the Rocky Mountains; then it went into service in Utah until the Central Pacific joined with the Union Pacific to transport Americans in those parts. In 1876 the coach was transferred to the death-defying run between Cheyenne and Deadwood, where it was attacked many times by the Sioux. Several drivers were killed in these attacks, but the marksmen riding shotgun were usually successful in driving off the attackers. Once, when the driver was killed, Martha Jane Canary, "Calamity Jane," seized the lines, whipped up the team, and escaped with the coach through whizzing bullets. The Deadwood coach was often used to carry treasure; so when it wasn't being menaced by Indians, it was often being menaced by bandits. At Cold Spring, outlaws killed one guard, wounded three others, and captured the stagecoach and its cargo of $60,000 in gold.

The problem with Buffalo Bill's Wild West was that too many of the old plainsmen who made up its cast looked upon the tour as an excuse to go on an epic drunk at the public's expense. Fellows said that "of the sixteen-car train one whole car was devoted to a stock of liquor." But that precaution probably wasn't necessary: every American town was filled with men who were honored to buy drinks for their boyhood heroes.

When they were sober enough to stay on their horses and hit their targets, the plainsmen put on an unforgettable show. When it played Hartford, Connecticut, the *Hartford Courant* said that Buffalo Bill had "in this exhibition, out-Barnumed Barnum."

Salsbury bided his time. He saw the show

when it played Coney Island, and he thought that it would be a money-maker if it were properly managed; but that it would probably go broke because no one was in control. A short time later, not surprisingly, Cody broke with Dr. Carver, and set up a new partnership among himself, Salsbury, and Bogardus.

With Salsbury managing the show for the summer season of 1884, it began to be more professional—and financially successful.

The New York press loved the show. Buffalo Bill invited reporters to ride with him in the Deadwood coach up Fifth Avenue to the Polo Grounds, where he held a barbecue for them in a tent carpeted with animal skins. There were six courses and free-flowing whiskey (not to mention champagne and beer) with every course.

Trouble struck when the Wild West chartered a steamboat at Cincinnati and began to give performances at towns along the Mississippi River. Their vessel collided with another steamer and sank. No people were killed, but all but a few of the horses perished, and all the equipment was lost except the bandwagon and the apparently unsinkable Deadwood stage.

There followed an exchange of telegrams between the Mississippi and Denver:

OUTFIT AT THE BOTTOM OF THE RIVER
WHAT SHALL I DO   CODY

GO ON TO NEW ORLEANS AND OPEN ON
YOUR DATE   HAVE WIRED YOU FUNDS
SALSBURY

After two weeks of heroic endeavors, Cody opened on time in New Orleans with enough animals, wagons, firearms, and equipment to put on a stirring show.

Then came the deluge. According to Fellows, the show ran into forty-four straight days of rain, and although that sounds too biblical to be true, whatever rain fell was enough to make Bogardus quit, sell his interest to Cody and Salsbury, and go home.

Cody himself begged Salsbury to give up on Buffalo Bill's Wild West, but the Civil War combat veteran turned manager insisted that they go on. They hired a new shootist to take Bogardus's place. She was a shy twenty-four-year-old who became so wildly popular that no one ever missed Bogardus. Her name was Annie Oakley, and she was one of the most phenomenal shots in the history of firearms. Buffalo Bill could shoot at tossed blue glass balls while on the gallop, and hit eighty-seven out of a hundred. Annie could sight with a hand mirror and shoot backward as her husband threw glass balls in the air and hit them all; or she could shoot from the back of a galloping pony—and hit them all. She nearly always hit them all. At thirty paces she could hit the thin edge of a playing card, or a dime tossed in the air.

She had been playing with the Sells Bros. Circus but didn't like the way she was being treated, so she showed up at Cody's tent during his last week at New Orleans and asked for an audition. When he saw her shoot, Cody hired her for the next season. Later, in the program for the 1894 season, her official show biography traced her incredible marksmanship back to her childhood:

This celebrated Girl Shot was born at Woodland, Ohio. Ever since a toddling child she has had an inherent love for fire-arms and hunting, and at the age of ten she, as often as ammunition was available, would smuggle her brother's musket and steal into the woods where game at that time was plentiful. Naturally, she was a good shot, and came home well supplied with game . . . although she has many times beaten all records, like the modest little girl she is she never uses the word Champion in connection with her name.

Annie Oakley was born Phoebe Anne Oakley Moses on August 13, 1860. As we know from the charming Irving Berlin musical *Annie Get Your Gun*, she first won a national reputation when she won a shooting match in Cincinnati against a crack shot named Frank E. Butler. The match was arranged by a local hotel keeper who knew of her skill. The musical's hit song, "You Can't Get a Man With a Gun" notwithstanding, Butler and Oakley got married and made successful tours of vaudeville circuits and circuses until 1884, when their dissatisfaction with Sells Bros. led them to Buffalo Bill. They stayed with Cody for seventeen years, though for much of that time, Butler acted as her manager and attendant rather than a shootist. He was the one who held a lighted cigarette in his lips so that she could shoot off the burning tip.

But because she projected her real-life shy sweetness, she had another role in the show that was at least as important as her marksmanship. Major John M. Burk, the publicist, once explained it to the press:

> It was our first thought, when we planned the show, that so much shooting would cause difficulty, that . . . women and children [would be] terrified. It was when Annie Oakley joined us that Colonel Cody devised the idea of graduating the excitement. Miss Oakley comes on very early in the performance. She starts very gently, shooting with a pistol. Women and children see the harmless woman out there and do not get worried.
>
> Gradually she increases the charge in her rifles until at last she shoots with a full charge. Thus, by the time the attack on the stagecoach comes, the audience is accustomed to the sound of shooting.

In other words, if it was all right with their Annie, it was all right with audiences. Har-

ANNIE OAKLEY. *At thirty paces, she could hit the thin edge of a playing card, or a dime tossed in the air, or the end of a cigarette. Once, in Berlin, she obliged Crown Prince William by letting him hold the cigarette in his lips. During World War I, when he had become Kaiser Wilhelm II, Annie was quoted as saying, "I wish I'd missed that day." The hole punched in complimentary tickets made people think of the bullet holes she fired into small cards, and free tickets became known as "Annie Oakleys." In 1901 she was severely injured in a train wreck but recovered and continued her performances. On stage and screen, she has been played by Ethel Merman, Mary Martin, Barbara Stanwyck, and Betty Hutton. The sweetness of her personality is reflected in the diary kept in 1896 by M. B. Bailey, superintendent of electric lights for Buffalo Bill's Wild West: "Piqua, Ohio, Saturday, July 4— Our own Annie Oakley was happy today; her mother, brother, three sisters, and their six children were at the show today." (Circus World Museum, Baraboo, Wisconsin)*

BUFFALO BILL AND SITTING BULL. The chief who united the Sioux tribes was born about 1831. As long as the buffalo inhabited the plains, his people thrived. Buffalo Bill, of course, was famous for killing buffalo to feed the crews building the first transcontinental railroad. To protect the settlers who came on these trains, the Sioux were ordered to settle on reservations by January 31, 1876. Sitting Bull performed the Sun Dance, then reported that he had seen soldiers falling into his camp like grasshoppers from the sky: a prophecy fulfilled at Little Big Horn. The Sioux were victorious in their battles but could not win a war that was destroying the buffalo. Famine forced Sitting Bull's surrender; he spent two years in prison. He was permitted to tour with Buffalo Bill partly to get him out of the way. Back on the reservation, and amid rumors of an impending uprising, he was ordered arrested as an "agitator." He was killed in the melee that followed on December 15, 1890. (Circus World Museum, Baraboo, Wisconsin)

monized by her calming presence, Buffalo Bill's Wild West hit its stride and enjoyed its first big triumphs. In fact, seeing that audiences were so in love with her, Buffalo Bill gave top billing to the name she selected for herself: "MISS ANNIE OAKLEY, the PEERLESS LADY WING-SHOT." He himself called her "Little Missy." Sitting Bull, the great Indian chief, who was with the show for five months in 1885, adopted her as a member of the Sioux tribe when he saw her shoot, giving her the name Watanya Cicilla, or "Little Sure Shot."

For the rest of the century, the show continued to be a legendary success. The person who, more than any other, deserved the credit was Salsbury, who brought money to the show, of course, but, more important than that, instilled in Cody the trouper's unbending resolve that the show must go on, come hell or forty-four days of high water.

In 1887, the Jubilee Year of Britain's Queen Victoria, Buffalo Bill's Wild West went to England, where there were two performances commanded by the Queen. The Prince of Wales gave a medal to Annie Oakley, and she would be shown wearing it in a famous 1901 poster devoted entirely to "the peerless wing and rifle shot." With that kind of royal reception, it was not surprising that two and a half million persons attended the show in London alone.

Buffalo Bill's letter to Louisa F. Cody, his wife, back in America, describing the highlight of the trip, gives the flavor of the man—all the boyish enthusiasm and naïveté:

What do you think, Mamma, I've just held four kings! And I was the joker! It wasn't a card game either. You remember the old stage coach? Well, I got a request from the Prince of Wales to let him ride on the seat with me, while inside would be the kings of

Denmark, Saxony, Greece, and Austria. Well, I didn't know just what to say for a moment. I was a little worried and yet I couldn't tell the Prince of Wales that I was afraid to haul around four kings, with Indians shooting blanks around. So I just said I was as honored as all getout, and we made the arrangements.

And, Mamma, I just had to have my joke, so I went around and told the Indians to whoop it up as they never did before. We loaded all the kings in there and the Prince got up on the seat with me, and then I just cut 'er loose. We sure did rock around that arena, with the Indians yelling and shooting behind us, fit to kill. And Mamma— I wouldn't say it out loud—but I'm pretty sure that before the ride was over, most of the kings were under the seat. It sure was fun.

When the ride stopped, the Prince of Wales said to me that he bet this was the first time that I'd ever held four kings. I told him that I'd held four kings before, but this was the first time that I'd ever acted as the royal joker. Well, he laughed and laughed. Then he had to explain it to all those kings, each in his own language—and I kind of felt sorry for him.

The Prince gave me a souvenir, a sort of crest, with diamonds all around it. It sure is pretty and I'm real proud of it.

Buffalo Bill's Wild West had become an international sensation. The show went back to Europe in the spring of 1889, and its fame endured. In Paris, they played for six months. In Rome, the Prince of Sermonetta saw the show and challenged Cody's cowboys to tame his horses. His own horsemen, using irons and chains, had failed, and had been badly bitten to boot. Twenty thousand people came to see Buffalo Bill's boys try. A reinforced corral was built on the show grounds. Even so, special barricades had to be set up because of the Ital-

ians' fears that the horses would get loose and charge the audience.

Two horses were released into the corral. Buffalo Bill's sister reported what happened next: "The wild equines sprang into the air, darted hither and thither and fought hard against their certain fate, but in less time than would be required to give the details the cowboys had flung their lassos, caught the horses, and saddled and mounted them. The spirited beasts still resisted and sought in every way to throw their riders, but the expert plainsmen had them under control in a very short time; and as they rode them around the arena, the spectators rose and howled with delight. The display of horsemanship effectively silenced the skeptics; it captured the Roman heart and the remainder of the stay in the city was attended by unusual enthusiasm."

The quick taming of the wildest horses in Europe by American cowboys caught the imagination not only of Rome but of the entire continent. Wherever they went, Buffalo Bill and his cowboys would offer to break and ride any horse given them, and they always succeeded.

The Wild West formula was unvarying—and unforgettable. Each show began with 400 riders at a full chase; then came the breathless moment of the triumphant entry of Buffalo Bill himself. As Rupert Croft-Cooke described him:

> His was the most imposing figure of all. Almost six feet in height, with the head of a stage musketeer, his greying hair fell from under a Stetson hat and curled luxuriantly about his shoulders. His brown eyes had the clear, steady gaze of the marksman; the straight classical nose was that of the old-time American frontiersman. His attire for these occasions was a hunting shirt made of deerskin, beautifully dressed and tanned, long leggings of the same material, the broad

collar and leg seams decorated with bright-hued fringes; he wore moccasins on his feet; around his middle was buckled a leather belt in which, besides ammunition pouches, were stuck a hatchet and a hunting knife.

A typical performance included an attack on an "Emigrant Train Crossing the Plains" and Buffalo Bill's dramatic arrival "in the nick of time" to save the Deadwood stage. (These hairbreadth rescues were often the subject of posters advertising the show, but Robert L. Parkinson, director of the research center at the Circus World Museum in Baraboo, Wisconsin, pointed out to me that every lithograph showing American settlers in danger also showed the rescuers close enough to save the day. Buffalo Bill's Wild West was always designed to bring reassurance and give a feeling of security to the Europeans who had come to settle this land.)

By including buffalo in his show, Buffalo Bill helped to draw attention to the fact that the American bison was even then in danger of extinction. The former buffalo hunter was now on the other side. (In 1986, to show that conservationists are saving the bison from extinction, Kenneth Feld included one in the circus parade of the 113th edition of Ringling Bros. and Barnum & Bailey Circus.)

When, in 1893, Cody recruited Cossacks from the Russian steppes, plus German, French, Irish, and Arab riders to augment his troupe, he cleverly billed them as the "Congress of the Rough Riders of the World." They not only became a permanent, popular feature of his spectacles, they inspired Theodore Roosevelt to call the men who followed him up San Juan Hill during the Spanish-American War by that same name: the Rough Riders.

One day in 1893, when Buffalo Bill's Wild West was playing on a lot across the street from the Chicago World's Fair, Annie Oakley demonstrated sharpshooting, of course; and Vicente Orapeza, a rope artist from Mexico, gave demonstrations of roping and lassoing. Seated among the 22,000 people in the huge horseshoe amphitheater was a boy of thirteen or fourteen, part white, part Cherokee Indian, who had come all the way from Oklahoma to see Buffalo Bill, but who now found himself more affected by Señor Orapeza.

Will Rogers watched Orapeza gracefully spinning his lariat, leaping in and out of its circling loop, snaking it out and smoothly lassoing a dashing horse by the front feet, then the back feet, then all four feet, then by the saddle horn and even the tail! To close, he spelled "Orapeza" in the air, one letter at a time, with a rope that seemed alive. "It might have been here at Chicago, with the freedom of the West luring millions to vicarious participation, that Rogers first thought of showing his own westernness to the public," wrote William R. Brown in *Imagemaker: Will Rogers and the American Dream*.

Later, as a cowboy in the Texas Panhandle, Will Rogers practiced rope twirling and steer roping for himself. By 1903, he was working with a Wild West show in South Africa. His American debut as an entertainer was made with a Wild West show appearing at Madison Square Garden in New York City in 1905. Then he began adding jokes and humorous political commentary to his rope-twirling act, and found a stage for his kind of showmanship in the Ziegfeld Follies. He was probably the greatest symbol of the American West after Buffalo Bill. And somehow his whole improbable, uniquely American career had snaked out like a lariat from seeing Buffalo Bill's Wild West.

The version of the American saga that Buffalo Bill brought to the world can be gathered from this program for 1895:

OVERTURE

"Star-Spangled Banner." Cowboy Band; William Sweeney, Leader.

1. Grand Review

Introducing the Rough Riders of the World, Indians, Cowboys, Mexicans, Cossacks, Gauchos, Arabs, Scouts, Guides, American Negroes, and detachments of fully equipped Regular Soldiers of the armies of America, England, France, Germany, and Russia.

2. MISS ANNIE OAKLEY

Celebrated Shot, who will illustrate her dexterity in the use of firearms.

3. Horse Race

Between a Cowboy, a Cossack, a Mexican, an Arab, a Gaucho, and an Indian, on Spanish-Mexican, Bronco, Russian, and Arabian horses.

4. Pony Express

A former Pony Post-Rider will show how the Letters and Telegrams of the Republic were distributed across the immense Continent previous to the building of railways and the telegraph.

5. Illustrating a Prairie Emigrant Train Crossing the Plains

It is attacked by marauding Indians, who are in turn repulsed by "Buffalo Bill" and a number of Scouts and Cowboys.

6. A Group of Riffian Arabian Horsemen

Will illustrate their style of Horsemanship, together with Native Sports and Pastimes.

7. JOHNNY BAKER

Celebrated Young American Horseman.

8. Cossacks

Of the Caucasus of Russia, in feats of Horsemanship, Native Dances, etc.

9. A Group of Mexicans

From Old Mexico, who will illustrate the use of Lasso, and perform various feats of Horsemanship.

10. HURDLE RACE

Between Primitive Riders mounted on Western Bronco Ponies that never jumped a hurdle until just before opening of present exhibition.

11. Cowboy Fun

Picking Objects from the Ground, Lassoing Wild Horses, Riding the Buckers, etc.

12. Military Musical Drill

By a detachment from the Seventh United States Cavalry from Fort Riley; detachment from the Fifth Royal Irish Lancers; detachment from French Dragoons of Republic Francaise; detachment from Garde Cuirassiers of His Majesty Kaiser Wilhelm II.

13. Attack on the Deadwood Mail Coach by Indians

Repulse of the Indians and Rescue of the Stage, Passengers, and Mail by "Buffalo Bill" and his attendant Cowboys. N.B. This is the identical Deadwood Mail Coach, famous as having carried many people who lost their lives between Deadwood and Cheyenne nineteen years ago. Now the most famous vehicle extant.

14. RACING BETWEEN INDIAN BOYS ON BAREBACK HORSES

15. TEN MINUTES WITH THE ROUGH RIDERS OF THE WORLD

16. COL W. F. CODY

("Buffalo Bill") in his unique feats of Sharpshooting at full speed.

17. Buffalo Hunt

As it was in the Far West of North America. "Buffalo Bill" and Indians. The last of the only known native herd.

18. Attack on Settlers' Cabins

Rescue by "Buffalo Bill" and a band of Cowboys, Scouts, etc.

19. SALUTE

Conclusion.

Buffalo Bill was always on the lookout for the best horsemen of every country, and he

also recruited talented acrobats. When the 1895 program promised that "A Group of Riffian Arabian Horsemen will illustrate their style of Horsemanship, together with Native Sports and Pastimes," that meant whirling and tumbling.

At least one Arab member of Buffalo Bill's Wild West stayed in the United States and became a very prominent American circus owner. His name was George Hamid, he was born in the village of Broumana, Lebanon, in 1896, and he always credited his success in the New World to Annie Oakley.

"Conditions were bad in Lebanon in those days," he wrote in *Circus*, his 1950 autobiography. "Any way you looked at it—food, shelter, education, opportunity—the picture was black. Our people schemed, plotted, and connived to get their children out of the country—to Europe or, better yet, to the United States."

George's mother had died when he was three; his grandmother encouraged him, his brothers, and his cousin in tumbling, since, as George said, in the Arab world "more than anywhere else, the practice of springing and whirling is a cherished art, virtually a national sport."

At the age of nine, working in Europe with his uncle's troupe of Arab tumblers, he charmed Annie Oakley. She took him to Buffalo Bill, who had also been known as a charmer as an orphan boy trying to get started as a dispatch rider. Buffalo Bill, too, sparked to Hamid, and took him to America. To make sure that he would succeed there, Annie Oakley taught this self-proclaimed "Arab ragamuffin" to speak, read, and write English. Thoroughly at ease in English, Hamid moved from his youthful career as an acrobat with Buffalo Bill's Wild West to become one of the leading theatrical booking agents in the United States. During the Great Depression of the 1930s, Hamid joined with Robert Morton, one of America's pioneers in the modern presen-

ROUGH RIDERS. *Buffalo Bill's Wild West shows were greeted with enthusiasm from their beginning as a permanent touring show in 1884 through the military pageant, "Preparedness," that Buffalo Bill and the 101 Ranch put on in 1916, the year before America's entry into World War I. In the 1890s Cody added to his shows a "Congress of Rough Riders of the World," who incorporated various kinds of trick and specialized riding. When Theodore Roosevelt abruptly resigned as assistant secretary of the navy under President William McKinley in 1897 and organized the First Volunteer Cavalry to go to Cuba and make an impulsive charge up San Juan Hill, he called his cavalry troop by the name Buffalo Bill's Wild West had made famous: the "Rough Riders." (Circus World Museum, Baraboo, Wisconsin)*

ARAB RIDERS. *Among the roughest of Buffalo Bill's Rough Riders were a group of Riffian Arabian horsemen from the mountainous coastal region of north Morocco, who put on the kind of galloping, rifle-firing, acrobatic display that in Morocco today is called a "Fantasia." There was also a Lebanese Arab in the troupe, a tumbler named George A. Hamid, who was taught to speak English by Annie Oakley and went on to become one of America's leading booking agents and a partner in the Hamid-Morton Circus. (Circus World Museum, Baraboo, Wisconsin)*

tation of indoor circuses. Morton had been in this business since 1918, when he arranged to rent Gentry Bros. Circus equipment to the Shriners, but he was having trouble weathering the Depression until joined by the hardship-inured Hamid. Together, they built a powerful route of engagements, playing annual benefits for Shrine temples, police departments, and others in such cities as Memphis, Milwaukee, Kansas City, Washington, Philadelphia, and Toronto, and Hamid eventually emerged as one of America's most successful circus owners.

Buffalo Bill's success wasn't lost on other eminent western figures. Gordon W. Lillie organized his Pawnee Bill's Wild West in 1887; outlaws Cole Younger and Frank James—Jesse's brother—went straight with a Wild West in 1903. Miller Bros. 101 Ranch Real Wild West was launched by the Oklahoma ranch empire of George Miller in 1908. Among its attractions was Iron Tail, the Indian who posed for the buffalo nickel, and black cowboy Bill Pickett, originator of bulldogging—throwing a calf or steer to the ground by seizing the horns and twisting the head.

It didn't take established circuses long to copy Buffalo Bill's Wild West. The combination of performing animals and feats of physical prowess and daring by human beings was an important part of the spectacle and pageantry that have always been the circus. W. W. Cole was probably the first circus to present a Wild West performance, in 1886. That same year, the Adam Forepaugh Circus presented a western display.

At the close of the 1894 season, Nathan Salsbury was struck with an illness that made him a semi-invalid for the rest of his life. With Salsbury's incapacitation began the slow but inexorable decline of Buffalo Bill's fortunes. Cody had no trouble putting on a show that could compete with any circus. But logistics was another matter. Trying to provide this necessity, Salsbury made a contract with James A. Bailey, who received a 50 percent interest in Buffalo Bill's Wild West in return for making himself responsible for providing rolling stock, financial support, and winter quarters. Bailey then sold half of his share to W. W. Cole.

In 1896, Bailey's three shows—Barnum & Bailey, Forepaugh-Sells and Buffalo Bill's Wild West—fought the Ringling Bros. for supremacy in the circus world. In 1897, Bailey took the Barnum & Bailey show on a five-year tour of Europe, leaving Forepaugh-Sells and Buffalo Bill's Wild West to compete with Ringling Bros.

Bailey died in 1906, leaving Barnum & Bailey Circus to his widow, who sold all of Bailey's assets to Ringling Bros. in 1907. Ringling Bros. sold the Wild West equipment back to Cody, now in his sixties, but the Colonel had neither the ability nor the strength to carry on alone. To the rescue came his old friend Pawnee Bill, who had helped Cody procure Indians for his first Wild West, and was now running a show of his own called the Far East Show. He suggested that they organize a "farewell tour" together. They would take three years, and visit every town and city in the United States and Canada. When Cody agreed, Pawnee Bill bought out the Bailey interest, and the two shows were combined in what came to be known as "the Two Bills' show."

Annie Oakley traveled with the show in its successful first season, 1909–10. She had been severely injured in the fall of 1901 when the Buffalo Bill show train crashed in a head-on collision near Lexington, Virginia, and her recovery was slow, but she came back just as her old boss's years of independence came to an end.

In his second "farewell" year, profits were

not great enough to keep Cody ahead of his creditors. Business in the next six months was disastrous. Sheriff's men attached the property of the Wild West and the Far East Show for debt. There was an auction.

The buyers were H. H. Tammen and Fred Bonfils. Tammen, who had started with a dog and pony show, wanted a big circus that could compete with Ringling Bros., and he had decided that he had the makings of such a circus if he controlled Buffalo Bill. At first, Cody hoped that they would help him make enough money so that he could liberate himself from them and start another Wild West show of his own. So he signed a two-year contract with the Sells-Floto Circus for $100 a day, plus 40 percent of the gross over $3,000 a day. By this time, Buffalo Bill's drinking had become a business problem, so in his contract, he had to agree not to take more than three drinks a day. He didn't, but he made the drinks whiskey— in oversized beer mugs.

At the end of the 1914 season, Cody wanted to buy Ranch 101, a Wild West show that had grown out of an exhibition put on in 1907 by cowboys of the Miller Bros. ranch at the Jamestown Exposition. But Cody couldn't raise the capital to buy the show; in the end, he merely joined it. Nevertheless, it was called Buffalo Bill (Himself) (The Military Pageant Preparedness) and The Miller Bros. 101 Ranch Real Wild West.

Cody was beginning to be seen as a pitiful figure. His linen was still immaculate, his boots were still gleaming, and he was as quick as ever in picking up the tab at the bars he frequented as much as ever—but these days, he often paid for the drinks with the last dollar in his pocket.

Dexter Fellows last saw Bill Cody in 1916, when Fellows was advance man for the Barnum show and Cody was being featured in a pageant on military preparedness. "He was seventy years old," wrote Fellows, "and, while his hair was thinner and crows had left their footmarks on his face, his eyes were bright. I spent most of the afternoon in his tent and talked of the great days of the Buffalo Bill show. His credit at that time was minus zero, yet he still hoped to raise money for another Wild West show."

But Cody confided in Fellows that he had fainted on several occasions after leaving the arena "and that he lived in mortal fear of dying in the saddle in front of an audience."

Night after night, Johnny Baker, a North Platte boy who had always worshiped Buffalo Bill and who had made himself a marksman in order to travel with the show, would help his hero onto his horse. Cody would sit slumped behind the curtains, gathering his strength, until Johnny would say, "Ready, Colonel." Then the curtains would part, and audiences would see a vigorous-looking man standing tall in the saddle, back straight, chin held high. By sheer willpower, he would ride out, doff his big Stetson, and bow like the Buffalo Bill of old.

But his fear of dying "before all those people" increased. Night after night, when the curtains closed, he would slide off his horse into the arms of Johnny Baker and wonder how long he could go on. Then in Portsmouth, Virginia, on November 11, 1916, he caught a cold in his chest and that night made his last appearance. Afterward, he set out for his beloved home in the mountains in his namesake town of Cody, Wyoming; but he felt so weak that he stopped in Denver to see his sister, May Cody Decker.

He made it home to Cody, but almost immediately he was back in Denver being cared for by his sister. Uremic poisoning was spreading rapidly through his system.

He died in bed at the home of his sister at noon on January 10, 1917, broke and defeated in his last desire to mount just one more Wild West show. The nation mourned, from schoolchildren, who immediately started sending pennies to the *Denver Post* campaign to erect a monument above Denver on Lookout Mountain, to Theodore Roosevelt, who wrote that "his name, like that of Kit Carson, will always be associated with old adventure and pioneer days of hazard and hardship. . . . He embodied those traits of courage, strength and self-reliant hardihood which are vital to the well-being of our nation."

Buffalo Bill was all right, in the end; for it turned out that it was the pitiful figure of the last years that had died and the legend that had survived, more vibrant and vivid than ever. The world forgave him his faults: forgave him his lifelong failure in any kind of business investment; forgave him his obsessive profligacy; forgave him his estrangement from his wife, who had complained constantly—and accurately—that he had failed to grow up and settle down; forgave him his weakness for beautiful women who took his help and his money and never looked back; forgave him the few drinks too many he increasingly took as his years and his troubles increased. They saw him instead as a courtly, openhearted, openhanded man who brought them the sense of unlimited possibilities for adventure and heroism that really did belong to the West of his youth but that could increasingly be looked for only on the exhibition grounds as he grew old. It is some sense of this Wild West, now no longer provided even by the circus, that tourists continue to seek at Buffalo Bill's burial site on the top of Lookout Mountain.

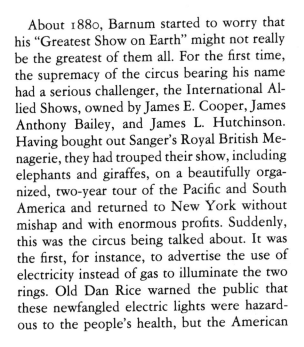

Jumbo!

About 1880, Barnum started to worry that his "Greatest Show on Earth" might not really be the greatest of them all. For the first time, the supremacy of the circus bearing his name had a serious challenger, the International Allied Shows, owned by James E. Cooper, James Anthony Bailey, and James L. Hutchinson. Having bought out Sanger's Royal British Menagerie, they had trouped their show, including elephants and giraffes, on a beautifully organized, two-year tour of the Pacific and South America and returned to New York without mishap and with enormous profits. Suddenly, this was the circus being talked about. It was the first, for instance, to advertise the use of electricity instead of gas to illuminate the two rings. Old Dan Rice warned the public that these newfangled electric lights were hazardous to the people's health, but the American public flocked to International Allied Shows anyway, and once again, there were no mishaps.

Barnum never discounted his competitors. He inquired as to who the managerial genius among the three owners of the rival circus really was. The answer came back: it was Bailey.

Then Barnum saw a half-sheet advertisement that, for appeal, was like a scene come to life out of Walt Disney's *Dumbo*—but sixty-one years before that baby elephant became America's "mammal-of-the-year."

"THE ONLY BABY ELEPHANT EVER BORN IN CAPTIVITY," the banner line proclaimed. "Hebe the Mother and Columbia the Baby / Born March 10, 1880. Weight 213 pounds."

The lithograph was a charmer: "Actual scene taken from Life, Mother and Baby Playing,"

JUMBO with Matthew Scott, his keeper for twenty years, in 1882. Scott coaxed him into an immense van on wheels, which transported him the six miles to the Thames. There he was hoisted aboard a lighter by steam crane, moved down the river to the steamer, and lifted to the deck by tackle. Calmed by English beer, with Scott snoring beside him, Jumbo sailed for America and the fame that lasts to this day. (Ringling Museum)

said the description of the elephant child romping around his pachyderm mom.

The baby elephant had been born with Cooper & Bailey's Allied Shows. Barnum, the genius at showmanship and publicity, apparently hoped that Bailey, the genius at logistics and organization, wouldn't realize what a bonanza he had. Figuring he could make a fortune with such a rare creature, Barnum dashed off a telegram offering Cooper & Bailey $100,000 for the infant.

To his dismay, the great Barnum was soon seeing his telegram blown up to circus poster size, under Bailey's headline: "WHAT BARNUM THINKS OF THE BABY ELEPHANT."

"I found that I had at last met foemen 'worthy of my steel,'" responded P. T. Barnum. He offered Hutchinson a free partnership in his show if he would persuade the shrewd Bailey to combine with Barnum. That very year, an agreement was reached, and the combined shows were organized under the firm name of Barnum, Bailey & Hutchinson.

James Anthony Bailey, who hated personal publicity, was the perfect partner for the self-glorifying P. T. Barnum. No one could draw attention to his individual attractions (and himself) like Barnum, and no one could get the whole show on the road like Bailey. Fred Bradna, an Alsatian who spent five years as a German cavalry officer before becoming Bailey's equestrian director, called his boss "a genius" and remembered in his book *The Big Top*, "While I was in the army at Dieuze, the German military staff sent its quartermaster general to travel with Bailey and learn how to move masses of men, animals and equipment by railroad car. His techniques for loading and unloading trains and laying out lots are still, with modern modifications, in use today."

They were opposites in character: Bailey was a nervous perfectionist who chewed rubber bands when he was perturbed; Barnum was a high-spirited optimist who made a fortune exploiting imperfection. In business relations, they were usually willing to complement each other.

Bailey had been born James A. McGinnis in Detroit on the Fourth of July, 1847. He was only a child when his father died in a cholera epidemic, and his mother died shortly thereafter, leaving him at the mercy of brothers and sisters whom he disliked intensely. His solution was to run away from home and get a job at the Pontiac Hotel. There, he met an advance agent for the Robinson & Lake's Circus who gave young McGinnis a job in the show. This benefactor was Frederick Harrison Bailey, and he claimed to be an indirect relation of Hackaliah Bailey of Somers, New York, who owned Old Bet.

Like Jimmy Gatz re-creating himself as Jay Gatsby, young McGinnis took a new name for his new identity, one with a circus resonance: James A. Bailey. He hated his old name so much that in later years, when an equestrian named Billy Dutton told it around the circus that he had played marbles with Bailey when his name was McGinnis, Bailey fired him on the spot.

During the Civil War, Bailey followed the Union army as a civilian, selling it provisions. In the violent post–Civil War period, he was working as a billposter for Bill Lake when Lake was killed by a gunfighter. Then Bailey acquired a half interest in the Hemmings, Cooper & Whitby Circus aftershow—but Harry Whitby was also shot to death. Bailey survived to become half owner of the Cooper & Bailey Circus at the age of twenty-nine. As active manager, he made good profits from 1873 through 1875.

For America's centennial year of 1876, when a giant centennial celebration was planned for Philadelphia, Barnum had responded by taking a wagon show on the road to give Americans "a Fourth of July celebration every day." Bailey, on the other hand, worried that with so many Americans saving their money to go to Philadelphia for the Centennial Exposition, circus business might suffer over most of the rest of the country. So he put the show on rails and struck out for California, then chartered a steamer and took his circus across the Pacific.

The first word of the boy wonder's awe-inspiring organizational ability came from that tour, when Bailey took his circus to California, Australia, New Zealand, Java, Peru, Chile, Argentina, Brazil, and the Dutch Indies—76,000 miles during a two-year tour—and came back to the United States with enough profits to purchase the Great London Circus, a railroad show since 1875, at a forced sale. Bailey went into winter quarters at Philadelphia in 1878, and when he came out, in the spring of 1879, the show renamed Great London, Cooper & Bailey's Allied Show was ready to do battle with the Barnum show, then the largest show on the road.

And then "WHAT BARNUM THINKS OF THE BABY ELEPHANT" brought the rivals into partnership.

Barnum, Bailey, Hutchinson, and Cooper first presented the results of their combined talents—P. T. Barnum's Greatest Show on Earth and the Great London Circus and Sanger's Royal British Menagerie, etc.—to New York City on March 18, 1881.

For the first time in history, three rings were used. As with Barnum's two-ring show, the aesthetic argument was heard. The *New York Herald* called the three rings "the only drawback to the performance" because "the spectator was compelled to receive more than his money's worth; in other words, that while his head was turned in one direction he felt he was losing something good in another."

But three-ring circuses were to become the American way. European and British circuses generally retained their one-ring format, but to American ears the term "*one-ring circus* soon sounded derogatory. "Perhaps nothing is more typical of America—the richest nation on earth—," explained one social commentator, "than the principle of overabundance, of planned waste, characterized even in its amusements."

If "Bigger Is Better" continued to be the American way in circus rings, it was preeminently the American way in circus elephants. In 1882, P. T. Barnum, the man who defined clowns and elephants as "pegs, used to hang circuses on," went after the biggest peg to which a circus could aspire.

"**Jumbo**; very large (after *Jumbo*, name of large elephant in Barnum's show)," says the *Random House Dictionary of the English Language*. "He was the largest elephant ever kept in captivity, a record undisputed to the present day," wrote James L. Haley in a study in *American Heritage* in August 1973. "It was the giant animal whose name was given to outsized objects," wrote Haley, "not the other way around. He himself was christened Jumbo when he was less than five feet tall."

The promotion of Jumbo was undoubtedly Barnum's greatest single achievement in the world of the circus, and, indeed, it stands to this day as the greatest in the history of circus promotion, bigger even than John Ringling North's promotion of the gorilla Gargantua or Kenneth Feld's promotion of "The Living Unicorn" in the twentieth century.

And yet, Barnum said afterward, "It never cost me a cent to advertise Jumbo. It was the greatest free advertising I ever heard of."

Jumbo had been captured as a baby, most probably in Ethiopia by a band of Hamran Arabs. For a time he was in the Jardin des

Plantes in Paris, which had plenty of elephants but wanted a rhinoceros. The London Zoological Society had an extra rhino but no African elephants, so it suggested a trade. The Paris zoo liked the idea so much it threw in two spiny anteaters.

When the baby elephant arrived in London, he was found to be severely ill and near death. An underkeeper named Matthew Scott was assigned to be his keeper, and "Scotty" spent so many months nursing him tenderly back to health that the two became inseparable.

The zoo called him Jumbo as a shortened form of Mumbo Jumbo, the name of a grotesque idol said to have been worshiped by certain African tribes. Since 1847, the term *mumbo jumbo* had been in the English language to describe any object of senseless veneration. Soon Jumbo would put his name in the world's dictionaries by growing into the very definition of a huge person, animal, or thing. Many a soldier in Great Britain's wars over the next century would be nicknamed Jumbo after this elephant, and the American advertising industry would make it one of its favorite words.

In London, Jumbo grew and grew—in size and popularity. He was the leading attraction of the London Zoological Gardens, a favorite of Queen Victoria and the royal family; a sight of the city seen by Theodore Roosevelt and by the young Winston Churchill, who was photographed with him. Barnum saw him many times, and once rode on his back.

By 1882, Jumbo was twelve feet tall at the shoulders, weighed six and a half tons, and could reach an object twenty-six feet from the ground with his seven-foot trunk. He was famous for his gentleness, and *Harper's Weekly* said he was "as gentle with children as the best-trained poodle dog, taking the proffered biscuit or lump of sugar with an almost incredible delicacy of touch. . . . The most nervous child,

having once overcome his alarm, never hesitated to hand a morsel to his waving trunk a second time." Literally hundreds of thousands of children had ridden in the howdah strapped to his back as he plodded the gravel paths of the zoo in Regent's Park.

So had Phineas T. Barnum—and Barnum knew that Jumbo, now the largest animal in captivity, would be an untoppable attraction in the circus, which has always been the ultimate repository of the most of almost anything.

Barnum offered $10,000 for Jumbo, over the objections of partner James L. Hutchinson. "What is the difference," Hutchinson asked, "between an elephant seven feet high and another eleven or twelve feet high? An elephant is an elephant."

Mr. Hutchinson has not gone down in history as one of the world's greatest showmen.

Barnum certainly has, and one of the reasons was luck. He did not know that the directors of the London Zoo had two excellent reasons for wanting to get rid of their most popular attraction.

The first reason was that Jumbo, near adulthood, might soon fall victim to musth, the periodic inflammation of the male elephant's temporal glands. Musth (the word for *drunk* in Persian) is a condition accompanied by the exudation of an oily substance from the glands between the eyes and mouth, which can drive an elephant into a violent and often destructive frenzy.

The second reason was Matthew Scott, who was to him more nanny than keeper. Jumbo could hardly bear to be separated from Scotty, and when Scotty went home at night, Jumbo would throw tantrums and try to damage the elephant house. What if Scotty were to die suddenly? In an animal so large, that grief could be destructive indeed.

So when Barnum's offer was made, the directors of the London Zoo hesitated for just two days before selling him Jumbo. (They didn't feel guilty; Barnum's circus, which had more than twenty elephants, knew about musth-crazed elephants and was equipped to deal with them.)

Enter Barnum the master psychologist. He shrewdly realized that getting the British to complain about what they were losing was the surest way to make Americans appreciate what they were gaining. Uncle Bob Sherwood, a great Barnum clown, said later that Barnum put some of his publicists to work in England, fanning the protest movement against him, particularly by getting schoolchildren all riled up, and put others to work in America letting his fellow countrymen know what he was taking away from the English for their delight.

Obviously, much of the protest was authentic. Queen Victoria's husband, Prince Albert, publicly condemned the transaction; the Queen, too, had ridden Jumbo, and it was said that she felt the contract should be broken. John Ruskin wrote icily that England was not in the habit of selling her pets.

Barnum succeeded so emphatically that 4,626 Jumbo lovers came to say good-bye in one day in March 1882, compared to 214 who visited on the same day the year before.

The editors of the London *Daily Telegraph* cabled Barnum: "Editor's compliments; all British children distressed at Elephant's departure; hundreds of correspondents beg us to inquire on what terms you will kindly return Jumbo. Answer prepaid, unlimited."

Barnum made sure that the world could read his reply:

My compliments to Editor *Daily Telegraph* and British Nation. Fifty-one million of American citizens anxiously awaiting Jumbo's arrival. My forty years' invariable practice of exhibiting the best that money could procure makes Jumbo's presence here im-

perative. My largest tent seats 20,000 persons, and is filled twice each day. It contains four rings, in three of which three full circus companies give different performances simultaneously.

BARNUM

Jumbo's departure was even more exciting. Halfway through the gate of the zoo, Jumbo lay down in the street, apparently refusing to leave England. Some Englishmen believed that Jumbo did this out of loyalty to English soil; others more realistically suspected that Jumbo lay down at a signal from Scotty.

Reporters wrote that the loudest noise making over Jumbo's leaving came from his mourning mate, an elephant named Alice. They got the wrong elephant, and Alice wasn't his mate, but it made a wonderful story.

"Jumbo is lying in the garden and will not stir," Barnum's head elephant keeper, William Newman, cabled from London. "What shall we do?"

The answer added to the legend: "Let him lie there as long as he wants to. The publicity is worth it.—BARNUM."

Farewell receptions for Jumbo at the zoo had grossed $50,000 for its treasury. Presents for Jumbo, presented to his keeper, were enriching Matthew Scott. But at last, in the Court of Queen's Bench, Mr. Justice Chitty ruled that public remorse over a perfectly legal transaction was not enough to cancel the contract, and the biggest elephant had to go to America. Since only Scotty could control him, Barnum hired Matthew Scott to continue to be his keeper.

On March 15, Jumbo was hoisted aboard the *Assyrian Monarch*. For much of the trip, Scotty perched on the front of the cage, holding Jumbo's trunk. Jumbo got a bit seasick crossing the Atlantic, but not too seasick to consume two tons of hay, three sacks of oats, two sacks of biscuits, and one sack of his favorite treat, onions.

Jumbo arrived in New York on Easter Sunday, 1882, in time for the annual opening of The Greatest Show on Earth at Madison Square Garden. The *New York Times* declared that there was more excitement in New York "than there would be in London if Queen Victoria's imperial knee was swelled to twice its royal size . . . the multitude burst into a roar of applause which almost shook the city to its foundations and caused the cobble-stones to grind against each other in the streets." Jumbo had cost Barnum and his partners $30,000 to buy him and bring to America, but he made that amount back in ten days; in six weeks, Jumbo had grossed $336,000 for his owners.

Even Thomas Nast, the caustic editorial cartoonist famous for his exposure of Boss Tweed, was charmed by Barnum's promotion of Jumbo. He drew a cartoon that showed Barnum hugging Jumbo's trunk and resting his head against it as he says, "You are a *humbug* after my own heart. You have even beat me in advertising."

Jumbo was the greatest circus attraction in American history, but he had only three and a half years to live.

He lived it to the hilt—or tusk. In the golden age, when the circus train itself had seemed the height of glamor, Jumbo went on the annual tour of The Greatest Show on Earth in a private railroad car, which Barnum called "Jumbo's Palace Car." It was a crimson-and-gold boxcar with huge double doors in the middle to give Jumbo easy access up a ramp.

Scotty rode in a bunk near Jumbo's head; their compartments were separated by a small door, but Jumbo never let Scotty close the door. As long as his nanny was near, he had no outbursts of temper, unless you count the time that Scotty forgot to share his daily quart of beer. Jumbo had grown used to this ritual, and when Scotty once guzzled the beer by himself, then fell asleep, Jumbo reached through the small door, picked Scotty up with his trunk and set him down meaningfully near the empty beer bottle. Scotty never again forgot to share his beer with Jumbo, as long as they were together.

For three and a half seasons, Jumbo was the greatest star of the circus. In the fourth season, the show had its traditional opening on March 16, 1885, and from there the circus train carried it through New York, Pennsylvania, New England, and the Maritime Provinces of Canada. After 8,000 miles and more than a hundred stops, the train pulled into the town of St. Thomas, Ontario, in the early morning of September 15, 1885. It rolled into the Grand Trunk Railroad Yards east of Woodworth Avenue, and was shifted to a siding.

The long circus train was uncoupled near the middle and the forward part pulled up a few yards, so that the animals wouldn't have to make the long walk around the end of the train to get to the circus grounds, making loading and unloading faster.

Even today, while the performance is going on during one-night stands such as at St. Thomas, or on the last night of longer engagements, anything that is no longer needed is being packed up and loaded on the train. So after the thirty-one elephants performed their military drill about halfway through the night show, twenty-nine of them were taken back to the train and loaded for the trip to the next town.

Fred R. Armes, the operator in charge of the Grand Trunk Railroad depot at St. Thomas that night, claimed later that he requested that the circus not reload its elephants until 9:55 P.M., long after a westbound express freight was due to pass through. At that time, Armes said, he would have a yard crew available to take the elephants across the track at a designated crossing, near the station.

In any case, the elephant handlers didn't

wait. They tore down a section of right-of-way fence directly between the Big Top and the circus train and marched the twenty-nine elephants up an embankment, across the main-line track, and into their cars.

The other two elephants were needed to close the act: the smallest, a dwarf clown elephant named Tom Thumb, and the largest, the famous Jumbo.

When they finished, Scotty led them through the dismantled fence and up the embankment and walked eastward with them down the track toward Jumbo's Palace Car.

The westbound express freight, Grand Trunk's Special Freight #151, pulled by high-wheeled, diamond-stacked locomotive #88, was not scheduled to stop in St. Thomas, so as it neared the rail yard it entered a downgrade and started gaining speed.

In the weak light of the kerosene lamp above the cowcatcher, William Burnip, the engineer of locomotive #88, thought he saw a hulking gray shape looming over the rails in the night. As the train moved closer, he made out a second shape, plodding toward him on the track.

They looked like—*elephants*! Burnip lunged for the Johnson bar to throw the engine mechanism into reverse, and he blew three short blasts on the whistle in a call for emergency brakes.

Matthew Scott, leading Jumbo and Tom Thumb up the track to the Palace Car, was just opposite the flagman when he heard the three blasts.

"What line is that train on?" Matthew Scott asked.

"My God!" cried the flagman. "It's on our track!"

Somehow, Scott managed to turn the elephants around on the track. His words have come down to us with their chilling, primerlike simplicity: "Run, Jumbo, run!"

The limitations of the biggest land animal and the biggest land vehicle combined to doom Jumbo. Elephants can't really run: at their fastest what they're doing is a fast walk. And the trains of 1885 couldn't stop quickly. The Westinghouse air brake would not be installed for two years yet, so a train still had to be braked manually by the brakeman, turning those great handwheels at the end of each car that had slowed down Coup's first attempts at the rear loading of circus wagons.

The high wheels of the locomotive began to churn backward as the engine reversed itself. The wheels of the cars locked with a screech of metal on metal, sending glowing sparks into the dark night. But it was a slow, car-by-car business, and the train, on the downgrade now, was still gaining speed. Burnip and his fireman leaped from the cab to save themselves.

Jumbo was moving as fast as he could, waving his trunk in the air and roaring and trumpeting as if he understood the danger he was in. Tom Thumb was following, but his dwarf legs couldn't keep up with Jumbo's giant ones, and he immediately fell behind.

Scott was running beside Jumbo, trying to get the leviathan to go down the steep embankment, but Jumbo stayed on the track as if determined to outdistance the train.

Suddenly, Scott saw a chance for Jumbo to survive. He had no chance of reaching the end of the circus train on the adjoining track and ducking behind it—the freight train, skidding fast on the downgrade even with wheels locked, would catch them before that. But there was that break where two cars of the circus train had been uncoupled to let animals pass through, and it was only about three car lengths ahead. If they could reach it, and the elephants would turn into it, the freight train could roar harmlessly past them.

But now the cowcatcher of the freight train hit Tom Thumb a glancing blow, which broke his left hind leg but saved his life by tossing him aside.

And then Matthew Scott and Jumbo reached

the break. Scott turned in, out of harm's way, and called to Jumbo to follow him. It was no use: the momentum of the mammoth animal was such that he was two cars past the opening before he could stop to turn. And just as he stopped, and before he could turn, the locomotive struck him from behind.

Jumbo dropped to his knees. The freight train went off the rails, and when it did, it shoved Jumbo under the heavy iron wheel-carriage of one of the circus cars on the next track. The circus car pulverized Jumbo's massive skull, driving one of his tusks back into his brain.

Jumbo was still conscious and groaning in agony when Matthew Scott crawled under the the circus car to comfort his companion of twenty years. Jumbo took Scott's hand gently in his trunk, as he had as a baby when he first arrived in London. Jumbo died quietly, and Scott wept uncontrollably on his corpse. A large crowd gathered. They felt they were doing the right thing to pull Scott away from his dead friend.

It was like a scene out of *Gulliver's Travels*. Jumbo was dragged to the edge of the steep embankment by 160 men who hauled with ropes, pried with crowbars, pried with stanchions, pried with timbers, and finally rolled Jumbo over the embankment.

Photographers arrived to take pictures of the corpse. Souvenir hunters with knives and scissors moved in to cut souvenirs from his body. Circus people tried to prevent the mutilations. Matthew Scott again lay down on his friend's remains, this time to protect them; but shock and grief had so exhausted him that he was soon fast asleep, and while he was asleep, someone cut a large slice from one of Jumbo's ears. When Scott awoke and saw the disfigured head of his friend, his grief was terrible. By morning, the St. Thomas police had mounted a twenty-four-hour guard that prevented further mutilation.

Barnum got the news in New York. "The loss is tremendous," he told the press, "but such a trifle never disturbs my nerves. Long ago I learned that to those who mean right and try to do right, there are no such things as real misfortunes. On the other hand, to such persons, all apparent evils are blessings in disguise."

The process by which Barnum unmasked the blessings disguised in this apparent misfortune was an important part of the golden age of the circus.

Step one was to publish his own version of Jumbo's death. In Barnum's version, Jumbo laid down his own life to save the little clown elephant, Tom Thumb. Jumbo, wrote the master publicist, "snatched the little elephant from in front of the thundering train and hurled the little fellow twenty yards to safety." After he rescued Tom Thumb, wrote Barnum, Jumbo turned to face the oncoming freight. "The leviathan of the rail and the mountain of bone and brawn came together with a crash that made the solid roadbed quake. . . . Jumbo . . . gave but one groan after being struck and then assumed an attitude of determination and composed himself to meet death with a becoming dignity and fortitude."

Millions of Americans, including many who had never seen Jumbo, mourned him as if they had lost a beloved pet and preferred to accept Barnum's version of his death; accepting it as Sir Winston Churchill, writing his *History of the English-Speaking Peoples*, accepted the legends about King Arthur's life: "It is all true, or it ought to be; and more and better besides."

Step two was when Barnum acquired and brought to America Alice, the dull and impassive old cow elephant from the London Zoo, mistakenly reported by the press as mourning Jumbo's departure. Alice was billed as Jumbo's widow, but although they had been acquainted, they had never mated and Alice had never even shown any interest.

· · · · · THE SCENE OF JUMBO'S HEROIC DEATH. · · · · ·

THE BARNUM VERSION OF JUMBO'S DEATH. *Three days after Jumbo died, Barnum wrote to a publisher: "PRIVATE. Gentlemen. Millions of children and adults (myself included) are mourning the death of Jumbo. Would you like to publish for the holidays—the life history and death of Jumbo, with many incidents and anecdotes not heretofore published By P. T. Barnum Profusely Illustrated? The title can of course be changed from the above. Probably numerous cuts now extant can be used. If properly written up, would it not be an interesting Christmas Childrens book—perhaps on both sides of the Atlantic?" The published book was illustrated with the above heart-rending drawing of Jumbo wrapping the baby elephant in his trunk and lifting him out of harm's way only seconds before being struck himself. Less romantic eyewitnesses said that the locomotive hit Tom Thumb a glancing blow, breaking his left leg but tossing him aside to safety. Not surprisingly, the public preferred the Barnum "Greater love hath no elephant" version. (Ringling Museum)*

In step three Barnum had all the other elephants in his circus trained to wipe their eyes with giant black-bordered handkerchiefs.

It was hard to out-Barnum Barnum. He no longer had the world's largest living elephant to exhibit, so he and Bailey created two necessarily smaller but more emotional exhibits: Tom Thumb, whom the world's largest living elephant gave his life to save, and Alice, Jumbo's "widow," who was actually exhibited alongside Jumbo's preserved carcass in a kind of prolonged mortuary visitation.

The poster advertising the tiny survivor read: "The Original, Famous & Only Diminutive Clown Elephant 'Tom Thumb,' to save whom Jumbo so nobly sacrificed his own life." It promised "Inimitable Displays of Elephantine Intelligence," and it showed Tom Thumb wearing a clown hat and spectacles, and beating a bass drum with his trunk, as well as riding a teeter-totter with a fat human clown, sitting at table and ringing a bell with his trunk, riding a tricycle, and crouching so that a clown could straddle him.

———

With a baby elephant able to do so much with The Greatest Show on Earth, it is perhaps not surprising that lesser talents were deserting the circus for the variety stage. Nonetheless, a very small circus began that year that had no elephants and yet lasted for a very long time. It was the Gentry Bros. Circus, founded by two poor farm boys from Bloomington, Indiana, who started out in 1885 giving matinee performances with twenty dogs. By 1889, they had added eight ponies and were giving two shows a day. Their first overland show was composed mostly of dogs, monkeys, and ponies, and in 1891, they entered the tent show field with a two-car show. In 1892, they put a second show on the road. For their two identical units, they had Sullivan & Eagles, master wagon builders of Peru, Indiana, make them two identical bandwagons, two identical ticket wagons, and a matched pair of calliopes. In their heyday, the Gentry family had four complete traveling shows, called Gentry Bros. Famous Shows, which required seventy-two railroad cars to transport them. Eventually, "Professor" H. B. Gentry's show became known as Gentry's Dog and Pony Show.

"The dog and pony format was highly successful," wrote Parkinson and Fox in *The Circus in America*. "The Gentrys' reputation, if not their size, was the equivalent of Ringling Bros." And they had something else, something that often got lost in the spectacle of the larger shows: they had charm. For example, when they gave a street parade, they would make a children's band out of the offspring of their performers, and mount the little band members on Shetland ponies. Sometimes they offered a women's band, which rode in a finely carved bandwagon hitched to a team of black-and-white spotted ponies. They would also "play the lots," giving a whole series of stands in a principal city. The little circus would appear for a day or two on vacant lots in each of a dozen neighborhoods. And seeing the trained dogs, ponies, and monkeys that had come to perform almost in their own backyards, audiences would find delight.

Dog and pony shows were true circuses, with a variety of acts including a clown performing in, above, and around that unifying ring. Sometimes dogs and ponies worked together in the same act; often, dogs were an integral part of the clown's routine—stepping between his legs each time he took a step, for example. Dogs climbed ladders and jumped off their topmost rungs into safety nets. Dogs walked on their hind legs and dogs jumped rope. And all the animals appeared in appropriate costumes: when the Gentry Bros. put on chariot races, a monkey dressed as Ben Hur "drove" a chariot pulled by two collies. The Gentry family lost control of their show in 1916, and others operated it until it was combined with the James Patterson show in 1922. In 1926, the King brothers acquired the Gentry-Patterson Circus, changed its name back to the Gentry Bros. Circus, and operated it until it failed in the Crash year of 1929.

The big circuses have trained dog acts, of course: the 113th edition of Ringling Bros. and Barnum & Bailey in 1983–84 had an excellent dog act in each ring. In Ring One were Eric Braun, a 1968 graduate of the Ringling Clown College (and a member of a circus family that dates back to the 1840s); his wife, Francine; and his children, Ricky, seven, and Neecha Torina, six. In one spectacular trick, a poodle was catapulted from a teeterboard and landed on its front paws in Eric Braun's hands. In Ring Two, fifth-generation circus performer Mickey Antalek and his wife Kveta presented a toy poodle named DoDo, who made a midair plunge from a fifteen-foot perch into the hands of Kveta. And in Ring Three, Gunther Gebel-Williams's twenty-year-old stepdaughter, Tina, made an elegant circus debut with a pack of Russian wolfhounds that balanced themselves on a rolling wheel, then climbed a ten-foot ladder and slid back to the arena floor. But with the three acts competing with each other for the attention of viewers, many of whom were far away in the vast arena, even spectacular tricks often failed to look spectacular, and charm was dissipated by space. Old-timers among circus fans say that it was in dog and pony shows that the trained dog act really sparkled.

———————

In the seasons of 1886 and 1887, Jumbo's skin and skeleton led Barnum and Bailey's grand parade. They rode in a custom-designed wagon and were followed by the Widow Alice and her attendants—the Barnum herd dabbing at their eyes with those black-trimmed sheets.

But the circus has always been a celebration of life, not death, and even before Jumbo was killed, Barnum was hoping to top him with another live elephant, an Asian totally unconnected with Jumbo. It would not be the biggest, but it would be the only sacred white elephant ever seen outside the Far East.

Almost as long as there had been a United States, Americans had been going to the circus to see the wonders of the world, human and animal. According to Barnum's biographer M. R. Werner, two of Barnum and Bailey's agents had been traveling in Asia in search of human types for a leading feature of The Greatest Show on Earth to be called the "Ethnological Congress of Strange Savage Tribes." An agent named Thomas H. Davis learned that the king of Siam (the son of the monarch that Yul Brynner made a career out of playing in Rodgers and Hammerstein's *The King and I*) could be induced to let a sacred white elephant leave the country—for a price. Accounts vary on what Barnum paid into the royal coffers for the elephant itself, but Barnum later estimated that it took him three years and cost him $250,000 to bring a sacred white elephant to America.

The day the white elephant arrived in New York must have been one of the blackest in Barnum's career. He had already given a word to the English language, *Jumbo*; he was about to give it a phrase. "White elephant: a possession entailing great expense out of proportion to its usefulness or value to the owner."

Toung Taloung, for such was the creature's name, had been shipped from Rangoon to London, and thence to New York, arriving aboard the steamer *Lydia Monarch* on March 28, 1884. Once again, as when Jenny Lind came to these shores, Barnum offered a prize for the best poem commemorating the arrival in America. No less a bard than Joaquin Miller, the poet of the Sierras, was among the three finalists who shared the $500 prize.

For fifty years good Barnum bought
  God's wondrous creatures every one;
And last, impossible! he sought
  To buy the "sun spots" of the sun—
The Sacred Elephant! as soon
Could silver buy the silver moon.

Twas daring much to gain the prize
  Where kings had failed, and more than bold,
And doubtful Europe rubbed her eyes
  To see him scatter heaps of gold!
But Barnum gold, and Barnum grit,
And Barnum wit accomplished it.

There were six more stanzas, but these two suggest the image that the public had of Barnum: he was a kind of Super Daddy who would get for us whatever we wanted to see, no matter the cost. (Forget the fact that only in his street parades did Barnum let us see these wonders for free.) He was the Walt Disney of his day; a Santa Claus for All Seasons, who brought wonderful gifts to children of all ages all over the land.

But when Barnum himself, followed by the press, went to the steamer to inspect his latest purchase in the "wondrous creature" line, he saw not the elephant of purest milk-white hue that he had already started advertising, but an elephant that was dirty gray, except for a few light pink spots and unprepossessing pink eyes.

Henry Lowenthal, who covered the story for the *New York World*, would never forget Barnum's chagrin—or his grace under pressure. When pressed by reporters for his reaction, he gave them a broad smile.

"Well," beamed Barnum, "it's whiter than I expected to find it."

But he couldn't get off that easy. He himself had scheduled a press reception in the ship's dining room after the first viewing of the elephant, and the free drinks that the famous teetotaler had provided emboldened a reporter to call out so that everyone could hear: "Mr. Barnum, I don't think your elephant is so very white."

Instantly, the room was so quiet you could have heard a Feejee Mermaid chatter. Barnum was standing beside Bailey, but it was Barnum's reputation on the line.

"My boy," said Barnum, "in my youth I was fond of attending sociables. At one such party I unwisely expressed the opinion that a young lady's extraordinary complexion was not genuine. Unfortunately she overheard my tactless remark. As she passed me she said, without introduction, 'God made these cheeks.' Now, sir, God made that white elephant, but I assure you had he been made by Mr. Bailey or myself he would be as white as the driven snow."

His reply was as graceful a riposte as Barnum could have hoped to make, but it didn't make his elephant whiter. And this fact provided an opening for Barnum and Bailey's chief rival in the circus world, Adam Forepaugh. A fierce publicity battle began.

Forepaugh was a crude Philadelphia meat dealer who got into the circus business when he sold some horses to the Tom King Circus and had to join the show to get his money. Like Barnum, Forepaugh believed that the public enjoyed being humbugged. But Barnum was a natural gentleman, whereas Forepaugh seemed to enjoy treating his employees cruelly and his patrons cavalierly, and scoring with deceptive advertising rather than presenting the real thing. Nevertheless, he prospered, not in small part because he knew his circus intimately, tent stake, baggage stock, and cage star.

Barnum believed that the sacred white elephant was the real thing, and he presented authentication from Siamese experts.

But Forepaugh had operated in ways that plagued Barnum for years. He had hired Dan Rice when Rice was still the nation's foremost clown by paying him $1,000 a week.

In 1881, just when Barnum finally made a truce and a merger with James A. Bailey, it was Adam Forepaugh's circus that had the attention of America because of Forepaugh's $10,000 contest to find "the handsomest woman in America."

A bosomy variety actress named Louise Montague won the contest; but, typical of Forepaugh, the contest was fixed. Miss Montague never saw the $10,000 she "won"; her agreement to put herself on exhibition by leading Forepaugh's street pageant and appearing in his circus's opening spectacle, "Lalla Rookh's Departure from Delhi," for the paltry sum of $100 a week was apparently as essential a qualification for "winning" as her undenied pulchritude.

But with this pageant, Adam Forepaugh invented the beauty contest. From Snow White to Lalla Rookh to Miss America, the idea of "the fairest of them all" has been the real winner, and the streets were packed wherever Miss Montague appeared. In Chicago, where the crowd shattered the windows of the Western Union office, one man who was trying to catch a glimpse of "beauty's tribute, the handsomest woman in America," fell out of a second-floor window and broke his neck. At the circus, receipts broke new records. Forepaugh netted $240,000 in 1881 and $260,000 in 1882. He was managing to out-Barnum Barnum.

Forepaugh's "Lalla Rookh" street parade was one of the most popular in circus history. It was like a scene out of the *Arabian Nights*, specifically *The Thief of Baghdad*, when a princess famed for her beauty is carried into the city as part of a great parade. But in *The Thief of Baghdad* anyone who looks on her must die, and the Wicked Wazir's soldiers go riding ahead of the pageant, firing arrows at any windows not yet shuttered. Forepaugh brought "The Lovely Oriental Princess, Lalla Rookh," or a reasonable facsimile thereof, into America's cities, and anyone might look, and no one need die—except for those who, craning to see, fell out of windows. It was the democratization of the fairy-tale search for the most beautiful woman in the world, and its appeal was to the part of us that believes in fairy tales.

But Barnum, as we have seen, came back strongly. In 1880, he had joined forces with Bailey. In 1882, they bought Jumbo.

It made no difference to Forepaugh that Jumbo was truly the world's largest elephant; he simply advertised that he had an elephant, Bolivar, who was the "largest & heaviest elephant in the world." Barnum practically screamed "Foul" with his "Jumbo, the Children's Giant Pet" poster, which said: "Barnum, Bailey & Hutchinson Challenge the World in $100,000.00, that JUMBO is the largest & heaviest Elephant ever seen by mortal man either wild or in captivity." Forepaugh couldn't collect, of course; and the public never accepted his claim, either, because they could see how big Jumbo was; but in the matter of this sacred white elephant, Barnum was vulnerable.

Assuming an air of religious indignation, Forepaugh advertised that he had secured in Siam, at terrific cost, *the only white elephant living*, and that Barnum, realizing that his own circus was inferior to Forepaugh's even without the white elephant, had faked an imitation. And now Forepaugh hit a nerve: Barnum had faked the white elephant, he concluded, just as, in the past, Barnum had faked the Feejee Mermaid and other so-called freaks of nature repudiated by natural historians.

Barnum's humbug had come home to roost.

The press embraced the controversy over rival elephants. They served a public who couldn't seem to read enough about P. T.

Barnum. As Barnum had, Forepaugh invited reporters to see his elephant, and, as Barnum had, he plied them with drinks. Then he showed them a white elephant, called Light of Asia.

Stealthily, Alexander C. Kenealy, a non-drinking reporter from the *Philadelphia Press* (and afterward editor-in-chief of the London *Daily Mirror*), moved toward the elephant with a water-soaked sponge. Suddenly he ducked under a barrier and gave the animal's hindquarters a long, quick swipe. Down the elephant's leg trickled streams of milky water, restoring the elephant's hide to its natural dark gray.

"The thing may be sacred," said Kenealy, "but I'll swear it's not white."

Instead of publishing his exposé in the *Philadelphia Press*, Kenealy sold it to Barnum, who advertised Forepaugh's deception as energetically as Forepaugh had claimed that Barnum was the deceiver. But despite the exposé, Forepaugh's white-painted elephant outdrew Barnum and Bailey's genuine gray-with-a-few-white-spots elephant.

No one has ever been able to document the legend that Barnum said: "There's a sucker born every minute." Maybe Forepaugh said it.

Then Barnum and Bailey had a falling-out. Barnum leased his name to a circus run by the notorious "Pogey" O'Brien and began trying to override Bailey in the circus that Bailey was supposed to be running for him. Disgusted, Bailey sold his interest to James E. Cooper and W. W. Cole.

With Bailey gone, Adam Forepaugh even got the lucrative Madison Square Garden engagement away from Barnum by taking a lease far in advance. The best that Barnum could do in 1887 was to agree to a joint appearance. He also agreed to a four-year route pact that divided the territory between Barnum and Forepaugh. In short, Adam Forepaugh was outmaneuvering P. T. Barnum, who was now almost seventy-six years old.

Once again, the public was the winner. In 1886, the year the Statue of Liberty was dedicated, New York saw an all-star circus in Madison Square Garden that combined the best of both the Barnum and Forepaugh shows, including a reported sixty elephants. There had never been so large a circus before, but Forepaugh, the former Philadelphia butcher, insisted that there would be again, the following spring, when the two shows combined under canvas in Forepaugh's hometown.

Escalating numbers of elephants now joined free street parades as the status symbols of the huge new circuses. In the 1870s, at the beginning of the golden age, a big circus might have five elephants. The first Barnum and Bailey circus boasted twenty elephants. Now here were Barnum and Forepaugh offering a giant exhibition in Madison Square Garden with as many as sixty elephants.

The destructiveness of the circus wars had reached its climax. Elephants, the largest land animals on earth, eat 150 pounds of food a day apiece. For the public, fascinated by their size, it was the best of times; for many circus owners, burdened by the cost of their elephants' appetites, it was often the worst.

Circus elephant herds peaked in the 1880s, although the largest herd ever employed by a single circus was the fifty elephants of the Ringling Bros. and Barnum & Bailey Circus, by then the undisputed big one, in 1955.

———————

Barnum missed Bailey. He didn't make as much money when Bailey was gone, and that was no wonder. No one could run a circus like Bailey. So in October of 1887, Barnum agreed to give Bailey control of the show and to add his name for the first time to the actual title of

JAMES A. BAILEY. *After Barnum's death, Bailey was holding his own against the upstart Ringling brothers until an insect bit him on the nose while he was inspecting his circus's menagerie at Madison Square Garden; he died a few days later, at the age of fifty-eight. Perhaps the best assessment of what Bailey means to the circus was made by Barnum's biographer, M. R. Werner, when he wrote in 1923: "If Barnum had not had the foresight to select Bailey as his partner, it is likely that the present generation would never have known his {Barnum's} name as a showman. Bailey was able to cope with every calamity quickly and efficiently. When the winter quarters were burned down on November 20, 1887, all the animals were destroyed except thirty elephants and one lion. Bailey ordered a new menagerie by cable, and in six hours he had purchased enough animals to form a better menagerie than the one destroyed." Barnum named The Greatest Show on Earth, but Bailey assured its continuity, so that it is now the oldest entertainment institution in America. (Ringling Museum)*

LOUISE MONTAGUE *was the Marilyn Monroe of the nineteenth-century circus, a big-bosomed variety actress who won America's first beauty contest. In 1881, Adam Forepaugh said that he would award $10,000 to the most beautiful woman in America—then fixed the contest so that the winner would be the most beautiful woman willing to put herself on exhibition in his 1881–82 pageant "Lalla Rookh." Miss Montague never saw the $10,000—Forepaugh gave her $100 a week—but Forepaugh out-Barnumed Barnum in getting publicity. In the twentieth century, the circus's Marilyn Monroe was Marilyn Monroe herself, who rode a pink elephant in Madison Square Garden to begin the 1955 season of The Greatest Show on Earth. (Circus World Museum, Baraboo, Wisconsin)*

ADAM FOREPAUGH *began circusing in 1863 and took delivery in Chicago of two elephants and other menagerie animals costing $42,000 on April 14, 1865—the day Lincoln was shot. Forepaugh had a show under his own name from 1866 through 1890. It was a major show and part of the time it was the nation's biggest. Often the billboards needed only to say: "4-PAW." His greatest triumph was his 1881 pageant based on Thomas Moore's "Lalla Rookh: An Oriental Romance." In this 1817 poem, the Irish poet says that Lalla Rookh means "Tulip Cheek," and that she is "a Princess described by the poets of her time, as more beautiful than Leila, Shrine, Dwilde, or any of those heroines whose names and loves embellished the songs of Persia and Hindostan." (Circus World Museum, Baraboo, Wisconsin)*

the circus. From the 1888 season on, it was officially the Barnum & Bailey Greatest Show on Earth.

Bailey immediately had to demonstrate his coolness during calamity. On November 20, 1887, the winter quarters of The Greatest Show on Earth at Bridgeport, Connecticut, burned to the ground. All the animals were destroyed except one lion and thirty elephants. Alice, who had played Jumbo's widow, perished in the flames. So did Toung Taloung, the sacred white elephant of gray, who had disappointed so many audiences that Barnum had sent him to winter quarters to keep him out of sight. One elephant survived by swimming in the dark, cold waters of Long Island Sound.

Nimrod, the sole surviving lion, was found by circus employees in a barn near Bridgeport. He had been eating sheep, and when the farmer's wife went into the barn to investigate the noise, she saw what in the dark looked like a large dog. She began to beat this animal with a broom, but the animal, busy eating, paid no attention to the blows. When the lion handlers arrived and informed her that the animal she had been beating was not a dog, she fainted.

The show went on. In six hours, Bailey had ordered by cable a new menagerie, better than the one that had been destroyed by fire.

———◆———

Barnum donated Jumbo's skeleton to the American Museum of Natural History in New York, and the stuffed skin to Tufts University near Boston, of which he was a founder and trustee. Jumbo's faithful friend, Matthew Scott, followed Jumbo's stuffed skin to Tufts, where he was often seen dusting it and talking to it.

But first, in 1889–90, Jumbo returned to England, skin and bones, for The Greatest Show on Earth made in those years an unforgettable English tour.

In November 1889, the Barnum & Bailey circus opened at the giant Olympia in London, and Phineas T. Barnum was there. Everyone wanted to see the individual who was as great a freak of nature in his own way as Tom Thumb the midget or Jumbo the elephant. There seemed to be general agreement that Barnum was the greatest showman that the show-loving human race had ever produced. Practically every idea the man had seemed to turn into a show and a way to make the public want to see it. Barnum began the age of publicity that is with us now more than ever. He embodied the greatest strength of that age: the satisfaction of man's natural curiosity. He also embodied its greatest weakness: the acceptance of "humbugs," of illusions, as if they could satisfy our curiosity as well as, or better than, reality.

About two hundred noblemen, politicians, and writers got to meet Barnum at a banquet given in his honor by the Earl of Kilmorey at the Victoria Hotel, but the general public was able to see him, too. Every afternoon and evening, Barnum's open carriage would enter the Olympia's arena drawn by two fine horses, driven by a coachman, attended by a footman in splendid livery.

It was Barnum who popularized the three-ring circus, but now, in its founder's honor, the activity in all three rings came to a stop, for the old man's carriage was slowly circling the arena and he didn't want anybody to miss *that*. At intervals in his tour of the hippodrome track, Barnum would stop his carriage, rise, remove his shining top hat, and call out to the audiences in his sharply Yankee-accented English: "I suppose you all come to see Barnum. Wa-al, I'm Barnum."

Then he would make a deep bow. Ladies would return his salute by emotionally waving their handkerchiefs at his celebrity; men would doff their hats; and Barnum's carriage would proceed a little farther, and he would do the same thing all over again.

Next to Karl Marx and Sigmund Freud, wrote the American intellectual Louis Kronenberger, the ideologue with the greatest impact on U.S. lives was Phineas Taylor Barnum. "The business of America is business," said Calvin Coolidge, thirtieth president of the United States, in a speech before the Society of American Newspaper Editors in 1925, and ballyhoo, the clamorous attempt to win customers (or, indeed, to advance any cause) by theater, by flamboyant, frequently exaggerated, sometimes sensational means, was Barnum's contribution to America's business. George Augustus Sala, toastmaster at the Victoria Hotel banquet, compared Barnum with Caesar, Napoleon, and Nero—to Barnum's advantage. All were entertainers, at least in part, he said, but Barnum shed no blood.

Indeed, the 1880s were years of peace and prosperity in America, and in that atmosphere, Barnum's circus flourished. His Greatest Show on Earth developed a custom of opening its thirty-two week season in New York in late March for a stand that varied from three to six weeks. Then it toured Pennsylvania and New Jersey for several weeks, returned to New York for a week in Brooklyn, then spent eight weeks touring New York State and New England. July 4 was a day off to celebrate America's Independence Day with a big circus dinner at winter quarters in Bridgeport. Then the circus swung west, visiting cities in Michigan, Indiana, Illinois, Ohio, Missouri, Iowa, Nebraska, and Kansas, and ended its tour in late October in Texas. This was the general pattern, although business took such a dip during the brief Texas tour in 1881 that the Barnum show did not go back to the Lone Star state for six years.

Total receipts for the 1881 season were $1,116,390. The circus normally played a six-day week, keeping holy the Sabbath by not showing on Sunday. Receipts for an average day were $5,864, or $34,887 each week. The "nut," the amount it cost to put on the show, was $755,888, so that profits in 1881 amounted to $360,510. Barnum got half; the other half was divided between Bailey and Hutchinson. Among them, they had a healthy 31 percent return on their money. There were only three years from 1881 to Barnum's death in 1891 when the show's annual business dropped below the million-dollar mark, and these were the years of his estrangement from Bailey. Barnum's last request, on the night before his death, was to know what the circus receipts had been during the day at Madison Square Garden. Even though he couldn't take them with him, they were evidence that, as the world's greatest showman, he had been successful to the end.

Death came to Phineas T. Barnum at 6:34 P.M. on April 7, 1891. It was said that the only Americans whose passing had been noted with more newspaper space were presidents of the United States. But it took *The Times* of London to express his importance best:

> Barnum is gone. . . . He created the *metier* of showman on a grandiose scale, worthy to be professed by a man of genius. He early realized that essential feature of a modern democracy, its readiness to be led to what will amuse and instruct it. He knew that "the people" means crowds, paying crowds; that crowds love the fashion and will follow it; and that the business of the great man is to make and control the fashion. To live on, by, and before the public was his ideal. For their sake and his own, he loved to bring the public to see, to applaud, and to pay. . . .

The golden age of the American circus was now at its height. Barnum left a country in which half a dozen railroad circus owners vied for his title of "Showman on a Grandiose Scale." Even in the era of the wagon show, the circus was America's most popular form of entertainment, because its traveling shows went to the people and gave them, often, the only entertainment they had all year. Hamlin Garland, in his autobiography, *A Son of the Middle Border*, said that the circuses that came to his community in Iowa in the 1870s were thought of as India, Arabia, and the jungle combined. It was "a compendium of biologic research," he wrote, "but more important still, it brought to our ears the latest band pieces and taught us the most popular songs. It furnished us with jokes. It relieved our dullness. It gave us something to talk about."

But now grandiose scale was possible, and there was a lot more to talk about. In the years between Coup and Barnum's first real railroad show in 1872 and Barnum's death in 1891, the nation's rapidly expanding railroad system had enabled the circus to bring to every corner of the continent much bigger shows with a much greater variety of wonders. As many miles of track were laid in the 1880s alone as in all the years from 1828 to 1870. By 1900 the nation had more miles of railroad track than all of Europe, including Russia. The effect of all this on the circus was easy to see. W. W. "Chilly Billy" Cole and Haight, DeHaven & Miles had followed Barnum's example by going on rails in 1873; John Robinson in 1874; Forepaugh in 1876; Sells Bros. in 1878; Batcheller & Doris in 1879; Burr Robbins in 1881; Sells Bros.' No. 2 show in 1882; Harris Nickel Plate Show at its beginning in 1884; Frank A. Robbins in 1884; Great Wallace in 1886; Ringling Bros. in 1890; and Walter L. Main in 1891. That year, the year that Barnum died, seven of the railroad shows were big ones: Barnum & Bailey was traveling on sixty-five cars that year; Adam Forepaugh on fifty-two; Sells Bros. on forty-two; John Robinson on thirty-five; and William Main on twenty-seven. Even the smallest of the big seven, the Great Wallace and the Ringling Bros. shows, had twenty cars each. And more railroad cars meant more elephants, more clowns, more horses, more circus wagons, more performers and exhibits of every kind in the lineup as that vital sign of the golden age, the free street parade, grew longer and longer.

Old John L. Sullivan, "the Boxing Elephant" (he walloped clown Billie Burke with a boxing glove tied to his trunk), with Fred E. Sterling, lieutenant governor of Illinois. In 1922, Old John walked fifty miles, from Madison Square Garden to Somers, New York, and laid a wreath at the granite shaft erected in memory of Old Bet. (William E. and Marian Culhane Sterling)

The Ringlings and Their Rivals

DISPLAY·10

In 1884, the year that the Ringling brothers came upon the circus scene, the United States had fourteen traveling shows. The golden age was approaching its moment of maximum glitter. Five years later, there would be twenty-two traveling shows. How these brothers from Baraboo, Wisconsin, who began without circus connections and without financial backing, outperformed, outmaneuvered, outacquired, or just plain outlasted all their competition—including Barnum & Bailey—is the greatest saga of all within the saga of the circus in America.

What inspired them to this gigantic effort? It sounds too good to be true, yet it has been amply documented that the Ringling brothers were inspired to become the circus kings of the twentieth century, while they were still boys, by the clown prince of the nineteenth-century circus, Dan Rice.

Continuity is the lifeblood of the circus. Hackaliah Bailey's tales of Old Bet inspired P. T. Barnum, and the eventual result of his efforts was Jumbo, the biggest elephant in the world appearing with The Greatest Show on Earth; the sight of Rice in action inspired the Ringling brothers to emulate him, and the eventual result was the Ringling Bros. and Barnum & Bailey Circus—the continuation into a new century of Barnum's Greatest Show on Earth.

The fateful encounter occurred in McGregor, Iowa, where the Ringling family was then living under its original German name of Rungeling. Rice brought his Great Pavilion Circus up the Mississippi by steamboat and played McGregor in May of 1870.

Al Rungeling, then eighteen and the eldest, took four of his six brothers down to the docks

KINGS OF THE CIRCUS WORLD. *A newspaper editor said, "John Ringling knows more about the United States than any man living . . . the Railway Guide is his Bible. Name any town in the United States and he can tell you offhand how large it is, what its train connections are, what factories are located there, when pay day comes and how much the circus netted on its last stand there." (Ringling Museum)*

on the Mississippi River to see the circus un-load from a side-wheel steamboat. Otto (1858–1911) was twelve; Alfred T. (1861–1919) was eight; Charles (1863–1926) was six; and John (1866–1936) was four. Six-year-old August G. (1864–1907) and Henry (1869–1918), less than a year old, were left at home.

"To the five Ringling brothers the circus boat, with its barge of tent-wagons and chariots alongside, seemed like the triumphant achieve-ment of a great genius, who had arisen out of the waters which hitherto had been inhabited by nothing more mysterious than a catfish," Alf T. Ringling would write in *Life Story of the Ring-ling Brothers.*

That book, published in 1900 when Alf was thirty-nine, and first offered for sale in the me-nagerie tent of the brothers' sixteen-year-old circus, tells how "With rapt attention they watched the one big elephant of the show ma-jestically tread down the gang-plank to the shore."

The Ringlings attended their first circus for free, because their father, August Rungeling, was a harness maker who did some work that day for Andrew Gaffney, a hometown boy turned acrobat who would be doing a balancing perch act in Rice's circus. Gaffney's job was supporting a fellow acrobat who performed at the top of a pole; he would hold the pole with the aid of a leather belt and socket, but the belt had broken. August Rungeling repaired it, and because the acrobat was from McGregor, refused to take payment. Not to be outdone in hometown courtesy, the local hero gave the harness maker a circus pass for his entire fam-ily—and the brothers were bitten by the circus bug forevermore.

According to Alf T. Ringling, after they had watched the circus unload, his eldest brother, Al, said, "What would you say if we had a show like that?" To his surprise, each of his brothers claimed to have been thinking the same thing.

Before 1870 was over, the Ringling brothers were already imitating what they had seen. They put on their first circus, a backyard affair, to be sure, but family tradition says that it had all the necessary elements. There was a ring, and Al was the ringmaster. There were feats of physical skill and daring. Al juggled his fa-ther's hats and his mother's plates. Charles rode a pony. Otto did an animal act with a goat named Billy Rainbow. And there was a clown. Four-year-old John Ringling did a raucous ren-dition of the song he had heard Dan Rice sing: "Root, Hog, or Die!"

In the fall of 1875, the Rungeling family moved to Baraboo, Wisconsin, in a region so starved for entertainment of any sort that even the brothers' primitive skills could bring forty people into the local opera house. This success was enough to convince five of them to plunge deeper into the world of show business. Henry and Gus decided that they could do better at something else, but Al, Alfred T., Charles, Otto, John, and three other local boys orga-nized "Ringling Bros. Classic and Comic Con-cert Co." Al was now a juggler. Alfred T. and Charles were fair on wind instruments, and Otto could beat the drums. As for John, he had not been inspired by Dan Rice in vain. He was still singing "Root, Hog, or Die!" and had become a passable clown.

Especially interesting about this show is the way the brothers saw themselves. On the play-bill, they called that first 1882 season their "Fourth Season," counting the backyard circus of their childhoods as the first, and the two years that Al had spent managing hall shows as the second and third.

While managing hall shows, Al met another hall show manager—a man with a magnificent spread of white whiskers and a passion for oys-ters. His name was Yankee Robinson, and he had been in the circus business off and on for thirty years.

In the early months of 1884, Al induced his new friend and mentor to show him and his brothers how to organize a circus. Robinson did, and in April the Ringling family received a letter from their showmen sons on the road:

Dear Parents, Bro and Sis:

It froze today. Will be in Baraboo Saturday. We bought a team in Waukon, Iowa. . . . Hoping this finds you in good health as it does us.

Yours,

RINGLING BROTHERS.

There was a portentous postscript:

The name of our show is Yankee Robinson's Great Show and Ringling Brothers Carnival of Comedy.

With this letter from Montello, Wisconsin, in the round, immature handwriting of eighteen-year-old John Ringling, began the first tenting season of the five brothers whose circus was to become, in name and fame, The Greatest Show on Earth and which the Ringling family continued to own and operate until they sold it in 1967.

"The most interesting aspect of it," John's nephew, Henry Ringling North, would point out in *The Circus Kings: Our Ringling Family Story*, "is that Uncle John, writing to his own family, signed it 'Ringling Brothers.' That indicates how proud were the brothers of their partnership, and how completely they regarded themselves as a single entity in which any one of them could speak for all."

On May 19, 1884, the Ringling brothers gave their first performance of Yankee Robinson and Ringling Bros. Circus in the Ringlings' hometown of Baraboo, Wisconsin, where they also established their first winter quarters.

Yankee Robinson walked to the center of the ring, doffed his stovepipe hat, bowed low to the audience, and made a little speech. He said that he had traveled in every state of the Union and had been associated with—or had competed against—every circus man of prominence in America, and thus was in a position to attest that the Ringling brothers were "the future showmen of America. They are the coming men!" He predicted that "this show is destined to become the greatest circus in the world."

One wonders if anyone in the audience even imagined that old Yankee's prophecy would actually come true. There was little enough indication that day of the kind of circus Ringling Brothers would become. The Ringlings' first ring was nothing more than a strip of red cloth staked out to form a circle. The tent was only forty-five by ninety feet with two center poles. The performance had no ring horses, no elephant, no wild animals, not even a dog act. The entire personnel, including performers, sideshow, workers, and owners consisted of twenty-four people, and the Ringling brothers were most of the show. Al did his juggling and plate-spinning act, then relieved Alf T. as bandleader. John, in clown costume, did a comedy routine with liberal borrowings from Dan Rice. The brothers led most of the acrobatic stunts and tricks (mostly contortionist, juggling, and balancing acts) interspersed with clowning and musical selections.

The biggest trick of their first circus was performed by Al, who balanced a plow on his chin. He may be the only circus performer who ever accomplished this feat, and he did it by achieving perfect balance. He used an old-fashioned wooden frame hand plow, which weighs about seventy pounds. Such plows have a brace—a wooden rod—extending between the handles. Somehow, Al Ringling had discovered that if he balanced the exact center of this rod on the exact center of his chin, the plow was supportable. So, before the show, Al would put a chalk mark in the middle of this brace; and in the ring, he would seize the plow by its handles, swing it into the air above his head, then lower it until the chalk mark was centered as nearly as possible on his chin. Farmers would catch their breath as Al moved the plow a little, this way and that, to attain that delicate balance, and some would gasp when he let go of the handles for a few seconds. Then there would be tumultuous applause.

In that first season, Yankee Robinson's health failed rapidly; so when their circus faced a forty-mile trek to Lake City, Iowa, Al Ringling persuaded him to ride the train rather than endure the discomfort of the circus wagon. (The show had nine.) He put Robinson aboard a passenger coach on August 27, but Robinson became so ill that he had to be taken off the train before he reached his destination. Yankee Robinson died in a hotel, and by the time Al Ringling traced him, he had been buried by his fellow Masons.

In their second season, the brothers quietly dropped Yankee Robinson's name, and called themselves Ringling Bros.' Great Double Shows, Circus, Caravan, and Trained Animal Exposition. The company also expanded from nine to twelve wagons.

From the beginning, the brothers let it be known that they would not allow the gambling, shortchanging of patrons, solicitation for prostitution, and other illegal and/or dishonest practices tolerated or even encouraged by some of their competitors. When they first went into the show business, their strict Lutheran grandmother expressed the fear that they were headed for "the bottomless pit"; but the brothers were sure that they could run a circus that would be both Christian and successful. The reaction of many of their competitors was fear that the Ringling example would deprive the circus business of a needed source of revenue: the kickbacks of tolerated

crooks. They derided the Ringling circus as "the Sunday School Circus," and the brothers themselves were called "The Ding-a-Ling Brothers." In fact, the moral atmosphere of the show turned out to be a great boon to its growth and prosperity. If a ticket seller was caught shortchanging a customer, he was fired on the spot. When a circus detective caught a pickpocket on the show grounds, he was handcuffed to a tent pole where all the patrons could see him, with a sign around his neck proclaiming his crime.

But success depended on more than morality. An equestrian act was a must—yet equestrians in those days were the most expensive performers. So Al's wife, Louise, a dressmaker who had made the costumes in the first season, decided that in the second she would become a bareback rider as well. She learned with a homemade version of a device called a riding mechanic or spider appliance, whose invention Earl Chapin May in *The Circus from Rome to Ringling* credits to Spencer Quinn Stokes of Cincinnati. (Stokes was the trainer of Ella Zoyara, the bareback rider courted as a beautiful equestrienne here and abroad until revealed in the 1860s as a young man named Omar Kingsley.) In the center of the ring, Al put an upright post that could revolve in a socket. About twelve feet from the ground, the post had an arm that extended as far as the edge of the ring. At the end of the arm was a pulley, and through the pulley was a rope that ended in a harness for the rider. An attendant kept the device turning, keeping the end of the arm right above the horse as it cantered around the ring. When Mrs. Ringling lost her footing on her horse's back, the harness would hold her suspended in the air. By the end of that second season she was able to jump through a flaming hoop, although it would be several years before she became a truly adept bareback rider. Like her husband and brothers-in-law, however, she combined tenacity with the resolve to give the circus whatever the Ringlings thought it needed.

In 1886, the brothers exhibited their first menagerie: a bear, monkeys, an eagle, and a hyena that they were able to buy cheap because it was blind. Alf T. Ringling, after consulting an encyclopedia and his own Barnum-like imagination, wrote the following copy:

HIDEOUS HYENA STRIATA GIGANTIUM

THE LARGEST OF ITS KIND TO BE SEEN ONLY WITH THE RINGLING SHOWS

The Mammoth, Midnight Marauding, Man-Eating Monstrosity, the Prowling, Grave-Robbing Demon of all Created Things, Who, While the World Sleeps, and no Hand is Raised to Stay His Awful Depredations, Sneaks Stealthily Under Cover of Darkness to the Cemetery, and with Ghoulish Glee Robs the Tomb.
His Hideous, Bloodcurdling Laughter Paralyzes with Terror the Bravest Hearts. He Leaves Behind Him a Trail of Blood, and the Wails of the Dying Are Music to his Ears.

The brothers also wanted a snake charmer in their sideshow—it was a must in the 1880s—and, once again, Louise, who didn't even like snakes, volunteered to help out.

Of course, nobody "charms" snakes. The Ringlings bought a couple of big but nonpoisonous snakes that were accustomed to being handled by human beings. Assured that snakes,

when well fed, are sluggish and not dangerous, Louise overcame her repugnance and taught herself to let them crawl around her body while she delivered a "lecture" about them.

By 1888, the Ringlings' fifth season, they had increased the size of the show and the price of a ticket from twenty-five cents to fifty cents. Then, the rains came. Deep mud en route to show dates made the circus late, again and again. ("Wagons continually pulled to pieces," the brothers would report.) Often, they missed their afternoon stands entirely. And even when they got there, wet and muddy lots kept the crowds away.

The situation became so desperate that the brothers wrote to a Baraboo bank, asking for a loan of $1,000 to carry them through. Their plan was to cut the size of their show, ship some wagons and equipment back to Baraboo, then drop the admission price back to twenty-five cents.

"We will give you any security you may ask for, houses or notes . . . ," they told the bank. "We will give you a bill of sale of everything we have, the big elephant which will sell for $2000 anytime, a bill of sale on the house or anything you may choose."

The bank sent them $1,000, but they didn't use it. On June 5, they left the rain and the mud behind. Their resources were down to $122 plus the bank loan, but in sunny Iowa they made $3,000 in eight days. They paid back the bank loan, and came home to Baraboo with a profit.

In 1889, the brothers leased the Van Amburgh title from the circus veteran Hyatt Frost (1827–1895), and the show went out as a wagon show for the last time, under the logo of Ringling Bros. and Van Amburgh's United Monster Circus, Museum, Menagerie, Roman Hippodrome and Universal World's Exposition. The Roman Hippodrome was an imitation of Barnum & Bailey's chariot races around the arena. If an act had horses in it, the Ringlings usually went for it.

To deal with their growing operation, Augustus and Henry joined the show. Gus, a gentle person, managed the advance car that went ahead of the circus and arranged for the advertising that told people it was coming. Henry, the baby of the family, became "superintendent of the front door."

By 1889, the Ringling brothers had decided that the only way to keep up with their powerful competitors was to start traveling by rail. By that time there were already eleven rail circuses: Barnum & Bailey; The Great Wallace Show; Sells Bros. Circus; John Robinson Circus; Adam Forepaugh; William Main; Lemon Bros. Circus; Frank A. Robbins Circus; Bob Hunting Circus; W. H. Harris Nickel Plate Shows; and Miles Orton Circus. The important thing was that from now on they would be in direct competition with the mighty Barnum & Bailey show. P. T. Barnum had only a year to live, but James A. Bailey was in his prime.

That fall, the Ringlings bought eleven railroad cars from the slippery Adam Forepaugh. The deal also included one cage, six baggage wagons, and three camels. In a letter to "Mr. Ringling Bros., Proprietors of Shows, Baraboo, Wis.," Forepaugh assured them that the equipment he was selling was in fine shape, but the camels turned out to be so badly infested with lice that they had to be isolated, and it took all winter to delouse them.

The Ringling Bros. Circus began traveling by rail in the spring of 1890. Its success could be attributed to the same two factors that accounted for much of the success of American industry: hard work and specialization.

Alfred T. Ringling did the publicity.

Gus arranged for the advertising.

Al picked the acts.

Charles produced the show.

Henry was the Ringling always at the performance.

Otto was treasurer.

In their wagon show days, John picked the routes and drove the leading wagon until, said the *New York Times*, "he became a human encylopedia on roads and local conditions, particularly as to localities where there were droughts or mills closed and no money was being spent."

In the railroad era, John made it his business to learn as much about railroads as he knew about roads and the communities they led to, and his routing expertise only increased.

"In the old opposition days," John once said, "when shows fought for territory and when the big fellows tried to starve us out, knowledge of railroads and routes was a big help. I learned my geography that way, and brother Charles still insists that I am able to name the counties of any State in the Union, and if the county is named, I can name the county seat, the road leading to it, and the license fee."

Gradually the expertise of "Mr. John" passed into legend. The apotheosis of the "Mr. John, Super Router" story has the circus train roaring through a pitch-black night in Ohio. Someone asks him as a joke if he can tell where they are. John Ringling stares out the train window for a moment, then speaks: "Fourteen miles east of Ada, Ohio, population 2,465. Northwest corner of Hardin County. Farming town, but I've never made it, though we showed Upper Sandusky—the town we just passed through— September 6, 1890, first season we had our show on the rails. We'll be coming into Lima soon. Showed that town September 8, 1893, and July 21, 1894. . . ."

Whether or not that ever happened, it is certain that John Ringling's skillful routing to small and/or neglected towns permitted the Ringling Bros. Circus to avoid direct clashes with their formidable competitors in all but five or six places yet do good business.

I have been hearing since I was a small child how Ringling routing and Ringling advertising won friends for the young circus. My grandfather, Dr. T. H. Culhane, after graduating from medical school in 1890, had become the first intern in the first hospital in Rockford, Illinois. His stated duties at Rockford Hospital included mowing the lawn when there weren't any patients to see.

That was the year Gus Ringling became head of the Ringling show's advance advertising. He created an image of the Ringling circus that remained in the minds of those who saw his advertising—including my grandfather—as long as they lived. "When he took over," wrote Gus Ringling's daughter, Alice:

the Ringling show was young, small and little-known. At that time and up to 1900 there were more big circuses criss-crossing America, elbowing and gouging each other at every turn, than at any other time before or since. It was a continuous free-for-all for the towns, the lots, the parade routes, but above all, for the billboards and the barn sides, the board fences and the store fronts, because outdoor advertising was the life blood of the circus of that era. Only the advertising brought in the customers and sold the tickets . . . the men in his crews were carefully chosen and properly directed; instead of angry farmers and irate citizens they left behind them friends and wellwishers. In this way the Ringling advertising was protected while they went on plastering the countryside with gorgeous, gigantic lithographs in lavish abundance, for my father, like all the Ringlings, thought "big."

When I was a little boy, my grandfather would tell me about the magnetic effect of those gorgeous Ringling lithographs—so stunning that they enticed him to get the hospital lawn mowed early and arrange for an afternoon off on May 9, 1891, so that he could see the Ringling circus for himself.

The Forepaugh-Sells Circus, a much better known show, was due in Rockford the same day, so the advertising must have been good to make my grandfather choose Ringling.

The advertisements Grandpa would have seen promised "Ringling Bros. world's greatest railroad shows, real Roman hippodrome, 3 ring circus and elevated stages, millionaire menagerie, museum and aquarium and spectacular tournament, production of Caesar's triumphal entry into Rome." And what he saw was almost as good as the ads.

The circus that year was made up of twenty-two railroad cars—two for Alf T. Ringling's advertising staff—three sleepers, eleven flatcars, five stock cars, and one elephant car that transported four elephants. The stock cars carried 130 horses and ponies, eighteen cages of "wild and ferocious animals," five camels, one hippopotamus, and three lions.

And it was a show that got through, come high water or even what is still the worst train wreck in Ringling's long history. On May 17, 1892, the show was en route to Washington, Kansas, when, said the route book:

An appalling crash awoke us. Pouring out into the night our men perceived a chaos of wrecked cars, some crushed to utter kindling wood; others hurled headlong into a lake of mad waters, whose undermining power had wrecked a trestle and our train. The lake was full of dead and drowning horses. With humane bravery our men plunged into the waters to pull the necks of the horses out of the water. Robert O'Donnell was found in a mass of bloodstained wreckage with a splintered piece of scantling [timber used in bridge building] driven clear thru his head. His brains were strewn in every direction.

The losses were terrible:

Twenty-six magnificent draft horses were floating dead in the river. Other horses had ripped bellies, or broken legs, and had to be killed. Two crowded sleepers just escaped

Behold the Old Hero of the Arena!
COMING WEDNESDAY, MAY 28.
OLD YANKEE ROBINSON
—AND—
RINGLING BROS.'
Double Show!!

The largest and most elegantly conducted and perfectly equipped Arenic Exposition ever witnessed. EVERY ARTIST A STAR.

Superior to any tent show now traveling, introducing all new and attractive features in the ring, by a host of artists, selected with care for their superior abilities.

Two and a half hours of solid fun. A classical and intellectual entertainment, endorsed by the clergy and religious press.

The Great 25 Cent Show!
Not 50 cents as was reported, but only 25 cents.

TWO PERFORMANCES DAILY, RAIN OR SHINE.
Doors open at 1 and 7 o'clock, p. m.

Free for everybody: The lady who visits the clouds, and our Grand Street Parade.

Remember, Our Admission is only 25 cents.

Wait for OLD YANKEE ROBINSON, who will positively in this city, Wednesday, May 28th, 1884.

IN THE BEGINNING. *In 1884, Barnum and Bailey were the kings of the circus world, the Ringling brothers were unknown, and Yankee Robinson was a has-been. From 1882 to 1885, Barnum and Bailey had Jumbo, perhaps the greatest circus attraction of all time; Yankee Robinson was to die during his first season as adviser to the young brothers. Yet, twenty-two years later, the Ringling brothers would be America's circus kings. They bought Barnum & Bailey in 1906 and combined it with their own show in 1919 to make Ringling Bros. and Barnum & Bailey, The Greatest Show on Earth. (Circus World Museum, Baraboo, Wisconsin)*

FORTY-HORSE HITCH THEN (1904). *In a day when nearly everyone was a judge of horse flesh, the first forty-horse hitch was used by the Spalding & Rogers Circus in 1848 to demonstrate in its street parade that it knew how to handle animals. When Barnum & Bailey opened the 1903 season the parade featured this forty-horse hitch pulling the new "Two Hemispheres" bandwagon. Master teamster Jake Posey died at ninety, but the Two Hemispheres bandwagon that he drove can be seen today, completely restored, at the Ringling Museum in Sarasota. (John Culhane Collection, gift of Charles Philip Fox)*

THE FORTY-HORSE HITCH NOW. *The forty-horse hitch was revived in 1972 by Dick Sparrow of Zearing, Iowa, who drove a hitch of forty Belgian horses in the Schlitz Circus Parade in Milwaukee, and, in this photo, in Indianapolis. A forty-horse hitch hadn't been seen in sixty-eight years, but Sparrow noted: "If it had been done before, it can be done again." Sparrow had been driving a twelve-horse team hitched four abreast in the Schlitz Circus Parade for several years; now he began to buy and trade stock to match forty horses in color, size, and temperament. There was no one to teach him, so he taught himself, practicing constantly from April to July. On the Fourth of July, more than one million people saw him drive three and a half miles, turning more than a dozen corners in downtown Milwaukee. Afterward, he was asked the question people used to put to Posey: "How do you know which rein to pick up?" He gave the same answer Posey used to give: "How does a musician know which chord to strike?" When Circus World Museum put on the 1989 Great Circus Parade in Milwaukee, it included a forty-horse hitch pulling the Two Hemispheres bandwagon for the first time since 1904—driven by Sparrow's son Paul. (John Culhane Collection, gift of Charles Philip Fox)*

VOLO THE VOLITANT. Bill Clarke, Eugene O'Neill's friend and drinking companion and the model for Ed Mosher in The Iceman Cometh, used the circus name Volo the Volitant when performing a daring bicycle stunt called cycling the gap. But he soon found himself sharing the tent with Italian sensation Ugo Ancillotti, who added a loop-the-loop to the trick. Clarke tried to regain the premier spot, but a fall broke his back and ended his career. (Circus World Museum, Baraboo, Wisconsin)

FRANK "SLIVERS" OAKLEY in his greatest comedy routine—the one-man baseball game. Oakley worked alone, without competition from other acts, earning up to $750 a week. Year after year he performed his pantomime baseball game for Barnum & Bailey, giving audiences in five minutes the clear and hilarious impression of eighteen players and an umpire going through a whole game. He began playing the catcher, and by his reactions audiences saw clearly that the batter had socked the ball, that it soared into the sky, that he needed a telescope to find it—and that he was giving the umpire a peep. Slivers, meanwhile, was running after that fly ball—outrunning it, in fact—and making a sensational catch, to retire the side. At bat himself, he walloped the ball, but was thrown out sliding into home plate on a very close call. The player's argument with the umpire, in which Slivers played both parts, convulsed audiences. Fellow clown Robert Sherwood quoted Slivers in 1905 on how painful such physical comedy could be: "'When I get through my work, I feel as if I'd been playing scrimmage against Yale. If people only would laugh at something nice and gentle! But no—not for theirs! We have to kick and get kicked, punch and get punched, get up, fall down, roll around, and get generally walked all over, trampled under and hoofed up, to make any sort of hit at all.'" The funny thing was, of course, that Slivers did it all to himself. (Ringling Museum)

destruction. Four seriously injured men were sent to a Kansas City hospital. The wives of the various Ringlings showed great womanly kindness in their constant ministrations to the striken. 40 head of horses were lost in all; which were replaced immediately by purchasing stock locally and ordering a carload from Chicago.

Yet the show missed only its Washington stand and went on to play Concordia, Kansas, the following day.

———————————

By the 1895 season, the Ringling brothers felt that they were ready to visit the second largest city in the United States. So they opened their season in Chicago, in the Tattersall Building. Signor A. Liberati was engaged for the entire season to conduct a concert for one hour prior to each circus performance. The special features of the show that year included "Speedy," who dived eighty feet into a tank of water about three and one-half feet deep.

The brothers were very satisfied with their big city opening: "Hundreds of thousands saw it; thousands were turned away," said the route book.

During that 1895 season, for the first time, the Ringling show invaded New England, long the stronghold of the Barnum & Bailey Circus. They were traveling on forty-four cars with three others in advance, which meant that they were formidable competition.

Bailey got the message. At his suggestion, the Ringling brothers agreed to divide the United States with him. They would make Chicago their headquarters; he, New York. Neither would intrude upon the other's metropolis.

But Bailey was not afraid of the Ringling brothers. He was moving with the times, if not

a little ahead of them. While touring New England in 1896, Barnum & Bailey exhibited a "Duryea, four-wheeled Motor Wagon, the identical horseless carriage that won the great ten-hour road race in Chicago last November."

By then, Barnum had been dead for four years, and Bailey, his surviving partner, was employing his enormous shrewdness and his own logistical genius to try to contain the growing power of the Ringling brothers. When Adam Forepaugh died in 1890, Bailey bought his show. W. W. Cole, the first man to make a million dollars in the circus business, auctioned off the W. W. Cole Circus in 1896 in order to accept an executive position with Barnum & Bailey. Then Bailey and Cole entered into a partnership with the two surviving Sells brothers. Like the young Ringling show, Sells Bros. Circus was particularly popular with midwestern farm communities. In 1885, Sells Bros. Circus had reached forty-five-car size and also ran a subsidiary with forty-four cars. But the two surviving Sells brothers were nearing eighty. So Bailey transferred most of the rolling stock of the Adam Forepaugh Circus to his Buffalo Bill's Wild West and combined the Forepaugh title with that of Sells Bros. to make a new major circus in 1896—the Great Adam Forepaugh and Sells Bros.' Shows Combined. Bailey now controlled three large shows with which to compete with Ringling Bros.: Barnum & Bailey, Buffalo Bill's Wild West, and Forepaugh-Sells. He made out their schedules for the 1896 season in such a way that Bailey-operated circuses would play the same towns at the same time as the Ringling Bros. Circus ("day and date," circus folk call it) forty-five times. He was observing the letter of the New York–Chicago deal—Barnum & Bailey itself did not play Chicago—but not its spirit.

Moreover, if the public wanted horses, Bailey was willing to go to the trouble and expense of reviving one of the most spectacular sights of previous street parades—the forty-horse hitch, driven by one man. Cost and complexity had kept it off the streets since Ben Maginley's Circus of twenty-three years before. In the nineteenth century, when practically every American considered himself a judge of horse-flesh and horse driving, a long-string driver who could maneuver teams and big wagons through narrow streets and around corners was a kind of hero. Charles Philip Fox and F. Beverly Kelley, in documenting the forty-horse hitches of circus history, say that the first recorded was the 1848 hitch with Spalding & Rogers Circus. Fox and Kelley counted ten more, including the hitches of Wm. Lake's Circus (1864), Yankee Robinson's Circus (1866), and the Dan Rice Circus (1872), before Bailey told boss hostler Tom Lynch to put a hitch together for the Barnum & Bailey season of 1897. The horses cost an average of $333 each and pulled a $7,000 bandwagon. The harness was made in Concord, New Hampshire, for $6,000. Plumes and other decorations brought the total cost of display to over $26,000—a small fortune in those days. Carl Clair's Grand Military Band rode in the wagon. Jim Thomas drove.

Incredibly, Ringling Bros. topped Barnum & Bailey by presenting something that could only be matched by the U.S. Cavalry. Their innovation for 1897 was to mount the entire circus band—comprising forty musicians—upon "matched white horses, fully caparisoned in the richest of habiliments. The members of the band are uniformed in the full dress of United States artillerymen," said the 1897 route book:

> Their accoutrements are all correct, even to the waving red plumes on their helmets. And, best of all, this band is not merely for display but it is a musical organization of the very highest order of merit.

Prof. Ganweiler, formerly band director in the Second United States Cavalry, which has the only mounted band in this country except the one now with the Ringling Brothers' Shows, is a director of a lifetime experience, and accredited with being one of the best arrangers and leaders in the country, as well as a cornet virtuoso ranking with the very best.

Their horses came in columns of twos and fours, "every man and horse in correct military position." The only member of the band who had any difficulty, reported the route book, was the bass drummer. "The heavy thud of his drumstick upon the drum, which is almost over the horse's head, made the animal restless, but as the days went on he got more and more used to it, and by the time the summer was half spent a cannon wouldn't startle him."

Forty bandsmen riding horseback, sitting on saddle blankets of red velvet with gold ribbing sewn on for flash, turned out to be an inspired way to let a city know that the Ringling Bros. Circus was here.

———

The Ringlings couldn't warm up to the automobile, but if modern technology was to be a battlefield, the brothers were prepared to fight there, too. In 1897, the Ringlings opened an annex, a special attraction exhibited in a separate tent on the circus lot. The previous year, Americans had had their first look at the invention that would eventually dethrone live and in-person entertainment as America's favorite kind. It was an early form of motion pictures called the cinematograph. Developed from an Edison Kinetoscope peepshow machine to project the pictures, it was in fact the first movie projector. The Edison people gave a public showing in New York in 1896, and in 1897, Ringling Bros. toured with a cinematograph in a black tent as an annex show. The tent was black to keep the interior dark enough for the projections to be sharp, and the public soon referred to it as the Black Top.

"More wonderful than the inventions of the past 100 years," said the banners in front of the tent, "Edison's latest and greatest invention—actual cost $10,000." The movie shown this first year was of the Corbett-Fitzsimmons heavyweight prizefight held March 17, 1897, at Carson City, Nevada. The following year, the route book contained a picture of what it called "The War Show." In the picture, banners in front of the Black Top headlined "EDISON'S LATEST / THE WAR GRAPH / SHOWING IN MOVING SCENES / THE STORY OF CUBA / REMEMBER THE MAINE."

At the end of the 1897 season, Bailey, a man who made few mistakes, made the biggest mistake of his career. He took Barnum & Bailey on a five-year European tour, leaving Buffalo Bill and Forepaugh-Sells to hold Barnum & Bailey territory against the growing Ringling threat.

The Barnum & Bailey show did big business in Europe, and the forty-horse hitch was a sensation in England and on the continent. Jake Posey took over the reins in Europe from the 1899 through the 1902 season, and he later explained how he did it:

I always had three men with me. One operated the wheel brakes, the second was available to quickly jump to the pavement in case a line got snagged on a plume or if a hame strap broke. This man could take care of most small emergencies. The third man was most important. He sat directly behind me and either pulled in lines or fed them out as I turned corners. When the team turned a corner 20 or more feet of lines slipped through my fingers. It was the job of the man behind me to feed the leather

smoothly as a twist in one line would force open my fingers and cause me to lose the line. When the team straightened out it was his job to pull back all the slack.

But when Barnum & Bailey came home in 1903, they would find that the Ringling Bros. Circus had become supreme in America. Moreover, the brothers' love of the soon-to-vanish America that looked to the horse as its primary means of entertainment as well as transportation was propelling them toward ever grander equestrian displays. Horse acts were always the main attraction in those years, and probably the grandest display of all was the Ringling sixty-one-horse finale of 1899. In order to accommodate sixty-one horses in the arena at one time—even in a three-ring circus—they were raised on stages into a great pyramid of horseflesh, with a single magnificent white Arabian at the very top.

In 1900, the Ringling brothers made their first continental round-trip, exhibiting in every section of the country. Dan Rice died that year, at seventy-seven. Seth B. Howes died in 1901, at eighty-six. And in November 1902, when the Barnum & Bailey Circus returned from Europe, Bailey found the still young brothers from Wisconsin the new circus kings of America.

With undiminished resolution, Bailey immediately put into effect plans for again outdoing the brothers from Baraboo. He enlarged his circus to ninety cars—and at that size found that he had difficulty moving, setting up, and tearing down the show. The Big Top and menagerie tent each had six center poles; the baggage stock stable, which sheltered the workhorses, had four; and the ring stock stable, which sheltered the performing horses, had three, as did the sideshow tent and the dining tent. Even the dressing tent, with two center poles, was the size of a Big Top for a smaller show. Bailey's opening spectacle, "Cleopatra," had a cast of 1,250 persons.

For his free 1903 homecoming season street parade, Bailey brought back the forty-horse hitch and saw to it that it was hitched to the largest, heaviest, and most ornate circus wagon ever constructed—the "Two Hemispheres" bandwagon, specially built for the occasion. There were also four specially built examples of a kind of circus wagon made first in England, the telescoping tableaux wagon. These floats had no practical use—what they carried was their own display—but they were beautiful to look upon. So Bailey had four built to represent the continents whose names were carved on their sides: "Africa," "Asia," "Europe," and "America." In the body of each wagon was a huge allegorical group carved in wood. For parades, these carvings could be cranked up onto the top of the wagons by a worm gear arrangement. Raised to the top of the "America" wagon, for example, would be carvings of a buffalo, an Indian chief, and two female figures. Fully extended, the floats towered fifteen to thirty feet above the ground. After the parade, the tableaux would again be lowered, or telescoped, into the interior of the wagon. They were the perfect symbols of the grandeur to which circuses aspired at the turn of the century.

Nor had they forgotten thrills. In the 1904 season, Barnum & Bailey introduced a daredevil who for an enchanted moment caused spectators to hold their breath. He called himself Volo the Volitant, and his name for his specialty was "Cycling the Aerial Arc." To do this trick, he rode a bicycle down a forty-five-degree incline that was forty-five feet high at the top and eighty feet long. The incline acted on the bicycle like a suddenly ending roller coaster: Volo and his bike would shoot off its end and fly through the air for a distance of fifty-six feet—"a bird-like bicycle flight

through space, describing an enormous aerial arc," said the circus poster. Then, if all went well, bike and rider would land on a seven-foot-high platform and descend to the ground by a second ramp.

In short, he leaped a gap on a bicycle.

Volo's real name was C. B. Clarke, and he was from Kansas City. The great difficulty of his feat was that it required tremendous skill to right the cycle, which sailed through space with the front wheel raised at a forty-five-degree angle. Each time he did the trick Clarke had to make a perfect touchdown, with both tires striking the landing stage at the same time. If his control was not perfect, if he landed on the rear wheel only, he would be thrown off backward, and could break his back—which is exactly what happened, eventually. But for a long time, his control was perfect.

And then, in Europe, an Italian named Ugo Ancillotti became the first person to loop-the-loop on a bicycle—not only leaping the gap, but making one complete somersault on his bike as he did it.

Still in the midst of his heated competition with the Ringling brothers, Bailey sent his European agent to Paris to hire the Italian for Barnum & Bailey's Greatest Show on Earth. So Volo and Ancillotti had to perform their unequal feats under the same tent. They even had to share the same circus poster. And with his better trick, Ancillotti got better ballyhoo, with Bailey promising a donation to charity if anyone could prove that the Italian cyclist's 360-degree loop was achieved by anything other than the power of centrifugal force. Volo tried so hard to be more thrilling than Ancillotti that he fell and broke his back.

But if his circus fame has faded, Volo the Volitant has at least achieved a kind of literary immortality.

Across the street from Madison Square Garden in the first decade of this century was a four-story red brick building called the Garden Hotel. It served as a rooming house for circus people, fight promoters, actors, gamblers, racketeers, and participants in the six-day bicycle races that were all the rage at the time. Eugene O'Neill used to go to that hotel to drink at the bar with his brother Jamie, and to visit their father, the actor James O'Neill, who put up at this slightly disreputable place when he was in New York without his wife.

"The circus men who stayed there I knew very well," Eugene O'Neill later recalled. "One of my old chums was Volo the Volitant, a bicycle rider whose specialty was in precipitating himself down a steep incline and turning a loop or so in the air," said O'Neill, airily exaggerating his friend's very real daring.

O'Neill remembered Volo, or Clarke, whom he called "Clarkey," as a good Catholic who had always said a Hail Mary before he began his perilous descent. Now recovered from his accident, he had become a guide with a Manhattan sightseeing bus service. He was also, like O'Neill, a drinker, and when his money ran out, he would drink wood alcohol flavored with Worcestershire sauce.

In those days, Clarke had more money than O'Neill and often paid for the drinks. Clarke also introduced O'Neill to his friend, Jack Croak, an old circus man who had been traveling with a tent show through the West Indies. Croak told O'Neill a story then "current in Haiti concerning the late President Sam. This was to the effect that Sam had said they'd never get him with a lead bullet; that he would get himself first with a silver one. . . . This notion about the silver bullet struck me, and I made a note of the story."

The note was made in the memorandum section of a bartender's guide and calendar of major sporting events that was distributed to good customers of the bar in the Garden Hotel. In addition, Croak gave O'Neill a coin with the image of the black president of Haiti on it.

O'Neill credited Croak with giving him the idea for his play *The Emperor Jones*, in which Paul Robeson played the character suggested by President Sam.

In later years, when his plays had made him rich and Bill Clarke was out of work, O'Neill gladly supported him. O'Neill even skipped the opening night of *Strange Interlude* in 1928 to spend the evening dining with Clarke in a suite at the Wentworth Hotel. "You were good to me in the old days, Clarkey," the author told the ex–circus man. "I've never forgotten it."

But the immortality that O'Neill conferred on his friend in return was essentially negative, if, as Barbara and Arthur Gelb say in their 1962 biography *O'Neill*, "Ed Mosher in *The Iceman Cometh* was based on a circus man named Bill Clarke [who used] the name Volo. . . ." Ed Mosher is not formerly a star daredevil with the circus; he is a former circus ticket taker who brags of shortchanging patrons. "You know, Harry," Mosher says to the proprietor of Harry Hope's bar at one point, "I've made up my mind I'll see my boss in a couple of days and ask for my old job. I can get back my magic touch with change easy, and I can throw him a line of bull that'll kid him I won't be so unreasonable about sharing the profits next time."

With friends like O'Neill, Clarke didn't need enemies.

Bailey knew that the vogue of the bicycle was quickly being eclipsed by the automobile. From a bicycle leaping a gap (Volo) to a bicycle looping-the-loop (Ancillotti), the thrill quickly accelerated to a car leaping a gap, then a car looping-the-loop (the Dip of Death).

The Dip of Death, or the Auto-Bolide (auto-meteor), as it was known in France, land of its invention, required a framework as high as a three-story house, divided into two sections. The first section consisted of a small platform at the top of a tower from which Mlle Octavie LaTour began her descent down a runway. The second section was the wooden receiving track. The gap between the two was about twenty feet. The car with Mlle LaTour strapped into it was hoisted to the platform and the brake released.

According to the Barnum & Bailey press release,

As the car descends the incline it gathers velocity. You are dimly conscious that its speed is so terrific as to be beyond comparison with anything you have ever seen. An express train is seemingly slow beside it. You think of a pistol shot; a speeding arrow; a meteor. It is all three in one. Before you can realize it, the car has descended the incline, turned upside down and still inverted, has shot into space. Twenty feet away, across a veritable chasm of death, is a moon-shaped incline.

Your breath comes fast. You gasp. Your heart seems to stop pulsating.

Will the auto strike the incline?

Will it be upright?

It did, it was—and there was a trick. The rubber-tired wheels of the car never touched the runway in the descent, although they revolved. Small wheels in the axles were fixed to the tracks under the incline. This prevented the auto from getting off the track until it reached the end of the car-throwing runway. The car-receiving runway was three times the width of the car-throwing runway—and its angle and distance were precisely calculated so that the car wheels would land at exactly the right spot, with hardly a shock to the occupant. It was much less dangerous than it looked.

Octavie LaTour herself admitted as much in three sentences buried in an article in the old *New York World* on April 8, 1905:

At present, I am courting death each day in La Tourbillon De La Mort, the supposed limit of human daring. But this act of plunging down the steep incline in an automobile that turns a back somersault in midair and lands on a runway is not really the limit of human daring. It is only the most perilous act that human imagination has so far devised for human daring. But it is the limit for only a moment. Hundreds of inventors are hard at work trying to perfect a machine that will make a double turn. . . . *For hairbreadth as the escape must seem, the probability of accident must be really small. No one wants to see people die. The game is one of mettle, not of death.* [Italics added.] So get your minds fermenting; give your imagination free play; and invent the real limit of human daring. Show us how to fly to the moon; direct the way to Mars; point the signboards down the roads of human daring. And I for one will go.

By that time, the once-adventurous James A. Bailey would not have gone with her. Mademoiselle LaTour's act was too much for him. Bailey, said Dexter Fellows, "hid himself in his private office and waited until the success or failure of the act could be reported to him." He was not the man he had been. He was growing old and weary of the constant struggle. He had made one last all-out effort against the Ringling brothers in the seasons of 1903–1904, with his double-threat daredevils and telescoping tableaux wagons and a forty-horse hitch pulling the "Two Hemispheres" bandwagon, the longest and most beautiful bandwagon of all time. (The next time a forty-horse hitch would pull it would be in the Great Circus Parade in Milwaukee in 1989.) But the broth-

A liberty act is a group of horses performing without riders—free, or "at liberty"—executing manuevers on the command or signal of a trainer who stands in the ring. When Ernest Hemingway saw this liberty act commanded by Czeslan Mroczkowski, he wrote: "The horses make the loveliest pattern of dreams." (Ringling Museum)

ers were clearly in their prime and he was past his, and future competition would be unrelenting. So he made them a peace offer—which they sensibly accepted. He sold them a half interest in the Forepaugh-Sells Circus, which was sent out under the management of Henry Ringling; and from then on, all three circuses were carefully routed to avoid any conflict of dates. The Ringling brothers had won over all their rivals.

A Rainy Day.

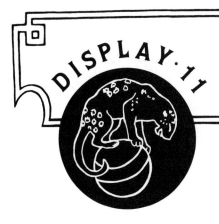

DISPLAY·11

The Golden Age

The competition among all these circuses created the golden age of the circus in America. Each show tried to outdo all the others with a Circus Day more delightful and spectacular than circusgoers had ever seen. Like the golden age of Hollywood half a century later, when there seemingly couldn't be too many movies, the country had room enough for all the shows—a brief, sunny period when there could never be too many circuses.

Circus Day at the turn of the century involved the whole community in a way that the small size of the average circus had not permitted before, and the sprawling size of towns and cities has not permitted since. This splendor lasted until too many American towns had spread and darkened into cities inhospitable to the amenities of Circus Day.

In those days, nearly every community had convenient open space, large enough to accommodate a circus and near enough for the circus to unload the train, give a free street parade through the center of town, and get back to the lot in time to give the matinee on schedule. There were no movies, radio, or television to compete with the glories of the circus ring; little traffic congestion to impede those who sought those glories; and no parking problems. The lots were almost always big enough to contain every buggy and the few automobiles that came. Labor and transportation costs were low; railroads found it profitable to bring the circus train to town; streetcar lines were usually there to bring the town to the circus.

You just had to let the townsfolk—and the people of neighboring farms, towns, and villages—know that the circus was coming.

Since the show would usually be in town for

LOVE STORY. Fred Bradna, equestrian director of Ringling Bros. and Barnum & Bailey Circus, carries his wife, Ella, star equestrienne, across a muddy circus lot. Nowadays the person who announces the show is called the ringmaster, but traditionally he was called the equestrian director, and the ringmaster was the monitor who, with a whip, kept the horses under control during riding acts. (Ringling Museum)

only one day, and give only two performances, word was spread ahead of time. About two weeks before Circus Day, the advance crew of the circus arrived to place ads in the newspapers and to say most courteously to shopowners, "Can I give you two free tickets to the circus for the privilege of putting some posters in your window?" The most popular way of advertising a circus was the colored lithograph or circus poster.

The drugstore, the barbershop, the hotel lobby, the cigar store—hundreds of business establishments all over town would have posters of half-sheet size (28" × 21") or one-sheet size (28" × 42"). Pasted on buildings, walls, and fences were posters of larger sizes, from 3-sheet (42" × 84") up through 6-, 9-, 16-, 20-, and even 28-sheet size. In fact, if you rode or drove around the countryside, you might find posters larger than 28 sheets, clear up to the rare 100-sheet circus poster, pasted on sheds and barns. If the billposters couldn't find the right kind of space, they would simply go to the lumberyard for boards, build a board fence around an empty lot, and cover it with posters.

Your town might be covered with 5,000 to 8,000 sheets. If two circuses were coming at about the same time, they might double that amount in an attempt to outpaper the opposition. Sometimes they covered over each other's paper. Sometimes fights broke out between the rival billposters. And all the while, the excitement mounted.

The posters were designed to catch the eye with their boldness and brightness of color and their cleanness and simplicity of line and legend, whether the potential circusgoer saw them from five feet away while walking along the sidewalk or from fifty feet away while riding on horseback or in a wagon or carriage or horse-drawn streetcar—or, later, from an automobile. Among the dozens of lithograph houses that specialized in circus posters, the leaders were the Strobridge and Enquirer Companies of Cincinnati, Ohio; Courier of Buffalo, New York; Donaldson of Newport, Kentucky; Riverside of Milwaukee, Wisconsin; and Erie of Erie, Pennsylvania.

When the circus train pulled into a local depot at 5:00 A.M., there would already be a crowd waiting for it at the crossing. Fathers would have set their alarm clocks for 4:00 A.M., wakened young sons and daughters and got them dressed, and hurried down to see the steam train chug in.

There would be an informal parade following the first wagons to the lot and watching the setting up of the cook tent and dining hall. The spectators had usually had breakfast at home, but their mouths would still water as the canvas men and grooms were given breakfast, the cook flipping great stacks of wheat cakes into the air as if he were the greatest circus juggler of them all.

The novelist Thomas Wolfe, born in Asheville, North Carolina, in 1900, would have delivered his paper route already, and gone home to get his kid brother out of bed, to be on the circus lot when the Big Top went up. As he remembered,

> Great flares of gaseous circus light would blaze down on the seared and battered faces of the circus toughs as, with the rhythmic precision of a single animal—a human riveting machine—they swung their sledges at the stakes, driving a stake into the earth with the incredible instancy of accelerated figures in a motion picture. And everywhere, as light came, and the sun appeared, there would be a scene of magic, order, and of violence. . . . Already in the immense cleared space of dusty beaten earth, the stakes were being driven for the main exhibition tent. And an elephant would lurch ponderously to the field, slowly lower his

great swinging head at the command of a man who sat perched upon his skull, flourish his gray wrinkled snout a time or two, and then solemnly wrap it around a tent pole as big as the mast of a racing schooner. Then the elephant would back slowly away, dragging the great pole with him as if it were a stick of match-wood.

Afterward, the elephants were given water. William Saroyan, born in 1908 in Fresno, California, was there to help. "We used to carry water to the elephants and stand around afterwards and try to seem associated with the whole magnificent affair," he wrote in *My Name Is Aram*, "the putting up of the big tent, the getting everything in order, and the worldly-wise waiting for the people to come and spend their money." Saroyan knew what the circus was: "The circus was everything, everything else we knew wasn't."

By about 8:30 A.M., the elephants, camels, ponies, and horses had been harnessed for the parade. The "artists," who had been called at 7:15, would have had breakfast, and would start dressing for "The Grand Street Pageant."

"The Glorious, Gorgeous Cavalcade" would start at 9:30, and Booth Tarkington, born in Indiana in 1869, was there. "The boys whooped in the middle of the street," he wrote in *The Gentleman from Indiana*:

some tossed their arms to heaven, others expressed their emotions by somersaults; those most deeply moved walked on their hands.

There was another flourish of music. Immediately all the band gave sound, and then, with blare of brass and the crash of drums, the glory of the parade burst upon Plattville. Glory in the utmost! The resistless impetus of the march-time music; the flare of royal banners, of pennons on the breeze; the smiling of beautiful Court Ladies and great, silken Nobles; the swaying of howdahs on

camel and elephant, and the awesome shaking of the earth beneath the elephant's feet, and the gleam of his small but devastating eye; then the badinage of the clown, creaking along in his donkey cart; the terrific recklessness of the spangled hero who was drawn by in a cage with two striped tigers; the spirit of the prancing steeds that drew the rumbling chariots, and the grace of the helmeted charioteers; the splendor of the cars and the magnificence of the paintings with which they were adorned; the ecstasy of all this glittering, shining, gorgeous pageantry needed even more than walking on your hands to express. Last of all came the tooting calliope, followed by swarms of boys as it executed "Wait till the clouds roll by, Jennie" with infinite dash and gusto.

The procession returned to the circus grounds about 11:15. The artists had dinner at 11:45, while visitors might watch a balloon ascension.

At 1:00 P.M., the doors opened to the menagerie and the sideshow, and Carl Sandburg, born in Galena, Illinois, in 1878, was there. "I hung around the midget and his wife," he wrote in *Always the Young Strangers*, "watched them sign their names to photographs they sold at ten cents—and they were that pleasant and witty that I saw I had guessed wrong about them and they were having more fun out of life than some of the men in the Q shops." Sandburg's father worked for "the Q"—the Chicago, Burlington and Quincy Railroad.

The main tent opened at 1:15. People who took their seats early saw the period before the show when the clowns pulled their tricks on the hippodrome track. W. Earl Aumann was there, and reminisced about it in the Venice, Florida, *Gondolier* when he was an old man:

One clown dressed in a Prince Albert suit and wearing a silk hat (but without clown makeup) carried an old fashioned camera on a tripod and would ask people coming in, especially large families, for permission to take their pictures. Quite flattered they would readily agree and the photographer would take infinite pains in posing them, frequently changing their positions and then putting his head under the black cloth again. After about five minutes of that when the family began to get restless, he would quietly pick up the camera and stroll unconcernedly away, leaving the family still posed.

At about 1:40, the band would begin its "Overture and Giant Steam Orchestration." And suddenly, at about 2:00 P.M., the big show, also called "the programme of soul-inspiring acts and achievements," began.

This performance always commenced with the "Grand Entry." Typically and traditionally, the Grand Entry was a glamorous parade into the Big Top or arena and around the hippodrome track that set the tone of high pageantry for which the whole circus aimed. A brassy fanfare would announce it, the backdoor curtain would snap open, and in would come the circus band, followed by circus performers on horseback, some carrying the national colors, followed by most of the rest of the company— "a prestigious potent potion of daring-doers from every corner of the globe plus pretty girls"—as many mounted as possible, but with those who walked perambulating at least in colorful capes or alongside such exotic animals as camels or zebras or sometimes a ponderous hippopotamus. This dignified procession would be punctuated, of course, by clowns attempting to break up the audience with sudden sight gags, like the clown who usually ran around the arena with a skeleton attached to the seat of his pants as if it were chasing him. As the first of the procession completed their tour of the Big Top, the last would just be coming in the other door. The band would step out of the line of march and up onto the band-

stand and play until the tail end of the Grand Entry—the elephants, caparisoned in their spangled blankets, moving along trunk to tail, with their attendants walking solemnly beside them—had exited. Then the equestrian director, immaculate in top hat and red coat, would take his place near the center ring and blow the blast on his silvery whistle that brought on the first act.

Then, as now, in what is called the "Program of Displays," there was everything a circus should have: feats of physical skill and daring and exhibitions of trained animals, counterpointed by clowns, in, around, and above a riding ring.

At the turn of the century, the horse was still the primary means of transportation, and the average American knew horses intimately and loved to see superior riders demonstrating the fine points of horsemanship. E. B. White, born in 1899 in Mount Vernon, New York, was there watching the performing horses and riders, since he belonged, as he later wrote, to "one of the oldest of societies—the society of those who, at one time or another, have surrendered, without even a show of resistance, to the bedazzlement of a circus rider. . . ."

Another member of that society was Frederick Ferber, a romantic young cavalry officer who in the spring of 1901 attended a performance of the Nouveau Cirque in Paris and saw a star equestrienne born. It was Ella Bradna's debut, and at the end of her act, her horse suddenly shied and tossed Ella into a ringside box—and into the arms of Fred. A year later, Fred was backstage at the Hippodrome trying to persuade Ella to marry him, when a representative of Barnum & Bailey Circus named George Starr offered her a contract. "Seeing me in Ella's dressing room, Starr mistook me for her husband, and included me in the contract as 'Fred Bradna,' " Ferber recalled. "I was to display fancy horsemanship and assist my wife. We were married the next day." After a start like that, is it any wonder that Ferber changed his name to Bradna, or that the Bradnas trouped happily ever after—for more than forty years, anyway. Ella enjoyed twenty-nine consecutive seasons of center ring stardom. Fred became equestrian director.

The clowns were there, and so was Ogden Nash, born in 1902 in Rye, New York, and a master of light verse for nearly half a century—though he later confessed: "I lack the adjectives, verbs and nouns, / to do full justice to the clowns."

The elephants were there, and so was Rachel Field, born in 1894 in Stockbridge, Massachusetts, and a distinguished poet who later wrote of one of them, "colored like city smoke he goes, / as gingerly on blunted toes / as if he held the earth in trust / and feared to hurt the very dust."

The jungle acts were there, and a newspaper reporter in Keokuk, Iowa, described what big cage historian Fred D. Pfening, Jr., says is the first wild animal act presented in a steel arena—in the Adam Forepaugh Show in 1891. (From 1835 to 1891, Isaac A. Van Amburgh and his followers did their act by entering a wagon cage or den of wild animals.) "After the imposing entry," said the Keokuk reporter,

came a startling novelty. In a steel bound ring forty feet in diameter and of sufficient height to prevent the escape of the animals that might be confined within it, appeared a gentleman and a lady, Col. Edgar Daniel Boone and Miss Carlotta, and two hounds. A moment later a big elephant came walking into the tent pushing a cage of three lions. The cage was backed up to the entrance to the steel ring. The door was opened and the three kings of the forest came bounding down into the enclosure. The people were startled, but apprehension soon gave way to the admiration and wonder at the exhibition

of the lion trainers' supremacy over their monster pets. The lions formed pedestals, held ropes for the hounds to jump over, played seesaw, rode a tricycle, fired a pistol, romped with Col. Boone and seemed to enjoy the whole performance.

The rare and exotic people were there—and none was rarer than "Zip, the What-is-it?" Actually, the "What-is-it?" was an intelligent black man named William Henry Jackson who had the misfortune to be born with an incredibly deformed skull whose crown was the size of a silver dollar and the shape of a cone.

Capitalizing on public interest in Darwin's theory of evolution, Barnum exhibited Zip as the missing link between man and ape, and said he had been captured in Africa by a party in pursuit of gorillas. People who persuaded themselves that they were higher on the evolutionary scale delighted in the antics of their "distant ancestor." Zip ate the cigars and coins that they offered him. His speech was limited to grunts and groans. But he obviously understood them, and he was a wonderful mime. Asked where he expected to go when he died, Zip would point upward. Asked where his colleague, South Sea Island Joe, would go, Zip would point in an equally positive manner toward the other place. Joe was billed as a Polynesian Warrior, but it was rumored that he was merely a fearsome-looking black man from Brooklyn. It was thought that Zip somehow divined and resented the imposture.

When the American Museum closed its doors, Zip went with Barnum's circus, then with Barnum & Bailey (and, finally, with Ringling Bros. and Barnum & Bailey). At the circus, Zip's best mimicry was of the bandmaster, and he always got a lot of laughs—and customers—when he pretended to lead the circus band as ballyhoo for the sideshow. His greatest moment, however, would come in 1924, when the

Ringling Bros. and Barnum & Bailey Circus put on a one-time-only show to commemorate the tearing down of Madison Square Garden Number Two, in which it paid tribute to P. T. Barnum and his principal attractions. Modern-day circus people impersonated Barnum, Tom Thumb, and Jenny Lind; but Zip played himself. When he began the circus's 1926 season he was in his nineties, and his career in show business was in its eighty-fourth year. But he was taken to Bellevue Hospital during the New York engagement, suffering from pneumonia. There, shortly before his death, Zip said to his sister, "Well, we fooled 'em a long time." He was buried where he was born, in Bound Brook, New Jersey.

The rare and exotic animals were there—although, sometimes, they were not quite as rare as the circus would have us believe. In 1895, a Ringling Bros. poster promised:

> THE LAST GIRAFFE Secured at the cost of a Fortune as a SPECIAL FEATURE . . . The one and only GIRAFFE known to exist in the entire world / To be seen at each exhibition of Ringling Bros.' Tremendous Triple Menagerie. The sole and lonely survivor of a once numerous family / The Last of his kind / Brought direct from Samona Land, Africa. He cost a fortune, But now is beyond all price for there is no other in the whole world. WHEN HE IS GONE, THE GIRAFFE WILL BE EXTINCT. Human eyes will never behold another. This is your last chance to see THE LAST SPECIMEN. See him now! You may never have another opportunity.

Robert Parkinson, research center director of the Circus World Museum at Baraboo, Wisconsin, has made a study of the use of this poster, and has determined that the Ringling Bros. did not use it in cities that had giraffes in their zoos.

The thrilling acrobats and aerialists were often unforgettable. Wallace Fowlie, born in Brookline, Massachusetts, in 1908, described as one of his earliest memories:

> a girl, an "artist" of the circus, hanging by her teeth, as the rope, which had been twisted an infinite number of times, uncoiled. The silence began as she was hoisted slowly through the air on the rope. She had grasped the rope with one arm and one leg, and thereby held herself erect as she moved upwards. She was dressed like a ballet dancer: a white ruff around her waist, which was crushed against the rope, legs and thighs covered with what seemed to be the same stockings or tights, and shining gold sequins over her breast. She appeared to me the ideal of beauty.

And the daredevils were often heart stopping. One can hear the note of genuine awe behind the circus hype of the anonymous publicist who wrote the copy for the Forepaugh & Sells Brothers Enormous Shows United circus poster picturing "DIAVOLO Looping the Loop" on a bicycle. He described the trick as "the extreme and absolute limit of sensationalism reached at last. Beyond the tremendously terrible temerity and illimitable, inimitable intrepidity of DIAVOLO, no man may go."

And yet, as we have seen, on the Barnum & Bailey show a "handsome girl" was already looping-the-loop not merely on a bicycle, but in an automobile!

The evening show began about 7:00 P.M. and would last until about 10:30. By 10:40, the crowd was piling into their carriages and buggies and buckboards, and the first few gas buggies in town (the doctor, usually, and the banker), and leaving the lot—except for those who wanted to watch the tear-down.

The last tent pole, baggage wagon, and vestige of the show were off the lot by midnight.

The circus train had pulled out of the depot by 1:00 A.M. In about four hours' time, another nineteen-hour day would begin. The roustabouts didn't get much sleep.

And after the circus was over? What effect did it have? In a memoir given to the Mothers' Thursday Club of Cambridge, Massachusetts, in 1970, Elizabeth Thaxter Hubbard, born in 1894 the daughter of Professor Roland Thaxter of Harvard College, remembered the circus fan and "constant playmate" who lived next door and became the poet e.e. cummings. "As I remember those years together," she wrote, "I spent most of my time admiring Estlin Cummings's feats of daring in swinging and jumping from the high branches in his apple trees. I probably contributed greatly to his ego. He planned to be in a circus, and I was to be his wife and mend his clothes."

Women, of course, had circus dreams of their own. Lucia Zora, growing up "in the sleepy little upstate town of Cazenovia, New York," first saw a circus elephant in a street parade when she was five. To Lucia, it was "the personification of dreams which are natural to childhood: far-away places, strange, mysterious happenings, adventures, and fields of golden fulfillment, just beyond the horizon." Her "comfortably fixed" parents' ambitions for her "took the usual line. I would be given the best education which they could afford, my natural talents would be heightened, and I would be made ready to become the educated and accomplished wife of some good man, according to the dictates of the average conservative American home." At nineteen, she rebelled, ran away to the circus, learned to break her own lion acts, and became the first featured female trainer of wild animals in America.

———————

Meanwhile, the competition of the men in charge of the dream machines was reaching its climax.

After the Ringling show opened its 1906 season in the Coliseum in Chicago on April 5, Mr. John went to New York City to try to buy Bailey's share of the Forepaugh-Sells Circus so that the Ringlings would own all of it.

Bailey was putting his own show together, as was his habit, in three days of intense rehearsals in the old Madison Square Garden. On the first day, he was inspecting his menagerie when an insect bit him on the nose. Bailey was too busy to pay any attention to the bite; but the next day he was delirious with fever and had to be taken to his home in Mount Vernon, New York. John Ringling, while he waited for Bailey to get well enough to meet with him, took some time to sample the luxury he loved with some of his New York friends. Mr. John was becoming well known now. He wasn't just one of the Ringling brothers who owned a circus in the Midwest. He was the wealthy businessman whose private railroad car, the "Jomar" (a contraction of the first names of John and his wife Mable, ending in r for Ringling), was one of the most opulent, in those days when opulence meant shining brass and sumptuous red velvet.

His friends included important people in high places, such as Stanford White, the most imaginative member of the prestigious architectural firm of McKim, Mead, and White. White had designed the second Madison Square Garden, on Twenty-third Street, a spectacular block-long building of yellow brick and terra cotta, topped by a controversial nude statue of the goddess Diana, that had become an instant landmark in New York.

There have been four buildings known as Madison Square Garden, and the circus that Barnum began has played in every one of them. The buildings on the first Madison Square Garden site were depots of the New York & Harlem and New York, New Haven & Hartford railroads. In 1873, wanting a Manhattan home for his three-year-old circus, P. T. Barnum acquired the entire square block between Fourth and Madison avenues, facing Madison Square. After almost a year of construction, Barnum's

Great Roman Hippodrome opened there in April 1874. The huge brick structure featured an oval track for chariot races that measured a fifth of a mile in length, inside of which was the circus ring. After one successful season, however, Barnum sold the Manhattan property and took his circus on tour. From late 1874 through early 1879, it was known as Gilmore's Gardens, and Barnum's circus paid it an annual visit as a tenant. In 1879, the building's name was changed to Madison Square Garden. In 1881, Barnum & Bailey's Greatest Show on Earth played its initial Garden date, boasting, for the first time anywhere, a three-ring circus.

Garden Number One was demolished in 1889 to make way for Stanford White's Garden. The first edition of Ringling Bros. and Barnum & Bailey Combined Circus would eventually play there, in 1919. Garden Number Two was torn down in 1925 to make way for the New York Life Insurance Co.'s skyscraper. By this time, Manhattan's entertainment center had moved uptown, so the third Madison Square Garden was erected, not on Madison Square near Twenty-third Street, but on Eighth Avenue, between Forty-ninth and Fiftieth streets. That building made way for a giant parking lot for the Broadway theater district in 1968. Ironically, the fourth and present Madison Square Garden stands on the site of McKim, Mead and White's monumental Pennsylvania Station, at Thirty-third Street, between Seventh and Eighth avenues. The trains still operate beneath the present Garden, which was formally opened on February 11, 1968, but no longer amid the grandeur of a great railroad station.

On the night of April 11, 1906, as Ringling and White were leaving Moquin's, a popular French restaurant of the time, Ringling bought a copy of the early edition of the *New York World*. He read the headline by the light of the streetlamp.

"Holy Christ!" Ringling said to White. "It's Bailey! James A. Bailey is dead!"

Bailey had died, within forty-eight hours of the insect bite, of erysipelas, an acute infectious disease.

So, instead of meeting with Bailey, John Ringling went to his funeral.

Bailey's true epitaph was the hole he left in the Greatest Show on Earth. Suddenly, the circus lost the knack of mounting a memorable street parade, while even the performances under the Big Top were often badly coordinated. Disappointing acts that Bailey would ruthlessly have cut after the New York engagement were permitted to last all season, while newly imported acts whose promise Bailey would have encouraged until they became American circus stars gave up in disgust with the circus's administration and went home.

Mr. John was continually on the telephone to his brothers in Chicago. He had been spending time since the funeral with Charles R. Hutchinson, treasurer of the Barnum & Bailey Circus, and he had gathered much information about the physical and financial state of Bailey's properties. His original notion of getting Bailey's share of Forepaugh-Sells had undergone a typical Ringling enlargement into the ambition to own The Greatest Show on Earth.

John and Otto voted yes; Al, Alf T., and Charles voted no; it was 3–2 against buying, and the way the Ringling brothers operated, they couldn't act until all agreed.

The nos argued that, with Bailey gone, his circus would be no match for theirs; that they had all they could handle running their own huge circus; and that the widow might eventually tire of the struggle and sell her property even cheaper. John's argument was that, even without the persons of Barnum and Bailey, the mystique of The Greatest Show on Earth was formidable competition. Besides, he said, "if we buy the whole thing at once, we'll control the circus field."

Charles switched sides, but Al and Alf T. continued to oppose the acquisition. Before Bailey died, John had had his brothers' permission to buy Forepaugh-Sells. He went back to New York to see if he couldn't do at least that much.

And there again a death seemed to be an omen. On June 25, 1906, Ringling and Stanford White were to attend the opening of the roof garden restaurant atop Madison Square Garden. John Ringling arrived at the Garden a little before 11:00 P.M. But he was too late to meet Stanford White: a few minutes before he arrived, White had been shot dead by Harry K. Thaw, the scion of a coke and railroad fortune, and husband of Evelyn Nesbit, the beauty who had once been Stanford White's mistress.

John Ringling, although shocked by his friend's murder, always counted it as fate that he had barely missed being a witness; he had no time for testifying at lengthy murder trials. In the coming months, while Harry Thaw was being tried and judged insane, the Ringling brothers would acquire The Greatest Show on Earth.

George Starr was just settling into the job of directing Barnum & Bailey in Bailey's place when the show ran into twenty-one straight days of rain during a tour of the Midwest. In those days, the only way a circus had to dry out shoes and costumes was to put them out in the sun; but for almost a month, there was no sun. Performers worked in damp clothing and muddy or even mildewed shoes. Ella Bradna wore rubber boots into the Big Top and changed into her ballet slippers just before mounting her horse, fearing all the while the accidents that might come from slippery slippers on a horse's slippery back.

Then, on September 15, 1906, wind and rain blew the tents down at Iowa City, Iowa. In the confusion after the storm, several thousand townspeople converged on the circus lot, and many of them took home souvenirs—red wigs, nose putty, oversized shoes and hats from clown alley; a leather box of clarinet reeds from the bandstand; gilt panels and statues from the circus wagons.

The night show was canceled; the circus train took the discouraged performers on to Muscatine. The sun came back the next day, and the show went on, but the season was a disaster. Barnum & Bailey, Limited, did not pay a dividend that year; the stock dropped from $5 to eighty-five cents a share. W. W. "Chilly Billy" Cole, a veteran circus manager, replaced Starr for the 1907 season. The weather was good and Cole struck a bargain with John Ringling dividing the territory so that their circuses would not compete. By mid-July the stock was up to a dollar a share. There were rumors that Mr. John had finally talked his brothers into buying the Barnum & Bailey stock.

The rumors were true. In October 1907, the Ringling brothers became the sole owners of Barnum & Bailey for $410,000—less than the profits of one good season.

The first result was that the Ringling Bros. Circus, rather than the Barnum & Bailey Circus, opened at Madison Square Garden in New York on March 25, 1909. Barnum & Bailey went west from Bridgeport to Chicago and opened in the Coliseum on April 1. Al and Alf T. had voted against the switch, arguing that their circus had always had good opening business in Chicago, and expenses would be higher to move the show all the way from winter quarters in Baraboo to New York. But the winning argument belonged to Mr. John: Ringling Bros. Circus might objectively be the biggest and the best in America, but it would never be considered a national institution until it played where the most money was: the East in general, and New York City in particular.

In the short run, it didn't pay off. The high

MAY WIRTH, *the world-famous Australian equestrienne, loved "performer's tricks," the feats that called for more skill and daring than most of the audience was aware of but at which other equestrians marveled. At left, she completes a back-backward somersault, which began with her back toward the head of the horse. She has thrown herself contrary to the forward motion of the horse, somersaulting and simultaneously twisting so that she is about to alight facing forward. Below, she does a backward somersault from one horse to another. A woman does not look her best when she is about to land on the back of a galloping horse, but the critic for the* New York Clipper, *while pointing out that "she does not rely upon her physical attractions for her success," also noted that "pretty of face and finely formed, she is the acme of ease and grace." From her debut in Madison Square Garden with the Barnum & Bailey Circus in 1912 at the age of sixteen, circus posters acclaimed her simply "The Greatest Bare Back Rider of All Time." There were no women and very few men who could even challenge that claim. (Ringling Museum)*

ELLA BRADNA'S "ACT BEAUTIFUL" employed three white horses, sixty pigeons, thirty dogs, three clowns, and twelve ballet girls as a backdrop for a bareback ballet dance by the lovely equestrienne. Add a pachyderm and you have John Ringling's fond definition of his institution's appeal: "Clowns, elephants, pretty ladies in fluffy gowns riding white horses. That is the circus!" (Ringling Museum)

MAKING PANCAKES. Famous for saying "you can't go home again," novelist Thomas Wolfe nevertheless re-created a time "when the greater circuses would come to town—the Ringling Brothers, Robinson's, and Barnum and Bailey Shows," and described "the circus performers eating tremendous breakfasts, with all the savage relish of their power and strength: they ate big fried steaks, pork chops, rashers of bacon, a half dozen eggs, great slabs of fried ham and great stacks of wheatcakes which a cook kept flipping in the air with the skill of a juggler." (Circus World Museum, Baraboo, Wisconsin)

cost of moving two big circuses to opening stands more than 800 miles from their winter quarters was not justified by the business they did in a nation just recovering from a recession; neither circus had a very profitable season. But in building prestige for the long run, John Ringling knew what he was doing.

Stories in the *New York Times* show the building excitement as the Ringling Bros. Circus came to New York for the first time in the spring of 1909.

"ONLY ONE BIG CIRCUS LEFT," said the headline on March 6. "The Ringlings Have Absorbed the Others—Will Be Here March 25."

"THE CIRCUS HAS STARTED," said another headline. "Coming All the Way from Wisconsin—Will Be Here March 18." (The early arrival date was to give them a week's rehearsal time in the unfamiliar Garden.)

"MEN AND ANIMALS REHEARSE FOR CIRCUS," said a Sunday article. "It is not only the men and women of the circus who are busy training for the opening night. The animals are all being put through their paces each day, and many times a day. Most of the animals were a trifle out of practice when the circus arrived at the Garden. . . . The lions and the bears and the elephants all have to be rehearsed almost every hour during the day in order to perfect them again in the old tricks or to make them learn the new ones."

Bears, for example, must be put through precisely the same schedule at every appearance or they become confused, refuse to perform, or even turn on their exhibitor. So as precious minutes passed, the trainer patiently waited for a ferocious bear to master one trick so that the act could proceed to the next. Nothing could be done to break the act or hurry it up.

And finally, on March 26, "RINGLINGS' CIRCUS OPENS TO BIG CROWD." The story began:

The Ringlings, the five brothers who in recent years have won fame as "Circus Kings" in the West, made their debut in this city last night. For a long time they have tried to enter New York. The Barnum & Bailey show kept them out. So the Ringlings bought the Barnum & Bailey Circus.

They promised long ago that if they ever did get into New York they would give a circus such as never was seen by a New York audience.

The 8,000 or so men, women and children who sat in Madison Square Garden at the first performance expected much. They were not disappointed. For three hours they laughed and marveled, and when the last act took place, when Mlle. La Belle Roche turned a double somersault in an automobile after the machine had run down a steep incline, the circus crowd went away many saying they had seen the best circus of their lives.

The automobile had captured the imagination of the public, so in the 1909 season the Ringlings offered not only a double-somersaulting automobile but the three Saxon brothers, strongmen who did an automobile-lifting act. Two of the Saxons supported a bridge over which passed an automobile containing six passengers. "The bridge itself was so heavy that it required twenty property men to lift it and put it in place," reported the *Times*. "The Saxons lay on their backs beneath the middle of the bridge, lifted the structure with their feet, and held it there without a quiver, while the heavily laden motor car chugged safely over."

But the hearts of the Ringling Brothers, as usual, were with the 650 horses of the show, especially the famous Schumann horses from Germany. The "Schumann Dynasty" had begun in Germany in 1844 when Gothold Schumann, a saddlemaker from Weimar, began performing as a bareback rider. In 1870, he created his own circus. In 1891, his son Max established the Circus Schumann in Copenhagen, Denmark. Albert, his other son, became one of the greatest of all trainers of liberty horses, riderless horses that execute maneuvers on the command or signal of a trainer who stands in the ring. Albert Schumann directed the Circus of Berlin until 1915. (Katja Schumann, who has been performing with the Big Apple Circus since 1981, is a fifth-generation Schumann circus rider.)

Despite the success of Ringling's New York engagement, poor business on the road in 1909 convinced the brothers that the bad business practices of some circuses were beginning to hurt all circuses. About thirty circuses were traveling by rail, ranging from two-car shows such as the little Mollie Bailey Circus in Texas to the eighty-four-car Ringling Bros. Circus. Charles Ringling proposed an organization of circus owners to try to eliminate practices that gave the circus as an institution a bad reputation.

In December 1910, representatives of more than a dozen circuses, including Ringling, Barnum & Bailey, Forepaugh-Sells, John Robinson, Hagenbeck-Wallace, Buffalo Bill, Sells-Floto, Miller Bros., Gollmar Bros., and Gentry Bros., met in the Chicago suburb of White City. They agreed not to cover one another's posters, to remove their advertising matter promptly after show dates, and to give the public "a square deal." With the dominance in the circus field of the Ringling brothers, their "Sunday School" approach to the business was becoming the dominant way.

On March 31, 1911, Otto Ringling died in brother John's apartment on Fifth Avenue in New York City. The first of the Ringling brothers to die, he was only fifty-three. He left his share in the circus to their youngest brother, Henry, and the older brothers immediately discontinued the use of their trade-mark portrait posters and programs. It was a valuable publicity asset, that portrait of the five founding brothers with their handlebar mustaches; but the brothers felt it would be unfair to Henry to use a family portrait in which he wasn't included.

They also discontinued the Forepaugh-Sells Circus at the end of the 1911 season and concentrated on the two giants: the Ringling Bros. Circus and the Barnum & Bailey show.

And then, in the 1912 season, the horse-loving Ringling brothers presented the American debut of what many regard as the greatest of all equestrian acts.

The rider's name was May Wirth. She was just seventeen, and when she made her debut in Madison Square Garden for the Barnum & Bailey Circus, "Mr. John" Ringling gave over the entire three-ring arena to her act. She was immediately acclaimed the finest equestrienne in the world—and she has never since been rivaled.

May Wirth did with ease things that few men and no women had ever done: not only the forward somersault but the back-backward somersault as James Robinson had done it, beginning with her back toward the horse's head, so that she was throwing herself contrary to the forward motion of her steed and had simultaneously to somersault and twist so that she could light facing forward. And she would do graceful somersaults from the back of one horse to another. Other equestrians would stand at the performer's entrances to the Big Top, marveling at her tricks, knowing most audiences could never appreciate their difficulty.

May Wirth was the adopted daughter of Maricles Wirth Martin, one of the world's great riders and a member of the family that ran the Wirth Circus in Australia, New Zealand, and throughout the world. May was an orphan who began performing at the age of five with a contortion act in the Wirth Bros. circus in Australia. A year later, she was adopted by Mrs. Martin and her husband, John, and her equestrienne training began. Many years later, May would give her first pair of pink practice pumps, the *W* on them initialed by the woman she called Mother, to the Ringling Circus Museum. In 1911, when she was seventeen, Mrs. Martin brought May Wirth to the United States and to the Barnum & Bailey Circus. Since 1906 the star equestrian of the Ringling Bros. Circus had been Orrin Davenport, later a pioneer of American indoor circuses, and, according to Barnum & Bailey's equestrian director Fred Bradna, he became May's mentor.

Bradna snobbishly called Davenport "the only product of American training who was commonly mistaken for a graduate of the traditional European school. He had continental style, grace as well as courage. To the standard repertoire he added a new sensation: a backward somersault from one horse to another, then a second somersault to a third horse, then a backflip to the ground, all in one series." Davenport taught May Wirth to somersault from one horse to another. But the pupil, said Bradna, "ultimately excelled her instructor." So easily did she perform three back somersaults and one forward, in series, on a bareback horse, that her contract required her to do this daring trick at every performance.

This peerless young horsewoman with the patrician profile was a lovely illustration of the continuity of the equestrian art. She wore the satin costume made in China for her foster mother, and carried a whip that had belonged to the great nineteenth-century rider Charles W. Fish, who had retired in 1889. Circus posters described her "jumping from the ground to her flying steed WITH BASKETS ON HER FEET!" and showed her lovely bare shoulders and her huge trademark hair bow.

A measure of her fame is the fact that when she was injured on April 22, 1913, it was front-page news in the next morning's *New York Times*: "MAY WIRTH BADLY HURT," said the headline. "Barnum & Bailey Champion Rider Dragged Around Circus Ring."

Bradna described it as "the most heart-rending accident I ever witnessed," and the horror of the eighteen-year-old woman's head banging against the ringbank comes through even in the newspaper account:

Miss May Wirth, who appears on the programmes of Barnum & Bailey's Circus as "the champion bareback rider of the world," was seriously injured last night when she was thrown from her favorite white Arabian horse, Juno. While the big crowd in the tent at Wyckoff and Myrtle Avenues, Brooklyn, where the show is now being presented, looked on helplessly, Miss Wirth was dragged around the ring four times.

Miss Wirth appeared in the center ring to do her act at 10 o'clock. She was greeted by a great outburst of applause when she successfully did a double somersault on the back of her horse. Then as she was bowing to the crowd and about to leave the ring her foot slipped. In falling she caught her right foot in a rope stirrup used by circus attendants who cling to the horse during part of the performance. The frightened animal started on a wild dash about the ring.

Before the attendants could stop the horse Miss Wirth was tossed a dozen times against the wooden embankment and dragged back into the ring. Once she was pulled beneath the feet of Juno; and half the people in the audience rose to their feet in horror. Miss Wirth was unconscious when she was rescued, and there was a deep wound over her right ear. Her body was a mass of bruises. Dr. Grabill, the circus physician, said that while no bones were broken, Miss Wirth would be unable to appear again for two or three weeks. . . .

In fact, she was not able to appear again for months, and for a long time it was thought that her riding days were over. But her spirit was indomitable. The following winter, she appeared before the Prince of Wales and the Queen Mother Alexandra at a command performance, a benefit matinee at the Olympia, London, on February 7, 1914. And in 1916, President Woodrow Wilson, on a visit to the circus in Washington, D.C., congratulated her personally.

Wilson had his own circus fantasy. He wanted to ride an elephant in the show. According to Fred Bradna, Wilson's advisers warned against a Democrat president riding on the symbol of the Republican party, but that might not have been a good enough reason to deter Wilson, who had come out on top of the GOP before. It was the Secret Service who frustrated his ambition by telling him that they could not protect a president atop an elephant in the center ring of the circus.

Nevertheless, on May 8, 1916, Wilson did manage to use the circus ring for political purposes. Nearly everyone thought that he would run again for president, but he hadn't yet announced his intent. Bradna escorted Wilson across the Barnum & Bailey arena from the performers' entrance to the reserved seats, the circus band began to play "Hail to the Chief." Wilson doffed his hat—and threw it squarely into the middle of the center ring. The crowd went wild, while the print media in those pre-television days ran for the nearest telephone to inform their papers that Woodrow Wilson had *literally* thrown his hat into the ring.

On New Year's Day, 1916, Al Ringling, the real founding brother, died at the age of sixty-three. A habit he had cultivated now came back like bread cast upon the water. Al had always remembered where old troupers were buried, and whenever his circus played near those places, he sent flowers to be laid on their graves. Now, when Al Ringling was being laid in his final resting place, the funeral cortege that trailed from his big stone mansion to the cemetery in Baraboo was swollen with mourning troupers: not just kinkers (as acrobats originally and, later, all circus performers were called), but ticket sellers, horsemen, cooks, and workmen. To his wife he left a fortune in cash and securities, as well as the Ringling theater and the mansion.

But Louise Ringling no longer wanted the expense of maintaining the mansion. She moved out, and the Ringling brothers' only sister moved in. In that mansion, Ida Ringling North and her husband, Harry North, would raise their three children: a daughter, Salome, and two sons, John and Henry. It was John Ringling North who would eventually take over The Greatest Show on Earth.

When the United States entered World War I in 1917, the Ringling Bros. Circus alone had more than 1,000 personnel, 335 horses, a zoo-like menagerie that included twenty-six elephants and sixteen camels; and it traveled aboard ninety-two railroad cars. The Barnum & Bailey Circus was about the same size.

Suddenly, circuses couldn't get enough help or acts. So many Ringling employees joined the armed forces, wrote Fred Bradna, that "Alf T. Ringling, as usual in charge of specs and tableaux, was unable for the first time in his career to extemporize adequately in the face of many canceled contracts. The show was ragged. We did not know that Alf T. was a dying man, with scarcely two years to live. But we could see that he was slowing down."

The military services and the war industries so depleted circus manpower that when Ringling Bros. left Madison Square Garden for the road, they had only eighty canvasmen instead of 250, and only twenty property men, all middle-aged to elderly, instead of the eighty husky men who did the job in peacetime. Few hostlers, grooms, or valets were left to the circus during the last war in which horse cavalry was still used.

"All the able-bodied men and some of the stronger women took turns morning and night getting the show up and down," wrote Bradna. "Great stars loaded trunks, seats and stringers; the slighter women carried such things as chairs."

Late in the summer of 1918, a global influenza epidemic, which would eventually claim twenty-two million lives, struck America. Patronage on both the Barnum & Bailey and the Ringling shows fell below the break-even point. Meanwhile, the railroads served notice that the war made it impossible to handle two big circuses. The three remaining brothers thought that the war would last at least another year, and that forced them to make a decision they had been postponing. As usual, the Ringling brothers kept their own counsel, but Bradna, relaxing with Charlie Ringling on a Lake Erie beach after an afternoon performance in Toledo the year before, had heard him say, "We would get around all these shortages if we combined the two big shows. Then we'd have help enough, and acts enough, to go on. What a show *that* would be!"

The Ringlings folded their tents a month early in 1918, but instead of putting their show in winter quarters at Baraboo, Wisconsin, as usual, they sent everything to Bridgeport, Connecticut, home of Barnum & Bailey.

The 1919 circus season opened with a front page headline in the *New York Times*:

SUPERCIRCUS DRAWS CROWDS TO GARDEN
Combined Ringling and Barnum & Bailey
Shows Open Season Here

ACTS STIR THE SPECTATORS
Thrills Abound in Performance Which Has
Best Troupes of Two Old Organizations

The name of that supercircus came trippingly to the tongue: Ringling Bros. and Barnum & Bailey Circus. Today, some seventy years later, it is the most familiar circus name in the world.

That first season of peace probably marked the highest point yet for the circus in America. The new circus opened in New York on March 29, 1919. The *Times* described some of the wonders of that show: "In number and variety of acts, in the size of the menagerie, and even in the case of the freaks the circus, as it is now showing in the Garden, is the biggest thing of the kind New York has ever seen. The circus people themselves call it the 'world's first super-circus.'"

It was an all-star circus if there ever was one. Performing horses and riders included the Hanneford Troupe from the Barnum & Bailey aggregation. In 1915, Edwin "Poodles" Hanneford had set a world record by making twenty-six running leaps on and off horseback, a record that was still in the *Guinness Book of World Records* seventy years later.

Rare and exotic animals included a pony that boxed, and a dog, Toque, who did a double somersault from a high perch to the arena. Among the exotic people was "Zip," Barnum's "What-is-it?," who was reportedly eighty-eight at the time.

The thrilling acrobats and aerialists included the trapeze artists Ernest and Charles Clarke. Ernest Clarke was the first male to accomplish the triple back somersault, throwing the trick to his brother Charles in an engagement with the Publiones Circus in Cuba in 1909 (a woman, Lena Jordan, had performed the world's first flying trapeze triple in Sydney, Australia, in 1897); but there is no record of Clarke doing the triple during the 1919 engagement.

There was an act in which, according to the *Times*:

seven troupes of aerial performers took part. Among them are three troupes of women aerialists who are hoisted to the top of the Garden, where, suspended by their teeth, and garbed in butterfly raiment, they are whirled at dizzy speeds, the result being, so far as color is concerned, the most gorgeous picture of the whole performance. But the stars of this act are the Cromwells and a little woman who is down on the program as Miss Tiny Kline. The act of the Cromwells is a double-trapeze feature, in which the woman member of the team is swung half way across the Garden suspended by her feet from the feet of the man. Miss Kline performs at the very top of the Garden. She uses a metal swinging trapeze, and brings the act to a close with a series of giant swings in which the trapeze itself revolves around the bar, while she stands rigid within it.

(Forty-five years later, Tiny Kline, seventy-two in 1963, was playing Tinker Bell at Disneyland in California. Every summer evening, wearing wings and carrying a wand, she would be harnessed to a cable and would "fly" from the top of the Matterhorn to the Skyway. As she seemed to soar past Sleeping Beauty's castle, fireworks would explode a shower of colors like fairy dust from her wand. But Peter Pan's good fairy, and Ringling's former star, traveled to work by bus. "I'm afraid to ride in a car on the freeways," she said. "They're not safe.")

The wire walker was Bird Millman from Barnum & Bailey whom Bradna called "the most beautiful performer" he had ever seen. "To appreciate her act you had to see her imitators," wrote Bradna. "They did the same tricks—but lacked that distinguishing asset of the true star, hypnotic charm." The first American wire walker to perform without the aid of a balancing umbrella, Bird Millman danced the waltz, the one-step, and the cakewalk on the wire, while a chorus of eight voices below her

sang popular songs. It was not that her tricks were so difficult, it was that she was a great personality performing them—and it comes across in Bradna's recollection: "She herself sang 'How Would You Like to Spoon With Me' with debonair insouciance, ending the number with a saucy flip of the shoulder as she stepped from the wire to the pedestal." Like May Wirth, Bird Millman had the Garden all to herself. No one else performed while she was performing. Because it was assumed that all eyes would be on these performers anyway, the other two rings stood empty when they came on.

The daredevil was Hilary Long, "a young man who performs what is perhaps the most dangerous feat of this year's circus," according to the *Times*. "He wears a tin hat with a groove in it. He climbs to a high perch in the western end of the Garden from which a slender solid steel wire is stretched a fourth of the way across the Garden. On this wire he stands on his head and in that position, while the audience gasps, he slides to the ground."

But if there was a star of stars, it had to be May Wirth.

"The first of the numbers in which the whole Garden is used is the equestrian act of Miss May Wirth, the Australian girl rider," reported the *Times*.

Six years ago Miss Wirth was the star of the Barnum & Bailey Show, and was seriously injured during the first performance under canvas that year, the place being Brooklyn. For a long time it was thought that her riding days were over, but she is back, and her act is as thrilling and as pleasing to look upon as it was in 1913. She uses two horses in the act, one of them a frisky spotted animal, upon whose back she executes a series of back somersaults through rings, ending her performance by a leap from the ground to

BIRD MILLMAN, *circus darling of the Jazz Age, danced on a tightwire thirty-six feet long—twice as long as all others—singing popular songs as she danced. She was the first tightwire artist to work without balancing pole or umbrella, holding only, at times, a tiny balloon as she trilled "Tip-toe Through the Tulips" or "Would You Like to Spoon with Me?" She leaped, pirouetted, and performed intricate dance steps as if she were on not a tightwire but a ballet stage. Her rivals for the hearts of circus audiences, such as Lillian Leitzel, were enraged that Ringling Bros. permitted her, in addition to the circus band, a mixed chorus of eight voices, "garbed," wrote Robert Lewis Taylor, "in vestments not dissimilar to the Vatican Choir." (Ringling Museum)*

MABEL STARK (*opposite, top*). *The first woman to break, train, and work tigers was famous for wrestling a three-year-old tiger as a regular part of her act. She would walk unarmed into a cage containing twelve Bengal tigers and a black panther. Without the aid of whip, gun, or iron fork she put her cats through their routines, apparently controlling them with her attitude and voice alone. Fred Bradna once heard another woman ask her what it took to be a tiger trainer. "Slowly the star thrust both legs from under her dressing gown," wrote Bradna. " 'This,' she said. From ankles to thighs she was covered with scars where the cats had clawed her. Indeed, her whole body is a scarred reminder that the way of the circus is hard." (Ringling Museum)*

LILLIAN LEITZEL *was the first to demand that the Ringling brothers give her a private railroad car on their circus train. Once they gave in to her, they had to give in to other stars; but Leitzel's car remained the flagship of the line. "She had a grand piano on her railroad car," Jenny Rooney, the equestrienne, said. "When in the humor, she would give concerts for what she considered the elite of the circus, and for distinguished visitors from outside." She also lighted them with electricity, cooled them with an electric fan, and entertained them with a wireless, all state of the art in the 1920s. "Leitzel was a little bit of a thing, four feet ten inches tall and weighing ninety-four pounds," recalled Fred Bradna, but Jenny Rooney added: "She was a storm center every day she lived. . . . Now and then I'd say, 'Leitzel, you ought to slow down—you're burning up your life in a hurry.' Her answer would always be, 'Jenny, I'd rather be a race horse and last a minute than be a plow horse and last forever.' " (Ringling Museum)*

the back of the fast-going animal, her feet encased in baskets. . . .

Display No. 9 was the big riding act. All three rings were filled with cantering horses. "The MacPherson Clan of Scotch Riders . . . have adopted as one of their team members the midget rider, Signor Bagonghi, who is so small they have to tie a rope to him to keep him from falling off." There were the Davenports, including May's mentor, Orrin Davenport. And, finally, there was the entire Wirth family, Miss May included.

May Wirth was the quintessence of the kind of horse-centered circus that the original Ringling brothers nurtured throughout their long reign, and they treated her like the treasure that she was. When later in 1919 she married another circus performer, Frank Edwin White, all the living Ringling brothers attended, and Robert Ringling, Charles's son, who was only three years older than May Wirth, served as best man.

She performed with the circus that had just become Ringling Bros. and Barnum & Bailey until 1927, toured outdoor fairs with Otto Griebling in 1929, when the great clown Otto was still an equestrian, then toured with her family in vaudeville until she retired in 1937. She died in a Sarasota, Florida, nursing home on October 18, 1978, at the age of eighty-four.

May Wirth seemed to epitomize the appeal of the circuses that the Ringling brothers put on. "In recent years," as John Ringling said in *American* magazine of September 1919, "I have been asked often whether the circus will be modernized, whether the universal use of the automobile will change it. It never will be changed to any great extent, because men and women will always long to be young again. There is as much chance of Mother Goose or Andersen's Fairy Tales going out of style as of the circus altering greatly. If we desired to change it, the people would not permit it.

"Clowns, elephants, pretty ladies in fluffy gowns riding white horses. That is the circus!"

Here is the definition of circus *in one sentence and one photograph: acts of skill and daring performed by talented humans and animals in, above, and around a ring, contrasted with the ineptitude of the clowns. (Ringling Museum)*

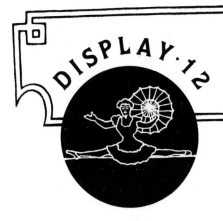

<figure>

DISPLAY·12

The Circus in the Jazz Age

</figure>

By all accounts, the circus in the jazz age was like America in the same era—confident, happy, outgoing, optimistic, sky's-the-limit—full of life and larger than life.

Empire building was the order of the day. Jerry Mugivan and Bert Bowers, who had gone into the show business in 1904 with a few rented cars and little equipment, had grown, and grown acquisitive. By 1920, they owned the long-lived John Robinson, Howe's Great London, Hagenbeck-Wallace, and Gollmar Bros. circuses.

In the fall of that year, Mugivan and Bowers bought the Yankee Robinson and the Sells-Floto circuses and acquired title to Buffalo Bill's Wild West. They took in Ed Ballard as a third partner, and in 1921 they organized the American Circus Corporation.

The nation's economy boomed; wages rose. Americans had money to spend and they still spent it on the circus. There were big shows—Ringling Bros. and Barnum & Bailey, Sells-Floto, Hagenbeck-Wallace, John Robinson, Walter L. Main, Sparks, Christy Bros., Al G. Barnes—and there were small ones, including those of the brothers Cole, Kay, and Wheeler. All were prosperous, and more and more they abandoned the railroad for the truck shows, beginning with the short-lived Great United States Motorized Circus of 1918. The Lindemann Bros. Circus of 1924 became Seils-Sterling, a major motorized circus until 1938. At first, most circus folk, who had lost their hearts to the railroad train half a century before, sneered at truck shows—until a few became so successful that they couldn't sneer anymore.

LILLIAN LEITZEL, QUEEN OF THE AIR. Speaking of circus joys to a meeting of the Old Guard of Westchester County in 1989, I showed this picture of Lillian Leitzel, and the faces of several retired businessmen lighted up. Afterward, they came to me to tell me what they remembered of her, and it was golden variations on what Robert Lewis Taylor wrote of her in Center Ring, *that she was "a beautiful little rag doll twirling far over our heads, charming her faithful, her smile filled with promise. Though then very young, I remember her very well, for I had planned to marry her right after the matinee, but forgot it during the Wild West show." (Ringling Museum)*

The twenties was a decade of superstars performing superfeats in every field. Naturally, in the birthplace of ballyhoo, Lillian Leitzel and Alfredo Codona were not merely superstars: she was "The Queen of Aerial Gymnasts"; he was "The King of the Flying Trapeze." By the time they were through, alas, they were best known as the star-crossed lovers of the circus; for, like the decade itself, they ended in a crash. They were a pair of lovers Scott Fitzgerald might have created as a cautionary tale of the Twenties, an echo of the jazz age.

Alfredo Codona was widely called the handsomest man ever to appear with a circus. His face had a boyish quality that made women want to take care of him, and Dexter Fellows reported, "He had a figure like a Greek God. Every muscle in his body seemed to sing in harmony as he flew from trapeze to trapeze. Catchers with whom he worked told me he landed as lightly as a swallow."

Alfredo was born in Hermosillo, Sonora, Mexico, in 1893, two years after his slack-wire-walking sister, Victoria, who has been called the most beautiful woman ever to appear in a circus. The father of this handsome family, Edwardo Codona, was a tumbler whose strength and timing had helped him rise to catcher in a flying act. When the flyer left his perch, Edwardo, swinging head down from the catch bar, would pull a watch from his pocket, look at it, yawn, pocket it again, and then casually receive the hurtling flyer. He also did the "heel catch" before Winnie Colleano made the trick famous: swinging in a wide arc on a high trapeze, he would let go with his hands, actually catching the bar with his heels.

In 1911, eighteen-year-old Alfredo Codona joined the Barnum & Bailey Circus, performing his father's heel-catching trick. In 1917, when Alfredo was twenty-four, the family act went on the Ringling show with the Siegrist-Silbon troupe of flyers. Alfredo was soon flying on the show, with his brother Lalo as catcher.

Back in 1897, in Sydney, Australia, a young Latvian woman named Lena Jordan had accomplished the first triple back somersault to the hands of the catcher—her adopted American father, Lew Jordan. Ernest Clarke threw the triple occasionally, beginning in 1909. But no one until Alfredo Codona was able consistently to accomplish the "salto mortale," or "somersault of death," as the Spanish called it. Codona threw his first triple in public in the spring of 1920, and continued to do this difficult and dangerous trick throughout the twenties. That consistent triple was the superfeat that brought him his fame.

"My job with the Ringling Brothers and Barnum & Bailey Circus hinges upon the fact that I can be depended upon twice daily, rain or shine, to turn a triple somersault from a trapeze into the waiting hands of my brother Lalo," he told the *Saturday Evening Post* in 1930. "My speed, when I leave my trapeze for the triple, has been accurately measured; I am traveling at the rate of sixty-two miles an hour. At that speed I must turn completely over three times, in a space not more than seven feet square, and break out of my revolutions at precisely the instant that will land me in the hands of Lalo, who, hanging to his trapeze by his hocks, has swung forward to meet me."

Once, Alfredo misgauged his time in leaving the bar by less than a hundredth of a second. Connecting, he was four inches off. His head struck his brother in the chin, knocking him unconscious from the catch bar. Alfredo landed first, facedown on the safety net, and Lalo, dead weight because he was still unconscious, fell on the small of Alfredo's back. Alfredo Codona spent two weeks in the hospital with three ribs broken on one side of his back and two on the other.

In the air, of course, Codona's timing was

seldom less than perfect, and his physical abilities were of a rare order higher than most circus athletes'. Making a high dive from a flying trapeze straight through a rotting net to the ground below, Codona lived to tell about it in these words:

> I drove my trapeze steadily higher, until the absolute limit was reached. Then I shot over the bar, curved into the air, and straightened into the bullet-like descent to the net. Two feet above it I jerked inward for the forward somersaulting position, struck the net—and went straight through! I was, at the most, eight feet from the ground, and in a position which meant my death. In that eight feet I jerked out of the forward somersault into a backward one, lit on my feet, instantly turning another and a third and a fourth, swung into a succession of roll-overs and came to my feet for my bow, absolutely uninjured.

He also lived to seek out the property man who had permitted a rotting net to be hung, and to beat the hell out of him.

And then this man who couldn't live with mistakes met Lillian Leitzel.

Lillian Leitzel was, of course, a superb aerialist; but there have been some others as good, and many others as daring. In truth, she probably succeeded on charm, an overused and ill-used word, but one that described Leitzel perfectly.

Leitzel's act had two parts. In the first part, she performed on Roman Rings, two metal rings hanging on the ends of ropes: rings for the performer to grasp and pull and push against to turn acrobatic tricks, as Dolly Jacobs does today.

But it was part two that made her the toast of the tanbark, an acrobatic maneuver called swingovers or one-arm planges.

Here is how she would do them: Leaving her Spanish web, that long, soft rope made of canvas filled with cotton that aerialists use for climbing aloft, Miss Leitzel would place her right hand and wrist in a rope loop attached to a swivel and ring hanging from the rigging, and the circus band percussionist would begin his drum rolls. As the drums rolled, she would throw her small body up and over her right shoulder again and again, to make broad circles, as if she were a human airplane propeller. The crowd would count them in unison, and their chanting in the darkened tent had the feeling of a magic incantation. The chanting crowd, we can see now, was a vital part of her act. In a sense, the crowd cast a spell on itself: "One . . . two . . . three . . ." up to "one hundred forty-eight . . . one hundred forty-nine . . . one hundred fifty . . ." That was in the early days; later she cut the number down to sixty a show. The most she ever did was 249.

At least one woman acrobat has done more one-armed swings than Lillian Leitzel: Janet May Klemke, who did 305 with the Medina Shrine Circus in Chicago, in 1938. I have seen her; she made her planges look like the punishing effort they were. Those who saw Leitzel's rope burns and scars could scarcely believe they came from her stunning performance.

Once, she got a bad infection, probably from something the rope ground into her flesh after it tore it. Charlie Ringling brought in a specialist, who warned that if the infection got worse, the arm might have to be amputated. He asked her if she could possibly do her planges with her left arm. Of course, she replied. Suddenly, the whole situation seemed to the doctor absurd. "Then in heaven's name why don't you give your right arm a rest?" he demanded.

"My right arm is already ruined," she answered, "but my left arm is pretty, and I'm a woman."

Lillian Leitzel was born in Breslau, Germany, in 1882. She hated her harsh father, a Hungarian army officer who became a theatrical impresario; her aerialist mother came from a family that had been circus performers for several generations. She was a niece of Adolph Pelikan, who clowned with the Ringling show under the name Bluch Landolf, and popularized the gag in which a workman walks briskly with a long plank on his head, does an about-face, then goes just as briskly in the opposite direction without disturbing the plank.

Little Leitzel disturbed everything. She was the perfect star for the roaring twenties. When the Ringlings came to her, she was already a star of the Palace and other vaudeville theaters, billed as "Lillian Leitzel, the World's Foremost and Most Daring Aerial Star." She had been married, but claimed she could never remember the man's name. To join the Ringling show for the 1919 season, she demanded $250 a week (soon doubled), a private car, and a private dressing tent. Ringling management had always rejected similar accommodation requests by explaining that space didn't permit such coddling. But this wasn't a request—it was a demand—and The Greatest Show on Earth had to have Leitzel. The result was better accommodations the next season for May Wirth, Bird Millman, and the Silbons, and the beginning of improved living conditions for all circus performers aboard an ever-lengthening train (but very few private dressing tents).

Leitzel was always willful, and she usually got her way. In 1920, having divorced the man she called "what's-his-name," she married Clyde Ingalls, the sideshow manager who also made the ring announcements. The marriage was troubled from the start. Leitzel liked to help the Ringlings engender goodwill for the circus by entertaining the rich and powerful in her tent. Ingalls was jealous. Then a Chicago sportsman returned the favor by throwing a party for Leitzel at the Stevens (later the Conrad Hilton) Hotel. There was a display featuring a mermaid swimming in vintage champagne, and a gold-plated statue of Leitzel as the centerpiece. The host passed out fifty-dollar bills to the guests; Leitzel herself was given a diamond tiara that one guest observed was worth only slightly less than the hotel. Ingalls's jealousy passed the point of no return. He and Leitzel were divorced.

Leitzel couldn't change her life-style. She loved to fill her private dressing tent with admirers and children. Railroad magnates, oil men, senators—once they had watched her under the Big Top, watched her slip off and kick aside her gold mules, watched her tiny figure in its sequined brassiere, her midriff bare, her trunks brief, her short skirt sheer—they longed to be invited to her private dressing tent. Henry Ford was admitted in Detroit, but he and his bouquet were kept waiting. The children got in easily: she remembered the birthdays of all the circus children, and loved to give them parties with ice cream and cake and lots of presents. The pop psychologists of the day said that she was trying to make up for a childhood that was all work and no play under the lash of a disagreeable father.

This was the Leitzel with whom Alfredo Codona fell in love.

A Chicago reporter gushed: "The marriage of these two comets in the galaxy of circus stardom would brighten heaven. And it will—it must—take place. It is preordained."

Preordained or not, it did take place, in July 1927. Certainly preordained were the passionate quarrels that alternated with equally passionate reconciliations. As a Latin male, Codona expected his wife to have eyes only for him. Fred Bradna, whose wife, Ella, was Miss Leitzel's attendant at the wedding, felt that La Leitzel, try as she might, "could not abandon the adulation of the masculine world."

Even Codona's act was not watched with the awe that greeted Leitzel. The Ringling brothers helped, of course. When Leitzel performed, they had all other circus activities stopped—not only acts in other rings, but even the candy butchers hawking their wares. (Many years later, Philippe Petit, the wire walker who walked between the twin towers of the World Trade Center to no sound but the wind, described how disconcerting it was to walk the wire to the sound of "Coca-Cola—ice-cold Coke!" But Ringling would not suspend all other activities for him.)

Underneath her, wearing the coat and trousers of a property man, would be the second greatest star of the circus world. Before her act, Alfredo had seen to it that her wrists were properly taped; now he was there in case something went wrong, to break her fall. He knew that she had been married twice before; that made no difference. What he wanted was for her to give him the same complete attention he was giving her *now*.

Sick with jealous love for Leitzel, Codona tried to make her jealous by having an affair with a sexy Australian bareback rider named Vera Bruce. According to Bradna, "Miss Bruce derived satisfaction from thrusting the knife into a woman to whom she must always defer professionally." As Bradna saw it, Vera Bruce would regard stealing Leitzel's husband as the kind of "triumph" she could never have in the circus ring over "The Queen of the Circus."

It was the wrong move on the ground for the man fabled for his right moves in the air. Previously, Leitzel and Codona had gone abroad together for winter bookings between Ringling seasons. After the 1930 season, they went separately. In his company, Codona included Vera Bruce, saying he was teaching her to be an aerialist.

And so we come to Friday the thirteenth of February, 1931. At the beginning of her February engagement at the Valencia Music Hall in Copenhagen, Leitzel had a nightmare that made her cry out and sit bolt upright in bed.

Weeping, she told her maid about it: she had seen herself giving a performance, being hoisted toward the top of the tent; then she saw her rope unraveling, strand by strand. Alfredo was standing beneath her, but she couldn't make her voice reach him. The last strand broke, and she woke up.

Now she was giving a real performance, and her prop boy, Frank McClosky, was standing beneath her. She was doing her famous planges, and a drummer was beating out the rolls that always accompanied them. It was just after midnight, and forty-three years later, McClosky, now president of the Clyde Beatty–Cole Bros. Circus, told me what happened next as if that moment had never completely ended for him.

"I was reaching for a rope for her when she fell. If I had seen her falling I could have caught her."

The brass swivel ring—heated and cooled, heated and cooled, by the constant friction as she turned—had crystallized and snapped like sugar candy. The fall was twenty feet. She landed on her head and shoulders but was not knocked out. She wanted to get up and go on with her act.

"I'm not really hurt," she told McClosky.

But he overruled the willful Leitzel and ordered her taken to the hospital.

Codona was in Berlin, performing at the Winter Garden. He quit his engagement and rushed to her side. On Saturday, she convinced him that she was not seriously injured and talked him into going back and finishing his commitment. The following morning, February 15, she died suddenly, of concussion and complications.

Two days later, at Madison Square Garden, the opening of a hockey match was delayed and the house lights were dimmed, as they had always been dimmed for the entrance of Lillian Leitzel. Someone skated out onto the ice and said, "To the memory of Lillian Leitzel—God rest her soul."

The crowd sang "Auld Lang Syne," and a drummer beat out the same kind of rolls that had accompanied her performance.

———

But the twenties were a lot more than Leitzel and Codona. The circus season of 1926, for instance, was the year the new Madison Square Garden opened in New York. Charlie Ringling negotiated a new contract for The Greatest Show on Earth's annual six-week stand at the new sports palace, a contract that promised an annual profit of about $150,000.

The show was well worth it. The Big One included half a dozen circus immortals that year: the Queen, Lillian Leitzel, and her consort-to-be, Alfredo Codona; May Wirth, the greatest of all equestriennes; Emil Pallenberg with his bears; Buck Baker, the producing clown (every show has a clown who supervises props and staff), who introduced his trick taxicab that followed him about like a dog but reared on its hind wheels like a horse; Winnie Colleano, who swung from the bar of a high trapeze and caught herself by the heels, then turned a somersault into the safety net (a trick done on the Ringling Show in the 1970s by Elvin Bale); and Winnie's sensational brother, Con Colleano, "Toreador of the Tight Wire," "The Wizard of the Silver Thread."

In the *Guinness Book of World Records*, only one circus record still stands from the twenties: the low wire (seven feet) record for the first feet-to-feet forward somersault. The record will stand until the unlikely day someone does a double forward. It was set by Con Colleano at the Empire Theatre in Johannesburg, South Africa, in 1923, but he performed it numerous times with Ringling Bros. and Barnum & Bailey Circus.

Colleano decided early on that he was going to become a star, and simply picked out a feat that no one had ever done before. The backward somersault was natural, and often done: the shoulder and back muscles flex naturally; the arms swing to give additional momentum; the acrobat can see the wire before he alights and make split-second adjustments in his landing position. The forward somersault, however, reverses these natural muscular reflexes. It throws the head down at the start of the turn, generating rapid gravitational pull. The arms are in the way and must be wrapped against the chest. Worst of all, you can't see the wire as you come out of your somersault: your feet are hiding it from you. The discouraging word about this trick is "your head may be slashed from your body by the taut wire."

But Con, born Cornelius Sullivan of Irish and Spanish ancestry, had a trick up his sleeve: the training in coordination he received from his grandfather, also a circus performer. When he was a boy, his grandfather used to seat him at a table on which stood a bowl of sugar. Con's job was to catch all the flies that attempted to light on the sugar, with both his right and his left hand.

When the flies were all caught, his grandfather gave him a jump rope and told him to jump in and out of a row of eggs without breaking any.

This training gave him the eye, foot, and body coordination, and the muscular precision, that eventually made him the star he wanted to be. "The flies helped the most," he said. "They really gave me the 'eye' for the forward somersault."

The first night he tried the forward somersault before a paying audience, he failed in his first three attempts, then struck the wire with his chest on the fourth. Blood spurted and the curtain was dropped, but Colleano begged the stage manager to let him try again. Since the audience still hadn't stopped applauding his courage, the stage manager complied. On his fifth attempt, his feet found the wire, and Con Colleano found his niche in the hall of circus immortals.

His act is still talked about. Colleano warmed up his audience and his own body for his acrobatics by dancing on the tightwire while the band played Ravel's "Bolero." Anyone who has ever tried gymnastic and balancing feats on a thin steel strand knows how difficult it is even when you use a pole or umbrella. Colleano was the first man not to use a stabilizing prop of any kind. (Bird Millman was the first person.)

Next, to introduce his tumbling on the wire, he threw a backward somersault—and removed his trousers in the air as he turned, alighting on the wire in his tights.

Soon he was ready to try the feet-to-feet forward somersault. He did not always accomplish this trick, but even when he missed it, the audience did not always know. Colleano didn't like to be applauded for courage in failure, as in South Africa; so in falling, he would usually seize the wire, turn a giant swing completely over it, and light on his feet. Many thought they had seen another trick; some thought they had seen the trick that was announced. With Colleano, the feet were quicker than the eye.

But when he accomplished the feet-to-feet forward somersault, there was a look of triumph that Fred Bradna could never forget. "Yet, aside from himself and perhaps a dozen observers," wrote Bradna, "none of the crowd realized what he had done, how much he had triumphed over gravity, muscles, fear and the laws of physics to do something that was a little beyond him."

It was the essence of the aspiration that the circus embodies.

"Mr. Charlie," who had always played Santa Claus at the Ringling family Christmas celebrations ("probably because he was the most fun," said his niece, Alice), died in 1926 at the age of sixty-two. "I'm the last one on the lot," said John Ringling, looking down at his brother's body. As last of the Ringling brothers, Mr. John was also absolute monarch of The Greatest Show on Earth. True, Charles's widow, Edith, had inherited a third share of the circus from her husband, and Richard, son of Alf T., also owned a third; but, as Henry Ringling North observed, "the Ringlings traditionally paid no attention to women in business," and Mr. John felt that he could control his nephew.

Some of the fun went out of the Big One when John ran it alone. He quickly abolished two major things about the show that he didn't like: "jungle acts" with lions, tigers, and other dangerous animals, and long clown solos.

For years, John and Charlie Ringling had clashed over the proper role of circus clowns. Mr. Charlie felt that the clowns should be permitted to develop their art in their own way. Mr. John maintained that the long buildups solo clowns required to establish rapport with the audience slowed the production, thereby hurting the circus as a whole.

The passing of the era of the long clown solo was a factor in the suicides of two of the circus's greatest clowns, Marceline and Slivers Oakley.

Before World War I, the great French clown Marceline was the rage of London. No less a connoisseur than Charlie Chaplin has lauded Marceline's "droll and charming comedy." Dressed in opera hat and rather sloppy evening clothes, Marceline would enter carrying a fishing rod, sit on a camp stool, open a large jewel case, bait his hook with a diamond necklace, then cast it into the water. Suddenly, he would

THE GREATEST. *Alfredo Codona (born in 1893, Hermosillo, Mexico; died in 1937, Long Beach, California), the aerialist considered the greatest trapeze artist in circus history and the first to achieve a consistent triple back somersault off the flying trapeze, was the son of circus acrobats and the brother of the tightrope walker Victoria Codona, one of the most beautiful women ever to perform with a circus (and the beauty pictured on the jacket of this book). Codona joined Ringling Bros. Circus in 1917. He became famous not only for the triple, but for the exceptional grace with which he performed all his tricks in the air. On the ground, his life was neither smooth nor balanced. This photograph was given by Victoria to his flying heir, Tito Gaona, who made me a copy. (John Culhane Collection)*

TWO SIDES OF A TRAGIC TRIANGLE. *Wavy-haired, handsome Alfredo Codona stands on a trapeze, giving flying lessons to two women. On the left is Vera Bruce. His grief over his wife Lillian Leitzel's accidental death unbalanced Codona, propelling him into marriage with Bruce; then into the accident that ended his career; then, on July 1, 1937, into the murder of Bruce and his own suicide. On the right is Antoinette Concello, soon to be mistress of an occasional, graceful triple somersault. Miss Concello gave a copy of this picture to Tito Gaona, Codona's heir as master of the triple. (John Culhane Collection)*

CLASSIC CLOWNING. *"Fifty years ago an audience would scream with laughter when it saw a clown chased up the center pole by a pig," wrote Ringling press agent Dexter W. Fellows in 1936, "but the guffaws are just as loud today when one of our clowns is pursued by a papier-mâché skeleton fastened to the back of his trousers." Here is that gag as practiced on the Sparks Circus in 1923. A skeleton was still chasing a clown in the 1973 edition of Ringling Bros. and Barnum & Bailey Circus. In all that time, there is no record of a skeleton ever catching a clown, but that Ringling show included a gag that might be called "The Skeleton's Revenge." A clown playing Hamlet and carrying Yorick's skull began the speech, "Alas, poor Yorick . . . ," when the skull reduced his recitation to a gargle by spitting water in Hamlet's face. There was also a hard-hat clown balancing a steel girder on his head. And two carpenter clowns who sawed a tall clown in half—and got two midgets. And there was a musician clown with a clarinet through his head (it went in his mouth and came out of his hair). Clown gags are sprinkled throughout a circus to make sure people remember that humanity's great feats of skill and daring go hand in hand (or foot in mouth) with a great propensity for screwing up. Thus, whenever wild animal trainer Wolfgang Holzmair carried a live lion on his shoulders and smiled proudly, a clown carried a stuffed lion on his shoulders—and stuck out his tongue. (Ringling Museum)*

SWAN BANDWAGON. "To tell the truth," wrote Walt Disney of his hometown, "more things of importance happened to me in Marceline {Missouri} than have happened since—or are likely to in the future. Things, I mean, like experiencing my first country life, seeing my first circus parade, attending my first school, seeing my first motion picture!" His love for circus parades led him to save a number of old circus wagons from destruction, including the one shown here, built in Baraboo, Wisconsin, by the Moeller Bros. Wagon Works. The Moellers were cousins of the Ring-lings. (Circus World Museum, Baraboo, Wisconsin)

ALFREDO CODONA FLIES! If Lillian Leitzel, Queen of the Rings, heard the circus band play a certain chord while she was being interviewed, she would lift a finger and say, "Listen! That's Alfredo's cue. You must go and see him work. He's wonderful." If the journalist said he had already seen the act, Leitzel would say, "You can never see too much of Codona"—and go herself to watch. "Every muscle in his body seemed to sing in harmony as he flew from trapeze to trapeze," Ringling-Barnum publicist Dexter Fellows recalled long after. "Catchers with whom he worked told me he landed as lightly as a swallow." Before he was caught by his brother, Lalo, seen here, or lightly grasped the bar, he always had time for little balletic movements, or for pantomiming a diver, as here. This photograph was given by Codona's sister Victoria to Tito Gaona, Codona's fellow Mexican and heir as master of the triple. (John Culhane Collection)

L'OS CODONA

Long Beach. Calif. Dec th. 193

Direction Wintergarten Theatre.
Dorotheen Str 16.
B E R L I N. Germany.

Dear Friends:--
It is with great regret that I write you now
to notify you that I will not be able to fullfill my Contract this
coming month of Feb. 1934.
You know of my injury which occured the 28th,of April last,
while doing the Triple Somersault, I cought the Trick but unfortunaly
with such a terrific jerk that my Right Shoulder was dislocated and
Two of the Main Muzzles of my Shoulder were snaped.
At the time I went to see several of the best Doctors in New York
and they all seem to agree that time would heal my Injury and that I
would be able to work again after six months time. But It is not so
I did not work for Six months and came out here to Reharse thinking
that I would be all right and able to go to Berlin. But Tho I felt
stronger and started to practiced easily as soon as I tried to do
some of my tricks my Arm was injured again and it is very weak now.
I have gone to see most of the Doctor here and they may operate
on my Shoulder,and saw up the torn muzzled, this may help,and again
it may not. it all depends on how the Muzzles were torn.
Therefor my Dear Friends I am obliged to stay home, I assure
you that it breaks my heart to think that I may not play ever again
in the Dear Old Wintergarten, that I had learned to Love,where its
Public was so Dear to me,and where I was shown so many many Favors
by its Wonderful Directors.
I have tried my best to make it,I have fought hard, but It can
not be this coming year. I hope and pray that I will be able to make
it next year.
All the Luck in the world to The Wintergarten, my love to the
Berliner Public, and my sincere best wishes, and thanks for past
favors to the Directors and all my Friends of The Wintergarten.

Home Add.   Your Friend
1825 Cherry Ave.
Long Beach. Calif.U.S.A.   Alfredo Codona

END OF THE JAZZ AGE. "He had come a long way to this blue lawn," wrote F. Scott
Fitzgerald of Gatsby, "and his dream must have seemed so close that he could hardly fail
to grasp it. He did not know that it was already behind him." Alfredo Codona was the
Great Gatsby of the circus world, an obscure Mexican aerialist who became an international
superstar, then won the heart of the Queen of the Rings; he did not know, when he wrote
the letter shown here, that he would never fly again—that all that was left was defeat
and murder and suicide. Tito Gaona would later seek inspiration for his own triples by
visiting the monument that Codona had erected after Leitzel's death. Twelve feet high, it
shows Codona and Leitzel, in their aerialist's costumes, embracing. (John Culhane Collection)

get a bite and throw himself into hauling it in. His pantomime of a fisherman struggling with a big catch was priceless. That catch, however, would turn out to be a small poodle, which proceeded to mimic everything Marceline did. If Marceline sat down, the poodle sat down. If Marceline stood on his head, so did the poodle.

When Chaplin was a child, he had actually done a small comedy bit with Marceline in a Christmas pantomime at the London Hippodrome. Charlie played a cat and wore a cat mask frozen into a look of surprise. Backing away from a dog, Marceline would fall backward over Charlie as he lapped milk from a saucer. Charlie would do a "take," turning his surprised cat face to the audience.

Marceline came to America, where he was also a success with a circus that played the New York Hippodrome. Then, says Chaplin, "In 1918 or thereabouts, Ringling Brothers' three-ring circus came to Los Angeles, and Marceline was with them. I expected that he would be featured, but I was shocked to find him just one of many clowns that ran around the enormous ring—a great artist lost in the vulgar extravagance of a three-ring circus."

Chaplin, by then a world-famous star, went back to Marceline's dressing room and reminded the clown that he had been the cat Marceline used to trip over. "But he reacted apathetically," said Chaplin. "Even under his clown make-up he looked sullen and seemed in a melancholy torpor."

About a year after that, said Chaplin, Marceline committed suicide in New York. "A small paragraph in the papers stated that an occupant living in the same house had heard a shot and had found Marceline lying on the floor with a pistol in his hand and a record still turning, playing 'Moonlight and Roses.'"

After Charles Ringling died, the principal use of clowns in The Greatest Show on Earth was in clown production numbers, big, broad, spectacular turns that could easily be seen and understood from the last row of the giant tents. The intimacy that a clown could establish with less than 1,000 spectators in a one-ring show was impossible when there was room for as many as 16,000 spectators—with many sitting several hundred feet from center ring. As usual, clown acts were also used to focus attention on the center ring for five minutes while setups for other acts were being changed. But circus rigging was getting better and better. The overhead flying frame used in the three-ring circuses now facilitated a smooth-flowing production and cut out empty spots where clowns could shine.

The elimination of the clown solos had a terrible effect on the great solo clowns. According to Dexter Fellows, Slivers Oakley had been as well known at the turn of the century as Chaplin was in the twenties, and he had the huge arena to himself while he played his one-man game of baseball. Then he left the circus. He took his one-man baseball act to London, "but since it wasn't cricket," Fellows cracked, "few appreciated him." He went into vaudeville but was not happy there. So he tried to come back to the circus. "He dropped into Otto Ringling's office at winter quarters in Bridgeport and asked for his old job." Mr. Otto offered him a place in the "walk-around" (that part of the show in which the clowns charge into the arena en masse and each repeats a certain sight gag as he walks around the hippodrome track). The proposed salary was that of a routine clown. Fellows insists that Otto was not trying to drive a hard bargain; since Oakley was not to be featured, he didn't merit more than any other clown.

"Friends of mine who saw Slivers come out of Mr. Otto's office said that he acted as if he were drunk or drugged," said Fellows. "He barged around the yard muttering: 'Fifty dollars! For Slivers Oakley, fifty dollars a week! Why, he doesn't know who I am.'"

Not long afterward people trying to rescue the great Slivers Oakley broke down the door to his room in New York and turned off the gas, but they were too late.

———

As the three-ring circus began to replace the one-ring show in America, the talking clown and the singing clown and the stars who demanded long solos were gradually phased out. In fact, as early as 1885, all the clowning with Barnum & Bailey was silent, and there was at one time a rule that any clown who spoke would automatically be fired. As the new style of broad pantomime and fast-moving slapstick spread to other circuses, clowns could no longer perform in the old styles of Durang, Pentland, Conklin, or Rice. Indeed, to Uncle Bob Sherwood, a Barnum clown who performed into the Ringling era, and did it their way, "the art of clowning gradually went out with the generation that followed Dan Rice." It wasn't only that they had to be silent; Marceline was a superb mime. But circus clowns were seldom given the time and the showcasing to develop a routine in the old style.

Talking and singing clowns hadn't disappeared, of course; they were just disappearing from the circus. There was now a greater outlet for the talking and singing clown than Dan Rice ever dreamed of. By 1924, there were 2.5 million radios in America. (By 1960, only 8.5 percent of the population would still lack radios.) A talking clown exchange like the following found a new medium.

RICE: Master, do you know that I can prove that an Irishman's mud cabin is better than heaven?

RINGMASTER: No, sir, you cannot prove it.

RICE: Now listen, ain't a mud cabin better than nothing?

RINGMASTER: Certainly, it is better than nothing.

RICE: And nothing is better than heaven; ergo, the Irishman's mud cabin is better than heaven.

Just compare that with the following exchange from a Joe Penner radio show:

PENNER: What's the best way to raise corned beef and cabbage.

MAN: I don't know, Joe.

PENNER: With a knife and fork!

MAN: Now listen, Joe—

PENNER: What kind of hen lays the longest? A dead one! *Yuk, yuk, yuk!*

You didn't need a marvelous visual medium like the circus for such exchanges; and the best radio couldn't give you Lou Jacobs trying and failing, again and again, to hang his oversized coat on an imaginary coat hook.

The circus clown survived by adapting to the size and pace of the three-ring shows—and this adaptation resulted in the enrichment of two other old clowning traditions: comedy acrobatics and pantomime. It was these traditions that would produce three of the greatest clowns of the three-ring circus. Otto Griebling, Emmett Kelly, and Lou Jacobs are all great mimes and acrobats. Griebling began as a bareback rider; Kelly as a trapeze artist; and Jacobs, who joined Ringling Bros. and Barnum & Bailey Circus as an acrobat in 1925, began his show business career as a contortionist. (It was the reverse of the situation for clowns in films: clowns who were superb mimes and acrobats, like Langdon and Keaton, gave way when sound came in to talking clowns and singing clowns, like W. C. Fields [a juggler who seldom juggled when the movies began to talk] and Groucho Marx [whose song, "Lydia the Tattooed Lady," would have been a sensation in a one-ring circus]).

Harry Ritley's wordless "table rock" was perfect in a big tent. Ritley built a tower by piling five tables on top of one another, each table smaller than the one below it. He climbed to the top of the tower to read his morning paper, then caused the tower to sway precariously back and forth, traveling a bit farther from the vertical each time. Eventually, he pressed his luck too far and toppled to the ring with a loud crash.

This is classic clowning: the fool who goes too far. Henry Miller has said of the clown that it is "his special privilege to reenact the errors, the follies, the stupidities, all the misunderstandings which plague human kind." No wonder we laugh with recognition at the clown who insists on opening the door marked DANGER!, who walks head-on into a mirror instead of going around it, and who peers into the business end of a loaded rifle. Yet the clown does not die. And he even gets his paper read.

———————

In 1927, John Ringling moved the winter quarters of Ringling Bros. and Barnum & Bailey Circus from Bridgeport, Connecticut, where P. T. Barnum had established the winter quarters of Barnum and Bailey in the 1880s, to Sarasota, Florida. Human beings could live more comfortably and cheaply there, but the main reason was the great cost of heating the block-long brick animal barns in Bridgeport: only the most delicate animals would need artificial heat in Florida.

There were always a lot of animals in a Ringling Bros. circus. The impulse to educate its audiences in natural history (and to be well paid for it, of course) was strong in the Ringling brothers. In the early 1900s, they had a circus

poster picturing all the different kinds of animals in their menagerie, and advertised their circus as "the only complete & perfect exposition of natural history on this continent." People in areas that didn't have zoos valued this aspect of the circus.

There was a walrus in that old poster but no sea elephant. Sea elephants (or elephant seals) are the largest pinnipeds, that suborder of carnivores whose limbs are adapted to an aquatic life. They are gregarious animals, named for their size and for the male's inflatable, trunklike snout.

On a trip to Europe, John Ringling had checked Hagenbeck's Zoo in Hamburg and found two of these great creatures for sale. To eliminate the possibility that a rival circus would acquire one and compete with Ringling, Mr. John bought both. He kept one as a backup at winter quarters in Sarasota. The other—a huge, blubbery creature named Goliath—made his debut in the 1928 season and immediately captured the imagination of the public.

Goliath's tank occupied half a railroad car. "Transporting his enormous bulk was more bother than getting one section of the show train under way," wrote Dexter Fellows. Each morning his attendants had to coax him to wiggle his great body from the railroad car to the flatbed wagon that would drive him to the show grounds. There he had to be induced to slither into a portable canvas tank in the rear of the Big Top, to wait for show time.

Goliath's "performance" consisted of riding around the hippodrome track on that flatbed wagon. After that, he was put back in his canvas tank until time for his "performance" at the night show. Then he was taken back to his tank on the railroad car. "During all these transfers," said Fellows, "Goliath moved under his own power, which was the equivalent of a steamroller operating on one cylinder." If he wouldn't move, the attendants dangled fish in front of his nose, then slowly moved the fish in the right direction. They were very patient handlers.

Americans who, as skirts rose above the knee in the twenties, were beginning to pay anxious attention to weight watching, seemed to find relief in admiring Goliath's don't-give-a-damn approach to eating. "Fifty or more fish were just an hors d'oeuvre to him," wrote Fellows, "and by the time he had finished his meal, several hundred pounds of herring, heads, tails, and bones, had passed down his gullet."

After Goliath died, the public demanded another sea elephant—and, of course, Ringling had one. As press agent for the show, Fellows said that he filled more personal requests from newspapermen for photographs of the two Goliaths than of any other circus animal that inhabited the menagerie during his tenure with the Big One.

There is some unfinished business to take up before this chapter on the circus in the twenties is done. The tragic epilogue to the love story of Leitzel and Codona occurred in the thirties, but it is the real ending to the story of the circus in the twenties.

Victoria Codona (center) washes clothes in the circus backyard. (Circus World Museum, Baraboo, Wisconsin)

Lillian Leitzel fell to her death on February 13, 1931. When the next Ringling season began, Codona's bosses began to sense that Alfredo was trying hard to die himself. His tricks now had a recklessness that chilled those who understood the chances he took.

In 1932, he married Vera Bruce. With Leitzel dead, Codona was now the unparalleled star of The Greatest Show on Earth. No matter; he remained depressed and withdrawn, tortured by his memories.

He had erected a twelve-foot marble monument to Lillian Leitzel in Inglewood, California. It shows a man and a woman embracing, and the man has the wings of an angel. It is called *The Spirit of Flight*.

Traveling with the circus now, Codona would often walk alone to the flap of his dressing tent and pull it back to stare at the spot where Leitzel's bright awnings would have been.

Even Codona couldn't do the triple for long in that frame of mind. On April 28, 1933, he dislocated his shoulder while throwing the triple, and tore two muscles beyond healing. He would never fly again.

He left the circus. For a while, he worked in the gas station owned by his sister's husband. There, Vera Bruce left him and went back to being a circus equestrienne. Codona followed her and for a while worked as her hostler. Then he vanished, turning up in various circus jobs over the next four years.

On June 28, 1937, Vera Bruce sued for divorce, charging cruelty and extreme jealousy. He met her and her mother in a lawyer's office in Long Beach, California, to arrange a property settlement. Codona asked attorney James E. Pawson if he could have a moment alone with his wife, and when the lawyer stepped out, Codona lit a cigarette for Vera Bruce.

"Vera," her mother remembered him saying to her daughter, "I guess this is the last thing I can do for you."

That was the only warning she had before he drew a revolver from his pocket. Rapidly, he fired four shots—into her head, her arm, her breast, and her abdomen, mortally wounding her. Then he fired one bullet into his own head.

Codona was buried, at his own request, beside the ashes of Leitzel, beneath *The Spirit of Flight*. Thirty years later, that monument would become an often-visited shrine for another young flier, who became the first since his idol to do the triple consistently.

The Dining Department and Blacksmith Shop of the Ringling Bros. and Barnum & Bailey Circus being transported by rail before World War II. In the 1990s, RBB&B is still moving its two units by rail—forty-two railroad cars with a total weight of about 750,000 tons. (Ringling Museum)

DISPLAY·13

The Great Depression

The 1930s was the decade that saw John Ringling, the last of the Ringling brothers, deposed as the circus king of the world. It was a fate that followed the boom-and-bust rhythm of the times.

"Eccentric, egocentric, and arrogant, able to impose his will on outsiders by the power of his wealth," said his nephew, Henry Ringling North, of willful Uncle John. In the spring of 1929 it was time to negotiate the usual circus contract with Madison Square Garden for the 1930 season. John Ringling set a date for the meeting with the officials of the Garden, then stood them up.

"He was quite accustomed to making engagements with important people and breaking them cavalierly," explained his nephew. After all, in the twenties, John Ringling was one of the richest men in America and a principal stockholder in Madison Square Garden, where the circus was the biggest single money-maker. The directors of the Garden corporation, however, were in no mood to be treated cavalierly. When the meeting finally took place, the other directors gave Mr. John the condition that the circus not play on Fridays, so that the very profitable Friday night prizefights could continue to be held. Unwilling to have his wishes opposed, Ringling announced that the circus would open at the Twenty-second Regiment Armory.

Not to be outmaneuvered by John Ringling, the other directors promptly made a contract with the American Circus Corporation, Ringling's only serious rival, to play the Garden in the spring of 1930. Jerry Mugivan said his cir-

CLYDE RAYMOND BEATTY. In one of the most dangerous acts in circus history, he mixed forty lions and tigers of both sexes in one cage. He also used daring combinations of tigers, lions, leopards, pumas, hyenas, and bears. "Personally, I believe you can teach an animal nothing," Beatty said. "They show you what they can do and then you develop it." From making tigers behave to making a dog sit up for a lick of an ice cream cone, Beatty developed it. (Ringling Museum)

cus would be delighted to close down on Fridays.

John Ringling was enraged. For more than half a century, Barnum & Bailey or Ringling Bros. or the Combined Shows had opened its season in Madison Square Garden. Many, not least John Ringling, considered it a New York tradition.

So Ringling purchased the American Circus Corporation outright in the fall of 1929. The price was $2 million, but he didn't pay much in cash up front. Instead, he gave his personal note for $1.7 million to the financiers, the Prudence Bond and Mortgage Company.

Said John Ringling, "I'm playing the Garden next year."

At the high tide of his power, he wasn't worried about the $1.7-million note: Ringling's Wall Street friends told him that if he would incorporate a new company, they would have no difficulty selling shares on the booming stock market. After all, the American Circus Corporation owned five medium-sized circuses—Sells-Floto, Hagenbeck-Wallace, John Robinson, Sparks, and Al G. Barnes. Their total assets included tents, 150 railroad cars, 2,000 animals (exclusive of the heavy draft or workhorses, the so-called baggage stock), not to mention 4,500 employees.

And then the stock market crashed.

The American dream had always floated on expectations of boundless prosperity, but during the last two weeks of October 1929, those great expectations seemed to be going down a drain on the floor of the New York Stock Exchange. Among the countless dreams that died that month was John Ringling's hope of selling an issue of circus stock.

The circus, dependent on discretionary dollars, felt the pinch quickly. Ringling Bros. and Barnum & Bailey had netted $1 million in 1929. By 1931, business was so bad that The Greatest Show on Earth ended its year on Sep-

tember 14, the earliest closing date in its long history.

John Ringling had lost a lot of money since 1926, when the Florida land boom went bust, but he could still have kept the circus going without great financial strain on himself had it not been for the necessity of paying off that note. As it was, his fortune was still so large that his financial survival was really a matter of closer attention to all his enterprises.

It was the smaller circuses that were hardest hit. Before the end of 1929, Howard King had closed Gentry Bros. Circus. In 1930, the Christy Bros. Circus, which had been traveling on twenty railroad cars before the crash, left its Houston, Texas, winter quarters on April 4, to find bad economic conditions and bad circus business everywhere it played. George Christy cut his show in half and sent ten cars back to Houston. But this left him with only two sleepers and no place for the workingmen to sleep except under the wagons on the flatcars. The show collapsed at Greeley, Colorado, on July 7. Christy borrowed money to pay those who were still with the show a small part of what they were owed plus transportation home, and then his circus, which had begun in 1910 as a tented vaudeville-movie show, went out of business forever.

Floyd King's Cole Bros. Circus lasted until August of 1930. In August of 1931, the Miller Bros. 101 Ranch Wild West Show collapsed in Washington, D.C. Robbins Bros. Circus gave up in September 1931 and was on its way home when the owners handed workingmen one dollar each and told them they could expect no more. Those who protested were thrown off the moving train—a revival of a bad old circus practice called "redlighting," apparently because as you look up from the ground, broken and bleeding, you can see the red light of the caboose disappearing down the track.

Several redlighted workers were seriously

injured and one of them died of his injuries at the Mobile, Alabama, City Hospital on October 17. The owner of the Robbins Bros. Circus was indicted for causing the death, but the case was never brought to trial.

"John Ringling's personal crash," as his nephew Henry called it, came at the end of the 1932 season. That spring Ringling suffered a clot in an artery in his leg. Fearing blood poisoning and amputation, he forgot all about his financial affairs and went for rest and recuperation to the Half Moon Hotel in Coney Island, which, along with the Dreamland Amusement Park there, was owned by Ringling's friend and sometime business associate Samuel W. Gumpertz.

While Ringling was recuperating, he defaulted on an interest payment on his circus note, which had been reduced to $1,017,000. The note was bought from the Prudence Company by two groups of businessmen under the corporate titles of Allied Owners and New York Investors. The man who organized the whole thing was Samuel W. Gumpertz.

In 1931, Richard Ringling, the only son of John's brother Alf T., had died at the age of thirty-five of injuries he received in an auto accident. Richard left the part of the circus he had inherited from his father to his widow, Aubrey Black Ringling, and their daughter, Mable. Edith Conway Ringling, Charles's widow, was already unhappy that John never consulted her about the running of the circus; now Gumpertz, according to Henry, succeeded in convincing Aubrey "that John Ringling had lost his grip and was bringing the show to ruin."

At a meeting of the circus creditors and his kinfolk partners, Mr. John was presented with an ultimatum:

1. The circus would be turned into a stock company, to be chartered in Delaware.

2. The creditor groups would receive 10 percent of the stock as a bonus for their work in forming the corporation. The remainder of the stock would be divided, one-third to each of the partners—Edith, Aubrey, and John Ringling.

3. The note for $1,017,000 would be assumed by the new corporation; but to secure it John Ringling would pledge all of his personal assets, a full, itemized list of which was appended. The banking group would hold them as collateral until the note was paid off.

4. Samuel W. Gumpertz would be in charge as senior vice president and general manager. John would still hold the title of president at a fixed salary but with no authority on or off the lot.

That was one way to try to survive the Depression. Other circus people in difficulties turned to little truck shows, some of which had themselves learned survival at the end of the wagon show days by switching to motor trucks. These included the Mighty Haag Circus, Atterbury Bros., Orton Bros., and a brief revival of the Gentry show. Then there were new shows started by showmen who saw railroad circuses go broke and decided with old-fashioned American optimism to move in on their abandoned routes. These included Barnett Bros., Russell Bros. Circus, Downie Bros., and the Tom Mix Circus.

The Tom Mix Circus was the first circus ever to travel from coast to coast by truck. It grew out of the remnants of the Gentry truck show, but there was really no comparison because Gentry didn't have Tom Mix.

Tom Mix was the favorite cowboy of my father, who first saw him in person in the Sells-Floto show in 1929 and 1930. Emmett Kelly, also on the show, said that that was when Tom

Mix became the first circus performer to get $10,000 a week. Even then, there were those who carped that Mix liked money too much, but out of that money he had to support his troupe of cowboys, cowgirls, and horses. The envious might have groused, but the cowpoke had shown he was big business, and he soon had a circus of his own. In 1937, its sixty-five trucks played a route that took it into some of the nation's largest cities, and my father took me to see him that year in Rockford, Illinois. Afterward he bought me a cowboy suit with real leather chaps—but not, alas, a horse.

Tom Mix certainly had a horse: Tony, the Wonder Horse! To my father, born in 1910, Tom Mix was a cowboy in the movies, the good guy in such "horse operas" or "oaters" as *Riders of the Purple Sage* (1925); to me, he was a cowboy on the radio, and I sent in a boxtop from Shredded Ralston breakfast cereal, receiving in return a deputy sheriff's star that made me one of Tom Mix's Straight Shooters. (I'll bet all of us Straight Shooters can still sing the anthem that ends: "Take a tip from Tommmmm, Go and tell your Mommmmm— Shredded Ralston cain't be beat!") For both my father and me, Tom Mix, not later-arriving Roy Rogers, was the King of the Cowboys, and my father impressed upon me the fact that Mix, unlike Rogers and Gene Autry, had been a *real* cowboy before he was a movie star. Seeing him was seeing in person an important part of our growing up.

In the era of the silent movie, Tom Mix was second only to William S. Hart as the world's favorite western hero; and the press always pointed out that he was only "carrying his real life into his reel life." Born in 1880, he had decided to become a cowboy at the age of ten when he saw Buffalo Bill's Wild West at a Pennsylvania fairgrounds. He learned to ride and practiced stunt riding and roping. When the Spanish-American War broke out, he en-

listed. A distant relative named Paul Mix wrote a book, *The Life and Legend of Tom Mix*, which says that Tom never saw action in Cuba, or later in the Mexican Revolution, as he claimed, and questions whether he was ever, as he also claimed, a deputy U.S. marshal. It has been established, however, that Tom Mix worked as a full-time cowboy on the 101 Ranch, and as a deputy sheriff and night marshal in Dewey, Oklahoma.

Whether or not he had ever been a real-life hero, Tom Mix was certainly a boy's idea of what a hero looked like. "To explain Tom Mix you have to go back to Buffalo Bill," the early film director Allan Dwan told Kevin Brownlow for his silent film history, *The War, the West, and the Wilderness*. "He set up the picture for the world. He said, 'That's the West'—tight white pants, a sharp coat, guns all over the place, and underneath, fancy white embroidered materials, with diamonds down the side of his pants." Dwan should have added mention of the tallest, whitest hat a "good cowboy" ever wore.

Working cowboys wear practical clothes, but Mix often got the jobs that required fancy get-ups. At the annual St. Louis Fair in 1899 (later confused with the St. Louis World's Fair of 1904), where he first met his friend Will Rogers, Rogers was a rodeo clown for Colonel Zack Mulhall's Wild West Show, while Mix was the resplendent drum major of the Oklahoma Cavalry Band. In 1905, when a Cowboy Brigade was formed to help celebrate the election of President Theodore Roosevelt, Mix went to the inauguration in Washington as a brigade member, in fancy cowboy duds.

Then, in 1909, the Selig Polyscope Company shot a documentary, *Ranch Life in the Great Southwest*, near Dewey, Oklahoma, and Mix was hired to handle stock and act as safety man. With his flair, he ended up being featured in the picture as a bronco buster. Soon he was the star of the early Selig westerns, and he was always careful to cultivate the image of the western hero, making the white hat his sign. When he went to New York he traveled on a handsome private railroad car, with a private boxcar for Tony. In New York, he rode Tony down Broadway, stopping traffic and inspiring those who looked down on them from skyscrapers to shower horse and rider spontaneously with paper from torn-up telephone books.

Mix made a fortune—but spent it fast, too. He knew that he was one of the last of a dying breed, and that there was always more money to be made in representing the American cowboy the way those of us who never saw them in action wanted to think of them. "There wasn't much real West left when I knew you back on the 101 Ranch," he told Herbert Cruikshank of *Photoplay* in 1928. "There ain't none at all now."

His fans thought they found it in Tom Mix. They were overjoyed when, in 1934, he bought an interest in the Sam B. Dill Circus & Tom Mix Wild West and went on tour. By the end of the season, he owned the show and had renamed it the Tom Mix Circus. It had a cast of 150, and those who were too young to see Buffalo Bill felt that they hadn't missed the Old West after all. In his movies, Mix had always scorned doubles and done his own stunts, and to see the way he rode and roped under canvas made small boys feel as if they were present at the last roundup.

For a time, the Tom Mix Circus did good business. But it failed in 1938, a bad year for most circuses. In 1940, Mix went back to his old studio, now known as 20th Century-Fox, looking for a job. He told R. Lee "Lefty" Hough, Fox's production manager, that he had lost a million dollars in the circus and there was no money left. John Ford, his old friend and former director, who was then shooting *The Grapes of Wrath*, took Mix to lunch, but neither Ford nor anyone else at the studio where Mix had once been top gun had any work for him. The cowboy was sixty years old.

Later that year, Tom Mix sped past a detour sign near Florence, Arizona, and crashed at a washed-out bridge. He was dead when rescuers dragged him clear of the wreck, but at first they couldn't find any wounds. Then it was determined that he had been struck in the back of the neck by a metal suitcase he was carrying in the car. It was filled with thousands of dollars in cash and checks. According to Brownlow, "Hollywood legend filled the suitcase with gold—twenty-dollar gold pieces—and fashioning a moral drama from this sad accident, saw Mix's life ended by the very element that, as far as he was concerned, gave it meaning."

But his fans knew nothing of that. We did know that, before his movie and circus career, he had been a real cowboy; and for years after his death, rushing home from school to listen to the largely fictional adventures of Tom Mix on the radio, I would remember that once I had seen him plain (and his huge Wonder Horse, Tony, even plainer). It was something the circus could do that movies couldn't—bring you the real thing.

———

But circus thrills usually had to take a backseat to survival in those years. Before the end of 1932, about one in every four workers—12 million able-bodied Americans—were unemployed. Many who had jobs were only working part-time. If people couldn't afford to pay their rent, they could hardly afford to go to the circus.

Those who did put aside the quarters that the circus cost in 1932 saw that the old institution was providing, once again, a great performer who was representative of his age.

His name was Clyde Raymond Beatty and he was a wild animal trainer. During the Depression, he suddenly burst on the American scene as a symbol of winning out against great odds.

"The boy from Bainbridge," as he was known, was born in that southern Ohio town on June 10, 1903. He became the master of what circus historian Robert L. Parkinson has called the "American style" of jungle act, just as Gunther Gebel-Williams, born in Germany a generation later, is the master of the European style. "In the American style," says Parkinson, "the trainer, with his gun blazing and whip cracking, is pitted against roaring animals, apparently on the attack, with the final outcome seemingly in doubt. By an apparent hair's breadth margin, the disciplined routine imposed by the trainer triumphs over jungle fury. . . . In the European style, the trainer endeavours to prove his mastery and skill by presenting his jungle charges in the role of obedient, even playful, pets. The wild character of the animals, however, is revealed just often enough to remind the spectator that what he sees is indeed the result of masterful training."

The image of a human being demonstrating his courage and mastery over ferocious animals first worked its magic on Beatty when he was only nine. On the side of a barn, a circus bill-poster emblazoned a colorful lithograph announcing the arrival of Sun Brothers' World's Progressive Shows in nearby Chillicothe on May 15, 1912.

On that poster, Beatty first saw the image he wanted for himself—a picture of a wild animal trainer, surrounded but not vanquished by killers from the jungle.

When Clyde was eighteen, the Howes' Great London and Van Amburgh Trained Wild Animal Shows came to Chillicothe. On show day he rode a mule from his home to the show grounds and "joined out" as a cage boy in the menagerie.

The job of cage boy, cleaning out the dens of tigers and lions, is hard work but vitally important to the safety of the trainer. If the dens aren't cleaned out twice a day, the cats get headaches from the high percentage of ammonia in their urine. A tiger with a headache is a tiger with whom a trainer doesn't want to be in a cage.

Young Beatty finished the season with the Howes show, and the following year, when the Howes equipment was being used by the Gollmar Bros. Circus, Beatty went to work on the Gollmar show. There, during the 1922 season, he saw a polar bear act as his chance to get into the steel arena. Before the season was over, he was helping Dorothy Asal with the act and demonstrating promise as a trainer. A year later, when Gollmar Bros. became the John Robinson Circus, its owners, the American Circus Corporation, brought over an act to enlarge the show, fourteen polar bears from the Hagenbeck show. They put the former cage boy in charge of the bears.

On the Robinson show, Beatty found his mentor: a wild animal trainer named Peter Taylor who spiced his cat act with showmanship. Beatty studied Taylor's act and later credited the older man with teaching him style—the essence of Beatty's success.

In the 1923 John Robinson route book, Clyde Beatty was finally listed as a performer. He was twenty years old.

Two years later, Beatty moved to the Hagenbeck-Wallace Circus—the first of ten straight years when he was featured in its center ring. He worked the polar bears and also took over the mixed animal act of lions, leopards, pumas, hyenas, and a black panther that John "Chubby" Guilfoyle had worked on the Robinson show in 1924. Before long he would be introduced as "America's youngest and most fearless wild animal trainer."

"All successful trainers know," Beatty would write, "that aside from a basic knowledge of animals, the two greatest factors in securing results in our little-understood profession are the kindly approach and a capacity for taking pains, plus a reasonably cheerful disposition, which helps absorb the inevitable disappointments one suffers in teaching certain types of animals that are very slow, deliberate learners."

But the public didn't see a kindly approach. I was part of that public, and I remember what we saw: a quick, authoritative, black-haired young man who carried both a pistol and a chair in his left hand and cracked a whip with his right; he was in the midst of creatures who would kill him if they could, but was always too quick for them, too smart for them; he was always in control. At three, I said to my father about Clyde Beatty: "Why is he so *mad* at them?"

Many assumed that this fierce-looking man must employ "cruel practices" in training his lions and tigers. Some individuals, and the Society for the Prevention of Cruelty to Animals, opposed Clyde Beatty's performances.

Raymond L. Ditmars, former curator of mammals and reptiles of the New York Zoological Society, came to his defense. Beatty did not declaw his animals; declawing changes an animal's personality, usually in ways that make him more dangerous for a trainer. Neither did Beatty, as some critics had whispered, use sharply pointed steel rods or red-hot irons in training his cats. "Only a trainer anxious to get himself killed would attempt such cruelties," said Beatty. "There are pleasanter ways of committing suicide." But Beatty would have to answer such complaints until 1937.

In 1928, Beatty set the record for a mixed animal act: twenty-eight lions and tigers in one cage. In 1929, now billed as "Captain Clyde Beatty," he broke his own record: now there were thirty animals at once in the cage with him, the world's greatest collection of African and Nubian lions and Royal Bengal and Si-

berian tigers. In 1930, he handled his greatest act: forty jungle-bred lions and tigers of both sexes.

Clyde Beatty's fearlessness was legendary. Once, he slipped and fell to one knee. One of his tigers immediately pounced on him. Fortunately, the cage also contained a lion that hated that tiger. The lion sprang from its pedestal and clawed the tiger. With the tiger distracted, Beatty escaped through the safety door. But even after such close brushes with death, he still had to go back to work in the same steel cage.

And then, in the depths of the Depression, this symbol of fearlessness became a symbol of recovery as well.

On a cold January Saturday in 1932, Beatty was rushing through his practice session in the Hagenbeck-Wallace winter quarters in Peru, Indiana. He was anxious to finish with the big cats and be on his way to Chicago, where he had a date with a young woman named Harriet Evans. She was a ballet girl on the Hagenbeck show whom he had met during the 1931 season. From the start, the two talked about the rare rapport between them.

Beatty was rehearsing his greatest act that day: a group of forty jungle-bred lions and tigers. The previous season its instant popularity had prompted Ringling Bros. and Barnum & Bailey, which also owned the Hagenbeck show, to bring Beatty to New York, put his name in lights on the marquee of Madison Square Garden, and to bill him as "the sensation of the century, greatest and most daring wild animal act ever presented."

The mere appearance of a wild animal trainer with The Greatest Show on Earth was eyebrow-raising. It was the first time that Ringling Bros. had presented a wild animal act since its 1924 season, when it had *four* steel arenas working at one time: Dutch Ricardo with lions; Rudolph Matthies with tigers; Christian Shroder with polar bears; and, of course, in the center ring, the famous Mabel Stark, working eight tigers—and wrestling her tiger Rajah. Historian Fred D. Pfening, Jr., has called it the largest display of trained wild animals performing at one time in the history of the circus.

In eliminating such displays, Ringling press agent Dexter Fellows admitted later, John Ringling took into consideration not only protests from people who could not be convinced that cruelty wasn't used to train the animals but also "the immense amount of work entailed in erecting and dismantling three steel arenas and transferring the animals to the shifting dens twice a day. . . . If the menagerie men did not get the shifting dens right up against the cages in the rings, there was always the possibility of an animal escaping."

But Clyde Beatty was one of those archetypal circus performers who come along only once or twice in a generation, a real-life Jungle Jim (though he seems never to have been in the jungle)—and how could a circus claim to be the Greatest Show on Earth when Beatty was around if it did not have him? So Ringling put Beatty in the Garden and in Boston. "His act was so big and spectacular that we could not play it on the road," said Fellows; so on tour, Beatty performed with the Hagenbeck-Wallace Circus, where he was allowed to dominate the smaller show.

And then, suddenly, on this rehearsal day, when all but three of the cats had left the cage, a lion named Nero caught Beatty off guard and knocked him to the ground. By coincidence, it was Nero that had saved Beatty's life only the year before by battling the tiger that had unexpectedly lunged. This time, however, Nero plunged his long sharp teeth into Beatty's thigh.

Every good wild animal trainer knows that there is no such thing as a lion tamer. Wild animals are never "tamed," and Beatty himself has written of the big cat: "No matter how

much affection I lavish on him he will never lose his basic primitiveness."

Besides the trauma and loss of blood, there's another danger from a lion bite. A Beatty protégé, Dave Hoover, told me that wild animal trainers particularly fear a fulminating infection from the injection into the wound of the rotting and rancid meat between a lion's teeth.

Six hours after the lion bit him, Clyde Beatty had a temperature of 104 degrees. Doctors determined that he had been infected by the disease-producing bacteria named *Pasteurella* for Louis Pasteur. For this infection, in 1932, no cure existed.

Clyde Beatty was dying. By telephone, doctors in Peru, Indiana, conferred with specialists across the United States. They tried the usual serum for blood poisoning, but to no avail. Their next hope—and they were running out of time—was to excise the seat of the infection deep in Beatty's leg. A surgeon cut clear to the bone before he found the pocket that held the infection. The radio and newspapers kept the nation informed as Beatty fought to recover. Six weeks after the lion attack, Beatty said he was about ready to leave his wheelchair and reenter the big cage. He was determined to make a return engagement with the Ringling show when it opened in New York that April.

Once again, the circus was functioning as a metaphor for America. In this Depression year of 1932, Clyde Beatty seemed to express the national longing for recovery, and the belief that an American boy could overcome the "Law of the Jungle."

The New York date had to be delayed, but Clyde Beatty did make it to the Garden in 1932, as well as in 1933 and 1934. These were the days in which Franklin D. Roosevelt would firmly assert that "The only thing we have to fear is fear itself." Was there a better example than Clyde Beatty?

In 1935, there would be a once-in-a-lifetime circus known as the Cole Bros. and Clyde Beatty Circus. Even without Beatty it would rank as one of the greatest circuses of the century because of the presence in its clown alley of two of the best clowns in all of circus history: Otto Griebling and Emmett Kelly.

That fine essayist and fellow circus lover Edward Hoagland has pointed out the connection between these two clowns and the times in which they first flourished.

"In America," Hoagland wrote in *The Tugman's Passage*, "the best character clowns were two hoboes invented during the Depression by Emmett Kelly and his good friend Otto Griebling. Kelly . . . wore blackish, reddish, grayish makeup on his cheeks and chin, white and black on his mouth, and a polka-dot derby. He was broke and sad and seedy— in short, a tramp. Griebling projected an angrier, 'crazier' idea of humanity and of those times, but both were men for the 1930s, not for our more prosperous, fast-paced decade."

Griebling, born in Germany in 1896, was brought to the United States by Albert Hodgini to be a part of the Hodgini family riding act. Among the very best stories that the Hodgini family has bequeathed to circus history is the story of the entrance into circus life, temporary exit, and reentrance of the incomparable Otto. They were playing Madison, Wisconsin, and Hodgini gave Griebling five dollars to go to a store in town for two quarts of milk and two loaves of bread. Instead, Griebling decided to give up the circus life. He pocketed the money and took a job on a dairy farm outside Madison, while the circus moved on.

Two years later, Ringling Bros. played Madison again. Griebling hitched a ride into town, bought two loaves of bread and two quarts of milk, and delivered them, with the proper change, to Hodgini. "All he does," Otto would later recall, "is carefully count the change."

It was apparently the correct change, for Hodgini let Griebling come back, and Griebling never left the circus again. Indeed, Otto became such a good bareback rider that when he worked the Sells-Floto show, and the great Poodles Hanneford became ill and couldn't work for several days, Otto donned his costume and took his place.

"I had to get well fast," said Poodles. Otto "was getting funnier than I was."

Then, in 1930, came the fall. Griebling broke his wrist, leg, and ankle, thus ending his days as an equestrian. During his convalescence, he reasoned that if he had been successful as a comic rider, he could be successful as a nonriding clown. As his bones knit, he worked on the character he wanted to create: he studied textbooks on psychology, and books and articles on the art of acting in general and comedy in particular, with primary emphasis on pantomime.

"In all comedy business," Charlie Chaplin has written, "an attitude is most important, but it is not always easy to find an attitude." Otto remembered the frustration of trying to get started in a country where he didn't speak the language. Now he had the frustration of having to start all over again in a different career. From these frustrations grew the classic Griebling attitude of aspiration gone sour, of hope curdled. Before the mirror, the man whose body had just betrayed his dreams practiced his unforgettable reactions to life's bad breaks: embarrassment and resentment and anger and outrage. Looking for a clown character who could best express such emotions, Griebling chose the tramp.

All circus clowns are of only three basic types. Every clown face in the world is a variation of the *whiteface* clown, the *auguste* (rhymes with "roost"), and the *character* clown.

The whiteface clown derives from the classic Pierrot, the white clown of French pantomime, and harlequin, the mischievous intriguer of French and Italian light comedy and English pantomime. His clown face is all white, with the features (eyebrows, nose, mouth) painted on in black and red, and other decorations, if wanted, in various other colors. When the features are life-size, the clown is called a *neat whiteface*. When they are larger than life, he is called a *grotesque whiteface*. Alone he may show, as Hoagland says, his "sunny, quick, boyish soul." But when interacting, the whiteface quickly becomes an authority figure—the adult or parent or boss.

The *auguste* is the scapegoat, the recalcitrant child, the foolish employee, the country bumpkin among city slickers. He is overtly funny, so he wears the most comic clown face, the face Lou Jacobs wears. The base color is pink or reddish instead of white. The features (red and black) are of enormous size—as witness Lou's mud puddle smile. The mouth is usually thickly outlined with white, and white is often used around the eyes. The *auguste* is the most slapstick of all clowns; his actions are wilder and broader, and he gets away with more. The name, according to Fred Bradna, inexplicably stuck during a performance in Berlin about 1850 when the fall guy's comic ineptitude "inspired someone in the audience to shout, 'Look at that *dummer Auguste*,' and 'silly *Auguste*' the type remains to this day."

Federico Fellini, a great student of the contrast between the whiteface clown and the *auguste*, points out that "in the circus, thanks to the Auguste, the child can imagine himself doing everything he is forbidden to do. He can dress up as a woman, make faces, yell in public,

and say just what he thinks out loud. No one condemns him; on the contrary, he gets clapped for it."

The whiteface represents order and authority and the *auguste* represents disorder and rebellion, the two most basic psychological postures of the human race. The whiteface and the *auguste* are parent and child, teacher and pupil, cop and citizen, boss and worker—any kind of leader, any kind of follower. The humor always comes when the follower doesn't want to follow where the leader wants to lead. Institutions—families, schools, cities, corporations, governments—all want unity and harmony; individuals all want freedom. In that basic conflict lies the comedy of the clown.

Whiteface and *auguste* are true clown masks, just as authority figure and mischievous child are universal types. In contrast, the character clown is a comic slant on some of the roles we play: cops, farmers, ethnics; and the makeup is a comic slant on the standard human face. Character clown faces make sport of mustaches, beards, whiskers, freckles, warts, odd-looking or large noses and ears, bald heads, strange haircuts or facial features and caricatures of various ideals of male and female beauty. As a psychological type, a character clown can be either whiteface or *auguste*.

The most well-known character clown is the tramp or hobo, and has been for decades. In the 1890s, jugglers on the vaudeville stage often dressed as tramps to burlesque the then-popular "salon jugglers," who wore white tie and tails and juggled top hats and canes. Tramp jugglers wore rags and juggled old plug hats and cigar boxes. When W. C. Fields performed as a tramp juggler in London in 1901, one critic stiffly labeled him "another of the apparently extensively patronised type of tramp which appears to be indigenous to American vaudeville entertainments."

Charlie Chaplin made the tramp character

clown universally popular with his film comedies, starting in 1914 and continuing through such masterpieces as *The Tramp* (1915) and *The Gold Rush* (1925) to *Modern Times* (1936), his last film using that character. "Charlie was a shabby Pierrot," Chaplin told Robert Payne. With this conception, Chaplin was free to embellish the comedy with touches of sentiment, and this sentimental clown was the "little tramp" the world loved—a victim who was a poet and a dreamer in the tradition of the melancholy whiteface Pierrot portrayed in France by Jean-Gaspard Deburau (1796–1846) in the 1820s. Deburau's biographer, Jules Janin, noted that his Pierrot was "always poor, just like the common people," another connection with Chaplin's tramp.

There were some tramp clowns in the circus in the 1920s, but they were not especially popular. Emmett Kelly tried to introduce the first version of his "Weary Willie" tramp character as early as 1924 while on the John Robinson show, but the boss clown, Kenneth Waite, said that a tramp clown looked dirty and told Kelly to stick to plain whiteface.

Then came the Great Depression. With so many Americans "on the tramp," the comic tramp was an idea whose time had come again.

———

In 1932, Otto Griebling was a tramp clown in the Hagenbeck-Wallace show when Emmett Kelly joined on as a whiteface. The next year, they were both tramp clowns and together worked out what is called a progressive clown stunt. Just before the show, they would get a twenty-five-pound cake of ice. When the show began, they would circle the hippodrome track, with Emmett carrying the ice on his back and Otto calling into the seats for "Missus Jones," who was supposed to have ordered the ice. Three or four times during the show, they

would search again for "Missus Jones." Each time, the block of ice would be more melted, until, on their last tour of the track, Emmett was licking a little ice cube while Otto was still calling in frustration for "Missus Jones."

They were both character clowns, both tramps—but Otto was behaving like a whiteface clown, determined to get the job done (though letting Emmett do the heavy work), whereas Emmett was an *auguste*, the naughty kid who ends up licking the ice.

In the winter of 1934–35, Griebling and Kelly played the Moslem Shrine Circus in Detroit, where they did a gag that stuck out like a tuning fork of the times, with vibrations felt across the country. It was the quintessential clown gag for the Depression, and it became known as the PWA Shovel Routine.

Once again, Griebling was the boss on the job. He carried blueprints and stakes and a measuring tape. Kelly, in his "Weary Willie" getup and carrying a shovel, was the worker. The boss busily scurried around staking out a plot of land. Kelly didn't lift a finger to help. He just leaned on his shovel and looked world-weary. It was a basic white clown–*auguste* confrontation: the white clown tries to get the *auguste* to do something; the *auguste* can't be bothered.

But when Emmett Kelly leaned on his shovel, he inadvertently became a symbol of Republican opposition to President Roosevelt's federal relief programs. A photograph of Kelly leaning on a shovel near a sign that said P.W.A. (Public Works Administration) circulated nationwide. Kelly said a member of a Republican committee in Detroit had it taken. "A lot of Roosevelt Democrats took offense," wrote Kelly in his 1954 autobiography, "but the circus got plenty of publicity and it had been conceived as an innocent, non-political gag."

It is hard to believe that the two master

clowns didn't know what they were doing. Roosevelt had signed the Federal Emergency Relief Act in May of 1933. Under various titles—Civil Works Administration (CWA), Works Progress Administration (WPA), and Public Works Administration (PWA)—federal relief was to continue until 1942. (Indeed, from 1935 to 1939 a W.P.A. Circus gave jobs each year to 375 unemployed performers and free shows for hospitals and for poor children. The salary was low, only $23.86 per week, and only one person in a family could draw a wage. So sometimes, whole circus families did their act for that fee.) The government funds went into over 30,000 New Deal projects, including paying teachers and building waterworks, post offices, bridges, jails, airports, sewers, playgrounds, and public swimming pools. "But to critics of the program," wrote William Manchester, "most of the jobs were boondoggles—'make-work.' To upper-middle-class critics, the symbol of the reliefer would always be a man leaning on a shovel or a rake. . . ."

And a circus clown had given them the most vivid image of that symbol.

———

The clown is one quintessential circus figure; the spangled lady is another. *The Billboard* for April 27, 1935, raved about the equestrian beauty in Display 15 of the Cole Bros. and Clyde Beatty Circus. "In the center ring Harietta (Harriett Hodgini) in a riding act of superb artistry. Miss Hodgini has beauty of face and form and as a rider she is unsurpassed. Graceful in the extreme, she makes a beautiful picture, and her work throughout was superb."

So let Harriett Hodgini stand in this history for all the spangled ladies of the circus to whom towners lose their hearts, and she and her celebrated love affair with a millionaire hotel owner will provide the occasion for a disquisition into the glamor of the circus.

Harriett Hodgini was in her twenties in the 1930s. Spectacularly beautiful, she was a member of one of the world's top circus families, which at that time had one of the world's top circus acts. They were Hodges when they got started in the English circus three generations before Harriett, through a trick-riding great-uncle named Tom Hodges. Tom went to Italy, operated a wagon show, married an Italian performer, and changed his name to Hodgini because it made his circus sound Italian. When his circus came back to England to perform, it was as Hodgini's Great European Shows.

First of the Hodginis to come to the United States was Albert, who joined the Ringling Bros. Circus in 1908. It was Albert who brought Otto Griebling to America in 1913.

In 1924, the Albert Hodgini riding act was in the Sells-Floto show. The riders wore Indian costumes, and the act ended with lots of Indian war whoops and sophisticated fire effects as their horses galloped around the ring.

In 1935, the first season of the Cole Bros. Circus under the ownership of Adkins and Terrell, the Hodginis in the show included Albert; daughter Harriett; sons Albert, Jr. (Bertie), and Joe; Joe's wife, Etta, and their sons Tom and Joe, Jr.

The Hodginis expected Harriett to marry someone in the circus. That's the way circus families usually do. But when the circus came to Springfield, Ohio, in the summer of 1935, Harold Van Orman, millionaire hotel-chain owner, threw a party for the officials and stars of the Cole Bros.–Clyde Beatty show in his very own Shawnee Hotel.

And there he saw Harriett Hodgini.

"Van Orman . . . one of America's ten best dressed men, was shaken to the toes of his $50 shoes," reported William Randolph Hearst's *American Weekly*. Why not? There were many rich men in America, but a circus queen then was a kind of royalty.

The editors of Hearst's Sunday supplement

HUNT BROS. CIRCUS PLAYS TARRYTOWN, NEW YORK. *It is June 14, 1933, during America's Great Depression. A circus doesn't have to be The Greatest Show on Earth: even the smallest true circus has all the ingredients that have been bringing people respite from their cares since Thomas Pool put on the first circus in America in 1785. The Hunt Bros. little smokestack circus (as those that confine their activities to the heavily industrialized eastern United States are called) has three rings and at least four equestrians to perform the feats of human skill and daring on which a circus is based; and a clown to send everything up. This clown is standing to the right of an elephant, the beast that is the best thing added to the circus since Pool's day. The Charles T. Hunt Circus was founded in 1892 and became a family show as Charles Jr., Eddie, and Harry Hunt grew up to assist their father. (Circus World Museum, Baraboo, Wisconsin)*

BOONDOGGLE. *Emmett Kelly's dream of being a trapeze star was smashed by the Great Depression, when the Sells-Floto Circus closed down. Kelly had no contract for the 1932 season when he received an offer to clown with the Hagenbeck-Wallace Circus. He created a clown who was a caricature of a type becoming all too familiar: the sad hobo. In 1935, Kelly took his hobo, "Weary Willie," to the new Cole Bros. and Clyde Beatty Combined Circus; his wife stayed behind with their two sons, and the marriage fell apart. Circus folk noticed that Kelly was increasingly melancholy, and it was affecting his hobo character—for the better. This photo shows the PWA (Public Works Administration) routine that brought Kelly to national notice. (Circus World Museum, Baraboo, Wisconsin)*

CLYDE BEATTY WITH LION AND CHAIR. *Here is the way we remember Clyde Beatty, standing alone in the Big Cage with a chair, a whip, and a pistol, holding a snarling lion at bay. His act can be seen in several movies, including* The Big Cage *(1933) and* Ring of Fear *(1957). His appeal to the psychology of Americans in the Depression, when* Time *magazine put him on its cover, was that he would not give in to fear—even after a serious mauling by a lion. (Circus World Museum, Baraboo, Wisconsin)*

SPANGLED LADY. *Harriett Hodgini stands in this history for all the spangled ladies of the circus to whom "towners" lose their hearts. She was a member of one of the world's top circus families. Her father, Albert Hodgini, had the riding act that brought Otto Griebling, a skilled rider who became a great clown, to America. Of Harriett's contribution,* Billboard *said: "Miss Hodgini has beauty of face and form and as a rider she is unsurpassed." Her 1930s love affair with a millionaire hotel owner, celebrated by the tabloids, revived one of America's loveliest dreams: the beautiful bareback rider you fall in love with and determine to woo—and win. (Circus World Museum, Baraboo, Wisconsin)*

ALFRED COURT AND THE RETURN OF WILD ANIMAL ACTS. *In 1926, John Ringling abolished wild animal acts and until 1938 the Big One had none—except for the appearances of Clyde Beatty in some of the big cities. In 1938, John Ringling North revived wild animal acts as all-season, three-ring features by bringing Terrell Jacobs from the Hagenbeck-Wallace Circus to work the largest number of lions and tigers ever presented as a feature of The Greatest Show on Earth—between thirty-eight and fifty-two in a seventeen-minute act. It was so popular that North imported Alfred Court from France to play the 1940 season. Court brought eighty animals, fifty tons of baggage, and four other trainers with him. A slight, suave Frenchman, he specialized in mixing species that were natural foes of one another. When the show opened, a total of sixty animals were working in three rings, including lions, tigers, black jaguars, snow leopards, black panthers, pumas, cougars, Great Dane dogs, polar bears, Himalayan bears, spotted leopards, mountain lions, spotted jaguars, ocelots, and black leopards—the greatest variety of trained wild animals ever presented in America. Court's original contract was for two years, but World War II kept him here "for the Duration." For the 1945 season, Court, with the assistance of his nephew, Willy Storye, broke a group of twelve leopards to work with six young women. His understudy, Damoo Dhotri, returned from the U.S. Army to display the act (Court was now sixty-two). Following the opening, Court retired from the show and from wild animal training, one of the few who had never been seriously hurt. Court's style, like that of Gunther Gebel-Williams today, followed the European "Hagenbeck method" instead of the "fighting act" of Clyde Beatty and other American wild animal trainers. Court used no pistol or chair, only a small pole and whip, and he always climaxed his act walking about the steel arena with a leopard as a neckpiece, just as Gunther drapes a leopard around his shoulders today. (Ringling Museum)*

knew the kind of story that would appeal to its vast readership. Details of the life-styles of the rich and famous have always been relished in America, but perhaps never more so than during the Great Depression; and the life of a spangled circus beauty has been the epitome of American glamor at least since frontiersmen fell in love with the various bareback riders who played Mazeppa. So what could be better than a love story of a rich man and a spangled lady?

Van Orman was then fifty-one years old, four years divorced from his first wife, "socialite Susie Beeler," who was the mother of his three sons.

The millionaire's courtship was a long-distance commuting affair. "Like the daring young man," reported the press, "he flew through the air for thousands of miles in short hops and long, to cities and towns and whistle stops—wherever the circus went—and in time every freak, clown and acrobat under the big top knew him and his ambition."

The wedding took place on November 9, 1935. Said the Sunday supplement: "A middle-aged Lochivar rode out of the Midwest by plane and automobile in pursuit of a beautiful bareback rider—and in three months Mademoiselle Hodgini was Mrs. F. Harold Van Orman, wife of Indiana's first hotel man and ex–lieutenant governor."

The headquarters of the Van Orman chain was the Hotel McCurdy in Evansville, and that is where F. Harold installed Harriett Hodgini Van Orman in splendor. However, the first Mrs. Van Orman was already in residence at the McCurdy. "One of the few conversations on record between the two wives ended with No. 2 flinging a letter tray at the suave head of No. 1," the American Weekly revealed.

Professionally, Van Orman continued to prosper. He was elected president of the American Hotel Association. He continued to

entertain circus people at his hotels. He named Bertie Hodgini manager of his Terre Haute House.

Privately, things seemed all right, too. There was a son born to Harriett, whom they called Richard Albert. But then, on October 13, 1944, after a little less than nine years of marriage, Harriett sued for divorce. Like his first wife, she charged cruel and inhuman treatment. The difference was that socialite Susie Beeler Van Orman asked for nothing but a divorce. Bareback rider Harriett Hodgini Van Orman wanted a quarter of a million dollars—and custody of their son.

The Hearst press of the period knew just how to sing of such a blighted love. "It was a heavy blow for the persuasive inn-keeper," wrote the American Weekly. "The big tent of love was down. The parade was over. The last calliope had gone."

In 1961, White Tops, the magazine of the Circus Fans Association of America, reported that Harriett was "now married to a prominent surgeon [and] resides at Chicago and Miami Beach. . . ." But in the 1930s, she was all America's sweetheart. In the style of the movie romances of the period, of course, this aspect of the truly happy dream that is the circus should end with the fade-out kiss at the altar. The American Weekly wrote the more cynical epitaph for such romances: "The Elderly Lochinvar's Spectacular Pursuit of the Beauteous Bareback Rider Was Like Poetry in Motion Until They Were Married—But, It Seems, They Couldn't Ride Double."

———————————

The circus has satisfied the public's ongoing curiosity about strange and exotic people for over two hundred years, and spangled ladies have remained high on the list of the public's perceptions of the strange and exotic—as witness the way that the country boy played by Henry Fonda looked on the spangled lady played by Dorothy Lamour in the 1940 circus film *Chad Hanna*. But the location of beauty in the eye of the beholder was never more exotically demonstrated than when John Ringling brought the Ubangi women to America in 1930.

The Ubangis—five men and eight plate-lipped women from the Congo—"drew a bigger gate than any freak the sideshow ever promoted," reported Fred Bradna.

"GREATEST EDUCATIONAL FEATURE OF ALL TIME!" shouted the Ubangi posters. "TRIBE OF GENUINE UBANGI SAVAGES. New to Civilization!!! From Africa's Darkest Depths! WITH MOUTHS AND LIPS AS LARGE AS THOSE OF FULL-GROWN CROCODILES!"

Well, crocodile-sized was barefaced ballyhoo; but their lips were undeniably plate-sized, and few customers ever felt their sense of wonder unexercised after beholding a Ubangi woman.

From the beginning, the circus was frequently the only institution that brought the cultures and traditions of far-off lands to parts of America remote from the big cities. But even big-city Americans had never seen Ubangis. They were even more popular than the so-called "giraffe-neck women" from Burma, who had their necks stretched by the gradual addition of metal rings, a 1931 attraction which was also presented as "the greatest educational attraction the world has ever known."

Ringling press-agentry provided an explanation of the origin of the plate lips that sounds fanciful, but Dexter Fellows still maintained it in his memoirs: "It seems that in the old days the tribe was constantly being bothered by pirates who stole the young women. After counsel it was decided to make the girls so homely that even the pirates would leave them alone. But in time the lip-stretching came to be con-

ZACCHINI X-15 DOUBLE HUMAN MISSILE ROCKET. *How were the Zacchinis "shot through space with violent velocity from the mouth of a monster cannon," as a 1930 Ringling Bros. and Barnum & Bailey circus poster said of Hugo Zacchini? Although the commands in Italian were followed by a terrific explosion, and the "human cannonball" emerged in a puff of smoke (photographs show the smoke; the poster showed his trajectory as a line of fire, making him look like a kind of human tracer bullet), the Zacchinis were not "fired" like explosive shells; they were pushed by compressed air out of the tube, some seventy feet up into the air and for a lateral distance of 135 feet at an initial speed of eighty miles per hour. When Zacchini men went off to fight in World War II, they were replaced in the cannon's mouth by Zacchini women.*

The circus-adoring film director Federico Fellini described how their garden in Florida was too small for the full trajectory. "They had to fire them across the road outside the house, landing them in a field beyond. Car drivers who didn't know this often had accidents when they saw men flying across the road; they thought they were having hallucinations and lost control of their cars. So the mayor of Tampa, the small town where the Zacchinis lived—which considered them a local marvel, like the Eiffel Tower—at last put up notices at either end of the road: 'If you see a flying man, do not be alarmed. It is just the Zacchinis rehearsing their stunts.'" (Ringling Museum)

sidered beautiful, and only the comeliest little girls were chosen for this adornment."

Whatever the origin of the practice, the enlargement of the lips was in fact accomplished by slitting the lips of girl babies and inserting wooden disks in the slits, then increasing the size of the disks as the children grew, until they had lips like plates: the larger the plate, it was thought, the more beautiful the woman.

The chief exploiter of the Ubangis, according to Fred Bradna, was a Frenchman named Dr. Ludwig Bergonnier. He saw his first Ubangi women at a Paris exposition of so-called colonial possessions and decided that they would have exhibition value throughout the world. So he went to the French Congo, traveled deep into the interior, and explained to the Ubangi chief, a man named Neard, how rich he could become by taking some of his people on a world tour.

The two questions most people in the audience asked were: "What do they eat?" "How do they eat it?"

Chief Neard provided the answer to the first question. From a pile of fresh fruit, he would toss oranges and bananas to his tribeswomen. They ate the bananas skin and all. The oranges they peeled. Neard would then ask in French for fish, which the Ubangis would tear apart with their fingers and gulp down raw. These remained their sole diet for the two years that they were with the Ringling show.

As to how they ate, we have the eyewitness account of Henry Ringling North: "They took the disks out of their lips, so they hung down like great fleshy awnings over their mouths. They lifted the awning with one hand and poked food in with the other."

The Ubangis were miserably unhappy in America—the women in particular. They had left behind a total of sixty-four children, and they wanted to go home. They couldn't, of course; a business deal had been made. So they asked that their children be brought from the Congo and allowed to travel with them. Good as it was, business wasn't good enough for *that* to be profitable. So the women remained separated from their children.

On their last night in New York, former New York governor Al Smith, who had been defeated by Herbert Hoover in his bid for the presidency only a few years before, came to the circus. Governor Smith was permitted to blow Fred Bradna's whistle to start the show, and was seated in a special draped box at the Garden. Chief Neard asked Bradna in French what kind of American was so honored, and Bradna explained that Smith had once been the king of New York and was still a powerful chief.

Marching in the Spec, the Ubangis suddenly bowed down before Al Smith's box. Smith acknowledged them with a wave of his cigar as if it were a scepter—but they did not move on. They seemed to have brought the parade to a halt to ask some favor of the American chief, and they weren't going to move until he answered them. Dr. Bergonnier was hurriedly summoned. According to Bradna, Bergonnier explained that the Ubangis "were asking the great king for a special boon: would he send for their children?"

Upon advice, Al Smith rose in a regal manner and commanded the Ubangis to move on, which they did. But they were not pleased. That night, Neard told Bradna: "That's no way for king to treat king. I king, too."

John Ringling paid the Ubangis $3,000 a week, according to Fellows; $1,500 a week, according to Bradna, who adds that Bergonnier "siphoned off all but a pittance, letting the Ubangis make what they could selling souvenir postcards."

In their desperation to go home, the women made tiny effigies of Dr. Bergonnier, which they stuck with pins and choked around the neck with strings. When Bergonnier found out what they were doing, he began to carry a revolver.

The Ubangi women first noticed the weapon as they were about to board their wooden Pullman car for the jump from Chicago to Milwaukee. They refused to go on the train with their "discoverer." Ringling management offered to send them by bus to Milwaukee, while Bergonnier remained with the train; but they were having nothing further to do with Bergonnier.

"One thing is inviolable in the circus—its railroad schedule," said Bradna. Ringling management ordered Bergonnier to leave the show. As soon as they saw his luggage removed from the circus train with their own eyes, the Ubangis boarded.

Bergonnier went to circus winter quarters in Sarasota, where he suddenly died in the last week of the 1932 season. American doctors said the cause of death was the bite of a tropical insect, but Chief Neard said that he was killed by the curses the Ubangi women put on him.

In any case, when the Ubangis returned to winter quarters, they asked to see Bergonnier's body. Satisfied that he was dead, they demanded to go home.

John Ringling arranged for them to ship back to the Congo at his expense, according to Bradna, who adds: "He had made a killing from their exhibition, and he was grateful to them." It was later said that even after the good doctor had taken the major part of the money they made from their tours, there was still enough left to buy a big Congo ranch, stock it with cattle, and live on it with their children and grandchildren.

Some say that the curse of the Ubangis not only did in Dr. Bergonnier but brought about the downfall of John Ringling as well—which is at least as plausible as your average Barnum humbug, and squarely in the tradition of the circus.

———

The Ubangis satisfied a quality found in every society: curiosity; and Clyde Beatty represented a quality prized in every society: courage. Sam Gumpertz must go down in circus history for a quality derided in every society: foolishness. He lost the greatest circus superstar of his time.

By 1933, Beatty was famous enough to be a film star. Twelve-year-old Mickey Rooney played a kid who looked up to Clyde Beatty in a film of that year called *The Big Cage*, with Beatty playing himself. There was a lot to look up to. In one scene, Beatty rescues an aerialist who has fallen into the big cage while Clyde is doing his wild animal act—all while the circus tent is being blown down by a storm! Whew!

For this film, Beatty used forty-three big cats owned by the Hagenbeck-Wallace show, and the Ringling coffers received the rental fee. Soon there was a Republic Pictures serial called *The Lost Jungle* that also used the cats—and included some scenes shot at the Peru, Indiana, animal barns. Again, the studios paid a handsome rental fee to the circus. After that, however, the Gumpertz team decided that Beatty was being "exposed" too much by the movies and that they would affect his drawing power. So his circus bosses forbade him to appear in any more films.

Beatty didn't like the way the order was handed down. He revered John Ringling, whom he considered "circus"; but the Gumpertz crowd to him were only businessmen.

In 1935, two men who were also "circus," Jess Adkins and Zack Terrell, asked Beatty to join them and to let his name be used in the title "Cole Bros.–Clyde Beatty Circus"—a potent name for advertising purposes. W. W.

"Chilly Billy" Cole was credited with being the first man to make a million dollars in the circus business, with shows operating under various titles from 1871 to 1886. In the twentieth century, several shows used Cole's name for its connotation of strong acts—and what act was stronger than Beatty's?

Beatty agreed; Adkins and Terrell bought railroad equipment from two Depression victims, Christy Bros. and Robbins Bros.; and a formidable competitor to Ringling Bros. and Barnum & Bailey was on the road.

Gumpertz struck back. Beatty's cats, though individually trained by Beatty, were owned by the Ringling interests. Beatty would have to build a completely new act. This was a difficult and dangerous task, as we have seen by his near-fatal accident in 1932, and it would have to be accomplished, not by the following spring, but by early in 1935, for a group of winter dates that had already been booked.

Beatty found many of the animals in the Los Angeles Zoo. These and others he shipped to the new winter quarters in Rochester, Indiana, just north of Peru. He "broke" the act, as circus people call the process by which animals, from horses to lions and tigers, are made tractable and trained to adjust to the service and/or convenience of human beings. He kept his winter dates, and he opened the first regular season of the new circus in the Coliseum in Chicago, April 20, 1935. It was dangerous for Beatty to train these new jungle animals so quickly, and it was dangerous for the Ringling animals already trained by him to be turned over to another trainer, but Gumpertz had forced the situation upon both animal trainers.

Remember the circus ballet dancer with whom Beatty had a date the day the lion called Nero almost killed him? The rare rapport between Clyde Beatty and Harriet Evans had resulted in their marriage, and Harriet had taken an increasing interest in her husband's big cats. During the winter of 1935 and 1936, Beatty and Eddie Allen, the elephant boss, broke a Siamese elephant to carry a lion and a tiger together on its back. When the 1936 season opened, this act was presented by Harriet Beatty, and she would continue to work with her husband on his shows until her death on the road at Kosciusko, Mississippi, during the 1950 season. Beatty later remarried, and he and his new wife, Jane, had a son, Clyde Beatty, Jr.

By 1937, Clyde Beatty was such an attractive symbol of the fearless American that he made the cover of *Time* magazine for March 29. On July 17 of that year, I saw him for the first time, appearing with the Cole Bros. Circus in Rockford, Illinois. I still have the newspaper clipping from the Rockford *Morning Star*, announcing that he would appear. The *Star* didn't interview him; they printed the circus press agent's handout just as it was under a picture of Beatty "with Menalik, full grown, jungle-born lion taught to sit up like a dog." It was tailored to the mood of the times, and the heart of it said:

A famous lion tamer, Beatty says even the most successful have their troubles.

You have probably seen him amble into a cage of 40 lions and tigers armed with only a light cane bottom chair and a cap pistol. Beatty says the reason he uses the chair is—it's a little protection and gives the animals four legs to chew on besides his own.

His slight, 140-pound frame is lacerated by the claws of the big jungle bullies—they've done everything but kill him.

"Aren't you frightened?" Put this query to him and he assures you in all earnestness that he never enters the cage without being scared to death.

"You see," he says, "you never know when they'll decide to feed on you. In my racket, it's impossible to get any life insurance."

This stripling who dominates tigers because he has the steady glance that brings fear to them used to be a pugilist. . . . "But I like cats better," he reminisces. "Pugs—they black your eyes and batter your nose. The cats only cut you into nice, clean strips."

Of course, no cat killed Beatty. I saw him again in the 1960s, a quarter of a century after I first saw him when I was a small, rapt boy. "Presenting the greatest wild animal trainer of all time," the announcer still intoned. And the name was still pronounced: "Cly-de Baay-tee." And Beatty, although chunkier, still appeared as a quick man with wavy black hair, white shirt, white jodhpurs, gleaming black boots, black belt, and low-slung gunbelt, who stood alone in a cage full of killers, and worked them with a fearless gaze.

Enter the Norths—and Gargantua

Robustious, luxury-loving John Ringling died of bronchial pneumonia at his home on Park Avenue in Manhattan on December 2, 1936. He was seventy years old. With him when he died was his only sister, Ida Ringling North, and his nephew and successor (though he didn't know it and didn't want it), his equal in the love of luxury, thirty-three-year-old John Ringling North.

In 1928, "Mr. John" Ringling had been one of the ten richest men in the United States. There followed an eight-year combination of bad luck and the wages of arrogance: the death of his beloved wife Mable; the world Depression and his personal depression; receivership; a disastrous second marriage that would have been dissolved by a final divorce decree if he had lived a week longer; and loss of control of his circus to its receivers. The final blow, a paralytic stroke, caught him with a telegram in his pocket ordering him to cease negotiations with the Cristiani equestrian troupe and threatening that if he tried to take any part in the operation of the circus he and his brothers had founded "we will hold a stockholders' meeting and turn you out." It was signed "Sam Gumpertz."

Mr. John had only $311 in the bank when he died, and his affairs were in a confusion the untangling of which would thread suspensefully through circus history for years, but his estate was officially appraised at $23.5 million. He owned a lot of land and many paintings, but little of his property was liquid. As for his North nephews, his avowed intention just before he died was to cut them off without a cent.

Whatever his faults, John Ringling's epitaph could deservedly have been the proverbial cir-

GARGANTUA THE GREAT made his debut in 1938, only five years after the premiere of the still-popular film King Kong, *and such ad lines as "The Largest Gorilla Ever Exhibited," "The World's Most Terrifying Creature," or, simply, "The Terror Is Coming!" seemed to promise that if Gargantua escaped somebody might get a free ride to the top of the new Empire State Building.* Life *put Gargantua on its cover. (Ringling Museum)*

cus wisdom, "Any boob can *run* a circus; it's the wise showman who knows where to *put* it." At his best, John Ringling knew better than anyone where to *put* a circus. He knew America as did few other Americans; and he knew that this knowledge could make the difference between a successful season and a failure. If, for example, a town's biggest industry was to get a fat contract the next year, Mr. John's circus would visit that town; if a strike had impoverished it, Mr. John's circus would go someplace else.

After a quarrel with his nephew some years before, Mr. John had cut Mr. Johnny out of his will. In fact, Johnny North and his younger brother Henry (Johnny was born in 1903; Henry in 1909) were to get nothing from the estate, and their mother was to receive only $5,000 a year for life. But Uncle John seemed to forget that he had named his sister and Johnny North as co-executors of the estate, and all three were to be trustees.

"So we Norths were struck out of inheriting what seemed unlikely to be worth anything," wrote Henry, "but given the whole responsibility for the administration of the estate." To be sure, the Norths received a large executor's fee.

Henry and Johnny were both, in Gene Plowden's phrase, "Baraboo-born and bred to the circus." As they were growing up, they both worked at circus jobs. Johnny had been boss of a candy stand when he was sixteen; Henry had been in the ticket window at eighteen. Then Johnny went to the University of Wisconsin and to Yale (1922 to 1924) but did not graduate; and Henry went to Yale (class of 1933) and did. Johnny became a customer's man on the stock exchange in New York, then a real estate salesman for his uncle in Florida, but he had a reputation as a playboy. Henry was a largely frustrated aesthete who went to work in 1936 for the Chronicle Publishing

Company in Marion, Indiana. And then Uncle John died, and the Ringling heirs elected Johnny—now called John Ringling North— president of the circus, and Henry Ringling North vice president and assistant to the president. With absolute control of the management, though as yet no stock, Mr. Johnny saw that his task was to pull "a disintegrating, has-been institution out of its doldrums and make it once again The Greatest Show on Earth."

One year later, John and Henry North were able to pay off enough debts and raise enough capital to restore family control of The Greatest Show on Earth. Samuel Gumpertz retired, and the North boys began immediately to revitalize the show.

Their first big move showed that John Ringling North had the same true showman's instincts as his uncles. He began his career by finding perhaps the greatest circus attraction of the twentieth century, second in history only to Barnum's Jumbo. Not surprisingly, the attraction would become a symbol for the last uneasy year of peace: a circus "mean machine."

More than Edward G. Robinson as Little Caesar, more than Jimmy Cagney as the Public Enemy, more even than Humphrey Bogart as Duke Mantee, he had the most famous sneer of the 1930s. He was not a movie gangster, but a real gorilla, and his name was Gargantua.

"WORLD'S MOST SUCCESSFUL ANIMAL LIVES FOR ONE PURPOSE: MURDER" was the headline for one story in *Life* magazine, which seemed to swallow the Gargantua legend whole. There was a famous circus poster picturing the gorilla seemingly about to dash an African native to death, but there was no real evidence that Gargantua had ever killed anybody. In fact, murder wasn't necessary. Gargantua made the cover of *Life*, with a double-page spread inside, by giving John Ringling North a bite.

The circus owner had gotten too close to the cage; Gargantua grabbed his arm and started biting on it. Dick Kroner, Gargantua's keeper, beat the gorilla over the head with a pole until he let go.

North was not too badly bitten—by the gorilla, at least. He had long before been bitten by the same ballyhoo bug that bit Barnum; so on his way to the hospital, North stopped by the advertising car to discuss the accident with the Ringling press agent, Roland Butler. The result was a gorilla-bites-man story that went around the world, capped by Butler's insistence that North had received "the most massive anti-tetanus shot ever given to a human being."

The facts in the phenomenal Gargantua saga seem to be these: John Ringling North and his brother found the gorilla, whom they would bill as "the most terrifying creature the world has ever seen," in "a quiet little lady's backyard shed in Brooklyn."

According to Henry Ringling North, the saga of Gargantua the Great began when "a small, middle-aged lady" named Lintz telephoned Johnny North at the Ritz Hotel in New York to ask if he would be interested in buying a full-grown gorilla that she owned. Johnny asked to see it, and she invited him and his brother Henry to come to tea at her home in Brooklyn.

She lived, said Henry North, in "a mansion of faded grandeur straight out of Charles Addams' macabre cartoons." Over tea, she warned them that her pet was not pleasant to look upon. Her late husband, a plastic surgeon, had tried to improve the gorilla's looks, but to no avail. According to the tale that the Norths said they got from her, the gorilla as a baby was being brought to America from Africa by ship when someone, reportedly a sadistic crew member, threw acid in its face, burning it horribly. Captain Arthur Phillips of the SS *Humbaw*, American–West African Line, thought that the disfigurement had ruined the animal's value, and sold him to Mrs. Lintz.

After tea that historic day, Mrs. Lintz took the Norths into her backyard to a shed that had once stabled the owner's horses. Inside the shed she introduced the brothers to Richard Kroner, a young German who used to show the Lintz St. Bernards when they won best of breed at dog shows. Now she was paying him to be her gorilla's keeper.

"Dear little Buddy lives in there," Henry North remembered Mrs. Lintz saying—and he was not pleased to hear it. Henry's nickname, bestowed by Uncle John, was Buddy. He did not want to share its sentimental associations with a gorilla.

When Kroner the keeper raised the sliding door on the cage in Brooklyn, and the North brothers looked for the first time on the scarred gorilla's face, Mr. Johnny saw his big chance. Plastic surgery had not improved Gargantua's looks much, the Norths realized thankfully. ("That acid was worth a million to us," Henry would later say.) There were ten or twelve gorillas then in captivity, and several were larger; others had big hairy heads and great dripping fangs, as this one did. But only this gorilla had the angry leer from the acid-twisted mouth that gave those who stared at him the shivers.

Although the acid story was probably true, Mrs. Lintz didn't just have this gorilla by accident; she was in the wild animal business. At the Ringling Museum of the Circus in Sarasota, Florida, there is a letter to John Ringling North dated Brooklyn, New York, December 4, 1937. It reads:

For one dollar and other valuable considerations I hereby give to you for the period of one week an option to purchase for the sum of ten thousand dollars ($10,000) my gorilla named Buddha and my two chimpanzees named Johnny and Maggie and the three steel cages two on trucks and one on a trailer now at the North Miami Zoo in North Miami, Florida. The price of the cages and trucks is not included in the price of $10,000.

Very truly yours,
Gertrude Davis Lintz

Buddy North thought it was risky to spend $10,000 on a disfigured gorilla even before they had a circus to show him in—but remember Hutchinson, P. T. Barnum's partner who couldn't see spending $10,000 on an elephant just because Jumbo was the biggest? As Buddy later wrote, he came to realize that his brother's "handling of the great gorilla showed that Brother John had the magic touch and the calculated recklessness that a successful circus man must have."

"We just can't afford to miss having the most terrifying creature the world has ever seen," is the way John Ringling North put it.

Henry finally agreed—but only on the condition that the gorilla's name be changed so that it was not the same as the nickname of the circus vice president. He always took credit for Buddha ("Buddy") Lintz's new name, attributing to his Yale education his familiarity with the sixteenth-century work by Rabelais in which there is a giant named Gargantua.

But that Gargantua was nothing like this. A picture of the gorilla's hand, twice the size of a large man's hand, appeared in *Life* and evoked vivid memories of King Kong, as did a full-page picture of his furious face. There was also a picture of his medicine shelf. Like many children at that time, Gargantua took cod liver oil every day so that he wouldn't catch cold.

He didn't look as if sickness—or anything else—could get him down. He was five feet seven and one-half inches tall, and in his prime weighed 550 pounds. And those enormously powerful arms had a total span of over nine feet.

Details like that made him famous overnight.

The international publicity got off to a great start when Arthur Brisbane wondered in his syndicated newspaper column whether Gargantua could beat the former world boxing champion Gene Tunney. Tunney, a personal friend of the Norths, gave an interview saying that he could indeed take Gargantua, that the gorilla could be knocked out by a solar plexus punch before he could bring his awesome arm reach and prodigious strength into play. But Tunney didn't try it.

Ernest Hemingway, back from the Spanish Civil War, got into the discussion. For a magazine called *Ken*, Hemingway wrote a piece called "My Pal the Gorilla Gargantua." He speculated on Tunney's ability to beat Gargantua, saying that "if any man could, Gene could, because he would not be afraid, because he can hit to the body, and because he is intelligent." Hemingway had just seen the current world champion, Joe Louis, knock out, in the very first round, Nazi Germany's Max Schmeling (at whose hands Louis had suffered his first defeat as a professional fighter), and Hemingway now wrote that a Gargantua-Tunney bout would in any case be prettier to watch than the second Louis-Schmeling fight, which was over almost as soon as it began.

Such publicity made certain that the names of Gargantua and the Ringling Bros. and Barnum & Bailey Circus would be mentioned everywhere. Whenever you got into a discussion of who was the greatest whatever, you were likely to find yourself invoking the name of Gargantua. Indeed, four years later, when it was announced that movie star Katharine Hepburn would appear on Broadway in *Without Love*, and all the seats quickly sold out, her press agent told her that she was the second greatest entertainment attraction in America—after Gargantua. For a time, Hepburn even referred to herself as Gargantua, and when the play opened, she started adding ruefully that the gorilla got better notices.

But John Ringling North was worried. What if "the mightiest monster ever captured by man" should get sick? As Henry North put it, "Living normally in germ-free jungles, gorillas are terribly susceptible to human respiratory diseases." John assuaged his fear in a way that would have made P. T. Barnum proud. Many chapters in the history of the circus have shown: find a way to make the latest technology part of the circus, and you have a new attraction. Talk of air-conditioning was much in the magazines (and the hot air) in those days, though it wouldn't become widely available to human beings until after the war. But John Ringling North asked his friend Lemuel Bulware of the Carrier Corporation in Syracuse, New York, to build an air-conditioned cage for his gorilla.

"Good publicity for us both," said John Ringling North.

Carrier did better. The company announced that it had made tests of climatic conditions in the Congo and fitted up a cage with thermostatic controls and humidifiers that reproduced those conditions exactly. With the phrase "jungle-conditioned cage," they won the advertisers award for 1938.

All over America, people longed for a look at the attraction billed as "the world's most terrifying living creature," "the most fiendishly ferocious brute that breathes," "the mightiest monster ever captured by man." Eleanor Roosevelt, the president's wife, had a reputation for being ubiquitous, so naturally there had to be a photograph of Eleanor staring at Gargantua through the bars of his famous cage.

The big gorilla's life-style delighted the public in those drab Depression days, as can be seen in this paragraph from *Life* magazine:

Gargantua started life in an African jungle, without even a name. Today, he rides about in an air-conditioned private car worth about five times as much as the amber-fitted Rolls Royce which John Ringling bought from the Czarina of Russia. Thermostats and strainers govern the humidity of the air that he breathes. His food could be served with pride by Oscar of the Waldorf. His health is the daily concern of three well-trained Yale alumni [the North brothers, presumably; but who was the third man from Yale who was concerned about Gargantua?] and a world-renowned scientist is his consulting physician.

While 1938 might have been a good year for advertising, it was a terrible year for circuses—the worst since the 1860s. Tim McCoy had been such a popular attraction with Ringling Bros. and Barnum & Bailey that he went out by himself with the Tim McCoy Wild West Show—and folded in four weeks. The Tom Mix Circus and Downie Bros. shows closed early. The leased Hagenbeck-Wallace Circus, once the showcase for Clyde Beatty, collapsed in California. Adkins and Terrell took their Cole Bros. Circus off the road after Bloomington, Illinois, on August 3. Some of the acts, including Beatty, moved over to the smaller Robbins Bros. show to finish the season. Robbins Bros. and Barnes–Sells-Floto were the only railroad shows that completed the season.

Even the Big One, Ringling Bros. and Barnum & Bailey Circus, could not finish the season—under that famous name, at any rate. Union organizers chose this year of setbacks to press their demands. On Tuesday, April 12, while the circus was playing Madison Square Garden, the animal handlers and roustabouts struck the circus.

"The Boss says we show," Director of Personnel (and former clown) Pat Valdo told Equestrian Director Fred Bradna.

Show they did. Management, performers, and freaks did the work of animal handlers. Gargantua, in his twenty-two-ton air-conditioned cage, with shatterproof glass and loaded with

THE COLE BROS. AND CLYDE BEATTY COMBINED CIRCUS (preceding pages). In 1937, Beatty-Cole had one of the greatest wild animal trainers and two of the greatest clowns in circus history—Clyde Beatty, Emmett Kelly, and Otto Griebling. On July 17, 1937, I saw it in my Illinois hometown, where it also put on one of the last circus street parades. Down a Rockford street still struggling out of the Depression rolled one of the wonderful Continent wagons from Barnum & Bailey's 1903 parade. During their European tour, Barnum & Bailey executives had seen the Prince Albert Memorial in London and noticed the symbolic stone sculptures at its outer corners representing each of the continents. "We'll do the same thing with circus wagons!" they said; and for their return to America, they built four tableaux wagons, named them Asia, Africa, Europe, and America, and covered them with carved busts representing the peoples of that continent. On the Asia wagon (above) were the faces of men and women of Arabia, Persia, Afghanistan, Ceylon, China, Korea, Japan, Siam, Borneo. . . . Many years later, on a journalistic assignment in Borneo, traveling in a temois, a native longboat, up the Baram river in Sarawak, I looked at my guide, remembered the faces on the Asia wagon passing weatherbeaten frame houses in Rockford, and thought of Emily Dickinson's lines: "Friday, I tasted Life./It was a vast morsel./A circus passed the house." (preceding pages, Ringling Museum; above, Circus World Museum, Baraboo, Wisconsin)

steel, was scheduled to circle the hippodrome track as a separate display. The draft power of six horses was called for. Without animal handlers, workhorses could not pull the cage, so fifty managers, performers, and freaks pushed and a light tractor pulled, and Gargantua moved out. Among those who pushed were John Ringling North, the Flying Concellos, and Ella Bradna in a ballet costume. Some of the spectators could not see Gargantua for the crowd of human celebrities pushing him, but the show did go on.

For those who knew the backyard gossip, the greatest moment concerned the two equestrian acts. The Cristiani troupe, which John Ringling had been trying to bring to his circus when he had his stroke, had come, but they had a bitter, almost Hatfield-McCoy-type feud with Ringling's other riding act, the Loyal-Repenskys. But since the grooms wouldn't work, the Loyal-Repenskys put aside the feud and groomed for their competitors, and the Cristianis returned the favor.

Such harmony among the performers only served to build union pressure against the circus. The recession of 1938 was in full swing, organized labor was boycotting the show, and John Ringling North was losing $40,000 a week. The showdown came at Scranton, Pennsylvania, a strong union community, on June 22.

The union made Fred Bradna's opening whistle the signal for another full-blown strike. Johnny North refunded admission money to the customers and ordered the circus back to winter quarters. The mayor of Scranton visited the circus lot to tell the union pickets that he was "behind them, one hundred per cent," and ordered the show out of town. But it couldn't move because the union members wouldn't move it.

On June 24, the performers voted not to join the strike. On June 26, heckled by pickets and townspeople, the nonstriking personnel loaded the show and The Greatest Show on Earth limped back to winter quarters in mid-summer.

Yet by August it was on the road again. John Ringling North had devised entirely new billing and publicity for a makeshift show which stated: (in small print) "The Al G. Barnes and Sells-Floto Circus PRESENTS [in larger type] RINGLING BROTHERS AND BARNUM & BAILEY'S STUPENDOUS NEW FEATURES."

———

As John and Henry North saw it, the American people were much more sophisticated in the late thirties. Compared to the public served by their uncles, Americans traveled much more widely, thanks to the automobile; and they heard and saw more of the world, thanks not only to cars but to the radio and movies with sound and color. When the Norths took over, in 1938, movies had been talking for only ten years, been in color less than seven, but in the view of the Norths, the musicals of Broadway and Hollywood had already accustomed the young parents who brought their children to the circus to themes that unified unrelated acts, to well-designed costumes and lighting, and to big production numbers with original music. The circus, they felt, must be a match for these spectacles. In short, the Norths were going to make the circus look more like a sophisticated Broadway show or a Technicolor Hollywood musical of the late 1930s and early 1940s. And they did.

They built the show in 1938 around Frank "Bring 'Em Back Alive" Buck. Johnny North "dreamed up" and Charles Le Maire designed an opening Spec called "Nepal," described in the program as portraying "in fantasy, splendor, and exotic opulence the royal welcome to 'Bring 'Em Back Alive' Frank Buck by the Maharajah of Nepal and his native court."

Frank Buck, in his famous pith helmet, was to arrive riding on a hunting elephant in a basket howdah, accompanied by a picturesque train of native hunters and beaters, dancing girls garlanded with hibiscus and wild orchids, and an odd assortment of jungle animals, including Lotus the hippopotamus and Edith the giraffe. There was also a Spec in which the circus's midgets and dwarfs were costumed as Walt Disney's Seven Dwarfs, nearly twenty years before such characters appeared at Disneyland. They paraded to "Heigh-Ho," the dwarfs' marching song from the first animated cartoon feature, Disney's *Snow White and the Seven Dwarfs* of 1937.

A midget clown named Paul Horompo, waiting to go on in that Spec, became a hero of the circus.

Just before showtime at the Garden one afternoon, a tiger named Lady escaped in the back of the building and slashed a donkey that was lined up for the Grand Entry. The tiger dodged the menagerie men who had come to capture her and headed down a corridor that opened into the main lobby.

The show hadn't started yet: the public was still milling around the lobby, and the place was full of children. Standing between the children and the tiger was Horompo—dressed as Dopey for the "Snow White" Spec.

Horompo had dressed early, shouldered the little papier-mâché pick that every dwarf except Doc carried in the walk-around, and was standing alone in that corridor when the tiger streaked down it heading for the lobby.

Instead of running for his life, the midget clown moved into the path of the tiger. In his head, he said, he was picturing the carnage if the beast reached the children. He struck the tiger sharply on the nose with his little papier-mâché pick. More surprised than stunned, let alone hurt, the tiger became confused, spun around, and headed back the way she had

come—straight into a net that the menagerie men dropped over her.

The story reached the newspapers and radio stations, and everybody wanted to hear how Horompo had faced down an escaped tiger. By the time the circus reached Boston, he was flown back to New York to be honored on a network radio show called "We, the People."

———

North and the union came to terms during the winter, and in 1939 the show went out again as Ringling Bros. and Barnum & Bailey Circus. This time, business was good. "Many days we played $50,000 gates," recalled Fred Bradna. Gargantua drew huge crowds, bigger than P. T. Barnum had attracted with Jumbo. But then, as John Ringling North had realized, it was a new era. Barnum didn't have the movies to ballyhoo Jumbo. *King Kong*, one of the most popular films of all time, had been getting people excited about a giant ape since 1933, and the film had just been reissued to big grosses in 1938. But Kong was a fantasy, created by the animation of a twelve-inch model; Gargantua was real.

That was the enduring attraction of the circus. Clyde Beatty was not a movie actor playing Tarzan while remaining carefully protected from his lions; he was a wild animal trainer who actually entered a cage with forty jungle cats. That has always been the appeal of the circus: it is life as heightened as imagination can make it. It is also, to be sure, life as carefully controlled as human precision can make it, but it is not special effects; it is real.

Nevertheless, the circus was no longer America's most popular form of entertainment; the illusions of the movies had replaced it. But though the decade of the Great Depression had been the most difficult for the old institution since the decade of the Civil War,

RINGLING BROS. AND BARNUM & BAILEY AND SIX DWARFS. Almost the entire cast of the 1938 edition of The Greatest Show on Earth was photographed in Madison Square Garden at the beginning of their tour. The man in white suit and sola topee with the cheetah on a leash is Frank "Bring 'Em Back Alive" Buck, who captured wild animals for the circus and was featured that year in a Spec called "Nepal." There are also six of the seven dwarfs from the "Snow White" walk-around, which came early in the performance. With a magnifying glass, I can make out five of the names on their caps: (from left) Sneezy, Grumpy, Bashful, Happy, Doc. The heavy-lidded guy, fourth from the left, must be Sleepy. But where is beardless Dopey? Was this the day that the midget clown, Paul Horompo, dressed as Dopey, helped corral an escaped tiger backstage? If so, he's excused. (Ringling Museum)

THE POLE CAR (overleaf) of the Ringling Bros. and Barnum & Bailey Combined Circus train, with attendant roustabouts, stopped at Rome, New York, on July 11, 1935. Parkinson and Fox, in The Circus Moves by Rail, *a treasure trove for circus train buffs, tell us that "Two car-building firms were responsible for nearly all of the circus flats. One was the Warren Tank Car Company of Warren, Pennsylvania; the other was the Mt. Vernon Car Manufacturing Company of Mt. Vernon, Illinois." In the 1920s the American Circus Corporation bought Mt. Vernon cars for its units—Hagenbeck-Wallace, John Robinson, and Sells-Floto. The Al G. Barnes show also bought Mt. Vernons, as did Christy Bros., Robbins Bros., and Sparks. On the Ringling-Barnum show, cars carried three-digit numbers, the first number designating the section in which the car was operated; so this car, 116, is in the train's first section. Ultimately, the idea behind flatcars gave rise to some of the most modern equipment in railroading, long piggyback and rack cars. (Ringling Museum)*

EY   COMBINED   CIRCUS   116

LY 11ᵀᴴ 1935.

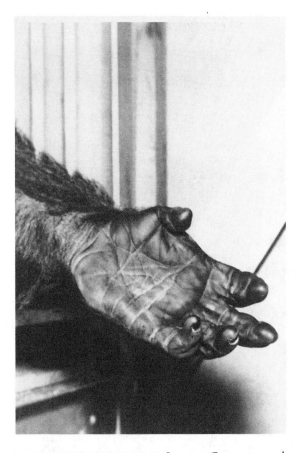

AN UNTRUSTWORTHY HAND. In 1941 Gargantua and Toto were married in a bower of flowers under a canvas canopy at circus winter quarters in Sarasota, Florida. Toto was M'Toto, which means "Little One" in Swahili, a gorilla who lived in Cuba on the grounds of her owner, Mrs. Stephen Hoyt. One day, having tea in the garden, M'Toto playfully broke both of her owner's wrists; Mrs. Hoyt sold M'Toto to the circus. The marriage was never consummated. Gargantua would have nothing to do with M'Toto. They toured in two cages, each with two compartments so that the gorilla could be shut in one end while the other end was cleaned. When the Ringling show got to Madison Square Garden in 1941, Mrs. Hoyt came to visit M'Toto. To get to her cage, wrote Henry Ringling North in his memoirs, Mrs. Hoyt had to pass Gargantua's cage. "Incautiously, she turned her back on him. He grabbed for her and just got her dress. A loud rip and there was Mrs. Hoyt in nothing but her bra and panties screaming bloody murder." (Ringling Museum)

the circus had come through. It was not unscarred, as we have seen: the majority of the old names had been wiped out by the Depression, and even some of the more promising of the new names were not able to survive. Most railroad circuses were too expensive for the times, but motorized circuses seemed a feasible new way. When circuses were motorized, baggage horses were everywhere giving way to tractors, and the old street parades had all but disappeared.

The Depression was ending, but largely because a new world war had begun. Mobilization for war in 1940 provided thousands of new jobs, though there would still be six million out of work in 1941. And as always, since George Washington relaxed from the cares of state in 1793, the circus provided the truly happy dream that transformed one's troubles into leaps, lion cages, and firecrackers in the pants.

Otis Ferguson, one of the best critics of popular culture that America has produced, caught Ringling Bros. and Barnum & Bailey in his hometown of Worcester, Massachusetts, during the 1940 season, at the end of its second month on the road. Then almost thirty-three years old, Ferguson sat at the circus "within a hundred yards of where, at the age of five, I missed most of my first Ringling show from being flat under my father's knees after the first clown fired the first horse pistol."

But he didn't miss a moment of this Ringling show; and he wrote a lovely picture for *The New Republic* of what it looked like, traveling on the railroad and playing under canvas, just before the war that would take his life:

I submit that a circus starts when the cars are shunted onto the siding at just daylight, and ends when the hoarse whistle for Off Brakes comes over the sleeping town from the yards, along about three the next morning; and that there was never anything under a tent so fascinating as the business of getting it up and knocking it down, unloading and loading back up, wagons and elephants and truly the most intricate and smoothly ordered job of rigging known to the world.

Even as shaken down for the long summer grind, the new Ringling-Barnum-Bailey is a show to put an end to all others. You never saw such a tent; nobody did; nobody ever saw so many elephants outside Kipling; they have a tiger that stretches down the block and around a corner, a lion who roars a little just to keep in practice and all the air in the big tent shakes gently; and they have the best acts, high, low, and flying, that money can buy, and clowns all over the place. Sometimes it's a furor, sometimes a ballet, sometimes your hands sweat freely, and sometimes it's an expensive bore. But always the show that is the true circus goes on underneath, the scene-shifters for the biggest show on earth working their quick miracles with rope and planks and metal—outside a sailing ship, the best example I have seen or heard of, of many men making haste and speed, too.

Of Clowns, Death, and World War II

As 1941 drew to a close, Emmett Kelly believed that he had "arrived" at last. "You can troupe all over the world, and you can listen to applause in far-away places and you can read flattering publicity from hell to breakfast," he was later to write, "but when you open with Ringling Brothers and Barnum & Bailey in Madison Square Garden, New York City, you have 'arrived.'"

In the last month of 1941, that once far-off event was about to happen to him. Emmett Kelly had his first contract to clown with the biggest circus in the world, and he was to join The Greatest Show on Earth at winter quarters in Sarasota in December. But first, he had to go to Cincinnati to play a nightclub date, and that's where he was on December 7, shaving with his little portable radio turned on.

"I almost cut my throat with my razor when I heard the news that the Japs had bombed our fleet in Pearl Harbor," he wrote in *Clown*, his autobiography. He ran down the hall to the room where a dance team was living. They had heard the news, too. What would the war mean for the circus—and for his career?

It took over three and a half years for history to give the full answer to that question. But in its broad outlines, the answer was this: with World War II bringing tragedy to so many American families, the U.S. government considered the circus of vital importance for the "sustainment of morale on the home front." The Office of Defense Transportation issued a general permit for operation of circus trains, and President Roosevelt personally expressed his appreciation that the show was going on.

The bombing of Pearl Harbor pushed Dumbo, Walt Disney's big-eared cartoon baby

A GAG IS BORN. It came about by chance. One day a boy offered Emmett Kelly a peanut, and Kelly pantomimed finding it too hard to crack. He looked around for something to break it with and saw a sledgehammer leaning against a clump of stakes. He put the peanut on the iron railing, picked up the sledgehammer, and gave the peanut a tap. The heavy hammer pulverized it. Weary Willie was disconsolate; the crowd was convulsed. (Ringling Museum)

circus elephant, off the cover of *Time* magazine; but *Time* still ran its story about Disney's new circus picture. In hindsight, *Dumbo* was a nostalgic farewell to the way the circus had been before the war but would never quite be again. Disney's animation artists captured, as no live-action movies do, the rhythm of the tented show in our collective imagination: the promise of the circus train leaving winter quarters; the early arrival of its wagonloads of wonder in one's commonplace hometown; roustabouts raising the tents at dawn to contain the spectacles to come; animal and human prodigies tantalizing us with a street parade; and then, in, around, and over the rings, extraordinary, marvelous, and unusual accomplishments, plus clowns to burlesque them—all exemplified in the film by a little defeat-into-victory fable about a baby elephant whose big ears make him a laughingstock and a clown until he learns to flap them to fly his way to stardom. "*Dumbo*," said *Time*, "could only have happened here. Among all the grim and forbidding visages of A.D. 1941, his guileless, homely face is the face of the true man of good will. The most appealing new character of this year of war. . . . He may not become a U.S. folk hero, but he is certainly the mammal-of-the-year."

———————

From John Bill Ricketts's "Festival Ballet Dance, in Honor of the President of the United States" in 1797, love of country had been a theme of the circus spec in America. During World War II, the circus pulled out all the stops. The Cole Bros. finale in 1941 and 1942 brought all the performers into its three rings for a giant tableau. The cast was dressed as soldiers, sailors, nurses, and war workers, and Uncle Sam, the symbol that Dan Rice inspired, held the place of honor in center ring.

In the last minute, a giant flag was unfurled, revolving wheels of colored fire were ignited, and huge pictures of General Douglas MacArthur and President Franklin D. Roosevelt were lowered from the ceiling.

But it was during World War II that traditionalists began objecting loudly that John Ringling North was turning the circus into a Broadway musical. Indeed, his show *was* full of Broadway showgirls—"North Starlets," he called them. North had begun by giving each circus a "theme"—one year it was "Candyland"; another year, "Dreamland"—interspersing traditional acts with production numbers. North argued, as Robert Lewis Taylor put it, that "his critics are not only wrong but broke"—in other words, the Ringling show was doing good business and traditional circuses were dying left and right.

Actually, this was not true. War in Europe and rearmament in the United States gave American industries a boost that not only ended the Depression but provided audiences with money to spend on circuses. Both of the two big railroad shows, Cole Bros. and Ringling Bros., were doing good business. Several new smaller shows came out and others were enlarged. Mills Bros. Circus, which had opened in 1940 as a small truck show, had adapted and developed a system of using local sponsors to ensure ticket sales, and was thriving. The Wallace Bros. Circus, founded in Canada in 1927 by Ray W. Rogers, combined with Clyde Beatty to become the Clyde Beatty–Wallace Bros. Circus in 1943. Rogers died that year, but the employees operated the circus themselves in 1944, then sold the equipment to the Beatty and King circuses. Russell Bros., which suffered a terrible blow-down of its Big Top in Richmond, Virginia, in 1941, moved its headquarters and its route to California that year, opened in Los Angeles in 1942, and took over the western route that was once considered the private preserve of the Al G. Barnes Circus.

Russell Bros. was sold to Ringling trapeze star Art Concello for 1944, and transformed into a railroad show for 1945, when it was Russell Bros. Pan-Pacific Circus. The new Arthur Bros. Motorized Circus was converted to railroad operation, utilizing Hagenbeck-Wallace equipment that had been stored in California. The tiny Davenport Society Circus became the new Dailey Bros. Railroad Circus in 1944 and also thrived, adding more cars to its train each year for the next several years. In 1945, in fact, it operated Austin Bros. Circus as a second unit. Unfortunately, the Dailey show, according to Parkinson and Fox, "thrived on trouble" as well, and was "permeated with petty gamblers and thieves."

Nevertheless, the first wartime Ringling show was a memorable success. Perhaps the truth is simply that John Ringling North gave the public the kind of circus *he* liked—a combination of traditional circus and Broadway musical—just as, later, Irvin Feld would give the public the kind of circus *he* liked, a combination of traditional circus and Las Vegas revue.

One of North's big ideas was a ballet for the elephants—choreographed by George Balanchine, with music composed by Igor Stravinsky. It was Balanchine who contacted Stravinsky, by telephone, to ask: "I wonder if you would like to do a little ballet with me. A polka, perhaps."

"For whom?" asked Stravinsky.

"For some elephants," answered Balanchine.

"How old?" asked Stravinsky.

"Very young," replied Balanchine.

"All right," said Stravinsky. "If they are very young elephants, I will do it."

Thus it was that when Ringling Bros. and Barnum & Bailey Circus opened at Madison Square Garden in the spring of 1942, the program listed as "Display No. 18: THE BALLET OF THE ELEPHANTS. Fifty Elephants and Fifty Beautiful Girls in an Original Choreographic Tour de Force. Featuring MODOC, premiere ballerina, the Corps de Ballet and Corps des Elephants. Directed by George Balanchine. Staged by John Murray Anderson. Music by Igor Stravinsky. Elephants trained by Walter McClain. Costumes designed by Norman Bel Geddes." They may have been inspired by Disney's film *Fantasia* of two years before, which featured both an elephant ballet to Ponchielli's *Dance of the Hours* and dinosaurs moving to Stravinsky's ballet music for *Rite of Spring*. But animated cartoon elephants (or even dinosaurs) are much easier to choreograph than the real thing.

At least one critic of the ballet claimed that Stravinsky's music was both confusing and frightening to the elephants. "It robbed them of their feeling of security and confidence in the world about them—so alien to their native condition of life. It would have taken very little at any time during the many performances of the ballet music to cause a stampede."

This is unlikely. In fact, it is about as likely that Stravinsky's music would cause elephants trained by Walter McClain to stampede as that it would cause ballerinas trained by Balanchine to run offstage in headlong panic. And, in fact, there were 425 performances of this circus ballet, with no reports of elephants behaving even as badly as the 1913 human audience who hooted and stomped at the premiere of Stravinsky's *Rite of Spring*.

At least one elephant may even have liked the music. Stravinsky himself is quoted as saying, "I received a congratulatory telegram from Bessie, the young pachyderm who had carried the *bella ballerina*. I never saw the ballet, but I met Bessie in Los Angeles once and shook her foot."

The poet Marianne Moore did see the bal-

STRAVINSKY, BALANCHINE, AND ELEPHANTS IN TUTUS. *When George Balanchine called Igor Stravinsky and proposed an elephant ballet, Stravinsky asked, "How old?"*

"Very young," replied Balanchine.

"All right," said Stravinsky. "If they are very young elephants, I will do it."

At Christmastime in 1939, Stravinsky and Balanchine had visited the Walt Disney studio together, where Stravinsky's "Rite of Spring" was being made a part of Disney's Fantasia. *Balanchine was photographed showing Stravinsky a clay model of a hippopotamus in a tutu for Ponchielli's "Dance of the Hours," and Stravinsky said afterward that he particularly enjoyed this part of the film. Now Stravinsky and Balanchine had an opportunity to put real elephants in tutus.*

A program for Balanchine's New York City Ballet said that music confused and frightened the elephants. Ringling old-timers such as the clown Prince Paul did not remember it that way. "They would have done what McLain {their trainer} told them to do, regardless of what the band was playing," he said. Robert Lewis Taylor wrote that "Stravinsky cranked out a number, filled with whistles, gargles, and moosecalls, that everybody said was among his best works, but there was never any evidence that the elephants understood it. . . ." The bella ballerina on opening night was Vera Zorina, the dancer and film star who was married to Balanchine. In all, there were 425 performances of the circus ballet, and the music, called "Circus Polka," is still played in an elephantless version. (Circus World Museum, Baraboo, Wisconsin)

PATRIOTISM AT THE CIRCUS *was displayed in the finale of Ringling Bros. and Barnum & Bailey's 1942 edition when huge pictures of President Franklin Delano Roosevelt and General Douglas MacArthur were lowered from the rigging to the center ring at Madison Square Garden. Cole Bros. donated a block of seats at each performance to war bond buyers and dressed performers as soldiers, sailors, nurses, war workers, and Uncle Sam—the U.S. symbol descended from a Thomas Nast caricature of the nineteenth-century circus clown Dan Rice. The Ringling-Barnum show in 1943 featured spectacles called "Let Freedom Ring," "Drums of Victory," and a third that featured the new Liberty Bandwagon, shown above. The 1943 poster for RBB&B read: "COMING SOON! to TOKYO and BERLIN!" In peacetime, The Greatest Show on Earth made it to Tokyo in 1987. (Circus World Museum, Baraboo, Wisconsin)*

let, and rhapsodized in *Dance Index* over the dancing elephants: "their deliberate way of kneeling, on slowsliding forelegs—like a cat's yawning stretch or a ship's slide into the water—is fine ballet."

What remains today of that elephant ballet is the music, of course: Stravinsky's "Circus Polka"; plus some motion picture film of the elephants in action; and a wonderful circus poster showing two elephants in pink tutus and cupcake hats dancing in a golden, star-studded spotlight. The "strong linear" poster with its frankly flat elephant shapes, "a radical departure in the history of poster art," according to poster connoisseur Jack Rennert, was designed by E. McKnight Kauffer (1890–1954), who is known in Europe for his many London Transport posters. During World War II, almost all Ringling posters had either "Buy War Bonds" or "Buy Defense Bonds" as an integral part of the design. Kauffer placed "Buy Defense Bonds" on the red, white, and blue elephant tub on which the ballerina poses.

———————

The acrobatic sensation of the 1942 season was a juggler named Massimiliano Truzzi, whom North found at the Cirque Royal in Brussels. North figured that Truzzi's technique would appeal to Robert Benchley, a humorist famed for being all thumbs physically, mentally, and spiritually, and Benchley's reaction did not disappoint him. Sitting in North's box on opening night, 1942, watching Truzzi put every object around him in orbit about his head without dropping anything, Benchley sighed: "Look at that son of a bitch, and I can't even get a cup of coffee up to my mouth."

Eventually, Truzzi got even better by dropping things. Emmett Kelly, who called Truzzi "a great juggler with a rare streak of comedy in his work," said that it was Truzzi's idea to let the clown burlesque not just jugglers' acts

in general, but his specific act. They worked out a routine in which Truzzi's good-looking wife, who assisted him, would give Kelly the eye while Truzzi was trying to hold the attention of the crowd with his juggling. Kelly would give a shy wave to Mrs. Truzzi with his red bandanna—and Mr. Truzzi would begin dropping the plates he had up to then had no difficulty keeping in the air.

Trying to be helpful, Kelly would come to Truzzi with an old burlap sack and offer to catch the plates Truzzi could no longer keep from dropping. Not surprisingly, Truzzi would reject the offer of help, and order Kelly out of the ring, making the eternally misunderstood Weary Willie sadder than ever.

On August 4, 1942—a "soft and sunny morning," remembered Henry Ringling North—the Big One had its tents pitched for a five-day stand on a lakeside lot in Cleveland, Ohio. At eleven-thirty that morning, before the crowds arrived, the menagerie top burst into flames. Zebras and giraffes, frantic with fear, ran for their lives. But the elephants, said Dr. J. Y. Henderson, the circus veterinarian, "wouldn't budge, burned or not, until he arrived." *He*, of course, was Walter McClain, boss of the bull men, who came running and shouted a command to his elephants. They pulled out their own front stakes (the workmen had already pulled out the back ones) and left the inferno in formation, trunk to tail, but they were terribly burned. The flesh was peeling off some elephants in long sheets, some had singed trunks, and some had had their thin, floppy ears burned off.

In three minutes, the tent was consumed. Dr. Henderson made immediate preparations to treat the animals who still had a chance for life. He filled spray guns with a healing preparation called Foille, and put assistants to work spraying those who might survive. Bull men saved many suffering elephants by climbing ladders put up against them and slathering Foille all over them with big paintbrushes.

Those he could not save Dr. Henderson had to shoot. Borrowing a pistol from a policeman, the grieving vet moved quickly among the still-burning cages, amid the charred poles and smoking bits of canvas, ending the torture of those that were not already cooked to death by the burning straw of their bedding.

None of the camels were saved. Perhaps searing heat did not seem a danger signal to them. In any event, they made no attempt to save themselves and resisted all efforts to lead them from the burning tent. In his book *Circus Doctor*, Dr. Henderson says that "They lay down, staring out off into space like old men looking out of a club window, and died."

The cause of the fire was never determined, but, in it, 65 animals died of burns, including: 4 elephants, 4 lions, 3 tigers, 2 giraffes, 12 zebras, 1 ostrich, 3 pumas, 16 monkeys, 2 black bucks, 1 sacred cow from India, and, of course, all 13 camels.

Walter McClain, the well-liked elephant superintendent, mourned the big animals that had burned. But he was too busy to grieve long. Once again, as in World War I, when business was booming but personnel was short, performers and workmen alike pitched in to do jobs that were not normally theirs. McClain had joined Ringling Bros. and Barnum & Bailey when the Barnes show closed in 1938, and brought with him its policy of using elephants to unload the train and pull wagons; when the war came, in addition to all this work, he substituted at the dangerous job of poler, handling wagon poles in loading and unloading at the runs. He was unloading the circus train at Jacksonville, Florida, in November 1942, when a wagon broke loose and crushed him to death.

No human beings were injured in the menagerie fire, but it had caused a terrible fear in

John Ringling North: what if it had been the Big Top? At the next stockholders meeting, North moved that they either offer the circus free to the government as a morale builder or retire it for the duration of the war. Fireproof canvas had been invented, but the process required chemicals that private companies could not obtain in wartime. If the government ran the circus, it could certainly get clearance to fireproof the tents.

The other stockholders rejected the idea. The North brothers voted only one of three blocks of Ringling stock. A second was owned by Mrs. Aubrey Ringling Haley, widow of Richard Ringling, son of Alf T. The third was owned by their Aunt Edith, widow of Charles Ringling. While John Ringling North owned only 7 percent of the stock outright, as executor of his uncle John's estate he also voted the 30 percent then owned by the state of Florida. He had been elected president each year through 1942, but now he tendered his resignation. It was quickly accepted, and the family elected his cousin, Robert Ringling, son of Edith and Charles. Robert was a sweet-tempered opera singer in ill health.

Under Robert Ringling, The Greatest Show on Earth came out in 1943 with a huge patriotic Spectacle called "Let Freedom Ring." For its finale, there was not only a giant-size cloth picture of President Roosevelt but enormous American flags that unfolded in sections from the thirty-foot-long trains of circus showgirls who climbed lofty rigging at the ends and center of the Big Top.

With the musicians' strike of the year before settled, the circus band rode in a brand-new bandwagon, called the Liberty Bandwagon. On its sides were carved representations of the Liberty Bell, its famous crack clearly delineated, flanked by carvings of fluttering American flags. The new bandwagon was filled with Merle Evans and his back-to-work bandsmen, and they were featured on a circus poster that year. So was the Spec, "Let Freedom Ring"—and that poster, appearing in store windows across America in the discouraging year of Salerno, Cassino, and Tarawa, of terrible losses in the air and on the ground, defiantly added the words: "COMING SOON! TO TOKYO AND BERLIN!"

The 1943 season is remembered by performers and workmen alike as one of those rare circus seasons when there were no disasters and business was good. The 1944 season started well, except for the manpower shortage. The invasion—the peak of the war effort in Europe—approached, and in the Pacific vast numbers of men and amounts of material were making a bloody "island-hopping" advance toward Japan. On every show, there was lots of "cherry pie," an old circus expression for the double duty everyone does when a show is shorthanded. Ticket takers, ushers, candy butchers, and performers had to pitch in to help the workers move the show. The expression is probably a pun: the circus gave you plenty of "chairy pie" every day, because you had to carry thousands of those folding grandstand chairs made of wood.

Ringling Bros. and Barnum & Bailey showed in Hartford, Connecticut, on Thursday, July 6, one month to the day after the D-Day landings in Normandy began the Allied invasion of Hitler's Europe. After the long Fourth of July weekend, most men were back at their offices or factories, while the majority of women with young children were at leisure; the good crowd of 6,789 people at the afternoon performance that day was mostly women and children.

The flame-resistant Big Top that had been used in lieu of the fireproof canvas they couldn't get had leaked badly, so for 1944 the new management had substituted an old-fashioned tent waterproofed with a solution of paraffin and benzene. The coating was good at keeping water out, but the canvas was also capable of being easily ignited and of burning with extreme rapidity.

The show had been on for almost twenty minutes. Emmett Kelly was sitting in clown alley, waiting for the waltz music that would announce Karl Wallenda's three-high human pyramid on the wire. That would be the signal for Weary Willie to walk into the center ring directly underneath the Wallendas and spread out a tiny handkerchief to catch anyone who fell.

The waltz music began, and the Wallendas started their high-wire act. Beneath them, May Kovar, having finished her performance with Alfred Court's lions, was driving the big cats through the steel-barred chute to their cages.

One of the first to notice the tiny flame traveling up a tent rope was bandleader Merle Evans, who was holding and fingering his silver cornet with his right hand and conducting with his left. As quickly as his brain took in the terrifying possibilities of what he was seeing, his breath made his cornet blast out the circus band's tent-clearing signal—Sousa's "The Stars and Stripes forever." The waltz was over.

With a shrill blast on his whistle, Fred Bradna stopped the Wallendas in midair and brought them sliding down the guy wires. He could see smoke at the entrance. Somebody made an announcement over the public address system asking the audience to leave quickly.

Recognizing the march that means "All out!," and remembering the terrible menagerie fire less than two years before, the bull men in the backyard didn't ask why, they simply shouted "Tails! Tails!" and the herd of forty elephants, forming the familiar trunk-to-tail queue, lumbered out of danger into the street.

A policeman on duty outside testified later how the roof of the Big Top burned in a tiny circle "like the glowing end of a cigarette" that slowly widened into a ring of flame, "then . . . suddenly burst through in a big common flame, and went roaring all around the place."

When that happened, the crowd broke into a stampede.

They could have gotten out under the tent flaps almost anywhere, but in their panic, many tried to leave the way they had come in, and they now found that way blocked by the steel-barred animal chute. May Kovar did not panic. She risked her life to get all of the lions back in their cages, fearing what would happen if they returned to the chute now surrounded by fear-crazed people.

Even so, the chute was blocking the escape of hundreds.

Outside, somebody ran by clown alley, shouting "Fire!" Emmett Kelly's first impulse was to try and put it out. Beside his trunk was a bucket of water for washing off his makeup after the show. He grabbed the bucket and ran outside in his big flapping clown shoes.

In this catastrophe, Kelly's bucket of water was as useless as his handkerchief would have been had the Wallendas fallen.

Despite many acts of heroism by performers and workers, their customers were giving in to chaos. Bradna screamed at the people blocked by the animal chute to leave through the side flaps. But too many of those who thought they were trapped were children, and in their mounting hysteria they continued to try to get out the same way they got in.

So hundreds of people were still piled up against those steel bars, trampling and grinding and squeezing and smothering and crushing the life out of those underneath and in front of them. Bradna, his hair aflame, smelling his own eyebrows and mustache burn, managed to drag eleven children from this "monstrous pile in front of the animal chute" and shove them to safety. By that time the inside of the tent looked like the inside of a furnace.

Even so, mothers who had gotten separated from their children in the chaos were trying to get back in.

"You can't get back in there!" Emmett Kelly was shouting. "Keep moving, keep moving!"

The tent burned for eight or nine minutes before the last of the six great center poles toppled and the last section of the Big Top fell with it. The band played throughout. They "blasted it," as they say in the circus, so that their music could be heard above the roaring flames and might provide a reference point of normality for the escaping crowd. Many people did seem to be steadied by the music, so Evans and his musicians kept playing, their faces blackened, their uniforms scorched, until the last center pole fell. They jumped off the bandstand just before a quarter-pole fell flaming onto the stand.

Then they reassembled outside and started to play again.

Within fifteen minutes after Merle Evans saw the single flame zipping up a tent rope, the place where the Big Top had been was an ugly oblong of scorched earth, with Alfred Court's steel cage and animal chute rising from the smoking embers. And there, piled up against that chute, was the most awful sight of all: blackened bodies piled four and five deep, including some still living who moaned and writhed under the dead.

In the fire, 168 persons were trampled or asphyxiated or burned to death—and at least 84 of them were children. Another 487 were treated for burns and injuries, including 60 circus employees. It was by far the worst disaster in circus history.

That night, Jim Haley, who had replaced Henry Ringling North as first vice president and assistant to Robert Ringling; general manager George Smith; tractor boss David Blanchfield; seat boss James Caley; and lighting boss Edward R. Versteeg were arrested and charged

THE WORST CATASTROPHE IN CIRCUS HISTORY. *On July 6, 1944, Emmett Kelly was sitting outside the Big Top in Hartford, Connecticut, waiting for a cue, when somebody ran by shouting, "Fire!" Within ten minutes on that terrible day, 168 people had been burned or trampled to death. Robert Ringling said that such a flash fire would never have occurred if his circus had been allowed to use fireproofing for canvas that had been reserved for war use. Clown Kelly said seriously: "We must forget the fire. We must entertain. In wartime, it's more important than ever." The show went on. In 1950, the Associated Press reported that a twenty-one-year-old circus roustabout had confessed to setting the fire, but he had a history of mental problems and investigators were never absolutely sure. What was sure was that the Hartford Fire of 1944 was the worst catastrophe in the world history of the circus. (Circus World Museum, Baraboo, Wisconsin)*

LOU JACOBS, *a contortionist before he was a clown, is famous for emerging, big foot first, from a midget car. Jacobs, born in Germany, emigrated to America in 1923, joined the Ringling-Barnum show in 1924, and was still being featured by The Greatest Show on Earth in the 1980s. Lou has a knack for creating cockeyed images of American society. His midget car, along with some other immortal foolery by Lou, Emmett Kelly, Otto Griebling, and movie star and frequent guest clown James Stewart, is on permanent display in Cecil B. De Mille's 1952 Best Picture Oscar winner* The Greatest Show on Earth. *(Charles Philip Fox)*

THE CRISTIANIS. *The horse and rider performing together are the first circus act, the clown burlesquing them the second. As Earl Chapin May observed, "Prior to the advent of motor cars all circus performances were centered on horsemanship because nearly all circus patrons owned or made frequent use of horses and understood the fine points of equine flesh and management." Even in this car-loving century, the American circus has seen at least six great riding families: the Cristiani family from Italy, pictured above in 1967; the Hodgini troupe from England; the high-riding pyramids of the Loyal-Repensky troupe, which began in France; the Davenports, who share with the Cristianis a knack for horse-to-horse somersaults; the Zoppes, who created their own circus in Italy more than 125 years ago; and, of course, the Hanneford family, with Poodles Hanneford's still-unequaled record of twenty-six running leaps on and off horseback. (Ringling Museum)*

SONG OF THE ROUSTABOUTS. *Walt Disney's tribute to the circus, his 1941 animated feature* Dumbo, *contains not only a cartoon evocation of the circus parade, but also a sequence called "Song of the Roustabouts," which evokes another potent circus lover's memory: seeing the roustabouts put up the Big Top. With the center poles in position, the giant bales of canvas are unrolled. Roustabouts with sixteen-pound sledges, such as the one Emmett Kelly used to pulverize a peanut in his most famous gag, pound into the ground the stakes that secure the canvas. Canvasmen spread the canvas sections, lace them together, and lash the canvas to bale rings at the center poles. At last, the tents are raised and filled with seats and rigging. This magical operation is preserved on film both in* Dumbo's *animated drawings and in the live-action footage that Cecil B. De Mille photographed for* The Greatest Show on Earth. *(Circus World Museum, Baraboo, Wisconsin)*

GENERAL MARSHALL, HIS GRANDSON, AND CLOWN EM-METT KELLY. *Just one season after the terrible Hartford fire, when the Big One came to Washington, D.C., in the spring of 1945, General of the Army George C. Marshall broke his rule against attending social functions while the war was on and brought his grandson, Jimmy Winn, to the circus. They were photographed with Emmett Kelly, and the picture appeared in almost every newspaper in the country the next day. "There was no further fear among the public," said Fred Bradna. " 'If the General thinks it's all right to take his grandson, I guess we can risk it, too,' was a refrain we heard over and over again as the season progressed. It is quite possible that the General's action saved trouping under canvas in America." (Circus World Museum, Baraboo, Wisconsin)*

with involuntary manslaughter. A warrant was served on boss canvasman Leonard Aylesworth when he returned from conferring with the ailing Robert Ringling. Robert Ringling, who hadn't even been in Hartford, was not charged with anything.

The courts attached all circus property and funds: not a single train, wagon, truck, or elephant could move. It was obvious to everyone that claims for damages would run into the millions.

"The Ringling family is not interested in escaping liability," said a spokesman. "It wants to help and it wants to carry on."

Haley acted decisively. If anybody was to get anything, the circus had to be on the road again as quickly as possible. The circus had a cash reserve fund of $500,000 for emergencies, and Haley had taken out a $500,000 insurance policy on the big show only months before. That million dollars was put up as security to enable the circus to leave Connecticut. Nine days after the fire, it returned to winter quarters to reorganize.

There were, in fact, so many damage suits that lawyers for both the circus and the claimants consulted together to draw up what was known as the Hartford Arbitration Agreement. By this agreement, the circus assumed full responsibility, and left to the lawyers' committee the task of fixing the amount of damages to be paid. The circus further agreed to pay a "receiver" out of earnings, the amounts necessary to pay off these claims—and not to enter into any unusual expenses until every penny was paid.

The circus executives came to trial in late 1944. All but Blanchfield were convicted and sentenced to short prison terms. They were permitted to go to winter quarters to get the show ready for the 1945 season, but then they had to report back to the Hartford authorities.

While the accountability for the circus fire

was being determined, the circus performers had to go on with the show. "We must forget the fire," said Emmett Kelly. "We must entertain. In wartime, it's more important than ever. It's going to be great in the open air."

And it was. One month from the date of the fire, Ringling Bros. and Barnum & Bailey Circus opened again in the Rubber Bowl at Akron, Ohio; then went on, in the blazing sun of ballparks and such open-air arenas as Soldier's Field in Chicago. The clowns, like all the other performers, were personally depressed by the Hartford disaster; but as performers, they had never been funnier.

Women whose men were away at war at least had the attentions of old Paul Jerome, whose nose lighted up whenever he saw a pretty girl. Then, if he was really smitten—and he was often really smitten—the neon heart that he wore over his real heart would begin to flash on and off, giving many a lonely woman uncontrollable giggles. Let it be noted that Paul Jerome wore a heart light long before ET; and it was hard work falling in love like that: he had to be wired before every performance.

Then there was Emmett Kelly, with his burlesque of the victory gardens we planted. The victory garden program was the most popular of all the civilian war-effort tasks: at its peak, there were nearly 20 million gardens producing 40 percent of all vegetables grown in the country, freeing farmers for a more direct role in the war effort. Naturally, Weary Willie wanted to help, too. He started out by setting up a little portable fence with its own little swinging gate. Inside this fence, he hoed a little plot of ground, and presently, started planting seeds out of paper packets. He planted with a lot of energy at first, but gradually, he slowed down. Kelly was the most subtle mime in the circus, and you could tell that he was dreaming of the delicious vegetables he was going to eat one day, and that all this thinking was making him hungry. Pretty soon, he sat down and ate all the seeds.

And there was Felix Adler, the greatest white-face of modern times, famous for bottle-feeding the suckling pig he carried around the hippodrome track in the walk-around. To earn its daily milk, the little pig would often climb a slide for Felix, and scoot down to the delight of the crowd. Dressed as the Big Bad Wolf, Felix got chased around the track by three of his little trained pigs. Get it? Who's Afraid of the Big Bad Wolf?

And Paul Jung, the great producing clown, built a steamroller one year; the gag called for it to run over the clowns who got in his way. The roller was hollow and built so that a clown in its path, while temporarily shielded from the audience's view by a gaggle of fellow clowns, could climb inside, leaving a perfectly flat, oilcloth copy of himself on the ground as "casualty." Then stretcher bearers would remove the oilcloth victim. The gag had been seen in a pantomime performed by the Byrne Brothers troupe (former circus acrobats James, Matthew, Andrew, and John) in the 1890s, but during World War II it was like a clown version of the way we were steamrolling the *Wehrmacht* in our drive for Berlin.

Come around again, clowns, for one last laugh, one last cheer: Harry Dan with his pet goose, and Frankie Saluto with his pet rabbit; and Charlie Bell with his little fox terrier dressed to look like a rabbit; and Lou Jacobs with his real, live dachshund that was dressed in a giant bun to look like a hot dog!; and Prince Paul Alpert, the dwarf driver of the little fire cart that Emmett Kelly rode in "Hold Your Horses," a 1943 Spec "recalling happy hours of bygone circus days."

One more, then: Paul Wentzel and his "break-away britches." His trousers were made to unsnap and go flying through the air when pulled by an invisible wire in the hands of one of his colleagues. In cities and towns across the war-weary land, from ocean to ocean and Great Lakes to Gulf, he lost his pants.

———

The 1945 season opened, of course, in New York's fireproof Madison Square Garden. That year, The Greatest Show on Earth held its first New York parade in twenty-five years, to promote the sale of war bonds (they put on one other street parade in 1945: in Rocky Mountain, North Carolina, for the same cause). In these two war-bond parades, and in the Spec that year, Robert Ringling allowed the appearance of the oldest and most widely traveled circus bandwagon in existence—the famous Five Graces Bandwagon. Built in 1878 for the Adam Forepaugh Circus, it was used by other circuses as a feature of their parades for two decades before it created a sensation during the European tours of the Barnum & Bailey Circus in 1898 and 1902. In Europe, this massive, ornate vehicle was pulled by a massed hitch of black horses—a sight that moved the people of the Continent to raptures worthy of a circus press agent. (It can be seen now in the Ringling Museum of the Circus in Sarasota, Florida.)

On May 8, while The Greatest Show on Earth was still playing in Madison Square Garden, V-E Day ended the war in Europe.

Ringling announced that it was going to resume tented operation. It publicized the fact that the war department had released the fireproofing chemical the day after the catastrophe, and that all the tents were now fireproofed. Moreover, the wooden folding chairs had been replaced by chairs of metal. But as Fred Bradna said, "No one knew whether Americans would ever again patronize a circus under canvas."

The nation's capitol was to be the first Big-Top stand of the Ringling Bros. and Barnum

& Bailey Circus season. Preparing for the Washington, D.C., engagement, management held a worried conference. How could they restore public confidence? Bradna suggested that if a public figure who inspired confidence were seen attending the circus, that image might do more good than "a million dollars spent advertising the new unburnable canvas."

The public figure whose attendance was hoped for was General George Catlett Marshall, U.S. Army chief of staff during the war that had just ended in Europe. Marshall was one of the public's favorite war heroes, a hard-working architect of the victory of America and her allies who had not even taken time out to attend public functions during the conflict.

General Marshall not only accepted the invitation to be present as a guest of the circus; he brought his grandson, Jimmy Winn. A photographer snapped a picture of Emmett Kelly shaking hands with little Jimmy, as he sat in the stands under canvas on his grandfather's lap. Grandpa was in uniform, with his general's stars and a chest full of ribbons.

The picture appeared in almost every newspaper in the country the following day. Again and again, as the season progressed, Bradna heard the hoped-for reaction from the public: "If the General thinks it's all right to take his grandson, I guess we can risk it, too."

Fear of another fire in a circus tent seemed to have been quenched by that photograph of a clown, a child, and a hero. "It is quite possible," wrote Bradna, "that the General's action saved trouping under canvas in America."

DISPLAY·16

The Big Top Folds

"Every clown gag ends with one or more of seven kinds of blow-off," said Glen "Frosty" Little, 1980s boss clown of The Greatest Show on Earth: "They are—they've always been— fire, water, smoke, explosions, slaps, falls, and surprise."

The Ringling show's finale, the first season after World War II ended, was entitled "Drums of Victory," and featured a giant-size model of the Statue of Liberty for a wow finish. But the surprise gag was the clowns' attempt to top the atom bomb.

Newspapers were full of stories about the "atom smasher," the popular term for the particle accelerator called the cyclotron. So Paul Jung, producing clown for Ringling Bros. and Barnum & Bailey Circus, pulled the venerable circus trick of cross-breeding old gags with current events and invented the "Adam Smasher."

"With the newspapers full of smashing the atom last winter, I got to thinking what I could

do with it," Jung would explain. "A clown is supposed to be a man with the mind of a child, so I figured that was the way a clown would see it: the atom as Adam, a man."

So a goofy-looking clown with a sign on him that read ADAM was confronted by clowns decked out in black academic robes. These clown "professors" coaxed Adam to enter the ADAM SMASHER, a large box covered with cranks, wheels, and dials, from which only his head stuck out. The professors would then pace around and around the box, cranking, wheeling, and dialing until a derrick had swung what appeared to be a heavy weight into a position directly above Adam's head. As Adam pulled his head into the hole, the "weight" dropped, and *bam!* its door flew open—and out ran four midget clowns, all dressed exactly like "Adam."

The postwar circus world was under way.

In the West, the Clyde Beatty Circus toured

TRUNK UP! A beautiful woman usually fronts the elephant act, in this case, Kitty Clark and Modoc. "Trunk up!" is the command for the elephant to lift her high in the air. (Ringling Museum)

aboard fifteen cars with its twenty-two lions and tigers. In the Midwest, Cole Bros. Circus was in good shape after profitable wartime seasons. When Midwesterner Harry Truman was reelected president in 1948, Cole Bros. took its steam calliope to Washington for the inauguration and played "Meet Me in St. Louis" and "The Missouri Waltz" in the Inaugural Parade.

Meantime, what one wag called "Ringling Wrangling"—the power struggle among Ringling heirs and once-and-future executives—continued unabated. Losses from the 1944 fire were at last reckoned in dollar terms; claims for damages were filed and the total eventually awarded came to something over $4 million.

In 1945, Johnny North called on James Haley, first vice president at the time of the Hartford fire, in jail. According to North's brother, Henry, Haley thought that Robert Ringling had "let him down" in his testimony after the fire, "that he was interested only in saving his own skin. He believed that had Robert's testimony been more forcefully in his favor he would have been given a suspended sentence." At the stockholders meeting in April of 1946, Robert Ringling was ousted as president: Haley would now carry that title. And John Ringling North was back as vice president and in charge of operations.

The Ringling family's neo-Byzantine plotting finally came to a temporary halt in 1947, when Haley and his wife, Aubrey Ringling Haley, sold John Ringling North the bulk of their stock for $200,000, which North raised the way he did most things—creatively. North knew his people, and he knew that the great flier Art Concello was a frustrated businessman. "Most of the time I was up there," Concello later said, pointing to the flying trapeze, "I was trying to figure out some way to get into the office." John Ringling North offered him a way.

In 1943, shortly after North had been replaced as president of The Greatest Show on Earth by his cousin Robert, Concello left the show. The star circus flier had bought, in partnership with his sister and with his wife and flying partner, Antoinette Concello, the Russell Bros. Circus, which operated in California. Then the Concellos added Clyde Beatty's act to their circus, and organized several new flying acts, which they placed with circuses in this country and in England and Australia. Altogether, they handled about fifty fliers, and the Russell Bros.–Clyde Beatty Circus was prospering as the Concellos were getting rich. So when North telephoned Concello and said, "Art, I can have the circus back if I can raise a hundred thousand dollars for stock," Art answered, "I'll have the money tomorrow noon, John." He was there the way his catchers were there when he did a three-and-a-half. He subsequently sold the Russell Bros. Circus equipment to Clyde Beatty (who operated it in the Clyde Beatty Circus until 1958) and became general manager of Ringling Brothers and Barnum & Bailey Circus.

Buckets of beluga caviar and five or six cases of vintage champagne were consumed by the celebrants in the M'Toto Room of the John Ringling Hotel in Sarasota when John Ringling North took charge of his uncles' circus again. At forty-four, John Ringling North at last owned 51 percent of the stock in The Greatest Show on Earth. He was the first individual in its history to hold a controlling interest. He could name himself president forever.

He brought his brother, Henry, back in again as vice president and assistant to the president. During the Ringling wrangling, Johnny had made a deal with his aunt Edith that he would drop all lawsuits and pay her son Robert a salary as chairman of the board if he, Johnny, got the job as president and was left alone to run the show. Johnny kept his part of the bargain; in any event, Robert lived only two more years. Then Edith took her son's place as board chairman and served until her death at age eighty-three in 1953, calling herself "Queen Mother of the Circus."

Following the pattern of his mentor, Uncle John Ringling, North traveled in royal comfort aboard the private railroad car, the "Jomar," slept late, and was attended by a valet. On his infrequent visits to winter quarters, he would take an hour's ride on a circus horse if it was sufficiently spirited, then appear in the ring barn with his brother, both of them elegantly tricked out in expertly tailored jodhpurs and Italian sports jackets, to confer with his executives on plans for the approaching season. De Mille has it exactly right in his film *The Greatest Show on Earth* when he shows Johnny North being brought a horse as soon as the executive meeting is over.

In the evening Johnny would review circus acts in the ballroom of the John Ringling Hotel. Once on the road, he left the day-to-day operation to his brother and their executives. What they looked to "Mr. Johnny" for was the great eye for the crowd-pleasing attraction that had brought them Gargantua before the war. Each year Mr. Johnny would climb into a custom-built Cadillac to be driven through Europe by a French chauffeur named Henri; his fellow passenger was a European agent who had changed his name at the end of World War II from Schichtholz to Umberto Bedini.

The excitement when word spread through a European circus that "John Ringling North is in the audience" was captured in Sir Carol Reed's fictional but truer-than-life 1953 film, *Trapeze.* An actor playing North sees a great flier played by Tony Curtis throw a triple to catcher Burt Lancaster, and North immediately signs him up to come to America and join The Greatest Show on Earth. That's the way North often operated in real life, and every circus,

from the best known to the most obscure, worried about keeping its top acts when John Ringling North was in town.

The film *Trapeze* remains an opportunity to see one of the great trapeze stars of the North era, Fay Alexander—although he was usually disguised as Tony Curtis. The catcher doubling for Lancaster in the film was Eddie Ward, the former catcher for the Flying Concellos.

Lancaster himself had started out in the circus. In 1932, at the age of eighteen, Lancaster had formed an acrobatic team, Lang and Cravat, with Nick Cravat, the little man who later was his sidekick in such adventure films as *The Flame and the Arrow* (1950) and *The Crimson Pirate* (1952). From 1932 to 1939, Lang and Cravat performed in circuses, carnivals, and vaudeville. Lancaster did a memorable trick on the horizontal bars in which he negotiated a series of giant swings on one bar and then, at the height of one swing, released his hold and sailed to the second bar, about six feet away, landing on his feet. Although he was not a trapeze artist, Lancaster continually studied aerialists' work.

"Back in the thirties," Lancaster told me, "Art Concello was throwing three-and-a-halfs in the Ringling show when Alfredo Codona was doing triples in the next ring. Art Concello was tremendous, but he was an awkward-looking flier. He didn't have the beautiful style and grace that Codona had. Anyway, it turned out that Art's wife, Antoinette, was the one who did the triples in their act, and Eddie caught for her."

But Eddie Ward's face took a beating from both Antoinette and Art Concello smashing into him in practice, said Lancaster; and, as a result,

he had all false teeth, and a terror of being hit in the mouth again. At the time of *Trapeze,* I was forty-one and he was about forty and he had been retired from catching for some years. I got him out of retirement, so to speak, and he was working on the film as a kind of technical expert. He hadn't caught in some years, but he went back into training with Fay for the film.

Eddie caught the double, and the two-and-a-half, and things of that kind. I caught a couple of cockamamie trips such as singles and a full-twister, where all you had to do was lay there and Fay Alexander would come right to you.

But when it came to the triple, what happened is that Eddie couldn't help himself, he had such a terror of being hit in the mouth again that he'd move out to the side, and then try to reach in from the side to snatch him. Consequently, Fay could never really get the right kind of a grip.

For the film, Fay Alexander did nineteen triples in a row that day. His back was all cut up and bleeding from landing in the net. All scraped. Nothing serious—it was just skin broken—but it looked terrible. And Eddie could never bring himself to come right to him.

So we had to do a cutting trick to split the screen and make it look like a triple.

For the real North, and with another catcher, Alexander had done triples on The Greatest Show on Earth, and would do so again. In those days, North had a knack of bringing the best out of performers.

Touring England, North spotted the reckless but exciting Harold Alzana walking the wire with an obscure show. Touring southern Spain he stopped to watch a band of roadside performers and saw a young woman with a phenomenal sense of balance . . . and apparently no nerves. She did a single-trapeze act without a net, and she could balance for ten minutes, first on her toes, next on her knees, then on one knee, and finally on her head, never reaching for support. He brought her to America and told the press that they had made their

contract in a gypsy cave, and that her name was Pinito Del Oro, "Little Pine Tree of Gold." A charmed media rushed to photograph Miss Del Oro pretending to read the morning paper while standing on her head on the trapeze.

Henry Ringling North called 1948 "that wonderful year in which John introduced for the first time in America such famous stars as Unus, 'Upside-down gravity-defying, equilibristic Wonder of the World'; the great juggler Francis Brunn; Cucciola, the midget equestrian clown; and nine other new imports from Europe and the Orient in addition to our grand old stand-bys."

Unus was by far the greatest success of the group. North saw him working in a nightclub in Barcelona in 1946 and knew that he belonged in the Greatest Show on Earth.

Unus (originally a Viennese named Franz Furtner) always wore white gloves when working, but before he performed the finale of his act, he would deliberately remove them and exhibit his bare hands to the crowd to show that he used no gimmick. Then he would put the gloves back on and climb to the top of a giant electric light bulb, made especially for him by General Electric. On the top of that bulb, he would balance himself on his index finger with his feet straight up in the air, and the crowd would go wild.

How did he do it? How did he manage to *stand* on his index finger? By combining his equilibrist's skills with the skills of a magician, apparently. For after exhibiting his bare hands to the audience, it was alleged that he would use sleight of hand to apply a brace to his palm when he put the gloves back on. If so, he wasn't balancing himself on his index finger at all— the finger belonged to the brace—but even standing on one's fist on a finger-sized device is a world-class feat of balance.

Ernest Hemingway paid tribute to Unus when he wrote: "In your dreams you watch

Unus standing on one finger and you think, 'Look at such a fine, intelligent and excellent man making his living standing on one finger when most of us can't even stand on our feet.'"

Cecil B. De Mille, Hollywood's veteran producer-director of movie spectaculars from *The Ten Commandments* to *Samson and Delilah*, "joined out" on the road in the summer of 1949. "At every show, every night," wrote Henry North, "he mingled with the circus crowds as they poured in, listening and making notes . . . squinting through his finder to study camera angles. . . . " At Madison, Wisconsin, on August 12, 1949, De Mille's sixty-eighth birthday, he had himself hoisted in a bosun's chair to the peak of the Big Top, where he remained for more than an hour, swaying giddily, as he peered down on the aerial and high-wire acts.

The result of all this was the shooting script of *The Greatest Show on Earth*, which De Mille filmed in the winter of 1949–50, much of it in Sarasota. For De Mille, the Ringling show even put on an old-time circus parade through Sarasota's main street.

Betty Hutton, one of the film's stars, insisted on learning how to fly, so Antoinette Concello put a "mechanic" on her and taught her some of the simpler tricks. Hutton got so she could do a crossover, flying from the swinging bar to the hands of the catcher, then swinging from his hands back to the pedestal, and you can see her do it in the finished film—with no mechanic. But for the more difficult tricks, she is doubled by Fay Alexander, wearing a blond wig. (He also doubled for Cornel Wilde, without a wig.) The fact that Alexander was a convincing double for Hutton led to his being chosen to double in *Trapeze*, not only for Tony Curtis but also for Gina Lollobrigida—this time wearing a brunette wig.

Some of the tricks were special effects, however. In one scene, the elephant girl played by Gloria Grahame lies down on the ground and allows an elephant to lower one foot over her head until it is only a few inches away. The script called for the trainer to threaten to command the elephant to crush her skull. These are the kinds of risks movie companies are not supposed to take with their actors. De Mille had special effects build a mechanical replica of an elephant's foot, which could be lowered almost to Miss Grahame's nose with no danger of mashing it.

The famous train wreck was also produced by special effects, accomplished by mixing trick photography of model trains with footage of the destruction of some real railroad coaches that De Mille had bought from the Southern Pacific Railroad. He had them painted to look like circus cars, then raised them high in the air with a huge crane and dropped them on the tracks with convincing crashes.

The true value of the film is as a record of the last years of The Greatest Show on Earth under canvas. We see the Big Top put up and taken down, and we see the circus train loaded and unloaded. Under that Big Top, no less than sixty performers or acts are shown in whole or part, including clowns Emmett Kelly, Otto Griebling, Paul Jung, and Lou Jacobs (Jacobs did his famous midget car routine with an assist from "Buttons the Clown," played by Jimmy Stewart); the bareback-riding Zoppes; and aerialists Antoinette Concello and Fay Alexander.

The Greatest Show on Earth's two hours and thirty-one minutes of spectacle, comedy, and drama won the Academy Award for the best picture of 1952.

———

Clown alley of the Ringling Bros. and Barnum & Bailey Circus was the answer to those who lamented the passing of the talking clown, the singing clown, and the style of clowning that fit best in a one-ring circus. Three-ring circus clowning—broad pantomime and energetic, even acrobatic, slapstick—had reached its height. In the 1953 show, for example, three of the greatest three-ring clowns were all on the same show.

Emmett Kelly convulsed the crowds by suddenly leaving the circus arena for a hobo vacation wearing a homburg instead of his trademark derby and carrying a battered golf bag. It was a typically quick and deft Kelly sight gag: President Eisenhower was always leaving the White House wearing his homburg hat . . . but with a golf game in view.

Otto Griebling and Fred Freeman gave "an exhibition of frivolously futile fisticuffs for the Championship of Clown Alley: 'Puncho' Griebling vs. 'Slugger' Freeman."

And Lou Jacobs, whose midget automobile routine was being seen by millions in *The Greatest Show on Earth*, now came up with a midget airplane. "Pint-sized Sorcery," said the program, "The World's Smallest Airplane Carrying the World's Most Double-Jointed Clown on a Flight of Fun."

Lou also rode around the arena in a motorized bathtub—supposedly so that he could bathe while he drove. With that one gag, he managed to sum up the old American spirit of invention and innovation that put a nation on wheels and gave it the best plumbing in the world—and yet to burlesque the immoderate America that can't rest until it has combined the two.

Other clowns could have stolen his bathtub gag. The midget car gag, however, was a routine that very few clowns were capable of. To perform it well, you had to be a contortionist, which Lou was.

He developed those skills as a youngster in Germany after excelling in school gymnastics. His parents were a song-and-dance team, and his first performance was at the age of seven,

when he played the hindquarters of an alligator to his older brother's head and forefeet in a Bremen variety hall. Twisted into the tail end of the alligator, Lou discovered that he was a natural contortionist, but his father disapproved of Lou's penchant for clowning. To discipline his son, the senior Jacobs apprenticed him to a hand balancer and tumbler.

It was as a tumbler that Jacobs was brought to the United States in 1923, for nearly two years of fairs, outdoor exhibits, and winter vaudeville. Late in 1924, he teamed with another contortionist named Michael Morris in a comedy "aerial" number. Their "trapeze" was a broomstick. Morris had a Ringling contract, so almost by accident Lou Jacobs found himself with The Greatest Show on Earth during the 1925 season. Midway through the season, Morris complained that Jacobs was usually difficult to find: he was continually donning disguises and working production numbers with the clowns. Truth to tell, Lou's heart was in clowning, but he was hesitant about giving up his sure thing with Morris to take a chance at being a solo clown.

But, in fact, The Greatest Show on Earth would hire him as a clown for the 1926 season, and in the 1989 season he was still with the Big One, as a master teacher at the Ringling Bros. and Barnum & Bailey Circus Clown College, and was generally acknowledged to be the greatest living circus clown.

During his first solo season, Lou gave up the whiteface and Pierrot suit he had worn as a contortionist and became an *auguste* clown in blackface, baggy pants, and big shoes. He walked around the track in a checkered suit of pink and lavender and a twelve-inch-high celluloid collar, carrying a tiny umbrella on a ten-foot handle.

He was the clown who teamed with the fey self-satirist Polidor to reconstruct the Dempsey-Tunney prizefight; he was a western sheriff;

he was the mother who threw her child into the fire and then jumped into a safety net in the burning-house gag; in drag, he was the bride in the clown wedding—or the woman in the red satin dress and ostrich-plumed hat who carried a cage containing an old shoe that sang like a canary.

But Lou's most famous gag was the midget car.

He started tinkering with it in 1944. He developed several models into which he could collapse his contortionist's body, but none of them would run. George Wallenda, whom Fred Bradna called "the mechanical expert of the high-wire Wallendas," suggested the installation of a washing machine motor. They made twenty-three cardboard mock-ups of chassis and body. Inside, Jacobs squirmed this way and that; outside, Wallenda marked off an inch of waste space here, an inch there. When Lou couldn't corkscrew another inch, they built a working model. In its test under street conditions, Lou discovered that he hadn't made enough allowance for visibility: he wound up contorted around a tree.

The next model was enough of an improvement to rate an audition at Ringling winter quarters in Sarasota. Climbing out, Lou caught his suspenders on a loose screw and ripped off his trousers. People laughed at that, but Lou wanted a car he could count on for laughs in the right places.

The midget car made its professional debut in the Spec during the 1946 opening in New York. It stalled on the track and had to be pushed out of the arena. Jacobs tried to salvage the situation by turning this into a gag. The next night the car was left on the track deliberately. After the parade had passed it by, Jacobs climbed out of the stalled car pantomiming his humiliation. The gag was judged too long and was cut.

Lou thought it would be hilarious if the first thing the audience saw when his big frame emerged from his tiny car was one of his feet, wearing the biggest clown shoe ever seen. For the 1947 season, Jacobs cobbled a new pair of giant shoes. Indeed, they were so big that his visibility again disappeared. When the car raced around the track, it knocked down a clown policeman, Jimmy Armstrong. The collision damaged the steering arm so that when Lou wheeled into the center ring, he crashed into a stage. The car was wrecked. Jacobs couldn't even climb out. He had to be towed from the arena inside the car, his big shoes still obscuring the windshield, and freed by a hacksaw.

And then came 1948. The honking of an automobile horn was heard in the Garden. A tiny sedan raced into the immensity of the center ring. It backfired loudly, then stopped at a filling station run by the irascible Italian dwarf clown Frankie Saluto.

Suddenly, a really big shoe emerged from the door, followed incredibly by six-foot-one-inch Lou Jacobs. He stood there wearing the biggest shoes in clowning while squeals of delight rose all over the Garden. Like all gas station attendants, meanwhile, the dwarf was insisting that Jacobs had parked too far from the gas pump. Lou did what we all want to do: he whacked the attendant on the head with a mallet, raising a rubber balloon welt on his head.

Jacobs did try to start his car to drive closer to the pump, but all he got was more backfiring. Looking for the problem, he removed the radiator cap—and loosed a snake and a geyser of water. He sat on the water to stop the geyser, but it merely kept spouting out the top of his head. When he tried to stop the flow with his hand, the torrent emerged from his mouth.

Finally, they pushed the car to the gas pump, and the routine accelerated to its insanely satisfying conclusion. Saluto climbed inside his gas pump. Jacobs tossed in a bomb. The explosion sent a dummy dressed like the dwarf to the top of the tent, which came gently back to earth in a parachute. Nevertheless, Armstrong the clown cop rushed forward to arrest Jacobs—who relied on quick contortions and the world's smallest car for the world's fastest exit.

———

If the best clowning in the post–World War II years was to be found in the Big One, some of the best tumbling and bareback riding could be found with a comparatively small circus. In 1954, the Cristiani family, famed for their dazzling bareback riding and spectacular acrobatics, joined with the little Bailey Bros. Circus (no kin to the Bailey of Ringling Bros. and Barnum & Bailey), which usually played ballparks and fairgrounds, and made an historic tour of Alaska four years before its 1958 statehood.

"Alaska never had a circus before," explained Lucio Cristiani, "so we went to Alaska with ten elephants, a lion act, the biggest show they ever had in Alaska. And we had Hugo Zacchini with the cannon." And they did great business.

The Cristianis' circus roots go back to Italy of about 1840, when Lucio Cristiani's grandfather, a gymnast and good amateur tumbler in Pisa, met and married a circus girl and ran away with the circus. To the tumbling son's surprise, the father, who had made some money as a blacksmith, invested it in the circus his son had run away with, and it became a combined circus with the Cristiani name.

That tumbler's son was an even better tumbler. He was Ernesto Cristiani, Lucio's father, and his skill carried him from Italy to France, Spain, and Yugoslavia. "And then, of course, the family got big, and it was too big to travel around as a performing group, and my father was the kind of a guy who didn't like to work

for somebody else if he could help it," said Lucio. "So he went back to Italy and started a little circus himself with his little family. And the circus grew with the family. We grew up and the circus became big, until it was the largest one in Italy. But then the war clouds started gathering."

"Tumbling is the key to everything," Ernesto Cristiani used to tell Lucio when Lucio was a little boy. Perhaps the most popular part of Papa Ernesto's act involved a little dog that Papa himself had found and trained. He called her Ninette, after the dark brown color of a popular Italian vermouth, and he pretended to quarrel with her when she got more applause than he did by imitating his acrobatics. In pantomime, he would challenge the little dog to a contest of flip-flops, or backward somersaults. There followed a contest in which man and beast flip-flopped all around the ring so that the audience could decide who was best. Ninette invariably won, joyously turning paws over rump as many as forty times, then acknowledging her victory with a flurry of barks.

Unsympathetic to Mussolini, the Cristianis went to France in 1931, and joined the Cirque Medrano in Paris for one season. There, Papa Ernesto set a record of eighty-three flip-flops executed without a pause. He would also spring through a hoop placed fourteen feet away from him and six feet high, which was soaked in kerosene and set on fire. Before he lit the hoop, Cristiani would demonstrate that it had a diameter only one inch wider than his shoulders. Then he would back up, take a short run, dive directly through the hoop, and tumble to his feet. He never missed, so he began trying to light a cigarette going through. Sometimes he didn't get the cigarette lit, but he always dived successfully through the fire.

The circus owner, Medrano, known to Toulouse-Lautrec in former days as the clown Boum-Boum, gave Ernesto Cristiani a special medal because of his skill and popularity.

But it was Ernesto's son Lucio whose elegant riding was the subject of a front-page article in *Paris Soir*. By this time, Lucio Cristiani was doing a full-twist backward somersault from the first to the third horse. He was soon dubbed "an equestrian Nijinsky." There followed engagements in England and Germany.

In the winter of 1933, Pat Valdo, Ringling clown turned Ringling talent scout, came to Europe and hired the Cristianis for the 1934 season—not for Ringling Bros. and Barnum & Bailey Circus, but for Hagenbeck-Wallace, which Ringling also owned.

The Cristianis spent two seasons with Hagenbeck-Wallace; then they went to another Ringling-owned property, the Al G. Barnes show. In 1938, the family made a movie short subject that was seen by John Ringling North. North decided that he wanted the Cristianis in The Greatest Show on Earth. Now began the big-salary years of the private railroad car that said "The Cristiani Family" on the sides.

But the Cristiani family grew and grew until finally John Ringling North said, "I can't pay you any more, because I need *many* families, and you make me go over budget."

So the Cristiani family went from show to show, but it became increasingly difficult to get the big money they were used to. The solution to the problem was to split up or start their own show; so in 1949 they formed King Bros. and Cristiani Circus with Floyd King.

"Floyd King was a man of two distinctly separate but simultaneous circus careers," wrote Fox and Parkinson in *The Circus in America*. "In one he was among the foremost general agents, the expert in deciding where shows should play and adept in not only contracting the difficult towns, but garnering strong publicity for his show. He had been agent for Cole Bros. Circus and its Robbins subsidiary. In his other career he was a circus owner and manager. But here his fortunes varied. Either his

show was scraping bottom, operating with no customers and no money, or it was coining profits at a merry rate. King thrived in either condition."

In 1950, the King-Cristiani partnership toured western Canada and successfully exhibited a giraffe, despite that animal's famous fragility. (Giraffes really are subject to king-size sore throats.) In 1951, the circus toured New England and the South, and profits were even bigger. In 1952, the show carried twelve elephants, the Zacchini cannon act, and had a street parade. Its advertising budget was large, and it also used local organizations as sponsors.

Sometimes it played "day and date" with the Big One, and the smallish King Bros. and Cristiani Combined Circus even made a respectable showing against the giant Ringling show.

By 1953, they were traveling on fifty-four trucks and had added a free balloon ascension to the free street parade as a way of bringing the crowds to the show grounds. At least they advertised a free balloon ascension; often, the ballon didn't get off the ground. No matter: the crowds still came to the show grounds.

According to Richard G. Hubler, the biographer of the family, they made these "partnership deals . . . chiefly because they did not feel that their name was strong enough yet to swing the patronage of the American public. To those who were circus aficionados, the Cristianis represented the best; but these were few compared to the number of tickets the box office needed to make a profit. In addition, they themselves lacked capital to go on their own."

In 1954, the Cristiani family dissolved their partnership with King and formed a one-year relationship with little Bailey Bros. Circus to play a territory that they correctly anticipated would be starved for any kind of circus entertainment: Alaska. That successful Alaskan tour was in the great tradition of circuses that had brought entertainment to *all* the territories of the United States even before they became states.

In 1956, the Cristianis started a show all on their own, which lasted until 1961. "By 1956," wrote Hubler, "the Christianis could boast a circus that cut close in principle to Papa's original, though it was vastly larger. It had none of the trappings and glitter of the Ringling organization, which had turned the circus tradition toward that of the Broadway extravaganza. It was streamlined, austere, and direct as pure circus could be."

It is well to remember, in this connection, that in 1955 Ringling Bros. and Barnum & Bailey actually presented Marilyn Monroe on opening night, riding into Madison Square Garden on a pink elephant.

The Cristiani show didn't even have a printed program. Its displays were the traditional circus acts: performing horses and riders, clowns, acrobats, animals, and daredevils. The band was lusty. The concessions were clean. The grounds were kept clear of anyone who would bother the customers. The Circus Fans of America voted it "Circus of the Year."

Thirty-six members of the circus—one-third of the performers—were Cristianis. Papa was the ringmaster. Mama supervised the cookhouse. Lucio managed the circus and led the bareback riders. Sometimes he counted fifteen relatives in the ring at once—brothers, sisters, and in-laws.

There were only three Cristianis in the ring for the show's grandest moment, however: the triple backward "suicide somersault." Lucio, Belmonte, and Paul, each riding a different horse, threw backward somersaults through hoops at the same time. At the end of the trick, the lead horse was riderless, the other two were occupied, and one Cristiani was already taking bows on the ground.

The Cristianis moved through the country in thirty-three trucks that carried 175 performers and roustabouts. They raised in two hours a tent that could contain 3,000 people, and they struck it at the end of the day in thirty minutes less. In this way, during the 1950s, they traveled from 11,000 to 12,000 miles between April and November, making as many as 188 appearances in twenty states.

"The circus will be finished when ice cream is finished," said Papa Cristiani; and in the 1950s, with the appeal of their tumbling at its height, the Cristianis were the Emperors of Ice Cream.

The secret of the famed Cristiani horse tumbling was actually their ability to tumble on the ground. Lucio, for example, perfected his back somersault on terra firma before he ever tried it on the back of a horse. Only when he was confident that he could return to the exact spot he had been standing before he made his tight circle in the air did he feel ready for horseback. He learned to use his legs as "adjusters," tucking them in to increase speed or pushing them out to slow down. "As for a full twist," he said, "even today less than five per cent of the professional acrobats can do it on the ground, much less on the back of horses."

Building on their tumbling background, the Cristianis were able to perform two stunts of surpassing difficulty: the three-man somersault on three horses, and the passing leap, where one rider jumps over the other from horse to horse. Lucio himself could leap from the first horse to the third, and he could perform a full twist from horse to horse.

For these feats, the horses are galloping at nearly ten miles an hour, one slightly inside the other, head to croup. What went on, in these moments, in Lucio Cristiani's head? Hubler tells us:

The performer must choose his moment of departure exactly, and know the rise of the horse's muscles and the force of his own spring backward. All this must be calculated beforehand—for once the stunt is launched, the performer has no more control over himself, his speed, or direction than a stone out of a sling. He must launch himself at a considerable angle toward the inside of the ring while whirling in the air and then, in the last minisecond before he lands, spot his rhythmically heaving pad for landing and adjust his legs to either the rise or fall of the horse's muscles. Such a leap covers about fourteen feet.

Circus historian J. S. Clarke has described the act as "synchronization brought to perfection." And that perfection was amply rewarded, in what was a dark decade for most other circuses. At the close of the 1953 season, John Ringling North fired Art Concello as general manager of the Ringling show. Henry North said that Concello wanted to cut drastically the 1954 show to a fifty-car presentation, while John insisted that it live up to its boast of being "bigger and better than ever." North replaced Concello with his assistant, Frank McClosky.

As it began the 1955 season, the Ringling show was $1 million in debt, which was too much debt for a circus that grossed only $6 million a year, and that had already been suffering substantial losses for several seasons. What was keeping it going was the more than $1.3 million in royalties that was its share of Cecil B. De Mille's film *The Greatest Show on Earth*, plus an annual fee of $100,000 from NBC for televising the Big One's dress rehearsal in Madison Square Garden.

As the executive director of the circus, John Ringling North hired Michael Burke, who had parachuted into occupied France during World War II with North's brother Buddy. (Their exploits inspired the 1948 Gary Cooper film *Cloak and Dagger*.) Johnny North, Burke later wrote, wanted someone to look after his circus (and his Florida real estate and Oklahoma oil wells) "while he, at age fifty-two, repaired to the south of France to embellish his well-established reputation as a bon vivant and epicure."

Johnny North told Burke to clean up the rackets on the circus: dice, whiskey, and beer, forbidden by show policy and by law. They were controlled on the Ringling show by a group called the Three Sneezes or the Sneeze Mob. What North didn't say, or didn't know, Burke says, was that the rackets on the Ringling show were run by Frank McClosky, North's new general manager. (He was the same Frank McClosky who, as the peerless Lillian Leitzel's prop boy, was standing beneath her when she fell, receiving the injury that caused her death.) Around the circus, McClosky was known as the Chief Sneeze.

A number of people were allowed to bilk the circus, Burke wrote in his memoirs, "as long as they paid the Sneeze for their bilking privileges." For example, "The menagerie superintendent bought the horsemeat for the wild animals; by a curious coincidence he was also the fellow who *sold* the horsemeat." Hamburger Jack, the head porter on the circus train, took aboard fifteen hundred cases of beer in Philadelphia, which were sold at 500 percent profit to the circus performers and workers who couldn't get off the train.

When Burke found that the circus was transporting and feeding a professional gambler assigned by Jimmy Blue Eyes, the Miami rackets boss, he had a showdown with the Big Sneeze. As Burke recalled the incident, he was not subtle and Frank McClosky was not forthright. The conversation went:

"Get the gambler off the lot, Frank."

"What gambler?"

"This is not a discussion. I want him off the show."

PINITO DEL ORO. *She was with a band of roadside entertainers in southern Spain when she was discovered by John Ringling North, or so said* The New Yorker *in an April 10–17, 1954, article called "The Triumph of Hoopla." The two signed a contract in a gypsy cave on the outskirts of Murcia, Spain, and a star was born. As a single trapeze performer, Pinito was good; as the star of what would later be called "photo opportunities," she was one of the best. (Ringling Museum)*

THE GREAT UNUS. *Ernest Hemingway wrote, "In your dreams you watch Unus standing on one finger and you think, 'Look at such a fine, intelligent and excellent man making his living standing on one finger when most of us can't even stand on our feet.'" The American debut of Unus was the sensation of the 1948 season of Ringling Bros. and Barnum & Bailey Circus; he was billed as the "Upside-down, gravity-defying, equilibristic Wonder of the World." Unus always wore white gloves while working, but for the finale of his act he would take them off and exhibit his bare hands to the audience to show that there was no gimmick. It was whispered that with sleight-of-hand he concealed a steel brace inside his white glove. Was that the answer? Even if it was, try doing a handstand on a little steel brace. (Ringling Museum)*

HUBERT CASTLE. *His high-wire routine was a variation on one of the oldest clown gags in the circus. The drunk who barges into the ring convinced he can do the riding act better than the circus equestrian and then proceeds to do so delighted Mark Twain when Dan Rice did it, and he later described it in* Huckleberry Finn. *Castle played a drunken gentleman in white tie and tails who barges into the ring convinced he can walk a high wire better than the circus performers. The act can be seen in Julien Duvivier's 1943 film* Flesh and Fantasy, *in which co-producer Charles Boyer plays (on the ground) the drunk who weaves, staggers, and stumbles on the wire. (Ringling Museum)*

BURT LANCASTER RETURNS TO THE CIRCUS. *A circus performer before he was an actor, Lancaster returns to the circus as a movie star and obliges photographers by adjusting a hat on an elephant's head. Lancaster joined a circus troupe at seventeen and performed an acrobatic duo with Nick Cravat, the little man who was his sidekick in such films as* The Flame and the Arrow *and* The Crimson Pirate. *In the 1956 film* Trapeze, *filmed at the Buglione Circus in Paris, Lancaster played catcher to Tony Curtis's flier. In the circus, Lancaster also performed on two horizontal bars. He would take off his shirt, displaying his seemingly iron-hard chest, jump up and catch one bar, then do a series of giant swings. At the height of one swing, he would release his hold and sail to a second bar about six feet away, on which he would land on his feet and remain in a standing position. Others who went from the circus to stardom on the stage, bandstand, and in films include Red Skelton, who clowned with the Hagenbeck-Wallace Circus; Wallace Beery; and Harry James, who first played his trumpet in a circus band. (Ringling Museum)*

THE LONG MOUNT. *The glory of the three-ring circus, and probably the most awesome of circus spectacles, is the Long Mount. This is a thrill that the one-ring circuses that are standard in most of the rest of the world cannot give. All of the elephants come out of the rings, gather around the hippodrome track in single file, and move at once to the front side. Then each elephant stands on its hind legs and puts its forelegs on the back of the elephant in front of it. Looking up to see more than a dozen elephants towering over you is to understand the meaning of majesty. Sometimes they even walk that way for a few elephant paces. At the conclusion of the act, trainers and animals run out the back door at a pounding pace that actually shakes some auditoriums. "The long mount," said Kenneth Feld, who has produced Broadway plays and ice shows as well as circuses, "is the kick-line of the circus." (Ringling Museum)*

McClosky did not get rid of the gambler; Burke had to do it personally. It was when he found out that the show was being cheated by the printing of duplicate tickets that he gave McClosky a final warning: "Frank, money is running down a hundred rat holes. You know them all better than I do. If it doesn't stop, this show just ain't going to finish the season. If it weren't for the million dollars from the deMille film, we'd be in the barn now."

When the situation continued, Burke reported what he had learned to John Ringling North; North came to Chicago to meet with the Three Sneezes, and McClosky came to the meeting drunk. In disgust, North told Burke to get rid of all three of them.

According to Burke, he fired the Three Sneezes between shows on the last night of the St. Paul stand, August 4, 1955. According to the account next day in the *Minneapolis Star*, "the three, sitting in a black Cadillac just as big as North's, and just as air-conditioned, had a different version. They said they'd quit, and flipped out resignations, dated July 23, to prove it. July 23 is about the date on which North hired Michael Burke as executive director to 'clean house.'"

That night, as about 8,000 people were watching the three wild animal acts that opened the show, the Three Sneezes went to their department heads and told them to pull their employees. Bob Reynold pulled out his property men, so there was no one to take the cages down. "David Blanchfield, head of the truck department, and Whitey Versteeg, the electrical boss, refused," wrote Burke, "not for any particular loyalty to me but because of an unbreakable loyalty to their own code. The show must go on."

If Whitey Versteeg had not refused to turn off the lights, three animal trainers would have been caged in darkness with lions and tigers and bears, and 8,000 spectators would have heard—but not seen—in terror whatever happened next.

As it was, the band played on, under Merle Evans's unflappable direction, and the Ringling clowns staged the longest clown walk-around in the history of The Greatest Show on Earth.

But the show couldn't go on without prop hands. The performance was canceled and refunds, or a seat for the following night's show across the Mississippi River in Minneapolis, were offered. Lloyd Morgan, a taciturn man who had been lot superintendent, got a "battlefield commission" to head the property department—and get the tent torn down. He sent back to the train one of the circus's oldest calls: "cherry pie," and once again, performers were called upon to do the work the circus workers usually do.

It galvanized the performers into action. "For them," said Burke, "Ringling Brothers Barnum & Bailey Circus was an institution, not to be sucked dry but to be cherished as a historic form of entertainment at its most sophisticated level." Most of them had started on small shows, where they had to do everything, and they knew how to move a circus as well as how to perform in one. And it turned out that they bitterly resented the Sneeze Mob.

So the show moved successfully across the the Mississippi to Minneapolis, where it played to capacity houses for two days, and then the circus went on to finish its season without missing a single play-date. It had been the longest season in the history of the Big One. When they reached winter quarters in Sarasota on December 4, they had traveled 20,000 miles and played to 2 million people in 170 cities.

But the troubles were not over. McClosky, Walter Kirnan, and an "assistant Sneeze," moved their liquor stock from their staterooms on the train—and Kirnan took an ax to the improvements he'd made in his. Then, as

Burke says, "they found their way to Jimmy Hoffa. . . . "

The 1956 season of The Greatest Show on Earth began on a very sour note. The Ringling family corporation's "Forty-niners" (the group holding 49 percent of the stock) filed a mismanagement suit for $20 million against John Ringling North, Henry Ringling North, and Art Concello. Soon the International Brotherhood of Teamsters and the American Guild of Variety Artists began in earnest to try to establish standard union-shop contracts with the Ringling circus. Johnny North and Michael Burke met with Jimmy Hoffa in February of 1956. Hoffa said he wanted a Teamster contract with the circus, and wanted the Teamsters recognized as the bargaining agent for all its nonperforming personnel. North said that although he used Teamster standby drivers when the show was playing the Garden in New York, the circus couldn't afford an across-the-board contract. Hoffa, according to Burke, "said he would put us out of business."

From this vantage point, what the unions were doing to a circus seems reprehensible. But circus employees, from the workers to the performers, have historically been underpaid for hard work carried on over long hours in frequently difficult conditions. The Sneeze Mob, in its anger, and the unions, in their desire to organize workers, were able to touch a live nerve. Even so, such workers as Whitey Versteeg refused to take any action that would endanger the public.

The indoor dates went all right. During the six weeks in New York at the Garden, Ringling added a ten o'clock morning show on Saturday, and the three performances that day grossed $110,000—the highest single day's receipts in Ringling history. Boston was no problem. But when the show went outdoors, under canvas, the Teamster harassment started. There was violence on the picket lines and truck and tractor slowdowns. The circus was late for nearly every date. There were matinees that went on at 9:00 P.M., and evening performances that started at midnight. Someone called it "The Latest Show on Earth." "To run against the Teamsters' costly harassment would have been self-defeating," Burke was to write; "to agree to Hoffa's demands was economically prohibitive. More fundamentally, it was a delusion to think that a three-ring circus playing under a big canvas tent, traveling the country in an eighty-car train, was viable in 1956. . . . Railroads were once allies; now the very presence of the huge Circus train was an irritant, and the cost of moving the Circus train had risen two hundred and fifty per cent in a decade. Convenient open space, large enough to accommodate the Circus, was increasingly difficult to find in spreading cities. . . . "

The circus arrived in Pittsburgh, Pennsylvania. And during the evening show on July 16, 1956, a clown took a little boy into his lap and told him to "put away a lot of memories tonight."

That day, John Ringling North had announced tersely: "The tented circus as it exists today is, in my opinion, a thing of the past." After the evening performance, The Greatest Show on Earth ended its season and returned to winter quarters.

To circus lovers all over America, it looked as if the circus itself was dying. According to North's statement, the circus as an institution was the victim of competition from television, and labor troubles, bad weather for the Big Top, traffic problems for audiences trying to get to it, and increased freight rates for railroad circuses.

"BIG TOP BOWS OUT FOREVER," keened *Life* magazine. "The Big Top Folds Its Tents for

Last Time," said the headline in the *New York Times*. "It looks like kids in the future won't know the circus, the thrill of greeting it at dawn—the sideshow, the walk thru the sawdust," wrote the Pittsburgh *Post Gazette*. A cartoon in the *Post Gazette* showed Uncle Sam with hat in hand and tears streaming down his cheeks, standing before a gravestone inscribed "Here lies Ringling Bros. and Barnum & Bailey."

Too many thought that the words "Big Top" and "tented circus" were synonymous with the circus itself, forgetting—or never knowing—that the circus in America didn't even show under canvas until the 1830s, when it was about forty years old.

To be sure, the circus was in deep trouble. Already that year, the Clyde Beatty Circus, by that time the only railroad circus other than Ringling, had gone bankrupt. Frank McClosky and Walter Kirnan acquired the show from the fifty-three-year-old Beatty, reopened it in New Mexico on August 29, and finished the season with Beatty as a performer only. The next season it went out as a truck show.

Next to go bankrupt was King Bros. & Cole Bros. Circus, which had toured on seventy trucks only the year before as the biggest truck show ever. Despite a big budget for advertising, telephone promotion, and operations, the people had just not come out. The Kelly-Miller Circus managed to keep going in 1956 but made things worse for the future by capitalizing on the idea that the circus as an institution was dying. It advertised itself as "Last of the circus—see it now or miss it forever."

There was, however, at least one man in the country who thought he knew how to arrange for the comeback of the circus in America. Six months to the day before The Greatest Show on Earth gave its final tented performance, a promoter of jazz and rock-and-roll concerts named Irvin Feld had written John Ringling

North a letter telling him that while the era of the gigantic canvas big tops was finished, a new era of arena circuses could begin. North's reply was a polite brush-off.

The day after he folded the Big Top, North telephoned. Now he was ready to listen to Feld's ideas.

Feld was born in Hagerstown, Maryland, on May 9, 1918. His father was a Russian Jew who had emigrated to this country with bitter memories of Cossacks and pogroms. When the Depression came, Ike Feld had six children to support on the profits from a modest men's and women's clothing emporium in downtown Hagerstown. Irvin's only brother, Israel (Izzy, to the family), born in 1910, was, from the beginning, his adviser, confidant, and trusted partner. The ideas usually came from Irvin; how to make them work financially was usually Izzy's department.

When Isaac Feld's clothing store went bankrupt in the Great Depression, thirteen-year-old Irvin and twenty-one-year-old Izzy went on the road to sell snake oil at summer carnivals. In the ranges of low mountains that lie north and west of Hagerstown in Maryland and Pennsylvania, they learned to sell in hamlets with such names as Shade Gap, Bean Soup, Claylick, Yellow Creek, Burnt Cabin, Shy Beaver, and Walnut Bottom. These were places too small for real theater or even the Chautauqua circuit; they were usually places without movie theaters, where not everybody had a radio yet; and, of course, it was long before TV. Some of these hamlets were even too small for the smallest circuses. The carnivals with their medicine shows were about the only kind of entertainment these country people ever got to see, and sometimes they bought whatever the medicine man was selling as thanks for the show.

So while Izzy sold the snake oil from a fold-up booth, Irvin gave a spiel that Barnum would not have spurned. If he had old people in his audience, he would stress how the snake oil smoothed out wrinkles; if he had middle-aged people with hands that were callused from working in the fields or mines, he would tell them that the snake oil was good for backaches. And after telling the folks that this snake oil was good for whatever he figured ailed them, Irvin Feld would launch into the entertainment: a terrifying account of the difficulty and danger of capturing just the right snakes to make just the right medicinal blend.

The Felds got the nostrum from Arthur Fraidin's supply house in west Baltimore, but Irvin was never sure if it was truly oil from snakes.

"Exactly what was in it? I never really wanted to know," he was once quoted by the *Chicago Tribune* as saying; for then, "I might not have been able to sell it."

Whatever it was, it enabled the Felds to save five hundred sorely needed dollars for their family. But it also taught Irvin Feld a lesson he would never forget: THINK BIG. "I told my father that those little stores he always had would never make it. Just from watching how much more money the bigger carney stands made than ours did showed me that you've got to do things on a large scale."

The next summer, Irvin Feld made his pitch from a brand-new collapsible stand that had "a circus awning on top, painted in red and yellow stripes." In 1939, the supply house that had provided Irvin and Israel with their snake oil loaned them $1,000 to open a variety store in a black neighborhood in Washington, D.C.

There are two things of note about this operation: when the NAACP urged Irvin to expand it into a drugstore luncheonette, he did so, leasing the prescription end to black pharmacists and giving Washington its first integrated lunch counter. This foreshadows the way that he would later integrate the circus.

The other thing to note is that this store, despite its name (Super Cut-Rate Drugs), was one of those little stores that Irvin Feld believed would never make it; so he thought of a way to make it a big store: he added a record department, which turned into a chain of record stores, which, in turn, led to the Felds' own private record company.

By 1954, *Time* magazine had noticed the Feld brothers, and ran an article in the June 21 issue called "Super Brother Act" which began: "Headquarters for one of the biggest entertainment enterprises in the U.S. are two crowded cubbyholes at the back of Super Cut-Rate Drugs on Seventh Street, N.W., in downtown Washington. The men who run it are two brothers from Hagerstown, Md., Irvin and Israel Feld, who opened the store in 1939 and spread out into music with the ease of an Alka Seltzer foaming through a glass of water."

That year, Irvin pioneered the packaging of rock-and-roll tours, with such artists as Chubby Checker, Bill Haley & the Comets, Fats Domino, Frankie Avalon, Fabian, the Everly Brothers, and Buddy Holly. Feld also discovered a fifteen-year-old Canadian boy who had composed and sung a song called "Diana," put him on tour, became his personal manager, and shared in the fortune that Paul Anka would make as a composer-singer.

"I had a complete list of cities throughout the United States and Canada in which there were big, beautiful new air-conditioned and heated indoor auditoriums," Feld said—and he got the idea that this list and his booking know-how could be the salvation of the faltering Ringling Bros. and Barnum & Bailey Circus.

———

After the Big Top folded in Pittsburgh, John Ringling North made the entire train trip from Pittsburgh back to Sarasota in his pajamas without sleeping. He may already have been thinking about the letter Irvin Feld had written him the year before, because he was suddenly giving The Gospel According to Feld, saying, as Michael Burke remembered it, that "to survive in the modern world the Circus must be restructured to move from building to building as new arenas appeared in cities across America. In the new beginning it would be forced initially to abandon the famous Circus train and shrink itself to a truck show, a Mud Show in Circus vernacular."

Back in Sarasota, North telephoned Irvin Feld to set up a meeting. In Irvin's words, The Greatest Show on Earth was "not in good financial shape. The budget was unbelievable. They told me what their expenses were and I told them what their expenses should be."

Feld told North and his people that the circus was really in six different businesses. They were in the construction business, because every day or so, they would erect a tent with 12,000 seats and then tear it down. To do this work, they had to hire hundreds of roustabouts all over America, and use twenty-five work elephants. This put them in the restaurant business, because to feed their human workers they had to serve at least 900,000 meals a year. It also put them in the hotel business, because they were providing sleeping accommodations for 1,300 people for eight months. They were in the sanitation business, because they had to have rest rooms for the customers and the workers, and they had to clean up after all the animals. They were in the railroad business, moving 67,000 tons of equipment, animals, and people 20,000 miles a year. And, finally, they were in show business.

But only the show business made any money.

So Feld proposed that North get out of every business but the show business—and, to a lesser extent, the railroad business. Irvin Feld proposed the deal: North's only obligation

would be to deliver his circus to the places that Irvin and Israel Feld would schedule. The Felds would have exclusive control of booking and promoting the circus, and they would pay for advertising and rent. In return, North would pay them a percentage of the gross ticket revenues. The Felds guaranteed that running the circus would not cost beyond a stated figure. "They said, 'Impossible,' Irvin recalled. "I beat the figure by $8,000 the first week of operation." The Felds were sure that their idea would work because they knew how many hard-top buildings there were in the United States that could contain the circus, and they knew how many would be built in the following five years—and where.

"Mr. North said, 'How fast can you get started?'" Irvin Feld recalled. "I said, 'We'll be back in business next month.' And we were."

North's deal with the Felds immediately saved the circus the salaries, feeding, and sleeping of the 1,500 to 2,000 roustabouts, and the care and feeding of the work elephants. "We cut out the freaks and the sideshow," said Feld, "because it was making fun of people and sickening to me." They cut out the menagerie. Henry Ringling North thought that this was a wise move: "The menagerie had been anachronistic for a long time," he agreed. "Gone were the days when people gaped in wonder at a polar bear—there were so many animals in zoos and moving pictures and TV shows that people were sated by the sight of them." The Ringling show loaned its menagerie to the Providence Zoo in Rhode Island and borrowed it back once a year for Madison Square Garden.

Instead of owning a great eighty-car train, Ringling Bros. and Barnum & Bailey now confined itself to leasing from the railroads the baggage cars in which the elephants and some other trained animals would ride. The show's equipment—rigging, properties, and costumes —now moved in ten big trailer trucks. The performers were given travel allowances, lived and ate in restaurants and hotels of their choice, and got from show to show in their own cars and trailers.

As agents, the Felds reduced the number of employees from 1,400 to 300, including about eighty performers, and cut the break-even point to $125,000. Once the circus had boasted fifty-five elephants, including the work animals. Now it carried only twenty show elephants. Moreover, moving the show indoors permitted forty-six consecutive weeks of performance, from the first week in January to the third week in November.

In 1957, for the first time in eighty-six years, the circus season began without a single railroad circus in operation.

Ringling Bros. and Barnum & Bailey would play mostly indoors. The old car barn in Sarasota was turned into an indoor arena for practice sessions.

The show moved out of Sarasota on March 28, 1957, on fifteen railroad cars—three sleepers, eight flats, four stock cars—for the April 3 opening in Madison Square Garden. About sixty railroad cars were left behind. They were being replaced by Ringling's new fleet of trucks.

Significantly, Emmett Kelly ran away *from* the circus that year, and joined the Brooklyn Dodgers as a clown mascot, doing sight gags out on the diamond between innings. Later, he would do a nightclub act, and television commercials.

The circus that North was heading and that Irvin Feld was selling was no longer The Greatest Show on Earth, except in copyrighted name. Germany's Gunther Gebel-Williams was generally considered the greatest wild animal trainer on earth, but North had been unable to induce him to leave the Circus Williams in his native land. Emmett Kelly wasn't with the Ringling show anymore. Of those who remained, Otto Griebling and Lou Jacobs were in their prime, but most of the other performers weren't. Their average age was forty-six, which is old in a profession whose very heart is feats of physical skill and daring, and where physical beauty has always been important. Some of the show girls were in their fifties. ("A fifty-year-old woman may be fantastic," said Feld, "but a show girl she isn't.")

Worst of all, the number of clowns—described by P. T. Barnum as "pegs, used to hang circuses on"—had been allowed to dwindle from more than fifty to only thirteen. Seven were in their seventies and eighties; the youngest was past fifty. "We know that clowns can fall down," lamented Irvin Feld, "but can they get up again?"

———

Television was the major factor in the decline of the circus in America. The Age of Television had dawned faster than the Age of Radio. In the summer of 1947, people in New York, Philadelphia, Schenectady, and Washington, D.C., had a choice between seeing the circus live and seeing the World Series on TV—the first World Series on TV! Of course, there were so few TV sets that only 3.9 million people saw the series, and 3.5 million of those saw the series on sets in bars. But by 1949 there were 1 million TV sets in the United States, and only ten years later, there were more than 50 million.

It seemed to be the medium itself—not what appeared on it—that fascinated people. The long streak of success that Cole Bros. Circus had enjoyed right through the war years was over by 1949, when Jack Tavlin sold the circus to Arthur M. Wirtz and Associates, owners of the Chicago Stadium. They hired William Boyd, the cowboy star whose Hopalong Cassidy films were then at the height of their popularity on television, but not enough people came out to see Boyd in person to keep the show on the road. On July 22, 1949, the sixteen-season career of Cole Bros. Circus came to an end.

It wasn't only live entertainment that suffered. The period when the Ringling show folded its Big Top was also the period when 5,000 motion picture theater marquees went dark and movie admissions plummeted. Suddenly, millions who went to the movies every week and the circus every year were staying home to see the latest novelty on the tube. After all, people could see circus acts every week on "The Ed Sullivan Show." A former circus clown named Red Skelton was on free every week in those years, and you could see lots of animals on "Disneyland" (*Dumbo* was on in 1955; and *The African Lion*, made for the movie theaters in 1955, was on television by 1958).

However, if your neighbor or a friend at work asked you to buy circus tickets for your family to benefit the work the Shriners do with their children's hospitals, you might bestir yourself and get away from the TV set for an afternoon. And that is basically why the period of the decline of the great independent circuses saw the sponsored circuses survive and even, in some cases, do well.

In 1957, there were only five middle-sized to big circuses touring America: Ringling Bros. and Barnum & Bailey, Clyde Beatty, Kelly-Miller, Mills Bros., and the new Cristiani Bros. Circus. Three major shows, Ringling, King, and Beatty, hadn't been able to make it through the 1956 season, so the Beatty show was an all-new operation, motorized and sponsored, and it netted $320,000 for the season, making it Beatty's best season since his record-breaking tour of Canada just after the war.

More and more, the circus in America was relying on the relatively new phenomenon of the "promotional" or "sponsored" shows. Back in 1906, when Orrin Davenport was a star bareback rider with Ringling Bros. Circus, he began producing indoor circuses in the winters for Shrine sponsors. He and his family continued their riding act until 1937, but his indoor route was proving so profitable that he started devoting full time to it. Of the thirty or so circuses operating in the United States when the Big One folded its tents, about half a dozen appeared throughout the season under the

Ringling Bros. Barnum, Bailey Circus
Last Stand Under Canvas
Pittsburg, Pa.   July 16 1956

LAST STAND UNDER CANVAS. On July 16, 1956, in Pittsburgh, John Ringling North, owner of The Greatest Show on Earth, announced tersely: "The tented circus as it exists today is, in my opinion, a thing of the past." With that, Ringling Bros. ended its tour in midseason and returned to winter quarters. To circus lovers all over America, it looked as if the circus itself were dying. "A magical era has passed," lamented Life *magazine. But thirty-three years later, Kenneth Feld, the son of the man who saved the circus in America by making it a success in arenas, said that he was considering a return to the Big Top in selected American cities in the 1990s. "The tented circus, as we use it to tour Japan, is, in my opinion, a definite possibility for the future," said Feld. "I already have architects designing new tents for the circus in America." (Circus World Museum, Baraboo, Wisconsin)*

sponsorship of some civic group or charity. The predetermined costs of the circus would be deducted from the gross, then the remainder would be divided between the circus and its sponsor on a sliding-scale plan by which the sponsor might receive as much as 75 percent of the profits.

You could see terrific acts in some Shrine circuses. Attempts at training camels for ring routines are seldom successful, but in the 1950s, on Polack Bros., Jack Joyce introduced a camel act that was particularly memorable. Joyce trained horses for Ringling Bros. and others, and he used his skill to break five camels. He dressed them in ornate Oriental blankets, which made them look like symbols of the Ancient & Arabic Order of the Mystic Shrine, and, as Fox and Parkinson put it, "they loped and lumbered through an elaborate routine with the turnabouts, countermarches, and other attributes of equine liberty acts."

In that same show, Mac and Peggy MacDonald presented an elephant called Baby Opal doing the one-leg stand, a feat that few elephants accomplish because it does not capitalize on a natural ability.

Into this world of the indoor circus came the Big One, Ringling Bros. and Barnum & Bailey Circus. Playing indoors, it was no longer so dependent upon good weather, so it could operate nearly all year. At first, however, it found many of the best arenas booked two and three years in advance, so it would be 1959 before the show's new routing pattern could be established. Fairground and ballpark dates were frequently rained out. In Syracuse, New York, for example, expenses were $20,868, while income was a pitiful $1,618. The 1958 season was stretched out by adding a month in Mexico. It opened in March, not at New York but at Charlotte, North Carolina.

By 1959, the Ringling show had worked out the basic routing pattern that it would still fol-

low in the 1990s. It would open in January in Florida and play its way northward to a long spring engagement at Madison Square Garden in New York. Then it would appear in arenas all around the country before closing in November. Over the Christmas season it would be in winter quarters rehearsing its new edition.

But the decline continued into the 1960s. Most of the surviving circuses were small and, worst of all, the few superstars who could perform crowd-pleasing superfeats were falling victim to age or tragedy. In 1961, the Great Wallendas made it into the *Guinness Book of World Records* by performing the greatest highwire feat of all time, a three-layer, seven-person "human pyramid" moving on a wire. But on January 30, 1962, while performing the pyramid in Detroit, the Wallendas fell. No law required a net, and their leader, Karl Wallenda, preferred to perform without one. Then fifty-seven, he saw his nephew and his son-in-law killed in the fall, and his own son paralyzed for life. In 1963, the Wallendas had another accident, and Mrs. Wallenda's sister fell to her death.

The whole circus in America was in trouble.

Take the Al G. Kelly and Miller Circus. Obert Miller had run it in the early forties as a very small truck show, but when his sons came home from World War II, they expanded it into one of the most innovative—and profitable—circuses on the road. It successfully carried a giraffe, a most fragile animal, by truck. It adapted motorized equipment to the circus the way that Coup adapted railroad equipment to the circus. It was the first to use an airplane to advertise the circus from the air.

In the 1950s, the Al G. Kelly and Miller Circus was a strong rival to Ringling. Its outstanding menagerie and large herd of elephants made it a pleasure to see.

D. R. Miller bought an old steamboat to take his show on a tour of the Maritime Provinces of Canada. It sank at Halifax, taking with it a lot of the circus's equipment. In the midst of this and other setbacks, the government wanted back taxes. The circus was forced to sell its rhinoceros, hippopotamus, and many of its elephants. Then its giraffe died. The circus had survived for over a quarter of a century, but now key department heads were retiring. The show shrank to the standard size of the small shows—traveling on about twelve trucks, performing under an 80-by-200-foot Big Top. Finally, Miller leased the circus to another operator, who was not successful. The Kelly-Miller Circus finally closed in August of 1968.

Cristiani Bros. had great success in the 1957 season, netting $100,000, and in 1958 it took over the former Ringling Bros. stand in Soldier's Field on the Chicago lakefront. But business was generally disappointing as the fifties ended, and in the sixties it got so bad that Cristiani Bros. began hiring out some of its most talented riders—such as Lucio and Belmonte—to other shows.

Even the sponsored indoor circus business was divided up so many ways that few of the circuses could any longer play a long, and hence profitable, route. Polack Bros. was losing dates to Clyde Bros. and the new Hubert

Castle Circus. Orrin Davenport died, and the dates of the Davenport Circus were divided among several rivals and some former employees. Mills Bros. Circus, which had been started in 1940 by three brothers who adapted and developed the system of using local sponsors to ensure ticket sales, did not go out in 1967. Some of those who did go out should have stayed in winter quarters.

"By the early 1960's," wrote Bill Ballantine in *Clown Alley,* "a visible slump in spirit and style took hold of most American circuses. Owners and operators became shiftless and contemptuous of the public. Sloppy, cheaply produced performances were presented. Many smaller circuses became nothing more than ragbag cheats. Since circus performers were embarrassed to work on them, professional pride unraveled. On most shows the clowns were pitiful—in some cases, just work hands with smeary, dash-on makeups, simple costumes, and gags of unbelievable ineptitude and confusion."

The malaise extended right to the top. In 1962, John Ringling North decided to leave the United States forever and live in Switzerland. As Irvin Feld said, "The next five years were horrendous. The quality of the show kept going down, yet the attendance figures kept increasing."

The public was evidently hungry for good circus; it was the circus that wasn't being good enough for the public.

*Hind Rassam, a student from Baghdad, meets an Arabian camel from Jack Joyce's magnificent camel act in the backyard of the Polack Bros. Circus in Rockford, Illinois. Americans first saw a camel in 1721, and two camels, a male and female, were shown at Stevens's Livery Stable, Wall Street, New York, in 1787, but attempts to train these aloof and temperamental animals had been largely unsuccessful until Joyce. (*Rockford Register-Republic *photo in John Culhane Collection)*

DISPLAY·17

Gunther Gebel-Williams and the Comeback of the Circus in America

As early as 1971, Richard Schickel, an astute observer of the American scene, wrote in *Harper's* magazine that Gunther Gebel-Williams, the wild animal trainer, was "something vital and reviving in an entertainment form that has been stylized and ritualized for time out of mind . . . he has indeed transformed the circus, made the anachronism seem a thing very much of our time."

The comeback of the circus in America is essentially the story of how Irvin Feld finally came to own The Greatest Show on Earth; how he at last got Gunther Gebel-Williams for America; how Gunther came, was seen, and conquered both the circus ring and the television screen; and how, together, Feld and Gebel-Williams began the revitalization of the circus in America that continues to this day.

On January 1, 1967, Irvin Feld made a New Year's resolution. He would either acquire Ringling Bros. and Barnum & Bailey Circus that year or he would sever his connection with it.

"I couldn't stand to let it go on in the state it was in then," he said. "I was really afraid that the American public was going to be permanently turned off. I felt I must do everything possible to purchase the circus. It became an obsession."

The Great Depression, World War II, the Hartford fire, and the competing lures of film and television with sound and color had all corroded the bright image of the live circus and lessened the public's desire for live entertainment. Since the 1950s, and particularly since 1962, when John Ringling North became

"A STAR OF THE CIRCUS IS TURNING IN HIS WHIP," said a headline in the New York Times *for February 7, 1989, over a three-column picture of Gunther Gebel-Williams. He gave his first U.S. performance in 1969. Since then, more than 150 million people have seen him in some 11,000 performances (he never missed a show). As for the whip Gunther is turning in, it's a spare, anyway. He presented his original whip to the Smithsonian Institution in 1981. (Ringling Bros. and Barnum & Bailey Circus)*

the absentee landlord of the circus his uncles founded, running it, after a fashion, mostly from Switzerland, Irvin Feld—and a lot of other circus aficionados—were seeing a serious decline in the quality, spirit, and style of the circus they had always called the Big One. It was still billed as The Greatest Show on Earth, but its program had fewer than a dozen acts, some of which might not have found a place in the golden age of the circus.

That first day of 1967, Irvin Feld telephoned John Ringling North in Rome, wished him a Happy New Year, and told him they had to talk. North replied that he would have to come to Rome if he wanted to talk, so Feld immediately hopped a plane to the birthplace of the ancient circus—the one that did without the counterpoint of the clowns.

When Feld met North at the Excelsior Hotel in Rome and told him that he wanted to buy Ringling Bros. and Barnum & Bailey Circus, North laughed. But Feld "sold" North for three solid hours, describing the ways in which the quality of the circus was declining. "We're doing business, but sooner or later the public is going to catch on," said Feld boldly. That seemed to have an effect on the nephew who had fought long and hard before 1962 to keep the family circus The Greatest Show on Earth his uncles had built. At last, John Ringling North set a price—$7.5 million—but he wanted it all in cash, "not one cent in a note." And what's more, even if Feld *could* raise the money and bring it back to Rome, North said, he still might change his mind: "I'm liable to go back to the U.S. and run the Circus again."

The following November, after protracted negotiations, Irvin Feld was back in Rome with his brother and partner, Israel Feld, and Judge Roy Hofheinz, builder of the Houston Astrodome, then America's largest indoor arena. They bought the circus from North for $8 million. (Before Judge Hofheinz entered the picture, Feld had lined up another backer who, to his horror, tried to talk North into reducing the purchase price. North's reaction was to raise the price by half a million dollars.)

Time magazine, in words that Feld had been waiting all his life to hear, said: "The deal, in a publicity stunt worthy of Barnum, was ceremoniously sealed in the center of the Roman Colosseum." Feld brought along a lion cub, which he had his daughter Karen present to North for a photo that ran in newspapers all over the globe. "I wanted to make sure the whole world knew," Irvin Feld told the *New York Times*, "that the circus had changed hands."

Old circus hands looked upon the purchase with skepticism. Ringling Bros. and Barnum & Bailey had been owned and operated by the same family for eighty-three years—and the Ringlings founded the circus by performing as well as managing. Neither Feld brother had ever trouped with a circus, so they were resented as money men who had bought, not earned, their position of power. To real troupers, running a circus was something you learned by doing, day and night, rain or shine. So along with the circus, the Felds had bought the traditional distrust that troupers have for towners, the word circus folk use for all outsiders.

Having bought the circus in late 1967, there was very little Feld could do with the 1968 show. But in February of 1968, he announced that come 1969 there would be a completely new unit of The Greatest Show on Earth—not a second unit but one that was the equal of the other in quality and quantity. One unit would be called the Red Unit and the other the Blue. The Felds would produce one new show each year and each show would run two years.

Feld believed that there were more communities in America that would provide profitable show dates for Ringling Bros. and

Barnum & Bailey Circus than the circus could get to in a season, even now that playing indoors had lengthened the circus season to eleven months a year.

Even his own employees were against the idea. Their negative attitude was shared by John Ringling North, who demanded that Irvin Feld come see him in Vienna for a meeting, at which he threatened to remove the Ringling name from the show.

"How can there be two Greatest Shows on Earth?" he asked Irvin Feld. "Which will be the greatest?"

Barnum would have loved the illogical logic of Irvin Feld's answer: "Both," he said.

To make good on his pledge, Irvin Feld went to Europe in March of 1968. In thirty-five hectic days, he scouted forty-six continental circuses for acts.

In those early years, his great competition for being the first to present European circus acts to American audiences was "The Ed Sullivan Show" on Sunday night network television. Feld would fly to Europe about six times a year to beat Sullivan to the talent. "Once in a while," Feld told *Time*, "after a couple of weeks on dusty lots in the midst of a blazing Italian summer, you get the feeling you've seen everything. Then, out of the blue comes an act so spectacular that you get shivers up your spine."

The circus star who had sent shivers up more spines than anybody since World War II was undoubtedly Germany's Gunther Gebel-Williams. From the morning in 1968 that Irvin Feld caught up with the great Gunther under canvas on a muddy circus lot in Salerno, Italy, the comeback of the circus in America was under way.

As Barnum had to have the greatest wild animal in the world in Jumbo's day, Feld had to have the greatest wild animal trainer. Virtually everyone agreed that Gunther was his

man—indeed, that Gunther was the greatest all-around circus performer of his time. John Ringling North had tried to get him, but Gunther had many reasons for not wanting to leave the Circus Williams in Europe.

Just as Barnum had paid a then-staggering $10,000 for Jumbo in 1882, Irvin Feld paid a staggering $2 million for the whole Circus Williams in 1968. And just as Jumbo proved to be one of the greatest attractions in the history of the circus, so too has Gunther Gebel-Williams—elephant trainer, horse trainer, tiger trainer, superstar performer.

It all worked out just as Feld planned. Gunther Gebel-Williams is not just a circus star, he is perhaps the greatest all-around star in circus history—and here is why. He is a star in the steel cage, making those mortal enemies, tigers, horses, and an elephant, perform together for the first time in history, or controlling the largest cage full of tigers (seventeen) ever seen. He is a star as an elephant trainer, capable of controlling a herd of nineteen elephants, spread over three rings, with the sound of his voice alone. And he is a star as a horse trainer or a horse rider, giving overall direction to his wife and stepdaughter as the three of them direct three rings of liberty horses (horses trained to work in the ring without any riders), or reviving all by himself the ancient, dangerous, and demanding art of Roman post riding, with one foot on each saddle of two galloping horses. He has even been a star as an acrobat, letting one of his elephants run from a standing start to stomp on the opposite end of a teeterboard, sending Gebel-Williams somersaulting through the air to land lightly on the back of a second elephant. To get The Greatest Show on Earth, and then to get the greatest for The Greatest Show on Earth, Irvin Feld wouldn't take no for an answer.

Yet all this leaves out the charisma of the broadly smiling wild animal trainer with the long golden hair and the hard-muscled physique, jaunty in bright red boots and tights and a jacket that glitters like gold. Tarzan in all his glory was neither arrayed as splendidly nor as abundantly talented as Gunther Gebel-Williams.

Gebel-Williams is not a child of the circus. In fact, he didn't even have circus-oriented ambitions until he joined a circus. His father had been a successful set designer for the theater, and Gunther's earliest memories are of seeing his father make sketches at home and then going with him to a theater and seeing up on the stage whole worlds produced from the sketches. So show business, at least, was there from the beginning, along with an example of how ideas are generated and produced. To see the living tableaus he has produced with his animals, such as two horses with tigers on their backs, flanking an elephant with a tiger on its back, and straddling that elephant-topping tiger, smiling triumphantly, Gunther Gebel-Williams himself, is to think of him as his own art director.

Gunther Gebel-Williams was born Gunther Gebel in eastern Germany on September 12, 1934, less than a month after the plebiscite that approved Hitler's assumption of the presidency and sole executive power. When Germany went to war, so did Gunther's father. He was sent to fight on the Russian front, was captured, and disappeared into the forced-labor camps of Siberia.

Gunther's first encounters with fear came during Allied bombing raids on Germany. He says that he never mastered his fear of random death by falling bombs. There was no opportunity to get to know a bomb so that you could predict its behavior. Perhaps in consequence, the extraordinary self-control and willpower that his coworkers were later to observe in him had not yet shown itself in his wartime school years. Even in school gymnastics, his prowess was no more than average.

As the war ended, Gunther and his mother and older sister fled from the advancing Russian army and came to West Germany "with nothing but what we could carry." His postwar adjustment meant learning to survive adolescence without his father, who did not get out of Russia until 1949. Before the war, his mother had not worked, but in postwar Germany, said Gunther, "she must work for us to live." It happened that the Circus Williams was starting up after the war in a town where the Gebels were staying. Mrs. Gebel saw a notice: "Seamstress Wanted," and she got the job.

It was 1946. Gunther was twelve. His sister was eighteen; she soon married and left her mother's charge, and Gunther has rarely seen her since. But Gunther's mother had to travel with the circus and Gunther had to travel with his mother, so he left school and never went back.

"I have not so much school in my time. Only from six to twelve I went to school. That's not so much. But I have a good feeling for animals, so I do OK." But it wasn't only his feeling for animals that permitted him to "do OK." If he didn't have much formal education, he turned out to have a real passion for learning.

"Not so many people like to take the time to learn something very well—and almost nobody wants to take the time to learn *everything* about anything. Many people today like to learn fast something, and that's all, so they don't know many things, and they don't know anything well."

The circus gave Gunther Gebel a direction and a purpose. He set out to learn the whole circus world, beginning with various types of acrobatics. He was surrounded by people who had been circus folk for generations. Like true professionals in any art or craft, they took a parental interest in the young outsider who not only appreciated what they did, but wanted to learn how to do it—and even do it better.

"My mother had not the feeling for circus life, and she didn't like traveling around so much, so she left the circus," says Gunther, "but I stayed. The Williams family took me like a son."

Herr Harry Williams, the stern circus director, was an expert horseman, and he was already raising his young daughter Jeanette to be the best equestrienne in the circus. Now he began to teach Gunther his method of horsemanship. "First I learned to stay on a horse standing up, like in cowboy movies," he said. Eventually, he mastered the dangerous and demanding art of Roman post riding, in which the rider stands astride two galloping horses.

Another pupil, Charly Baumann, has written that Harry Williams provided "a basic understanding of animal training. It happened to be with horses, but the education was applicable to all animals. By example he demonstrated that infinite patience was the true secret of success in training an animal. He was methodically persistent in developing even the most minute movement of his own horses. He never struck an animal to accomplish his purposes, but instead constantly repeated his instructions, using rewards for accomplishments and mild rebukes for failure." It was, in short, the method Gunther Gebel-Williams has used with tigers, horses, elephants—even goats and giraffes.

One evening, illness prevented Herr Williams from going on, and Gunther appeared alone with the animals. He displayed such competence that his foster father started him immediately in animal training. Even those whose whole lives had been the circus were astonished by the boy's self-control and ability to communicate with wild animals.

The animal that Gunther began with as a trainer was the horse—and he still maintains that horses are the most difficult to train. "Horses are just not too bright," he says.

Next, Herr Williams entrusted him with the show's herd of performing elephants, which were, and are, Gunther's favorite animals. "You don't have to know me long before you understand how much I love elephants," he says. "People think they are good-natured and dumb. But no! It is easy to get across what you want with elephants because they are very smart animals, but also very clever. [The only two animals rated higher in intelligence by zoologists are chimpanzees and orangutans.]

"Elephants can be taught to listen, to do what you tell them," he says. "I don't think it's necessary to push them or shove them around. All you have to do is work with them until they understand what's expected. Then you just remind them of their act and they do it."

Proof of their intelligence is provided by one of Gunther's most famous acts, "Propulsion by Pachyderm Power." In it, Gunther makes a backward leap from a teeterboard onto the back of an elephant. The wonder of it is that the performer who applies the pressure to the other end of the teeterboard is a second elephant, which runs across the ring and stomps the teeterboard down.

By the time Gunther was sixteen, his mentor considered him competent enough to drive horses in Roman-style chariot races. And in 1951, Gunther went with Circus Williams on its first visit to England after World War II. One afternoon in London, four Roman chariots, each pulled by four large, fast Arabian stallions, raced around the rings, with Herr Williams among the drivers. "It was *very* fast driving," Gunther recalled, "and, at one turn, Mr. Williams's horse went around OK, but a chariot wheel hit the corner of the ring and Mr. Williams was thrown out." The wheel of the chariot behind him, driven by a man named Barley, struck Williams as he lay on the dirt track.

In a few minutes Williams regained consciousness, sat up, shook his head, and suddenly commanded, "Get that boy out of that wagon!" Gunther had taken Williams's chariot, which had righted itself after the fall, and was walking the horses to prevent their cooling off too fast. Williams brushed himself off, returned to the chariot, and finished his act.

That night, however, Harry Williams woke up screaming because of a severe pain in his head. Neurosurgery was performed, but he died fourteen days later in a London hospital.

Mrs. Williams took over the business end of the circus. "You see," said Gunther, "she was an Althoff, and they, too, are an old circus family; so she knew the business. But she asked me to take over the technical side. And it was at this time that she gave me the family name, and I became Gunther Gebel-Williams."

Originally, said Gunther, the name was intended to give him more authority in dealing with adults. He was, after all, only seventeen. "She would say, 'There's *Mister* Williams—you see him about that.'" But gradually, Gunther took his authority from his actions rather than his name. And his devotion and fidelity did, indeed, make him seem like one of the family.

In 1960, Frau Williams married her daughter, Jeanette, to her adopted son, Gunther Gebel-Williams, who had become the circus's operating head. "Everyone thought it was a good idea," Gunther said in 1973. "Jeanette and I have a very good friendship—but it was not good for a marriage. It was too much brother and sister." The marriage broke up in 1967.

Gunther Gebel-Williams was no longer the promising protégé of the Williams family. He was a man standing on his own two feet—on top of galloping horses. In 1964, for his outstanding horsemanship, he was awarded the Ernest Renke-Plaskett Award, the coveted "Oscar" of the European circus world; then won this highest European honor an unprecedented twice more, the second time as the trainer of a herd of twenty elephants—the herd

he would bring with him to America and The Greatest Show on Earth—and then yet a third time as an all-around circus performer.

And he was gradually changing the Circus Williams. In 1960, he bought his first tiger. "I got him from India for $1,000." What did he want with a tiger? "I have the idea to have two elephants and a tiger together in the cage."

By this time, the Circus Williams was a prosperous, middle-sized circus. "We had a Big Top tent that seated 3,500 people, and we went to Italy, France, and Spain—though never to America." But in the circus, whether indoors or under the Big Top, the big topper is the name of the game. No matter how good an act is, the true circus professional wants to top it. "I saw for the first time one horse and one tiger done by another guy in Germany," said Gebel-Williams, "and I say to myself, 'OK.—I'll do it, also—but with *two* horses and *two* tigers.'"

Gebel-Williams married again in 1968, to a girl he had spotted in the audience the year before. "I talk to many girls in the audience, but I don't marry them," he said—until Sigrid. She was a slim, blond high-fashion model who had also been married before. She had a daughter from her first marriage named Tina.

"When she traveled with me for the first time, I say to her, 'Everybody has something to do here.' Starting in 1969, I'm teaching her everything, and at the beginning, she was very scared of everything. She was frightened just to be near a horse. But when she sees that I am not frightened, it makes her less frightened."

But first there was the move to America. Lucrative offers were coming to him from all over the world; Gunther turned down John Ringling North, but Irvin Feld made him an offer he couldn't refuse. Feld bought the entire Circus Williams and merged it into Ringling Bros.

Gunther had Feld buy everything except

Circus Williams's winter quarters in Cologne and give him a five-year personal contract. This arrangement, said Gebel-Williams, made his foster mother a wealthy woman while giving him both money and comparative freedom. His first contract ran from his first American tour in 1969 until 1973, when he was free to negotiate for himself without also being responsible for the whole Circus Williams. He signed his second five-year contract as a performer with the Ringling circus for $1,000 a week. (When he took over as operating head of Circus Williams in 1951, he had been making about $1,000 a year.) Every five years since then, there has been a new and more lucrative contract.

Still, he earns his money the hard way. He has only three weeks a year off—and, even then, he is tied to his tigers. He won't let anyone else feed them because his safety depends on their absolute acceptance of him as the man from whom all blessings flow.

For the 1973 season, he got three tigers, two horses, and an African elephant to perform together in the same cage, and seemed to be enjoying his feat as much as the audience. Behind the smiles, however, Gunther Gebel-Williams was constantly aware that in this act he had to be particularly careful. "Only people who understand how much horses and elephants fear beasts of prey will realize how much time and effort went into the act," he told me afterward. It took him three full years to train the three species to fraternize as they do. He hand-picked the horses from a ranch near Waco, Texas. He trained Kongo, the only performing African elephant in the United States at the time, from the age of six months. But the tigers were the toughest job. He and his wife hand-raised and bottle-fed the three from birth. When the cubs were six months old, he began taking them on daily visits to Kongo and the horses. "I must be very careful

that the tigers make no unexpected movements which might panic the elephant," he said.

Unexpected movements had already covered Gebel-Williams's arms with scars, though he has no other wounds on his body. He showed me the worst: the scars on his right arm where one of his tigers slashed an artery in 1968. He had returned to Trier, Germany, from negotiations with the Ringling circus in America and found the tiger very sick. "I was tired from the jet lag when I brought a doctor to give my tiger a shot. I went into the cage to back him up with a little stick to the bars, where the doctor could shoot him in the rump, and when the needle went in, the tiger struck out at me. A tiger doesn't retract his claws, you know—I had to pull my arm off them. I got a tetanus shot right away, but tigers have old, decayed meat under their claws, so the infection put me in the hospital. Now I know what's possible and not possible, and I don't go in the small cages with tigers anymore."

As his first act of each show, Gebel-Williams controls up to a dozen tigers at once. (Danger aside, try to control the movements of one house cat, if you want to measure his accomplishment.) He coaxes one big cat into leapfrogging another; he makes seven at once walk forward on their hind legs; he makes another dance backward on its hind legs. He makes them roll over together.

The first time I saw this act, the man next to me gestured at it with his foot-long hot dog and said to his wife, "Of course, you know they've been fed just before the show, and the *last* thing they want is another meal."

"My tigers are never fed until the act is over," said Gebel-Williams when he took me along one night at tiger-feeding time. "I don't like sleepy tigers, ready for a snooze after a big meal."

These tigers were not sleepy. Smelling the meat, they began to growl and pace their cages nervously. An attendant followed us, pushing a wheelbarrow piled high with horse meat. The lions and tigers in the Ringling Bros. and Barnum & Bailey Circus consume more than 168,000 pounds of meat each year. "One week they get horse meat; one week, beef," said Gebel-Williams.

In addition to feeding his tigers himself, he is careful to pay personal visits to his tigers and elephants before and after every performance of the circus. During the preshow visits, he carefully inspects each animal, checking its health and general well-being, and—most important—its mood. "I can see on my tigers' faces if they are angry or don't feel well," he says. He wants to understand what he will be up against when he meets them in the arena. One time, for example, he had to replace a male tiger because it had incurred the dislike of a female, a situation that could be dangerous with Gunther in the middle.

Taking such care meant, until just recently, that Gunther could never take a vacation. In 1986, eighteen years in America, he did take a trip away from his tigers, to Germany to visit his aged mother—since he could at last leave his sixteen-year-old son in charge of his animals.

At each cage, Gebel-Williams spoke to the tiger by name as he poked a stick through the bars to get it to move back. Then he raised the feeding door high enough for the attendant to toss in a hunk of raw red meat.

"It is in the after-show visit," said Gebel-Williams, "that I thank the animals who have done well and scold the ones who haven't. All of my animals have come to expect me after the show. One night, a few years back, I was in a hurry and decided to skip the visit. But the tigers roared so loudly and the elephants trumpeted so much that I had to stay twice as long to calm them down."

This little touch of Gunther in the night

places him, as a wild animal trainer, in the tradition begun by Karl Hagenbeck (1844–1913), animal dealer and founder of the Stellingen Zoo at Hamburg. Karl Hagenbeck completely revolutionized the presentation of wild animal acts in circuses by inventing new and humane methods of training and sustaining wild animals in captivity.

In Hagenbeck's classic *Von Tieren und Menschen* (*Of Beasts and Men*), published in Berlin in 1908, he wrote: "In the popular estimation, carnivores conjure up a vision of all that is faithless, savage, and cruel. But it is certainly a mistake to call them cruel. It is their nature in the wild state to hunt living prey, and they have to kill in order to live. We are prone to forget how many millions of animals are hunted and slaughtered both by land and sea, to provide food for human beings; and it is as reasonable to accuse mankind of cruelty on this score, as it is to accuse carnivores. . . . Of course, one often comes across black sheep, but that is due either to their having been caught when adult, or to their being the victims of bad rearings."

It is Gunther's practice to rear his tigers lovingly from the time they are babies. "Since Gunther and I were married, I've mothered dozens of baby tigers," said Sigrid Gebel. She and her husband will often bottle-feed babies around the clock until they grow up enough to make it on their own.

I once saw Gunther go over to a cage containing two baby tigers, one ten months old, the other only seven months. They immediately rushed over to him like suburban kids greeting their daddy at the train station. Gunther caressed the little tigers, crooning, "Hey, kids, come here, *Schatz*." I have frequently watched him affectionately cuffing a grown tiger in the center ring after a good performance.

Prior to Hagenbeck's time, trainers generally believed that only fear could force animals to perform tricks. Hagenbeck called this the "brute-force system," and derided trainers who terrified cats into jumping over barriers by poking at them with sticks and firing blanks near their ears with pistols. He claimed—and Gunther Gebel-Williams, Charly Baumann, and others have abundantly proved—that the brute-force system couldn't achieve "one-hundredth part of what can be done by humane and intelligent methods."

The catch was that the Hagenbeck method called for more time and patience than most trainers were willing to give. As Gunther says,

> Every kind of animal is different. Before any kind of training can begin, you first have to establish a friendship, a mutual trust. Then anything is possible.
>
> It's very difficult to begin training a new cat. At first you never know how smart he is, what his personality is all about. When I start with a cub, the first thing I do is give him a name. It must be short, easy to call and not close in sound to any other animal's. Until he's named, the newcomer doesn't feel part of the family.
>
> Once he's named, then he must learn who I am—the boss! Several times a day, I visit the new cat in his travel cage, always bringing a little food. After a few weeks, I take him into the big cage in the morning—not to work, just to play around and get him acquainted with the cage and props. He must be comfortable there, it must be home. Then and only then can serious training begin.

Gunther carries the trainer's whip, but, more important, his belt also holds a pouch filled with small chunks of meat to reward his carnivores for obedience to his commands, which he gives in both English and German.

> The language I speak to him doesn't matter. What matters is the tone of voice. The an-

imals must be able to hear me and understand me.

> Animals, you must understand, are very like children. You must have very great patience with them, praising them when they behave, scolding them when they don't. In that way, they learn to respect you and learn that it is to their advantage to do what you tell them.
>
> The first thing a cat must learn is his place, his set in the cage. After that, I must find what tricks are natural for him, the kinds of things he will have fun performing.

Gunther finds that some animals have great potential as performers, while others are a waste of time or can't get along with the other cats. These are weeded out as quickly as possible so that Gunther can concentrate on adapting the personalities of the most willing and cooperative animals to the tricks he has in mind.

"From the beginning of my work with cats, I always tried tricks that were not the usual. I took a little from liberty horse routines and even borrowed something I'd seen a chimp perform. I have no interest to just copy what other tiger trainers have accomplished already."

Each animal's part in the performance has to be so thoroughly drilled that the animal will do the right thing at the right time without variation.

Richard Schickel, who was fortunate enough once to watch Gunther introduce a new tiger into his cat act, has written a vivid picture of the trainer's famous patience. This tiger, named Futzi, had been brought up as a house pet in Florida, said Schickel,

> a business for which Gebel-Williams has a well-honed contempt. "She has no respect for the whip," he complains. "It's just something more to play with. And I have to

watch—Thomas [another tiger] does not like her." It's quite funny to observe him with her. She's always hopping up proudly on some other cat's stand, turning happily to Gebel-Williams for his praise—"brava, Futzi, brava"—and receiving instead a smart tap on the nose with the butt of his whip. When she gets on the right stand she invariably turns away from the trainer and stares vacantly out into the arena. Nor will she consistently do the first thing Gebel-Williams requires of his cats, which is to sit up in unison. What Futzi does instead is half-turn, hook the claws of one paw into the bars of the cage and haul herself halfway into the sitting posture. "Futzili, Schatzi, no, no," Gebel-Williams croons, poking at her to regain her attention. "Six months I have her," he says, "and still she does not know what I expect." He gestures to another cat. "*This* one, he learns in thirty days." Poke, poke goes the hockey stick and Futzi finally manages some kind of unaided, if graceless, sit-up. "Brava, Futzi, brava," Gebel-Williams sighs. He fixes a bit of meat to a long stick, hands it to her, then turns his attention elsewhere. "Two, three times you can push a tiger, no more."

Schickel concluded that the animal trainer's problem lay in finding "the right combination of words, rewards, attitudes" that will reach the animal. "Females are anyway more trainable," Gebel-Williams told him. "Males have the attitude, 'My God, now I'm going to have to do something.' "

These are the discouraging, sometimes frightening, days behind the scenes. "To the audience," Gunther told me, "it must all look easy. Even when I am scared—believe me, I am scared sometimes—the people must never suspect.

"But I know that, no matter how long you work with an animal, how well you think you know him, there's always a chance that, one day, when you least expect it, he may revert to his natural instincts, and turn on you. A wild animal trainer who puts total trust in his animals is very foolish, very foolish."

The wild animal, on the other hand, must learn to trust the trainer absolutely. Trust is a key concept in the circus. It is developed in tiger cubs in the same way that it is developed in human children: by assuring them that they can rely on the trainer's integrity. In the circus world, the young child on the trapeze dares to fly through the air because he feels an absolute assurance that the hands of the catcher will be there when he needs them. Circus people usually develop this certain reliance on each other's integrity by training their own children, almost from infancy, to carry on their craft.

It is all a far cry from Clyde Beatty, who made his animals fear him by poking the legs of a chair in their faces, snapping their rumps with a whip, and shooting off blanks from a pistol in their faces.

"For me, the pistol and the chair and the noise just aren't right. Audiences know that the animals can kill the trainer. I know it, too. But my job is to make every time a smooth performance." So in an age when television and films are filled with phony violence and fake defiance of sham death, Gunther Gebel-Williams defies real death but seeks to avoid actual violence, turning the old man-over-beast act into an act of love between God's creatures.

Nothing shows Gunther's communications skills better than the human members of his various acts. In his first years with The Greatest Show on Earth, Gunther supervised a liberty horse act that had his first wife, Jeanette Williams, in Ring One; his second wife, Sigrid Gebel, in Ring Three; and John Herriott and his wife between them in Ring Two. "When people asked who did the Liberties," Herriott told *Sports Illustrated*, "I always said Gunther, me, and our three wives." The running gag

"PROPULSION BY PACHYDERM POWER" *is one of Gebel-Williams's greatest feats: an elephant stomps on a teeterboard with just enough force to propel Gunther into a somersault onto the back of another elephant. Too little force and he wouldn't make it; too much and he would fly into the audience. "To get inside the head of animal and communicate—that is wonderful," says Gunther. His son Mark Oliver, assisting here, is himself an accomplished performer, in the tradition of all great circus families. (Ringling Bros. and Barnum & Bailey Circus)*

GUNTHER GEBEL-WILLIAMS AND TIGERS. *Gebel-Williams made his American debut in 1968 with a tiger act that featured just eight tigers. In his farewell tour in 1989–1990, he had eighteen tigers with him in the Big Cage. Here six of them prepare to sit up and beg like pet dogs. Two will then get down and play leapfrog with each other, sometimes managing six flowing, consecutive leaps. (Ringling Bros. and Barnum & Bailey Circus)*

THE CIRCUS WITHOUT THE BIG TOP. *By the mid-twentieth century most circuses were playing for large urban crowds in indoor arenas, ballparks, or athletic fields. Many were staged for promotional reasons by civic or charitable organizations. Shown here is the Clyde Bros. Circus appearing at Beyer Stadium, a ballpark and athletic field in Rockford, Illinois, in August 1959, under the aegis of the Shriners. The young man "leading" the elephants is me. As a reporter and daily columnist for the* Rockford Register-Republic *in the late fifties, I was usually invited to play a part in circus performances, and, of course, I wrote about the circus in return. In 1956, I was a guest clown with the Polack Bros. Shrine Circus and got to appear in the same circus with the fifth generation of Riding Hannefords. Polack's publicist, William B. Naylor, first became a circus press agent when he joined the Sells-Floto show in 1921, so I also got to watch an old-time "tub thumper" at work. Ringling Bros. and Barnum & Bailey had folded its tent and returned to winter quarters the month before, but Naylor told me enthusiastically: "Only the Big Top died— circuses are coming back. Why, auditoriums and ballparks are great places to have circuses. The psychology of the circus in the ballpark is the best yet. Our rings and acrobats are in the infield, because fans are used to looking down at the infield for close plays. The aerial acts are in the outfield, because fans are used to looking up for flies hit into the outfield." And, in fact, the circus in a ballpark thrived in Rockford. The year after I was Clyde Bros.' elephant man, I was a guest clown carrying out the gags of Clyde Bros. producing clown Jack LaPearl. My clown partner was Eddie Arvida. In 1958, Arvida was a Clyde Bros. aerialist. On opening night he fell forty feet from his trapeze and spent three months in the hospital with a severe arm injury. He never flew again.* (Rockford Register-Republic, 1959)

AN ELEPHANT NEVER FORGETS. *In the wild, tigers often kill baby elephants, so elephants grow up naturally fearing them. Only people who understand this will appreciate how much time and effort goes into training an elephant to carry a tiger on its back. "I must be very careful that the tigers make no unexpected movements which might panic the elephant," says Gunther Gebel-Williams. (Ringling Bros. and Barnum & Bailey Circus)*

GUNTHER GEBEL-WILLIAMS WITH DICKIE THE GIRAFFE. *Feld bought the entire German Circus Williams for $2 million to get its star, the world's greatest wild animal trainer, for his Ringling Bros. and Barnum & Bailey Circus. Gunther trained Dickie the giraffe for the 1982 edition of The Greatest Show on Earth. Giraffes are so fragile that they are seldom seen on circuses and almost never subjected to training. (Ringling Bros. and Barnum & Bailey Circus)*

around the circus was that "working with horses, elephants, and even tigers is nothing, compared to working with wives." But Gunther handled the situation as gracefully as he has handled the rest of his life, and soon Jeanette Williams married Elvin Bale, and the Bales moved to Ringling's Blue Unit, where they collaborated on an aerial act, and Jeanette commanded her liberty Lippizaner stallions in the center ring, flanked by Charly Baumann and Axel Gautier. (Jeanette and Elvin Bale have since divorced.)

Gunther soon had children of his own to train. A son, Mark Oliver Gebel, was born to Gunther and Sigrid in Houston, Texas, in 1970, and Gunther adopted Sigrid's daughter, Tina.

"I am a very lucky man," said Gunther, with his famous broad grin. "Not only do my animals listen to me, but my family pays attention also."

At the time of the 107th Edition of The Greatest Show on Earth, in 1977, Mark Oliver Gebel was seven years old and still answering to his nickname of "Buffy." But he was beginning to play little parts in his father's routines. In his elephant act, Gunther would stand on the low end of a teeterboard and let an elephant stomp on the high end, catapulting him into a backward somersault so that he would be politely facing the audience when he landed on the back of another pachyderm.

Each time his father made it safely, Buffy would stuff whole loaves of bread into the mouths of Gunther's fellow performers, sender and receiver, in eloquent thanks for Dad's happy landing. And each time Buffy gave the elephants their food reward, his father would jump down and affectionately cuff both elephants and his small son.

There have always been circus tricks that capture the imaginations of audiences, and audiences never seem to tire of seeing them re-peated. Every second season, when his unit was back in circus winter quarters to prepare a new show, Gunther Gebel-Williams would come up with new tricks and new routines for his jungle cats, his horses, his rare and exotic animals, and himself. But, in addition, audiences wanted to see again and again that trick that Curry Kirkpatrick, writing in *Sports Illustrated*, called "the magnificent teeterboard number."

"That move right there takes Gunther out of the realm of trainers and into the acrobats, equilibrists," said John Herriott, himself an esteemed animal trainer.

Believing that a bull, or male elephant, would be too aggressive for the act, Gunther trained a female elephant named Nellie to launch him into space. Nellie broke several thousand pieces of wood before she learned just the right amount of pressure to put into her stomp, and even after she learned, she had relapses. In Baltimore one year, Nellie stomped that teeterboard so hard she sent Gunther hurtling end over end into the rigging above the audience.

"I think I am out of the building that time," Gunther said.

But Gunther kept doing that teeterboard stomp, with its small role at the end for his young son.

Before Buffy and Tina could be stars, with acts of their own, they would get, in the circus way, experience with their father in both performing and training, not to mention cleaning up after and caring for the animals.

Gunther has often pointed out the only way to become an animal trainer: "You try to find out what's possible, what's interesting, what you can do with yourself. Now for me this time is over; but for anyone else that is what he must do. For many years."

Throughout the seventies, Gunther was training his son and stepdaughter as well as elephants, horses, and tigers, and in 1977, Tina

Gebel made her debut, commanding one of the three rings of liberty horses. (The horses in the other two rings were exhibited by her mother and another of Gunther's protégés, Henry Schroer.)

In the Ringling show for 1979, Gunther had filled the hippodrome track and all three rings with elephants for a production number called "Gypsy Fandango." Horses worked with the elephants, which wore a gorgeous pachyderm wardrobe designed by Don Foote. And Gunther had worked both Buffy and Tina into the act. Buffy held tight to the headdress of a rapidly turning elephant to perform the "airplane spin" from its forehead, letting the elephant turn him like a propeller. Tina executed a split between two elephants. As a climax to this elephant extravaganza, Gunther and his elephants again did their crowd-pleasing teeterboard stomp.

Once you've done an airplane spin from the head of an elephant, there's no place to go but up. In 1981, when Buffy would be eleven, Gunther Gebel-Williams intended to introduce a trained giraffe into the Ringling show, with Buffy as the world's first giraffe jockey.

"There's never been a trained giraffe in America," Gunther told the Felds several years before. And in his native Europe, he said, "they are only trained to walk around." By so saying, Gunther had, in effect, challenged the Felds to challenge him to train one.

The Felds decided to display the giraffe with four African elephants.

Even those who see a lot of circuses don't see a lot of African elephants. "They are taller, with larger ears and longer tusks, than their Indian cousins, but the Indian elephant is much easier to work with," said Gunther the wild animal trainer.

"But," added Gunther the performer, "the Africans are much more impressive in the big arena, so I want four Africans. I have to get the idea and Mr. Feld and Kenny [Feld's son] have to come up with the money, because new ideas usually mean new animals."

And so, in anticipation of the 1981 show, the Felds bought in 1979 two more African baby elephants.

"And then we took an option on an unborn giraffe."

"Giraffe futures?" I asked Kenneth in September 1980. "How do you deal in giraffe futures?"

Kenneth laughed.

It *is* like dealing in commodities. You survey Busch Gardens and all the zoos and animal men around until you find a pregnant giraffe. Then you say, I want the first male born, at such and such a price.

And the reason we wanted an unborn giraffe as opposed to one six months old was so that we could train it our way. As soon as it was born, we sent our vet down to Busch Gardens, took it away from the mother, and put a groom with it from Day Two.

Six months later, we took the baby giraffe up to Washington, introduced it to Gunther, who had never worked with a giraffe before, and built a special truck for it so that the giraffe could go on the road. That was Easter of 1980, and Gunther would work with it from that time right through the month-long rehearsals for the 1981 show at winter quarters in December, 1980.

We had to build a special truck for it because it quickly grew to be about nine feet tall, and it was still a baby. A giraffe is not a terribly expensive animal as circus animals go—it's in the $7,000 to $10,000 range—but we then had to spend $80,000 on a truck with a hole in the top.

After Gunther stuck his neck out by saying he could train a giraffe, he then came up with a way to top the trained giraffes in Europe that "are only trained to walk around." Irvin and

Kenneth Feld had decided that the theme of the Spec in the 111th edition would be "The Old-Time Circus Parade," which most American cities hadn't seen since before World War II. It would be a sight to remember, they all agreed, if, in that parade, the giraffe would come striding with ungainly vitality down the track as he used to stride down America's streets—but this time with Buffy Gebel on his back.

So Gunther trained his son and the giraffe, and it came to pass just as he and the Felds had envisioned it.

Giraffes are traditional in the circus. I saw them in Ringling's pre-Feld era—but in the menagerie. You went up to the keeper and you said, "What do you do if he gets a sore throat?" So many people have asked that question that it inspired the Ringling giraffe's big scene in the film *The Greatest Show on Earth*, in 1952.

"Same old trouble?" asks Charlton Heston, playing the performance director, when he comes upon a man who has climbed a long red ladder propped against the enclosure fence to examine the giraffe within.

"Yeah, sore throat—all the way down."

"Well, get a billiard cue and swab it out," says Heston.

Actually, giraffes are such rare zoological features that they don't need hyperbole, and the sight of a ten-year-old boy riding on a giraffe was new, unusual, and energetic.

Buffy Gebel grew up riding that giraffe in the Spec, and so did the giraffe. By the second year of the 111th edition's tour, Buffy was twelve years old and Dickie, the giraffe, was about eighteen feet tall.

But Dickie was retired before the 1983 show. The problem was Gunther, not Buffy. Kenneth Feld told me, "Gunther is so concerned about his animals that he won't let anybody else drive the truck. And I don't want to kill Gunther having him drive a truck all around the country." Gunther's nature as a human being who cares deeply for his wild animal charges was in conflict with his role as a circus performer. He was wearing himself out before he even got to the arena, transporting his fragile giraffe from city to city. The only solution was to take the responsibility for the giraffe away from him.

In a sense, Buffy Gebel's two years as giraffe boy were his good-bye to childhood. When he reappeared in the 1983 edition, it would be with an act of his own, officially announced over the loudspeaker by the ringmaster for the first time, and his childish nickname would be no more.

This act was not Gunther's idea; it was Kenneth Feld's. But Gunther had learned to trust Kenneth's instinct for helping the audience see the circus with fresh eyes by coming up with something new, or with new ways to present the great traditional acts—with new costumes, new music, or simply in a new order on the circus program.

"The white tiger I work with was an idea from Kenneth," Gunther told me. "It was a female tiger and I had to put it on a horse and also an elephant, and an elephant is not so easy with a female. Then I put her also inside the cage with the other tigers in the cat act, so that the audience can see much better the difference between the normal tiger and the rare white."

Kenneth Feld followed up that exotic idea with the homespun suggestion that Gunther train some goats with his son.

"Who wants to train goats?" was Gunther's immediate answer. "There really is nobody in America who has a goat act," Kenneth coaxed. Gunther then considered the possibilities: "Goats are good jumpers. They're good climbers. They might do the hind-leg walk." He decided that although audiences wouldn't want to see Gunther Gebel-Williams with goats, a thirteen-year-old animal trainer with ten or twelve goats in a fast-paced billygoat revue should appeal to audiences.

I was at dinner with Gunther and his family and the Felds at the beginning of the December 1982 rehearsal period when Irvin Feld told Buffy that he would be making his formal circus debut in the 113th edition of The Greatest Show on Earth, which meant that the ringmaster would announce him. And by what name did he want to be announced?

"Mark Oliver Gebel," replied the young performer-cum-trainer, as if he had already given the matter sufficient thought. The nickname Buffy belonged to the green years before he commanded a ring full of animals in his own act. He would share the show's fourth display with the Mickey Antalek Chimpanzees in the center ring and Hall's Baboons in Ring Three. The act would be called "Mark Oliver Gebel's Goats," and the program would add: "First time anywhere."

Mark Oliver was assisted by twelve-year-old Michelle Antalek, whose own parents were animal trainers, presenting both the chimps who always made monkeys out of their trainers and the poodles known as Miss Lona's Dogs. The two were dressed in Swiss costumes as if they were a latter-day Heidi and Peter whose herd had strayed from the Alps. Audiences found the debut charming.

There was in that same show the first Gebel Family Equine Display in which Gunther in Ring Two, flanked by Sigrid and Tina in Rings One and Three, simultaneously presented three rings of liberty horses. The snow-white Arabians of Sigrid and Tina, caparisoned in bridles trimmed with feathers, trotted riderless to the commands of their trainers. The center ring was filled with the Lippizaner stallions of Gunther. Without the help of lines or reins, solely with low-toned commands and by occasionally waving a whip, the three Gebels made their twenty white chargers wheel and canter, abruptly change direction, and dance and prance to the center of the ring. All the family's horses waltzed, circled the ring in synchronization, and executed a tandem hind-leg stand to the accompaniment of the circus band. Once, watching a training session on that tandem hind-leg stand, I saw Sigrid having trouble controlling her ring full of rearing Arabians. Gunther was in the center of his own rearing Lippizaners at the time, but out of the corner of his eye he saw her difficulty, darted under the air-pawing hooves of his own horses, brought her horses into line with a crack of his whip and a shouted command, and as swiftly returned to his own ring. I asked Gunther how he did it. "Horses are not so intelligent," he said. "Before they know I am gone I am back."

As for those most intelligent elephants, Gunther believes that they enjoy performing. "I think they love the music and the spotlight. I don't think they miss the jungles at all. In the jungles, they must walk miles and miles every day, just to find something to eat. In the circus, they get plenty of food and have a lot of people around to take care of them."

He also believes the old saw that "an elephant never forgets." "Sometimes I try a trick an elephant hasn't done in ten years. She does it right away. And we perform in seventy buildings on each two-year tour. I don't remember all the details—which way to turn for this or that. The elephants do."

His family shares his feelings. "Of all the animals I grew up with, I always loved the elephants most," says Mark Oliver. "They were always my favorite playmates. And my father saw to it that I learned everything possible about them—their attitudes, their personalities, the best methods of approaching them."

Mostly, Gunther reminds them to be patient. "Elephants need to understand completely what you want them to do. Sometimes that takes a while." And not to be timid or speak too softly. "If you do, you will get nowhere. Fast."

"Training is beautiful thing, I think," he said. "When animal's brainpower is enhanced, life becomes more natural, easier, more pleasant. To get inside the head of animal and communicate, that is wonderful. That is what I live for."

There are ways of dealing with wild animals, he has taught his children, that give a person the confidence that overcomes fear. Some writers have suggested that Gebel-Williams has mystical ties to his animals. "That is very romantic," he replies, "but it is not so. No man can have a mystical relationship with a wild animal. All I can do is love them, respect them, and, above all, try to understand them." What Gunther does trust is that, because his intelligence and experience are greater than theirs, he can anticipate the expected and react quickly and wisely to the unexpected.

The psychology of fear is something that Gunther Gebel-Williams has thought a lot about during his life—the humans' fear of the animals and the animals' fear of the humans. His childhood fear of bombs was terrible, he points out, because, with a bomb, no relationship was possible. With animals, however, relationships are not only possible but easy if nurtured with love and patience. But he warns: "Very easy to make an animal afraid—and an animal afraid doesn't want to train in a cage. If I hurt them by hitting them, I lose our rela-

tionship. So all my hits are light, just to hurt the animal's pride. The ASPCA has a right to look at the circus and inspect us. I welcome this. If I am doing something wrong, tell me, I change it. If any other people are handling animals bad, take animals away from them. Boom. Absolute. But I don't think I do anything wrong. I give animals feeling for joy and fun."

Gunther also used love and patience with his family. "Gunther used to say, when I was starting out, 'Relax. Enjoy yourself!'" recalled Sigrid Gebel. "I took his advice— he's a smart man—and now our whole family performs together, and it's glorious being out there with my family. That's what circus is all about!"

———◆———

Trusting in his love and understanding of animals and people to see him through, Gunther Gebel-Williams bounded, in 1968, into a tired era of ersatz circus in America, of playing it safe in brilliant costumes, and with his light and rapid movements revived the original magic of the circus: the therapy of watching real men and women overcome humanity's age-old fears of wild animals and of falling from high places. The delight that his audiences and his family and his fellow performers took in his joyous example, more than any other single thing, has brought about the comeback of the circus in America.

"*Tiger, tiger, burning bright / In the forests of the night, / What immortal hand or eye / Could frame thy fearful symmetry?*" From Blake's generation on, the circus has been the place where many people experience the tiger's terrible and unforgettable beauty.

DISPLAY · 18

The Quest for the Quadruple

On July 10, 1982, performing with Ringling Bros. and Barnum & Bailey Circus in Tucson, Arizona, Miguel Vazquez, seventeen years old, became the first human being ever to achieve the quadruple somersault from the flying trapeze to the hands of the catcher. Tucked in a ball and spinning through the air at over eighty miles per hour, then stretching out his arms blindly and feeling the hands of his brother Juan clamp, viselike, on to his flesh, Miguel Vazquez reached the top of a profession that had its origin in 1859 when a French gymnast named Jules Leotard let go of one metal swing, flew through the air above a startled crowd at the Cirque Napoleon in Paris, and grabbed on to another metal swing, thereby inventing trapeze flying. (Leotard simultaneously gave his name to the garment he wore.)

The *New York Times* reported Vasquez's unique feat on page one: "A QUADRUPLE FOR THE FLYING MIGUEL VAZQUEZ." *Times* reporter Glenn Collins wrote of the quadruple as "a goal that has eluded generations of performers throughout the 123-year history of trapeze flying."

The quest for the quadruple is, in miniature, the history of the circus. From a 1786 handbill promising New Yorkers that Thomas Pool, at each performance, "mounts two horses in full speed, standing on the saddles, and in that position leaps a bar," to a 1984 circus poster urging New Yorkers to "Be There When the Flying Vazquez Perform the Quadruple Somersault," the circus has always presented superstars aspiring to superfeats. Audiences take heart from their performances, because although these accomplishments are superfeats, they are not supernatural feats: circus excel-

THE QUADRUPLE. *In the 1970s, Don Martinez, master of the "triple-and-a-half" back somersault, came close, then hurt himself and dropped out of competition; Tito Gaona, first to do a consistent triple since Alfredo Codona, came closer. But the first to complete the quadruple somersault before a paying audience was Miguel Vazquez (shown here connecting with his catcher brother Juan). (Ringling Bros. and Barnum & Bailey Circus)*

lence is human excellence, based on practice and perseverance, mastery and self-reliance; and circus history is the history of the cage boy who becomes the king of the big cats.

Dangerous circus tricks are usually calculated risks in which the odds favor the skillful athlete who keeps his head. "For hairbreadth as the escape must seem," wrote Octavie LaTour, who turned somersaults in an automobile in the circus in 1905,

> the probability of accident must be really small. No one wants to see people die. That game is one of mettle, not of death.
>
> Courage, not merely moral courage that copes with ethical problems and wins the battles of the soul, but physical courage, is a primitive instinct with us humans. Persons who are not called upon to be brave themselves satisfy their natural inclinations with the admiration of another's thrilling feat.
>
> So we professional heroes and heroines fill a necessary bill in life's vaudeville. We foster the spirit of bravery and daring, and we risk our lives every day and think no more of it, probably less, than a lawyer does of his case at the bar.

They risk their lives, but usually not on tricks that are so dangerous as to be foolhardy. For example, even a double somersault is considered too dangerous by most trapeze artists if it is a *forward* double somersault. "Fay Alexander did a beautiful double forward somersault over the bar to the catcher," said Tito Gaona, one of the great artists of the trapeze, "but he finally hurt himself doing it, and he quit. It's very dangerous because, going forward, you don't have much control —physical or mental. I did it and landed standing up on the catcher's bar, so I said, 'Forget it.'"

Occasionally, circus performers keep trying a trick in which the odds of escaping serious injury or death are against them—which is not appreciated by circus owners, who have a show or two to put on every day.

By the twentieth century, the *quadruple* back somersault from the flying trapeze to the hands of the catcher was the most difficult and dangerous, though theoretically possible, circus feat still not accomplished. For thousands of years, acrobats had been thrilling crowds and honing new tricks. Ropedancing can be traced back to ancient Greece. When Pompey provided five days of performances in the Circus Maximus for the Roman populace circa 52 B.C., the program included "acrobatic feats of great daring and dexterity." After the fall of the Roman Empire, adventurous groups of acrobats wandering about Europe, Africa, and Asia found that, wherever they went, the arts of jumping, tumbling, and balancing were known and loved. When Astley in England founded the circus, it didn't take him long to add such wandering acrobats to his programs of equestrians and a clown; and Ricketts in America followed Astley's lead.

Circus historian Earl Chapin May wrote that the question of which acrobat would throw the first triple somersault from a circus springboard before a paying audience

> was quite as engrossing from 1840 to 1874 as the early twentieth-century argument over which aviator would first fly across the Atlantic. In 1859, an acrobat named Johnny Aymar, renowned for having turned a double somersault over four horses, tried a triple, landed on his forehead, broke his neck, and died before the crowd. Broken necks killed several other contenders before John Worland successfully threw a triple from a springboard in St. Louis in 1874. Worland pushed his luck by doing it at least three times more, then retired and became a coal merchant in upstate New York under his real name, John Comash.

Now the question became: could an acrobat throw a triple off the flying trapeze?

The flying trapeze was a breathtaking improvement on an old Spanish circus act called "casting," which involved two strong acrobats who hung head down from stationary trapezes while they threw a small acrobat back and forth through a few feet of space. The small acrobat gradually improved the "flying" part of the casting act by doing body twists and even somersaults in midair. To give the "flier" more room to maneuver, the casters widened the distance between them.

In the 1850s, at the "Gymnase Leotard," a gymnasium and swimming bath in Toulouse, France, the owner's son was ready for a swim one day when he noticed parallel cords hanging from each of two roof ventilators, which were used to open and shut them. It occurred to young Jules Leotard that if a wooden bar were fixed between each set of parallel cords, he could swing from one set to the other. If he fell, he would simply plunge into the pool below.

At this point, there were no somersaults, just flying leaps; but those who saw him swing from trapeze to trapeze found the spectacle so enjoyable that Leotard decided he had a circus act.

At the Cirque Napoleon in Paris in 1859, Jules Leotard presented the first flying trapeze act. A contemporary account marveled at Leotard's "reckless breakneck flights from trapeze to trapeze like some tropical bird swooping from branch to branch."

In case he fell, a padded mattress was spread the whole length of the stage. Eventually, the mattress was replaced by a net, and although air bags have long since become the method used by movie stuntmen to break their falls, the old-fashioned rope net is the form of protection still used in the circus. "The net itself can be very dangerous," said Tito Gaona, "but it's a circus tradition. Our fans love to see us bounce from the net."

Circus historian Tom Parkinson credits the invention of the net to acrobats Fred Miltemore of Bloomington, Indiana, and his partner, Charles Noble. Miltemore and Noble saw a flying trapeze act and decided it was too dangerous to do without a safety device. So they went to an Illinois River fisherman for help in making a net.

Their amused fellow performers dubbed them "The Fishermen"—and with a Barnum-esque knack for knowing the publicity value of being noticed in any way at all, they called their act "The Fisher Bros."

Broken necks, the cause of so many deaths to acrobats who turned somersaults off a springboard, were not entirely prevented when nets were put under trapezes. No less an expert than Alfredo Codona has warned that the

> great spread of knotted rope which stretches across the breadth of a big top during a flying-trapeze act is not the beneficent thing which it appears to be. It is dangerous, a friend indeed if you fall into it properly, but otherwise a lurking enemy, waiting to snap the bones of an arm or a leg—or a neck. Persons have been killed by falls into the net, and even on many tumbles which the audience classes as uneventful, it seems to possess satanic joy in gouging the flesh out of one. A net is made by a succession of spaces between square knots. Those knots can flay one like a whip if the fall is not accurately gauged.

So fliers—as they began to call themselves—had to learn how to land in a net. They had to practice bundling protectively for their falls until it became instinctive, keeping the arms close to the body and the chin jammed down onto the collarbone, and throwing their weight in order to land on shoulders and hips. When a flier misses a trick, watch how he immediately snaps his head forward, locks his arms to his body, and twists his back and hips to bring himself into the net in the right position. Landing on the head can snap the neck, net or no net. (Elvin Bale, who switched from nets to air bags to break his fall when he was shot from a cannon, overshot the air bag performing in Asia in early 1987 and was paralyzed when he slammed into a wall.)

Circus casters were quick to adopt the flying trapeze, because the momentum from swinging allowed for more elaborate flying tricks. The act changed from two casters and a flier to one flier and one catcher. Toto Siegrist and Walter Silbon did it this way about 1900, with the flier grabbing hold of the catcher, dangling from his hands, then simply dropping to the net. But the flier then had to climb aloft again for a new trick, and this slowed down the act.

So a new third man was added to the act. This performer waited on the pedestal board to catch the flier's bar on its backswing and send it forward again to where the flier dangled from the catcher's hands. Fred Bradna, who got his information on earlier fliers from Antoinette Concello and Mayme Ward, said that it was Eddie Silbon who first timed the trapeze's arc so that he could be flung back to it by the catcher for a flying return to his original pedestal. And that's what they called their crowd-pleasing new trick: "the flying return."

This is how the basic structure of the trapeze acts we know today evolved. At first, the credo of "more is better" was in force. Freed of the necessity to climb back up to the trapeze after every trick, the Silbons had six fliers—three flying simultaneously toward three catchers, with three other fliers waiting to fling back their trapezes so that they could make their flying returns. Soon circus arenas and big tops were filled with flying acrobats, crisscrossing as they switched from flybar to catcher to flybar.

The next great innovators were the Clarkonians, who added twisting tricks to the somersaults of the flying trapeze act. The Clarke family went back six generations in the entertainment world. John Clarke had a circus in London in Astley's day; his son and successor, known as Old John Clarke, was born in 1786, the year after the circus came to America. Old John's sons, Alfred and Charles, each had their own circus, and one of Alfred's sons was called the greatest bareback rider of his time in continental Europe. Charles, who had watched the development of aerial flying acts since Leotard's day, decided that *his* sons, Ernest and Charles F. Clarke, would be trapeze artists. Ernest was the flier or leaper, and Charles F. was the catcher. They practiced in secret for seven years before daring to present their act, including a double somersault, in the Coliseum in London. The family continued to ride under the name of Clarke, but the aerial act became known as the Clarkonians. In 1903, Barnum and Bailey brought the Clarkonians to America. After four and a half more years of practice and experimentation, Ernest Clarke added a pirouette to his double somersault. "The Marvelous Mid-Air Pirouette or 'Twisting Double Somersault'—a feat never before attempted by the most intrepid aerialists," said the Barnum & Bailey circus poster. But no matter how many fliers flew through space at one time (in 1950, appearing with the Polack Bros. Circus, the Ward-Bell Flyers featured nine aerialists flying through space at one time) or how many pirouettes they did, the aerial somersault was always the crowd's favorite trick.

Eddie Silbon had accomplished the first double back somersault at the Paris Hippodrome in 1879. But the golden goal of all trapeze fliers was the feat they then considered the limit of how far the human body could go—the triple somersault.

Alfredo Codona explained better than any-one why this feat was so difficult:

The reason lies in the terrific speed at which the act must be accomplished. At a propul-sion of more than sixty miles an hour, the body is traveling so fast that by the time the second revolution is reached, the space gauges of the brain have ceased to function properly. The body is going faster than it can be controlled, and for a split instant one loses all knowledge of time, space, distance, or surroundings. Then, in another split in-stant, as the body begins to fall and slows slightly with the third somersault, that ability to gauge must be regained, so that when the performer breaks out of the third revolution and toward the hands of the catcher, his brain can be clear again. It is a lack of clarity here which causes death; the performer has spun so fast that he has lost all knowledge of where he is, and plunges downward to the net or onward to the mat—if the turn is from a springboard—without being able to pro-tect his body properly in the fall. The impact, therefore, comes not on his back but at the base of the skull, in as much as the natural whirl of the fall almost invariably carries him toward that position; and the net or mat snaps his neck.

Despite the specter of the broken neck, the triple somersault from the flying trapeze was accomplished in 1897—and the first person to do it was a woman.

She was Lena Jordan of the Flying Jordans, a renowned American flying act that also ap-peared, during the 1890s, in Europe, South Africa, and Australia. The personnel consisted of Lew Jordan, his wife, Mamie, and three chil-dren: their own daughter, Nellie, and a girl and boy who were apprentices taken on by the Jor-dans while they were performing in Russia.

The Johannesburg, South Africa, *Times* for March 16, 1898, reported of Lena, "She was born in the city of Riga, on the Baltic, in Russia. She sprung from a humble Russian family and was christened Lena. When 14 years old, she was what is commonly termed 'a weak, puny child.' A troupe of celebrated American aerial performers happened to appear about this time at Riga, who, desiring to add to the variety of the gymnastic act, advertised for a child, a girl, to be apprenticed to them for a term of years to learn the profession of aerial gymnastics. Amongst the numerous applicants was our lit-tle Russian maiden, who, being selected from all the other applicants as being most suitable, was then and there apprenticed and left her parents to travel with her new employers to America."

In an interview with the Sydney, Australia, *Truth*, dated May 23, 1897, Lew Jordan ex-plained that he had viewed Lena's very puni-ness as a desirable characteristic: "I chose her for the very reason of her lightness, as I had in view a 'catching act' from my wife to myself, and I wanted a girl we could play catchers with good and easy."

In other words, the Jordans at first had a casting act, not a flying trapeze act.

By the time Lena performed in Australia with the Flying Jordans she was no longer weak or puny.

At the age of eighteen, she stood about four feet ten and weighed 94.5 pounds. A reporter spoke of her "extraordinary biceps . . . forearms as hard as that of a cast-iron god . . . and when she threw back her shoul-ders, a regular ravine was created between the rolls of muscles on each side of her spine."

There had already been times in circus his-tory when a male who could perform certain feats requiring great physical strength was passed off as a female to make the feat seem even more difficult. Lew Jordan apparently had Lena submit to a medical examination in New

York in 1896, probably to forestall such speculation, for the newspaper asserts that "at a recent exhibition before the medical faculty in New York, the leading surgeons of Gotham gave it as their firm opinion that little Lena Jordan is the most absolutely perfect and healthy female that ever came under their notice."

What this "absolutely perfect and healthy female" now accomplished was described by the Sydney *Mail* on May 22, 1897: "20 years ago, a single somersault from a trapeze was regarded as a feat. Walter Silbon, who was in these colonies, created a sensation by demonstrating the possibility of a double somersault, and it was generally felt that anything further would be physically impossible. Yet this little girl [Lena Jordan] actually performs the previously unheard of feat of turning three somersaults in mid-air while diving from a high trapeze to Mr. Jordan on a lower one." (The "Walter Silbon" who did a double in Australia may have been Eddie Silbon, who accomplished the first double back somersault in Paris in 1879—or another member of his family.)

The Flying Jordans had apparently achieved the feat before, because the Sydney *Daily Telegraph* for April 24, 1897, speaks of them "presenting for the first time in Australia, their famous triple somersault and catch. These are the only artists in the universe who have ever accomplished this breath-suspending act."

Lena Jordan executed a triple to Lew Jordan in the customary fashion from a flybar, except that, instead of taking off from the pedestal, she launched herself into her swing by hanging from her knees from a trapeze bar suspended high over the pedestal board.

But she also did a "flying-casting" triple, as this description from the Australian *Star*, April 27, 1897, indicates:

The principal in the act is a pretty, petite brunette girl, about 15 years old. She is held by the hands of Mrs. Jordan, who is suspended by her feet from the trapeze at one end of the auditorium. They swing to and fro in the air a number of times, gradually increasing the force of their momentum. When the proper point is reached, the little girl is flung out into space, spins around like a ball, making three distinct somersaults, and, as she comes down the last time, she darts out her stretched arms, and her hands are grasped by Mr. Jordan, who is hanging by his feet from the trapeze suspended just above the stage. It is a hair-raising performance, the like of which has never been seen in this country.

But Lena Jordan's triples were gradually forgotten. A picture of the Flying Jordans in 1910 no longer shows Lena with the troupe. By that time, the first triple was being credited to the Clarkonians' Ernest Clarke, who threw three back somersaults to his brother Charles, while performing with the Publiones Circus in Cuba, in 1909. For years, Clarke's feat was listed as the world's first triple.

But the triple was as dangerous as ever. It was not a trick that just any good flier could do. The Spaniards, who invented *casting*, which the French turned into *flying*, called the triple *salto mortale*—the somersault of death.

Ernie Lane turned a triple in 1916 and kept doing it for a short time. Charles Siegrist did it off and on for a long time. But both eventually broke their necks doing the triple.

And then came Alfredo Codona.

Looking back from 1930, Codona said that "the long, fatalistic history of the triple deterred me from its accomplishment for years. Then, in 1919, I determined either to accomplish it, get killed, or quit trying. My brother Lalo and I fitted up our rigging in a building in Shreveport, Louisiana, and with my father 'patting' [calling directions] for me and aiding me in my timing, we set to work."

At the Coliseum in Chicago, in the spring of

1920, Alfredo Codona went into performance "with the triple somersault as a climax of my regular routine." Codona was the first aerialist ever to do the triple *regularly*. He was such a graceful, charismatic flier, that the trick seemed to belong to him. Soon selective amnesia set in, and people who should have known better were asserting that Codona was the first ever to do the trick.

Codona attributed his triple to his timing—and to "the reestablishment of brain coordination following that dazed second in which the body is turning so swiftly that the mind apparently loses control."

Then, on April 28, 1933, Codona dislocated his shoulder while doing the triple, tore two muscles beyond healing, and never flew again.

Despite Codona's warnings about the dangers of the triple, the opening performance of The Greatest Show on Earth in Madison Square Garden in 1937 featured a husband-and-wife team—Antoinette and Arthur Concello—both performing the triple on the same bill.

Antoinette Concello never did the triple consistently (Ringling's posters only bragged about her double). The Concellos' great crowd-pleaser was their passing leaps, she and her husband both working from a single trapeze, one grasping it as the other left it. Her first teacher, Eddie Ward, apparently unaware of Lena Jordan, considered the triple beyond feminine strength, and wouldn't even let Antoinette try for it; but Arthur Concello, her second teacher and eventual partner on the trapeze and in marriage, actually challenged her to do it. It took her two years before she would attempt it in public. In addition to overcoming gravity, she had to overcome the psychological barrier that Codona had erected by warning that the mind loses control during the body's second revolution, and that if brain coordination could not be reestablished, a broken neck might swiftly follow.

Codona may have lost consciousness during his second somersault, but Mrs. Concello didn't, and she told me she later suspected that Codona might have made up this hazard because "he wanted to deter anyone else from trying it."

The Concellos were not deterred: they tried, they succeeded, and they dominated circus flying from the time of Codona's injury until Arthur went into management in 1947 and Antoinette pulled a muscle in her shoulder during the 1951 season and retired from flying to become the Big One's aerial director.

When Betty Hutton and Cornel Wilde played rival trapeze artists in the 1952 film *The Greatest Show on Earth*, Hutton insisted on learning to fly for real, and "Tony" Concello taught her. The stars had doubles for the more difficult feats, but Hutton learned a crossover, which is a trapeze swing from the pedestal to the catcher and back to the bar, and the "bird's nest," in which the flier, bracing the trapeze from behind with both hands and both feet in such a position that the knees are threaded through the arms, lets go and dives toward the catcher.

The man who doubled for Cornel Wilde was the next great circus flier to manage an occasional triple—Fay Alexander.

But the first flier to do the triple consistently since Alfredo Codona was a joyful, charismatic young Mexican flier named Tito Gaona.

In 1962, at the age of fourteen, Tito was a member of a family trampoline act called "The Titos." The act consisted of Tito, his fifteen-year-old sister, Chela, and their big brother, Armando, seventeen. Their father and teacher, Victor Gaona, was a thirty-eight-year-old acrobatic clown who had been many things in the circus but never yet a star. At 4:00 A.M. one day in that year, Victor Gaona took his family to a dingy all-night theater on Forty-second Street in New York City to see a six-year-old film called *Trapeze*. It was a fictional dramati-

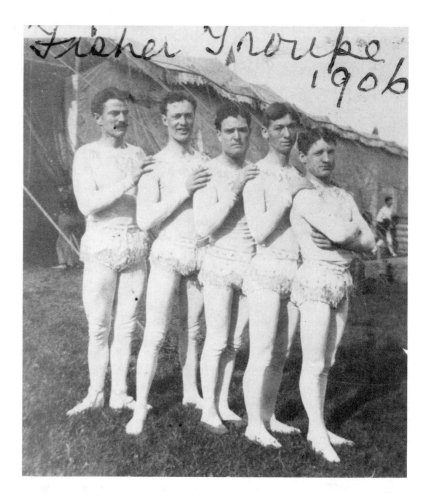

Fisher Troupe 1906

THE FLYING TRAPEZE. *Jules Leotard of France introduced the flying trapeze at the Cirque Napoleon in Paris in 1859. (Yes, parents, the garment that your young ballet student/gymnast/acrobat wears was named after Jules.) In the United States, in 1868, circus clowns were singing to audiences and selling the sheet music of the song Leotard inspired. "The Flying Trapeze" by Gaston Lyle, with music by George Leybourne, contained the familiar refrain:*

He flew through the air with the greatest of ease,
This daring young man on the flying trapeze,
His movements so graceful, all girls he could please,
And my love he purloined away.

The effort to achieve such graceful and pleasing movements has increased over the years. In the 1870s, the first double somersault was performed by another Frenchman, Eddie Silbon. Lena Jordan (second from left) threw the first triple somersault with the Flying Jordans (left) in 1897.

The Flying Fishers (opposite, top), originally Miltemore and Charlie Noble, got their name from hiring a fisherman to make them the first trapeze net used in the United States—hemp rope tied with knots. Charlie Noble was the first American to do a double somersault and catch. Charlie's wife, Minnie Noble, was the first woman in the United States to do the Iron Jaw Act, hanging suspended by a rope with only a leather strap in her mouth, holding on "by the skin of her teeth" while she was swiveled. Ernie Lane did the triple somersault for a short time, and Charles Siegrist (above) did it off and on for a long time. But both eventually broke their necks doing the triple. The original Siegrist-Silbon aerial troupe starred with Barnum & Bailey during its five-year European tour (1897–1902). "It seems that nothing can stop Siegrist," said one newspaper account. "He broke his neck in New York City along about 1933 in an aerial act, and in 1936 was back flying again. He is five feet, five inches in height and made of brawn, nerve, energy and stamina." Ernie Clarke was the first (with his brother Charles as catcher) to do the triple regularly in performances, beginning in 1909, but they missed as many as they achieved. With Alfredo Codona came the consistent triple, a feat that Tito Gaona, in the 1970s and 1980s, could do blindfolded. (Ringling Museum)

TITO GAONA. *Antoinette Concello (right), the great flier who became aerial director of Ringling Bros. and Barnum & Bailey, said Tito Gaona (with sister Chela, left) is "commanding in technique, brilliant in pirouettes, and his control of his body permits him to maneuver his arms and legs like a ballet dancer. It isn't just that Tito does the tricks. Lots of fliers can do the tricks. It's the grace with which he does them." His "double-double" was, in his own words: "Out-back-out on the trapeze, then UP: twisting and somersaulting once; then DOWN, twisting and somersaulting again. Then slap! Papa {his catcher-father Victor Gaona} and I would get a solid lock on each other's wrists." So great was his control, in fact, that when Tito dropped from the trapeze to the net at the end of a performance, he would bounce back up and sit on the trapeze again—sometimes again and again. He soared and floated and looked for all the world like a man who must recently have been a bird. (Leonard Kamzler)*

zation of the quest for the legendary triple—"thrown" in the movie by Tino Orsini (Tony Curtis) to Mike Ribble (Burt Lancaster) at the Cirque d'Hiver in Paris.

Two hours later, as the four Gaonas walked into the Manhattan dawn, an awestruck Tito had no doubt that he had just seen his destiny—in Technicolor. Ever after, he could quote from memory the lines that gave him the key to doing the triple: "In the beginning, the catcher, Mike—Burt Lancaster, you know—he tells Tino, 'Remember, there's a little clock inside of you and a little clock inside of me—and we've got to keep those clocks ticking alongside of each other.' And in the end, Tino is going to New York, to the Garden, see, to try the triple, but not with Mike, because of their fight over Gina. And Burt Lancaster warns the new catcher, 'Now that he's got it, don't let him lose it.' "

The exuberant Tito did his first triple in 1966, with Circus Scott in Göteborg, Sweden. He was eighteen and handsome and full of charm and high spirits. "I did a belly-balance on the flybar for my warmup trick, blowing a kiss to a gang of teenage girls in the box seats," he remembered. "They squealed and waved. Every trick we turned brought a vigorous response from the crowd." So he held up three fingers to his father to indicate that he wanted to try the big trick.

When they locked wrists in midair, he heard his father whisper, "The triple is yours, Tito."

With his father as his catcher, their rhythms seemed uncannily in synchronization. John Ringling North came to see this triple in Stockholm, and brought the Flying Gaonas to the Ringling show.

Fay Alexander, Tito's hero, was past his prime as a flier by 1966, the second season in which Tito did the triple consistently, but after studying Tito's triple from the ground, he asked to catch it.

"That's a circus first!" Alexander said afterward. "Do you realize that I'm the first flier ever to throw a triple and to catch one too?"

But Fay Alexander had another reason for wanting to be Tito's catcher. He had noticed that Tito flew so high above the rigging when he went up that he did the triple with time to spare. He would complete two somersaults going up and the third as he peaked and started to come down.

Codona and Alexander and the Concellos all straightened out directly into the arms of the catcher without a fractional instant's margin. But Tito Gaona's triple was different, and Fay Alexander wondered, since Tito had time, height, and power to spare, whether he might not be able to do a trick that, up until then, existed only in the imagination of fliers: the double-double, a full twist inward and a full twist outward as one turns a double somersault.

Tito's father figured out a way to coach him to do it, and Tito threw the first double-double in circus history to him at the HemisFair in San Antonio in 1968. Tito remembered every moment: "Out, back, out. Up-twisting and somersaulting once. Down-twisting and somersaulting again. Slap! Papa and I get a solid lock on each other's wrists. And we hold on."

Some fliers consider the double-double a more difficult trick than the triple. To the public, however, the triple still sounded like the untoppable trapeze trick—unless, of course, it was humanly possible to do the quadruple.

Having conquered the double-double, Tito resolved to try for the first quadruple—a reach for immortality, a permanent place in the record books: "Then I will always be remembered." But he waited for ten years, to get more experience, before making his all-out try; and it was probably while he was waiting that Tito Gaona really missed the quadruple. Perhaps it was when he was an inexperienced but fearless teenager that he could have set the ultimate trapeze record. Perhaps it was only his father, who had been retired from catching by a bad knee by the time Tito started his quest, whose internal clock ticked in absolute synchrony with his. Instead, Tito mastered the double-double, did the triple so consistently that he did it blindfolded to keep from getting bored, and became famous among fliers and an idol of audiences for his sensational rebounds. He would fall to the net from the flying trapeze, then bounce back to sit on the catch-bar, or sometimes *stand* on the catchbar, or even rebound to dive right through the trapeze and catch himself by his ankles! In 1973, the Gaonas won the Circus Oscar in Madrid for having the best flying act in the world. In April 1974, *Sports Illustrated* said that Tito "may be the finest athlete in the world." And still Tito waited to be completely ready for the big one.

Manuel Zuniga was Tito's catcher on the Ringling show for the first year after Papa Gaona retired, but Zuniga didn't want to travel, so Tito's cousin, Lalo Murillo, became his catcher. On the road in the fall of 1977, they began to record their tries for the quad with a videotape machine, so that they could study the tapes and find out what went wrong—and so that there would be a record if they succeeded.

Tito was practicing the quadruple at the end of long days on the road in which he had already done two shows—and two triples in performance. In Cleveland in November, he told me he had a nightmare:

> The show's over at 11 P.M., and we start practice, usually, at 11:30, and stay around practicing till 1 A.M. or so. At 1:30, I went down to the circus train, to my compartment, and I fell asleep on the couch watching the videotape of the quadruples I missed, over and over. In my dream, I dreamed that I got the catcher—and I took his arms with

me to the net. I looked up, and he had no arms, and I cried, "Lalo! Look—in my hands—your arms!" and Lalo said, "Well, OK—we'll try it again." And I woke up, and I said, "Jesus! What's happening?"

Since Tito was achieving adequate height on his four revolutions, his family attributed his inability to complete the trick to his fear that, if the catch was bad, one or the other of them might have his arms torn from their sockets. It was a psychological barrier, like the fear of blacking out, falling wrong, and breaking one's neck, which Codona instilled. Nevertheless, Tito decided to devote the whole month of December, when the circus is rehearsing at winter quarters for the next year's show, to mastering the quad.

Tito always did the four somersaults, and he frequently touched the catcher briefly, but he was never held.

I was there one Thursday when Tito threw nine quadruples in the afternoon and fifteen in the evening. On the fifth try in the afternoon, he came so close to catching the trick that the knot of the tape on his left wrist came undone from the force of his catcher's hand.

Full of hope that evening, he would sing from his pedestal to Lalo on the catchbar, in paraphrase of his beloved Beatles, "I want to hold your hands!" And he did, for a fraction of a second, before dropping to the net.

The next day, he found that the unremitting pressure of practicing so hard had popped open some of the calluses on his hands. His brother Armando, who had once gotten blood poisoning this way, canceled the family's regular Friday practice and made Tito take a couple of days off to let his hands heal. On Sunday, Tito tried the quadruple twice more, and seemed very close, but on the third takeoff from the pedestal, he did not do any more somersaults.

He just swung back to the pedestal. He looked at his hand. All the skin had come off the upper part of his palm.

"We're so close, so close," he mourned.

So close, yet so far. He had to stop practicing even the family act for a week, until his hand healed.

His basic optimism buoyed him. He knew that it was just a matter of relaxing and letting the catcher catch him; of letting Lalo adjust his rhythm to Tito's rhythm. "Once the catcher finds the right moment," said Tito, "it's done."

And Lalo knew it, too:

> When I see Tito leave the platform, I have to decide if the trick is in time with my swing, or if he's late or early. Then I have to adjust. If he's too soon, I have to rush on my swing. If he's late, I have to swing higher, so we meet at a certain point. Now my problems are when he lets go of the bar. He's traveling toward me. I have to back up my body. I can't stop the swing, but I can back up my body. I'm coming in sort of slow motion, and he's spinning and traveling at the same time. I have to find his wrist. We contact first, and then we grab, and then we grip. . . .

It was the hardest part of the quadruple: it takes two people to make it work; and if it doesn't work, injury or even death for one or both may result. Has there ever been a greater test of trust devised than the quadruple somersault from the flying trapeze?

In the 1978 season, Tito Gaona became the first flier in trapeze history ever to try publicly for the quadruple; but he could never catch it—not on opening night for the 1978 season, December 29, 1977, in Venice, Florida; not on opening night in Madison Square Garden, March 22, 1978; and not in the hundreds of tries afterward, in the Garden and on the road. Eventually, he stopped trying. In 1979, he left the Ringling show and went to Japan with an-

other Feld-produced show, the Cirque International de Monte Carlo. In 1980, their Ringling contract up, the Flying Gaonas went to Sweden, where their international fame had begun fifteen years before, for two seasons with Circus Scott. In 1982, they flew with the Circus Knie in Switzerland. Since then, the Flying Gaonas have divided their time between Circo Giganta Modelo, which tours South America, and the Big Apple Circus in North America, where Tito's triples of surpassing grace are the high points. He is, by common consent, the most charismatic trapeze artist since Alfredo Codona. But the quadruple had eluded him.

———————

By 1978, another Mexican family had developed a superior trapeze act, and in this one, all three brothers could do the triple.

The Vazquez family had been involved with circuses in Mexico for at least five generations. Papa Vazquez now doubles on drums and trumpet in small circus bands. He and his wife had nine children, and in the mid-eighties, seven were in circuses in the United States, Europe, and Latin America.

In the mid-seventies, brothers Juan and Felipe were performing with two uncles on horizontal bars. Horizontal bars call forth considerable acrobatic skills, but the acts are not really popular with circus crowds. The spectators usually applaud politely, but they are waiting for the glamor acts.

"Like everybody else," said Felipe, "we wanted to fly,"

Unlike most everybody else, Juan and Felipe did something about it. They asked the flying acts to let them practice some tricks. They started out wearing the safety harnesses called "mechanics" to keep from getting hurt, but it wasn't long before Felipe was throwing simple flips, and the more sturdily built Juan was catching him.

By the end of 1977, they were calling themselves a flying act. A younger brother, Vinicio, was taken into the act as a secondary flier, and so was Miguel, the baby of the family, who was only twelve at the time.

Flying didn't really appeal to Miguel when he was that age. He had spent most of his childhood in Mexico City, where a cousin owned a small traveling circus. The only place it traveled was around Mexico City, which meant that the members of the family could do a show every day and sleep at home every night. Miguel liked to *play* at circus under those circumstances, imitating tumbling tricks and jumping on the trampoline; when he got bored, he liked to be able to drift off. But his older brothers were serious about flying. They learned to do the triple, and soon they were both flying with U.S. circuses.

In the beginning, Miguel was an awkward flier, and his brothers didn't think he would ever be anything special; still, when Miguel got discouraged and wanted to quit, they insisted that he stick with it.

Suddenly, Miguel took a great leap forward. At the brink of adolescence, he was spindly in build and not very muscular, but he was a natural athlete and the most flexible flier of them all. Within weeks, he was performing a double somersault. In March of 1978, at the age of thirteen, he threw his first triple in Toledo, Ohio. Now they were the only family in the world with three brothers who could do the triple.

Juan, the steady, practical brother, was keeping a little black notebook in which he recorded the result of each trick that he and his brothers performed. In 1978 and 1979, the Flying Vazquez played what circus people call "spot dates" at short-run shows. The money was all right, but the routine was terrible for sustained improvement. They would work for four or five days, then have many days off, just when they were getting good. The way to make improvements—and to be consistent in performing them—was to work every day.

In 1980, the brothers worked for fifteen weeks straight with the Hubert Castle Circus. In that one stretch of nearly four months they improved enough to attract the attention of Ringling Bros. and Barnum & Bailey Circus, and now, with characteristic confidence, they began talking about going to The Greatest Show on Earth.

In 1981, the Flying Vazquez made their Ringling debut. There were two aerial acts: the Flying Farfans above Ring One and the Flying Vazquez above Ring Three. Both Gino Farfan, seventeen, and Tato Farfan, twelve, could do the triple. So could Miguel Vazquez, then sixteen; but the connoisseurs of flying around the Ringling show were not very impressed. "He was just an ordinary flyer," Antoinette Concello told the Chicago *Tribune*. "He was light and got off the bar very quickly. He did some good tricks. He did show promise. But his form was bad. He was all over the place when he flew, an arm sticking out here, or a leg sticking out there."

And the souvenir circus program for that year spotlights Tato Farfan as the young flier likely to conquer the quad. Miguel Vazquez, meanwhile, was having trouble with his triple. "Miguel was doing his triple too high," Juan told me. "I had to take all my swing to get him, up there. And some of the teeterboard people were watching, and they said, 'Hey, c'mon, man! You're goin' so high—why don't you do the quad?'"

Something in Miguel Vazquez leaped at the challenge. He started trying for the quad during practice sessions in Miami in January of 1981, working at it late at night after doing two and sometimes three shows during the day; and he kept on trying as the 111th edition of the Big One wended its way north to the Garden.

As Tito had, they videotaped their practice sessions and studied the films later, looking for flaws in Miguel's technique, or Juan's.

They started by having Miguel concentrate on perfecting the four somersaults. "We weren't trying to catch it then," said Juan. "We just wanted to get him up as high as he could go and do his spins as fast as he could. He did them over and over again, falling into the net." They had seen film of Tito's tries, and now they saw that Miguel's highest point was thirty-seven feet off the ground, about a foot higher than Gaona normally ascended. Miguel went so high that he was three feet above the frame of the trapeze rigging. He sometimes hit the crossbars, until they were raised another six inches. Juan thought that the extra twelve inches of height would be the key to Miguel's success.

The falls to the net were dangerous, and they hurt. If he hit the net at a slightly wrong angle going that fast, the skid across the net would rip open his tights and give his naked buttocks a bad skin burn. He started wearing soccer trunks.

When the brothers agreed that Miguel had the height and speed just right, Juan started to try to catch him. Bradna has written: "The ideal specifications [for fliers] are a height of . . . 5 feet 6 inches, and a weight of 155 pounds for men." Those were Tito Gaona's specifications exactly. Miguel Vazquez was 5 feet 7 inches, and weighed only 137 to his brother Juan's 155. But Juan thought being lighter should make his brother easier to hold on to.

For flexibility, Miguel jumped rope vigorously every single day. Two or three times a week, he lifted weights. He didn't want muscles that would be too stiff—they are not fast enough in the air. He did one hundred push-ups every morning and another one hundred every night.

And he and Juan boxed almost every day, because it was good for their reflexes and be-cause it got them used to feeling sudden, jarring blows on the face, shoulders, or chest—in case they should collide in midair and be forced to think fast.

"We were getting close," said Juan, "but it didn't happen."

Miguel said he was going to practice until Chicago, and if he couldn't get it he was just going to forget about it. By August, they were beginning to think it was never going to happen.

On August 19, 1981, when Ringling Bros. and Barnum & Bailey Circus was playing Long Beach, California, the Flying Vazquez, who had been trying the quad unsuccessfully for over seven months by now, scheduled yet another practice session. Once again, Miguel Vazquez climbed the twenty-one Lucite rungs of the slender rope ladder to the pedestal board, thirty-seven feet above the ground. He ascended with the aerialist's distinctive sideways climb, grasping only one of the side ropes of the ladder and going up on the outside, placing each slippered foot carefully around a side-rope onto a rung.

Juan Vazquez, his brother and his catcher, was now hanging upside down from the catch-bar of the trapeze in the catcher's end of the flying rig. Aerialists call that end the catch trap, and there are two popular misconceptions about what goes on there. Contrary to common belief, a catcher does not hang by his knees from the catchbar but wraps the ropes supporting his bar tightly around his legs. If he were hanging by his knees, a flier traveling as fast as Miguel would be by then would pull him off the catchbar as if he'd been yanked by an elephant hook. The second misconception is that the flier and the catcher grab hands. Hands alone are not strong enough to keep the two together when the flier is traveling that fast. So the catcher grasps the flier's wrists, the flier grasps the catcher's wrists, and both hold on tight.

On the ground, another brother, Felipe Vazquez, set up the video recorder.

"In those days Miguel used to throw, sometimes, fifteen to twenty quadruples each time we practiced," said Juan, "depending on how tired we felt, because he wanted to do it so bad." Miguel would nearly always "throw the quad," meaning that he would successfully turn four somersaults, but he had never yet "caught the quad."

Miguel swung forward, hanging full length from the bar. His back was arched, his toes were pointed. He pumped himself up three full feet higher than the rigging, to the very peak of the trapeze arc, thirty-seven feet above the floor.

Miguel swung back. He was hanging from the flybar with his full weight, to bring it back as fast and as far as possible. On his backswing, too, he went higher than the rigging.

Forward again—fast.

"Break!" shouted Juan.

Miguel pulled his knees up to his chest, tucked his head down, let go of the bar, grasped his legs, and revolved like something out of *Star Wars*.

He spun with increasing velocity. During his second revolution, his body seemed several feet higher than in the first. The third revolution was fastest of all. During the fourth revolution, his muscles tensed to open his arms and slow the fall—and to reach out, blindly, for the hands of the catcher.

"Open!" shouted Juan.

Less than one second had elapsed since Miguel let go of the trapeze. Coming out of that fourth somersault, traveling at an estimated eighty miles an hour, the young man would be too disoriented to find his brother. So it was up to Juan, who was swinging slowly forward to meet him, to find Miguel—and he had only a few microseconds to grasp the taping on Miguel's wrists.

Juan did grasp Miguel after Miguel's fourth revolution, as I saw the great Tito Gaona's catcher do so many times; but Tito's catcher, though he sometimes gripped him briefly, always failed to swing him and stay with him.

Juan did not fail; Juan stayed with his brother—and Miguel succeeded.

The realization was as shocking to the brain as the absorption of any other fact that has never, ever, in the history of the world, been a fact before.

They clung to each other, asking each other again and again if it had really happened, while down below the realization had already sunk in to the few spectators, and the clapping and the cheering had started. The Farfans, Ringling's other flying act that year, were working out on the other rigging in the arena in Long Beach that day. Now they all climbed down to congratulate the Vazquez brothers—the sudden kings of their profession.

It wasn't a quadruple for the record books, of course. For that, it would have to be done in performance in front of a paying audience. But for the skeptical, it was on videotape.

For the second time in five years, Irvin Feld decided to *announce* the quadruple on opening night in the Garden.

The Vazquezes knew all the possible consequences if they failed. On February 20, a little over a month before, their sister Marguerite had broken her neck performing with Ringling's Red Unit in Atlanta.

In her act, Marguerite, who performed under the name Marguerite Michel, did a balletic display of midair gymnastics and juggled flaming torches twenty-five feet above the ring—while hanging by her hair.

Her husband, Miguel Ayala, a wire walker, plaited her hair to a safety harness before each performance. But on the night of February 20, somehow her hair pulled free, and during her finale—a rapid body spin—she fell to the tanbark. Though her neck was broken, they rejoiced at the news that her spinal cord was uninjured.

"In the circus," said Patricia Segrera Vazquez, Juan's wife and the third member of the Flying Vazquez, "we are always prepared for tragedy, and it affects us like any other family: we worry and we grieve. But maybe the difference is that we have to go out the same night and perform as if nothing has happened."

And so Miguel tried for the quadruple on opening night in the Garden, in front of Irvin Feld and a packed house; and—like Tito—he failed.

For two months he tried—and failed two hundred times. Everyone knew that the odds were building up against him: one clumsy move, one flicker of inattention could cripple or destroy him. For example, he could lose control of his spins and crash into the catcher, perhaps killing them both. Gino Farfan of the Flying Farfans, trying in Dallas for a much less complicated trick that year of 1982, crashed his head against the catchbar and the catcher's

QUADRUPLE SOMERSAULT—BY THE NUMBERS. *Circus history was made on July 10, 1982, at the traveling Ringling Bros. and Barnum & Bailey Circus in Tucson, Arizona, when Miguel Vazquez turned over four times in midair as he launched himself from the flying trapeze into the hands of his brother Juan. He leaves the bar* (left) *and completes the first somersault immediately; he makes the third revolution* (center); *and he comes out of his fourth somersault and is caught* (right). (Ringling Bros. and Barnum & Bailey Circus)

knee, suffering a concussion and breaking his neck.

During another show, the Vazquezes were attempting the quad and their timing was off: Juan swung in too low, and Miguel slipped out of his hands—"but before I dropped him," said Juan, "I could feel a pain like my arm was being pulled out of my shoulder. The pain went all the way down to the bottom of my back." They remembered Tito's nightmare in which he pulled his catcher's arms off.

But the reputation of Irvin Feld and his Greatest Show on Earth was now on the line as well as that of the Flying Vazquez. "Mr. Feld came to see us in Phoenix," Juan Vazquez told me, but the only information he gave me on the meeting was that "Mr. Feld said we got to try harder."

The Flying Vazquez went on to Tucson, which to them was a fateful place. Julio Farias, a cousin of Juan's wife, had dreamed of doing the quad before Miguel had, and by 1980, he was very close. Julio had begun flying at a much earlier age than Miguel, and had completed his first triple at the age of nine. In the spring of 1980, he was already throwing four somersaults to the net, and he hoped to throw one to the catcher by the end of that year. And then in June he came to Tucson with the Flying Farias—himself, his father, and his younger brother, Tata (who had done the triple at age eight). Julio was practicing a trick he had accomplished dozens of times—the three-and-a-half somersault, Don Martinez's old trick, in which he was caught by his feet. A slight injury had kept him out of the air for about a week. His father insisted that he was out of practice and must wear a safety harness so that he wouldn't injure himself further. One of the ropes on the harness got caught on a pulley, and as Farias fell, the snagged rope pulled him too far to one side. He missed the net, landed on his head, and died a few days later. His grief-stricken father announced that the rest of the family were retiring.

So on Saturday, July 10, in Tucson, the city where Julio was killed, Miguel tried extra hard at all three shows. He failed at the first and second, but the third show was different.

"When I come out of the fourth spin, I just float there for a second before I really start to fall," Miguel told me afterward, "and my brother caught me at just that moment, and everything was very smooth."

There were 7,000 people in the Tucson Community Center. Most of them seemed to think at first that—ringmaster's announcement to the contrary—this was a routine part of the show. But then they saw Miguel Vazquez's fellow performers racing out to Ring One, heard them shout and scream, saw them pound Miguel on the back and hoist him to their shoulders. And then they added public acclaim to circus tribute for the first public quadruple somersault from the flying trapeze to the hands of the catcher in circus history.

Glen "Frosty" Little (left), an alumnus of the very first Ringling Bros. and Barnum & Bailey Clown College class in 1968, discusses the rich history of circus clowning with author and frequent guest clown, John Culhane. Little is now master clown for both units of The Greatest Show on Earth and teaches at the Clown College, whose dean, Bill Ballantine, calls him "master of jimcrackery, expert in explosive effects." (Ringling Bros. and Barnum & Bailey Circus)

DISPLAY·19

A Thousand Clowns

Barnum called clowns and elephants "pegs, used to hang circuses on." But from over one hundred clowns in the late 1930s, John Ringling North permitted the clown alley of the Big One to dwindle to only thirteen—and half of them were in their seventies or eighties. Other circuses were in even worse shape.

Irvin Feld's response was to start the Ringling Bros. and Barnum & Bailey Circus Clown College in 1968. He saw in three of the old-timers—Lou Jacobs, Otto Griebling, and Bobby Kay—the nucleus of a renaissance in circus clowning, and he made them master teachers, so that their grand tradition of buffoonery could be passed on to young and energetic aspirants. In 1984, he added boss clown Glen "Frosty" Little to that happy few. By that time, every clown performing in both units of Ringling Bros. and Barnum & Bailey Circus—with the exception of Jacobs and another vet-

MASTER CLOWN AND RUBBERNECKING GIRAFFE. The neck of a giraffe arches gracefully over one of the most famous funny faces in the history of the world—Lou Jacobs. When I was two years old, I went to the circus and fell in love with this clown. As a grown man writing a magazine article on clowning, I was assigned to be one of nineteen clowns shoehorned into the clown car. When I wriggled out, a clown cop, played by Lou, hit me on the head with his billy club. I felt as if I'd been knighted.

Mark Twain would have understood. He repeatedly told the great nineteenth-century clown Robert Edmund Sherwood that his ambition was to be a clown. "At first I thought he was joking; later I found he was really in earnest," Sherwood wrote in his memoirs, Here We Are Again. *"I ridiculed the idea, and inquired of him why a man who could write such books as he, wanted to become a common clown. 'Well, Bob,' he replied, 'I think it would be a very satisfying sensation when you come to a ripe old age, to feel and know that you had made people happy—children especially.'" When Lou Jacobs reached a ripe old age, he kept right on clowning—he has clowned with The Greatest Show on Earth for over sixty years—but for eight weeks every year, at the Ringling Bros. and Barnum & Bailey Circus Clown College, he reveals his secrets on how to make people happy—children especially. (Ringling Museum)*

eran comedy stylist, Duane Thorpe—were Clown College graduates.

This was probably the most signficant move for the preservation of the traditional circus that anyone has made in the twentieth century. Feld's clown college is the only professional school in the entire world devoted exclusively to clowning. Its purpose is to give young people the opportunity to learn the art of circus clowning as a worthwhile career. The application form is designed to reveal the emotional life of the applicant with such questions as "When was the last time you cried?"

As a master teacher Lou Jacobs would perform his entire repertoire for the students, so that they could study him close up, and then he would lead them through a classic routine, correcting their mistakes as they went along, like a musician teaching a master class.

For example, he would assign four aspiring clowns to a classic ring gag involving a baby in a buggy, the baby's nurse, a tramp who tries to kidnap the baby, and the cop who catches the kidnapper.

"I show them how I would act, and they get the idea," Lou explained at one session. Then he walked over to the student who was playing the tramp.

"You didn't take the slap too well," said Lou; and then, instead of telling how to take a slap, he took one, recoiling from a fake blow as if he'd been hit by a speeding Mack truck. You could see from the top of the grandstand that he'd been slapped.

Then Lou bent over the baby carriage, in which a small student was waiting to play the baby.

"*Waaaa!*" Lou demonstrated, contorting his mouth into a whale of a wail.

Lou turned to the man who was playing the nurse.

"You realize that the baby wants the bottle and you give it to her," said Lou, and the clown nurse handed the bottle to the clown baby in a straightforward, uninteresting way.

"That's right," said Lou encouragingly. "But everybody has a different way of reacting to a baby. You have to find a funny way of realizing that the baby wants the bottle. You have to have a funny attitude toward the baby. Watch this. . . ."

Lou Jacobs tapped his temple as if he were pressing a doorbell and raised his eyebrows until his eyes looked like upended eggs.

" 'I got an idea!'—that's what I'm pantomiming," Lou told the clown nurse—as if there was anybody in the arena who couldn't tell what Lou Jacobs was pantomiming. Then Lou pushed his thumb toward his pursed lips in short jabs.

" 'She wants a bottle!' That's what I'm pantomiming," said Lou Jacobs. "Now *you* try it."

With a flurry of gestures, the student pantomimed "I got an idea—she wants a bottle!" Then he looked to Lou.

"Don't make a lot of gestures without any reasons for them," said Lou. "Two gestures for two ideas—one at a time."

The student tried it again. This time, it was funnier because he was beginning to find his funny attitude toward the baby and to communicate it to the audience with simplicity and clarity. But Lou Jacobs was still funnier demonstrating each of the parts separately than all four of the students put together.

"They'll be all right," Lou told me. "They have their minds too much on the routine yet." And he added, "If it wasn't for the Clown College I don't know where they'd get any clowns."

In addition to the classes in clowning, which are given throughout each day of the ten-and-one-half-week session, and from which everything else in the college derives, there are courses in clown makeup, choreography, stilt walking, acrobatics, unicycling ("to develop balance and the basic skills of unicycling as well as techniques of falling along with the importance of equipment maintenance"), juggling, wire walking, improvisation, prop building, costume construction, music, and magic. "This course deals in visual comedic magic and how to amaze comically," says the course guide. "In the only course of its kind in the world, students are taught comedic presentation of stage illusion, as well as how to build and create magic props. Students are sworn to secrecy, as are all magicians, and cannot divulge the secrets of the art." The instructor in clown magic was the late Bobby Kay, who was renowned as a circus clown (forty-two years) as well as a magician.

John Russell put on his first pair of stilts at Clown College. They were three feet tall. He got a contract to the clown alley of The Greatest Show on Earth in 1976. In 1981, he made the *Guinness Book of World Records* for walking in performance on stilts that were thirty-one feet high. In addition to clowning, Russell became an instructor at Clown College, introducing students to the three-foot stilts on which he learned to walk. Most of the Clown College instructors can do as well as teach.

In 1970, for the first time, there were women in the Clown College class, seven of them. Among them was Peggy Williams, five-foot-nine-inch graduate of the University of Wisconsin, who had been working with children as a speech therapist when she decided that clown mime was a good way to reach kids.

Midway through the course, Peggy Williams tried a cartwheel in acrobatics class, landed badly on the edge of a tumbling mat, and broke a bone in her foot. She continued her college work on crutches, hobbled through as much of the course as she could, and was back on both feet by the next-to-last week.

Irvin Feld liked Peggy's personality, admired her persistence, and was amused by her grad-uation performance as a clumsy ballerina in a shocking-pink tutu. In Peggy's clown "number," her outsized ballet slippers, which she had made herself out of foam rubber, stubbornly refused to cooperate in her efforts to achieve steps *en pointe*. Feld chose her to be the first woman clown on the Ringling Bros. and Barnum & Bailey Circus in twenty years.

Peggy Williams was officially the "First Lady of clowning's American renaissance," because she was assigned to the Red Unit, the first show to get on the road that year. Another woman from the class of 1970 also got a contract and was assigned to the Blue Unit: Maude Flippen, a former exercise groom on a Michigan racetrack.

How do clowns develop their distinctive characters? After all, no two clowns look alike. An unwritten honor code that most clowns have observed throughout the history of the circus in America prohibits one clown from copying another's dress, makeup, and special gimmicks. (Felix Adler, for example, had a monopoly on a nose that lighted up.)

A Clown College makeup class is a class in circus tradition as well as the techniques of clowning. Students learn three basic clown faces—the traditional whiteface, the character clown face, and the *auguste* or grotesque face. Whiteface Bobby Kay and *auguste* Lou Jacobs, who had more than a century of experience between them, demonstrated the makeup of their clown types. Then the students got the benefit of their advice when they tried it themselves in the makeup room.

Peggy Williams experimented by drawing a checkerboard pattern on her face with a soft pencil, then contorting her features to see which were most expressive. When her mirror said "eyes," she put on the creamy white zinc oxide base, powdered it to chalk white with powder from a sock, drew on a smiling red mouth, a pert, red-tipped nose (her own, no rubber or putty), and then accented each eye by outlining it in black and then placing a blue teardrop glistening with a rhinestone beneath it.

"Professor" Lou Jacobs added the final touch: a long black oval in the middle of her forehead.

"It's me!" she exclaimed with delight. "I feel at home in this face."

In years to come, when she herself would be teaching makeup to Clown College students, Peggy Williams would say, "A clown's makeup isn't supposed to be a mask to hide behind but a projection of his personality."

By the 1980s, there was scarcely a circus in America that didn't include Clown College graduates in its ranks. Others were raising the level of the part-time clown who is paid to bring laughter to hospitals and schools and private parties. One graduate, William C. Witter, after three years as a clown and ringmaster for Ringling Bros. and Barnum & Bailey Circus, got the featured role of the ringmaster in the Broadway musical *Barnum*, where nightly he showed the kind of skills students learn in Clown College: he juggled rings and clubs, spun a large metal basin on a stick, rode a tall unicycle, balanced on an unsupported ladder, slid down a rope from the top of the proscenium, and even did a back flip from a teeterboard.

In the days when there was no Clown College, said Jacobs, "I learned to be a clown by watching and studying the old-timers. I'd watch how they'd polish up their acts. Watch the old-timers and polish it up—that's the way to do it."

And that's the way they do it at Clown College.

———

In 1968, in addition to founding Clown College, Irvin Feld introduced to the circus a troupe of basketball-playing unicycle riders, the King Charles Troupe, and proudly billed them as "the first all-black circus act in America."

Jerry King, architect of the act and father of the group's leader, Charles King, traced the act's origin back to 1916, when he went to a small circus in Florida and saw a man riding a unicycle on a high wire. "That stayed with me all my life," he said. Forty-two years later, Jerry King decided to teach his six-year-old son to ride the unicycle—which he did, in a narrow hallway in the Bronx. Warmer weather took young Charles King and his unicycle into neighborhood parks. When Charlie came home again, he had a lot more pupils for his dad. Daily practice made these pupils a close-knit, well-disciplined troupe. When they added their neighborhood know-how as basketball players to their skill on unicycles, they had a very special act—a kind of Harlem Globetrotters on wheels.

The circus's seeming nemesis, the television screen, scooped them up. They appeared on "The Tonight Show" when it originated in New York. Irvin Feld decided that America should have an all-black circus act.

He had long been sensitive to the feelings of blacks in American society. Super Cut-Rate Drugs, the drugstore-luncheonette that he and his brother ran in the 1940s and 1950s, had the first integrated lunch counter in Washington, D.C., and Feld insisted on integrated performing groups and audiences for his arena concert tours—even in the South—in the fifties and sixties.

In 1968, Irvin Feld auditioned the King Charles Troupe on the sidewalk outside Madison Square Garden—and signed them up.

In Europe, according to A. H. Saxon, "a surprising number" of black performers "flourished in the early nineteenth century, and several rose to prominent artistic and managerial positons. Thanks to its international character and emphasis on physical skill, the circus—in Europe, at least—was always open to them." Not so, apparently, in American circuses, except as freaks (Zip, the What-is-it?; the Ubangis)—until the era of Irvin Feld.

When he hired the King Charles Troupe, Feld told me, "there wasn't a black person in the circus." One of his executives from the North era said, "Kid, you're gonna have total rebellion. You can't have niggers in the circuses." But that closeminded executive had not noticed the times changing: major league baseball had already been integrated for twenty-one years; the American circus, traditionally open to performers of any nationality if they had the necessary skills, was now opened without great problems to black performers. By 1984, when Ringling Bros. and Barnum & Bailey Circus had black clowns, black showgirls, and, since 1983, Satin, the first black aerial act, the following paragraph appeared in Richard F. Shepard's *New York Times* review of the Big One's 114th edition:

> Among the very best of the acts is the King Charles Troupe, nimble and versatile young basketballers who whip through a game while riding unicycles and shamelessly, and magnificently, flaunting a dexterity and showmanship that might arouse envy in a choreographer. They are, in a way, to basketball, what Peter Brook's *Carmen* is to the opera, short and sweet and exceedingly dramatic.

Racial integration had been very, very good for the American circus.

The Spec for "The Centennial Edition of Ringling Bros. and Barnum & Bailey" was called "The First 100 Years." The press and public did not find the comparison odious.

"The Greatest Showman on Earth," *Time* magazine called Irvin Feld in its May 4, 1970, profile of that title, explaining: "In this, the 100th year of the road show originated by Phineas T. Barnum, the Ringling brothers' ex-

travaganza is so healthy that it is actually a six-ring circus—two separate, full-scale circuses traveling two different itineraries. Last week the 'Blue company' was playing Madison Square Garden while the 'Red company' was packing them in in Birmingham. Each, naturally, was billed as 'The Greatest Show on Earth.'"

The article was the second-best answer to John Ringling North's reservations. The best answer was given in the August 15, 1970 issue of *Amusement Business*: "Ringling Revenues Zooming." "We earned more in this year's first half than in all of 1969, which was the best year in history," said Feld. Gross revenues were listed as $11 million, 20 percent ahead of the 1969 period. "Income after taxes rose to $949,117, about 99 percent over the comparative year-ago total of $476,358, . . ." the article continued. "It was the first comparison available with both the Red and Blue Units touring for the two periods."

The main reason for success was the time-honored one: superstars performing superfeats. On the Blue Unit were "The Flying Gaonas, the first family of the air," with young Tito Gaona trying the triple every time he went aloft—and doing it almost every time he tried. Circus veterans like Antoinette Concello were comparing him favorably to the unquestioned greatest, Alfredo Codona. There was also a "thrilling demonstration of the skills of acrobats and aerialists"—with a difference: "Death-Defying Jose Guzman," who rode a motorcycle up a wire to the roof of the auditorium, carried with him a trapeze on which his wife Monique did acrobatic maneuvers. And the Blue show had one of the great daredevil acts of all time: for a finale, two Zacchinis, "Famed and Fearless Team of Human Missiles," were fired almost simultaneously from a double cannon, so that they sailed across the amphitheater together.

(The dangers, as ever, were real. At the beginning of February, the trajectories of the two

FELIX ADLER AND LOU JACOBS, TWO GREAT CLOWNS, CELEBRATE WITH ANTOINETTE CONCELLO, *who became in 1937 the first woman to do the triple somersault from the flying trapeze to the hands of the catcher since Lena Jordan, who did the first triple back in 1897. (Ringling Museum)*

THE GREATEST CLOWN. *That's what Fred Bradna called Slivers Oakley in his memoirs. "A clown who can stop the circus before sixteen thousand spectators probably will not be seen again," he wrote. Even clowning around outside the Big Top, as Slivers is doing here with a clown named Seabert (right), the drollness of the tall, lanky Scandinavian can be seen. His customary costume included a huge bustle on his rear, a white blouse, whiteface makeup, and a hat from which he flew the American flag. (Ringling Museum)*

OAKLEY & SEABERT

Zacchini "human cannonballs" intersected and they collided in midair. One Zacchini broke her back. Her replacement would subsequently break her leg.)

The Red Unit, of course, had Gunther Gebel-Williams; plus Bulgaria's Silagis, generally acknowledged as the world's most impressive teeterboard act, and Sweden's "Unbelievable Lindstroms," riding the high wire with all three Lindstroms balancing on a single unicycle.

———————

A financial report on the circus in the *San Francisco Chronicle* for August 28, 1970, reported that the gross revenues of the combined shows had doubled from 1967, when the Felds took over, to 1969, reaching $15.7 million. Net income had risen in that period from $125,000 to $832,000.

What it all meant, in terms of people entertained, was simple: at the end of North's reign, Ringling Bros. was playing to under 2 million people a year. "Each year since 1967, I have played to many more people," said Feld, "but the big jump occurred when I started the Blue Unit in 1969. Since we produce one completely new show each year, no city sees any act that they saw the year before." In 1974, Ringling Bros. and Barnum & Bailey Combined Shows played to 6 million people.

Individual engagements were getting longer. When Feld bought Ringling Bros., it was playing in New York for five weeks at Madison Square Garden; this engagement would gradually be increased to nine weeks, yet business was good enough to add a second New York engagement—two weeks at the Nassau Coliseum. Before Feld, Ringling Bros. never played Cleveland or Detroit longer than six days; under Feld, it began playing those cities for two weeks. Naturally, when Ringling Bros.

played longer in one city, others had to be dropped—and the smaller circuses began moving in. For example, when Ringling Bros. dropped Amarillo, Texas, from its itinerary in 1973, the revived Clyde Beatty–Cole Bros. circus came in. Indeed, Clyde Beatty–Cole Bros., the second largest circus in the United States, and the largest still under canvas, had the longest season in its history in 1974, playing 212 cities in twenty-five states. *Amusement Business* magazine's annual survey of carnivals and circuses for 1974 listed forty-six indoor and grandstand circuses and thirteen circuses under canvas that had actually played performances in the 1973 season, meaning that there were about nineteen more circuses on the road in the Feld era than there had been in the last years of the North era.

The circus was, indeed, coming back.

———————

In 1969, The Greatest Show on Earth went public at sixty-four times earnings. And being the circus, it went public with the first four-color stock prospectus in the history of the Securities and Exchange Commission and the first four-color stock certificates. "How can you do the circus in black and white?" asked Irvin Feld. He got enough money from going public to pay back the bank loan with which he had bought the circus plus $2 million to operate it better.

But as always, Irvin Feld's dreams were bigger than his pocketbook. On December 22, 1970, it was announced that Mattel, Inc., the largest toy company in the world, had bought, for $47 million, The Greatest Show on Earth.

Having acquired a large share of the ownership of the circus, having shaped it the way he wanted, why did Irvin Feld and his brother Israel sell to Mattel?

No matter how much money he made, Irvin

Feld could always think of great things to spend more on. In addition to owning and personally running the biggest circus in the world, he wanted to build the biggest theme park in the world, which he would call Ringling Bros. and Barnum & Bailey Circus World. For that, he needed financing from a giant corporation.

The man who had always wanted to out-Barnum Barnum now wanted to out-Disney Disney as well. Circus World would be a multimillion-dollar entertainment complex and school, for which he purchased land in Polk County, Florida, ten miles from Walt Disney World. "We'll have a university of circus arts there," said Feld. Not just a college anymore; a university. "For the first time we're going to teach circus arts to young Americans. In Europe, they are trained in circus; over here, it's a lost art. It's been years since we had an American wild-animal trainer, but plenty of young Americans would like this. Instead of importing acts, we'll be exporting."

"I have great respect for the Disney organization, but it's all animation, it's not real. We're live, real people, real animals performing, and you know they're real because there's a guy with a bucket and broom following them." But such a dream would cost $75 to $80 million, "which I was afraid I would never live to see." So they sold the circus to Mattel in return for stock and Mattel's promise to build the park. Unfortunately, financial woes at Mattel prevented that dream from being realized. The theme park was opened but soon sold, and quickly lost the Feld touch.

———

The 1971 season of The Greatest Show on Earth was the longest in its history. If you added the schedules of both units together, they gave Ringling Bros. a year of eighty-four weeks and three days—twelve days more than in 1970. No more did Ringling Bros. performers have to find winter engagements for their acts if they wanted to be paid for a full year's work.

But The Greatest Show on Earth very nearly blew the biggest opening of the season, the first night at Madison Square Garden in New York. In this saga, we have seen the circus battle train wrecks and floods and blow-downs. Now it faced one long tunnel.

The Blue Unit train was in New Jersey, heading for Manhattan, when the Brotherhood of Railroad Signalmen went on strike, leaving the circus train stranded in the South Kearny yards, more than ten miles short of the Garden. The question was, how do you get all those circus animals across the Hudson in time for the big show?

Irvin Feld telephoned his senior vice president, Allen J. Bloom, who had been with him since Allen was a fifteen-year-old pasting labels on the early rock records that the Feld brothers put out.

"The strike's started," said Feld to Bloom, early that Monday, May 17, 1971. "What are you going to do about it?"

It was the sixth birthday of Bloom's son, and Allen had planned to take his family to the Bronx Zoo. Instead, he spent the day on the telephone. Transportation was found for most of the animals. Flatbed trailer trucks carried Charly Baumann's tigers into Manhattan. Large semitrailer vans moved the horses. Other trucks and vans carried two gorillas, nine lions, and eight black panthers. Across the George Washington Bridge and through the Lincoln and Holland tunnels, most of the menagerie converged on the Garden. But what about the elephants? The train had always taken them to a Manhattan siding, and they had walked the rest of the way to the Garden.

Hugo Schmidt, the elephant trainer, felt that hauling the herd one or two at a time by truck would be difficult and dangerous. Difficult, because Hugo would not allow anyone else to accompany the animals, so nine or more separate trips would be required, with Schmidt riding with the van each time to keep the huge animals calm. Dangerous, because separating the herd might upset the animals.

The herd had to move intact, and that left only one solution. The elephants would have to walk. There was, in that, a great risk also. The most direct route would take the elephants through the Lincoln Tunnel, which is a mile and a half long. For elephants, who often refuse to go through underpasses—or even doors—a tube that long might be a frightening place. Schmidt worried that one elephant or another would be alarmed by the unusual noises of a long, echo-filled tunnel, and start an elephant stampede.

He decided that he could take all of his elephants through the long tunnel if he was in complete control. And what he wanted from Allen Bloom was a right-of-way through New Jersey plus one tube of the tunnel reserved for the exclusive passage of the herd.

First, Bloom telephoned the governor of New Jersey, who said that the problem was outside his jurisdiction. Then he telephoned the mayor of a New Jersey city that the circus would have to pass through, but the mayor was in jail; so he made arrangements with other New Jersey officials. Then he called the top authority over New York's bridges and tunnels.

"I need to walk our elephants through the Lincoln Tunnel," Bloom said.

"Why not?" chuckled the tunnel chief.

"It'll cause a long delay," Bloom warned him.

The chief chuckled again. "We're used to long delays. Just don't do it during rush hour."

The last step was to get the necessary permits from the office of the mayor of New York City for that menagerie to come strolling across Manhattan. Bloom was told that the permits would take two weeks. The exasperated Bloom told the mayor's office to start making arrangements to stop twenty elephants because they were on their way.

So the herd of elephants, led by a female named Targa, were taken on their long march by Captain Schmidt and an entourage of assistants and grooms. Schmidt led Targa by the ear with a bull hook, barking commands at the five-and-a-half-ton beast in German and English. The other elephants marched in pairs, tethered by chains and following each other with trunks linked to tails. Bringing up the rear was the youngest elephant, Karen, twenty-two months old, weighing about 1,000 pounds, followed by a pony, a zebra, and a llama.

The animals left South Kearny at 8:50 P.M. and arrived at the Jersey side of the Lincoln Tunnel one hour and fifty minutes later, averaging about six miles an hour for the ten-mile trip. The tollkeeper collected $9.50 for the nineteen elephants—fifty cents apiece, the same as for automobiles. The zebra, llama, and pony were allowed into Manhattan for free.

The circus opened on time the next day. And the Garden was filled with children of all ages who had been delighted by the front page of the New York *Daily News*. Under the lead headline there was a photograph of Irvin Feld at a Lincoln Tunnel tollbooth, paying the toll for the elephants, as Hugo Schmidt kept Targa calm before her mile-and-a-half-long journey underground.

"TRUNK LINE," said the caption. "How would you like to be the driver of a car at the end of this lineup of elephants? And do you think the little woman would believe your story for arriving home late? Well, missus, believe . . . believe. The pachyderms, derailed by strike, are taking Lincoln Tunnel to Madison Square Garden for circus. Toll wasn't peanuts."

Among the Clown College Class of 1971 there was a music student from New Jersey named Ron Severini who wrote on his application that he considered Harpo Marx "the greatest person who ever lived." Severini played harmonica, guitar, violin, bass, and piano.

Severini loved his master teacher, Otto Griebling. He watched with never-flagging delight whenever Otto wandered into a circus ring juggling pie pans while balancing a feather on his nose. Otto would drop some pie pans and bend over to pick them up. When he bent over, the audience would see that the feather was stuck into the putty of his nose. Otto would always mime a tantrum at being found out—and Severini would always break up.

Severini also loved an old-time gag called "The Balloon Chase" that Otto had started teaching the students as soon as he became a "perfesser" in 1968. No one was doing it on any circus at that time, but soon it had been reintroduced into The Greatest Show on Earth. Otto taught "The Balloon Chase" to Severini.

"We became friends the last year of his life," said Severini. "Of course, he couldn't talk by that time. He was dying of cancer of the throat. But he could communicate."

Otto was a balloon vendor, and Ron was the clown who would snatch Otto's cluster of balloons and run off with them, with Otto in hot pursuit. Huffing and puffing, Otto would be just about to grab back his stolen balloons when Ron would hand them off to a fresh racer, whom Otto would have to chase. And so it would go, with ever fresh relays keeping the balloons from an ever more tired, ever more frustrated Otto—until one of the clowns would trip and fall on the stolen balloons, popping them, every one. Otto would slap this last thief, and when he tried to escape, Otto would grab his shirt—a clown prop called a long shirt, a tube of fabric that keeps unraveling until it is about twenty feet long.

Ron found the perfect hat to wear when he did the gag. "I bought an old Milwaukee Road trainman's cap from an old Milwaukee Road trainman for two bucks. Then Otto saw it and he told me in sign language that he wanted to borrow it. Well, he kept it and wore it as part of his costume for three months, until his last illness."

On March 28, 1972, the 102nd edition of Ringling Brothers and Barnum & Barley Circus opened at Madison Square Garden, with Otto Griebling up to all his old tricks except the ones that required him to speak. His larynx had been removed, and he carried a notepad in his pocket to write, in his own phonetic combination of German and English, the communications he couldn't handle by pantomime alone.

There wasn't much Otto Griebling couldn't handle by pantomime alone. There were lots of great acts that year, but, for me, the 1972 edition will always be mainly Otto Griebling, walking slowly from section to section, wearing a borrowed Milwaukee Road trainman's cap, scanning faces in the audience, carrying a well-thumbed book.

What was he looking for?

A name in his well-thumbed book, you figured. And, sure enough, he would see a certain woman in the grandstand, and look at her as if hers was the face that belonged with the name he had in his book. He would climb to her row, cross over pair after pair of obtrusive knees, then perch at last on the railing right in front of the object of his quest. Ignoring the woman's husband and children, the tattered tramp would close his eyes and purse his lips for a kiss, but the woman, with all the goodwill in the world, would be too embarrassed to meet him halfway.

Otto's eyes would open finally, and you

would see it dawn on him that he wasn't going to get that kiss. His prideful indignation was hilarious. "Not kiss me!" his eyes would shout. He would unpurse his lips suddenly, draw himself up as if to say, "I wouldn't kiss you now if you *threw* yourself at me!" And he would walk away with his red rubber nose in the air, flipping his handkerchief dismissingly at the woman as if *he* had rejected *her*.

He would try other women in the audience—and none of them would kiss him.

Later in the show, he would return to all their sections and fix each and every one of them with his famous resentful stare, furiously crossing out in his well-thumbed notebook the name of every woman who had rejected him.

Otto died on April 19. Mrs. Griebling returned to Ron Severini his Milwaukee Road trainman's cap. She also gave him Otto's feather and his pie plates. Later that year, Severini married Sandra Hayes—a fellow student in the class of 1971—in the center ring at the Los Angeles Forum, in full clown makeup. In 1975, Ron became boss clown of the Blue Unit. In 1977, he and Sandy became deans of the Clown College (they were later divorced). From time to time, Ron would perform Otto's old pie plate gag for the new generation of would-be clowns. It was a demonstration of the role that Clown College was playing in preserving the continuity of the circus.

During these same years, Lou Jacobs was doing a hunting routine in which his little dog played a rabbit. It was a routine that Lou remembered from years before, when it was done by another little dog and the late Charlie Bell. Thus have routines and gags that George Washington laughed at been passed on from generation to generation to the present day.

Israel Feld died suddenly of a heart attack on December 15, 1972. But Irvin Feld was not

to be alone in running the circus. He had a son, Kenneth, born on October 31, 1948. During Kenneth's vacations from Boston University, where he studied business administration, his father had taken him on his worldwide circus talent searches, so that the son could study the way the father ran the circus. When Kenneth Feld graduated, in May of 1970, Irvin Feld let him prove himself by sending him alone behind the Iron Curtain to negotiate for circus talent.

By the 1970s, Iron Curtain countries had become great suppliers of talent for American circuses. In 1973, Kenneth negotiated the arrival of the first circus act ever to come to America from the German Democratic Republic. The 1974–75 engagement of the Samel Mixed Animal Act was such a rousing success—critically and financially—that the East Germans became amenable to sending their greatest circus act abroad: "Beauty and the Beasts," meaning Ursula Bottcher and the largest group of performing polar bears in the world, ten snow-white Arctic giants. They played Ringling Bros. and Barnum & Bailey for six years, beginning with the 106th edition in 1976.

In Irvin Feld's constant quest to out-Barnum Barnum, he had been looking for several years for a human being who would be smaller than Tom Thumb. The word went out that Irvin Feld was thinking big by thinking small, and the word came back that there was a circus performer in Hungary who was amazingly small. Precisely where in Hungary was not at first known.

Irvin and Kenneth found the person they were looking for in February of 1973, in a small village outside Budapest. The two men walked through an unlit alleyway and up a flight of stairs, Kenneth leading his father hurriedly past two snarling Doberman pinschers. A drug that Irvin Feld took to lower his cholesterol level had made him completely blind for a time in

1962; subsequent treatment had partially restored his sight, but he had no side vision, so the experience was doubly unsettling for him. They next passed carefully in front of a bear that was tied up on the porch. Then they entered a darkened kitchen, where Irvin became aware that the pattern on the linoleum that seemed to be moving was in fact an eight-foot boa constrictor that was crawling toward them.

"We were ready to get out of there fast when I first saw Michu," Irvin Feld later recalled. "His amazing size made me forget everything else."

He was just what Irvin Feld wanted: thirty-three inches tall—taller than Tom Thumb at his shortest, but seven inches shorter than Tom Thumb at his tallest; he weighed twenty-five pounds and was already versed, as a child, in circus skills.

His parents, both about six inches taller than Michu, were members of Budapest's Lilliputian Theatre, a legitimate company of small people who presented plays for children as well as light comedies.

They called their son Mihaly Mezaros, and sent him as a child to a state-run school with a curriculum of circus skills that included juggling, acrobatics, and pantomime. For fifteen years, he was employed by a small traveling circus in Hungary as a clown, unicyclist, dancer, and announcer.

Like so many small people, Michu had found a home in the circus, and he hastened to sign up with the most prestigious circus in the world. "In the ring," he said later, "I am a performer. Only my abilities are measured, not my height. The share of laughter and applause is the same for any size person."

When he arrived in the United States, he created quite a different image from Barnum's midget. Tom Thumb was so decorous that he was a great favorite of the British queen who gave her name to Victorian prudishness and observance of conventionalities. Unconventional Michu was a lusty man who loved to smoke, drink, and pepper his conversation with obscenities in both Hungarian and English.

Irvin Feld's favorite Barnumesque dream was to stage a wedding for his midget that would be as memorable as Tom Thumb's wedding, and to that end he brought a little woman, Juliana, from Hungary. Feld hoped that she and Michu would marry in real life, as had Tom Thumb and his midget wife, Lavinia Warren. But his attempt at matchmaking was a failure. Juliana was reportedly shocked by Michu's ribaldry. Michu tried to charm her, but Juliana was not amused.

For two seasons, 1976 and 1977, each copy of the Blue Unit's souvenir program included a wedding "invitation": "Irvin Feld and Kenneth Feld, producers of Ringling Bros. Barnum & Bailey Circus, request the honor of your presence at the Event of the Century, the Circus marriage of Michu, the Smallest Man in the World, to his Lilliputian lady love, Juliana, in a Circus-spangled spectacular. Ringmaster Harold Ronk officiating . . ."

At each "Circus marriage," a young girl and boy were chosen from the audience to be flower girl and ring bearer for the tiny couple, and dozens of other children rode in the wedding procession. Unfortunately, the one person Irvin Feld couldn't get involved in the wedding was Juliana. After two seasons of "marrying Michu," the "Modern-day Mrs. Tom Thumb" went her own way, still single.

In his pint-sized private railroad car, where everything from the bed to the washstand was at his level, Michu went on alone, enjoying the pleasures of the table, occasionally having a small dinner party for Irvin or Kenneth Feld, at which he would cook some Hungarian delicacy, served with the appropriate imported Hungarian wine.

OF LAUGHTER AND LENNON. *"To make people laugh,"* Ron Severini, *dean of the Ringling Bros. and Barnum & Bailey Clown College, told me, "clowns generally do six things. They take falls, strike blows against something or somebody, mimic, dispense foolishness (usually with overtones of stupidity), engage in trickery or chicanery, and top it all off with a surprise ending." And Frosty Little, Ringling-Barnum's boss clown, told me and my sons, Michael and T.H., when we did our yearly stint as guest clowns on* The Greatest Show on Earth, *"Every clown gag ends with one of these seven kinds of blow-offs: fire, water, smoke, explosions, slaps, falls, and surprise." These simple rules have been used to cause laughter from ancient Greece and Rome to that day we clowned in Madison Square Garden in 1979 when John Lennon and Yoko Ono brought their four-year-old son, Sean, to the circus. You can see the moment in the 1988 film* Imagine. *Someone asks Lennon what he thinks of the circus. "I love it," says the former Beatle, and smiles happily. "My favorite part is the clowns." (Ringling Bros. and Barnum & Bailey Circus)*

And two or three shows a day, he acted out, with his offbeat timing, countless variations of the David and Goliath theme. If, for example, he came upon a damsel in distress, he repaired immediately to a tiny telephone booth, and came out costumed as the world's smallest Superman. The rest of the act consisted of the little man of steel vanquishing the biggest and toughest-looking clowns in Ringling's alley and then, adding insult to injury, bending weightlifter's bars around them.

One of the best insights into the way that Irvin Feld managed his circus, coaxing ever greater feats out of his performers and their animals, can be seen in the way that he goaded his Red Unit tiger trainer, Charly Baumann, into giving him a tiger trick that had never been seen before—and then to top it.

Baumann started in show business as a child actor in Hitler's Germany, "only to find myself beaten down by the war to the point of picking garbage." A job shoveling horse manure and cleaning around the few animals of little Circus Busch emboldened Baumann to answer a trade paper advertisement for an assistant horse trainer with the more prestigious Circus Williams. For five years, Baumann was one of a number of young people who received their basic training in circus production and operation—including horse training—from the owner, Harry Williams. Another of William's young pupils was future superstar Gunther Gebel.

One day, three male lions attacked the Circus Williams lion trainer, Jean Michon, during his act; the lion act's backup froze, but assistant horse trainer Baumann saved Michon's life by rushing into the cage and attacking the lions with a club and a five-foot wooden fork. Michon and his lions were under contract to a zoo in Holland owned by Eric Klant, who promptly sent Baumann $50 for saving Michon's life and offered him a job as a wild animal trainer. So with no previous experience except his act of heroism, and only two weeks to learn the routine, Charly Baumann became the trainer for six huge male lions.

Eventually, Baumann worked up a superb tiger act, which included one of the most difficult circus tricks of all time; the simultaneous, multiple rollover of several tigers. The problem with this trick is that the tiger is a solitary, unsociable cat that resents rubbing fur with its fellow tigers.

Baumann started with a common circus trick, one tiger rolling over. Then he got two tigers to roll over together, which, as far as he could determine, was the top limit for tiger rollovers. But he had circus in his soul, and he had to beat the limit. After many hours of painstaking practice, he trained three tigers to roll over together.

Naturally, Irvin Feld ballyhooed the trick as the first and only three-tiger rollover, to the point where Baumann began to fear loss of face if any of his tigers refused to cooperate. To save himself embarrassment, he trained a fourth tiger to roll with any two of the other three.

"How many of your tigers can roll over in that trick?" Feld asked Baumann one day.

"Three."

"No, you have four," said Feld. "I saw you training four. So why don't you do a four-tiger rollover?"

In reply, Baumann used a word that Irvin Feld hated to hear. He said that the trick was impossible—not that he couldn't get four to roll over together, but that he couldn't get them to do it on cue at every performance. Three was already more than anyone had ever done before, he pleaded.

"Come on, Charly, you can do four," Feld replied. "Don't tell me it's impossible."

Charly Baumann gave special training to the pinch hitter until he was able to enlarge the tiger rollover trick to four. "The boss was full of praise, and I was proud of my accomplishment," Baumann said. But he was also full of anxiety again: what if one of the four refused to cooperate? When Irvin Feld wasn't around, and Baumann thought he wouldn't hear about it, Charly began training a *fifth* tiger as pinch hitter.

Out on the road that season, the four-tiger rollover fell apart. It wasn't just one tiger who wouldn't cooperate, it was two; show after show, his act was ending in dangerous tiger fights. Baumann had to take the troublemakers out of the act and was back to a two-tiger rollover. Between shows, however, he retrained the four—plus the pinch hitter.

By the time NBC was ready to film "Highlights of Ringling Bros. and Barnum & Bailey Circus" in Florida in January of 1974 for its annual circus special, the four tigers were rolling over beautifully. During rehearsals for the show, Baumann did a little who-cares-if-it-doesn't-work entertaining of the camera crew by adding the substitute. He didn't realize that a live camera was feeding a monitor in the NBC camera truck where Irvin Feld was checking on the progress of rehearsals.

Suddenly, Irvin was in the arena.

"Hey, Charly, you've been hiding something again. . . . A five-tiger rollover! Beautiful! How about it for the TV special?"

Baumann knew what was coming. He tried to decline on the grounds that the trick could fall apart on camera, but Feld answered that if the trick didn't work, it was only on tape: he could do it over.

Sure enough, the five tigers did a beautiful rollover, and sure enough, Irvin Feld wanted the trick for the opening in Madison Square Garden a few weeks hence. Sure enough, Charly Baumann protested that the trick would never hold together, and sure enough, Irvin Feld "didn't wait to hear any more of my protests."

Through January and February and most of March, Charly Baumann wore himself out doing practice sessions as well as his regular act, but by the time the trick reached Madison Square Garden on March 28, 1974, it was a beauty.

Baumann's next topper with tigers was the "fire trick," in which arena lights were lowered and two enormous and velvety cats bounded simultaneously through blazing circles of flame onto twin pedestals. The trick created a poetic image—a kind of visual evocation of Blake's "Tiger, tiger, burning bright, in the forests of the night."

But how do you teach a tiger to jump through a flaming hoop?

You start by teaching a tiger to jump from one pedestal to another. Baumann would begin by placing two unusually large pedestals called "jump" pedestals side by side, with the tiger on one pedestal and a piece of meat on the other. He would allow the tiger to step over to the other pedestal, eat the meat and get down; but, gradually, he would move the pedestals farther and farther apart until the tiger would be forced to jump from pedestal to pedestal if he wanted the meat.

When the tiger was jumping well, Baumann would place an object between the pedestals, often another pedestal. Although it was lower or of the same height, it would stop the tiger in his tracks until Charly reduced the distance so much that the tiger could again be coaxed to jump—but this time over the intervening object. The purpose of the intervening object, of course, was to prepare the tiger for the moment when a hoop would be introduced between the two pedestals. Gradually, Baumann separated the jump pedestals until the leap was perfected, then he started raising the middle object.

In the wild, a tiger is a natural jumper, and a magnificent sight as he sails through the air. His circus training capitalizes on this natural ability, and soon he is making beautiful jumps over objects between pedestals. Eventually, the object for Baumann's tiger to jump over became Charly Baumann himself, and then a hoop he held over his head. When Charly had the tiger jumping easily through hoops, he brought in an asbestos-wrapped hoop with just a spot of gasoline applied and lighted on the lower edge of each side.

It takes less than a minute to read this, but it takes hours and hours and days and days to do it. Training periods for animals are limited to about forty-five minutes a day. Any longer, says Baumann, and the session becomes counterproductive. "My nerves fray, I lose patience, and the animal's education can even slip into reverse."

The amount of fire on the hoop must be kept very small until the tiger dares to jump through it, then very slowly increased as the tiger becomes more at ease with the flames. When he sees that he will not hurt himself, he will leap without fear through a hoop whose entire top three-quarters is ablaze.

Irvin Feld's reaction to the attention to detail and infinite patience of Charly Baumann was to name him performance director of the Blue Unit starting with the 1971 season. The announcement was greeted by the performers with silence, then mild applause with a scattering of boos. Baumann was not well liked by his fellow performers.

Irvin Feld conceded that Charly Baumann was "a rough guy" more used to training tigers than working with people, but that his principal objective was a good show—"and that's for the benefit of all of us." Charly, in his short acceptance speech, told his colleagues that hard work and teamwork were the way to make the Blue Unit the best of the two Ringling shows, so "I'm still going to be a mean S.O.B., but I'll do my best to get along."

For the next twelve years, Charly Baumann did his tiger act and was performance director, too. Gradually, his stiff insistence on discipline and attention to detail was recognized as a recipe for safety as well as excellence, which brought him a kind of grudging approval. At the close of the 1983 season, he retired his tiger act and became, simply, performance director of the Blue Unit. In 1989, he was executive performance director of both units. No more the classical elegance of Baumann's tiger act. "If Charly could have his way," Kenneth Feld had often said, "he'd do his act in white tie and tails." Now, at least, Charly could wear black tie throughout the show.

———

The moist, misty morning of August 7, 1974, just after 7:00 A.M., thousands of astonished New Yorkers looked up from the sidewalk in disbelief: a man seemed to be dancing and juggling on a wire strung between the twin towers of the World Trade Center, the tallest building in the world.

It was true: they were seeing a superfeat that would go into the *Guinness Book of World Records* as "the tightrope walk over the highest drop"—1,350 feet above the street. Television immediately broadcast news of the event around the world, and the tightrope walker, a twenty-four-year-old Frenchman named Philippe Petit, became world famous.

Petit was then unknown in America, but he had been an overnight sensation in France at the age of twenty when he gave an unscheduled three-hour performance on a wire suspended between the 226-foot-high towers of Notre Dame Cathedral in Paris. He came to New

York after seeing a photograph of the World Trade Center towers and deciding that he must walk between them because "When I see three oranges, I juggle. And when I see two towers, I walk."

The feat required ten months of secret, meticulously detailed preparation. He rented an apartment near the towers, surveyed them for weeks dressed as a construction worker and as a tourist, flew over the towers in a plane, and, finally, sneaked equipment up to the top and rigged it, shooting the wire from tower to tower by bow and arrow. Then he took that legendary 200-foot walk, 1,350 feet high. As soon as he had performed the feat, he was taken away by the police for psychiatric examination. But instantly, news reports made Philippe Petit the Blondin of the twentieth century.

This was not the humble *funambule*, or rope-walker—a word derived from the Latin *funis* ("rope") and *ambulare* ("to walk"). A person who walks, dances, or otherwise performs on a rope raised several feet above the ground is not a high-wire walker. His rope can be tight or slack; it can bounce or be completely loose; he can work with or without a balancing pole— any way he does it, if he does it on a rope, he is a *funambule*.

But if he uses a thin wire of brass or steel at a low height, he becomes a low-wire artist. And if he dares to stretch that tight steel cable without elasticity or movement at great heights, he is a high-wire walker.

Jean-François Gravelet, a.k.a. Charles Blondin, walking a tightrope across Niagara Falls, had been the perfect symbol of the precarious position of human beings in the mid-nineteenth century, when nature was still untamed over vast stretches of the globe. Petit walking the tightwire between the towers of a skyscraper office building was as perfect a symbol of the precarious position of human beings in the perilous urban world of the late twen-

tieth century. (For his illegal jaywalk high above New York City's streets, the judge sentenced Petit to put on a free show for New York's children, climbing an inclined wire to Belvedere Castle in Central Park at night, which he gladly did.) Philippe Petit was born August 13, 1949, in Nemours, France, the son of a French army officer. He started walking the wire at the age of seventeen. At nineteen, he wrote, directed, and played a ropedancer in "a highwire play" called *L'IF* at the Theatre de l'Amicale in St. Germain-en-Laye. In 1971, he walked a wire at Vallauris, France, for the celebration of the ninetieth birthday of Picasso. While making his living as a street entertainer, juggling and doing close hand magic, he planned and executed a series of ever more spectacular clandestine walks—at Le Grand Palais and Notre Dame in Paris, and on the Sydney Harbour Bridge in Australia. Then came the World Trade Center.

To Irvin and Kenneth Feld, it was a case of "We see a star attraction, we sign. . . ."

Philippe Petit made his circus debut with The Greatest Show on Earth in Venice, Florida, on January 3, 1975. Because of what happened in St. Petersburg four nights later, the front-page review in the *Sarasota Journal* is ironic:

Philippe Petit is the capping act of the first half, walking up a slant wire to the high wire and doing most of the rest of his act without bothering with such mundane items as net below or pole in his hands.

He stands on one foot in the center of the wire and juggles three Indian clubs. He walks across with a rod balanced on his forehead. He does a drum major step barefooted. He does backward somersaults the length of the wire, then walks back down the slant wire to the ground—all going to show that the man who crossed between the two towers of the tallest building in New York is a rising star, and deservedly so, in the circus world.

Then two brothers, the Carrillos from Colombia, take up Petit's aerial challenge and in some ways go him one better. Also working without a net and mostly without balance pole, they leap and leapfrog, they jump rope. One walks across his reclining brother in a frightening finale: a leap without balance pole from shoulders to wire. . . .

Whatever aerial challenge there might have been ended abruptly when the circus moved from Venice to the next stand, the Bayfront Center in St. Petersburg. On January 7, while practicing for the opening performance, Petit declined to use rosin on his soft shoe soles, and while descending the slant cable between his thirty-four-foot-high circus tightwire and the arena floor, he slipped. He fell, and his chest hit the wire. As his body whipped around, he grabbed the wire, but the friction burn made him let go, and he dropped twenty-five feet to the cement. He landed on his right side about four feet from the grandstand seats, writhing in pain.

Petit was hospitalized for nearly a week with a broken rib and wrist and internal injuries. He was determined to be completely recovered and back on the wire in time for opening night at Madison Square Garden on March 25, but when he auditioned for the Felds on the day before the opening, they didn't feel that he was physically ready and grounded him.

And so, on opening night in the Garden for The Greatest Show on Earth's 1975 edition, Philippe Petit stood on the ground watching another high-wire act in midair, the Carrillo Brothers from Colombia, and the tears streamed down his cheeks.

He rejoined the circus on May 8 while it was still playing its long engagement at the Garden.

But he was not the big hit in New York that everyone had anticipated.

The problem was that Petit wasn't enough of a showman to make his act look as difficult, dangerous, or dramatic as it was. When he walked between the towers of the World Trade Center, every foot of the vast 1,350-foot height seemed to proclaim the difficulty, danger, and drama of what he was doing. But at a height of only thirty-four feet the Carrillo Brothers knew how to make wire-walking look as dangerous as it really is.

To make matters worse, Petit did not take the advice of Don Foote, the show's costume designer, on how to dress for a walk on the wire. Foote dressed the Carrillos like toreadors, visually reinforcing the idea that they were defying death. Petit insisted on an all-white effect of tights and short-sleeved leotard. He looked like a moonstruck Pierrot, not a death-defier. But death-defier he undoubtedly was. "I demand to be allowed to end my life on the wire," he wrote. "I have the patience of those who have fallen once, and whenever someone tells me of a high-wire walker who fell to the ground and was crushed, I answer: 'He got what he deserved.' For that is clearly the fate and glory of the aerial acrobat."

Circus old-timers remembered that Karl Wallenda, like Petit, got started with noncircus stunts. At the age of seventeen, he had ridden his bicycle on a cable strung between two church steeples in his native Germany, and a year later had bicycled across the Oder River at Breslau, on a wire eighty-five feet above the water.

But when Wallenda joined the circus, he learned as well as anyone ever had how to make his act look as dangerous as it was. Take the seven-person pyramid. Four members mounted bicycles and rode out onto a tightwire forty feet aloft—without a safety net below them. Shoulder bars connected them in pairs,

THE MAN WHO SAVED THE CIRCUS. *When Irvin Feld, chairman and chief operating officer of what he would only refer to as "the greatest show on earth," died on September 6, 1984, the* New York Times *honored him with an editorial headed, simply, "The Man Who Saved the Circus." It began: "No one has ever been able to explain what happens in the hearts of some children when they see their first circus. Whatever it is, it happened to Irvin Feld."* (Ringling Bros. and Barnum & Bailey Circus)

"AND THEN SOMEBODY SAID, 'SEND IN THE CLOWNS'" (Life *magazine). "It is meat and drink to me to see a clown," wrote Shakespeare. Well, here's a banquet for Will: 482 of the 1,000 graduates of the Ringling Bros. and Barnum & Bailey Clown College returned in 1988 to the "campus"—circus winter quarters in Venice, Florida—for the school's twentieth anniversary. Top students in each graduating class get jobs with The Greatest Show on Earth and, as* Life *put it, "$180 a week for 11 months on the road and all the laughs they can steal." I can spot both of my sons in this group: Michael and T.H. were fourteen and thirteen when they graduated, the youngest graduates in the history of the college. Both now work as entertainers and speak with warmth of "the great clowns who were great clowning teachers— Lou Jacobs, Frosty Little, Peggy Williams," and of the classmates they visit each year, not only on the Ringling show, but on the Big Apple and other circuses across the country.* (Ringling Bros. and Barnum & Bailey Circus)

BACK FROM
THE
CORONATION

THE CLOWN ALLEY *of Ringling Bros. and Barnum & Bailey Circus in 1937 included the greats Lou Jacobs; Paul Jerome, whose neon heart lighted up whenever he fell in love with a circus patron; and Felix Adler, who wore the birthstone of each month in the end of his putty nose. (Ringling Museum)*

and another performer stood on the bar above each pair. These two second-story men were connected by a second bar, to which one of the Wallenda girls ascended. At its midpoint she sat on a chair as the pyramid slowly rolled across the cable. All this was very difficult and very dangerous, but the Great Wallendas made it look very easy. When the pryamid stopped, the balancing pole wobbled—and that wobble sent an electric shock through the crowd. From then on, the crowd was working on a collective coronary as the girl on the chair slowly rose to a standing position atop the balanced pyramid.

Philippe Petit had walked the wire higher even than Karl Wallenda, and without a net. During his season with the Ringling Bros. and Barnum & Bailey Circus, he set another record—for the longest indoor tightrope walk—by walking a wire across the Louisiana Superdome in New Orleans, at the building's opening celebration. The walk that inaugurated the largest covered stadium in the world was 700 feet long, 200 feet high, and repeated six times—sometimes twice an evening. But his circus walks didn't generate either the suspense of walks by the Wallendas or the Carrillos, or the awe of his own World Trade Center walk.

And he knew it.

"What makes me different from other wire walkers is that they—maybe because they were born in the circus—try to sell the act," he told the *New York Times* in the summer of 1979. "They think they have to show it's dangerous. They fake slips. I don't. I think the courage of a high walker is beautiful if he can hide it.

"I'm trying to get rid of all the equipment, the unicycle, even the balancing pole. I want to bring choreography, juggling, even comedy to the high wire, to make it more pure and simple, almost forgetting the wire is there."

Petit told the *Times* that he earned $2,000

a week during his season with Ringling Bros. "But I didn't want another season," he said. "When you were up on the wire and you could hear them yelling 'Popcorn! Coca-Cola!' below you, you wanted to kill the poor guy selling it. I designed my own costumes, lighting and music, but they didn't want to change for them."

So Petit left The Greatest Show on Earth, but soon returned to the circus. It was, however, a new, European-style one-ring circus, created by Paul Binder and called The Big Apple Circus after its origins in New York, where it first opened on July 20, 1977. In 1981, at last, the French *ascensioniste*, or high-wire walker, had found a circus in America whose more intimate style suited his own. Walking above the one ring in a Big Top small enough for the entire audience to see him well, he would kneel in a pose that the more sophisticated in the audience would identify immediately as Rodin's statue, *The Thinker*. He would stop the band music, take off his elkskin slippers and, dangling them between thumb and forefinger, walk barefoot through the silence. And he would juggle a ball, six hoops, and Indian clubs like the street entertainer that he essentially was. He was not, ultimately, a three-ring circus star. He was the wire-walking clown that Richard Basehart played in Fellini's *La Strada*, come to the streets of America.

The three-ring tradition of high-wire walkers included, in the Feld era, such memorable wire walkers as the Great Doval, who crossed the high wire on stilts in the 1971 edition; and Gene Mendez, who made spectacular leaps from the shoulders of his partner, Joe Seitz, to the steel cable in 1971 and 1972. Then there were the Lindstroms from Sweden, whose act included a unicycle rider counterbalanced by two men on trapezes suspended below the wire. (Because of the heavy load under the wire, the center of gravity is so low that whatever is on the wire remains in balance.) Switzerland's Pio Nock rode his bicycle over a cage full of Wolfgang Holzmair's lions (interrupted briefly in 1973 by his fall into that cage, from which he escaped without serious injury).

As with trapeze artists, dangerous tricks in circuses are usually calculated risks in which the odds favor the skillful athlete who keeps his head. Pedro Carrillo of the so-called "Carrillo Brothers" was for a long time attracted to unattractive odds, even though the fate of his "brothers" kept reminding him of the perils of their profession. His first partner, whose real name was Daniel Acosta, fell in Los Angeles and gave up wire walking. Pedro's second partner, Werner Guerra, also fell. In 1980, working with his third partner, Luis Possa, Pedro Carrillo tried to do a nearly impossible trick while Irvin Feld was in the stands.

"Luis is sitting on the wire and Pedro jumps over both Luis and a jumprope that Pedro has in his hands and then does a twist in midair so that he lands backward facing Luis. He didn't fall but he didn't make it.

"I really gave him hell," Feld told me. "I said, 'Pedro, I don't want you to take those chances. You're the best high-wire act in the world, and I don't want you killing yourself. And the fact of the matter is, I'm not going to give you a new contract if you're going to do things like that.' "

Pedro agreed to eschew foolhardy tricks, and the Felds gave him the new contract. A few days later, he decided to try it just once more. He fell thirty-five feet, injured his spleen, broke his right arm, fractured his hip, and injured his neck. When he returned to the circus two months later, he understood the Felds' philosophy about the difference between courage and foolhardiness.

The high-wire walker goes far back in history. He is the *voleur* of the Middle Ages, the *ascensioniste* of Blondin's time. How do these people feel about going up on the wire after a fall? Philippe Petit has said the last word on falls: "A fall from a wire, an accident up above, a failed exercise, a false step—all this comes from a lack of concentration, a badly placed foot, an exuberant overconfidence. You must never forgive yourself." At the same time, says Petit, "You are a high-wire walker. You cannot go for long without visiting the sky."

———◆———

One thing that Philippe Petit did love about Ringling Bros. and Barnum & Bailey Circus was the circus train. "I loved the travel across America on the train," he said. "You would cross deserts at five o'clock in the morning. I would be looking out the window, and children would wave or throw rocks, whatever they felt like."

In this regard at least, Petit was the beneficiary of Irvin Feld's vision of what a circus should be. In 1957, for the first time in eighty-six years, the American circus season had begun without a single railroad circus in operation, and the experts said it was unlikely that any circus would ever again move totally on rails. But to Irvin Feld, The Greatest Show on Earth meant two units moving totally on two complete circus trains, and here, too, Feld confounded the experts.

Ringling had returned partially to rails under John Ringling North, but when Feld bought the circus, the circus train consisted of only sixteen cars, and those were mainly for moving heavy equipment. Performers got from stand to stand on their own.

"Of course, the railroad life is an easier life. You can sleep while you're being moved; you don't have to drive," I was told in 1975 by Frank McClosky, when he was president of the motorized Clyde Beatty–Cole Bros. Circus.

McClosky had been general manager of Ringling Bros. in the early fifties when it was still a railroad circus. "Last night," McClosky said, sitting in the white ticket wagon in Philadelphia's Liberty Bell Park, "we drove in the rain from Aberdeen, Maryland, and came in at 2:30 A.M. This morning, we were setting up the tents in the mud at eight."

Feld wanted his performers fresh. In 1969, he sent out the already established show, which he called the Red Unit, on twenty-five cars; and then the new Blue Unit moved out on twenty cars from the Penn Central's Twentieth Century Limited and the Rocket of the Rock Island line—great trains that have since been discontinued.

In early 1972, Feld purchased enough cars from the Union Pacific Railroad to give the Red Unit a new train. That year, the two units had a total of sixty-two cars, almost identical to the number the Barnum show had when the first circus train took to the tracks exactly one hundred years before. But the engine was powered by diesel, not steam. The cars were lighted by electricity, not kerosene. Aluminum had replaced iron. Still, the coaches and flatcars didn't look so different from those that Barnum knew. And the passengers were exactly the same: clowns and elephants and aerialists and wild animals and their trainers. By 1983, the Red Unit would have forty-three cars and the Blue Unit thirty-nine, for a total of eighty-two double-length railroad cars.

My sons, Michael and T. H. Culhane, who were Ringling clowns earning money to go to college, have described the circus train way of life in the 1970s:

The center was the pie car, [said T.H.]. Located halfway down the body of the train, it conveniently separated the circus castes— the more mundane clowns and showgirls and Eastern European teeterboard acts and ac-

robats on one side, the exotic animal training and death-defying superstars on the other. But it also served as a meeting ground, where new ideas and friendly conversations could occur over morning coffee, allowing the tension-smoothing and bond-building process of social eating to take place.

Michael remembered the elephant car at the back of the train:

You were always keenly aware of the fact that you were linked by a dozen tin cans on wheels to stockcars full of the greatest behemoths on earth, because you could hear them trumpet their frustration on long train rides, and at every city you would watch their arduous loading and unloading because it is impossible to sleep with the shouts of animal handlers yelling, late into the night, "Now MOVE, Targa!"—punctuated by the bellowed refusal of a giant pachyderm.

T.H. added:

It was like walking across a continent whenever you would wander down the tracks in search of a restaurant on Monday nights when the pie car was closed. At each train yard in the bleak outskirts of some city, the train would have been dismantled and its various cars parked side by side. The Poles would string their laundry across the spaces between the cars and would sit on the metal boarding steps like friendly villagers from the Old Country having a doorstep chat in their native dialects. The Hungarians would light small fires on the gravel between the tracks—some plump woman would be cackling from her window while the men played cards and smoked—and you got the curious sensation that these were real Gypsies you were mingling with. The Mexicans and South Americans would be cooking and joking in quick Spanish as you continued your multinational, multilingual journey down the tracks, and invariably you would get lost trying to find your own car out of the dozens of dismantled pieces of circus train bunched up in the surreal landscape of the trainyard. That is when you would discover the true international reality of the circus, for when you stumbled into someone else's car and asked directions, you would be greeted by silent and sometimes hostile tribal suspicion of families who spoke no English. The circus train in America's largest circus is a world unto itself, a world of gypsy mystery, of xenophobic clans and live and animal totems, of exotic cultural and mixed animal interplay.

———————

Irvin Feld saw the coming U.S. Bicentennial as an opportunity to combine, as Barnum had, his equally heartfelt patriotism (in what other land do storekeepers like Barnum and Feld rise to become the familiar of a Queen Victoria or the business partner of a Prince Rainier and a Princess Grace?) with his equally avid desire to do sensational business.

Since each show that he produced toured for two years, Feld decided to start his Bicentennial celebration a year early, on the night of January 3, 1975, when the 105th edition of Ringling Bros. and Barnum & Bailey Circus opened at winter quarters in Venice, Florida. I was there, and I saw and heard to my surprise the crowd giving a standing ovation to the *Spec*!

None of the old-timers present could recall ever seeing, hearing, or reading about a standing ovation for the Spec. If Barnum ever got a standing ovation for his Centennial Spec, he didn't mention it in his autobiography—and it was never Barnum's way to hide his ovations under a bushel.

The Spec is the only display in the circus in which every member of the troupe and every performing animal (except the big cats) has a part, and Irvin and Kenneth Feld had dressed them all in red, white, and blue, from the clowns to the patriotic pachyderms. They went further: they had the band play the music of John Philip Sousa and George M. Cohan. And even further: they put Uncle Sam in the center ring, walking tall on stilts to the beat of "It's a Grand Old Flag"; beautiful girls in red-white-and-blue sequins spun by their teeth from the clappers of airborne Liberty Bells; and a performer dressed as an astronaut rode an elephant, standing up and waving Old Glory. (The performer who appeared as the All-American Astronaut was an acrobat from Eastern Europe, possibly a dedicated communist, but in an astronaut's helmet he looked as American as anybody else.)

Throughout 1975 and 1976, as the 105th edition of Ringling Bros. and Barnum & Bailey Circus made its way across the country, the standing ovation for the Spec was repeated again and again. It wasn't just that the Bicentennial Spec was a rousing Spec—there had been plenty of rousing Specs before; it was the irresistible combination of circus and patriotism that has been a mainstay of the circus since John Bill Ricketts celebrated the firm resolve of President George Washington with a Spec about the Whiskey Rebellion back in 1797. And it was the timing: America's unpopular war in Vietnam was over at last; the Watergate scandal had been resolved with the first resignation of a president of the United States in history. Approaching the 200th birthday of their country, Americans seemed to want to stand up and cheer its symbols of continuity again, and the circus provided that opportunity as wholeheartedly as it had in Barnum's day.

One of the symbols of continuity, of course, was the American circus clown, from the joey who entertained George Washington at John Bill Ricketts's Circus when New York was the nation's capital, to Dan Rice, who gave Lincoln the respite of laughter during the Civil War, to the clowns who cavorted before President Ronald Reagan when he came to the circus in Washington, D.C., in 1985. Two years later, the Ringling Bros. and Barnum & Bailey Clown College marked its twentieth anniversary, and Kenneth Feld invited all the Clown College alumni—1,000 graduates—to a gigantic reunion in Venice, Florida. Of the fifty-two clowns on the Ringling show's two units, fifty were alumni. The exceptions were two holdovers from the show's pre-Feld history: a splendid whiteface named Duane Thorpe, and Lou Jacobs himself, eighty-four years old, sixty-four years a clown, still clowning and still teaching the new generation.

Master Clown Otto Griebling, veteran of the Hagenbeck-Wallace and Cole Bros. circuses, spent his last twenty years with The Greatest Show on Earth, and was one of the first teachers at Ringling Bros. and Barnum & Bailey Clown College.

Legends

All over America, as the circus approached its Bicentennial birthday, circus people were demonstrating the staying power that had given the institution its two-hundred-year run. In the 1780s, there was only one circus in America: the first, Thomas Pool's. In the 1880s, there were about seventeen. Now, in the 1980s, there were about seventy circuses showing in the United States, carrying on the traditions and incarnating the never-say-die spirit of the original traveling tenters.

Take, for example, "Hoxie" Tucker.

In Geneva, New York, on June 5, 1983, Leonard Basil "Hoxie" Tucker, the king of the ragtag mud shows that travel by truck and continue to show under canvas in frequently muddy lots, was badly stomped by Janet, one of the elephants on Hoxie's Great American Circus. This was sorry news, indeed, for Hoxie

Tucker was a symbol of the little circus in America just as Irvin Feld was a symbol of the Big One. And Tucker had been putting on a fine show that season, including the Loyal riding family, which topped its act with a backward somersault from one horse to another, a sight seldom seen in modern circuses. When one of Hoxie's own pachyderms broke Hoxie's pelvis and severely and painfully bruised his back two months before his seventy-third birthday, he decided to sell his show, including four years' right to the title, to his manager, Allan C. Hill. It seemed that Hoxie Tucker's long association with the world of shows under canvas was over. But at least the show would go on.

So Hoxie's Great American Circus did not fold, and neither, as it turned out, did Hoxie. So far, the saga of the circus in America has

THE APOGEE OF RISK-TAKING. Seventeen years ago, aerialist Karl Wallenda, patriarch of the Great Wallendas, watched his son-in-law plummet to his death. The next day, the old man was back on the high wire, no net beneath. Six years later, Al Pacino recalls, Karl himself plunged to his death as he attempted to walk the sky between two high-rise hotels in Puerto Rico. " 'I can never get that out of my mind,' Pacino says softly. 'His grandson said everyone would continue {walking the wire} . . . "Life is always on the wire," he said "The rest is just waiting." And that's true for me. Anyone who cares what he does has got to take a risk.' " (Circus World Museum, Baraboo, Wisconsin)

had no ending, and the ending of one story is frequently the beginning of another. As it turned out, it took more than being stomped by an elephant to end Hoxie Tucker's forty-year love affair with the circus.

Born August 7, 1910, in Somerset, Kentucky, to a father nicknamed Big Hox, Leonard Tucker added the *ie* in honor of the Western star Jack Hoxie (who played Deadwood Dick in thirties serials) and went into show business at fifteen. Eventually, he was taking stars of the Grand Ole Opry on tour under canvas during the week, always getting them back to Nashville for the Opry on Saturday night. He was what they called a "kerosene circuit man," because he knew how to get a touring show to the crossroads and the backwoods and to light the tent with lanterns when there wasn't any electricity.

In 1943, he went to visit a friend in Georgia who had an ailing circus. First thing he knew, Hoxie said, the friend had talked him into taking over the circus. He changed its name to Hoxie Brothers, not because he had any brothers in with him but because the public, since the Ringling brothers, liked to think of a circus as a family operation.

It was a one-ring show with horse acts and clowns and a sixty-foot tent, but no elephants. He advertised it as the world's largest one-ring circus, but as quickly as he could afford it, Hoxie added rings and elephants. Sometimes, when he had a bad season, he had to subtract an elephant or so, and maybe a ring or two.

In the early fifties, he had two rings but no elephants. Even in straitened circumstances, he could keep going, however, because he was the kind of circus owner who knew how to do just about everything himself that a small- to medium-sized tented circus needs—except perform, of course. As performers, he liked to hire circus families, particularly those in which a couple of family groups could do a whole show's worth of acts.

With this philosophy, Hoxie began to prosper again, but taking on more help didn't seem to allow him to relax more.

Fred Powledge, a writer who traveled with the Hoxie Brothers Circus for its full 1974 season, wrote of him that he knew

where every rope went, where every piece of wood should go, how to set up the Big Top, the sideshow tent, and the cooktent properly, how to move props, how to talk a crowd into a sideshow, how to read the clouds for rain, how to drive any of the seventeen trucks, how to avoid highway weight stations, how to talk to elephants, how to run the light plant. For years he had run around doing a lot of these things himself, for he was short on patience and it bothered him to see a green or lazy man *fool* at doing something when Hoxie knew how to do it twice as fast.

Over the years, this attitude had cost him three heart attacks and a nervous breakdown that once put him into the hospital for three weeks. But the result, as Edward Hoagland pointed out in a review of Powledge's 1975 book, *Mud Show: A Circus Season*, in the *New York Times*, was that little cities and towns still got good circus. "For example," Hoagland said, "the voters of a good circus burg, Greenville, S.C., rejected a bond issue to build a coliseum such as Ringling Bros. and Barnum & Bailey requires nowadays. They would have been left with no circus at all if Hoxie Brothers . . . hadn't agreed to come in and fill the bill."

And now an elephant had stomped him, bad. Yet by July 1983, Hoxie Tucker was up and around again. He made provision for the show to go on by selling the Great American Circus, including his most famous African elephant, named Hoxie after himself, to Hill, and he retired to live the life of a legend. In 1986, Hoxie the Elephant retired, too. Hoxie Tucker had been the stuff that "Tents"—as the chapters of the Circus Fans Association of America are called—are named after, and, sure enough, the one in Orlando, Florida, is called Hoxie Tucker Tent #137.

For Hoxie Tucker, as for Irvin Feld, the game was gambling on a dream. "If you want to learn something in the circus business," Hoxie told Powledge, "you can be whatever you want to be if you put your mind to it, whether it's a clown or a trapeze artist or an elephant trainer or whatever you want to be. First of all, you can't be afraid. If you gamble your life to do what you want to do, I think anybody in the circus business can achieve what they want."

In the 1980s, the three big tent shows were Clyde Beatty–Cole Bros., whose traditional territory is the East Coast; Circus Vargas, traditionally a West Coast circus; and D. R. Miller's Carson and Barnes Circus, whose traditional territory is the Midwest.

Wayne Franzen's Franzen Bros. Circus, founded in 1973, starred Wayne Franzen himself, who proved himself the Gunther Gebel-Williams of the small circuses by doing acts with the show's one elephant, its jungle cats, its twelve liberty horses, its camel, and its llama.

The roll call of circuses showing in the 1980s includes many a name known to circus buffs: Roberts Bros.; Lewis Bros.; Roller Bros.; Oscarian Bros.; Jules and Beck; Martin and Downs; Super Circus International; the American Continental Circus, owned by the Matthew J. Gatti Circus; Alberto Zoppe's Circo Italia or Circus Europa; Eddie Zacchini; Sam T. Polack; Grace McIntosh's M&M Circus; the Coronas Circus; Paul Kaye's Continental Circus; James M. Cole's All-Star Circus; Bill Garden's Holiday Hippodrome Circus; Lucio Cristiani; the Hubert Castle Circus, produced by John Zerbini; and Tommy Hanneford's Royal Hanneford Circus. The John Strong Circus folded in 1983, but much of its equipment was back in 1984, and with it returned a very famous circus title, when the Al G. Kelly and Miller Bros. Circus took to the road again after a long absence. Alaska was toured by John "Gopher" Davenport's Ford Bros. Circus out of Cut and Shoot, Texas.

In 1983, Henry Ringling North saw the 112th edition of Ringling Bros. and Barnum & Bailey Circus when it showed in Cincinnati, and probably reflected that he had been seeing Ringling circuses for seventy-one years, since his mother, the only sister of the Ringling brothers, took him to his first circus at the age of three. The 1980s show was much like the first he ever saw, though the world that he saw it in had changed considerably. The Red Unit of Ringling Bros. and Barnum & Bailey did a "gay night" in San Francisco that year—a date sponsored by local homosexuals. Dave and Judy Twomey's Happytime Dog & Pony Show performed in Glen Eden nudist camp in Riverside, California, though dressed in standard circus attire.

Two legendary performers who had once seemed nearly immortal were gone forever from the circus scene. With eerily appropriate timing, Karl Wallenda and Emmett Kelly died on the days in 1978 and 1979 respectively when The Greatest Show on Earth, scene of their greatest triumphs, opened in Madison Square Garden in New York.

Legendary circus performers tend to embody qualities that are prized by the generations that turn them from center-ring attractions into stars of the global arena. Karl Wallenda embodied balance—and the concept of "balance" has obsessed twentieth-century man. While Wallenda walked and rode bicycles on high wires around the world, the nineteenth-century "Balance of Power" was destroyed by world war and replaced by a "Balance of Terror" among nations with nuclear weapons.

The Wallendas achieved the seven-person pyramid shortly after the U.S. realized it would have to share the atom bomb with the USSR. Sixty or seventy feet below the Wallendas' symbolic cable, a strand only five-eighths of an inch thick, we in the crowd looked up fearfully as it slowly sank in: There was no safety net to save them from the unthinkable. And when this moving human pyramid had made it across the abyss, we cheered with a depth of relief that comes only when one is secretly cheering oneself.

And then, in 1978, Karl Wallenda, walking a wire alone, fell to his death in Puerto Rico on the day that the 108th edition of Ringling Bros. and Barnum & Bailey Circus opened in the Garden. Fifty years before, the Great Wallendas had been the sensation of the Garden opening of the 58th edition of that same circus.

In an unbalanced world, the Great Wallendas had stood for half a century as a human beacon of balance; and Karl Wallenda, the seventy-three-year-old founder, patriarch, and star of the troupe, fought his slowing reflexes and waning strength to maintain that symbolic image.

Born in Magdeburg, Germany, in 1905, Wallenda had an infallible sense of balance that was seemingly innate. He was the third generation in the European circus tradition: his grandfather, also named Karl, founded the dynasty in 1874 with an act involving twelve Russian wolves; his father was a catcher in a flying trapeze act.

By the time the third Karl Wallenda was nine, he and his brother Herman were doing acrobatic feats in public, performing for the patrons of provincial restaurants who threw money for tricks they liked.

His high-wire career began in 1921, when Karl did a handstand on the shoulders of Louis Weitzman while Weitzman walked the wire.

Young and proud of his strength, quickness of reflex, and presence of mind, Karl Wallenda was gripped by a compulsion to push human balance to unheard-of heights, a compulsion that would not leave him as long as he lived.

At seventeen, he went beyond Weitzman by rigging a bicycle with cupped rims to overlap a tightwire and riding between two church steeples sixty feet above the ground, then making the crossing with brother Herman riding on his shoulders.

At eighteen, he strung the wire across the Oder River at Breslau and bicycled above the water at a height of eighty-five feet.

By the time Karl was twenty-two, Herman weighed one hundred eighty-five pounds. Karl's search for a lighter "topper" for the act led him to a very poised Bavarian wire walker named Helen Kreis. Wallenda trained her to climb to his shoulders as he walked the wire.

Another brother, Joseph, joined the act, and airborne human pyramids became possible. But they were not popular. Many exhibitors feared that the Wallendas might fall, possibly injuring spectators—and causing lawsuits. But there was a booking in Havana, Cuba, and it was there that John Ringling witnessed a Wallenda high-wire pyramid, and immediately engaged their act for the 1928 season of Ringling Bros. and Barnum & Bailey Circus.

"The first time we made airborne pyramids, we used big nets," recalled Karl later, "but we took the net away in 1928 when we came to the United States."

That legendary Madison Square Garden opening night was one of the most exciting in the history of the circus. For a finale, Joseph and Herman Wallenda rode bicycles in tandem across the wire, with a pole braced across their shoulders. On the pole stood Karl and Helen. And when the bicycles reached the center of the arena, Helen mounted to Karl's shoulders.

"In forty-two years, I never heard an ovation of half the decibels," wrote Fred Bradna, Ringling's equestrian director on that unforgettable night.

Bradna went on to describe how the crowd would not stop crying and whistling and stomping for the Wallendas to take another bow; how the audience stopped the circus for fifteen minutes until Mr. Bradna had to go get the Wallendas; how he found them sitting glumly silent in their dressing room.

In Europe, whistling and stomping are expressions of derision: Karl Wallenda thought that the extraordinary risks that his family had taken, without even a safety net, had been received with contempt. Mr. Bradna explained what the tumult really meant, and escorted them back to the center ring and into a love affair with the American public that was to last half a century.

To do such an act in the comparatively controlled conditions of an indoor arena is one thing; but the Wallendas presented their vision of perfect balance in the tent circus, and even the open air. In 1952, their friend Bradna described some of the hazards: "The intense heat of the tent top may cause a fainting spell at a critical moment. Lightning may strike nearby, or a photographer's flashbulb explode at a time when concentration on technique is the difference between life and death." They were particularly wary of heat, which affected the tension of the wire as well as the clearness of their thinking. Herman carried a thermometer to register the temperature at the top of the tent, where they would have to stay for twelve minutes. In the Midwest in the summer, it was often 110 to 112 degrees.

But it was rain that nearly killed them all in 1934. A downpour made muddy ground that gave way just as Helen mounted to the shoulders of her new husband, Karl, causing the weight sustaining the wire to shift. The wire trembled violently, and all four Wallendas began to fall.

But twenty-nine-year-old Karl, in the prime of his life, caught the wire with both his hands, and thrusting out his legs as she fell past him, caught his wife's head between his ankles. So tight was this ankle scissors hold that Helen lost consciousness. Herman, meanwhile, had also grabbed the wire with his hands, while Joseph clung to Herman's legs. With Joseph hanging beneath him, Herman went hand-over-hand to the platform. Not even Karl Wallenda could go hand-over-hand while pressing another person between his ankles. But he could keep her from falling until a safety net was spread below them. Karl dropped his wife to the net, then followed her himself, and neither of them was injured.

Karl was almost forty when the worst disaster in circus history struck. They were performing at the top of the tent during the Ringling show's Hartford, Connecticut, engagement of July 6, 1944, when Bradna frantically motioned them down. Within minutes, fire had swept through the Big Top and 168 persons were dead. But again, the Wallendas had acted in time.

At fifty-six, Karl pushed human balance to the most spectacular equipoise ever achieved: the seven-person pyramid, three tiers high. This is the one listed in the *Guinness Book of World Records* as the greatest of all high-wire feats. No one but the Wallendas could ever do it, and two Wallendas died trying. Four men, linked to one another by shoulder bars, stood on a cable holding balancing poles. Above them, two more men stood on the shoulder bars holding shorter poles. Above the two men on the middle level, a woman sat on a white chair whose rectangular legs were balanced on their shoulder bar. In her lap she held a balancing pole of her own.

This three-layer, seven-person pyramid, first performed in 1961, burned an image of perfect balance into the minds of the thousands who saw it in person, and the millions who saw it on film.

THE WALLENDAS COME TO AMERICA. *This photograph of the Great Wallendas was taken in the Ringling-Barnum lot just after their arrival in the United States in 1928. Helen Kreis Wallenda's future husband Karl stands at left, holding Helen's hand; to her right is Karl's brother Joseph; behind them is his brother Herman. Together, the Wallendas were the sensation of the 1928 season, when they first exhibited their bicycle pyramid on the high wire. "Several generations of my own family and that of my husband have had the circus in their blood," said Helen. "We ourselves were performers for over sixty years." Karl saw Helen Kreis perform in Vienna in 1927, and engaged her as a "topper." "After carrying her on his shoulders for seven years in this act," wrote Esse Forrester O'Brien, "he assumed the carrying charge for life, and they were married." (Helen Kreis Wallenda)*

KARL WALLENDA OVER A BALLPARK *(opposite, bottom). Sometimes he would stand on his head, shouting to the crowd, in his thick German accent, "For Ez-dur Zeels" (Easter Seals), or "For der boys in Vietnam." (Circus World Museum, Baraboo, Wisconsin)*

THE WALLENDA AND ZACCHINI ORCHESTRA, 1936.
The Zacchinis are playing the mandolins. This is in the
"backyard" on the Ringling Bros. and Barnum & Bailey
Circus lot. There is an evocative re-creation of the backyard
in the Ringling Museum, which pictures such as this one
helped to get just right. (Ringling Museum)

But they didn't do it long. On January 30, 1962, Dieter Schepp, a young nephew of Karl's wife who was making his first appearance in the pyramid, cried out: "I can't hold on anymore . . ." and, for the first time since 1934, Wallendas began to fall.

This time, Karl clung to the wire with his legs while holding his niece Christiana safe in his arms. But Dieter Schepp and Richard Faughan, husband of Karl's daughter Jenny, fell to their deaths on the concrete forty feet below. Karl's adopted son, Mario Wallenda, was paralyzed from the waist down.

"We can't lose our nerve," said Karl Wallenda afterward, but his wife, Helen, never again could watch him perform. He dropped the human pyramid from the act, but he continued to tour.

"Rather than being discouraged and withdrawn following the tragedy, Karl seemed to bask in the fame it created," said Walt Hohenadel, editor of The White Tops, who had known him since the 1930s. "And I honestly feel he capitalized on what had happened. He vowed to continue the act. . . . I told Karl many times that he was going to kill himself on the wire. But he had a devil-may-care attitude."

More and more, Karl Wallenda's most spectacular feats of balance were accomplished alone.

At the age of sixty-five, in 1970, Karl took a 1,000-foot walk across the Tallulah Gorge in Tallulah Falls, Georgia. He did it in seventeen minutes and made $10,000.

"How long do you think you can go on?" he was asked about this time.

"I have to ask the good Lord," he replied. "He'll let me know."

"Is there anything that could happen that could make you say, 'No, never again. I'm not going back up'?"

"Well, I—I don't think so," he replied. "I always said, 'God takes care of me.'"

It was a typical conversation with a great daredevil. It is hard to get such people to think the unthinkable; to imagine what might happen if they had a bad day. They seem to focus their minds on thoughts of discipline and technique and to leave the rest to God.

"During subsequent long solo walks across ballparks, sports stadiums, and natural gorges—an obsession as Karl grew older," wrote Bill Ballantine, "usually he would stop at several spots along the cable stretch and do a headstand, dedicating each one to some person, cause, or organization. 'Und now,' he'd announce over his wireless mike, 'I do headstand for the boys in Vietnam,' or for 'Eazder Zeals' or 'Muzkellar Diztrophy,' or for the local sponsor of that particular exhibition in which the reconstructed (and smaller) Wallenda act was then performing. Pure circus hokum; Karl was standing on his head to rest his legs."

But it wasn't pure circus hokum. As he grew older, he did indeed find an occasional headstand on the wire restful, but Wallenda was also beginning consciously and publicly to give his balancing acts symbolic importance.

Reminders of the possible penalties of what he was doing were never far away. He was sixty-seven in 1972 when he watched another son-in-law, Richard Guzman, touch a high-voltage electric wire and plunge to his death during a circus performance in Wheeling, West Virginia.

When he did a nationally televised Miami Beach walk in 1977, he had already pursued his compulsion beyond the biblical threescore years and ten, and his comments afterward sounded as if he were beginning to imagine the end. On January 31, 1977, he walked 720 feet between the Fontainebleau and Eden Roc hotels through a chilly Atlantic breeze.

"It was a very dangerous walk," he said when it was done. "It was pitch black. I couldn't see anything and it was very windy. But I had to do it. The whole United States was waiting. When you chicken out, you're not a showman anymore."

He had admitted the compulsion: he had to do it. And so his path led him, at the age of seventy-three, to the wire between the Condado Holiday Inn and the Flamboyan Hotel in San Juan, Puerto Rico. On March 22, 1978, he began a 750-foot-walk twelve stories high to promote the Pan American Circus, where he and his seventeen-year-old granddaughter Rietta were performing nightly on a wire only fifty feet high. He was full of the future: after being away from Ringling Bros. and Barnum & Bailey Circus since 1946, he had signed with coproducers Irvin and Kenneth Feld as one of the acts that would represent them at the 1978 International Circus Festival of Monte Carlo, where annually the finest acts in all the circus world compete for the Golden Clown Award presented by Prince Rainier.

The gust of wind that blew him off the wire was not as strong as others he had walked through, but he was not as strong as he had been when he walked through them. If he had dropped his balancing pole and grabbed the wire with both hands he might have made it hand over hand back to the platform, as his brother did forty-four years before.

But he no longer had the strength, quickness of reflex, and presence of mind to serve his compulsion to be the beacon of balance; and so the greatest high-wire artist since Blondin fell one hundred feet to his death in a parking lot; and his granddaughter had to watch helplessly, as he had watched members of his family die.

"It was inevitable it was going to happen this way," said Hohenadel. "Deep down, I think he wanted to die performing. It was in his blood."

At Madison Square Garden that night, the media had gathered to see if Tito Gaona could accomplish the quadruple. Tito made the four somersaults but failed to connect with his catcher, and he fell to the net. Karl Wallenda's death earlier that day was the banner headline in the newspapers, and film of his fall, of the terrible bounce of his body off a parked car, was repeated endlessly on news broadcasts. His fatal fall made everyone conscious that circus risks are not movie or television risks, faked by stunt doubles and special effects.

Two years later, Enrico Wallenda, grandson of Karl, returned to San Juan and successfully completed the walk which took his grandfather's life. In 1983, young Wallenda taught a former news reporter to top-mount the famous Wallenda chair pyramid, and married her that same year. "Debbie Wallenda is the first and only female performer in the world to leap from a two-high column to the wire," reported *White Tops* in 1986, "a feat considered to be among the most dangerous in high-wire history." So that legend continues, too.

———

The next year, it was Emmett Kelly who died on opening day. On March 28, 1979, while taking out the garbage, he suffered a heart attack and died in the front yard of his home in Sarasota, Florida. He was eighty years old. How characteristic of Kelly that he died performing a homely act; he was never the type to keel over at a Hall of Fame banquet. When they told his good friend, the film and television clown Red Skelton, who had once been a clown on the Hagenbeck-Wallace Circus and had sometimes clowned with Emmett, too, Red said: "I guess the angels needed a laugh."

Emmett Kelly was the best kind of clown, for his gags were therapeutic. None of us loses more often than did his Weary Willie; yet he always tried again. And Kelly understood the good his clowning did. "By laughing at me, they laugh at themselves," he said of his audiences, "and realizing that they had done this gives them a sort of spiritual second-wind for going back into battle."

I'll always remember the time that Emmett Kelly made me cry. It was in 1953 in Rockford, Illinois. I had seen Kelly many times before, but never walking so slow, never looking so sad. He was dragging a limp broom, and I guessed he was going to do his famous spotlight gag. Yes, there was the spotlight, shining into the ring, and now he had seen it, and was trying to sweep it up.

At first, he seemed to be succeeding. As Weary Willie swept, the circle of light grew smaller and smaller. Finally, only a flicker was left. From somewhere in his oversize tattered black coat, he produced a dustpan, and swept up even this tiny residue of light.

Successful at last, he slung the broom over his shoulder and started to leave the ring— only to see, in front of him, another circle of light, just as large as the last one. Patiently, he started sweeping all over again.

And then Willie added the little extra that touched audiences to the heart. He blew up a balloon too big, and it burst. His expression made me think of all the children who lose something beautiful. With the broken balloon, he did exactly what a child would do: he gave it a little funeral and buried it, right there in the dirt under the Big Top.

Much later in the show, during an act involving high-flying trapeze artists such as Kelly had once dreamed of being, I thought of that balloon, buried like so many of our dreams, and my eyes filled with tears. I laughed at myself for being so sentimental—and realized suddenly that Emmett Kelly's Weary Willie was the sentimental dreamer in us all.

———————◆———————

Karl Wallenda was dead, but the celebration of human aspiration that is at the heart of the circus was made manifest by another high-wire walker, in 1982. To celebrate the resumption, after forty-one years, of construction on the world's largest Gothic cathedral, St. John the Divine, begun in New York City in 1892, Philippe Petit walked to the church across a 250-foot wire slung fifteen stories above Manhattan. In reporting the event, *Time* magazine called thirty-three-year-old Petit "that soaring seraph of acrobats."

The inspiration for having an aerialist commence the rededication of the cathedral, said Dean James Parks Morton, came from an eighteenth-century painting by Guardi depicting circus performers outside San Marco Cathedral in Venice. Dean Morton added that having an aerialist perform "is proof of faith, like nothing else."

Faith is as characteristic of the circus as the ring, and a center ring in the United States in 1983 featured a faithful trouper who was probably the oldest active circus performer in history, ninety-four-year-old Katherine Hanneford. As ringmistress for the riding act with the Royal Hanneford Circus, owned by her son Tommy, it was her role to keep the horses running at a steady pace around the circumference of the ring—a vital task, since a change of pace or direction could result in serious injury to one of the somersaulting riders. Nevertheless, she admitted to me, "I have never felt truly comfortable around horses, even though I have been in the act for over fifty years." But she was a Hanneford, albeit by marriage; and in the circus, Hanneford means horses, so she simply had faith that all would be well.

The year that Katherine Breen Hanneford was born, 1889, the Ringling brothers, P.T. Barnum, and Bailey were all alive—and so, for that matter, was Dan Rice. But the family into which she married goes back in the entertainment business before all of them.

Hannefords have been performing in public

for well over two hundred years, or longer than there has been circus in the world. Since 1915, there has not been a season without a Hanneford appearing in one or more of the leading American circuses—including their own.

Hanneford family tradition tells of a juggling contest held by King George III to determine the greatest juggler in his kingdom. According to the legend, the winner was their ancestor, Edwin Hanneford of Ireland, who prevailed over another juggler named Walter Scott.

Edwin Hanneford II, named after his grandfather, at one time managed a circus that toured Scotland. His son, Edwin III, performed with circuses as a knife thrower and bareback rider. Working on one of these circuses, he met Elizabeth Scott, a descendant of the Walter Scott who supposedly competed with the first Edwin Hanneford for the title of greatest juggler.

When they announced their intention to marry, the Scotts were not delighted to give a daughter to the Hannefords. But Elizabeth defied them, and she and Edwin left to join the Lord George Sanger Circus. Edwin III threw his knives; Elizabeth walked the wire and presented trained pigeons; both were accomplished riders, so their featured act was bareback riding.

Not content with merely performing, Edwin and Elizabeth were determined to own their own circus. Putting money aside every chance they got, they were able, in 1903, to form one. Not wanting to compete with their parents, they decided to make Ireland their territory; and knowing the Irish resentment of English organizations, they named their circus The Hanneford Royal Canadian Circus. A circus may carry the appelation "Royal" if its proprietors or their ancestors have performed before the King or Queen. The Hannefords, of course, gave their first royal command performance before King George III; and with the

EMMETT KELLY AND OTTO GRIEBLING. *Charles Dickens, who began his career editing the memoirs of the peerless nineteenth-century English clown Joseph Grimaldi, wrote in his introduction (1838): "It is some years now since we first conceived a strong veneration for clowns, and an intense anxiety to know what they did with themselves out of pantomime time, and off the stage." On the lot, they sit around a great deal, as two clown legends are doing here. But in case of a sudden mishap during a show's performance—a fall from a trapeze, an accident with a wild animal—the ringmaster will quickly "send in the clowns," so they have to have their comedy props near the ring. Clowns stow them as near as possible to the back entrance of the Big Top or in an arena close to the hippodrome track. In France, the ringmaster sent in the clowns with the command "Clowns allez!" ("Clowns go!"). In America, allez got corrupted to alley, so the props area where clowns hang out offstage became known as "clown alley." Soon the clowns' dressing area, too, was known as clown alley. It is usually curtained off by a stretch of canvas fly. Inside, the funnymen can be themselves in the intervals between being the creations of their fantastic imaginations—and the objects of ours. (Ringling Museum)*

exception of one generation, the family has repeated this tradition of honor in each succeeding generation.

The Hanneford Royal Canadian Circus flourished in Ireland from 1903 to 1910. Edwin III and Elizabeth had three children, called, not surprisingly, Edwin IV, George, and Elizabeth. The family has always felt that it was because these children were raised together that they developed the sensitivity to one another that enabled the split-second precision of their bareback act, and this is probably true. The circus world abounds in family acts in which performers almost seem to have the same pulse, from the Hannefords in the ring to the Wallendas on the high wire to the Codonas, the Gaonas, and the Vazquezes on the flying trapeze.

Edwin IV, called Poodles, was a natural clown. We have seen that the first thing a circus clown ever did was to mimic the acts of skill and daring, so those who burlesqued the rope-dancers were called "clown to the rope," and those who burlesqued the equestrians were "clown to the horse." By Poodles's time, these designations were no longer used, yet there has probably never been a better "clown to the horse," including Dan Rice, than Poodles Hanneford. Buster Keaton called him "the only trained acrobat I ever saw who could take a fall and make it look funny."

Together, the Hannefords looked funny, beautiful, and incredibly skilled all at once. In his full-length raccoon coat, Poodles would dive on and off the horse, ride backward, and sometimes hold on to the horse's tail for dear life, while the other members of his family stood comfortably on its back. Elizabeth, his dark-haired sister, got the *ooohhs* for her beauty; George, the somersault rider, got the *aaahhhs* for his daring; and Poodles got the big *hahas*. When he stepped off the back of the horse in such a way that he gave the impression

of being momentarily suspended in midair, crowds would scream with laughter.

For horse lovers, the Hanneford act took an unusual step in the direction of beauty. They used only fast, thoroughbred horses instead of the more plodding draft horses usually seen in such acts. This combination of skilled riding, comedy, and extremely fast horses soon got the act talked about all over Europe.

In 1910, Edwin III died while the show was in Penzance, England. The family decided not to tour Ireland in 1911 and accepted a tour of England under the directorship of E. H. Bostock, a famous British circus producer.

Traditionally, in England, the major cities have indoor circuses at Christmastime. The Hannefords toured only in the summer, showing under a tent and moving between towns by horse-drawn wagons. During the winter, they would shut down their own circus and appear as star performers in these big indoor Christmas circuses.

The biggest was the one produced at the Agricultural Hall. In 1913, the Hannefords were the feature act, and in the audience was John Ringling. Mr. John was so impressed that he tried to bring them to the United States immediately, but the Hannefords were already booked through 1914.

That was the year the riding act played the Black Pool Tower Circus at a summer resort. George met a beautiful girl named Katherine Breen, who belonged to a family juggling act called the Breens. Then the guns of August blasted the world into war. Soon after, the British government started commandeering all horses for the war effort. The Hanneford Circus was dependent on horsepower, so the Hanneford riding act signed with John Ringling to open in 1915 in Madison Square Garden and to tour America with his Barnum & Bailey Circus.

At their hotel in New York, George Hanneford got aboard the elevator—and there was Katherine Breen. Her family act was playing New York, too. The courtship that began culminated in their marriage.

The debut of the Hanneford family riding act with the Barnum & Bailey Circus on April 1, 1915, is one of the great debuts in the history of the circus in America. They were still with the show when it combined with the Ringling show, and when Ringling Bros. and Barnum & Bailey Circus had its premiere season in 1919.

A great new era of family equestrian acts was under way. In addition to the Hannefords, there were the Davenports, an American family; the Cristianis and Zoppes, from Italy; the Hodginis, an English family with an Italian name; the Schumanns, from Germany and Denmark; and the Loyal-Repenskys, who first became circus riders in France when Napoleon gave one of their ancestors some horses.

The acts were similar. First there would be graceful riding, usually featuring the family's beautiful young daughters, such as Elizabeth Hanneford or Harriett Hodgini, doing pirouettes and other tasteful ballet movements on horseback. Then there would be exciting riding, usually featuring young sons such as George Hanneford, doing feats like equestrian somersaulting. Everyone did forward and backward somersaults. Some acts brought on a second mount for horse-to-horse somersaults. Orrin Davenport did a backward somersault from one horse to another, then a second somersault to a third horse, then a back flip to the ground, all in one series. Lucio Cristiani, incredibly, did a somersault from one horse entirely over the back of a second to the rump of the third.

Elizabeth, wife of Edwin III, played the role of ringmistress that would become Katherine Breen Hanneford's part. "Prancing and strutting . . . in the latest Parisian evening gown and

stunning jewels, crowned by an ostrich-plume tiara," said Fred Bradna in fervent remembrance, "she became one of the most sensational figures of her time. She moved about the ring with dance steps and graceful gestures which made her an attraction equal in interest to her virtuoso children."

The third phase of the family riding acts featured sensational equestrian pyramids. In the beginning, most family acts employed one horse. All the turns were accomplished as solos until this finale, when everyone in the family stood on the same mount. Then two rosin-back horses (so-called from the resin placed on their backs to prevent the riders' feet from slipping) would be brought into the ring, and would circle it at their familiar, rhythmic pace while the whole family leaped up to form a high-riding pyramid. Then three; then four; until the Loyal-Repensky family combined *five* horses, four standing riders (the so-called Roman post riders, and the three riders who stood on them (the so-called top-mounters) into a galloping pyramid of seven persons.

But no family could match the Hannefords for, as the 1916 Barnum & Bailey poster put it, "combining hilarious humor with unequalled skill and daring." Left behind, Poodles would run for the horse, make a desperate dive, sail clear over the beast, and collide with a popcorn vendor. Even when he managed to get aboard the family mount, there was so little room left for him that it looked as if he were holding up the horse's tail to give himself a place to sit. Whatever the rest of the family riders could do, Poodles could do as well or better—and make you laugh at it besides.

After the comedy came the jockey act, and remember that the Hannefords had been expert jockey riders since Edwin III. Faster horses were used, and they ran around the hippodrome track at a much greater speed, while the jockey rider leaped to and from the horse's back, silver bells jingled thrillingly on the horse's halter, and the circus band kept up with the pace until the dizzying running leaps were done.

Incredibly, the *Guinness Book of World Records* shows that the unique, still unbroken record for these running leaps on and off a horse was set in 1915 by the equestrian who is also the most famous riding clown in circus history—Edwin "Poodles" Hanneford, who did twenty-six in one New York City performance.

After the running leaps, it was all over but for the tumultuous applause as the family riders took their bows and the grooms trotted their horses back to the stables.

In 1920, the Hannefords left the circus to play vaudeville dates. They were among the feature attractions for a number of years in the major spectacles at New York's Hippodrome. When they returned to the circus, it was to Sells-Floto, where they were paid $1,250 a week. It was said to be the largest sum paid to an act in the circus business; still, members of large acts could often make more by splitting up and going to work as singles and doubles on the stage, in films, or even with other circuses.

Elizabeth Hanneford married Ernest Clarke, the first male flier to accomplish the triple back somersault from the flying trapeze to the hands of the catcher. It was more than a marriage: it was an alliance of two of the greatest circus families.

Poodles married Grace White, a circus performer from Brooklyn who had a bicycle and roller-skating act in the Barnum & Bailey Circus. His mother stayed with him to serve as ringmistress, but George, and George's wife, Katherine Breen Hanneford, left to form their own act.

The George Hanneford Riding Act continued to play circus and vaudeville and eventually returned to the Ringling show for a season.

Poodles went to Hollywood to make two-reel comedies. The career of Roscoe (Fatty) Arbuckle, one of the most popular slapstick comedians in silent films, had been ended abruptly by a scandalous manslaughter case concerning a girl who had died following a party in Arbuckle's hotel suite. Arbuckle was cleared by the courts, but the public no longer wanted to see him in films. So Arbuckle hired Poodles to appear under his direction. Poodles returned to the circus but made films throughout his career. Part of his act can be seen in a movie that Shirley Temple made in 1935 called *Our Little Girl*.

Elizabeth and Ernie Clarke had a daughter, Ernestine Clarke, who became a riding and trapeze star of the Ringling Bros. and Barnum & Bailey Circus in the 1940s.

Poodles and Grace had a daughter, Gracie, who became a bareback rider. Poodles spent his last years at Frontier Town in North Hudson, New York, a place designed to acquaint today's children with early American ways. He died at his family home in Glens Falls, New York, in 1967. His wife and daughter stayed on, Grace running the weaving shop, Gracie crafting pottery and presenting her performing dog act.

George and Katherine Breen Hanneford had three children. When the children became old enough, George decided to form a new act based on the original act that he had performed with his brother and sister. It debuted in 1945 and success repeated itself. But so did breaking up. George Jr. and Kay Frances each left to form their own acts. Tommy and his wife stayed with their parents to continue the original George Hanneford Family Riding Act.

George Sr. died in 1962. His wife, Katherine, continued to tour with Tommy, serving as the ringmistress for the riding act.

By 1975, Tommy Hanneford, who inherited the "Riding Fool" mantle of his uncle Poodles, had formed his own circus, the Royal Hanne-

POODLES HANNEFORD. *He holds the oldest circus record still standing—twenty-six running leaps on and off horseback, set in 1915. That was the year that the Hanneford riding family, which dates back in circus history at least to England's Wombwell Menagerie of the 1820s, came to the United States. Edwin "Poodles" Hanneford (1891–1967) performed a version of the most popular equestrian act in American history, in which a clown disguised as a drunken spectator tries to ride a horse bareback. Joe Pentland (1816–1873) did it disguised as a drunken sailor. Dan Rice (1823–1901) transformed the sailor into a backwoodsman he called Pete Jenkins from Mud Corners in the act that delighted the young Mark Twain and, consequently, Huckleberry Finn. Clad in a full-length coonskin coat and carrying a huge walking stick, pretending to be falling-down drunk, Poodles would stagger into the ring, climb clumsily onto a horse, ride backward, take terrible falls, sometimes hold on to the horse's tail to stay connected, and dive back on (and fall back off) the horse as he gradually shed a series of coats and pants. Wonder of wonders, he would eventually emerge in tights to give an unparalleled riding performance. Often the rest of the Hanneford Riding Troupe would be standing comfortably on the back of the same horse. Poodles was most famous for stepping off the back of a horse as if he were an animated cartoon character—Disney's Goofy in "Clock Cleaners," say—giving the impression of being momentarily suspended in midair. (Ringling Museum)*

ford Circus, and was playing Canada with it. His brother, George Jr., had a small, one-ring circus under canvas and was touring the United States with the Deggeller Carnival. And their sister, Kay Frances Hanneford, was performing with Clyde Beatty–Cole Bros. Circus, where I caught her act in 1975 at the Liberty Bell Park circus lot outside Philadelphia. Because she was married to Jimmy Ille, then the musical director of Beatty-Cole, her act, not surprisingly, was a marvel of equestrienne skill synchronized with circus music.

I can see Kay Frances Hanneford now, galloping in a circle while standing on her horse's back, just as Philip Astley and Thomas Pool and John Bill Ricketts—and her great-grandfather, Edwin Hanneford II, used to do—but Kay Frances added little ballet kicks, and the band played "Over My Shoulder," from the old Hanneford Family Act.

Equestrienne acts can be divided into three main groups. There is high-school, a spectacular form of dressage, in which a horse is trained to execute all the standard steps of the Spanish riding school; *voltige*, in which a rider vaults on and off a horse's back; and trick riding, in which the rider spends more time turning somersaults, dancing pirouettes, and balancing on a horse's back. The most spectacular part of Kay Frances Hanneford's act that year was a trick riding exhibition, in which she skipped a hoop while standing on the back of a running horse.

Kay Frances Hanneford said that she was the only woman other than May Wirth, her mentor, to do the "back across," somersaulting from one galloping horse to another; but by 1975, no woman was doing it, because May Wirth had retired and Kay Hanneford, at forty-one, had considered herself too old for that trick for about six years.

She introduced me to her five-year-old daughter Nellie and told me that Nellie had made her debut two years earlier in Houston, Texas, doing a running jump onto the back of a horse with her two cousins, Cathy, then eight, and Georgie, then four, daughter and son of her uncle, George Hanneford, Jr.

"My cousin Georgie was so little he could hardly walk," said Nellie, "so Uncle George, he'd throw little Georgie up last. Then Uncle George jumped up and he used to jump on my leg all the time and hurt my leg."

Like a true Hanneford, she said this cheerfully.

Tommy had married Gertrude Zimmerman, called Struppi, who, growing up in Germany during and just after World War II, lost her father and suffered the hardships of a dislocated society. To help support her family, Struppi joined an act called the Luva Sisters, who performed on the trapeze for American soldiers. In 1953, an American circus owner brought them to the United States, where they appeared on "The Ed Sullivan Show" and the Super Circus.

In 1975, when Tommy Hanneford formed his own circus, Struppi did her single trapeze act, billed as Tajana. Then she took up and mastered the high wire, and later developed a trained tiger act.

In 1979, Nellie Hanneford, now nine years old, was working in her uncle Tommy's Royal Hanneford Circus, presenting her dancing pony and a boxer dog act, and working in the elephant act and, of course, the riding act. Tommy told me that Kay Frances had died of cancer in New Orleans a few seasons before and that Nellie now lived and traveled with him, her aunt Struppi, and her grandmother. She was enrolled in a professional children's correspondence school, and Elaina Slonin, a showgirl from a Long Island suburban family, was acting as her tutor, so she spent a good part of each day on her schoolwork. But being Hannefords, they were not neglecting her riding.

I had written, back in 1975, "Nellie can now stand on a moving horse, which makes her a member of the *fifth* generation of bareback riders in the Hanneford Family. ('And I ride elephants,' she adds.) I saw Kay Frances Hanneford the year that she joined the family act, when we were both eleven, and I am looking forward to seeing her daughter ride in a show. To see a Hanneford ride is to feel the whole history of the modern circus."

That day in 1979, I saw Nellie Hanneford ride at the age of nine, and I saw her grandmother, Katherine Breen Hanneford, perform as ringmistress at the age of ninety, and I came away feeling that I knew something about continuity in the circus.

Katherine Hanneford, matriarch of the Royal Hanneford Circus, died on October 22, 1985, after a stroke suffered while performing in the ring in Charlotte, North Carolina. Joseph Theodore Clown, a fellow performer, said, "Before she went to the hospital she told everybody to go on with the show." She was ninety-six years old.

The Return of Barnumesque Ballyhoo

"From the haunting shadows of the Himalayas comes a beast that will pierce the very fabric of your imagination!" intones a stentorian voice on the TV set.

Whispers are heard: "TUSK!"

Stentorian tones again: "The world's largest living land mammal!"

Louder whispers: "KING TUSK!"

The stentorian voice is positively awestruck: "Not since the Mighty Jumbo has a creature so awesome stalked the earth!"

Loudest whispers: "THE COLOSSAL KING TUSK!"

All the while, through the mists of our home screens, we have been glimpsing giant tusks, mighty legs with mammoth toenails, an eye, a trunk, an Asian ear—in a mini-epic of sound and color hype that makes a big elephant look like a cross between the Loch Ness Monster,

the Creature from the Black Lagoon, and the last parade of the British Raj in India.

There follows the sound of an elephant trumpeting wildly, then that voice again: "See King Tusk and seventeen acts never seen in America, plus the greatest wild animal trainer of all time. . . ." His name isn't mentioned, but at this moment, Gunther Gebel-Williams appears on the screen, walking insouciantly with a leopard draped around his neck. ". . . AT RINGLING BROS. AND BARNUM & BAILEY CIRCUS."

In three recent seasons, a combination of commercials and news coverage has helped make media events of King Tusk, the Shanghai Acrobats, and, most especially, the Living Unicorn. As the circus enters its third century, television has brought about the comeback of Barnumesque ballyhoo.

Once upon a time, Americans confidently

KING TUSK. Kenneth Feld sits on the giant tusks of "the largest living land mammal." That may be true; in any case, King Tusk is much more massive than Jumbo (billed as "the largest brute on earth" in the 1880s). Barnum's elephant was thirteen feet four, however, much taller than twelve-foot-six King Tusk. So the pachyderm puts his best feature forward: those tusks are six feet six and seven feet long. (Ringling Bros. and Barnum & Bailey Circus)

expected to be astonished every spring. They knew that, drab as reality might sometimes seem, P. T. Barnum and his rivals were on the job. And, sure enough, just about the time that the crocuses peeped through the snow and the voice of the cuckoo was heard in Central Park, the circus that Barnum called "The Greatest Show on Earth" would bring marvels, wonders, prodigies, sensations, and "gadzooks!"-inspiring gazingstocks before the hard-to-dazzle eyes in seen-it-all Madison Square Garden—and then transport these numinous nonpareils the length and breadth of the United States. Barnum & Bailey press agents and billposters would spread the word, and all the other circuses would compete to out-Barnum Barnum by somehow bringing their circuses more prominently to public notice.

This history has also been a compendium of the ways of ballyhoo, from the 1786 handbill that announced "Mr. Pool, the first American that ever Exhibited the following FEATS OF HORSEMANSHIP On the Continent . . ." plus the clown who would join Mr. Pool to "entertain the Ladies and Gentlemen between the Feats," to Barnum's barkers, broadsides, billboards, couriers, handbills, and newspaper squibs proclaiming the biggest and best of them all.

So the circus, which is already credited with the development of the outdoor advertising business, has finally begun using its vast experience to produce what should be called "moving circus posters" for television. As early as 1833, huge, colorful, but unmoving posters that measured seven or eight feet in length were cheaply printed and widely distributed. These posters might incorporate woodcuts representing the ferociousness of the lion or remarkable feats on the tightrope.

By midcentury, urban firms such as The Courier Co. in New York produced lithographs of circus scenes that are now social documents,

providing details of early circus performers and audiences as well as styles of dress, interiors of theaters and concert halls, and outdoor scenes of urban and rural America.

In the 1870s, advance cars carried billposters who would paste colored lithographs on the sides of sheds, fences, and barns. They traveled thousands of miles and posted hundreds of thousands of lithograph sheets with a paste made of flour and water cooked together with steam heat in the paste room of the advance car as it streaked through the night. (Lockers or "possum bellies" under the car carried the ladders and brush handles.)

In 1882, when Jumbo arrived in New York City aboard the *Assyrian Monarch*, Barnum had the Strobridge Lithograph Co. create a "welcoming poster" showing Jumbo stopping on his walk up Broadway so that a lady in a third-floor window could feed him peanuts. Thus inspired by wonder and delight, thousands of New Yorkers joined Barnum in meeting Jumbo at the boat and parading with the big elephant up Broadway to Madison Square Garden, where the circus was playing. There is no record that any third-floor lady was actually able to feed him peanuts, but Barnum later told a reporter that in six weeks Jumbo had attracted $336,000 to the circus.

That poster was the fulfillment of Barnum's dream of advertisements that could be seen by millions.

In the late nineteenth century, as competition for space forced advertisers to construct their own structures for displays, billboards largely replaced bills posted on walls and fences. With the development of the automobile and the improvement of highway systems, these large, freestanding panels increased in popularity as an advertising medium with high-volume exposure. About 1915, Strobridge paid the great animal artist, Charles Livingston Bull, the then-munificent sum of

$1,500 to paint the lunging tiger that once adorned billing stands all over the country.

But even Barnum didn't dream of a box that could ballyhoo the circus in every dwelling in the nation.

The age of TV ballyhoo began with a basic insight by Irvin Feld. Feld believed that seeing a picture of a wild animal trainer or an elephant or a clown—even a moving picture in color with sound—makes an audience only more anxious to see a real wild animal trainer, elephant, or clown. This was a direct contradiction of the then-prevailing wisdom.

The old theory that audiences wouldn't go to the circus to see a performer they could see on a screen had its greatest proponent in Samuel Gumpertz, who, when he took control of Ringling Bros. and Barnum & Bailey Circus, forbade his wild animal trainer, Clyde Beatty, to appear in any more films. The great Beatty, always a formidable box office attraction, later gave this as one of his main reasons for quitting The Greatest Show on Earth.

When television replaced the movies as the most popular form of mass entertainment, circus impresarios at first regarded it as even more threatening than the movies. Millions of Americans stayed home for more of their entertainment. Thus, television seemed to be playing a major role in the decline of circusgoing. John Ringling North listed competition from television as one of the major reasons for the demise of the tented circus. Attendance at live circuses kept falling.

But Irvin Feld knew, from his days as a rock promoter, that numerous appearances of, say, Elvis Presley or the Beatles on television only increased the public's desire to see Elvis or the Beatles live. What worked for the Beatles and rock concerts, Feld reasoned, would work for Gunther Gebel-Williams and circuses.

Television was only a flat, two-dimensional representation of a three-dimensional wonder; the sounds and colors were at best an approximation of the real thing, and there could be no appeal at all to the senses of touch and smell. Still, television could suggest the wonders of the circus even better than the best circus posters did, because it had sound and movement.

Beginning in 1970, Feld put highlights of each new edition of Ringling Bros. and Barnum & Bailey Circus on television as part of the Bell System Family Theatre, sponsored by AT&T, with hosts ranging from Richard Thomas to Bill Cosby. In addition, before and during the engagements in each city, Ringling Bros. aired commercials that gave quick previews of the show. And the circus publicists became masters at dreaming up ways to involve television news programs, inviting TV reporters to ride an elephant from the newly arrived circus train to the amphitheater, or to audition as a clown or a circus showgirl. Ringling Bros. circus performers were also made available for television talk shows, in full regalia.

In 1977, as part of Feld's ongoing campaign to make television work for the circus rather than compete with it, Gunther Gebel-Williams became the first circus performer in history to headline his own television special. And, indeed, growing attendance figures showed that Gunther's television special only whetted the big audience's appetite for seeing the celebrity live, life-size, and in person.

Gunther Gebel-Williams had, in fact, become a contemporary circus legend. "Do you know me?" he asked, staring out of an American Express television commercial that year, a leopard named Kenny (after Irvin Feld's son and coproducer) draped around his neck. "When I travel with my cats, people recognize me . . . but without them, they don't. So I carry the American Express Card." That image would henceforth identify him as quickly as the pistol, whip, and upturned chair identified Clyde Beatty forty years before.

As it entered its second century, Ringling Bros. and Barnum & Bailey was making the claim that it had played to more Americans than any other show in history; but through television it touched a larger audience than had seen all the live circuses that ever played since the circus began.

In 1985, the year after his father's death, Kenneth Feld, now the sole producer of The Greatest Show on Earth, presented the Living Unicorn—and the adroitly enflamed controversy over whether it was a real unicorn or a goat whose horns had been tampered with made it the most successful case of circus hoopla since The Greatest Show on Earth promoted a bad-tempered, scar-faced gorilla cleverly named Gargantua into a *Life* magazine Cover Primate in 1938.

When the circus came to town in 1985, it was preceded by television spots showing a creature it called "The Living Unicorn." Then the media revealed that there were actually four "living unicorns." Then the American Society for the Prevention of Cruelty to Animals stepped in, charging that the four "unicorns" were really horn-altered goats.

Investigations, well covered by the media, were begun on several fronts by state and federal agencies. Sidney H. Schanberg of the *New York Times* devoted his column to "The Great Circus Hornswoggle," reporting that "the Food and Drug Administration examined the creatures and, with the city frozen in suspense, proclaimed that they were goats. But, the F.D.A. said, 'there is nothing wrong with the goats. We found them to be in good health and very well taken care of.' Meanwhile, inflamed by the headlines, circus attendance soared. Circus officials adopted a look of hurt innocence and said they were astonished at the old meanies who would try to take the fantastical out of life and rob little children out of their dreams."

"Well, old P. T. Barnum sure would've loved it," said Charles Osgood, anchor of "The CBS Early Morning News"—and the debate continued to rage on the Johnny Carson show and all three network news shows.

It took New York's Mayor Edward Koch to get, in Schanberg's words, "the fantasy vote and the humane vote in one swoop." Koch said that he believed in unicorns but that belief "doesn't mean that they exist. Unicorns are just a part of fantasy that every child has had at some point or the other." On the other hand, he added, "if it develops that the animals have been tortured or ill-treated, then obviously action should be taken to prevent that."

Barnumesque ballyhoo was indeed back. Not content with all this free publicity, these same circus officials—whom many suspected of calling the ASPCA in the first place—paid a lot of money for a full-page ad in the *New York Times*. The heading said: "Children of all ages believe in Santa Claus, Peter Pan, the Wizard of Oz, and the fabled Unicorn. DON'T LET THE GRINCHES STEAL THE FANTASY."

The grinches, meanwhile, were persisting. The State Consumer Protection Board called on the circus to cease and desist its unicorn advertising. Kenneth Feld reported that *unicorn* (from the Latin, *unus*, "one" and *cornu*, "horn") means "one-horned" and that these beasts indubitably had one horn.

"ABC World News Tonight" accepted the circus's defense in an ode to the unicorn recited by Steven Geer: "A boycott is needed, claimed the SPCA, / till the truth is revealed, let the crowd stay away, / 'Ah ha,' said the circus, 'you can't get our goat, / it's this kind of hype keeps old Barnum afloat.'"

Old Barnum would have loved the bottom lines, too: attendance during the two-month New York engagement rose by 55 percent.

(The "unicorns" were in fact Angora goats bred in northern California and sold to the circus by their naturalist owners. Shortly after birth—in a procedure said to be painless—each kid's horn buds were surgically moved to the center of his forehead and fused, so that a central, single horn would grow. These one-horned creatures had already appeared at San Francisco's annual Renaissance Fair without creating any controversy at all. It took Barnumesque ballyhoo to do that.)

The 1986 edition of the Ringling show could not top the Living Unicorn, but it did handle the Shanghai Acrobatic Troupe much as Barnum promoted his circus's rare and exotic people. ("Direct From the People's Republic of China! By Special Arrangement! First time ever!") Ringling publicists made sure that the acrobats' days off became photo opportunities for the press to see Chinese communists watching the Yankees play baseball, visiting the Liberty Bell and Constitution Hall in Philadelphia, Colonial Williamsburg in Virginia, a Hollywood film studio in Los Angeles, America's largest Chinatown in San Francisco, and their very own giant pandas, Hsing-Hsing and Ling-Ling, at the Washington National Zoo.

The bottom line again: When Irvin Feld died in 1984, yearly attendance at the circus was 8.5 million people. In 1986, with the Living Unicorn in its second year with the Blue Unit and the Shanghai Acrobats in their first year with the Red Unit, attendance had risen to 11.8 million.

In 1987, Kenneth Feld took the circus into the VCR era by selling videocassettes of the highlights of the show that had just concluded its two-year run.

Bringing acrobats from China was very much in the tradition of Barnum, who, sharing the public's curiosity about the world outside the United States, made great efforts to get the permission of King Theebaw of Siam to exhibit the sacred white elephant in 1884. Therefore, soon after the United States and the People's Republic resumed diplomatic relations in the

early 1970s, Irvin and Kenneth Feld began negotiating to bring some of its artists to America. "The People's Republic had never before allowed their acrobats to perform in a show with other acts," said Kenneth Feld. "Nor had the performers ever been permitted to stay on foreign tour so long."

From the standpoint of circus skills, of course, the acrobats were much more important than the unicorns. Kenneth Feld persevered in overcoming all the obstacles because acrobatics, a primary ingredient of any circus, reached one of its earliest and finest flowerings in ancient China. Indeed, the tradition of acrobatics in China can be traced as far back as 200 B.C., when the Han Dynasty emerged as the vast kingdom often called "the Roman Empire of the East." According to the great historian of the first century B.C., Sima Qian, acrobatics were first developed by rural peasants in the Wuchao District in China's northern Heibei Province. To celebrate good harvests, weddings, and other occasions, farmers devised entertainments in which they took common household utensils or farm implements—tables or barrels or hoops, for example—and juggled them or tumbled with them or balanced themselves with them or on them.

When word of the astonishing acrobatics of the north reached the ears of the emperor, acrobats were summoned to perform at court and for visiting heads of state. Marco Polo described Chinese acrobatics when, near the end of the twelfth century A.D., he visited the court of Kublai Khan in the land that was then called Cathay: "When the repast was finished, persons of various descriptions entered the hall, and amongst them a troupe of comedians and performers on different musical instruments. Also tumblers and jugglers, who exhibit their skills in the presence of the Great Khan, to the amusement and gratification of all the spectators."

In those ancient times, the best of the acrobats were permitted by the emperor to abandon farming and spend full time perfecting their skills. Similarly, the People's Republic of China today supports about 300 acrobatic troupes. The Shanghai Acrobatic Troupe, which today numbers about 350 members, including performing artists, technicians, and staff, was founded in 1951 by the Shanghai Municipal Bureau of Culture to preserve and promote the traditional acrobatic arts. To get into its special school, superior students from eight to ten years of age are nominated by gymnastic schools throughout the province. For those accepted, the first two years emphasize fundamental tumbling skills, dancing, flexibility, and strength conditioning. Typically, the school day runs eight hours, six days a week. Mornings are generally devoted to acrobatic training; afternoons to academic subjects. "We are not interested," said a faculty member, "in people with empty minds."

Not until the age of fifteen or sixteen does the acrobat appear in performance with the troupe for the first time. Those who make it through the rigors of training are assured of a job with a regular salary, medical care, and a pension upon retirement.

The result? Young Chinese acrobats of the 1980s dived back and forth through hoops mounted three high on a cart as if they were flying. Jiang Zhengping and Li Yueyun shaped themselves into a "Pagoda of Bowls" by performing pretzel-like contortions while balancing, on their heads and hands and feet, stacks of ordinary bowls. Liu Peili and Xin Xiaoping performed the Celestial Mural Contortion Act in which, through contortion and oriental dance, they imitate the drawings on the ancient walls of the Dun Huang Cave in the Gansu Province of China, depicting people's imaginings of the movements of fairies in paradise. And a "Barrel Plunger" named Zhang Lianhui

walked on his hands with his rear end seemingly stuck in a red barrel and his legs sticking out, then passed through and in and out of the barrel like a turtle that could play with its own shell. (To do this, Zhang Lianhui bends his five-foot-seven-and-one-half-inch body to fit within the confines of a barrel that measures fourteen inches in diameter and is twenty-eight inches tall.)

Perhaps the highlight was "The Lion Dance," the most traditional entertainment, as performed by Lu Lei and six male acrobats. The two acrobats who create the illusion of each lion are trained blindfolded, since the acrobat who forms the rear of the lion cannot see anything while performing. To see an acrobat in human costume standing on two acrobats costumed as a red-maned lion, while that "lion" rolls on a big red ball up a teeter-totter—and then inevitably down the teeter-totter—is to see one of the greatest marvels of balance that the circus has ever presented.

I had a dizzying realization that the entire two-hundred-year history of the circus in the United States was only one-eleventh of the time represented by this acrobatic tradition.

But the 1986 edition of The Greatest Show on Earth was also probably the most successful in circus history in combining acts from faraway places and long-ago times. There were acts from ten other countries besides China, including Morocco (The Ali Hassani Troupe of tumblers), Spain (The Quiros Troupe, high-wire walkers), Mexico (The Flying Vazquez trapeze act), France (Daniel Suskow, who trained bison, camels, horses, and zebras to perform together in the same exotic animal act), Poland (Captain Christopher and Commander Henryk, who were fired consecutively from the Ringling Repeating Rocket), the Netherlands (The Peters Brothers, who walked the Wheel of Destiny—a more optimistic renaming of Elvin Bale's old Wheel of

Doom), Bulgaria (The Lilov Bears), Hungary (The Raskis, equestrians), Sweden (Axel Gautier, head of the Gautier family of elephant trainers), and the USA (most spectacularly The King Charles Troupe, which now added to its basketball playing on unicycles the American black folk art of jumprope double-dutching adapted to the unicycle, and Wade Burck and his white Burmese tigers, an endangered species of which these nine examples are insured by Lloyds of London for $150,000 apiece). The theme of the television spots: "We Bring You the World!"

Then, the Red Unit's 1987 edition presented "King Tusk—the Largest Land Mammal on the Face of the Earth." Circus publicists shrewdly ignored the fact that, at twelve feet six, Feld's Asian elephant is ten inches shorter than Barnum's thirteen-foot-four African. They concentrate instead on the undeniable fact that King Tusk's twenty-seven-foot girth and weight of 14,762 pounds make Feld's elephant much more massive than Barnum's. (Jumbo weighed only 13,000 pounds, which Barnum always called "six and one-half tons.") And then there are those tusks: one, six foot six; the other seven feet long. Jumbo was tall but not tusky.

The selling of King Tusk amounted to a new encyclopedia of circus hype. There had, for instance, long been the "good housekeeping" angle. The private railroad car that Jumbo shared with a baby elephant named Tom Thumb was itself one of the curiosities of the 1880s. In 1938, when air-conditioning was new, magazine and newspaper readers knew that Gargantua traveled in a "jungle-conditioned" private railroad car. So King Tusk would travel in a "Royal Coach—a 45 foot custom tractor trailer with appointments fit for royalty, complete with awning to shade the mastodonic mammal while he is not performing."

The "gourmet" angle was older than Jumbo. In 1797, the Philadelphian named Owne who exhibited the elephant he bought from Captain Crowninshield printed up handbills describing the beast's drinking habit ("Some days he has drank 30 Bottles of Porter, drawing the Corks with his Trunk"). Jumbo, according to *Leslie's Illustrated News*, drank five buckets of water a day and an occasional bottle of whiskey. (He could take down a quart in one gulp with no apparent effect.) In addition, Jumbo's daily fare consisted of:

Hay	200 pounds
Onions	Three Quarts
Biscuits	Two Bushels
Oats	Two Bushels
Bread	Three Loaves

Also uncounted apples, oranges, figs, nuts, cakes and candies.

By 1928, the nation's press was enthusiastically helping the circus disseminate the information that Goliath, old John Ringling's three-and-a-quarter-ton sea elephant, ate 150 pounds of fish every day. So the promoters of King Tusk carefully measured their big elephant's daily food consumption:

Hay	300 lbs.
Carrots	50 lbs.
Apples	50 lbs.
Grain	25 lbs.
Water	100 gallons

But no liquor or sweets.

And King Tusk has something that neither Gargantua nor Goliath had; *that not even Jumbo had!* The "esquire" angle: CLOTHES!

Ballyhoo got the media to report that King Tusk wore a gilded robe weighing 1,200 pounds that required twelve attendants to carry its train adorned with thousands of gold and purple sequins, brass studs, gold and silver mirrors, and gold cording. He was described as "a pachyderm Liberace."

Perhaps the most amazing thing about King Tusk is that no one paid any particular attention to him when he was almost as large but was prosaically called Tommy and was appearing practically without ballyhoo on several of America's smaller circuses. "I was the first girl to do any mounts on his tusk," said the veteran leopard and elephant lady Barbara Woodcock, who "worked with Tommy in '47 on Dailey Bros., and again on Diano Bros. Circus in '53. Those tusks were good sized when he was a punk, but when they really started to grow, I used to think that one day they would be too broad to go on a railway car. Well, it's happened—he has to have a specially built car."

In his first three years as president of The Greatest Show on Earth, Kenneth Feld took a goat with an altered horn that had caused little excitement in the Renaissance Fair in San Francisco and a big elephant called Tommy that had been lumbering around hippodrome tracks for years, and promoted them, largely through the skillful use of television, into those mythological marvels, the Living Unicorn and King Tusk! It is an old technique, ballyhoo, in the selling of the circus in America, but the Ringling Bros. and Barnum & Bailey Circus under Kenneth Feld has already given it two new twists.

———————◆———————

One of the most important new developments in the circus in the 1980s was the rise of New York City's traveling Big Apple Circus. The Big Apple not only wove superior circus acts into a unified presentation, but through the brief but illuminating comments of its director and ringmaster, Paul Binder, it placed these acts in the continuity of circus tradition.

Here, for example, is Binder's explanation

of the 1987 edition, when the Big Apple saluted the world's carnivals—Mardi Gras in New Orleans; Carnival in Rio, Venice, and the Caribbean; and a Mexican Fiesta—so that the circus performers became again what most of them evolved from, street performers, going from festival to fair:

> Circus, when done right, has the capacity in its magic circle, to create a briefly intensified collective "life." Its roots are deep in the community rituals that evolved from spontaneous popular street fairs and marketplace festivals of the earliest known cultures. Those festivals—anarchic, antiauthoritarian, bawdy, and rowdy, survive today—the most prominent around the world takes place from Twelfth Night (remember "The Twelve Days of Christmas"?) until Ash Wednesday. They culminate on Mardi Gras—literally, "Fat Tuesday"—the day before Lent begins. Carnival, Fiesta, Fastelavn, Carnavale, Fasching, et al. . . . a worldwide phenomenon.
>
> The circus is the single theatrical force that most closely keeps faith with this original exuberant ritual: music, clowning, processions, animals, sexuality, joy, and most importantly, personal triumph over life's obstacles.

Binder also teaches audiences that nearly every act in a circus has its own tradition—and many of those traditions are very old and very complex. The tradition of the equestrian act, for example, can be traced to the very first circus, Astley's, in England, in 1768. "I have heard it said in six languages," said Binder, " 'The circus begins with horses.' Well, in fact, the modern circus is a direct descendant of the great horse shows of Europe of the eighteenth century. For example, the mixture of fine soil and sawdust in the ring is to protect the hooves of the great performing horses. Even the clothes I'm wearing are the costume of the great equestrian masters of those eighteenth-century shows": high black boots, white breeches, a red jacket trimmed with black velvet lapels and red vest, a frilly ruff white at his throat—and, of course, a golden whistle hung around his neck.

Binder's wife, Katja Schumann, is a fifth-generation circus equestrienne. The famous Schumann Dynasty goes back to 1844, when a saddlemaker named Gothold Schumann, from Weimar, Germany, started performing as a bareback rider. Gothold created the circus that bears his name in 1870. In 1891, his son Max established the Circus Schumann in Copenhagen, Denmark. Albert, his other son, became one of the great trainers of horses "at liberty" and directed the Circus of Berlin until 1915. Katja Schumann made her first appearance in the ring at the age of ten, as a ballerina on horseback, before becoming an outstanding high-school rider and one of the finest liberty horse trainers of her generation. She won the Gold Medal at the Circus World Championship in London in 1976, and the Prix de la Dame du Cirque at the International Circus Festival of Monte-Carlo in 1974. In 1981, she began performing with the Big Apple Circus, and she became a resident company member in 1983. She has since married Binder and they have, says their 1987 program, "started a new circus lineage with their daughter Katherine Rose."

"To me," wrote Honoré de Balzac in the nineteenth century, "the equestrienne in full possession of her skills is superior to all the stars of the ballet, the opera or the theatre, to a Cinte Damoreau or to a Jejazet, to a Taglioni or a Dorval." Indeed, the fascinating Marguerite Turquet, better known under the sobriquet of Malaga, who figures in four novels of Balzac's *Comédie Humaine*, is an equestrienne star of Balzac's imaginary circus, the Bouthor Traveling Hippodrome. It is this tradition that Katja Schumann and others are continuing in the late twentieth century.

Since 1827, no more than two dozen equestrians have presented a complete version of the dangerous and spectacular act called "The Courier of St. Petersburg." It was created by Andrew Ducrow (1793–1842), who is still considered the most creative trick rider in circus history, and it was first performed on May 7, 1827, at Astley's Circus in London, of which Ducrow had become the director. The act told the story of a courier riding from St. Petersburg to London, and Ducrow simultaneously rode five horses, each bearing on its back a flag of the country through which he was imagined to be riding. Ducrow considered the exercise so exhausting that he refused to perform it two nights in a row. Only three women have presented the act. The first and second were Milly Yelding-Huzarinas, in England, and Martine Gruss, in France. The third was Katja Schumann, at the Big Apple Circus in the United States, in 1985.

(It should be noted that Ducrow, according to his biographer, eventually increased the number of horses he could ride simultaneously to nine.)

In Europe, the one-ring circus has remained the most popular circus form, with an enduring appeal to sophisticates, from Balzac, Maxim Gorki, and Henri de Toulouse-Lautrec in the last century to Picasso, Thomas Mann, and Heinrich Böll in this, and it was the European-style circus that inspired Binder in 1977 to try to reintroduce the one-ring circus to New York.

Binder graduated from Dartmouth College, earned an MBA at Columbia University, and headed to San Francisco—to be a juggler. There he met Michael Christensen, a street clown, and before long they were traveling through Europe, earning their living as street entertainers. They were soon elevated, however, to the stage of France's Casino de Paris, and it was here that they were discovered by Annie Fratellini, a daughter of Europe's most famous family of clowns. She invited them to join her Nouveau Cirque de Paris.

Binder returned to New York two years later with a dream: "I would create an American one-ring circus with the same dedication to theatrical quality and artistic intimacy that I had experienced in Europe."

In 1977, the Big Apple Circus was born. Then, as now, Binder is its core—founder, artistic director, and ringmaster—and he knows precisely why he prefers the one-ring format: "Your appreciation of the circus is heightened because of the intimacy," he says. "You see clearly how difficult and dangerous it is because it's not happening a quarter-mile away, like in those big circus extravaganzas, and your attention is not divided among three rings. You can focus on the performers in their power and in their frailty. You can see the sweat and straining muscles. And you can clearly see the grace and beauty of a perfectly executed trick."

A case in point is the performance of the Carrillo Brothers, from Colombia, South America, an act that was brought to the United States in 1975 by Ringling Bros. and Barnum & Bailey Circus, and was a great success in the three-ring format for ten years. Nonetheless, in a one-ring setting, more can see them better.

As the strings play tremulously, Luis Posso blindfolds Pedro Carrillo as they stand on the pedestal, then Pedro picks up the balancing bar with his left and right hands while simultaneously lifting a chair with the fingers of his left hand as he steps out on the wire. As Pedro carefully sets the chair on the wire, the trumpet plays slowly and passionately, as if to give Carrillo courage with a transfusion of Spanish bullfight music. Reaching out cautiously with his white-slippered foot, and holding the bar with a delicate balance, Pedro climbs up on the chair

that sits precariously on the wire . . . slowly stands up on the chair on the wire . . . raises the bar over his head . . . and the chair wobbles and wobbles on the high, thin wire. Pedro sits down tentatively on the back of the chair, then puts his feet warily on the lower rungs of the chair, then sits down alertly on the seat, then prudently takes off his blindfold, then triumphantly stands up, then unhurriedly lifts the chair off the wire with his left hand, while still holding the bar with both hands, then breathing easier but still vigilant, walks backward on the wire to the platform . . . while the trumpet and the audience scream in unison.

To give the background for another Carrillo Brothers trick, the Big Apple Circus tells the story of a German wire walker named Kotler:

> In 1818, an English wire walker, Jack Barred, entertained the kings of Europe gathered at Aix-la-Chapelle in Germany. Jealous, the State Minister Hardenberg asked for the German wire walker Kotler to compete with the Englishman on the same high wire. When the two acrobats eventually found themselves facing each other in the middle of the wire, neither agreed to step back. Kotler solved the problem by jumping over Barred. Circus legend? Impossible? Watch the Carrillo Brothers. . . .

And Pedro Carrillo leaps over Luis Possa and lands on the thin steel strand.

The tradition of circus acrobatics goes back to 1770, when Philip Astley hired acrobats, jugglers, and wire walkers from London's Sadler's Wells Theatre to perform in his equestrian show. At this time, explains Dominique Jando, associate director of the Big Apple Circus, there were two sorts of theaters in Europe: "Patent theaters were granted the right to perform plays with dialogue; others, such as London's Sadler's Wells and Paris's Theatre de Nicolet, had no such privilege. They relied on

THE LIVING UNICORN (with Tina Gebel). It was the biggest brouhaha over a circus attraction since P. T. Barnum bought a sacred white elephant from King Theebaw of Siam, brought it to America, and faced widespread disappointment as the slate-gray elephant proved fodder for his chief competitor, Adam Forepaugh. Similarly, scoffers tried to get Kenneth Feld's goat, but he prevailed, pointing out with a smile that unicorn, from the Latin, means "one-horned" and that these well-kept creatures indubitably had one horn. Barnum would have loved the bottom line, too: attendance during the two-month New York engagement of Ringling Bros. and Barnum & Bailey rose by 55 percent. (Ringling Bros. and Barnum & Bailey Circus)

"WE BRING YOU THE WORLD" was the ballyhoo on the 116th edition of Ringling Bros. and Barnum & Bailey Circus in 1986. There were acts from Morocco, France, Sweden, Mexico, Spain, the Netherlands, Bulgaria, Hungary, Poland, the United States, and China, which sent the Shanghai Acrobatic Troupe. "When President Nixon opened the door to the People's Republic of China in 1972, I began a campaign to bring performers to The Greatest Show on Earth," said Kenneth Feld. "It took fourteen years." (Ringling Bros. and Barnum & Bailey Circus)

TAHAR. *Also in the 116th edition was a group of classic Moroccan tumblers, the Ali Hassani Troupe. Feld was so impressed by the strongman who held up the others that he asked if he would like to learn to be the star of his own act— wrestling alligators. True to the traditions of circus ambition, Tahar didn't blanch. Feld hired a Seminole Indian wise in swamp ways to catch the alligators and teach Tahar how to handle them. The result was an act in which Tahar not only messes with six alligators, but throws one into a tank of water and jumps in after him for an underwater wrestle.* (Ringling Bros. and Barnum & Bailey Circus)

OVER THE GARDEN WALL *(opposite, bottom). That's what elephant men call this trick, says Buckles Woodcock, shown here with the Big Apple Circus in New York City in 1983. "One elephant lays down and the other elephants just crawl over the top of him. My dad saw this many years ago, and he named it, but in the version Dad saw, after the standing elephants crawl over the one that is lying down, they just go about their business. In this version, we have our elephant Toto sitting on the head of our elephant Peggy with my daughter, Dalilah, sitting on Toto and my son, Shannon, standing on Peggy's side; then we have my wife, Barbara, standing in front of Peggy; and our elephant, Mac, with his right leg on Peggy's rump." When this picture was taken, Shannon was fourteen and Dalilah was eleven. When you see how close the children in the front row are to the Big Apple Circus's single ring, you get a good idea of the intimacy of a one-ring circus, as opposed to the spectacle and grandeur of a three-ring circus. In 1988, Dalilah, then almost seventeen, did a handstand on Toto's forehead while Toto stood on his right front leg, a feat I hadn't seen since Mac and Peggy MacDonald presented Baby Opal on Polack Bros. Circus in 1960.* (Buckles Woodcock)

CIRQUE DU SOLEIL ("Circus of the Sun"), created as part of Canada's 450th anniversary celebration, is an illustration of the basic definition of a circus: feats of human skill and daring performed in, above, and around a ring, counterpointed by the buffoonery of the clown. There are no animals in this Montreal-based circus; there is just one ring inside the blue-and-yellow tent that seats 1,756 spectators. But there are thirty-two acrobats, aerialists, trick bicyclists, teeterboard flippers, jugglers, and clowns, including one of the best clowns of the twentieth century, rubber-faced Denis Lacombe. In five color pages on "The Sight Fantastic," Life said: "Steve Martin, who knows all about being funny, declared master clown Denis Lacombe a genius. . . . 'What is really special about the Cirque,' says Lacombe, who idolizes Buster Keaton and Disney's Donald Duck and Goofy, 'is that we went back to the roots of the circus 200 years ago and brought it into the 1980s.'" (Cirque du Soleil)

FAREWELL TOUR. *On December 27, 1988, in Venice, Florida, Gunther Gebel-Williams began his two-year farewell tour with Ringling Bros. and Barnum & Bailey Circus. His twenty years with The Greatest Show on Earth constitute the most amazing twentieth-century chapter in the saga of the American circus. In Europe, he has been awarded the Ernst Renke-Plaskett Award, the European circus world's highest honor, an unprecedented three times: for his outstanding horsemanship, for his elephant act, and as an outstanding all-around circus performer. In the United States, circus aficionados have found him, as essayist Edward Hoagland wrote, "the Nureyev of show business . . . a Circus by himself." (Ringling Bros. and Barnum & Bailey Circus)*

pantomime, wire walking and acrobats. . . . In the 1970s a movement started in Europe which aimed to bring back to the circus performance its characteristic poetry and theatricality."

One sees the poetry and theatricality of the presentation when Binder has the performers arrive in the ring in an authentic Irish gypsy wagon such as the first circus performers lived and traveled in during the late eighteenth and early nineteenth centuries. The performers descend from the wagon into morning mists created by new circus special-effects machines, wearing eighteenth-century costumes for the prologue to a presentation of "The Courier."

The tradition of comedy acrobatics, says Binder, goes back in Europe to Saunders and Fortunelly, the first clowns in circus history, who were acrobats as well as clowns. "For many decades, comedy and acrobatics went along well together," said Binder, "but at the turn of the century, gentleman circusgoers discovered the virtues of gymnastics and sport, and their exclusive interest for horsemanship faded away. Acrobatics became a serious matter, and clowns were asked politely to do something else. However, the tradition of comedy acrobatics remained in small circus families, where it is still possible to see the 'table rock' routine being performed."

On the Big Apple Circus, the tradition has been carried on by Jim Tinsman, a 1975 graduate of the Ringling Bros. and Barnum & Bailey Circus Clown College, who has developed into an acrobat in that old tradition. Tinsman joined the Big Apple Circus in 1981 to perform in a unicycling act with the Bertini Family. He has since created a new acrobatic act nearly every year, either as a solo performer or with his wife, Tisha, a former Ringling showgirl turned acrobat.

In clowning, the Big Apple returns to the tradition of the talking clown. "In the American One-Ring Circus era, when clowns were still able to speak and establish a relationship with their audience, Dan Rice became such a star that his weekly salary was twice that of President Lincoln," says the program.

The Big Apple clowns are Michael Christensen as Mr. Stubs, Jeff Gordon as Gordoon, and Barry Lubin as Grandma. Christensen and Gordon banter with Ringmaster Binder exactly as clowns teased ringmasters when George Washington went to the circus. Lubin, however, is mute. He is also a graduate of the Ringling clown school, where he and his friend Tinsman developed a routine in which Tinsman was a ventriloquist and Lubin was "Schnitzel," his dummy. From 1975 through 1979, Lubin and Tinsman toured with the Ringling show.

Lubin brought his "Grandma" character, created for the Ringling show, to the Big Apple in 1982. This gray-haired busybody with the outsized handbag, kibitzing on every circus activity, spilling popcorn over everything from a seemingly bottomless box, blunders into the performers' acts but with surprising proficiency—for an eighty-four-year-old woman.

The tradition of the aerialist reached its apogee in the 1920s with Lillian Leitzel, and Binder introduces the modern-day Leitzel: "Ladies and gentlemen, watch now as Dolly Jacobs prepares herself for one of the most extraordinary and unique tricks that we have ever seen. She will attempt a midair, flyaway somersault, completely releasing from the Roman Rings. Silence, please!"

In 1978, *Newsweek* magazine called her Queen of the Rings, and sportswriter Peter Bonventre wrote that "her act transcends mere aerial razzle-dazzle—it is a swirling exhibition of grace and flexibility that marks Dolly Jacobs as one of the world's finest women athletes."

The circus tradition of rare and exotic performing animals was represented in the Big Apple Circus in the 1984 season, and again in

1988, by Adolf and Taxi, two sea lions, presented by Roby Gasser. In 1810, "Captain" Joseph Woodward became "the first trainer to present a full circus act with sea lions—as opposed to a simple exhibition," said Binder. "This English gentleman soon inspired many competitors, as sea lions became a favorite feature in circus programs. For almost one hundred years, these acts were built more or less on the same model. Then came Roby Gasser. . . ."

In Gasser's act, the sea lion named Adolf would waddle into the single ring of the Big Apple Circus balancing a flaming torch on his bewhiskered snout. Once in the ring, Adolf would toss the torch away to his Swiss trainer, seemingly so glad to have that part of the routine over that the audience would explode in laughter. With that, Adolf and his smaller female partner, Taxi, got down to their act in earnest, proving, wrote Nan Robertson in the *New York Times*, that Adolf and Taxi "will stoop to anything for a guffaw and a gulp of raw fish. They play dead, do flipper-stands, head down and tail up; roll over and over; fan themselves with a flipper; lounge languorously with one flipper under their heads; put another coyly over an eye; balance a bottle and full wineglasses on a tray; bounce balls and shamelessly applaud themselves at every turn. Adolf also likes to spread his flippers, winglike, as he graciously acknowledges the hysteria of the fans."

The circus tradition of the flying trapeze has been traced in detail, but, as Barnum might have said, the apotheosis of the quintessence of the elegance of the flying trapeze may have been set at the Big Apple Circus in New York City at ten minutes to midnight, December 31, 1986, starting with Paul Binder's introduction: "Ladies and gentlemen, Yehudi Menuhin once said that gymnastics is the music of the body. The king of the circus gymastic acts is the flying

trapeze. And the king of the flying trapeze is— Tito Gaona!"

A capacity crowd of 1,650 celebrants—including the kind of sophisticated New Yorkers usually seen ushering in the New Year at an opera gala, private party, or night club—were gathered close around the one ring under the midnight-blue tent, right next door to the Metropolitan Opera House at Lincoln Center. From sixty-five feet to eight feet away they watched as Tito Gaona made the 12,600th triple somersault of his trapeze career—the 77th out of 77 tries in the first forty-one days of the Big Apple Circus's engagement. Then, as clocks struck midnight, the Big Apple audience swarmed into the ring to be served champagne by the performers.

———————

In the past twenty years, the circus has again become a popular place to go. This enthusiasm is being met, even among the circuses that can afford little or no television time to ballyhoo their shows, and which still rely on the print media, the radio, and local charities and promoters to fill their tents and arenas, with an abundance of great performers performing great feats all over the United States.

I began this history by recalling how Robert Lewis Parkinson, the chief librarian and historian of the Circus World Museum, explained the decline of the American circus in the fifties and early sixties by saying: "To audiences everywhere, a circus means performing horses and riders, clowns, jungle acts, rare and exotic animals and people, thrilling demonstrations of the skills of acrobats and aerialists, daredevils, and, of course, elephants. Experience has proved that when these basic acts aren't done in a way that captures the imagination of the public, the public is disappointed."

In the 1980s, all seven of these basic acts are

once again being performed with panache on one circus or another all over the country.

———◆———

There have been, for example, at least two trapeze artists who have accomplished the quadruple somersault since the famous first quad of Miguel Vazquez in the Ringling Show in 1982.

On May 20, 1985, Ruben Caballero, Jr., completed a quadruple somersault from the flying trapeze to the hands of the catcher, his father and the leader of The Flying Caballeros Trapeze Troupe, while performing with the Carson & Barnes Circus. By 1987, the Flying Caballeros were offering an opening double-double by Luis, age thirteen; a triple twist by Ruben Jr., eighteen; a double layout and full twist by Veronica, nineteen; a double layout by Elizabeth, twelve; a triple by Luis; and sometimes, a quadruple by Ruben Jr. There was then a two-and-a-half somersault by Veronica in the start of a passing leap trick with a single somersaulting Ruben Jr.; followed by all five performers in net come-downs, with a bounce back or two to the catchbar by young Ruben. (Most of the tricks also featured a pirouette back to the flybar.)

In late 1985, Jim Judkins, general manager of the Carson & Barnes Circus, advised *White Tops* that Ricardo Morales successfully completed three midair quadruple somersaults in performances with his family's Flying Morales Trapeze Troupe—the first time one show had two fliers successfully catching the quad. As for Ruben Caballero, Jr., he accomplished the quadruple about 30 percent of the time for Carson & Barnes. Before the decade was over, he was hired away by the Big One: on Ringling Bros. and Barnum & Bailey Circus in 1988, Caballero and Miguel Vazquez, the first flier to do the trick, presented quadruples during the same performance in Ring One and Ring Three. And this was the feat that, at the beginning of the 1980s, was considered "the impossible dream."

———◆———

D. R. Miller celebrated his fiftieth anniversary of circus ownership in 1986. His Carson & Barnes Circus features a seventh-generation artist, Mme Luciana Loyal, with the Alfonso Loyal-Repensky Troupe of bareback riders. Lalo Murillo, onetime catcher for Tito Gaona, was the performance director and announcer, and when he called for a volunteer to travel with the circus to learn the art of bareback riding, Lucy Loyal, planted in the audience, came forward. As has usually been the case for more than 150 years, the audience was in laughing tears at the plant's ineptness, when she suddenly began giving an exhibition of incredible riding skills. This act is a variation, of course, on the Dan Rice routine of the early nineteenth century in which a clown disguised as a drunken spectator tries to ride a horse bareback.

———◆———

In a routine called "The Maestro," ham-chinned, wild-eyed Denis Lacombe does the funniest caricature of a symphony conductor since Mickey Mouse burlesqued Leopold Stokowski in "The Sorcerer's Apprentice" section of Walt Disney's *Fantasia*. The biggest difference is that Lacombe "wears" his podium, a homemade prop consisting of ski boots secured to a miniature trampoline, so that he can bend completely over—backward, forward, and sideways. The Maestro conducts a tape-recorded "1812 Overture" that slows down to nothing in some passages and then, without warning, speeds up to warp speed. He eats a sandwich pulled from his pocket while keeping time with a yellow-and-red barber pole of a baton. Then he pulls handfuls of gift batons from inside his tuxedo pants and tosses them to the crowd, and, as a finale, pulls a flask from his trousers—which somehow causes his sleeves to come off and his pants to fall down.

As a member of Quebec's one-ring Cirque du Soleil, Lacombe in 1984 won a Bronze Medal in Paris at the Festival Mondial du Cirque de Demain, a worldwide competition reserved for young circus artists. He performed with the Big Apple Circus in the United States through August of 1987, then rejoined the Cirque du Soleil in Los Angeles for its first United States tour in the fall of 1987.

The Cirque du Soleil began with French Canadian youths trying to revive the almost forgotten traditional street performance arts in Quebec. In 1981, Guy Laliberté, a fire breather who had successfully and safely exhaled his way through Europe and Hawaii, organized them into "The Fun Fair of Baie St. Paul," which was a success for three seasons. In the summer of 1984, the organizers of Quebec City's 450th anniversary observances approached the group about turning their fair into a circus to celebrate the anniversary.

They attracted immediate attention—first, because the thirty-three artists are very young (the average age is twenty-six); second, because of the show's "look": each act is designed to be a light and music show as well as a demonstration of the skills of acrobats and aerialists or the zaniness of clowns.

"The traditional circus doesn't match the visual quality that we see every day on TV, in films, in magazine advertisements, or the sound of films," said Guy Laliberté, general director of The Cirque du Soleil. So René Dupère, the music director, working with nine synthesizers and two electronic drums, composes, arranges, and performs original scores for each act, and each is choreographed to a wide range of spe-

cial effects, including black lights, smoke effects, and pyrotechnic explosions.

The willingness of hundreds of thousands of Americans to go to one-ring circuses again shows the same fascination with close-up scrutiny of feats of physical skill and daring that is bringing ever greater numbers to the Olympics and to gymnastics events. (Of course, the circus adds clowns, lest we take ourselves too seriously.)

As the Olympics show, the fascination is worldwide. A new Cirque du Soleil act called "Le Cicyclette Artistique" won the Bronze Medal at the 1987 Festival Mondial du Cirque de Demain in Paris. To create this act, three acrobats from the People's Republic of China came to Canada to train and team up with eleven Canadian acrobats in order to show what can be done with fourteen human beings on one moving bicycle. In the Orient, according to Laliberté, the Chinese have set the world's record for this sort of thing by putting nineteen persons on one bike, but fourteen is so far the occidental record.

European acrobatic traditions are also well represented on this continent. From early in the nineteenth century, the Liebel Family Circus made its home in Budapest, Hungary, but traveled throughout Europe performing spectacular acrobatic feats. In 1977, they came to America, offering high trapeze, low wire, unsupported ladder, juggling, stilt walking, and a counting pony. In 1986, the Liebel Family Circus appeared at Pennsylvania's York Fair, and the family's contribution to the circus included juggling, unsupported ladder, and a new act, four miniature liberty ponies.

The "Risley act," or foot juggling, said to have been introduced to North America by Richard Risley Carlisle (1814–1874) around 1843, was featured in the 1986 edition of Dave and Judy Twomey's Happytime Circus, which has played annual dates at the Los Angeles County Fair since 1983. Chester Cable, lying on his back, juggled with his feet a six-foot cylinder, a wagon wheel, and a ten-foot-long, 100-pound table.

Another form of Risley act involves a number of performers lying on their backs passing a teammate along by the feet. In a review of the appearance of "Prof. Risley" and his son, the *New York Herald* of May 4, 1843, said: "One of the chief attractions, if we may judge from the applause bestowed, was Prof. Risley and his boy. . . . The somerset, in which he alights upon his father's feet, is a brilliant performance, and we believe never before attempted in this city." It was that form—the foot juggling of fellow humans—that was practiced by the Shanghai Acrobats with Ringling Bros. and Barnum & Bailey Circus in 1986 and 1987. In one trick, a woman starts out standing on the foot juggler's feet, does a somersault while another acrobat dives through the foot juggler's legs, and comes down to sit on the foot juggler's feet.

The Space Age has seen a revival of interest in human cannonballs, now often called human missiles.

Old-fashioned posters announcing Captain Henry Munoz, the human missile who gets shot out of a cannon, appeared in the windows of Hilander Fine Foods stores and at the Tom Harmer's Sports store when the George Carden Circus International came to Rockford, Illinois, in the summer of 1987.

It was a "show must go on" story. Henry's brother, Human Cannonball Christopher Munoz, suffered eye and face injuries in August 1985, when the explosive device inside his cannon misfired during a performance at Pittsburgh's Kennywood Amusement Park. Henry, normally a comedy bounding-rope artist, took his place as the cannon act projectile all during the fall of 1985, then went on

to fulfill bookings with the George Carden Circus.

Elvin Bale, the famous "Human Space Shuttle" of the Ringling Show in the 1970s, was seriously injured when he was fired from a cannon on tour in the Orient in 1986. Bale was experimenting with air bags to break his fall, but the cannon was accidentally set as if it were firing him into a net. His trajectory went right over the air bags and smashed him into a wall. The news was a shock to circus fans all over the world, for Bale, known as "The Phantom of Balance," was the greatest circus daredevil of the second half of the twentieth century, famous for walking "The Wheel of Doom" for Ringling Bros., and he was the son of a risk-taking wild animal trainer of the first half of the century, Col. Trevor Bale, who survived to retire from the Big Cage.

"Thrillers at the close of the nineteenth century and during the early twentieth followed the curve of mechanical invention," old-time Ringling press agent Dexter Fellows used to say. So bicycles looping-the-loop were superseded by automobiles looping-the-loop. But as the turn of the twenty-first century approaches, daredevils follow Age of Leisure lifestyles. In its 1989 edition, Ringling Bros. and Barnum & Bailey presented the debut of the R&T Aerial Ski Squadron, "free-style hot dogers . . . on skis." Four Canadian athletes ski-jump off a ramp in the arena, then perform double inverteds, back flips, and spinning 1060s as they soar across all three rings to another ramp.

On the same show, the wire-walking Carrillo Brothers—Colombia's Pedro Carrillo, Pedro Jr., and "brother" Louis Posso—dance, skip, jump, and leap-frog on a tightly wound, five-eighths-inch steel strand suspended forty feet above the hard arena floor, without a net.

And on Ringling's other unit is Tahar, who puts his head in an alligator's mouth. Between an alligator's jaws are seventy to eighty conical teeth, with a "spare" set in waiting. The closing power of that jaw has been measured at up to 1,200 pounds.

"Human daring has but one limit," said Octavie LaTour, who did back somersaults in an automobile in 1904. "Human imagination."

———

Animals are fundamental to the circus's celebration of human survival. They are part of its demonstration that we can learn to coexist with nature, whether in the form of wild animals or "the elements" or situations where we might fall; and even learn to live with our prideful, envious, covetous dumb selves (hence, the clowns).

Thus the pleasure we take in seeing, for example, Wally Naghtin, his wife, Doris, and their son, Wally Jr., working with one of the world's largest collection of uncaged bears: eleven performing bears including Syrians, blacks, Himalayans, and Syrian grizzlies, ranging in weight from twenty to seven hundred pounds. For the Naghtins, they dance, somersault, walk on their front paws, twirl flaming batons, balance on balls, and ride on motorcycles with intelligence and charm, and no special effect can touch them.

There is danger in Digger, the Boxing Kangaroo, presented in the 1986 season by Allan C. Hill's Great American Circus. George C. Bingaman, reviewing the act for *White Tops*, wrote, "Helge Dam [the trainer] gets my vote for the most courageous animal presenter this season. His vulnerability as he is exposed to Digger's deadly glove and leg blows not only continually threaten his sexuality and survival, but make you wonder how this miracle can be repeated daily without them carrying him out."

But the best opportunity to see the rare and exotic animals of the circus is probably at the Great Circus Parade in Milwaukee, Wisconsin,

produced each summer by the Circus World Museum in Baraboo, Wisconsin. Greg T. Parkinson (son of Robert L. Parkinson) is the museum director.

Here is also the only opportunity to see the circus parades that were an American institution for the eighty years between the end of the American Civil War and the end of World War II. In 1986, there was one parader in Milwaukee who had participated in the daily circus street parades of sixty-seven years before: Merle Evans, ninety-two years old, who for fifty years was the bandmaster of Ringling Bros. and Barnum & Bailey Circus, famed as "one of the few men in modern history who could blow high C on a cornet while eating popcorn."

The star of the 1986 parade was "Tutall," the giraffe of the grand menagerie of the Circus World Museum, shown off in a brand-new giraffe wagon, a replica of the Ringling Bros. Circus giraffe wagon of 1893, pulled by six Belgian horses. Then there was Miss Patricia White, "World's Foremost Lady Animal Subjugator," presenting her liger, a cross between a lion and a tiger, Lady and liger both featured on Carson & Barnes Circus of Hugo, Oklahoma. Also from Carson & Barnes came llamas and circus camels and a Royal Bengal tiger, caged in a Barnum & Bailey wagon pulled by four Percheron horses driven by Jeanne Jackson of Howard, Ohio. (Female team drivers hark back to 1857, when a woman driver drove a forty-horse hitch for Nixon & Kemp's Circus.) There was a mule with a clown on him, and a pony pulling the traditional circus cart of Sicily, and the pony "April" pulling Milwaukee's "Jolly the Clown" driving cart, and two oxen pulling a covered wagon of the 101 Ranch Real Wild West show. There were three cougars and three bears.

There was a mounted elephant crier—nostalgia in the 1980s, necessity at the turn of the last century—crying out, "Hold your horses!

The elephants are coming!" And there was a herd of circus elephants marching trunk to tail, complete with attendants and a "harem princess" in a howdah, in traditional circus parade style, courtesy of Carson & Barnes Circus and William Woodcock.

———

"The first elephant ever to perform in a circus ring was called Baba," says Big Apple Circus's Paul Binder. "In 1812, he appeared in a pantomime at the Cirque Olympique, in Paris. Baba was billed as an 'elephant comedien.' He presented a lady in the audience with flowers, performed some dance steps, and waved a handkerchief before leaving the ring." We do know that an elephant appeared with an American circus in 1812; it was the female known as Crowninshield's elephant, and it appeared with Cayetano's Circus in 1812, but there is no record of what it did, if anything.

The first performing elephants appeared in the United States in the 1870s. A man named Carter was one of the first trainers to present such an act. Ever since then, you have usually been able to gauge the health of the circus by what the elephants are up to, and in this, the beginning of the circus's third century, we see more than ever the old man-over-beast act being turned into an act of love between God's creatures.

On Ringling Bros. and Barnum & Bailey Circus, as we have seen, the Gautier Family commands the herd on the Blue Unit and Gunther Gebel-Williams and his son, Mark Oliver, are in charge of the herd on the Red Unit, which has, in addition, King Tusk, the biggest elephant alive today. The late Clifford E. Vargas, president and producer of Circus Vargas, presented the Circus Vargas Elephants with Ted Polke: three elephants in Ring One; two elephants in Ring Two, and three elephants in Ring Three. The Tarzan Zerbini Circus has Zerbini's Elephants. Dianne Hanneford Moyer, who starred with the George Hanneford Circus for twenty-six years before going on her own in the 1986 season, presents an African elephant, as well as her liberty ponies and canines, with the Bentley Bros. Circus. The four Cristiani Elephants, meanwhile, are presented by Pete and Karin Christiani Mortenson with Ed Migley's Circus Odyssey; and there are the three performing Barrada Elephants presented by LuAnn Jacobs, former aerialist and daughter of Ringling clown Lou Jacobs, with the Royal Hanneford Circus.

Which brings us to the Woodcock Elephants—a good stopping place for this ongoing saga of the circus in America, for no human beings and no animals alive today better represent the circus in America than the Woodcock family and their elephants.

The most talented elephant of all is probably a Burmese woodland elephant named Anna May, 46 years old, with superb coordination, an incredible memory, and a gentle disposition. Trained by the Woodcock family, she has starred in every major circus in America and on dozens of national television shows, and on each she has somehow communicated to her audience the closeness of this living being to ourselves.

Anna May made her memorable Ringling debut in 1978 when the Woodcock family presented a herd of twenty-two elephants. She would stand on her hind legs on an elephant tub holding Barbara Woodcock in her mouth by Barbara's right leg. She would skip and kick the tambourine in syncopated rhythm as she danced to an upbeat tempo with her titian-haired human partner.

Many elephants learn dance steps. Such tricks are taught, said her chief trainer, "Buckles" Woodcock, by tapping an elephant on the leg with a stick to indicate which leg she is to lift, and giving vocal commands such as "Lift!" When the elephant responds properly, she is rewarded with a piece of bread, a carrot, or an apple.

"It's the reward system," said Buckles. "Without food, you're outta business."

Each dance step appears to be in time to the music. Actually, the band sets its rhythm to the series of movements taught the elephant by the trainer.

"But what Anna May does is very, very complicated," said Buckles. "It takes an elephant with terrific coordination to be able to do so many things at once. And an elephant with a terrific memory to remember it all."

When Anna May and two other elephants appeared with the Big Apple Circus, Clive Barnes, former dance and drama critic for the *New York Times*, wrote that the Woodcocks "have, without exception, the best elephants—there are three of them—I have ever encountered." From Balanchine to Dame Margot Fonteyn, Barnes always had an eye for great dancers.

The training and presentation of Anna May is probably the greatest triumph of a family that has one of the most distinguished ancestries in the American circus. In this history, we have seen the Cooke family, which brought a circus from Scotland in the early 1800s, intermarry with the Coles and the Ortons, two other well-known circus families.

The Orton family started in the circus business with Hiram Orton, a Great Lakes sailor who opened a show in 1854. Upon his retirement in 1862, the show was continued by his son, Miles Orton, through 1895. Miles and his brother R. Z. had the Orton Bros. Circus until 1898, when they split into two Orton circuses. One or the other was on the road until Miles's death in 1903. R. Z. Orton continued by railroad, wagon, or truck, into the early 1930s. Several members of the family went on as performers with other shows. The name Orton was by this time one of the great names among the smaller circuses.

R. Z. Orton had a spunky daughter, Sarah, who liked to say, "My family was in the Circus when the Ringling Brothers were still wearing wooden shoes." She married William Woodcock, a legendary elephant trainer whose prolific and animated correspondence is one of the best primary sources for American circus history. As an eminent authority on elephants, he also began a detailed record of the origins and personal history of almost every elephant that ever came to America.

William "Buckles" Woodcock, Jr., was born in 1935 in Lancaster, Missouri, to Sarah and William Sr. Buckles got his nickname from his mother's insistence on keeping him buckled to her on a little harness so that he wouldn't run off and get in trouble with the elephants. His parents firmly believed that their son would be better off in the business end of the circus, and should "get out there and handle money," as opposed to following in his father's footsteps and training animals. So Buckles began his career as a candy vendor at age eleven.

"My father said an elephant trainer should have a strong back, a weak mind and a savage disposition, and I didn't qualify on any of these accounts," Buckles recalled.

In 1951, at the age of sixteen, Buckles ignored his father's objections and got a job as an animal handler with another elephant trainer, Eugene "Arky" Scott, who worked on the Ringling show. Two years later, Woodcock father and son were reunited when the elder Woodcock's vision became so poor that he needed Buckles to drive his animal van to his circus dates around America.

By 1956, William Woodcock, Sr., was resigned to his son's determination to become an elephant trainer like Dad. Indeed, Buckles even began carrying on his father's detailed records of elephants in America. Together, father and son ran the gamut of circus experience—from tent blow-downs and elephant stampedes to train wrecks. And Buckles developed a reputation for being able to handle the difficult elephants.

Buckles Woodcock married redheaded Barbara Ray, a leopard trainer and the daughter of Lalea Ray, who trained chimps and spider monkeys. Barbara was divorced from another elephant trainer, Rex Williams, and had a son, Ben, who had been working with elephants since the age of five.

In 1978, when the Woodcock Elephants were featured on The Greatest Show on Earth, the family included Buckles, Barbara, and their two children, Shannon Woodcock, seven, and Dalilah, six; as well as Ben; Ben's wife, Karen Williams, who did an act with a leopard named Odin; and their son, Shane, seven.

It was a sensational act. The twenty-two elephants in their herd included six males, though such experts as Gunther Gebel-Williams consider males too aggressive and unpredictable to be trained successfully for the circus.

In one of their displays, Buckles and Barbara supervised a quintet of elephants in a hind-leg stand. Buckles would give a command and two elephants would sit down on elephant tubs; two more elephants would lie down between the tubs; a fifth elephant would stand on the two lying elephants, and Barbara would sit astride this two-elephant high.

Their finish charmed the crowd. Little Dalilah would grab a baby elephant by the ears to mount her, then wave to the crowd as the baby elephant sat down on the ring curb between Dalilah's mother and father.

Dismounting, Dalilah took a bow with her parents, and the band gave them a fanfare. Her parents and the baby elephant started to exit, but Dalilah took another bow—and the band gave her another fanfare. Dalilah was bowing yet a third time, milking the applause to win a third fanfare when the seemingly disgruntled elephant ran back, wrapped its trunk tip around her hand and pulled her out of the ring.

In 1982, the Woodcock Elephants joined the Big Apple Circus, with various members of the family to supervise them while other family members appeared with other American circuses. In my favorite of Anna May's routines, the circus ring becomes a barbershop. Buckles has trained Anna May to lather and shave another elephant at his commands, and then to brush that elephant off with a whisk broom as the pachyderm "customer" is leaving.

But every member of the Woodcock family has played in, on, with, and around the infinitely adaptable Anna May. "On Circus Vargas in 1972," said Barbara Woodcock, "I would do a straight jump from the teeterboard to Anna May's neck, then Ben would stand on the teeterboard with his back to Anna May, and Anna May would stomp on the raised side of the teeterboard, propelling Ben into a back somersault over me to Anna May's back."

Those who have seen the Big Apple Circus over the years have watched, close up, as Shannon and Dalilah Woodcock have grown up on the backs and necks of such Woodcock elephants as Mac, Peggy, Toto, and Anna May. Ben is now the father of Stormy Ann Williams, who made her debut the year she was born, 1985, when Ben carried her into the ring when the Big Apple Circus played Lincoln Center. In 1987, when the Woodcock Elephants appeared with the permanent one-ring circus at Circus World Museum in Baraboo, Wisconsin, Stormy Ann Williams, one and a half years old, made her debut under her own power.

Such are the intimate delights of a one-ring circus. But for the full wonder of the circus one needs the energetic synergy of the three-ring circus as well.

Intimate a three-ring circus can never be, particularly when it is designed to play to 10,000 people at a single performance, but it does provide the circusgoer with the kind of spectacles that the fewer than 2,000 spectators at a one-ring circus will never see, close up or otherwise. Greatest among these is probably the Long Mount, which is to the circus what the kick line is to a Broadway musical. Indeed, the finale of *Chorus Line* itself is no match for the sight of a dozen or even two dozen elephants rumbling around three rings, before each, on a single command, stands on its hind legs and puts its forelegs on the back of the elephant in front. America is full of people who first experienced awe looking up at two dozen elephants towering over them in that famous three-ring finale. It is, in fact, a paradigmatic image of awe that ties us to our grandfathers and grandmothers.

In 1989, the great Gunther Gebel-Williams began his final, two-year American tour as a performer, accomplishing new wonders with horses, elephants, and tigers on the 119th edition of Ringling Bros. and Barnum & Bailey Circus. But the show will go on. In fact, television has already acquainted the public with the grooming of one of Gunther's successors. In 1981, NBC-TV presented "My Father, The Circus King," focusing on the relationship between Gunther and his then eleven-year-old son, Mark Oliver Gebel. The son has since grown into a fine elephant man and works with horses, too, though he does not intend to train and perform with the big cats. All-around Gunther will even play the clown to his own wild animal trainer, as when he tugs in mock desperation on a tiger's tail, in a vain attempt to move the beast. Of all the performers in this history, only Dan Rice before him has been what the essayist Edward Hoagland called Gunther: "a circus by himself."

Yet if continuity is the lifeblood of the circus, transcendence is its tonic. In the early nineteenth century, Hackaliah Bailey's tales of Old Bet, the first circus elephant, inspired P. T. Barnum with wonder and delight, and the eventual result was Jumbo, the biggest elephant in the world, appearing twice a day with The Greatest Show on Earth. The sight of Dan Rice and his circus inspired the Ringling brothers with wonder and delight, and the eventual result was the Ringling Bros. and Barnum & Bailey Circus—the continuation into the twentieth century of Barnum's Greatest Show on Earth. And now, Kenneth Feld, who, having been born as recently as 1948, seems likely to lead The Greatest Show on Earth into the twenty-first century, presents King Tusk, the biggest elephant of his time, to the wonder and delight of who knows who all. So the thread that ties Old Bet to Jumbo, and Jumbo to King Tusk, and includes a thousand and one attractions in between, is always and everywhere that same desire to transcend the ordinary, to exceed, excel, surpass—and thus to provide that same precious, hard-to-come-by wonder and delight that continually give the circus, as Hemingway wrote, "the quality of a truly happy dream."

Chronology of the Circus in America, 1785–1990

1785   Aug. 27: First circus in America: native-born Thomas Pool, horse, and clown play Philadelphia.

1786   July 8: Pool plays Boston.

       Sept. 21–Nov. 6: Pool plays New York with clown and trick horse.

1787   Sept. 7: Two camels, a male and female, shown at Stevens's Livery Stable, Wall Street, New York.

1788   Sept. 11: Trained birds and "little dogs, dressed in uniform" presented by Willman, from Augsburg, Germany, in New York. [*New York Journal*]

1789   Aug. 4: Two Arabian camels exhibited near the town pump in Salem, Mass.

       July 22–29: Donegani & Co., an Italian company of wire dancers, appear in Salem, Mass.

1790   Jan. 8: "Last evening one Bennet pretending to be the first American wire dancer" appears in Salem, Mass. [Rev. Dr. William Bentley's diary]

1791   July 21: A "tractable and docile" African lion shown in New York. [*Daily Gazette*]

1792   Aug. 10: Messrs. Placide and Martine dance on the tightrope in Boston, at the New Exhibition Room, Board Alley.

1793   April 3: John Bill Ricketts presents his first circus in his Philadelphia amphitheater with riders, leapers, tightrope dancers, and "Mr. McDonald," a clown.

       April 22: George Washington visits Ricketts's circus.

       Aug. 7: Ricketts's circus plays New York City.

1794   Nov. 19: Ricketts moves to Broadway for larger New York quarters.

1795   March: Ricketts, playing New York, adds mounted Indian chiefs to his performance, "drest in the character of warriors," anticipating Buffalo Bill's Wild West of 88 years later.

1796   A young elephant, believed to be the first elephant to reach the New World, brought to New York from India by sea captain Jacob Crowninshield. It is exhibited in New

York, then sold to Mr. Owen, who exhibits it in Philadelphia, Baltimore, and other Atlantic seaboard cities until about 1822.

Trained dog performs card tricks at the Assembly Room, New York.

1797   Jan. 24: George Washington sees Ricketts's circus again.

Washington sells Ricketts his Revolutionary War horse, Jack, for $150.00.

March 16: Ricketts performs with trick horse, Cornplanter.

First street parade.

Whisky Rebellion Spec.

April 8: Ricketts's one rival, Philip Lailson, opens his own building in Philadelphia with a performance of his small French circus, Lailson and Jaymond, and advertises "Miss Venice" as the first woman circus rider in the U.S.

1798   Ricketts in lawsuit.

July 18: Lailson's circus offered for sale in the *Commercial Advertiser*.

1799   Feb. 19: Lailson's circus again offered for sale in the *Commercial Advertiser*.

Feb. 26: Lailson's circus revived in New York as "The New Circus," though with same performers, and runs to mid-March; Lailson then embarks for the West Indies.

Nov. 21: Fire destroys Ricketts's circus in New York, then (Dec. 17) his circus in Philadelphia.

1800   Langley does a one-hand stand on a moving horse.

1801   Ricketts, after working briefly for Lailson's circus, boards ship for England, is lost at sea.

1802   Robertson and Franklin Circus appears in New York's Vauxhall Garden in the new arena.

1803   Robertson and Franklin give only circus performance in U.S.

1804   No circus performances in U.S. this year.

1805   Old Bet comes to U.S., according to circus tradition reported by Gil Robinson in his book *Old Wagon Show Days*.

1806   Messrs. Peppin, Breschard & Guitana's Circus appears in Boston.

John Durang, wire walker, and Lewis DeGraff, with Cornplanter, named after Ricketts's famous horse, perform at Baltimore.

1807   The circus troupe of Victor Pepin and his partner, Breschard, arrives in Plymouth, Mass., and revives the circus in America.

1808   Pepin, a dashing rider, appears in Philadelphia at the Walnut Street Theater, opened by Pepin, Breschard & Guitana.

Hackaliah Bailey is showing Old Bet.

1809   Dec. 11: Pepin & Breschard appear in Baltimore.

1810   Cayetano & Co. perform in Newburyport, Mass.

First circus in Charleston, S.C.

1811   Actor John Howard Payne predicts that the circus in America will be a lucrative business.

1812   June 13: Crowninshield's elephant joins Cayetano, Codet, Menial & Redon's New York Circus at Broadway and White Street. May be the first elephant shown with a circus in America.

Rolling shows begin to tour America.

1813	Pepin returns to New York: beginning of "Grand Entry."
	Crowninshield's elephant displayed at Cooperstown, N.Y.
1814	Astley dies.
	Pepin, Breschard & Cayetano play Pittsburgh.
	Circus showmen reach Ohio, gain access to the American West.
1815	Feb. 28: Lion shown at Nassau Street, New York. Most animals previously shown individually have joined menageries by this year.
1816	Old Bet, traveling with Nathan Howes Menagerie, is shot to death in Maine.
	John Rogers (father of Charles) among first to introduce still-vaulting from a springboard.
1817	Cayetano plays New Orleans.
	Thomas West brings spotted horses from England.
	Clown Campbell leaps over 5 horses.
1818	Rufus Welch manages a wagon show.
1819	James West goes west.
1820s	Circuses begin to merge equestrians, acrobats, and clowns with menageries.
1820	First circus advertising cut used in America.
c. 1820	The Zoological Institute settles permanently in its own building at 37 Bowery, New York, where it exhibits its menagerie in the winter and leases the animals to traveling caravans or takes some of them on the road in the summer.
1821	Blanchard marries Mlle Adolph and their family circus begins.
	Isaac A. Van Amburgh becomes an animal keeper.
1822	English equestrian James Hunter introduces bareback riding to American audiences.
	Clown Williams clears a stage wagon.
1823	Price and Simpson buy out West's Circus; Hunter rides for them at their Broadway Circus, New York.
1824	American dwarf Joseph M. Stevens, 37 inches high, exhibited at Washington Hall, and later at Park Theater, New York City.
1825	J. Purdy Brown puts up the first circus tent, in Wilmington, Del.
	Hackaliah Bailey builds the Elephant Hotel in Somers, N.Y.; puts statue of Old Bet on granite pillar in front; still standing in 1989.
	LaFayette attends circus in New York.
	Andrew Jackson goes to Pepin circus in Louisville, Ky.
1826	Menageries are all the rage.
1827	May: the pre-Barnum American Museum exhibits a trained dog, Apollo, who plays cards. On July 7, Peale's Museum has two trained dogs: Toby will tell any card, Minetto will climb a ladder.
1828	P. T. Barnum meets Hackaliah Bailey.
1829	James Hunter, last European-born impresario, leaves U.S.
	American-born Rufus Welch tours the West Indies with his own circus.
	Last use of canvas sidewalls by larger circuses; erection of wooden arenas in sharp decline.
1830	Circuses and menageries begin to merge.

1831 Early menagerie poster advertises American National Caravan featuring "The unicorn, or one horned rhinoceros."

1832 Selectmen of Worcester, Mass., license a company calling itself "Circus Riders" to exhibit its skills in their village.

1833 Isaac A. Van Amburgh enters a cage of wild animals at the Zoological Institute in New York.

1835 Poster advertising the Zoological Institute in New York for winter 1834–35 says that Van Amburgh enters the cages of various jungle beasts there; no attempt as yet to teach the animals to perform.

1835 Jan. 14: The Zoological Institute formed as a joint stock company at the Elephant Hotel, Somers, N.Y., to limit competition in the growing menagerie and circus businesses.

1836 Circus debuts of P. T. Barnum, secretary, treasurer, and ticket taker, and Barnum's client, Signor Vivalla, juggler, with Aaron Turner Circus.

Cooke's Royal Circus arrives in U.S.—the earliest known circus to move complete across the Atlantic.

William A. Delavan opens circus.

1837 Giraffe arrives in U.S.

Benefit for Victor Pepin in Louisville.

1838 Sept. 4: Nathaniel Hawthorne sees a man put his head in a lion's mouth at a menagerie performing in North Adams, Mass.

Bedouin Arabs give exhibitions.

Thomas Cooke loses many horses in Baltimore fire.

1839 Levi J. North turns the first full feet-to-feet somersault on the back of a running horse.

Elephant fight in New Orleans costs management $21,800.

1840 Levi J. North is leading principal rider in U.S.

The Sweeney brothers, Joe and Dick, travel with the Robinson Circus; Joe Sweeney, "the father of the banjo," makes his first by stretching strings over an old cheese box.

1841 Van Amburgh in England.

Earliest circus route book published.

Barnum buys American Museum; exhibits "freaks of nature."

1842 Dec. 8: Tom Thumb makes his debut.

Zip begins 84-year career with Barnum ventures; Dickens names him the "What-is-it?"

Sands Circus is first with American horses and horsemen to go to England.

Minstrel show develops from Joe Sweeney's act and will be included in circus performances.

June, Titus & Angevine: first American circus to travel to Continent.

First Risley act.

Many circuses playing New York season.

1843 Tom Thumb a sensation at Barnum's museum.

1844 Fabulous success of Tom Thumb's European tour.

1845 Hackaliah Bailey dies.

   Equestrian acrobatics: first 5-high act done on 3 horses, with Welsh & Lent Circus.

1846 Van Amburgh's bandwagon is the largest ever seen in North America.

1847 Barnum and Tom Thumb return to U.S.; visit President Polk.

c. 1847 Sam Clemens, 12 years old, sees Dan Rice do Pete Jenkins routine; will describe it in *Huckleberry Finn.*

1848 Circus spectator says: "Look, Dan Rice is on Zachary Taylor's bandwagon," and political language gains a phrase.

   Tom Thumb tours with circus.

1849 Feb. 22: Wild Animal Exhibitors' Ball celebrates Washington's birthday at the Elephant Hotel, Somers, N.Y., in display of wealth of area menagerie owners.

1850 Dan Rice, in Blue Eagle Jail, wins sympathy of the nation.

   Dan Rice tours with his famous One-Horse Show.

   April: Congress adjourns to attend benefit for Dan Rice.

   Ezra Stephens founds the sideshow.

1851 Barnum, Seth B. Howes, and Sherwood Stratton, father of Tom Thumb, organize P. T. Barnum's Great Asiatic Caravan, Museum and Menagerie and begin 4-year tented tour. There are no ring acts, but the show features General Tom Thumb, 10 elephants, and a Mr. Pierce in a den of lions.

1852 Spalding & Rogers *Floating Palace* launched.

1853 "Hippodrome Track," a racecourse, introduced; circuses hold chariot races.

1854 Dan Rice buys elephant, Lalla Rookh, from Seth B. Howes.

   Hiram Orton, Great Lakes sailor, starts Orton Circus.

1855 J. C. Stoddard invents steam calliope.

1856 James Robinson, 21, turns 23 consecutive somersaults on horseback.

1857 Pete Conklin, having quit Mabie Bros. Circus, invents pink lemonade.

   James Robinson wins the title of greatest bareback rider in the world.

1858 Lincoln and Douglas use Spalding & Rogers Circus tent to run for U.S. Senate.

   Howes & Cushing's Circus has a great success in England.

1859 June 30: Blondin crosses Niagara Falls on a tightrope.

   Earliest flying trapeze act: Jules Leotard, of France, at the Cirque Napoleon in Paris.

   Yankee Robinson (1818–1884) driven from Charleston, S.C., for northern sympathies.

1860 Civil War begins.

   Lincoln caricatured as Blondin in *Vanity Fair.*

   Spalding and Rogers features Tom Watson in a washtub pulled down Mississippi River by 4 geese.

   Oct. 13: The Prince of Wales, later King Edward VII of England, visits Barnum's American Museum, shows great interest in the Siamese twins Chang and Eng, and Zip, the What-is-it?

1861 Robinson & Lake's Circus and Menagerie raises Stars & Stripes; forced to move north of the Ohio River.

   Some Philadelphians demand that Dan Rice be shot as "Johnny Reb."

1862	Spalding & Rogers tie up the *Floating Palace*; take a circus to South America.
	General Tom Thumb and Commodore Nutt received by President Lincoln at the White House.
	Hiram Orton retires; Orton Circus continued by his sons, Miles and R. Z. Orton.
1863	Feb. 10: Wedding of Tom Thumb to Lavinia Warren pushes war news off front pages.
1864	Nov.: Confederate agents set fire to Barnum's museum.
1865	April 14: Lincoln shot; Dan Rice cancels performances until further notice and goes into mourning.
	Two elephants and other animals costing $42,000 delivered to Adam Forepaugh in Chicago.
	Spring: *Floating Palace*, idle during war, burns to the waterline.
	July 13: Barnum's American Museum burns.
1866	Adam Forepaugh starts his circus.
1867	Equestrian star Adah Isaacs Menken, famous as "Mazeppa," meets Swinburne, British poet, who becomes her lover.
1868	March 3: Barnum's new American Museum burns.
	Orton Bros. Egyptian Caravan tours.
1869	Golden Spike driven at Promontory Point, Utah.
	Oct. 16: The Cardiff Giant, 10-foot stone man, "unearthed" on farm of "Stub" Newell, who buried it. Exhibiting a copy of this fake and advertising it as real, Barnum makes thousands.
	William Lake, proprietor of Lake's Circus, shot to death by frontier badman.
1870	October: Contracts for new circus drawn up by P.T. Barnum, Dan Castello, and William Cameron Coup.
	Young Ringling brothers see Dan Rice's Great Paris Pavilion at McGregor, Iowa.
1871	April 10: P. T. Barnum's Circus, Menagerie, and Museum opens in Brooklyn, N.Y.
	Barnum's freaks travel with W. C. Coup.
	Dan Rice gives benefit for victims of Chicago fire.
	Cole & Orton Circus founded.
1872	Barnum and Coup go to 2 rings.
	The first circus train developed by Coup for the Barnum show.
1873	Barnum show nets $250,000 in bad economic year.
	W. W. Cole Circus first to go to California and back by rail.
1874	John Cornish Worland (1855–1933) of the U.S. does the first running forward triple back somersault from a giant springboard, in St. Louis.
	Jan. 24: Deaths of Chang & Eng, Siamese twins.
	Pedestrians vie for walking records in Barnum's hippodrome.
	April: Barnum's Great Roman Hippodrome opens facing Madison Square in New York.
1875	George F. Bailey Circus, last Flatfoot show, closes.
	Prof. Donaldson, balloonist, vanishes over Lake Michigan during 139th ascension from Barnum's hippodrome.
1876	Barnum's circus, now called P.T. Barnum's Greatest Show on Earth, celebrates U.S. centennial with "a Fourth of July celebration every day."

James Bailey takes his circus to California.

"Parisian Circus" outside Philadelphia Exposition does good business.

1877 War of the "rat sheets": Barnum & Forepaugh battle each other with scurrilous advertising.

1878 The Sells Bros. wagon show becomes the Sells Bros. Great European Seven Elephant Railroad Show; a brother-in-law uses the old wagon equipment for the S. H. Barrett Circus.

1879 Flying trapeze: Eddie Silbon, performing at the Paris Hippodrome, throws the first double back somersault.

James A. Bailey's Great London Circus exhibits an electric light; Dan Rice calls it hazardous to health.

Gilmore's Garden becomes Madison Square Garden.

1880 First baby elephant born in America.

Bested by Bailey's baby elephant, Barnum offers to merge his show with Bailey's and Bailey accepts.

"Mademoiselle Zazel, the Human Projectile," "fired" from cannon; actually, Rosa M. Richter of England was discharged by a spring from the cannon, flung 40 feet in the air, and caught by a colleague dangling from a trapeze.

1881 March 18: Barnum and his new associate, James Anthony Bailey, first present their combined Barnum and London circus to an audience of 9,000 in Madison Square Garden. For the first time, 3 rings are used. In the show are 338 horses, 14 camels, 20 elephants, 370 costumed performers, 4 brass bands, and the midget couple, 41-year-old Tom Thumb and his wife, Lavinia, who come out of semiretirement to help Barnum launch his new enterprise.

Forepaugh invents beauty contest with "$10,000 prize" search for Lalla Rookh, "the most beautiful woman in America."

Ella Zuila called "the female Blondin."

1882 Easter Sunday: Jumbo, bought by Barnum from London Zoo, arrives in America.

Ben Lusbie (1839–1884), called "The Lightning Ticket-Seller Champion of the World," sells 6,153 tickets in 1 hour, 3 minutes.

Nathan Salsbury proposes Wild West show to Buffalo Bill.

1883 Barnum and London Circus goes on the road.

U.S. frontiersman W. F. "Buffalo Bill" Cody (1846–1917) stages Wild West show in Omaha.

1884 Buffalo Bill's Wild West founded as permanent touring show.

Barnum shows "only genuine white elephant outside Siam."

Forepaugh shows fake white elephant; hoax exposed.

1885 Jumbo rammed to death by train in Canada.

Sitting Bull tours with Buffalo Bill.

Annie Oakley joins Buffalo Bill.

H. B. Gentry founds first "dog and pony show" circus.

1886 Statue of Liberty dedicated.

W. W. Cole first to add Wild West performance to a circus, then auctions his circus in order to accept a position with Barnum and London.

1887   Joint appearance of Barnum and Forepaugh shows in Madison Square Garden: 60 elephants; fish riding; worland leaping; Billy Burke clowning.

Robert Sherwood signs $200-a-week Barnum and London clown contract.

Queen Victoria's Golden Jubilee; she sees Buffalo Bill's Wild West.

1888   John L. Sullivan (1858–1918), heavyweight boxing champion 1882–1892, tours with the Great Inter-Ocean Circus.

Bailey takes control of circus now known officially as the Barnum and Bailey Greatest Show on Earth.

1889   P. T. Barnum appears at every show of Barnum & Bailey at London's Olympia, shouting to crowd: "I suppose you all come to see Barnum. Wa-al, I'm Barnum."

John V. "Pogey" O'Brien, dishonest circus owner, dies in poverty.

Madison Square Garden #1 demolished to make way for Garden #2, designed by Stanford White.

1890   Bailey engages Imre Kiralfy to produce Barnum & Bailey's Spec: "Nero and the Destruction of Rome."

Adam Forepaugh & Sells Bros. present the Ty-Bell Sisters in "Aerial Butterflies."

1891   April 7: P. T. Barnum dies; Bailey now monarch of the circus world.

Ringling Bros. expand from 1- to 3-ring show.

RB has worst "clem" (battle with rowdies) in its history at Boliver, Mo.

Four Gollmar brothers, cousins of the Ringlings, launch a little wagon circus with help from Ringlings; it lasts 25 years.

Wild animal trainer Jack Bonavita, student of Frank C. Bostock, first presents his famous act with 27 grown lions.

1892   "Billing Fights": Ringling Bros. vs. Barnum & Bailey.

Charles W. Fish is champion principal bareback trick act with Ringling show.

Nine clowns on Ringling show, including Jules Turnour, a general clown; Lew Sunlin, a talking clown; and a German immigrant clown.

Ringling Bros.: trestle collapses, train falls into river, 2 men and 26 horses killed outright.

Barnum & Bailey Spec: "Columbus and the Discovery of America," celebrating 400th anniversary.

1893   Buffalo Bill's Wild West appears successfully outside the World's Columbian Exposition of 1893 in Chicago.

Hagenbeck Zoological Arena at Chicago World's Fair features wild animal acts imported from Germany.

Frank C. Bostock, English trainer, plays 14 weeks with wild animal show under canvas at Fifth and Flatbush avenues in Brooklyn, N.Y.

1894   Financial panic in U.S.; Al Ringling reduces number of rings in Big Top from 3 to 2.

1895   Ringling Bros. plays New England for first time.

Barnum & Bailey has one of first women clowns, Evetta.

March 4: Coup dies.

1896   Bailey exhibits Duryea automobile with Barnum & Bailey Circus.

Ringling Bros. introduces mounted circus band.

1897	In Sydney, Australia, Latvian-born Lena Jordan throws the first triple back somersault from the flying trapeze; the catcher is her foster father, Lew Jordan.
	Bailey takes Barnum & Bailey to Europe for 5-year tour, opening at the Olympia, London, Dec. 27, 1897, closing in France on Oct. 26, 1902; leaving Forepaugh-Sells and Buffalo Bill in U.S. to battle Ringling Bros.
1898	Orton Bros. Circus splits into 2 Orton circuses, one run by Miles Orton, the other by R. Z. Orton.
1899	Etta Lake, "the Elastic Lady," featured by Ringling Bros.
1900	Feb. 22: Dan Rice dies at 77 in Long Branch, N.J.
	Thomas Patton invents "Fairy Floss," by 1990—as "cotton candy"—the most popular confection of the circus.
1901	Seth B. Howes, brother of Nathan and founder of Howes' Great London Circus, dies at 86. American circus parades began their major period of development when he imported from England wagons that looked like wooden wedding cakes.
1902	Bailey returns from Europe; finds that Ringling Bros. now dominates the American circus scene.
	Floto Dog & Pony Show started by owners of the Denver *Post*.
1903	"Reformed" outlaws Frank James (brother of Jesse) and Cole Younger tour with a circus.
	"America" wagon built by Bailey for 1903 season.
	Ernest and Charles Clarke, trapeze artists, make American debut.
	Historic Wild West—the Buckskin Bill Wild West Show.
	Miles Orton dies; R. Z. Orton continues small Orton circus under a new name.
1904	Barnum & Bailey: Volo the Volitant cycles the aerial arc; Ugo Ancillotti loops-the-loop with a bike.
	Carl Hagenbeck Wild Animal Show appears at St. Louis World's Fair of 1904, then becomes a circus that tours unsuccessfully for next 2 years.
1905	Octavie LaTour loops-the-loop with a car.
1906	Ringling Bros. opens its season in the Chicago Coliseum.
	April 11: James A. Bailey dies.
	Floto Dog & Pony Show enlarged to Sells-Floto Circus.
1907	Oct: Ringlings purchase Barnum & Bailey and operate it separately from the Ringling Bros. Circus.
	Carl Hagenbeck Wild Animal Show sold by Hagenbeck's U.S. partners to Ben Wallace; becomes Hagenbeck-Wallace Circus.
	Cowboys of Miller Ranch put on Wild West show at Jamestown Exposition.
1908	Miller Bros. 101 Ranch Wild West Show founded by Edward Arlington, circus man, and the cowboys of the Miller ranch in Oklahoma.
1909	Trapeze: Ernest Clarke, with Publiones Circus in Cuba, becomes first male to throw triple back somersault, to his brother Charles.
	Ringling Bros. Circus, rather than Barnum & Bailey Circus, opens season in Madison Square Garden for first time.
	Schumann horses from Germany make American debut with Ringling Bros.

1910   William Main Circus train wreck: panther escapes.

1911   Mabel Stark joins Al G. Barnes Circus; will wrestle full-grown Bengal tiger.

1912   May Wirth, called the greatest bareback rider that ever lived, makes sensational debut at Madison Square Garden with Barnum & Bailey Circus.

1913   April 22: May Wirth badly hurt while performing in Brooklyn with Barnum & Bailey.

1914   Emil Pallenberg, German bear trainer, makes sensational Ringling Bros. circus debut, working with wife, Catherine, and Russian bears without a cage on a platform, where bears roller-skate and ride bicycles.

1915   Equestrian feats: Richard "Poodles" Hanneford sets record for running leaps on and off running horse (26) in Madison Square Garden, with Barnum & Bailey Circus.

1916   Al Ringling dies.

        May 8: President Woodrow Wilson attends Barnum & Bailey Circus, throws hat into ring.

        Buffalo Bill and the Miller Bros. 101 Ranch put on the military pageant "Preparedness."

1917   March: Capt. Jack Bonavita crushed to death by a bear.

        Buffalo Bill dies.

1918   Global influenza epidemic. Patronage on both Barnum & Bailey and Ringling Bros. circus falls below break-even point.

        Biggest train wreck in circus history: Hagenbeck-Wallace circus train rammed by troop train in a major railroad disaster.

1919   Merged into super-circus, Ringling Bros. and Barnum & Bailey Combined Shows opens in Madison Square Garden for the first time.

1920   Sells-Floto Circus features Princess Victoria—beautiful wire dancer and sister of Alfredo Codona.

1921   American Circus Corporation formed.

1922   Mabel Stark makes her RBB&B debut with her trained tigers.

1923   Con Colleano throws a feet-to-feet forward somersault on the low wire (7 feet) at Empire Theatre, Johannesburg, then repeats the feat in circus in America.

        Era of Wonderful Nonsense: Funeral of Elephant Tillie with elephant pallbearers.

1924   RBB&B: Four steel arenas working simultaneously: Mabel Stark, tigers; Dutch Ricardo, lions; Rudolph Matthies, tigers; Christian Shroder, polar bears.

        RBB&B puts on farewell to Madison Square Garden #2; actors play Barnum, Tom Thumb, and Jenny Lind; Zip, the What-is-it?, plays himself.

1925   RBB&B: Charles Ringling dies; John Ringling abolishes long clown solos.

        Madison Square Garden #2 torn down to make way for New York Life Insurance Co. skyscraper; Garden #3 built on 8th Avenue, between 49th and 50th streets.

1926   RBB&B: John Ringling abolishes wild animal acts.

        Zip, the What-is-it?, who began with Barnum in 1842, begins season with RBB&B, then dies of pneumonia at Bellevue Hospital, in his nineties.

1927   Marceline, clown, shoots himself to death; had clowned with the young Charlie Chaplin.

        RBB&B moves winter quarters from Bridgeport, Conn., to Sarasota, Fla.

1928   RBB&B: American debut of the Great Wallendas.

1929   RBB&B nets $1 million.

Black Diamond, killer elephant with Al G. Barnes Circus, is executed.

1930   Great Depression under way: Christy Bros. folds.

John Ringling brings from Africa plate-lipped Ubangis.

1931   Lillian Leitzel, wife of Alfredo Codona, falls in Copenhagen, on Friday the 13th of Feb.; dies Feb. 15.

Clyde Beatty, Hagenbeck-Wallace star, makes RBB&B debut.

RBB&B: Bad Depression business forces Sept. 14 season end—earliest in history.

1932   John Ringling loses control of Ringling Bros. Circus.

Samuel W. Gumpertz, owner of Dreamland Amusement Park in Coney Island, becomes general manager of RBB&B.

1933   Flying Concellos replace Alfredo Codona over center ring of RBB&B.

1934   Clyde Beatty quits RBB&B; Jess Adkins and Zack Terrell, manager of the defunct Sells-Floto show, hire him and form the Cole Bros. and Clyde Beatty Combined Circus, to start touring in 1935.

American debut of Cristianis on Hagebeck-Wallace.

1935   Tom Mix, western star, forms own circus, tours with Tony the Wonder Horse.

1936   Dec. 2: John Ringling dies—last of Ringling brothers leaves estate of $23,500,000.

1937   Trapeze legend Alfred Codona murders second wife, Vera Bruce, and commits suicide.

Cole Bros.: Otto Griebling's Studebaker coupe gag packs in 15 clowns and performers.

1938   RBB&B: Production number based on Disney's *Snow White and the Seven Dwarfs* costumes real dwarfs as fantasy dwarfs.

Tiger loose in Garden; dwarf dressed as Dopey turns it back toward its capturers with a rap on its nose from his papier-mâché pick.

Depression hits circus hard; Tom Mix Circus folds.

John Ringling North introduces Gargantua the Great.

RBB&B Spec: "Nepal," with "Bring 'Em Back Alive" Frank Buck.

Medina Shrine Circus, Chicago: Janet May Klemke (U.S.) sets record for one-arm swings or planges (no net).

W.P.A. Circus gives jobs to 375 unemployed performers and free shows for hospitals.

1939   RBB&B: Opening Spec: "The World Comes to the World's Fair."

Sells-Floto–Al G. Barnes Circus does not go out; its best act, Mabel Stark and the riding lion, joins RBB&B.

1940   RBB&B: Alfred Court, French wild animal trainer, presents 3 rings of mixed animals: lions, tigers, mountain lions, black leopards, a Kodiak bear, Himalayan bears, polar bears, Great Danes, and a white snow leopard.

RBB&B: Tiger walks tightrope.

RBB&B: Francis Brunn spins hoops while balancing balls.

RBB&B: "Old King Cole" Spec.

Mills Bros. Circus opens as small truck show by 3 brothers.

1941   Disney's *Dumbo* includes his tribute to the old-time tented show and street parade.

Russell Bros. has a blow-down in Richmond, Va.

1942   RBB&B: Igor Stravinsky writes ballet for circus elephants; George Balanchine choreographs it; Norman Bel Geddes costumes it; John Murray Anderson stages it; and Vera Zorina dances with the elephants in the center ring on opening night.

Musicians' strike affects circus bands.

RBB&B: Menagerie fire.

1943   Cole Bros. Circus: Pitt, last of the John Robinson herd of military elephants, killed by lightning Aug. 6 at age of 102.

1944   July 6: RBB&B fire in Hartford, Conn.: 168 dead, 487 burned or otherwise injured; worst disaster in circus history.

1945   First street parade in New York in 25 years.

General Marshall takes his grandson to a tented circus, helping to restore public confidence in circus safety.

Beatty Circus features "Big Otto, the blood sweating hippopotamus from the Nile."

1946   RBB&B: "Adam Smasher" gag.

1947   RBB&B: John Ringling North returns to presidency.

1948   RBB&B: Debut of the Great Unus and his one-finger balancing act.

Lou Jacobs perfects smallest car gag.

1949   Gargantua dies; baby gorillas starred.

1950   Joe Louis, former heavyweight boxing champion (1937–1949), tours with Daily Bros. Circus, a railroad circus founded in 1944, which folds later in 1950.

1951   Two railroad circuses: RBB&B and Clyde Beatty; Beatty tours western Canada.

Sam Dock, a Pennsylvanian who operated small shows from 1887, usually under his own name, makes his final appearance with his grandson's small show, the Sam Dock Circus.

1952   Cecil B. De Mille's circus film, *The Greatest Show on Earth*, wins Oscar as best picture.

The Cristiani family of bareback riders tours with King Bros. Cristiani Circus.

1953   RBB&B: Emmett Kelly kids President Eisenhower with homburg and golf gag.

RBB&B: Gloria Vanderbilt Stokowski raises $100,000 for cerebral palsy with benefit circus in Madison Square Garden.

1954   Jan. 17, Flint, Mich., Polack Bros.: Opal, trained by Mack MacDonald (1900–1983), becomes first elephant to accomplish the one-leg stand in U.S. [*Billboard*, March 1954].

The Cristiani family starts its own show, Bailey Bros. & Cristiani, playing ballparks rather than in a tent, traveling by truck, and becoming the first circus to appear in Alaska, which it reaches by the Alcan highway.

1955   RBB&B: Marilyn Monroe rides pink elephant in Spec.

Fred Bradna, equestrian director of the Barnum & Bailey Circus, 1915–1919, and of RBB&B, 1919–1945, dies.

Kelly-Miller, America's second largest circus, features a giraffe.

1956   July 16: Final performance of RBB&B under Big Top.

RBB&B President John Ringling North: "The tented circus as it exists today is, in my opinion, a thing of the past."

Clyde Beatty, only U.S. railroad circus on tour after Ringling closing, goes bankrupt as a railroad show, but reorganizes as a truck show.

1957	Clyde Beatty Circus, still under management of Frank McClosky and Walter Kirnan and featuring Beatty in his wild animal act, continues touring as a tented show.
1958	Clyde Beatty and Hamid-Morton Combined Circus plays Palisades Amusement Park in New Jersey.
1959	The heyday of the smaller sponsored circuses such as Hamid-Morton, Orrin Davenport Shows, Tom Packs Circus, Clyde Bros., Polack Bros., and others playing for Shrine temples, police benefits, etc., in ballparks and arenas.
	Circus World Museum opens in Baraboo, Wis.
1960	Bill Ballantine: "By the early 1960s, a visible slump in spirit and style took hold of most American circuses."
1961	High wire: The Great Wallendas achieve 3-layer, 7-person pyramid.
1962	John Ringling North, president of RBB&B, decides to live abroad.
	High wire: Karl Wallenda's 7-person pyramid collapses in Detroit; two young men are killed: Karl's daughter Jenny's husband and a nephew of Karl's first wife; Karl's adopted son is crippled for life.
	Flying trapeze: Triple and a half back somersault: Tony Steel to Lew Strath Marilees in Durango, Mexico.
1963	American circus composed of RBB&B acts tours USSR in July; Moscow State Circus tours U.S. in Sept.; Americans see Russian clown O. Popov.
1964	Merle Evans, who became leader of the RBB&B band in 1919, celebrates forty-fifth year with circus.
1965	Clyde Beatty dies of cancer.
1966	Dave Hoover takes over the Clyde Beatty wild animal act on the Beatty-Cole show.
1967	Irvin Feld heads a group that buys RBB&B. Feld era begins with signing in Roman Colosseum.
1968	Irvin Feld founds Ringling Bros. and Barnum & Bailey Clown College.
	Irvin Feld buys the entire German Circus Williams for a record $2 million to ensure that its star, Gunther Gebel-Williams, will perform in America exclusively with RBB&B.
	Feb. 11: Madison Square Garden #4 opens.
1969	Gunther Gebel-Williams makes American debut with 99th edition, The Greatest Show on Earth.
	Clifford E. Vargas, grandson of Portuguese circus owners, founds Circus Vargas in America.
	Flying trapeze: triple back somersault with one and a half twists by Terry Caverette Lemus at Circus Circus, Las Vegas.
	Billed as Prince Bogino, Manual "Junior" Ruffin, former Beatty cage boy, becomes the first black man to present a trained wild animal act in America.
1970	RBB&B: Centennial Edition, Spec: "The First 100 Years."
	RBB&B: Gunther Gebel-Williams brings together "three snarling tigers, two giant horses and a mammoth African elephant" in the same cage.
	Dec. 22: Mattel, Inc., buys RBB&B for $47 million.
1971	Train strike forces RBB&B circus to walk through tunnel to New York.

1972 April 19: Otto Griebling dies.

    Billy Stebbing family founds Stebbing Royal European Circus to revive the one-ring circus in America.

    Dec. 15: Israel Feld dies suddenly of a heart attack.

1973 RBB&B: American debut of Michu, world's smallest man.

    Dec.: Kenneth Feld becomes coproducer of RBB&B.

    Pio Nock and bicycle fall off tightwire into Wolfgang Holzmair's lion cage; quick thinking prevents serious injuries.

1974 Aug. 7: Philippe Petit walks the tightwire between twin towers of World Trade Center.

    Circus World Showcase opens near Orlando, Fla.

    RBB&B feuds with Circus America.

    One-ring Pickle Family Circus founded in San Francisco.

1975 Jan. 7: Philippe Petit, featured with RBB&B, falls and is injured.

    Petit inaugurates the largest covered stadium in the world, the Louisiana Superdome in New Orleans, with the longest indoor tightwire walk in history: 700 feet long, 200 feet high. He repeated the walk 6 times—sometimes twice an evening.

1976 Jan 3: Standing ovation for RBB&B Bicentennial Spec.

    RBB&B: Gunther Gebel-Williams, working with a herd of 20 elephants and 12 horses, creates an act called "Elephant Roundup" that spans all 3 rings and is controlled by his single spoken command.

    RBB&B: debut of Axel Gautier and his elephants.

    Charly Baumann achieves 5-tiger rollover.

    Flying trapeze: Denise La Grassa (U.S.) performs 306 downward circles or "muscle grinding" at Circus World Museum, Baraboo, Wis.

    RBB&B: Frosty Little's Japanese compact car gag packs in 19 clowns.

1977 Debut of Gunther Gebel-Williams's mixed cat act, bringing together, after 3 years of rehearsal, 15 leopards, 3 panthers, and 2 pumas in one cage.

    Gebel-Williams becomes the first circus performer to headline his own network television special.

    Paul Binder founds Big Apple Circus.

1978 March 22: Karl Wallenda falls to his death.

    May Wirth, called the greatest bareback rider of all time, dies.

    Newsweek calls Dolly Jacobs "Queen of the Rings."

1979 March 28: Emmett Kelly dies; Red Skelton: "I guess the angels needed a laugh."

1980 RBB&B: Gunther Gebel-Williams trains and presents circus's first white tiger, Maharanee.

    RBB&B: "Globe of Death" debuts.

    RBB&B: Boss Clown Frosty Little revives "Burning House" routine.

    Hanneford Circus, appearing in White Plains, N.Y., presents Nellie Hanneford, a 6th-generation Hanneford rider.

1981 Equestrian Katja Schumann performs with Big Apple Circus.

    Triple twisting double somersault: Tom Edelston to John Zimmerman, Circus World, Fla.

Full twisting triple somersault from the flying trapeze: Miguel Vazquez to Juan Vazquez, RBB&B, Chicago Amphitheater.

April: ABC television special, "My Father the Circus King," focuses on a circus family; particularly Gunther Gebel-Williams and his 11-year-old son, Mark Oliver.

April 3: Gebel-Williams and the Felds present a collection of circus memorabilia to the Smithsonian Institution in Washington, D.C.: elephant harness, Gunther's bull hook and costumes, and selected circus posters and costumes become part of the museum's History of American Entertainment collection.

1982   July 10: First quadruple somersault from the flying trapeze: Miguel Vazquez to Juan Vazquez, RBB&B, Tucson, Ariz.

Irvin Feld and Kenneth Feld buy RBB&B for $22.8 million cash.

Gunther Gebel-Williams trains and presents a giraffe named Dickie, a herd of elephants, and his son, Mark Oliver, now 12, in Spec called "Jungle Dreams."

1983   RBB&B: Debut of "Satin," first black aerial act.

Big Apple Circus: Bill "Buckles" Woodcock presents elephant act with wife, Barbara, and children, Shannon, 14, and Dalilah, 11, great-great grandchildren of Hiram Orton.

1984   Sept. 6: Irvin Feld dies.

1985   The Living Unicorn in RBB&B object of biggest circus ballyhoo since Barnum.

Oct. 22: Katherine Breen Hanneford dies at 96.

Big Apple Circus: Katja Schumann re-creates Ducrow's equestrian classic "The Courier of St. Petersburg."

1986   Shanghai Acrobats, troupe from the People's Republic of China, tours with RBB&B.

Spoleto Festival, Charleston, S.C.: Circus Flora re-creates first circus to visit Charleston, in 1810.

Merle Evans, 92, leader of the Ringling circus band for 50 years, takes part in the annual Great Circus Parade in Milwaukee, Wis.

1987   King Tusk, largest elephant since Jumbo, tours America with RBB&B.

RBB&B makes its Japanese debut in Tokyo, tours Japan performing under a Big Top.

1988   RBB&B: Tahar, Moroccan acrobat, puts his head in an alligator's mouth, wrestles alligators in the ring and in a tank of water.

From 40 states, 482 alumni travel to RBB&B winter quarters in Venice, Fla., for the 20th anniversary of the RBB&B Clown College; make television special on the education of a circus clown.

Canada's Cirque du Soleil makes New York debut.

Big Apple Circus tours for 20 weeks, April–Oct., entertaining over 285,000 people from Vermont to Washington, D.C.; founder, director, and ringmaster Paul Binder receives honorary Doctor of Fine Arts degree from Dartmouth for bringing America "classical" 1-ring circus.

Big Apple Circus: Dalilah Woodcock does handstand on forehead of elephant standing on one front leg under direction of father, Bill "Buckles" Woodcock.

Dec. 27: Gunther Gebel-Williams begins final tour with the 119th edition of RBB&B, scheduled to tour the U.S. for 2 years. He has played live to over 120 million people—5 million a year for 20 years, more than any other performer in history.

1989 RBB&B: Free-form skiers loop-the-loop on skis.

Sept. 4: Clifford E. Vargas, founder of Circus Vargas, dies at 64.

Big Apple Circus, 1989–1990 edition, presents the Wild West show "Grandma Goes West," built around the clown character Grandma created by Barry Lubin, 1975 graduate of RBB&B Clown College.

Katja Shumann (Mrs. Paul Binder), who in 1985 became the first woman to perform a complete version of the European equestrian classic "The Courier of St. Petersburg" in America, does a Wild West version, "The Pony Express."

The Rios brothers, Michel and Mehdi, do the rarely seen Risley Act (acrobatic foot juggling of a human partner) in the Big Apple Circus.

Ben Williams, son of Barbara Woodcock and Rex Williams, performs with 46-year-old Burmese Woodland elephant Anna May, trained by "Buckles" Woodcock.

Construction and renovation boom in U.S. stadiums where circuses play, including 21-year-old Madison Square Garden in New York. All feature private suites or other luxury seating, which attracts corporate customers and wealthy investors.

RBB&B President Kenneth Feld considers a return to the Big Top in selected American cities. Says Feld: "The tented circus, as we use it on tour in Japan, is, in my opinion, a definite possibility for the future. I already have architects designing new tents for the circus in America."

1990 The Loyal-Suarez Troupe features Timi Loyal, seventh-generation rider in one of the world's oldest circus dynasties and son of Giustino, who came to America in 1932 with the Loyal-Repensky Troupe. Mexico's Suarez family has been circus for over a century.

RBB&B: Italy's Flavio Togni presents a leopard riding on the back of a rhino.

NOTES

Principal collections consulted are abbreviated as follows:

AAS   American Antiquarian Society, Worcester, Mass.
Baraboo   Circus World Museum, Baraboo, Wis.
Harvard   Harvard College Library, Theatre Collection
NYPL   New York Public Library
RPL   Rockford, Ill., Public Library
Ringling Ringling Museum of the Circus, Sarasota, Fla.
SAPL   Harry Hertzberg Circus Collection, San Antonio Public Library
Somers   Somers Historical Society, The Elephant Hotel, Somers, N.Y.

PREFACE

Page

xvii   "To audiences everywhere": Robert Lewis Parkinson to author, Baraboo, June 15, 1983.

DISPLAY 1

Page

1   The history of the early circus in England and Europe is dealt with most thoroughly by Isaac J. Greenwood in *The Circus: Its Origin and Growth Prior to 1835* (New York, 1898); Maurice Willson Disher in *Greatest Show on Earth,* (New York, 1969), a history of Astley's circus and its artists; A. H. Saxon's *Enter Foot and Horse: A History of Hippodrama in England and France* (New Haven, 1968), which deals with

Astley's and the Cirque Olympique in Paris; Thomas Frost in *Circus Life and Circus Celebrities* (Detroit, 1970); and Jacob Decastro in *The Memoirs of J. Decastro, Comedian* (London, 1824), which includes Decastro's "History of the Royal Circus." For Antonio Franconi: "Le Cirque Franconi: Details Historiques sur cet Etablissement Hippique et sur ses principaux ecuyers, recrueillis par une chambriere en retraite," pp. 41–49. For Charles Hughes, see also A. H. Saxon, *The Life and Art of Andrew Ducrow & The Romantic Age of the English Circus* (Hamden, Conn., 1978), pp. 23, 414, *n*1. Jacques Tourniaire was "a disciple of the Franconis, who also brought the circus to Germany and Scandinavia" (John H. Towsen, *Clowns* [New York, 1976], p. 87).

2 Pool's equestrian exhibition and burlesque, without a clown, on Saturday, August 20, 1785, as announced in the *Pennsylvania Packet* for August 15, is noted in Greenwood, *The Circus*; Leonidas Westervelt, *The Circus in Literature* (1931); R.W.G. Vail, *Random Notes on the History of the American Circus* (Worcester, Mass., 1934); and Earl Chapin May, *The Circus from Rome to Ringling* (New York, 1963), p. 21. See also George C. D. Odell, *Annals of the New York Stage* (New York, 1927–1949), p. 248, and *Billboard*, March 15, 1930, p. 59.

3 The history of the form of equestrian clowning known as the tailor's ride and its variations can be found in Greenwood, *The Circus*, pp. 20–22; Saxon, *Andrew Ducrow*, pp. 22, 80, 198–99; and Towsen, *Clowns*, pp. 90–94. The history of the early American circus is covered in most detail in Greenwood, *The Circus*, and in John Durang, *The Memoir of John Durang (American Actor, 1785–1816)* (Pittsburgh, 1966); Westervelt, *The Circus in Literature*; May, *From Rome to Ringling*; Vail, *Random Notes*; John and Alice Durant, *Pictorial History of the American Circus* (New York, 1957); George Chindahl, *History of the Circus in America* (Caldwell, Id., 1959); Esse F. O'Brien, *Circus: Cinders to Sawdust* (San Antonio, 1959); Charles Fox and Tom Parkinson, *The Circus in America* (Waukesha, Wis., 1969); and Stuart Thayer, *Annals of the American Circus, 1793–1829* (Manchester, Mich., 1976).
The *Pennsylvania Packet* noted "Between the different parts a Clown," and this addition was recorded by Greenwood, who said: "Not until the summer of 1785 did the United Colonies rise to the dignity of a full-blown circus." See also Westervelt, *The Circus in Literature*. Pool took essentially the same show to New York the following year, and a handbill for his exhibition on September 21, 1786, is reproduced in Durant and Durant, *Pictorial History*, p. 21, and credited to Harvard. It contains the decisive words: "A CLOWN will entertain the Ladies and Gentlemen between the Feats."
Pool in Boston: Vail, *Random Notes*, p. 62.

4 Ricketts in Philadelphia: Clipping at Baraboo, RKTS-N45-93-2.
Jefferson on Washington as "the best horseman of his age": In letter to Dr. Walter Jones, from Monticello, Jan. 2, 1814, in Andrew A. Lipscomb and Albert Ellery Bergh, eds., *The Writings of Thomas Jefferson* (Washington, D.C.: Thomas Jefferson Memorial Association, 1903), vol. 14, pp. 48–51; and in Bernard Mayo, *Jefferson Himself* (Charlottesville, Va., 1970), p. 51.
On Custis: May, *From Rome to Ringling*, p. 17.

Washington's visit to Ricketts's circus on April 22, 1793: Greenwood, *The Circus*, p. 78.

Washington's Neutrality Proclamation: May, *From Rome to Ringling*, p. 18.

What did Washington see?: Notice of Ricketts's circus, April 3, 1793, Baraboo, RKTZ-N45-93-2; Notice of Ricketts's circus, May 15, 1793: "Mr. McDonald will Perform several COMIC FEATS (Being his First Appearance in America)," Baraboo, RKTS-N45-93-1; May, *From Rome to Ringling*, pp. 18–19.

5   Pantheon, Philadelphia: Thomas Clark Pollock, *The Philadelphia Theatre in the Eighteenth Century* (Philadelphia, 1933), p. 58, contains detailed, documented history of Ricketts's and Lailson's circuses in Philadelphia. See also C. G. Sturtevant, "The Circus in Philadelphia," *White Tops*, Nov.–Dec. 1949.

Ricketts presents his circus in Philadelphia in 1794: Baraboo, RKTS-N45-94-2.

Yellow fever in New York: Odell, *Annals of the New York Stage*, vol. 1, p. 417.

Durang joins Ricketts: Durang, *Memoir*, pp. 35, 42–45.

Ricketts in Philadelphia, 1795–1799: Pollock, *The Philadelphia Theater;* Odell, *Annals of the New York Stage*, vol. 1, p. 473: "The Harvard Theatre Collection possesses a bill for the evening of the 21st [of October, 1797], by which it would appear that President [John] Adams sought relief from the cares of state on that night in the solace of the circus."

Whiskey Rebellion Spec: Ibid., vol. 1, p. 443.

Cornplanter notice: Ibid., vol. 1, p. 441.

Washington's horse, Jack: Ibid., vol. 1, p. 442, quotes the *New York Gazette* for April 29, 1797; see also Vail, *Random Notes*, p. 64.

6   Ricketts's Canadian tour: Durang, *Memoir*, pp. 46–93. Durang tells of performing with Ricketts's circus, pp. 42–103, and names its members on pp. 43, 47, and 94.

Lailson and Jaymond Circus: Thayer, *Annals of the American Circus*; Pollock, *The Philadelphia Theatre*.

9   First street parade: Ibid.

"First woman rider in the country": Vail, *Random Notes*, p. 66.

"Embarked for the West Indies": George Stone cited in ibid., p. 166.

On Dec. 26, 1798, Ricketts opened his winter season. The Spec with the American astronaut planting a flag on the moon was the Ringling Bros. and Barnum & Bailey Bicentennial Spec in 1975–76. See RBB&B 1975 Program.

"this new field": *Quebec Gazette*, quoted in Thayer, *Annals of the American Circus*, p. 36.

9–10   Ricketts's circus burns, 1799: Durang, *Memoir*, pp. 95–96; Vail, *Random Notes*, p. 65; Thayer, *Annals of the American Circus*, p. 37.

10   Ricketts's last season, April 1800: Durang, *Memoir*, pp. 98–101.

Ricketts lost at sea: Reminiscences of George Stone, veteran circus acrobat, in *Albany Morning Express*, 1860, in Joel Munsell scrapbook in AAS library, as reported in Vail, *Random Notes*, p. 65.

Pepin and Breschard: Vail, *Random Notes*, pp. 67–68; Odell, *Annals of the New York Stage*, vol. 2, pp. 305, 346.

"The Battle and Death of General Malbrook": Vail, *Random Notes*, 68; original bill at Harvard.

Cayetano, Codet, Menial & Redon: Vail, *Random Notes*, pp. 68–69; additional material in Sturtevant, "Circus in Philadelphia," p. 5.

11   "The third of May": Sarah Anna Emery, *Reminiscences of a Nonagenarian* (William H. Huse, 1879).

DISPLAY 2

Page

13   My primary research for this chapter was at Somers and the AAS. See also May, *From Rome to Ringling*, chapters 4, 5, and 6, dealing with Hackaliah Bailey and the Flatfoot Syndicate. Vail, *Random Notes*; Greenwood, *The Circus*; Westervelt, *The Circus in Literature*; Thayer, *Annals of the American Circus*; and Gil Robinson, *Old Wagon Show Days* (Cincinnati, 1925), were also consulted.

Barnum, "Clowns and elephants": Dexter Fellows and Andrew Freeman, *This Way to the Big Show* (Garden City, N.Y., 1938), p. 211.

"The elephant is the largest animal": Emmett Kelly to author, Rockford, Ill., summer of 1953.

Crowninshield's elephant: Vail, *Random Notes*, p. 13. Vail says the elephant's arrival is recorded in Greenleaf's *New York Journal*, April 13, 1796.

14   First elephant's progress in the New World, through newspaper advertisements and handbills: Vail, *Random Notes*, pp. 13–16.

"Crowninshield's elephant made the vital link-up": Vail, ibid., p. 16, says that on June 13, 1812, "she joined Cayetano, Codet, Menial and Redon's New York Circus at Broadway and White Street."

Old Bet: See ibid. Old Bet was never actually exhibited with a circus. In 1816, Nathan Howes had a menagerie. He did not have a circus until he became a partner in the Aaron Turner Circus in the 1830s. See Durant and Durant, *Pictorial History*, p. 39, and the note on Aaron Turner's Circus on p. 321. Nevertheless, it was Old Bet who showed future circus owners such as P. T. Barnum that an elephant was the most profitable of menagerie attractions.

Robinson's claim that Old Bet arrived in America "in 1805, three years after the birth of my father": Robinson, *Old Wagon Show Days*, p. 32.

15   Confrontation between Bailey and Howes over Old Bet: Irving Wallace, *The Fabulous Showman* (New York, 1962), pp. 42–43. Based on a newspaper account and cartoon ("I'm Only Aiming at My Half") in the Somers collection.

Press accounts of the death of Old Bet from the *New York Post* for April 16, 1817, and the *Evening Post* for Christmas Eve, 1821, are to be found at Somers.

16   Diary of the Rev. Dr. William Bentley: Quoted in Vail, *Random Notes*, pp. 16–17. The diary is in the AAS.

Volcano of Tambora: Haraldur Sigurdsson and Steven Carey, "The Far Reach of Tambora," *Natural History*, June 1988, pp. 71–72.

For the activities and incorporation of the Zoological Institute, my primary sources were the original documents kept at Somers. Many were reproduced in *Petition to the Postmaster General . . .* (Somers, N.Y., 1966).

17   Nonconflicting routes: The Zoological Institute, Branch No. 7, Noell E. Waring, manager, published a booklet giving the route of the show during 1835. Chindahl, *History of the Circus in America*, p. 276, calls this the "first known instance of a route book." It shows that the "Menagerie and Aviary" operated by Branch No. 7, upon arriving in New York, was combined with the show of Macomber, Welch & Company for exhibitions at 37 Bowery. A copy of this first route book is in SAPL. Since then, hundreds of route books have been issued by various shows. In addition to the itinerary, they contain much detailed information on the show and thus constitute one of the most valuable sources of circus history. *White Tops*, vol. 9, nos. 2–3, contains a list of 235 route books compiled by Colonel C. G. Sturtevant, national historian of the Circus Fans Association of America. Volume 14, nos. 6–7, lists nineteen more. A later and amplified list was published by Col. Sturtevant in *Hobbies*, Jan. 1942, p. 15.

"We put our foot down flat": May, *From Rome to Ringling*, p. 36.

Jackson at Pepin's circus: Thayer, *Annals of the American Circus*, p. 142.

"Brilliant": *Louisville Public Advertiser*, cited in ibid.

On Isaac A. Van Amburgh: See O. J. Ferguson, *Biographical Sketch of I. A. Van Amburgh* (Booth & Co., 1865).

20   "The effect of his power": Ibid., p. 49.

"enough money": Thayer, *Annals of the American Circus*, p. 79.

"completing the picture of the triumph of faith over the savage beast": Ibid.

20–21   *Passages from the American Note-Books of Nathaniel Hawthorne* (Boston, 1898).

Tallahassee newspaper ad (Feb. 14, 1832) and announcement (Dec. 27, 1834): Thayer, *Annals of the American Circus.*

21–22   Travels of menageries and circuses: Ibid. In 1811, only Victor Pepin and James West had circuses traveling about the United States. Nevertheless, after seeing one or the other, the actor John Howard Payne predicted in a letter to J. H. Dwyer, which is now at Harvard: "Some accidental turn of fashion, or that insatiable thirst for novelty which constitutes a predominant feature in our national character, may make the [circus] popular and lucrative" (ibid., p. 148). By 1825, there were nine American circuses; by the time Payne died, in 1852, there were thirty. The elephant was the novelty the circus was seeking.

22   The innovation of using portable canvas tent is attributed to Brown by Thayer. Documentation from the Delaware *Gazette* for Nov. 22, 1825, is in his *Annals of the American Circus.*

23   "The North Star": *New York Clipper*, July 11, 1885.

On Levi J. North: See Robinson, *Old Wagon Show Days*; and May, *From Rome to Ringling*, particularly chap. 22.

24   "fame spread through civilization": Ferguson, *Van Amburgh*, p. 66.

"there have already been several cases": *Age*, Aug. 26, 1838, cited in Saxon, *Andrew Ducrow*, p. 321.

"He sticks his head in the lion's mouth": *Bartlett's Familiar Quotations*, ed. Christopher Morley, 11th ed. (Boston: Little, Brown, 1938), gives the line as "He puts his head in the lion's mouth" and says (p. 952) that it is from "Menagerie, or Showman's Song," a song "of unknown authorship" that was "Popular at Eton and in American colleges in the 1860s. There are various versions." The first two lines are:

> *Van Amburgh is the man who goes with all the shows,*
> *He gets into the lion's cage, and tells you all he knows.*

However, Vail (*Random Notes*, p. 38) says that "It was Van Amburgh who inspired the greatest of all circus songs, 'The Menagerie,' by C. T. Miller of Providence . . ." And Vail gives the line as I learned it in childhood: "He sticks his head in the lion's mouth . . ."

"The Grand Showman's Ball": Waldron Baily, who says he is a direct descendant of Hackaliah Bailey (though their surnames are spelled differently), quotes this account, which he says he copied from an unidentified newspaper clipping in his possession, in his memoirs, *The Autobiography of Waldron Baily* (New York, n.d.). The same newspaper account is found in May, *From Rome to Ringling*, p. 41, although, curiously, May quotes the correspondent as calling it "The Great Showman's Ball."

DISPLAY 3

Page

27　My primary source for this chapter is Barnum's autobiography, *Struggles and Triumphs: or, Forty Years' Recollections of P. T. Barnum Written by P. T. Barnum* (Buffalo, 1877). Between the years 1855 and 1888 at least nine versions of Barnum's autobiography were published. The first edition was called *Life of P. T. Barnum Written by Himself*. As did Irving Wallace in writing *The Fabulous Showman: The Life of P. T. Barnum*, I have referred to the 1871 edition, published by the American News Company, brought out when Barnum was sixty-one, because, as Wallace said, "It proved more comprehensive than his first edition and less expurgated than his last" (Wallace, 1962, p. 262). However, the 1877 edition covers his life to 1876 and includes the centennial edition of his "Museum, Menagerie and Circus of immense proportions" (Barnum, 1877, p. 770), so my quotations are from this edition unless otherwise noted. I also found Wallace's 1959 life of Barnum and Morris Robert Werner's *Barnum* (New York, 1923) particularly valuable, though Wallace has no footnotes and Werner few. A thoroughly documented book on Barnum is *Humbug: The Art of P. T. Barnum*, by Neil Harris (Chicago, 1973), which is particularly valuable for its bibliographic essay and twenty-four pages of footnotes. The memories of W. C. Coup, Barnum's sometime partner, in *Sawdust and Spangles* (Chicago, 1901) was also very helpful.

Barnum's spiel for Tom Thumb: In Robert Sherwood, *Here We Are Again* (Indianapolis, 1926), as is Sherwood's estimate of Barnum that "He was a wonder."

28   "Small peddler of molasses candy": Barnum, *Struggles and Triumphs*, p. 26.
Barnum's father dies: Ibid., p. 39.
Barnum to Brooklyn: Ibid., p. 48; returns to Bethel, ibid., p. 50.

29   On Hack Bailey: Wallace, *Fabulous Showman*, 1962, pp. 41–43.
"My store had much to do": Barnum, *Struggles and Triumphs*, p. 52.
"If I had waited": Ibid., p. 61.
Herald of Freedom for Dec. 12, 1832: Ibid., p. 65.

30   "an omnibus": Fox and Parkinson, *Circus in America*, p. 138.
"One hundred and twenty years": Joice Heth quoted in *Evening Star*, cited in Wallace, *Fabulous Showman*, 1962, p. 18.
"unwilling to tell their age": Editorial in *Daily Advertiser*, cited in ibid., p. 18.
Dissection of Joice Heth: Ibid., p. 28.
New York Sun editorial by Richard Adams Locke: Cited in ibid., p. 28.
"ANOTHER HOAX!": *New York Herald*, cited in ibid., p. 29.
On Turner: Werner, *Barnum*, pp. 36–39.
"In April, 1836, I connected myself with Aaron Turner's . . .": Barnum, *Struggles and Triumphs*, p. 80.

31   "We began our performances": Ibid., p. 80.
Criticism from preacher at Lenox, Mass., church service: Ibid., p. 81.
Rev. E. K. Avery incident: Ibid., pp. 82–85.

32   Musicians jailed at Camden, South Carolina: "A Scotchman named Cochran," ibid., p. 91.
Joe Pentland hired: Ibid.
Barnum disbands: Ibid., p. 101.
Barnum on show business: Ibid.

34   Barnum decides to buy a museum: Ibid., p. 111.
Meeting with Olmstead: Ibid., pp. 111–12.
"Messrs. Welch, June, Titus, Turner, Angevine": Ibid., p. 112.
"The American Museum was the ladder": Ibid., p. 133.
"The Cincinnatians": Mrs. Frances Trollope, *Domestic Manners of the Americans*, ed. Donald Smalley (New York, 1949), pp. 278–79.

34–35 "It was only necessary": Barnum, *Struggles and Triumphs*, p. 119.

35   "To awaken curiosity": Ibid., p. 130.
"We risk being": Daniel J. Boorstin, *The Image: or, What Happened to the American Dream* (New York, 1962), p. 59.
"They had the whole Museum": Barnum, *Struggles and Triumphs*, p. 125.
Goshen "was not an Arabian": Coup, *Sawdust and Spangles*, p. 51.
"Look here!": Barnum, *Struggles and Triumphs*, p. 162.

36   "Sure, an I'm not going out": Ibid., p. 140.
"TO THE EGRESS": Ibid.
"I confess": Ibid., p. 135.

37   The Tom Thumb story, "The smallest child I ever saw": Ibid., p. 163.
"A defective pituitary": Wallace, *Fabulous Showman*, 1962, p. 80.

38 Mrs. Stratton surprised: Barnum, *Struggles and Triumphs*, p. 163.
    "His stature but an inch in height": Werner, *Barnum*, p. 74.

39 General Tom Thumb in England: Barnum, *Struggles and Triumphs*, chap. 11.

41 Tom Thumb in France: Ibid., chap. 12.
    Journal des Débats, May 23, 1845, in Wallace, *Fabulous Showman*, 1962, p. 93.
    Tom Thumb visits President Polk: Ibid., p. 102.
    On Iranistan: Barnum, *Struggles and Triumphs*, pp. 261–63. A room from Iranistan
    has been re-created in the new Barnum Museum in Bridgeport, Conn., which opened
    in 1989.

42 "projected a great travelling museum": Ibid., p. 354.
    Jenny Lind's second New York visit: Ibid., p. 356.
    "P. T. Barnum's Asiatic Caravan, Museum and Menagerie": Ibid., p. 355; also Durant
    and Durant, *Pictorial History*, p. 60.

43 Barnum's plow elephant: Barnum, *Struggles and Triumphs*, pp. 357–62.

DISPLAY 4

47 Dan Rice has been the subject of three full-length biographies, numerous magazine
    and newspaper articles, and is the only professional clown in the *Dictionary of
    American Biography*, eds. Allen Johnson and Dumas Malone (New York, 1958).
    W. F. Wallett, a man who knew him and clowned with him, makes him come alive
    again in *The Public Life of W. F. Wallett, the Queen's Jester*, published in 1870, while
    Rice was still alive. Maria Ward Brown, author of *The Life of Dan Rice* (Long Branch,
    N.J., 1901), was Rice's cousin, and Rice was the direct source of her book's infor-
    mation. John C. Kunzog's *The One-Horse Show: The Life and Times of Dan Rice*
    (Jamestown, N.Y., 1962) is a well-researched biography. Don Carle Gillette gave
    Rice a more journalistic treatment in *He Made Lincoln Laugh: The Story of Dan Rice*
    (New York, 1967). May devotes chap. 8 of *From Rome to Ringling* to Rice, "A Jester
    Who Yearned to Be President." O'Brien includes a sketch of Rice in *Circus: Cinders
    to Sawdust* (p. 25). See also Chindahl, *History of the Circus in America*, pp. 61–64,
    and Joseph S. Schick, "Early Showboat and Circus in the Upper Valley," *Mid-
    America*, Oct. 1950. Also helpful in getting to know Rice are the Harvard photo-
    graphs, pictures, and drawings.

48 "A drunken man": Mark Twain [Samuel Clemens], *The Adventures of Huckleberry
    Finn* (New York, 1882; reprint, New York: Modern Library, 1985), pp. 424–
    25.

49 *Dictionary of American Biography*, eds. Johnson and Malone, s.v. "Rice, Dan."
    "a wonderful trainer": Sherwood, *Here We Are Again*.
    "He had the happy attribute": Ibid.

50 Lincoln's version of "Root, hog, or die!": Carl Sandburg, *Abraham Lincoln: The War
    Years* (New York, 1939), vol. 4, p. 44.
    "A successful clown": Rice quoted in Brown, *Life of Dan Rice*, p. 107.

51 "all through the circus": Twain, *Huckleberry Finn*, Modern Library, 1985, p. 424.

52   Henry Clay story: Brown, *The Life of Dan Rice*, in Mildred Sandison Fenner and Wolcott Fenner, *The Circus, Lure and Legend* (Englewood Cliffs, N.J., 1970), p. 206.

53–55   Groom-Rice dialogue: Towsen, *Clowns*, pp. 138–39.

55   Wallett's account of his appearances with Rice are in his memoirs, *The Public Life of W. F. Wallett*.

58   "Is that a beefsteak I see": Billy Burke, the singing clown who was born in Knox County, Ohio, in 1844, was inspired by Rice's Shakespeare-quoting clowning. His daughter, actress Billie Burke, wrote in her memoirs, *With a Feather on My Nose* (New York, 1949), p. 5: "Dan Rice was the most celebrated circus entertainer of his day. Probably he was the greatest clown who ever lived. Dan Rice undoubtedly made an enormous impression on my father. To some extent he modeled his clowning after him, and the habit of quoting Shakespeare followed him all his life."

58–60   On James Robinson and Charles Fish, bareback riders: May, *From Rome to Ringling*, pp. 201–6; Durant and Durant, *Pictorial History*, pp. 84–85.

58   "The Man Who Rides": Durant and Durant, *Pictorial History*, p. 85.

59   "that something which distinguishes circus genius": Fellows and Freeman, *This Way to the Big Show*, p. 232.

60   Lincoln and Douglas speeches in circus tent: R. S. Dingess, *Memoirs*, unpublished manuscript in the SAPL. Dingess was general agent for Spalding & Rogers in 1858.
"Although the people were all anxious": Coup, *Sawdust and Spangles*, p. 199.
"The John Brown excitement": Robinson quote cited in Gene Plowden, *Those Amazing Ringlings and Their Circus* (New York, 1967), p. 47.

61   "no nerves to speak of": Vincent Starrett, "Blondin—Prince of Manila," *Saturday Evening Post*, Oct. 26, 1929.

62   "the swaying rope": Ibid.
Prince of Wales to Blondin: Ibid.
Cartoon: Captioned "SHAKY / Daring Transit On the Perilous Rail" in *Vanity Fair*, June 9, 1860, reproduced on p. 41 of Durant and Durant, *Pictorial History*.

DISPLAY 5

Page

65   The best accounts of the circus during the Civil War are Robinson's *Old Wagon Show Days* and Coup's *Sawdust and Spangles*. Coup tells of some of Dan Rice's experiences during the war in chap. 11, "Stories of Old-Time Shows and Showmen." Chindahl's *History of the Circus in America* has a chapter with footnotes, "The Civil War Period" (pp. 81–87), and May, *From Rome to Ringling*, devotes chaps. 10 and 11 to "Trouping Out of War-Torn Dixie" and "Trouping Into Post-War Dixie."
" 'My opinion,' said Tom Thumb": Sandburg, *Abraham Lincoln: The War Years*, vol. 2, p. 292.
"No other nation paid so high a price": Daniel Boorstin and Brooks Mather Kelley, *A History of the United States* (Lexington, Mass., 1981), p. 274.

66   Circus census as war began: Robinson, *Old Wagon Show Days*, p. 195.

The *New York Clipper*: Quoted in Chindahl, *History of the Circus in America*, p. 82.

67   "I have never met" and other quotations: Coup, *Sawdust and Spangles*, p. 219.

68   "THE TWO AMERICAN HUMORISTS": Sandburg, *Abraham Lincoln: The War Years*, vol. 2, p. 300.

68–71   The full story of Tom Thumb's wedding and gifts is told by Theodore James, Jr., in "Giant Wedding of the Little People," *White Tops*, Jan.–Feb. 1975, pp. 9–12; reprinted in *Smithsonian*, Sept. 1973; adapted from Theodore James, Jr., *Fifth Avenue* (New York, 1972), pp. 90–94. Also see Saxon, *Andrew Ducrow*, pp. 22, 80, 198–99; Wallace, *Fabulous Showman*, 1962, p. 93; Werner, *Barnum*, pp. 265–71; Sandburg, *Abraham Lincoln: The War Years*, vol. 2, p. 291; and Carlton Brown, "Have Midget, Will Travel," *Cavalier*, Sept. 1958, quoted in Fenner and Fenner, *The Circus, Lure and Legend*, pp. 114–17.

70   "the elite": *New York Times*, cited in James, "Giant Wedding of the Little People." All *New York Times* quotes are from James. Carlton Brown notes (Fenner and Fenner, *The Circus, Lure and Legend*, p. 116) that "Readers of the *New York Times*, the staid grey old lady of the nation's newspapers, will be amazed to learn that almost ten percent of the February 11, 1863, paper was devoted to a description of the wedding."

71   Sources for wedding gifts: Werner, *Barnum*, pp. 268–69; Wallace, *Fabulous Showman*, 1962, p. 93; Sandburg, *Abraham Lincoln: The War Years*, vol. 2, p. 291.

Tom Thumb and Lavinia visit the White House: Grace Greenwood quoted in Sandburg, *Abraham Lincoln: The War Years*, vol. 2, p. 292.

Tad Lincoln story: James, "Giant Wedding of the Little People."

72   In Robinson, *Old Wagon Show Days*, see also p. 119 for the tale of the "furloughed soldier" with greenbacks who sends two farm boys to the circus, and pp. 173–74 for the clown-become-Yankee artillery sergeant, Archie Campbell, who was sent to Andersonville prison.

"It was a common occurrence": John H. Glenroy, *Ins and Outs of Circus Life* (1885), quoted in Chindahl, *History of the Circus in America*, p. 84.

73   Copperheads plot: *New York Times*, Nov. 27, 1864, and Nov. 30, 1864.

75   "THE TALLEST, SHORTEST AND FATTEST": *New York Times*, Nov. 30, 1864.

DISPLAY 6

Page

79   The best books dealing with the circus on the wild frontier are Coup's *Sawdust and Spangles* and Robinson's *Old Wagon Show Days*. George Conklin's memoirs, *Ways of the Circus* (New York, 1921), have good tales of the times. May's *From Rome to Ringling* is helpful, and Chindahl's *History of the Circus in America* is more helpful because fully documented. To put the circus on the frontier in context, I used *History of the Westward Movement* (New York, 1978) by Frederick Merk, Gurney Professor of History at Harvard and one of America's great historians of

the West. "The Circus in Early Rural Missouri," by Elbert R. Bowen (*Bandwagon*, May–June 1972), is well documented. Sheridan Logan's *Old Saint Jo: Gateway to the West, 1799–1932* (St. Joseph, Mo., 1979) gives a fine picture of the period. Greg Parkinson's "The Wild West: Pageantry of the Plains" (RBB&B 1982 Program) was very helpful. See also my "Star-Spangled History of the Circus" in *Argosy*, April 1975.

Migration to the west: Merk, *History of the Westward Movement*, p. xv.

Boon's Lick Times on Seeley Circus: Quoted in Bowen, "The Circus in Early Rural Missouri."

80   "the city was packed": Logan, *Old Saint Jo*, p. 46.

"Mr. Rowe's circus entertainments": Quoted in Durant and Durant, *Pictorial History*, p. 35. See also *California's Pioneer Circus*, ed. by Albert Dressler (San Francisco, 1926).

81   "One night . . . we strolled out": Wallett, *The Public Life of W. F. Wallett*.

82   "those two small words, 'bad roads' ": Coup, *Sawdust and Spangles*, p. 76.

Romeo to the rescue: Ibid., p. 77.

82–84   Prairie fire episode: Ibid., chap. 5, "The Prairie Fire," pp. 86–103.

84   Tony Pastor jumps the show: May, *From Rome to Ringling*, p. 80.

Pink lemonade story: Conklin, *Ways of the Circus*; and May, *From Rome to Ringling*, p. 81.

84–86   Mollie Bailey story: Olga Bailey, *Mollie Bailey* (Dallas, 1943); May, *From Rome to Ringling*, chap. 27, pp. 274–76; and O'Brien, *Circus: Cinders to Sawdust*, pp. 37–41.

86–93   Story of Agnes and Emma Lake and Wild Bill Hickok: Gil Robinson, who married Emma Lake, daughter of Agnes Lake by William Lake, tells the story in *Old Wagon Show Days*, pp. 127–32, from the point of view of the Lake family. Joseph G. Rosa, in *They Called Him Wild Bill: The Life and Adventures of James Butler Hickok* (Norman, Okla., 1964), tells the story from Hickok's point of view, pp. 132, 164–70, 196, 202. Van Matre tells the story as it relates to circus history in "Agnes Lake and Emma Lake," *Circus Banner Line*, Oct. 1, 1978.

90   On Jake Killian: Matre, "Agnes Lake and Emma Lake." See also Robinson, *Old Wagon Show Days*, p. 127. Jake Killian didn't surrender to the authorities until his victim's widow had moved the William Lake Circus to its next engagement in another town. At the trial, Matre tells us, Killian's friends testified that he had a good local reputation and that his eye had been shot out during the war. Killian was sentenced to only three years, ten months in prison, and circus people were enraged that someone could get such a light sentence for murder. So it was with evident satisfaction that Gil Robinson wrote in his memoirs (p. 127) that Jake Killian "was subsequently killed by Bill Norton, a sutlers clerk during the war."

92   "As soon as he learned of her presence": Rosa, *They Called Him Wild Bill*, p. 167.

Hickok's letter: Ibid., p. 213, which Rosa takes from Frank J. Wilstach, *Wild Bill Hickok, The Prince of Pistoleers* (New York, 1926), p. 282, and adds in a note on p. 213, "Wilstach no doubt saw the original; but perhaps this, too, was edited."

93   Front-page story on Agnes and Emma Lake: *Cheyenne Daily Leader* (Aug. 3, 1880) quoted in Rosa, *They Called Him Wild Bill*.

DISPLAY 7

Page

95 The invaluable book on the railroad circus is *The Circus Moves by Rail* (Boulder, Colo., 1978) by Tom Parkinson and Charles Philip Fox. Barnum and W. C. Coup tell conflicting stories in their autobiographies of how they came to take the train, but Coup's version is corroborated by impartial witnesses.

96 "Under the old regime": The description of wagon show life is from a Spalding & Rogers advertisement for "A New Railroad Circus!" in the collection of the New-York Historical Society, as reproduced in *The Circus Moves by Rail*, p. 10. The year, say Parkinson and Fox (p. 3), was 1856.

97 "the man who was trying": Wallace, *Fabulous Showman*, 1962, p. 124.
American Museum fire of March 2–3, 1868: Barnum, *Struggles and Triumphs*, pp. 698–700; Werner, *Barnum*, p. 303; Wallace, *Fabulous Showman*, 1962, p. 227.
American Museum fire of July 13, 1865: See Barnum, *Struggles and Triumphs*, chap. 39, pp. 638–48; Werner, *Barnum*, pp. 291–92; Wallace, *Fabulous Showman*, 1962, pp. 197–201.

98 "a fountain of delight": Horace Greeley's *New York Tribune* editorial for July 14, 1865, is quoted in Wallace, *Fabulous Showman*, 1962, pp. 200–201.
On Coup: My primary source was Coup's memoirs, *Sawdust and Spangles*. The most thorough research on Coup has been done by Parkinson and Fox for *The Circus Moves by Rail*. See also May, *From Rome to Ringling*, chap. 13, as well as Barnum's autobiography and the biographies of Barnum by Werner and Wallace.

98–100 On the founding of the Barnum Circus: Chindahl, *History of the Circus in America*, pp. 92–96.

100 Barnum to Coup, Oct. 8, 1870: Coup, *Sawdust and Spangles*, pp. 38–39.
On the "great show enterprise": Barnum, *Struggles and Triumphs*, p. 741.

101 The Cardiff Giant: Coup, *Sawdust and Spangles*, pp. 36–39. Coup credits the making of the "giant" to "a certain George Hull. He lived, I think, at Binghampton, New York." See also Wallace, *Fabulous Showman*, 1962, pp. 121–22. Hull was William "Stub" Newell's cousin, says Wallace, and he it was who shipped the "giant" to Newell's farm, where it was buried for a year, then dug up. "The entire hoax," says Wallace, "had cost Hull $2,200, and had earned him $35,000. Barnum's hoax of this hoax—at one point the showman was calling his replica of the Cardiff Giant the original, and the original a fake—had cost Barnum considerably less and earned him much more."

101–3 Barnum takes credit for the circus train on p. 742 of *Struggles and Triumphs* and adds insult to injury on p. 741 by calling Coup "my very able but too cautious manager." For the true story, see Parkinson and Fox, *The Circus Moves by Rail*, p. 19: "Coup's persistence had created the railroad circus, proved its worth, and set it forth on a course that would require no change for a hundred years."

103 "This was my reason": Coup, *Sawdust and Spangles*, pp. 61–62.
"the crew found waiting": Parkinson and Fox, *The Circus Moves by Rail*, p. 18.

104 "clowns and acrobats": Werner, *Barnum*, p. 312.

105   Ben Lusbie (1839–1884): Durant and Durant, *Pictorial History*, p. 81 (also contains "lightning ticket seller" poster); O'Brien, *Circus: Cinders to Sawdust*, p. 44.
Coup and Charles Reiche: Coup, *Sawdust and Spangles*, p. 227. Coup tells the story of his falling out with Reiche in chap. 12, "How the Great New York Aquarium Was Made and Lost," pp. 247–62; May's *From Rome to Ringling* continues the story to Coup's death, p. 118.

106–7   Barnum's United States Centennial Circus: Barnum, *Struggles and Triumphs*, pp. 770–71; Werner, *Barnum*, p. 318.

DISPLAY 8

Page

109   The most dependable works on Cody are those of Richard John Walsh and Milton S. Salsburg, *Making of Buffalo Bill: A Study in Heroics* (Indianapolis, 1928), based upon the Cody papers and with the help of Johnny Baker and others who knew Cody best; Don Russell, *The Lives and Legends of Buffalo Bill: A Study in Heroics* (Norman, Okla., 1960); and R. Croft-Cooke and W. S. Meadmore, *Buffalo Bill: The Legend, the Man of Action, the Showman* (London, 1952). Other sources are the sketches by William J. Ghent in *Dictionary of American Biography*, eds. Johnson and Malone; and by Robert R. Dykstra in *Encyclopedia of American Biography*, eds. John A. Garraty and Jerome L. Sternstein (New York, 1974); and in *Who's Who in America, 1916–17. The Life of Hon. Wm. F. Cody, Known as Buffalo Bill; An Autobiography* (1879) has been republished in many guises: Helen Cody Wetmore (his sister) and Zane Grey, *Last of the Great Scouts* (1899); Louisa Frederici Cody (his wife) and Courtney Ryley Cooper, *Memories of Buffalo Bill* (New York, 1919); Frank C. Cooper, *The Stirring Lives of Buffalo Bill and Pawnee Bill* (New York, 1912); and H. B. Sell and Victor Weybright, *Buffalo Bill and the Wild West* (New York, 1955). See also the bibliography in Walsh's work.

On Annie Oakley, see *Rolling Stone* (New York, 1945), the reminiscences of her friend, comedian Fred Stone, pp. 148–50. Courtney Ryley Cooper wrote *Annie Oakley, Woman at Arms* (New York, 1927), a biography based on the autobiographical notes and scrapbooks that Annie Oakley gave to Stone, but as Gilbert H. Barnes says in his sketch in *Dictionary of American Biography*, eds. Johnson and Malone, "The material has been carelessly used." Walter Havighurst's *Annie Oakley of the Wild West* (Chicago, 1954) is reliable.

On Buffalo Bill's Wild West, see Fellows and Freeman, *This Way to the Big Show*, the reminiscences of the show's publicist; and Sarah Blackstone, "Buffalo Bill's Wild West Show: Images a Hundred Years Later," *Bandwagon*, Nov.–Dec. 1983.

To picture the way it all looked, look at the five posters and read the excellent notes in Jack Rennert's *100 Years of Circus Posters* (New York, 1974), pp. 47–52. And there are three films: *Annie Oakley* (1935), with Barbara Stanwyck as Annie and Moroni Olsen as Buffalo Bill; *Buffalo Bill* (1944), with Joel McCrea as Cody;

and *Annie Get Your Gun* (1950), with Betty Hutton as Annie and Louis Calhern as Buffalo Bill.

"I have seen your Wild West": Letter from Samuel L. Clemens to William Cody quoted in Greg Parkinson, "The Wild West: Pageantry of the Plains," 112th Edition Souvenir Program, RBB&B, 1982, p. 8.

Aftershows: See chap. 6, "Wild West Stars and the Aftershow," in Fox and Parkinson, *The Circus in America*; also Durant and Durant, *Pictorial History*, pp. 222–23, 317.

110   Cody's background: S.v. "Cody, William F." in *Dictionary of American Biography*, eds. Johnson and Malone, and *Encyclopedia of American Biography*, eds. Garraty and Sternstein.

110–11   Killing of Yellow Hair (mistranslated as "Yellow Hand"): Dexter Fellows says (in *This Way to the Big Show*, p. 140) that he saw Cody show "Yellow Hand's scalp" to English reporters in Taunton, England, in 1903, and heard Cody tell how he scalped Yellow Hand. "In substance he told the story as it appeared in his autobiography," says Fellows, and on p. 141 he reprints that account, from which I quote.

111   "Nobody's ever done it before": Fellows and Freeman, *This Way to the Big Show*, p. 65.

112   "a faker in the show business": Ibid., p. 67.

112–13   History of the Deadwood Stage Coach: Ibid., pp. 67–68; Fellows says he takes his information from "the printed program of the Wild West."

112   "of the sixteen-car train": Ibid., p. 69.

"In this exhibition, out-Barnumed Barnum": Ibid.

113   "OUTFIT AT BOTTOM OF THE RIVER" and the deluge: Ibid., p. 71.

"This celebrated Girl Shot": Quoted from the official Buffalo Bill program for 1894 in Rennert, *100 Years of Circus Posters*, p. 9.

"It was our first thought": Burke, quoted in Cooper, *Annie Oakley, Woman at Arms*, p. 57.

115   "PEERLESS LADY WING-SHOT": Havighurst, *Annie Oakley of the Wild West*, p. 61.

Relationship of Sitting Bull to Buffalo Bill: See Dee Brown, *Bury My Heart at Wounded Knee* (New York, 1972), pp. 401–2, 410–12.

"Little Sure Shot!": Stone, *Rolling Stone*, p. 149.

"What do you think, Mamma": Cody and Cooper, *Memories of Buffalo Bill*, quoted in Fenner and Fenner, *The Circus, Lure and Legend*, p. 165.

116   "The wild equines": Wetmore and Grey, *Last of the Great Scouts*, p. 261.

"His was the most imposing figure": Rupert Croft-Cooke and Peter Cotes, *Circus: A World History* (New York, 1976), pp. 81–82.

117   Vicente Orapeza: William R. Brown, *Imagemaker: Will Rogers and the American Dream* (Columbia, Mo., 1970), pp. 112–13. See also Fellows and Freeman, *This Way to the Big Show*, p. 89: "Vincent Orapeza, leader of our Mexican group, who gave a performance with a lariat."

117–19   Buffalo Bill's 1895 program: Ibid., pp. 76–78.

119–21 The full story of George Abou Hamid can be found in his autobiography, *Circus, as told to his son George A. Hamid Jr.* (New York, 1950).

119 "Conditions were bad": Ibid., p. 18.

122 The relationship between Cody and Harry Tammen and Fred Bonfils, and the battle between Sells-Floto and Ringling Bros., is described in Fellows and Freeman, *This Way to the Big Show*, p. 160; Gene Fowler, *Timber Line: A Story of Bonfils and Tammen* (New York, 1934); Fox and Parkinson, *The Circus in America*, pp. 92–95; and Tom Parkinson in Durant and Durant, *Pictorial History*, p. 320.

"He was seventy years old": Fellows and Freeman, *This Way to the Big Show*, p. 161.

123 Roosevelt quote: "Col. Cody is praised by Col. Roosevelt who accepts Vice Presidency of memorial association which proposes to erect monument on Lookout Mountain, which is to be renamed Mt. Cody," *New York Times*, Feb. 11, 1917. The death of Buffalo Bill is also reported in the *Times* on Jan. 11, 1917: career, p. 14:2; editorial, p. 15:3. Body lies in state in Denver and funeral: Jan. 15, 1917, p. 9:4.

DISPLAY 9

Page

125 Following Jumbo's death on Sept. 14, 1885, an account of Jumbo's career appeared in the *New York Times* for Sept. 18, 1885, p. 1:6. The biographies of Barnum by Werner and Wallace and Neil Harris's *Humbug: The Art of P. T. Barnum* are all good on Jumbo. See also H. A. Ardman, "Phineas T. Barnum's Charming Beast: Jumbo the Elephant," *Natural History*, Feb. 1973, and J. L. Haley, "Colossus of His Kind," *American Heritage*, Aug. 1973.

Bailey as competitor: See Chindahl, *History of the Circus in America*, on James A. Bailey, pp. 96–101.

Use of electricity: A poster for Cooper, Bailey & Co.'s Great International Allied Shows, Great London Circus and Sanger's Royal British Menagerie advertising "all our vast pavilions lighted by electricity" in an appearance at St. Joseph, Mo., July 23, 1879, is reproduced in Durant and Durant, *Pictorial History*, p. 75. The poster is in the SAPL Harry Hertzberg Circus Collection. Bailey's circus was the first to use electric light.

"Mammal-of-the-Year": *Time*, Dec. 29, 1941, pp. 27–28.

"THE ONLY BABY ELEPHANT": Lithograph described in "James A. Bailey," *White Tops*, Aug. 1929.

"WHAT BARNUM THINKS OF THE BABY ELEPHANT": Wallace, *Fabulous Showman*, 1962, p. 242.

126 Bailey "a genius" and "While I was in the army": Fred Bradna and Hartzell Spence, *The Big Top* (New York, 1952), p. 32.

Firing of Billy Dutton: Wallace, *Fabulous Showman*, 1962, p. 244.

127 "a Fourth of July celebration every day": Barnum, *Struggles and Triumphs*, p. 770. Cooper & Bailey routes, 1876–80, are in Ringling Bros. and Barnum & Bailey Route Book for 1947.

P. T. Barnum's Greatest Show on Earth and the Great London Circus and Sanger's Royal British Menagerie, P. T. Barnum, James L. Hutchinson and James A. Bailey, owners: Full title given by route books and newspaper ads in Baraboo.

New York Herald on three rings: Quoted in Wallace, *Fabulous Showman*, 1962, p. 245.

"Perhaps nothing is more typical of America": Robert C. Toll, *On with the Show* (New York, 1976), p. 62.

"He was the largest": Haley, "Colossus of His Kind," p. 63.

"It never cost me a cent": Quoted in Wallace, *Fabulous Showman*, 1962, p. 247.

128 "What is the difference": Hutchinson quoted in ibid., p. 248.

128–29 Barnum's purchase of Jumbo from the London Zoological Society: References in the *New York Times* in 1882 on March 7 (p. 1:6 and p. 7:3); March 18 (p. 3:2); March 20 (p. 1:7); March 23 (p. 1:4); March 24 (p. 1:3); March 25 (p. 1:4); and March 26 (p. 1:5). In short, Jumbo was front-page news in the *New York Times* for a month. Jumbo's departure from London is described in the *New York Times*, April 8, p. 5:1.

129 *Daily Telegraph* and Barnum cables: "P. T. Barnum's London Telegraph Dispatch," *New York Times*, Feb. 24, 1882, p. 2.

130 Jumbo's arrival in New York: *New York Times*, April 10, 1882, p. 1:4, and April 11, 1882, p. 8:1. See also *New York Sun*, April 10, 1882; and Odell, *Annals of the New York Stage*, vol. 11, p. 541.

Jumbo's first trip in America: *New York Times*, April 23, 1882, p. 9:2.

130–32 Jumbo killed: *New York Times*, Sept. 17, 1885; also the *New York Clipper*, Oct. 3, 1885.

132 The account of Jumbo's death by a Barnum publicist is given in Matthew Scott, *Autobiography of Matthew Scott, Jumbo's Keeper; also Jumbo's biography, by the same author* (Trows Printing and Booking Co., 1885), p. 95. Haley, "Colossus of His Kind" (pp. 82–85), contrasts the Scott account published by Barnum, in which Jumbo supposedly "snatched the little elephant from in front of the thundering train," with "several totally irreconcilable versions [that] have been published." The steps in Barnum's "post-mortem Jumbo campaign" are analyzed by Haley on pp. 84–85.

"It is all true": Winston Churchill, *A History of the English-Speaking Peoples*, vol. 1: *The Birth of Britain* (New York, 1956), p. 60.

134 "The dog and pony format": Fox and Parkinson, *The Circus in America*, p. 98; see also pp. 58, 60, 160, 185, 190–91, 200, 255.

135 Jumbo's skin and skeleton: The work of mounting Jumbo is described in the *New York Clipper*, Oct. 3, 1885, p. 452.

Two agents look for sacred white elephant: Werner, *Barnum*, pp. 348–49.

136 Joaquin Miller's poem: Ibid., pp. 350–51.

The U.S. exhibition of Toung Taloung is documented in the *New York Clipper*, Feb. 23, 1884, p. 831; and Odell, *Annals of the New York Stage*, vol. 12, pp. 387, 540.

"Well, it's whiter than I expected to find it": Fellows and Freeman, *This Way to the Big Show*, p. 272. Fellows says he had it from "Henry Lowenthal, who covered the story for the *New York World*." Fellows was thirteen when the "White Elephant War" erupted, but he retells it beautifully in his book's "Display No. 8: Elephants I'll Never Forget." See also Wallace, *Fabulous Showman*, 1962, p. 252; Harris, *Humbug*, pp. 256, 266–71, and 328 *n*58; and "White Elephants," *New York Times*, March 22, 1884, p. 4.

"I don't think your elephant is so very white" and "My boy": Wallace, *Fabulous Showman*, 1962, p. 252.

On Adam Forepaugh: Chindahl, *History of the Circus in America*, pp. 103–6. See also: Durant and Durant, *Pictorial History*, pp. 90–95; May, *From Rome to Ringling*, pp. 122–23; and Wallace, *Fabulous Showman*, 1962, p. 253.

137 Louise Montague: Durant and Durant, *Pictorial History*, p. 92. A full-page photograph of "The $10,000 Beauty, Louise Montague" is in May, *From Rome to Ringling*, facing p. 270.

"Lalla Rookh's Departure from Delhi" poster and Chicago accidents during parade: Durant and Durant, *Pictorial History*, p. 92.

"Jumbo, the Children's Giant Pet" poster: Reproduced on p. 22 of Rennert's *100 Years of Circus Posters*.

138 Exposé of Forepaugh's "white elephant" by Alexander C. Kenealy: Fellows and Freeman, *This Way to the Big Show*, pp. 276–77.

The compromise between Barnum and Forepaugh is described in *White Tops*, May–June 1939, p. 6:2; See also *New York Sunday Mercury*, April 2, 1887. The courier used for the road tour is described in *Billboard*, March 6, 1943, p. 39. See also Odell, *Annals of the New York Stage*, vol. 13, p. 339.

140 Fire at Bridgeport: Werner, *Barnum*, p. 360.

Jumbo's skeleton and skin: Photographs of both, courtesy of the American Museum of Natural History and the Barnum Museum, Tufts University, are in Harvey A. Ardman's "Phineas T. Barnum's Charming Beast," *Natural History*, Feb. 1973, p. 85.

"I suppose you all come to see Barnum": Werner, *Barnum*, p. 362.

141 Marx, Freud, and Barnum: Louis Kronenberger, *Company Manners: A Cultural Inquiry into American Life* (New York, 1954), p. 25.

"The business of America": Calvin Coolidge, speech before the Society of American Newspaper Editors, Jan. 17, 1925, see *Bartlett's Familiar Quotations*, 13th ed., p. 859a.

Business done by Barnum's circus: Harris, *Humbug*, pp. 249–54, analyzes the diary and ledger of Henry Eugene Bowser, Barnum's confidential secretary.

"Barnum is gone": Obituary in the *Times* of London is quoted in Wallace, *Fabulous Showman*, 1962, pp. 258–59.

142 "a compendium of biologic research": Hamlin Garland, *A Son of the Middle Border* (New York, 1920), p. 137.

"Spread of the railroad show: See Parkinson and Fox, *The Circus Moves by Rail*, for a complete account.

Free street parade grows: See Charles Philip Fox and F. Beverly Kelley, *The Great Circus Street Parade in Pictures* (New York, 1978), p. viii.

DISPLAY 10

The best source on the Ringling brothers is Charles Philip Fox's *A Ticket to the Circus*, a pictorial history of the Ringlings that Fox published in 1959. Chappie Fox has photographed so many primary sources for this book that it saves circus researchers an enormous amount of time. Next, I would list Gene Plowden's 1967 biography, *Those Amazing Ringlings and Their Circus*. Roland Butler, who wrote the introduction, was general press representative of Ringling Bros. and Barnum & Bailey Combined Circus for more than thirty years, until June 1954, and Butler wrote shortly before his death on Oct. 20, 1961, that Plowden's book was "the first completely authentic history of the Ringlings and their circus ever put on paper." The book is not documented, but Plowden, a reporter for both the United Press and the Associated Press, knew John Ringling from 1927 until his death. Plowden's book was recommended to me in 1982 by Tim Holst, then performance director of the Ringling Red Unit, former Ringling ringmaster and clown, and now associate producer of Ringling Bros. and Barnum & Bailey Circus.

The Circus Kings (New York, 1960), by Henry Ringling North and Alden Hatch, tells the Ringling story from the vantage point of one of the two nephews who took over the operation of the circus from the original brothers. Fred Bradna and Hartzell Spence's *The Big Top: My Forty Years with the Greatest Show on Earth* (New York, 1952) tells of the Ringlings from the point of view of their equestrian director; and Fellows and Freeman's *This Way to the Big Show* gives the view from the publicist's car. Chindahl's *History of the Circus in America*, the only fully documented history of the American circus until this one, is valuable on the Ringlings as on every other aspect of the circus. Durant and Durant, *Pictorial History*, contains many good pictures of the era of the Ringlings and their rivals. *The Circus in America*, by Fox and Parkinson, has much information on the Ringlings, as does *From Rome to Ringling*, by May. May includes, as chap. 31, a personal reminiscence of "Mr. John [Ringling] . . . The Circus King."

Much can be learned about the Ringlings from their circus posters. See *American Circus Posters* (New York, 1978), edited and with notes by Charles Philip Fox; Rennert, *100 Years of Circus Posters*; and Fox and Kelley, *Great Circus Street Parade*.

Even more can be learned from Ringling route books. At the end of each season many circuses would issue a route book in which appeared an entire list of the show's personnel and their jobs; the program; the entire season's route; statistics of the circus's size and equipment; photos and stories. In the early days, the route book was written in the form of a diary. Route books constitute one of the best sources of circus history. Baraboo and SAPL have good collections of route books.

The Ringlings: Wizards of the Circus (New York, 1952), by Alvin F. Harlow, a professional biographer and frequent contributor to the *Dictionary of American Biography*, benefits from a research trip to Baraboo and interviews with Ida Palmer Ringling, widow of Al Ringling; the Ringling's cousin Henry Moeller, who was the circus wagon builder; and others. Alf. T. Ringling's *Life Story of the Ringling Brothers* (Chicago, 1900), to which Florence Oliver, Somers town historian, directed me in the circus collection at the Elephant Hotel, is a compromise between biography and ballyhoo, signed by one of the brothers.

146 "With rapt attention": Alf. T. Ringling, *Life Story of the Ringling Brothers*, quoted in Fenner and Fenner, *The Circus, Lure and Legend*, p. 20.

"What would you say": Alf. T. Ringling, quoted in ibid.

Ringlings move back to Baraboo in 1875: Harlow, *Wizards of the Circus*, p. 45.

147 "Dear Parents" and "The most interesting aspect": North and Hatch, *The Circus Kings*, pp. 76–77.

For an account of Ringling Bros. Circus, year by year, 1884 to 1918, see John P. Grace, "The Ringling Bros. Circus, 1884–1918," *White Tops*, July–Aug. 1933, p. 16. The routes are given in Ringling Bros. and Barnum & Bailey route book for 1946, in the collection of Ringling Bros. and Barnum & Bailey Clown College, Venice, Fla.

"the future showmen of America" and "this show is destined": What Robinson said that day is variously reported by North and Hatch, *The Circus Kings* (p. 79), May, *From Rome to Ringling* (p. 147), and Harlow, *Wizards of the Circus* (p. 100), but all three agree that he called the Ringlings "the future showmen of America," and North and Harlow add "They are the coming men!" Fox attributes his version (in *A Ticket to the Circus*, p. 21) to "Henry Moeller, who witnessed this first performance," and who remembered Yankee Robinson "ending with, 'this show is destined to become the greatest circus in the world.'" Moeller was a wagon maker who married Mrs. August Ringling's sister.

How Al Ringling balanced a plow on his chin: Harlow, *Wizards of the Circus*, p. 47, and the information card in a 1983 diorama picturing this feat at Baraboo.

148 Spencer Quinn Stokes's riding mechanic: May, *From Rome to Ringling*, pp. 206–7; Peter Verney, *Here Comes the Circus* (New York, 1978), p. 96.

149 "HIDEOUS HYENA STRIATA GIGANTIUM": North and Hatch, *The Circus Kings*, p. 83.

Louise (Mrs. Al) Ringling, snake charmer: Fox, *A Ticket to the Circus*, p. 31.

"Wagons continually pulled to pieces" and "We will give you": North and Hatch, *The Circus Kings*, p. 88.

Brothers lease Van Amburgh title from Hyatt Frost: Ibid., p. 61.

150 Camels with lice: Forepaugh letter, and recollection of Mrs. Henry Ringling, reported in Fox, *A Ticket to the Circus*, pp. 24–25.

"he became a human encyclopedia": Obituary of John Ringling, *New York Times*, Dec. 2, 1936.

"In the old opposition days": Fellows and Freeman, *This Way to the Big Show*, p. 182.

On John Ringling, "Super Router": Ibid., p. 181.

151 "When he took over": Alice Ringling Coerper, "The Ringlings of Baraboo," in Fox, *A Ticket to the Circus*, p. 19.

Advertisement: "1891 Show Is Recalled As City Awaits Circus," *Rockford* (Ill.) *Morning Star*, Aug. 8, 1937, p. 1.

"An appalling crash awoke us": O. H. Kurtz, comp., *Official Route Book of Ringling*

Brothers' World's Greatest Railroad Shows, Season of 1892 (Buffalo, 1892). Kurtz was a juggler on the show. A copy of the route book is at Baraboo. Fox and Parkinson, in *The Circus in America*, summarize its contents in chap. 3.

155   "Hundreds of thousands saw it": Kurtz, comp., *Official Route Book . . . 1895*.

"Duryea . . . horseless carriage": C. P. Fox, "The Circus in America: A 200-Year Tradition," RBB&B circus program, 1975, p. 5. I saw the 1896 poster in Fox's personal collection in 1975. A photograph of the Duryea is in Durant and Durant, *Pictorial History*, p. 156.

156   The 1848 forty-horse hitch: Fox and Kelley, *Great Circus Street Parade*, p. 84.

"matched white horses . . . their accoutrements": *1897 Route Book, Ringling Bros. and Barnum & Bailey Circus*, quoted in Fox, *A Ticket to the Circus*, p. 85. A photograph of the Ringling mounted band of 1897 is in Durant and Durant, *Pictorial History*, p. 156. See also "Evolution of the Circus Band," by W. N. Merrick, a circus bandleader, *Billboard*, April 15, 1911; "Circus Band Music," by Col. C. G. Sturtevant, *Billboard*, March 19, 1927; and "Circus Bands and Leaders of the Past," by H. H. Whittier, a circus bandleader, *Billboard*, Dec. 7, 1929. In the twentieth century, the outstanding bandmasters have been Merle Evans, who led the RBB&B band from 1919 to 1955, and William Pruyn, who has arranged and conducted its music in the Feld era. Evans is remembered for facing the arena with his back to the musicians and conducting them with his left hand while playing the cornet he held in his right. Pruyn has led the Big Top bands in every state in the union.

Cinematograph: At Baraboo in the summer of 1983, Robert L. Parkinson, director of the research center there, showed me the Ringling route books for 1896 and 1897, containing pictures of the cinematograph and the information I have used here.

157   "More wonderful" and "EDISON'S LATEST": Fox, *A Ticket to the Circus*, p. 111.

"I always had three men": Jake Posey, *Last of the Forty Horse Drivers* (New York, 1959), pp. 332–33.

158   Bicycle daredevils: See the study by Willard D. Coxey recounted in Fellows and Freeman, *This Way to the Big Show*, pp. 241–46; also "A History of Circus Cycling: Deeds of Daring Deftly Done," *108th Edition Souvenir Program & Magazine*, Ringling Bros. and Barnum & Bailey Combined Shows, 1978. This article reproduces the 1904 Barnum & Bailey circus poster showing Volo the Volitant "describing an enormous aerial arc" with his bicycle and The Great Ancillotti "looping the gap" with his. For information on the friendship between Volo the Volitant (C. B. Clarke) and Eugene O'Neill, and for the fact that O'Neill got the idea for his play *The Emperor Jones* from another circus man named Jack Croak, I am indebted to Barbara and Arthur Gelb for their 1962 biography, *O'Neill*. (I used the edition published in New York by Dell, 1964.)

159   "One of my old chums": Gelb and Gelb, *O'Neill*, p. 297.

The idea for *Emperor Jones*: Ibid., p. 438.

"You were good to me": Ibid., p. 659.

"Ed Mosher in *The Iceman Cometh*": Ibid., p. 297.

"You know, Harry": Eugene O'Neill, *The Iceman Cometh*, in *Best American Plays*, third series, 1945–1951, ed. by John Gassner (New York: Crown Publishers, 1952), p. 114.

Bicycle being eclipsed by automobile: See Fellows and Freeman, *This Way to the Big Show*, pp. 241–46.

160   "As the car descends": Ibid., pp. 243–44.

"I am courting death each day": Octavie LaTour, "The Limit of Human Daring," *New York World*, April 8, 1905, quoted in Fenner and Fenner, *The Circus, Lure and Legend*, pp. 104–5.

Bailey "hid himself in his private office": Fellows and Freeman, *This Way to the Big Show*, p. 246.

Bailey growing old and weary: See Harlow, *Wizards of the Circus*, p. 144. Harlow interviewed Mrs. Ida Palmer Ringling, widow of Henry, who managed the Forepaugh-Sells Circus when Bailey sold the Ringling brothers a half interest.

DISPLAY 11

Page

164   "Great flares of gaseous circus light": Thomas Wolfe, *Only the Dead Know Brooklyn* (Signet, 1947), p. 33.

165   "We used to carry water to the elephants": William Saroyan, *My Name Is Aram* (New York, 1938), pp. 133–34.

"The boys whooped": Booth Tarkington, *The Gentleman from Indiana* (New York, 1902), p. 135.

"I hung around the midget": Carl Sandburg, *Always the Young Strangers* (New York, 1953), p. 145.

"One clown dressed": W. Earl Aumann, Venice, Fla., *Gondolier* clipping, n.d.

166   "a prestigious potent potion": circus poster in possession of the author.

"one of the oldest of societies": E. B. White, "The Ring of Time," in *The Points of My Compass*, reprinted in Fenner and Fenner, *The Circus, Lure and Legend*, p. 142.

Fred Ferber and Ella Bradna: Bradna and Spence, *The Big Top*, chap. 2, "Sixty-four in a Car; or, Love on Wheels," pp. 14–28. See also the unpaginated picture caption in that book: "Ella Bradna, exhibiting White Eagle in the center ring during her farewell season, 1942, at age sixty-eight. Madame Bradna holds the record for consecutive years of center-ring stardom, 29 seasons."

167   "I lack the adjectives": Ogden Nash, "The Big Tent Under the Roof," in *Verses from 1929 On*, reprinted in Fenner and Fenner, *The Circus, Lure and Legend*, p. 177.

Rachel Field poem: "Gunga," in *Three Owls*, ed. by Anne Carroll Moore, reprinted in Fenner and Fenner, *The Circus, Lure and Legend*, p. 174.

"After the imposing entry": Quoted by Fred D. Pfening, Jr., in "Masters of the Steel Arena," *Bandwagon*, May–June 1972.

167–68   On the length of Zip's career as the "What-is-it?": Apparently, Zip was on exhibition, intermittently, from at least 1842 until 1926. Bradna and Spence say (*The Big Top*, p. 242) that Zip "worked intermittently from 1865 until 1926, when he died at the age of eighty-one." The Durants (*Pictorial History*, p. 114) say that he "was first shown in 1859 and trouped continuously for sixty-seven years." However, Fellows and Freeman write (*This Way to the Big Show*, p. 308), "Barnum first exploited him as the 'Wild Boy,' and the story among show folk is that, when Charles Dickens saw Zip at the American Museum, he turned to a companion and exclaimed: 'What is it?' Word was quickly relayed to Barnum, and thereafter the wild boy became 'Zip, the What-Is-It.' " According to Wallace (*Fabulous Showman*, p. 124), Dickens saw Zip while being shown the American Museum by Barnum on his 1842 visit to the United States. "Dickens blinked up at him, and turned to Barnum. 'What is it?' asked the English author. Barnum clapped his hands with delight. 'That's what it is—a What-is-it!' " Wallace gives no source for this story, but Bradna, without knowing what year Dickens visited the American Museum, accepted it.

Charles Dickens visited the United States in both 1842 and 1867–68. (See J. B. Priestley, *Charles Dickens and His World* [New York, 1961], chronology, pp. 130–31.) If it was Dickens who named Zip the "What-is-it?" as Fellows and Wallace recount, the visit must have been in 1842, for Barnum writes in *Struggles and Triumphs* (1877 ed., pp. 543–44): "On the 13th of October, 1860, the Prince of Wales, then making a tour in the United States, in company with his suite, visited the American Museum," and during his inspection of the museum, "the 'What is it?' grinned." Fellows and Freeman say (*This Way to the Big Show*, p. 308) that Zip began the 1926 season, then went to Bellevue Hospital suffering from pneumonia and died. Therefore, if Zip could be seen by Charles Dickens at the American Museum in 1842 and by those who patronized Ringling Bros. and Barnum & Bailey Circus in Madison Square Garden in 1926, his career spanned at least eighty-four years.

168   "Well, we fooled 'em": Zip quoted in Bradna and Spence, *The Big Top*, p. 242.

"THE LAST GIRAFFE": John Lentz showed me this poster at the John and Mable Ringling Museum of the Circus in Sarasota, Fla., in 1983. It is also reproduced in Fox, *A Ticket to the Circus*, p. 71.

Parkinson to author, Baraboo, summer 1953.

"hanging by her teeth": Wallace Fowlie, *Pantomime* (Chicago, 1951), pp. 7–8.

Diavolo poster: Baraboo collection.

169   "constant playmate": Elizabeth Thaxter Hubbard, "Life Was Lovely," *Harvard Magazine*, Nov.–Dec. 1988, p. 62.

"the personification of dreams": Lucia Zora, *Sawdust and Solitude* (Boston, 1928), in Fenner and Fenner, *The Circus, Lure and Legend*, p. 140.

Bailey's insect bite: Werner, *Barnum*, p. 372n.

169–70   History of Madison Square Garden: John Culhane, "Take Me to the Garden," *New York Times Magazine*, Feb. 11, 1973.

170   "James A. Bailey is dead!": Plowden, *Those Amazing Ringlings*, p. 93.

170–71   "if we buy the whole thing at once": Ibid., p. 96.

171   Murder of Stanford White: Ibid., p. 99.

1907 and 1908 season: Ibid., p. 101.

Ringling brothers' vote on Garden opening: Ibid., pp. 102–3.

171–75   1909 season headlines: See the *New York Times*: New York City arrival set, March 6, p. 14:3; circus starts from Wisconsin, March 14, p. 11:2; arrives New York,

March 18, p. 18:1; care of elephants described, March 20, p. 12:2; article on circus, March 21, pt. 5, p. 11:1; rehearsal, March 22, p. 7:1; Ringling Bros. opens at Garden, March 26, p. 9:1.

174–75 The "Schumann Dynasty": See the Big Apple Circus 1984 Program; also the biographies of equestrienne Katja Schumann in the programs for 1983 through 1988–89. In the 1985 season of the Big Apple Circus, Katja Schumann re-created "The Courier of St. Petersburg," which Andrew Ducrow, considered the most creative trick rider in circus history, created on May 7, 1827, as director of Astley's Circus in London.

175 Meeting of circuses: Plowden, *Those Amazing Ringlings*, pp. 104–5.

Otto Ringling dies: North and Hatch, *The Circus Kings*, p. 150; Plowden, *Those Amazing Ringlings*, p. 127; Fox, *A Ticket to the Circus*, p. 62.

On May Wirth: See Bradna and Spence, *The Big Top*, particularly pp. 307–11.

175–76 On the Wirth Circus in Australia, see George Wirth (one of Philip Wirth's sons), *Round the World with a Circus* (Victoria, Australia, 1925).

176 "the only product of American training": Bradna and Spence, *The Big Top*, pp. 370–71.

"MAY WIRTH BADLY HURT": *New York Times*, April 23, 1913, p. 1.

May Wirth's subsequent career: From clippings at Ringling.

"the most heart-rending": Bradna and Spence, *The Big Top*, p. 257.

177 President Wilson's hat in the ring: Ibid., pp. 118–19.

Death of Al Ringling: Robert L. Parkinson to author, Baraboo, 1983; see also: North and Hatch, *The Circus Kings*, pp. 169–170; Bradna and Spence, *The Big Top*, p. 92; Plowden, *Those Amazing Ringlings*, p. 128.

177–78 RBB&B during World War I: Bradna and Spence, *Those Amazing Ringlings*, pp. 90–95.

178 1918 influenza epidemic: Ibid., p. 95.

Charlie Ringling, "What a show *that* would be!": Ibid.

"SUPERCIRCUS DRAWS CROWDS": *New York Times*, March 30, 1919, p. 1. See also *New York Times*, March 14, 1919, p. 18.

179 On Tiny Kline: Robert De Roos, "The Magic Worlds of Walt Disney," *National Geographic*, Aug. 1963. A photograph of the former Ringling aerialist flying as Tinker Bell at Disneyland is on p. 198. Her act can be seen in *Disneyland After Dark*, the April 15, 1962, program of Walt Disney's Sunday night series on NBC-TV, which was released theatrically in Europe.

182 May Wirth dead: Obituary in Sarasota, Fla., *Herald-Tribune*; clipping included in May Wirth display at Ringling.

"In recent years": John Ringling, "We Divided the Job—But Stuck Together," *American*, Sept. 1919; reprinted in Fox, *A Ticket to the Circus*, pp. 39–46.

DISPLAY 12

Page

186–90 The person who told me the love story of Leitzel and Codona with such passion that it brought tears to my eyes was Tito Gaona, the first trapeze artist since

Codona to perform the triple somersault consistently. Gaona had the story from Victoria Codona, Alfredo's sister, whose image is on the dust jacket of this book. A number of others have told their versions, notably Bradna and Spence in *The Big Top*, pp. 179–97; North and Hatch in *The Circus Kings*, pp. 182–90; and Robert Lewis Taylor in *Center Ring* (Garden City, N.Y., 1956), pp. 215–50. The denouement, of course, was front-page news in the newspapers of the day.

186   "My job": Alfredo Codona, as told to Courtney Ryley Cooper, "Split Seconds," *Saturday Evening Post*, Dec. 6, 1930.

187   "I drove my trapeze steadily higher": Taylor, *Center Ring*, p. 245.
Of the doctor and Leitzel's infected arm: Ibid., p. 209.

188   "The marriage of these two comets": Quoted in Bradna and Spence, *The Big Top*, p. 192.
"could not abandon": Ibid., p. 193.

189   "Miss Bruce derived satisfaction": Ibid.
"I was reaching": Frank McClosky to author, May 16, 1975, interview in Liberty Bell Park, Philadelphia.

190–91   Con Colleano: See Bradna and Spence, *The Big Top*, pp. 10, 61, 104–5, 131, 303, 313; North and Hatch, *The Circus Kings*, p. 179; O'Brien, *Circus: Cinders to Sawdust*, pp. 134–35.

190   "The flies helped the most": O'Brien, *Circus: Cinders to Sawdust*, p. 135.

191   "Yet, aside from himself": Bradna and Spence, *The Big Top*, p. 303.
"He was the most fun": Alice Ringling Coerper, "The Ringlings of Baraboo," in Fox, *A Ticket to the Circus*, p. 18.
"I'm the last one": North and Hatch, *The Circus Kings*, p. 205.
"The Ringlings traditionally": Ibid., p. 207.
John Ringling abolishes long clown solos: Bradna and Spence, *The Big Top*, p. 217.

196   Death of Marceline: Charlie Chaplin, *My Autobiography* (New York, 1966), pp. 38–39.

196–97   Death of Slivers Oakley: Fellows and Freeman, *This Way to the Big Show*, p. 211.

197   "the art of clowning": Sherwood, quoted in Towsen, *Clowns*, p. 259.
Rice–Ringmaster exchange: Ibid., p. 137.
Joe Penner–straight man exchange: Jim Harmon, *The Great Radio Comedians* (Garden City, N.Y., 1970), p. 65.

198   On Harry Ritley: Bradna and Spence, *The Big Top*, pp. 131, 217.
"His special privilege": Henry Miller, *The Smile at the Foot of the Ladder* (New York, 1948), p. 29.

198–99   On Goliath, the sea elephant: See Fellows and Freeman, *This Way to the Big Show*, pp. 261–62; Fox, *A Ticket to the Circus*, p. 126.

199–200   On Alfredo Codona and Vera Bruce: "Wounds ex-wife, kills self," *New York Times*, July 31, 1937; ex-wife dies, Aug. 1, 1937.

199   "I guess this is the last thing I can do for you": AP report in *Rockford Register-Republic*, July 31, 1937, p. 1.

200   An often-visited shrine: Tito Gaona to author, March 22, 1978.

DISPLAY 13

The decline and fall of John Ringling is best told by Plowden, *Those Amazing Ringlings*. See also North and Hatch, *The Circus Kings*; Bradna and Spence, *The Big Top*, particularly pp. 136–37; Fellows and Freeman, *This Way to the Big Show*; and Harlow, *The Ringlings*.

Page

203   "Eccentric, egocentric": North and Hatch, *The Circus Kings*, p. 217.
"He was quite accustomed": Ibid., p. 218.

204   Purchase of American Circus Corp., and "I'm playing the Garden next year": Ibid., p. 219.

205   "John Ringling's personal crash": Ibid., p. 222.
"John Ringling had lost his grip": Ibid., p. 223.
The Ringling-Gumpertz struggle: See ibid., pp. 222, 224; also Fellows and Freeman, *This Way to the Big Show*, p. 292.

205–7   The Tom Mix story: See Emmett Kelly, *Clown* (New York, 1954), pp. 108–9, Kelly's reminiscences of Tom Mix on the Sells-Floto Show. See also Olive Stokes Mix, *The Fabulous Tom Mix* (Englewood Cliffs, N.J., 1957); Paul Mix, *The Life and Legend of Tom Mix* (New York, 1972); Kevin Brownlow, *The War, the West, and the Wilderness* (New York, 1979); and Ellsworth Collings, *101 Ranch* (Norman, Okla., 1938).

206   A distant relative: Mix, *The Life and Legend*.
It has been established: Ibid., and Collings, *101 Ranch*, p. 218.
"To explain Tom Mix . . .": Brownlow, *The War, the West, and the Wilderness*, p. 309.

207   "There wasn't much real West left": Mix to Herbert Cruikshank, *Photoplay*, July 1928, p. 112.
Mix lost a million dollars in the circus: Brownlow, *The War, the West, and the Wilderness*, p. 309.
Death of Tom Mix: Ibid., p. 312.
"In the American style": Parkinson quoted in "Circus" entry, *The New Encyclopedia Britannica*, 15th ed. (1974), vol. 4, p. 636.

208–10   The story of Clyde Beatty: Clyde Beatty, *The Big Cage* (New York, 1933); Clyde Beatty and Edward Anthony, *Facing the Big Cats* (Garden City, N.Y., 1965); "Clyde Beatty & Captive," *Time*, March 29, 1937, cover story; Fred D. Pfening, Jr., "Forty Years in the Center Ring," *Bandwagon*, July–Aug. 1965, pp. 4–8.

208   "All successful trainers know": Beatty, *Facing the Big Cats*, quoted in Fenner and Fenner, *The Circus, Lure and Legend*, p. 44.

209   "Only a trainer": Beatty, *Facing the Big Cats*, quoted in Fenner and Fenner, *The Circus, Lure and Legend*, p. 46.

210   "the immense amount of work": Fellows and Freeman, *This Way to the Big Show*, p. 238.
"His act was so big": Ibid., p. 239.
"No matter how much affection": Beatty, *Facing the Big Cats*, quoted in Fenner and Fenner, *The Circus, Lure and Legend*, p. 44.

211   "the best character clowns were two hoboes": Edward Hoagland, "There Go the Clowns," in *The Tugman's Passage* (New York, 1982), pp. 177–78.
Griebling story of bread and milk: Towsen, *Clowns*, p. 301.
"In all comedy business": Chaplin, *My Autobiography*, p. 150.

212   Origin of name *"auguste"*: Bradna and Spence, *The Big Top*, p. 215. Spence, in his acknowledgments, says that he got a great deal of information about circus clowns from Lou Jacobs and Otto Griebling. In *The Circus Book*, edited by Rupert Croft-Cooke (London, 1947), W. S. Meadmore quotes Nicolai Poliakoff, England's great twentieth-century *auguste* Coco, the Clown (p. 71): "Unlike the true clown, an auguste must be funny at first sight, and funny all the time. He can wear whatever style of clothes or makeup he likes, but it must be grotesque."
"in the circus, thanks to the Auguste": Fellini, *Fellini on Fellini* (New York, 1974), p. 126.
"another of the apparently": from London review in *Black and White Budget*, March 16, 1901, quoted in Towsen, *Clowns*, p. 288.

213   "Charlie was a shabby Pierrot": Robert Payne, *Charlie Chaplin* (New York, 1952), p. 42.
"always poor": Janin quoted in Payne, *Charlie Chaplin*, p. 48.
PWA Shovel Routine: Kelly, *Clown*, p. 122.

214   "But to critics": William Manchester, *The Glory and the Dream* (Boston, 1973), p. 86.
Story of Harriett Hodgini: Bob Taber, "The Hodgini Family," *White Tops*, May–June 1961.

218   "Like the daring young man": *American Weekly*, Jan. 14, 1945, p. 9.
"End of the Circus Romance," *American Weekly*, Jan. 14, 1945.
"Now married to a prominent surgeon": "The Hodgini Family," *White Tops*, May–June 1961, p. 20.

219–21   Story of the Ubangis: Fellows and Freeman, *This Way to the Big Show*, pp. 14, 294–6; Bradna and Spence, *The Big Top*, pp. 243–51. The circus poster for the Ubangis is reproduced in color on p. 23 of Fox and Parkinson, *The Circus in America*.

221–23   End of Clyde Beatty story: Beatty, *The Big Cage*, and Beatty and Anthony, *Facing the Big Cats*; Pfening, "Forty Years in the Center Ring."

222   Cover of *Time*: "Clyde Beatty & Captive."
"Clyde Beatty Here July 17," *Rockford* (Ill.) *Morning Star*, July 8, 1937.

225   The death of John Ringling: Harlow, *Wizards of the Circus*, pp. 169–70; Bradna and Spence, *The Big Top*, pp. 136–37; Taylor, *Center Ring*, p. 32.
Ringling had been one of the ten richest men: Bradna and Spence, *The Big Top*, p. 136.
Gumpertz telegram: North and Hatch, *The Circus Kings*, p. 226.
John Ringling's estate: Ibid., pp. 247–48.
Cut them off without a cent: Ibid., p. 248; Plowden, *Those Amazing Ringlings*, p. 238.

DISPLAY 14

More has been written about the circus gorilla named Gargantua than about most circus owners or human circus stars. There is a whole book, *Gargantua the Great* (New York, 1959) by James A. Ware. A cover story in *Newsweek* ("Gargantua the Great: Star of the New Ringling Show," April 11, 1938) preceded numerous other articles in such top-flight publications as *Colliers* (J. Bryan III, "Wife in Fame Only: Toto, the Female Animal as a Mate for Gargantua," May 3, 1941) and *Life*. Indeed, J. B. T. Scripps's Feb. 26, 1940, *Life* article has one of my all-time favorite magazine titles: "Gargantua, World's Most Successful Animal, Lives for One Purpose Only: Murder." Even Ernest Hemingway wrote a piece: "My Pal Gargantua," *Ken* magazine, July 28, 1938. Not until the Living Unicorn in the 1980s would circus ballyhoo again reach such heights.

Henry Ringling North tells the family's story of Gargantua in *The Circus Kings*, chap. 21, "The Most Terrifying Creature the World Has Ever Seen," pp. 264–74. A poster billing Gargantua as "the largest gorilla ever exhibited—the world's most terrifying living creature! Gargantua the Great" is at Baraboo, RBB-NL37-38-IF-1. Gargantua is billed as "The Terror" on a page from a 1938 booklet about Gargantua, reproduced in Fox, *A Ticket to the Circus*, p. 121.

Page

226   John and Henry Ringling North and their mother named executors and trustees: John Kobler, "Close-up: John Ringling North," *Life*, Aug. 8, 1948.
        "So we Norths were struck out": North and Hatch, *The Circus Kings*, p. 249.
        "Baraboo-born and bred to the circus": Plowden, *Those Amazing Ringlings*, p. 269.
        "A disintegrating, has-been institution": North and Hatch, *The Circus Kings*, p. 255.

228   "handling of the great gorilla": Buddy North quoted in North and Hatch, *The Circus Kings*, p. 265.
        "We just can't afford": Ibid., p. 267.
        Henry Ringling North names Gargantua: Ibid.

229   Gargantua's air-conditioned cage: Ibid., p. 271.
        On the ballyhooing of Gargantua and other circus attractions by John North and Ringling publicists Roland Butler and Frank Braden, see "Fiendish" in Taylor's *Center Ring*, pp. 87–131. Also "Gargantua and Toto" and "The Gorilla Babies: Gargantua II and Mlle. Toto," in O'Brien, *Circus: Cinders to Sawdust*, pp. 191–200.
        "Gargantua started life": Scripps, "Gargantua, World's Most Successful Animal . . ."
        Gargantua died in 1949: "Our last stand of the season was Miami and that night Gargantua died. Even his passing was publicity-timed, for our press agents wrote that he had waited until the last night of the season to die like the good trouper that he was." North and Hatch, *The Circus Kings*, p. 274.
        1938 was a terrible year for circuses: Fox and Parkinson, *The Circus in America*, p. 106.
        Labor troubles: See North and Hatch, *The Circus Kings*, chap. 22, "Labor Pains," pp. 275–88; and Bradna and Spence, *The Big Top*, pp. 138–45.
        "The Boss says we show": Bradna and Spence, *The Big Top*, p. 140.

233   Loyal-Repenskys and Cristianis put aside their feud: Ibid., p. 141.
North's new billing and publicity: Henry Ringling North describes this ad in *The Circus Kings*, p. 285; for my hometown, in the *Rockford* (Ill.) *Morning Star* for July 31, 1938, it appeared this way: "The Al G. Barnes and Sells-Floto Combined Circus presenting RINGLING BROS. AND BARNUM & BAILEY STUPENDOUS NEW FEATURES including the world's most terrifying living creature GARGANTUA THE GREAT." The clown face in the ad belonged to Lou Jacobs. On Aug. 1, 1938, my father took me to see the afternoon show. One of the trains, carrying the Big Top and the 10,000 seats, had been incorrectly routed and didn't arrive in Rockford until almost noon—which permitted us to see the raising of the Big Top in broad daylight, though the 1:00 P.M. show didn't get under way until about 3:30. The boss man had a wonderful chant as he directed the tightening of the guy ropes around the tent: "Heave it—weave it—shake it—take it—break it—make it. Move along." (See Fox, *A Ticket to the Circus*, p. 91.) The visual poetry of the raising of the Big Top is preserved in "The Song of the Roustabouts" in Disney's *Dumbo*; but it was the show itself, which cannot be preserved, that defined for me the true meaning of *stupendous*.
Frank Buck in "Nepal": See RBB&B program for 1938; North and Hatch, *The Circus Kings*, pp. 278–79; and Bradna and Spence, *The Big Top*, pp. 139–40.

234   Horompo and the tiger: Kelly, *Clown*, pp. 257–58.
"Many days we played $50,000 gates": Bradna and Spence, *The Big Top*, p. 145.
Gargantua compared to King Kong: John S. Culhane, *Special Effects in the Movies* (New York, 1981), p. 100.

238   "within a hundred yards": Otis Ferguson, "The Circus on the Road," *The New Republic*, July 8, 1940, reprinted in *The Otis Ferguson Reader* (Highland Park, Ill., 1972), p. 143.

DISPLAY 15

Page

241   "You can troupe all over the world": Kelly, *Clown*, p. 175; "I almost cut my throat": Ibid., p. 172.
"Sustainment of morale": North and Hatch, *The Circus Kings*, p. 315.

242   "*Dumbo* could only have happened here": *Time*, Dec. 29, 1941, pp. 27–28. For the influence of the circus on one of the creators of Walt Disney's *Dumbo*, see Bill Peet, *An Autobiography* (Boston, 1989), pp. 64–66, 112–13, and 185–90. "With all my years of sketching and painting the circus I was well prepared for Dumbo," wrote Disney storyman Peet (p. 112), "and I contributed so much to the production that Otto [Englander, story supervisor] allowed me to present my story boards to Walt one day."
"his critics are not only wrong": North quoted in Taylor, *Center Ring*, p. 43.

243   "thrived on trouble": Fox and Parkinson, *The Circus in America*, p. 111.
Balanchine and Stravinsky, "It robbed them of their feeling of security": Rennert, *100 Years of Circus Posters*, p. 12. Rennert quotes the 1971 souvenir program of

the New York City Ballet, detailing the fifty-year collaboration between choreographer Balanchine and composer Stravinsky, in which this assertion is made.

"I received a congratulatory telegram": Stravinsky quoted in ibid., p. 12.

246   "their deliberate way of kneeling": Marianne Moore, review in *Dance Index*, June 1946, in Patricia C. Willis, ed., *The Complete Prose of Marianne Moore* (New York, 1986), p. 145.

E. McKnight Kauffer poster: Rennert, *100 Years of Circus Posters*, p. 12.

"Look at that son of a bitch": Robert Benchley, quoted in Taylor, *Center Ring*, p. 39.

"soft and sunny morning": North and Hatch, *The Circus Kings*, p. 317.

246–47   Dr. J. Y. Hendersen and his Foille preparation: Ibid., p. 318.

247   "They lay down": Henderson, *Circus Doctor* (Boston, 1966), quoted in Bill Ballantine, *Wild Tigers and Tame Fleas* (New York, 1958), p. 157.

The number of animals burned to death in the 1942 Cleveland fire is given in North and Hatch, *The Circus Kings*, p. 319.

248–53   The Hartford fire: Kelly, *Clown*, pp. 216–29; Bradna and Spence, *The Big Top*, pp. 261–63. Circus bandleader Merle Evans gives his account of the fire in Taylor, *Center Ring*, p. 69, which maintains, "No valuable animals were lost in the terrible fire; as far as they were concerned, at least, Evans' cornet, the circus's warning tocsin, had sounded the alarm in time."

248   "like the glowing end of a cigarette": North and Hatch, *The Circus Kings*, p. 327.

253   "The Ringling family": Ibid., p. 329.

"We must forget the fire": Emmett Kelly quoted in "Fire Destroys the Big Top," *Life*, July 17, 1944.

254   "recalling happy hours": 1943 RBB&B circus poster at Baraboo, RBB-NL12-43-½F-3.

"No one knew": Bradna and Spence, *The Big Top*, p. 263.

255   "If the General thinks": Ibid.

DISPLAY 16

The decline of the circus in America in general, and Ringling Bros. and Barnum & Bailey Circus in particular, in the early fifties, leading up to the folding of the Big Top in 1956, is best told by Bill Ballantine in *Clown Alley* (Boston, 1982) and Michael Burke in *Outrageous Good Fortune* (Boston, 1984). Burke devotes a chapter of his memoir, called "The Greatest Show on Earth" (pp. 173–207), to this decline. It was the subject of my first article on the circus, a newspaper interview in 1956 with William B. Naylor, an old-time circus press agent then touring with the Polack Bros. Circus. See also North and Hatch, *The Circus Kings*, p. 360: "Nineteen forty-eight was the last of the really good times."

Page

257   "Every clown gag": Boss clown Glen "Frosty" Little to author and sons, as we clowned with Ringling Bros. and Barnum & Bailey Circus in Madison Square Garden, between first and second shows on April 23, 1977.

Paul Jung on his "Adam Smasher": Quoted in Wyatt Blassingame, "Let's Meet the Clowns," *Family Circle*, Aug. 1953, p. 91. See also Kelly, who calls the gag "Paul's best," in *Clown*, p. 262.

258   North visits Haley in jail: North and Hatch, *The Circus Kings*, p. 333. See also Taylor, *Center Ring*, pp. 35–36.

"Most of the time I was up there": Art Concello quoted in Taylor, *Center Ring*, p. 164.

Buckets of beluga caviar: Ibid., p. 36.

The Ringling wrangling: See *Fortune*, July 1947; also Kobler, "Close-up: John Ringling North."

259   Johnny North's life-style is delightfully rendered by Robert Lewis Taylor in "The Triumph of Hoopla" in *The New Yorker*, April 10 and 17, 1954, and reprinted as part of *Center Ring*, pp. 21–50.

259–60   Burt Lancaster on the circus: Telephone interview with author, 1982.

260   On Harold Alzana: Taylor, *Center Ring*, p. 39.

On Pinito Del Oro: O'Brien, *Circus: Cinders to Sawdust*, p. 143; Durant and Durant, *Pictorial History*, p. 259; North and Hatch, *The Circus Kings*, pp. 39–40.

1948: "that wonderful year": North and Hatch, *The Circus Kings*, p. 347.

On Unus: Ibid., p. 348; O'Brien, *Circus: Cinders to Sawdust*, pp. 144–45.

261   "making his living standing on one finger": Ernest Hemingway, "The Circus," 1953 RBB&B Program, p. 7.

De Mille with circus: North and Hatch, *The Circus Kings*, pp. 355–59. See also De Mille's 1952 film, *The Greatest Show on Earth*; and Culhane, *Special Effects in the Movies*, pp. 74, 127. (A photograph of the simulated circus train wreck appears on p. 127.)

262   Description of 1953 RBB&B show: RBB&B 1953 Program, p. 68.

Emmett Kelly gag with golf bag and homburg: Kelly, *Clown*, p. 122.

262–64   On Lou Jacobs: For a biographical sketch, see John Culhane, "School for Clowns," *New York Times Magazine*, Dec. 30, 1973. Over the years, as a guest clown, I have been hit by Lou many times as I emerged from the clown coupe or jumped from the burning house and encountered him in the guise of a clown cop, and we have had many a discussion afterward about the daffy art of clowning. See also Kelly, *Clown*, pp. 262–63; O'Brien, *Circus: Cinders to Sawdust*, pp. 184–85; and many references in Bradna and Spence, *The Big Top*, and Towsen, *Clowns*. The latter gives a fine description on pp. 268–69 of Lou's hunting routine with Knucklehead, the little fox terrier he dressed to look like a rabbit. Lou told me that he took over this great routine from his late colleague, Charlie Bell, and his trick dog, Peanuts.

263   Washing machine motor for midget car: Bradna and Spence, *The Big Top*, p. 218.

264–67   On the Cristianis: Richard G. Hubler, in *The Cristianis* (Boston, 1966), tells the full story of this family up to 1966—"a narrative," as Hubler says, "of loyalty and talent which covers more than a century of continuous performing before the public from Austria to Alaska." See also Lawrence Lader, "The Cristianis," *Coronet*, Sept. 1947; and "Big Top's Royal Family," *Cosmopolitan*, Aug. 1955.

265   "I can't pay you any more": John Ringling North to Cristianis, quoted in "Big Top's Royal Family," p. 80.

On King Bros. and Cristiani Combined Circus: Fox and Parkinson, *The Circus in America*, pp. 116–18.

"Floyd King was a man": Ibid., p. 118.

"partnership deals": Hubler, *The Cristianis*, pp. 263–64.

266   "the Cristianis could boast a circus": Ibid., p. 270.

"The circus will be finished when ice cream is finished": Ernesto Cristiani to author, telephone interview, 1956.

"As for a full twist": Hubler, *The Cristianis*, p. 78.

"The performer must choose": Ibid., p. 80.

267   "synchronization brought to perfection": J. S. Clarke quoted in ibid., p. 78.

"Bigger and better than ever": Author's interview with the late Frank McClosky, Liberty Bell Park, Philadelphia, May 15–16, 1975.

267–73   On the conflicts and unrest on the Ringling circus, see Fox and Parkinson, *The Circus in America*, p. 123. Ballantine tells of RBB&B's decline during the 1953 and 1954 seasons, when he was with the show, in *Clown Alley*, pp. 19–24. Michael Burke gives a close-up view from management's perspective in *Outrageous Good Fortune*, chap. 9, "The Greatest Show on Earth."

267   "Their exploits inspired . . . *Cloak and Dagger*": John T. McQuiston, "Michael Burke, Ex-Executive with the Yankees, Dies at 70," *New York Times*, Feb. 7, 1987.

"While he . . . repaired to the south of France": Burke, *Outrageous Good Fortune*, p. 173.

"As long as they paid the Sneeze" and "The menagerie superintendent": Ibid., p. 183.

"Get the gambler off the lot, Frank": Ibid., p. 184.

272   "the three, sitting in a black Cadillac": *Minneapolis Star*, Aug. 5, 1955, quoted in Ballantine, *Clown Alley*, p. 23.

North hired Burke to "clean house": See ibid.

"David Blanchfield": Burke, *Outrageous Good Fortune*, p. 187.

an institution, not to be sucked dry: Ibid.

273   "they found their way to Jimmy Hoffa": Ibid., p. 188.

"he would put us out of business": Ibid., p. 197.

"To run against the Teamsters": Ibid., p. 204.

"The tented circus as it exists today": John Ringling North, quoted in "Ringling Bros.–Barnum & Bailey Gives Last Performance . . . ," *New York Times*, July 17, 1956, p. 1. For the folding of the Big Top, see John Culhane, "Comeback of the Circus," *Holiday*, March 1976, and in condensed version in *Reader's Digest* that same month. The 1956 quotes from *Life*, the *New York Times*, and *Pittsburgh Post-Gazette* were researched for those 1976 articles. See also Fox and Parkinson, *The Circus in America*, p. 123, and Ballantine, *Clown Alley*, p. 24.

274–77   My account of Irvin Feld's background and the beginning of the Feld era of Ringling Bros. and Barnum & Bailey Circus is based on numerous interviews and conversations with the late Irvin Feld over an eleven-year period; with Allen J. Bloom, now executive vice president of The Greatest Show on Earth; Shirley Feld, widow of Israel Feld; Kenneth J. Feld, Irvin's son and heir; and many others. See my articles "Dreaming the Impossible Dream: Irvin Feld" in the 1976 RBB&B Souvenir Program; "Barnum to Ringling to Feld" in the 1983 Souvenir Program; and "Lords of the Rings: Irvin and Kenneth Feld Are Making The Greatest Show on Earth Even Better" in *Signature*, March 1981. The Felds can be seen in action in the three cover stories I wrote on the circus in the 1970s for the *New York Times Magazine*: "The Lord of the Ring," on Gunther Gebel-Williams, May 13, 1973; "School for Clowns," Dec. 30, 1973; and "Trapeze—the Quest for the 'Impossible' Quadruple Somersault," March 19, 1978. Also helpful were Bill Ballantine's account in *Clown Alley*; "The Feld Brothers," *Business Week*, April 13, 1968; "Super Brother Act," *Time*, June 21, 1954; and "Greatest Showman on Earth," *Time*, May 4, 1970.

275 "Exactly what was in it?": Irvin Feld quoted in *Chicago Tribune*, in Ballantine, *Clown Alley*, p. 27.

276 "to survive in the modern world": Burke, *Outrageous Good Fortune*, p. 205.
Irvin Feld's meeting with John Ringling North: Interview with author in Feld's office in Washington, D.C., May 29, 1975.

277 Kelly ran away from the circus: Durant and Durant, *Pictorial History*, p. 310.
"We know that clowns can fall down": Feld quoted in Culhane, "School for Clowns," p. 10.

277–80 The decline of the circus in America in the 1950s and early 1960s can be seen in the sad attrition rate detailed in the list of circuses compiled by Tom Parkinson in 1957 for John and Alice Durant's *Pictorial History*, and in Fox and Parkinson, *The Circus in America*. The emotions of sadness and anger that greeted the decline are evident in Ballantine's *Clown Alley*, Burke's *Outrageous Good Fortune*, and, particularly, Hubler's *The Cristianis*. Live and in person, even the greatest of riding troupes couldn't compete against television in the 1960s. And yet, writes Hubler, "No professional performer can really claim the honor of such a title on a single lucky feat; he must perform his act day after day, time after time, perfecting and polishing—making his mistakes and conquering them. Too often, in the world of mechanics, a pitifully inadequate performance is made to seem professional simply by a pair of scissors and repetition" (p. 303).

278 "promotional" or "sponsored" shows: Durant and Durant, *Pictorial History*, p. 240; Hamid, *Circus: as told to his son*, pp. 224ff.

279 "they loped and lumbered": Fox and Parkinson, *The Circus in America*, p. 266.
Wallendas fall in Detroit: Leonard V. Farley, introduction to Dover ed. of May, *From Rome to Ringling*, p. xiii.

280 Cristianis hired out to other shows: Hubler, *The Cristianis*, pp. 305–6.
"By the early 1960s": Ballantine, *Clown Alley*, pp. 32–33.
"The next five years were horrendous": Irvin Feld to author, interviews in Venice, Fla., Nov. 17–18, 1973.

NOTES

DISPLAY 17

My primary sources on Gunther Gebel-Williams are himself and his employers and friends, Kenneth Feld and the late Irvin Feld. I interviewed Gunther perhaps a dozen times between 1973 and April 7, 1989; Irvin Feld, every year from 1973 to his death in 1984; Kenneth Feld every year from 1973 to 1989. I also interviewed Gunther's wife, Sigrid Neubauer Gebel; his son, Mark Oliver Gebel; and his stepdaughter, Tina Gebel. Excellent profiles of Gunther have been written by Richard Schickel in *Harper's* (Aug. 1971), Edward Hoagland in *Esquire* (July 1971), and Curry Kirkpatrick in *Sports Illustrated* (Sept. 26, 1977); and Elizabeth Hall did a fascinating interview with Gunther on animal behavior for *Psychology Today* (Oct. 1983). I profiled Gunther as "The Lord of the Ring" in the *New York Times Magazine* (May 13, 1973). Tenth Avenue Editions, Inc., produced for Ringling Bros. and Barnum & Bailey Combined Shows, Inc., a picture book on Gebel-Williams's life and career called *Lord of the Rings: Gunther Gebel-Williams* (New York, 1988), with an introduction by Kenneth Feld, President and Producer, Ringling Bros. and Barnum & Bailey Circus. It includes photographs from throughout Gunther's career and a chronology of Gunther's life, which Gunther himself now uses to refresh his memory. In addition, as one who has seen Gunther every time he has come to New York, I want to mention the many fine anonymous accounts of the circus's annual visits in *The New Yorker*'s "Talk of the Town."

Page

283 "something vital": Richard Schickel, "Gebel-Williams Burning Bright," *Harper's*, Aug. 1971.
"I couldn't stand": Irvin Feld to author, 1973.

284 "The deal": "Greatest Showman on Earth: Irvin Feld," *Time*, May 4, 1970, p. 74. See also "To the Feld Brothers, It's All a Big Circus," *Business Week*, April 13, 1968.
"That the circus had changed hands": *New York Times*, March 25, 1970, p. 38:2.

285 "dusty lots . . . blazing Italian summer": "Greatest Showman on Earth," p. 74.

286 "Not so many people": Gebel-Williams to author, in Culhane, "The Lord of the Ring," pp. 63–64.

287 "a basic understanding of animal training": Charly Baumann, *Tiger Tiger* (Chicago, 1976), p. 32.
"Horses are just not too bright": Gebel-Williams to author, Madison Square Garden, New York, April 2, 1973.

288 On the Ernest Renke-Plaskett Award: *Lord of the Rings: Gunther Gebel-Williams*, pp. 13–14.
"When she traveled with me": Gebel-Williams to author, Madison Square Garden, New York, April 2, 1973.

289 "horses and elephants fear beasts of prey": Gebel-Williams to author, in Culhane, "The Lord of the Ring."
"In popular estimation": For drawing my attention to the quote from Carl Hagenbeck's autobiography, *Von Tieren und Menschen (Of Beasts and Men)* (Berlin,

441

1908), I am indebted to Charly Baumann, a disciple of his method. See Baumann's *Tiger Tiger*, p. 60.

291–92   "a well-honed contempt": Schickel, "Gebel-Williams Burning Bright."

292   "who did the Liberties": Curry Kirkpatrick, "The Greatest Showman on Earth," *Sports Illustrated*, Sept. 26, 1977.

296   "the magnificent teeterboard number": Ibid.

297   "like dealing in commodities": Kenneth Feld to author, in Culhane, "Lords of the Rings: Irvin and Kenneth Feld."

300   "Training is a beautiful thing": John Culhane, "World's Greatest Showman," *Reader's Digest*, Nov. 1989, p. 95.

DISPLAY 18

In "Comeback of the Circus" (*Holiday*, March 1976; condensed in *Reader's Digest* that same month), I wrote: "The duel for the quadruple generates the kind of excitement that the circus—at its best—has provided." I traced the history of that competition in "Trapeze—the Quest for the 'Impossible' Quadruple Somersault" (*New York Times Magazine*, March 19, 1978). By 1988, Ringling Bros. and Barnum & Bailey Circus was offering two quadruples at some performances, one by Miguel Vazquez, of the Flying Vazquez, who had a 65 percent completion rate, the other by Reuben Caballero, Jr., of the Flying Caballeros. Unless otherwise noted, the story of that quest is drawn from my *Holiday*, *Reader's Digest*, and *New York Times Magazine* stories.

My original understanding of flying acts came from spending nearly two weeks at Ringling winter quarters in Dec. 1977 with Tito, Armando, and Victor Gaona of the Flying Gaonas, and with Antoinette Concello, formerly of the Flying Concellos. Mrs. Concello also told me about the flying career of Alfredo Codona as she had witnessed it, and suggested that I read chapters in two books to which she had also contributed her expertise: Bradna and Spence, *The Big Top*, chap. 12, "Leapers, Tumblers and Flyers," pp. 162–78; and Taylor, *Center Ring*, "Family Under Canvas," pp. 163–95. In 1982, after Miguel Vazquez became the first flier to achieve the quad, I interviewed him, his catcher and brother Juan, and their sister, Patricia.

Page

303   Glenn Collins, "A Quadruple for the Flying Miguel Vazquez," *New York Times*, July 11, 1982, p. 1.

304   Octavie LaTour, "The Limit of Human Daring," *New York World*, April 8, 1905.
"Alexander did a beautiful double": Tito Gaona to author, Dec. 1977.
"was quite as engrossing": May, *From Rome to Ringling*. The Worland story is told in chap. 26, p. 249.

305   On Jules Leotard (1838–1870): Norris McWhirter and Ross McWhirter, *Guinness Book of World Records* (New York, 1975), p. 450; and *The New Encyclopedia Britannica*, 15th ed., vol. 4, p. 636. See also: O'Brien, *Circus: Cinders to Sawdust*, p. 111.
"The net itself": Tito Gaona to author, 1977.

"The Fisher Bros.": Col. C. G. Sturtevant, "The Metamorphosis of the Flying Act," *Billboard*, Dec. 8, 1928, and "The Flying Act and Its Technique," *White Tops*, May 1932.

"great spread of knotted rope": Alfredo Codona, as told to Courtney Ryley Cooper, "Split Seconds," *Saturday Evening Post*, Dec. 6, 1930.

305–6   How to land in a net: Tito Gaona not only told me how, he showed me how, at Ringling winter quarters, Venice, Fla., in Dec. 1977.

306   "the flying return": Bradna and Spence, *The Big Top*, p. 167.

The Clarkonians: O'Brien, *Circus: Cinders to Sawdust*, pp. 115–16.

307   "The reason lies in the terrific speed": Codona to Cooper, "Split Seconds."

Pierre Couderc, Installment No. 9 of "Truth or Fiction, Legend or Fact: Important Trivia," *Bandwagon*, July–Aug. 1965, contains documentation of the fact that Lena Jordan accomplished the first triple somersault from the flying trapeze in 1897. Nellie Jordan, a natural daughter of Mrs. Lewis Jordan, Lena's adoptive mother, left her old traveling trunk in the Saginaw, Mich., attic of Ray and Buster Melzora of the Flying Melzoras, a trapeze act of the 1920s. It contained the newspaper clippings substantiating the claim that now appears in the *Guinness Book of World Records*.

Lena Jordan's "extaordinary biceps": Interview in *The Truth* (Sydney, Australia), May 23, 1897, in Couderc, Installment No. 9, "Truth or Fiction," p. 27.

308   "20 years ago, a single somersault": Sydney *Mail*, May 22, 1897, quoted in Couderc, Installment No. 9, "Truth or Fiction," p. 28.

"for the first time in Australia": Sydney *Daily Telegraph*, April 24, 1897, quoted in Couderc, Installment No. 9, "Truth or Fiction," p. 28.

"The principal in the act": *Star* (Australia), April 27, 1897, quoted in Couderc, Installment No. 9, "Truth or Fiction," p. 28.

Ernest Clarke's triple: *Guinness Book of World Records* prior to the 1970s. In the 1975 Bantam edition (p. 450), Lena Jordan is credited with the record, but Clarke continues to be listed for the "first back somersault (male)"!

Lane and Siegrist break necks: Antoinette Concello to author, Venice, Fla., 1977. See also: Bradna and Spence, *The Big Top*, p. 178; Taylor, *Center Ring*, p. 172.

"long, fatalistic history of the triple": Codona to Cooper, "Split Seconds," p. 98.

309   Codona dislocated his shoulder: See Codona's letter about his injury, the illustration on page 195 of this book.

On Antoinette Concello: Author interviews with Antoinette Concello in Venice, Fla., Dec. 1977. Born Antoinette Comeau and educated in a Canadian convent, she got her trapeze training in Bloomington, Ind., from the Flying Wards. This Bloomington-based troupe starred in a number of Ringling-owned shows, such as Hagenbeck-Wallace, and trained many of the great fliers of the thirties, including Antoinette and her husband, Arthur Concello. The greatest female flier of the twentieth century, she performed the two-and-a-half consistently throughout the 1930s and 1940s and also successfully performed the triple on numerous occasions over her long career. In her seventies, she choreographed the aerial ballet for the 1980s' RBB&B. See also Taylor, *Center Ring*, pp. 15, 179–85.

309–15   The story of the Flying Gaonas was pieced together for the author by every member of the family on many occasions, at their home in Venice, Fla., and in their trailers on the road, over a period of fifteen years, 1973–1988.

315   "Like everybody else, . . . we wanted to fly": Felipe Vazquez to Jim Gallagher, "Flyin' High: The Magic of Miguel Vazquez," *Chicago Tribune Magazine*, Dec. 5, 1982, p. 34.

316   Miguel took a great leap forward: Juan Vazquez to author, Venice, Fla., Dec. 1982.
"just an ordinary flyer": Antoinette Concello to Gallagher, "Flyin' High," p. 36.

317   "Miguel was doing his triple too high": Juan Vazquez to author, Dec. 1982.
"The ideal specifications": Bradna and Spence, *The Big Top*, pp. 173–74.
"We were getting close": Gallagher, "Flyin' High," p. 37.

318   The very peak of the trapeze arc: Gallagher continues, "Miguel's highest point is 37 feet off the ground, about a foot higher than Gaona normally ascended, and Juan thinks those 12 inches are the key to his brother's success. Miguel goes up so high that he is three feet above the frame of the trapeze rigging, and he used to make contact with the crossbars until they were raised another six inches" (ibid., p. 38).
Miguel does first quad in practice, August 19, 1981: Juan Vazquez to author, Venice, Fla., Dec. 1982.

319   "always prepared for tragedy": Patricia Segrera Vazquez to author, Venice, Fla., Dec. 1982. See also: "Marguerite Michele, who hangs by her hair in her act for Ringling Bros. Barnum & Bailey Circus, interviewed," *New York Times*, April 3, 1979, sec. 3, p. 12.

320   "Mr. Feld came to see us in Phoenix": Juan Vazquez to author, Venice, Fla., Dec. 1982.
Death of Julio Farias: Patricia Segrera Vazquez to author, Venice, Fla., Dec. 1982.
"When I come out of the fourth spin": Miguel Vazquez to author, Venice, Fla., Dec. 1982.
Heard them shout and scream: Charly Baumann to author, Venice, Fla., Dec. 1982. It was Baumann who, as performance director of Ringling's Blue Unit that night in Tucson, called Irvin Feld to tell him that Miguel Vazquez had accomplished the quadruple.

DISPLAY 19

The founding of the Ringling Bros. and Barnum & Bailey Clown College by Irvin Feld in 1968 and its first six years are covered in Culhane, "School for Clowns." Those Clown College graduates in action are described in John Culhane, "Clown for a Day . . . You Gotta Be Kidding," *Signature*, July 1974. Billie Burke, the actress daughter of nineteenth-century singing clown Billy Burke, says in her memoirs, *With a Feather on My Nose* (p. 6), "Clowns, I have heard, owe their origin to the religious plays of the Fourteenth Century when roving troupes of players, like the famous Lupinos, [film actress] Ida Lupino's direct ancestors, used to travel Europe; the clowns of today sprang from the Devils in those plays. At least, that is what Billy Burke thought, although more precise historians may trace the ancestry of clowns much farther back than that." A more precise historian, John H. Towsen, an RBB&B Clown College graduate, provides in *Clowns* a comprehensive survey of the clown throughout history and throughout the world, plus notes, glossary, selected bibliography, and index. Towsen precisely locates the medieval Feast of Fools that Burke talked about, in a tradition he traces back at least to the early Greek and Roman mimes and oriental theater clowns. Bill Ballantine, dean of Clown College from the class of 1970 through the class of 1977, has written his view of the history of the college in *Clown Alley*. Ringling Bros. and Barnum & Bailey Circus published a *Media Guide* in 1982 that includes a brief history of clowning and a short biography of Master Clown Lou Jacobs. Other good books are George Bishop, *The World of Clowns* (Los Angeles, 1976); Toby Sanders, *How to Be a Compleat Clown* (New York, 1978); Lowell Swortzell, *Here Come the Clowns* (New York, 1978); Ian Woodward, *Clowns* (London, 1976); Lawrence Senelick, *A Cavalcade of Clowns* (San Francisco, 1977); Charles R. Meyer, *How to Be a Clown* (New York, 1977) (also *How to Be a Juggler* [New York, 1977]; *How to Be a Magician* [New York, 1978]; *How to Be an Acrobat* [New York, 1978]), from Ringling Bros. and Barnum & Bailey Books. And, of course, the outstanding circus clown autobiography of the twentieth century is *Clown: My Life in Tatters and Smiles*, by Emmett Kelly with F. Beverly Kelley.

Page

323   "pegs, used to hang circuses on": Quoted by Kelly in *Clown*, p. 51. See also Fellows and Freeman, *This Way to the Big Show*, p. 211.

      Irvin Feld's response: See Ballantine's *Clown Alley* for a book-length account, and the 1982 Clown College brochure for a short version.

324   "You didn't take the slap too well" and "If it wasn't for the Clown College I don't know where they'd get any clowns": I attended Jacobs's Clown College Master Class on Nov. 6, 1973, and described it in detail in "School for Clowns," pp. 19–20.

324–25   In addition to the classes: Course description from the 1982 Clown College *Media Guide*.

325   "In the only course of its kind": Ibid. The clown magic instructor, Bobby Kay, is profiled with an accompanying series of photographs in Bishop, *The World of Clowns*, pp. 110–17. See also Ballantine, *Clown Alley*, pp. 197, 307–8; and Kay's capsule biography in the *Media Guide*, p. 15.

      First woman clown . . . in twenty years: Ballantine, *Clown Alley*, p. 170.

325–26   Peggy Williams makes up: Culhane, "School for Clowns," p. 18. See also Glenn Collins, "Well-Flung Pies a Smash at School," *New York Times*, Oct. 15, 1987: "According to the alumni, Clown College also hastened the arrival of women as clowns. 'When I began performing, female roles were only conceived of as men in drag,' said Peggy Williams, a 1970 alumna who was the first woman to get a Ringling contract after graduating from the college. Currently, 8 of the circus's 52 clowns are women. 'Now we've created real feminine clown characters, from ballerinas to truck-stop waitresses,' said Ms. Williams."

325   The three clown faces: See *Ringling Bros. and Barnum & Bailey Circus Presents How to Make Your Own Clown Face*, RBB&B, 1974.

326   "A clown's makeup": Peggy Williams to author, Venice, Fla., Nov. 5, 1972.
Clown Bill Irwin: "Some of the college's alumni have achieved recognition that clowns of a previous generation wouldn't have dreamed of," wrote Glenn Collins in the *New York Times* for Oct. 15, 1987. "For example, Bill Irwin, a 1974 Clown College graduate, has performed at Lincoln Center and received a 'genius grant' from the MacArthur Foundation." In 1988, Irwin played with Robin Williams, Steve Martin, and F. Murray Abraham in a New York production of Samuel Beckett's *Waiting for Godot* directed by Mike Nichols.
"I learned . . . by watching": Lou Jacobs, in Culhane, "School for Clowns," p. 20.
"That stayed with me all my life": Jerry King to T. H. Culhane, 1976.
"a surprising number . . . flourished": Saxon, *Andrew Ducrow*, p. 333. (See also Saxon's notes 40, 41, and 42 on p. 463.)

327   "Among the very best": Richard F. Shepard, review in *New York Times*, April 4, 1984, sec. III, p. 23.

329   "Each year since 1967": In Sidney P. Allen, "Ringling 1970 Financial Report," *San Francisco Chronicle*, Aug. 28, 1970.
"AB's 1974 Survey of Carnivals and Circuses," *Amusement Business*, 1974, pp. 20–40.
"How can you do the circus": Irvin Feld to author, 1973.

330   "We'll have a university" to "I would never live to see": Ibid.

330–31   "The strike's started": The story of how Bloom, now RBB&B executive vice president for marketing and sales, got the circus animals through the Lincoln Tunnel in time for opening night comes from a personal account by Bloom and Feld, and the *New York Daily News*, May 18, 1971; it is told in more detail in John Culhane, "Barnum to Ringling to Feld," RBB&B 1983 Program.

332–33   On Severini and Griebling: John Culhane, "Clown for a Day . . . You Gotta Be Kidding," *Signature*, July 1974.

333   "Otto Griebling Dies": *Bandwagon*, May–June 1972, p. 3; Ballantine, *Clown Alley*, pp. 225–28, a moving account!
Israel Feld dies: Irvin Feld to author, 1973.
Samel Mixed Animal Act: RBB&B 1974 Program.
"Ursula Bottcher, Beauty and the Beasts," RBB&B 1976 Program; see also C. P. Fox, "Awesome Arctic Ice Bears," in the same program. Fox points out that polar bears, unlike big cats, have no facial expressions, which can warn of impending attack. This is especially dangerous because they give what is known as a "series" bite: "They can bite ten times where a big cat bites once. If a bear grabs the ankle he will work right on up the leg with his series biting."

334   On Michu: Culhane, "Barnum to Ringling to Feld."

338   "I'm still going to be a mean S.O.B.": Baumann, *Tiger Tiger*, p. 255.

339   "When I see three oranges": Philippe Petit to author, Ringling Bros. and Barnum & Bailey Circus winter quarters, Venice, Fla., Dec. 1974.

340   "I demand to be allowed": Philippe Petit, "Two Towers, I Walk," *Reader's Digest*, April 1975.

345   "Luis is sitting on the wire": Irvin Feld to author, 1981.

On the Carrillo Bros.' U.S. debut: Gary Williams, "Circus Goes 'Glitter' in New Show," *Sarasota Journal*, Jan. 3, 1975, p. 1. With Ringling: RBB&B Program, 1975 and 1989. With the Big Apple Circus: Big Apple Circus 1984 Program.

"A fall from a wire": "Petit, Aerialist Figure Famous for His High Wire Walk Between Towers of World Trade Center Interviewed on His Upcoming Plans," *New York Times*, Aug. 13, 1979.

"I loved the travel": Ibid.

"railroad life is an easier life": Frank McClosky to author, Liberty Bell Park, Philadelphia, May 15, 1975.

346   Feld wanted his performers fresh: Revival of Ringling as a railroad circus from the close of the tented show in 1956 to 1977 is discussed in Parkinson and Fox, *The Circus Moves by Rail*, in the chap. "Modern Moves," pp. 287–322.

Red Unit's new train: Ibid., pp. 289, 297, 307.

"The center was the pie car": T. H. Culhane to author, 1976.

"You were always keenly aware": Michael Culhane to author, 1976.

347–48   On the Bicentennial Spec: Described at greater length, with color photographs, in John Culhane, "Star-Spangled History of the Circus," *Argosy*, April 1975.

Symbols of continuity: See Towsen, *Clowns*, chap. 4, "The American One-Ring Clown," and chap. 9, "The Three-Ring Clown." See also Glenn Collins, "Ringling Brothers Celebrates the Classic Clowning Moments," the *New York Times*, March 23, 1988. As Collins says, "Perhaps the most robust demonstration of clown choreography occurs during the three and a half minutes of the firehouse gag. It is a melee, first presented by Ringling in 1924, that involves 25 clowns, 2 firetrucks, 4 ladders, assorted hoses and one huffing, puffing, human fireplug." In the 1970s, when my two sons were Ringling clowns, I took part with them in such classic clown routines as the firehouse gag from 1924 and the clown car gag from 1940. When the burning house was temporarily retired after the 1982 season, Frosty Little and Lou Jacobs presented me with the megaphone that Lou used as clown fire chief to direct (misdirect, actually) the firefighters. When I first saw the gag, as a child, Lou was the big-bosomed, red-hot mama who utters the gag's immortal line, "Save my baby!"

348   The Twentieth Anniversary Clown College Reunion at RBB&B winter quarters in Venice, Fla., on Oct. 14, 1987: Michael Culhane to author; T. H. Culhane to author; Glenn Collins, *New York Times* staff writer, to author. See also Collins's article, "Well-Flung Pies a Smash at School." Collins covered the three-day reunion for the *Times*, including what he described as "the world's largest pie fight: 120 costumed clowns in top hats, chef's toques and other outlandish headgear galumphed around, aiming assorted pastries at one another in an apocalyptic mock battle. Few people in the vicinity were left un-pied. 'We had our cake and ate it too,' said a well-meringued T. H. Culhane, a 1975 Clown College graduate. . . . 'It's incredible, being with people who think like you and talk like you,' said Michael Culhane. In 1975 he and his brother, T. H., became the two youngest clowns (at 14 and 13 years old respectively) ever to graduate from the Clown College. . . . Even non-alumni have felt the pull of the school. 'When I was growing

up, I believed I was the only one in the world who thought and felt as I did," said the comedian Dick Van Dyke, who was attending the reunion as the host of a special CBS-TV program on Clown College. "I've felt very much at home, being here."

DISPLAY 20

This chapter deals primarily with four circus legends of the present day: Hoxie Tucker, the circus owner; the wire-walking Wallendas; Emmett Kelly, the circus clown; and the equestrian Hanneford family. In 1937, when I was three, Otto Griebling brought me into the ring of the Cole Bros. Circus with Clyde Beatty in Rockford, Ill., and did a little routine with me. I also met Emmett Kelly that day, and I never forget a clown face.

In 1953, I renewed my old acquaintance with Kelly during an interview in the backyard of Ringling Bros. and Barnum & Bailey Circus. Drawing on these experiences and research into his life, I wrote "Unforgettable Emmett Kelly" for the Dec. 1979 issue of *Reader's Digest*, illustrated with a great painting of "Weary Willie" by Donald Rust, from the private collection of Emmett's widow, Elvira Gebhardt Kelly. Evi, as she is known, had been one of the Four Whirlwinds, an acrobatic act Ringling found in Germany. In 1982, I had the pleasure of spending an evening at the home of Evi Kelly Lentz and her new husband, Jack Lentz, an old friend of Emmett and Evi's and the director of the Ringling Museum of the Circus. I am most grateful to both of them for the help they gave me with this book.

I am similarly grateful to Helen Wallenda, widow of Karl Wallenda, who provided me with an early photograph of the Wallendas. Several generations of her own family and that of her husband have had the circus in their blood. Helen and Karl Wallenda were performers for over sixty years, and I first saw them in Rockford with RBB&B in 1937. Within a week after Karl's death on March 22, 1978, I was asked to write appreciations of his career by the *New York Times* syndicate, the *Baltimore Sun*, the *Miami Herald*, and *The New Times* magazine. I have drawn on that research for this section on the Wallendas, particularly the memoirs of Fred Bradna, who wrote in *The Big Top*: "the warmest personal friends Ella and I made during our circus lifetime were the Wallenda family" (p. 264).

Hoxie Tucker has been memorably brought to life by Fred Powledge in *Mud Show: A Circus Season* (New York, 1975) and in a fully illustrated *National Geographic* article, "On the Road with an Old-Time Circus: Hoxie Bros. Gigantic 3-Ring Circus," by J. Fetterman, in the March 1972 issue, pp. 410–34. In addition, Toby Ballantine, son of an RBB&B Clown College dean and a Clown College graduate himself, was a clown with Hoxie Brothers and shared with me reminiscences of the experience.

Page

351   Hoxie Tucker stomped by elephant: *White Tops*, Nov.–Dec. 1983.

352–53   Tucker biography: Powledge, *Mud Show*, pp. 41–50.

352   "he knew where every rope went": Ibid., p. 42.

      "the voters of a good circus burg": Edward Hoagland, *New York Times Book Review*, Nov. 9, 1975.

353   "If you want to learn": Tucker quoted in Powledge, *Mud Show*, p. 47.

The roll call of circuses showing in the 1980s: See issues of *White Tops* in the NYPL collection at Lincoln Center.

Two legendary performers: See John Culhane: "Final Tribute: A Delicate Balance," *New Times*, April 17, 1978, p. 92; see also "Emmett Kelly Dies," *New York Times*, March 29, 1979, p. 34.

354   "In forty-two years": Bradna and Spence, *The Big Top*, p. 265.

355   "The intense heat": Ibid., p. 266.

Herman carried a thermometer: Ibid., p. 267.

Hartford fire: Ibid., pp. 269–70.

The seven-person pyramid, three tiers high: *Guinness Book of World Records*, 1982, p. 327.

358   "I Can't Hold On Anymore: Accident of the Great Wallenda Troupe," *Newsweek*, Feb. 12, 1962.

"We can't lose our nerve": Karl Wallenda, quoted in "Famous Artist Dies in Fall from High Wire," *New York Times*, March 23, 1978, p. 1.

"Rather than being discouraged": Walt Hohenadel, publisher of *White Tops*, phone interview with author, March 1978.

"How long do you think you can go on?": Ibid.

"Eazder Zeals": Ballantine, *Clown Alley*, p. 79.

358–59   "It was a very dangerous walk": Ibid.

359   "It was inevitable": Walt Hohenadel to author, phone interview, March 1978.

Repeated endlessly on news broadcasts: As I reclaimed my car in the Madison Square Garden parking garage after seeing the opening night of the 108th edition of RBB&B, March 22, 1978, I saw the fall on the television set of the parking lot attendant, who was reading a newspaper with giant front-page headlines telling of Wallenda's death.

"I guess the angels needed a laugh": Culhane, "Unforgettable Emmett Kelly," p. 138.

"By laughing at me": "Emmett Kelly's Woes Make Millions Laugh," *Life*, July 21, 1947.

360   "that soaring seraph of acrobats": *Time*, May 25, 1982, p. 6. Still the soaring seraph as the decade ended, Philippe Petit, back in Paris on Aug. 26, 1989, walked a wire from the Palais de Chaillot across the Seine to the Eiffel Tower.

360–67   This biography of the Hanneford family draws on the family biography in the program of the Royal Hanneford Circus for 1979, supplemented by interviews with Katherine Breen Hanneford; her son, Tommy; his wife, Struppi; and his sister, Kay Frances Hanneford Ille. See also the sketch of the "Hannaford family" in England, including Poodles, George, and Lizzie, in W. S. Meadmore's "note on the tenting show" in *The Circus Book*, ed. by Rupert Croft-Cooke, p. 18. Bradna, in a note to *The Big Top*, says that "Poodles has spelled his name Hannaford since he became a solo star, but on his passport it was Hanneford" (p. 77).

362   "The only trained acrobat": Buster Keaton, *My Wonderful World of Slapstick* (Garden City, N.Y., 1960), p. 149.

363   A great new era of family equestrian acts: The Zoppe Troupe didn't come to the United States until 1948, when their bareback act made its RBB&B debut, although they created their own equestrian circus in Italy more than 125 years ago. Since then, they have remained in the United States, producing many equestrian acts that have performed all over the continent. The fifth generation includes James Zoppe, whose American debut in 1978 caused Billy Barton to write in the *Circus Report* for Sept. 25 that year, "Not only is the young man a peerless rider, he is a beautiful one, with uncanny balance, superb form and style. He stands back on the horse's rump where he belongs, up on the balls of his feet, handles his body with the grace of a ballet dancer, and lands from pirouettes, leaps, jerks and somersaults as lightly as a falling leaf." In 1984, the Big Apple Circus Rosinback Riders presented a combined group of James Zoppe's troupe (Gary Borstelman and James's wife, Mafalda Zoppe) with the Big Apple Circus Company, including Marie-Pierre Benac, David Dimitri, Heidi Herriott, Sacha Pavlata, Jim Tinsman, Tasha Tinsman, Tady Wozniak, Teresa Wozniak, and Katja Schumann, wife of director Paul Binder. Wrote Binder in the 1984 Big Apple Program: "To my mind, James is the best bareback rider in America. Besides the classic and almost impossible somersault from horse to horse, I have never seen anybody who can turn a pirouette on horseback the way he does. His ability inspired us as a company (whom he trained) to create the special riding act in this show."

       "Prancing and strutting": Bradna and Spence, *The Big Top*, p. 79.

       "unequalled skill and daring": 1916 RBB&B poster at Baraboo.

364   Elizabeth and Ernie Clarke had a daughter: At Ringling, one can see a sculpture of Lou Jacobs, the *auguste* clown, on bended knee to Ernestine Clarke, the beautiful bareback rider, presenting her with a bouquet of flowers.

       Poodles spent his last years: "Edwin Hanneford, 75, Is Dead; Noted Bareback Riding Clown," *New York Times*, Dec. 11, 1967. The *Times* obit identifies Edwin as Poodles, the clown known as the Riding Fool. Early sources often misidentified Poodles's given name as Richard. The career of the Hanneford family of equestrians (then spelled Hannaford) in the British Isles is traced in *The Circus Book*, ed. by Croft-Cooke.

366   Their sister, Kay Frances: My visit to the Beatty-Cole Circus in Philadelphia was on May 15–16, 1975, and was recounted in John Culhane, "Superstars, Superprofits, Superfeats," *Holiday*, March 1976. Kay Frances Hanneford's husband, Jim Ille, who first joined the circus in 1970 as solo cornet player in Merle Evans's RBB&B circus band, was for a time musical director of The Greatest Show on Earth (RBB&B 1970 Program).

367   Death of Katherine Hanneford: Associated Press dispatch from Charlotte, N.C., Oct. 23, 1985, reprinted in the *New York Times*, Oct. 24, 1985, p. D31.

DISPLAY 21

In surveying the whole American circus scene today, I am indebted to *The White Tops*, the official publication of the Circus Fans Association of America, James G. Saunders, editor, for its individual circus reports. Karl Kae Knecht founded the CFA in 1926, and began its official bimonthly publication in 1927 as a four-page sheet called "Chatter from Around the White Tops." Renamed *The White Tops* in 1932, it is still going strong in its sixth decade.

The story of the founding of the Big Apple Circus, which first opened in New York on July 20, 1977, has been told in Peter Angelo Simon's *Big Apple Circus* (New York, 1978). Since then, it has been reviewed by Brendan Gill in *The New Yorker* under "Theatre" (Dec. 28, 1981) and been the subject of several magazine articles. But the best source of information on this one-ring European-style circus is the programs of its annual editions.

The best book on circus publicity is *This Way to the Big Show*, the life of Dexter Fellows, who ballyhooed both Buffalo Bill and the Ringling brothers. P. T. Barnum began as his own ballyhooer; then he took on Richard F. "Tody" Hamilton, graduate of Bennett's *Herald*, Wall Street, and Coup's New York Aquarium, as his press agent, beginning the long, colorful line that extends through Willard D. Coxey, Jimmy de Wolfe, Fellows, Frank Braden, Roland Butler, and others to the present day. The first to enchant me with his spiel was William B. Naylor, circus press agent from the Sells-Floto Circus (1921) to Polack Bros. Shrine Circus (1950–1956). Since then, I have known many fine publicists, as they are called today, including Lee Solters, Joan Tramantano, Nini Finkelstein Crangle (and her husband, former RBB&B marketing and sales manager Thomas Crangle), Pat Marcus, Patty Britt Johnson, Rodney Huey, Debbie Linde, Keri Menacho, Cathy Wales, and the "Media Coordinator for Gunther Gebel-Williams," Romulus B. Portwood, Jr.

Where this chapter deals with the return of Barnumesque ballyhoo in the Kenneth Feld era of Ringling Bros. and Barnum & Bailey Circus's long history, I have taken particular note of M. E. Recio's "Ladies and Gentlemen, Presenting—Kenneth Feld" in *Business Week*, June 8, 1987, and "The Story of Ballyhoo," in the RBB&B 1979 Program. Susannah G. Smith, vice president for RBB&B corporate communications, made available to me the files on the ballyhooing of the Living Unicorn. Allen J. Bloom, as RBB&B senior vice president, marketing and sales, is in overall charge of ballyhoo under Feld.

Page

369　"From the haunting shadows": Television commercial for RBB&B starring King Tusk, 1987.

In three recent seasons: See RBB&B programs for 1985 (the Living Unicorn), 1986 (the Shanghai Acrobatic Troupe), and 1987 (King Tusk).

370　"A CLOWN will entertain the Ladies and Gentlemen": Reproduced in Durant and Durant, *Pictorial History*, p. 21.

As early as 1833: Fox, *A Ticket to the Circus*, contains a fine chapter on advertising (pp. 59–62), plus illustrations and captions. See also the Introduction and Notes to Rennert, *100 Years of Circus Posters*.

1882 Jumbo poster: Reprinted from a circus pamphlet in Werner, *Barnum*, p. 345.

$1,500 to paint the lunging tiger: Rennert, *100 Years of Circus Posters*, p. 11.

371　The old theory: "Forty Years in the Center Ring," *Bandwagon*, July–Aug. 1965, p.

6: "However after this film the Ringling management decided that Beatty was being 'exposed' too greatly in movies and that it was affecting his drawing power in the circus."

RBB&B on television: Irvin Feld to author, 1975.

"Do you know me?": Frames from this American Express commercial are pictured in RBB&B's *Lord of the Rings: Gunther Gebel-Williams.*

372   Sidney H. Schanberg, "The Great Circus Hornswoggle," *New York Times*, April 13, 1985, sec. I, p. 23; Charles Osgood on "The CBS Early Morning News," April 9, 1985; "The Tonight Show," April 9, 1985.

New York Mayor Edward Koch quoted in Schanberg, "The Great Circus Hornswoggle."

"DON'T LET THE GRINCHES STEAL THE FANTASY": Full-page ad in the *New York Times*, April 7, 1985.

Steven Geer on *ABC World News Tonight*, April 8, 1985.

373   "Direct from the People's Republic of China": RBB&B 1986 Program.

On the Shanghai Acrobatic Troupe: "Shanghai Acrobatic Troupe dazzles audiences at Ringling Brothers and Barnum & Bailey Circus performances in New York City; Ringling pres. Kenneth Feld describes rigorous training and his long struggle to win Chinese Government permission for US tour," *New York Times*, April 2, 1986, sec. III, p. 19.

"The People's Republic had never before": Kenneth Feld to author, New York, March 25, 1986.

The tradition of acrobatics in China: Shanghai Acrobatic Troupe, RBB&B informational brochure, 1985, and RBB&B 1986 Program.

Bringing acrobats from China: Big Apple Circus 1988 Program. The Big Apple Circus presented the Nanjing Acrobatic Troupe in the United States in 1988–89. Dominique Jando, associate artistic director, in the article "The Chinese Acrobatic Theatre," says that "Historical records, carvings, and mural paintings in tombs and grottoes (such as the brick carvings discovered in the Han Dynasty tomb of Changdu, in the province of Szechuan) date the origin of Chinese acrobatics more than two thousand years ago, during the Warring States period."

375   Jumbo statistics: Wallace, *Fabulous Showman*, 1962, p. 247. See also H. A. Ardman, "Phineas T. Barnum's Charming Beast; Jumbo the Elephant," *Natural History*, Feb. 1973, and Haley, "Colossus of His Kind."

King Tusk statistics: Courtesy of Susannah G. Smith, RBB&B.

376   "I was the first girl": Barbara Woodcock to author, Big Apple Circus lot, Westchester County, N.Y., May 29, 1988.

On the Big Apple Circus: See the Big Apple Circus programs, 1983–1988. Many contain valuable essays on the circus by historian Dominique Jando.

"Circus, when done right": Paul Binder, quoted in The Big Apple Spring/Summer Tour 1987 Program, p. 5.

"The circus begins with horses": Ringmaster Paul Binder to audience at the Big Apple Circus, New York City, Dec. 11, 1984.

377   The Schumann Dynasty: Big Apple Circus 1984 Program.

"the equestrienne": Quoted in Big Apple Circus 1985 Program. For Balzac's equestrienne, Marguerite Turquet, see his novels, *The Imaginary Mistress*, *The Muse of the Department*, *A Man of Business*, and *Cousin Bette*.

"The Courier of St. Petersburg" is described at length in Saxon, *Andrew Ducrow*. When it was performed by Katja Schumann with the Big Apple Circus in 1985, the circus program gave a short description of its history. Reviewing it for *White Tops* (Nov.–Dec. 1986, p. 32), George C. Bingaman wrote: "A major portion of my motivation to travel to see this summer's edition [of the Big Apple Circus] was for another look at Katja Schumann's 'The Courier.' I was not disappointed as she recreated Ducrow's equestrian classic . . . first appearing at Astley's London Circus in 1827. Roman riding two steeds, she entered and as she circled one horse is added on each turn first passing beneath her arched legs at which point she grabbed the new set of reins. This continues until she has four horses in front in a six equine thriller. Never before seen in America in our time!"

On Paul Binder: Profiled by Meg Dooly in "In the Middle of the Magic," in the university magazine *Columbia*, Oct. 1984. Binder also received an honorary doctorate from Dartmouth.

378   "Your appreciation of the circus is heightened": Binder to author, interview in his trailer at Lincoln Center, New York City, Dec. 6, 1984.

On the Carrillo Brothers: See RBB&B 1973 Program; Big Apple Circus 1984 Program; and RBB&B 1989 Program.

"In 1818, an English wire walker": Big Apple Circus 1984 Program.

Two sorts of theaters: Dominique Jando, "Roots: The Art of Classical Circus in America," Big Apple Circus 1985 Program.

383   An authentic Irish gypsy wagon: Big Apple Circus 1985 Program.

"comedy and acrobatics went along well": Paul Binder introducing Jim Tinsman's "table rock" routine, Big Apple Circus 1984 Program. See also Harry Ritley's table rock in Bradna and Spence, *The Big Top*, p. 217.

"In the American One-Ring Circus era": Big Apple Circus 1984 Program.

"aerial razzle-dazzle": Peter Bonventre, "Queen of the Rings," *Newsweek*, July 31, 1978, p. 73.

"Ladies and gentlemen, watch now": Paul Binder introducing Dolly Jacobs at the Big Apple Circus, Dec. 1985.

384   Adolph and his smaller female partner, Taxi: Nan Robertson reviewing Big Apple sea lion act in the *New York Times*, Nov. 1984.

"Yehudi Menuhin once said": Paul Binder to Big Apple audience, New York City, Dec. 31, 1986.

The 12,600th triple: Tito Gaona to author in his trailer in Big Apple Circus lot, Lincoln Center, New York City, Jan. 3, 1987.

"To audiences everywhere": Parkinson to author, Baraboo, June 15, 1983.

385   Quadruples by Ruben Caballero, Jr.: William B. Hall III, "Tanbark Topics," *White Tops*, Nov.–Dec. 1986, p. 44.

Two quadruples at the same RBB&B performance: Kenneth Feld to author in telephone interview, Dec. 31, 1988.

The Carson & Barnes Circus and Luciana Loyal: Francis E. Sanders, "Carson & Barnes Circus," *White Tops*, Nov.–Dec. 1986, p. 32.

386   On Cirque du Soleil and Denis Lacombe: Guy Laliberté, executive director of Cirque du Soleil, phone interviews with author, 1977. "Le Cirque du Soleil, circus from Quebec that will make its East Coast debut at Battery Park City, Manhattan," *New York Times*, May 25, 1988, sec. 3, p. 15. Anna Kisselgoff reviews performance of Cirque du Soleil in Manhattan, *New York Times*, May 27, sec. 3, p. 5. Mel Gussow reviews Cirque du Soleil, *New York Times*, June 5, sec. 2, p. 5. See also Cirque du Soleil official programs, 1985 tour and 1986 tour.

      On the Liebel Family Circus: See review by Bingaman in *White Tops*.

386–87   On "Risley acts": Pierre Couderc, "Risley," *Bandwagon*, Jan.–Feb. 1965, pp. 18–22.

387   "One of the chief attractions": *New York Herald*, May 4, 1843, quoted in Chindahl, *History of the Circus in America*, p. 205.

      On daredevils Henry and Christopher Munoz: *Rockford* (Ill.) *Register-Star*, July 1, 1987.

      On Elvin Bale: Kenneth Feld to author, Madison Square Garden, New York, April 7, 1987.

      "Thrillers": Fellows and Freeman, *This Way to the Big Show*, p. 241.

      On the R&T Aerial Ski Squadron: RBB&B 1989 Program.

      On the Carrillo Brothers: Ibid.

387–88   On Tahar: *Guinness Book of World Records* honors Tahar Douis of the Hassani Troupe for supporting the largest human pyramid in recorded history, in Birmingham, England, in 1979. As "understander," Tahar supported a three-high tower of twelve men on his shoulders: total weight, 1,700 pounds.

388   "Human daring": Octavie LaTour, *New York World*, April 8, 1905, quoted in Fenner and Fenner, *The Circus, Lure and Legend*, p. 105.

      On the Wally Naghtin bears: RBB&B 1979 Program.

      On Digger, the Boxing Kangaroo: George C. Bingaman, review of Allan C. Hill's Great American Circus in the *White Tops*, Nov.–Dec. 1986, p. 29. That same issue gives detailed coverage to the 1986 Great Circus Parade in Milwaukee.

      "One of the few men": Taylor, *Center Ring*, p. 51. Taylor profiles Merle Evans in this book.

      The 1989 Great Circus Parade in Milwaukee presented a forty-horse hitch pulling the "Two Hemispheres" bandwagon for the first time since Barnum & Bailey's 1903 season. The "Two Hemispheres" was built for that entirely new 1903 parade, and Bailey wanted a forty-horse team to draw it in a style befitting its magnificence. Sebastian Wagon Works in New York City built the wagon, and it is the longest (twenty-eight feet) and one of the most beautiful ever constructed. One side says "Eastern Hemisphere," the other, "Western Hemisphere"; where the twain meet sat the handsomely uniformed "windjammers," as circus bandsmen were called. (Robert L. Parkinson to author, 1989. See also Fox and Kelley, *The Great Circus Street Parade in Pictures*, pp. 22–23, 86.)

389 "first elephant ever to perform": Carter's act, Big Apple Circus 1984 Program.
Cayetano's Circus in 1812: Vail, *Random Notes*, p. 16.
On Clifford E. Vargas: The founder of Circus Vargas died of heart disease on Sept. 4, 1989, at his home in Hollywood Hills, Calif., at the age of sixty-four. According to the Associated Press dispatch in the *New York Times*, Sept. 7, 1989, p. B17: "The grandson of Portuguese circus owners, Mr. Vargas founded Circus Vargas twenty years ago with three trucks and eight animals. In the early years, he was ticket taker, ringmaster and truck driver. The circus grew to include 150 animals and up to 300 employees, and is billed as the largest traveling tented circus in the world."
The Woodcock Elephants: See Fox and Parkinson, *The Circus in America*: "Bill Woodcock, Sr., one of the top elephant trainers of this century, knew nearly every elephant in every circus herd—the bad ones, the hard workers, the leaders" (p. 276).
Anna May's Ringling debut: See RBB&B 1978 Program.

390 "It's the reward system": Buckles Woodcock to author, interview in the Big Apple Circus lot "backyard," Lincoln Center, New York, Dec. 28, 1983.
"The best elephants": Clive Barnes, *New York Post*, Nov. 25, 1983.
On the Orton family circus: See Tom Parkinson's list of circuses in Durant and Durant, *Pictorial History*, p. 317.
"My family": Sarah Orton Woodcock to author, interview at the home of William Schultz in Baraboo, Wis., June 14, 1983.
Buckles got his nickname: Ibid.
"My father said": Buckles Woodcock to author, June 14, 1983, Baraboo, Wis.

390–91 Buckles developed a reputation: RBB&B 1978 Program. See also Big Apple Circus 1984 Program, Paul Binder: "Bill demonstrates a firm but gentle hand with his charges. His world-wide reputation is well founded: that of a trainer of difficult elephants. On top of that, he is a pleasure to work with. If I were an elephant, I'd choose Buckles as my trainer."

391 "On Circus Vargas in 1972": Barbara Woodcock, interviewed on the Big Apple Circus lot in Westchester County, N.Y., May 29, 1988. Barbara also provided the information on her granddaughter, Stormy Ann Williams.
Such are the intimate delights: On the revival of the one-ring circus in America see John Culhane, "The One-Ring Circus Revival," *Signature*, April 1987. The Stebbing Royal European Circus, founded in 1972 by Billy and Lillian Scott Stebbing (the "royal" referring to the command performances both sides of the family used to do in England), was the first in this country to re-establish a one-ring, intimate show on the order of English and European circuses. The Stebbings couldn't afford a tent those first months, but by Sept. 1973, when the circus began doing annual shows at the Virginia State Fair in Richmond, it had made enough money to put up its own big top—a new $17,000 red-and-white-striped canvas. The Stebbings were followed by the San Francisco–based Pickle Family Circus, founded in 1974 by Larry Pisoni and Peggy Snider as an offspring of the San Francisco Mime Troupe. Bill Erwin and Geoff Hoyle were Pickle clowns; the star clown in 1989 was Joan

Rankin as Queen Moon. The New York School for Circus Arts (and its performing company, the Big Apple Circus) was founded in 1977, also, according to its 1984 program, "to revive the classical tradition of the one-ring circuses for American audiences." Cirque du Soleil was founded in Quebec in 1984 by the Club des Talon Hauts Inc., a nonprofit corporation organized in 1981 to promote the circus arts and street performance. In 1986, Ivor David Balding, the founder and artistic director of Circus Flora, created in one ring at the Spoleto Festival in Charleston, S.C., a reenactment of the first circus to perform in Charleston, in 1810, with musical instruments and costumes of the period. See John Culhane, "The Stebbing Circus: All in the Family," *GEO*, Aug. 1979, pp. 72–92; Jennifer Dunning, "Stage: Spoleto's Circus (Circus Flora)," *New York Times*, June 4, 1986, p. C24; and "A Show by the Pickle Family, Starring Clowning," *New York Times*, July 24, 1989; the Big Apple Circus 1984 Program; and the Cirque du Soleil 1986 Program.

392   "a circus by himself": Edward Hoagland quoted in *Lord of the Rings: Gunther Gebel-Williams*. After Gunther's retirement, announced for the end of the 1990 season, his son, Mark Oliver Gebel, will continue to perform with elephants and horses. Of the young Gebel's debut in 1983, theater critic Mel Gussow wrote in the *New York Times* (April 1, 1983, p. C1): "While his father is chumming around with tigers, snuggling up to them as if they were teddy bears and tossing one around his neck as if it were a feathered boa, the son is beginning his career with goats. But he is a good goat tender, and when one proves to be recalcitrant, he deftly pushes it down a slide as if it were a timid child in a playground. . . . Later the young Gebel joins his father and 'thundering pachyderms' in the center ring." An old family photograph in *Lord of the Rings* shows that Gunther himself began his animal training and performing career as a goat tender.

"a truly happy dream": Ernest Hemingway, "The Circus," RBB&B Circus Magazine & Program, 1953, p. 7.

CAPTIONS

40   "The loss of Waterloo": Tom Thumb quoted in Barnum, *Struggles and Triumphs*, 1877, p. 184.

44   "The General left America": Barnum, ibid., p. 257.
"The keeper was furnished": Ibid., p. 357.

45   "As long as there is a child": Thorpe to author.

54   "The comic element of Lincoln" and "something of the cartooned figure": Sandburg, *Abraham Lincoln: The War Years*, vol. 3, p. 300.
"While the boys were traveling": Alf. T. Ringling, *Life Story of the Ringling Brothers*, p. 53.

57   The *Floating Palace*: See Durant and Durant, *Pictorial History*, pp. 48–49.
"The boss of all riders": Robinson, *Old Wagon Show Days*, p. 165.

63   "Our big outing": Marian Anderson, *My Lord, What a Morning* (New York, 1956), pp. 6–7.

65   "No, sir": Tom Thumb quoted in Werner, *Barnum*, p. 265.

74   "Five Great Clowns": Robinson, *Old Wagon Show Days*, p. 135. See also Billie Burke, *With a Feather on My Nose*, in which she remembers her father.

77   On Jackie Onassis: C. David Heymann, *A Woman Named Jackie* (New York, 1989), p. 18.

79   Grizzly Adams: Barnum tells the story of James C. "Grizzly" Adams in *Struggles and Triumphs*, 1877, pp. 529–42.

87   Orton-Woodcock connection: Sarah Orton Woodcock and Buckles and Barbara Woodcock to author.

88   William Lake: See Robinson, *Old Wagon Show Days*, p. 115.
"Col. Cody considered my wife" to "In after years": Ibid., p. 125.

89   "Representing the last": Ibid., p. 192; also contains the letter from Taft giving his memories of John Robinson.
History of the John Robinson Circus: Tom Parkinson in Durant and Durant, *Pictorial History*, p. 319.

95   "He created the metier": The London *Times* obituary of Barnum is quoted at length in Wallace, *Fabulous Showman*, 1962, pp. 258–59.

99   "Hallo! Barnum's Museum is burned": Barnum, *Struggles and Triumphs*, 1877, p. 698.

102   Death of Chang and Eng: J. P. McEvoy, "The Siamese Twins," *Kiwanis* magazine, Sept. 1943, quoted in Fenner and Fenner, *The Circus, Lure and Legend*, p. 120. See also the 1874 report of the *Annual Register*, reprinted in Wallace, *Fabulous Showman*, 1962, p. 107; Durant and Durant, *Pictorial History*, pp. 100–101, 112; and Werner, *Barnum*, pp. 242, 305.
"La-deez and gen-tul-men": Sandburg, *Always the Young Strangers*, reprinted in Fenner and Fenner, *The Circus, Lure and Legend*, pp. 121–22.
"a Maiden Dwarf": *Massachusetts Spy*, reprinted in Vail, *Random Notes*, p. 49.
"I can't make money out of human misery": Feld to author, 1973.

107   "No one but a country boy": Hamlin Garland, *Boy Life on the Prairie* (New York, 1907), p. 39.

109   On Fred W. Glasier: Born in Adams, Mass., in 1865, Glasier developed a great interest in the American Indian, eventually being adopted into the Massasoit tribe. He took advantage of his profession as photographer of circus life to photograph Indian life as well; and on his own time, Glasier traveled around America giving lantern slide lectures on both circus life and Indian life. Hundreds of Glasier's prints and negatives were acquired in the 1960s by the Ringling Museum, whose director in 1983, John Lentz, made some of them available for this book.

114   "Piqua, Ohio, Saturday, July 4": Reprinted in Fellows and Freeman, *This Way to the Big Show*, p. 346.

115   Buffalo Bill and Sitting Bull: See Vine Deloria, Jr., *Custer Died for Your Sins* (New York: Macmillan, 1970), written by a Standing Rock Sioux, a former director of the National Congress of American Indians, which tells the story from the Indian point of view. For the white man's view, see "Buffalo Bill's Medal Restored," an Associated Press dispatch from Cody, Wyo., dated July 8, 1989, which appeared on p. 23 of the *New York Times* for July 9: "Seventy-two years after Congress stripped Buffalo Bill Cody of his Medal of Honor, it has been restored. William F. Cody, the Buffalo Bill who later became a famous Western showman, received the medal in 1872 for gallantry as an Army scout in the Indian wars, but it was revoked in 1917, along with medals of 910 recipients, when Congress retroactively tightened the rules for the honor. Among the other changes, Congress held that only military personnel could receive the award. A scout was considered a civilian; in all, five scouts lost medals in 1917. Now, however, the Army Board for Correction of Military Records, which has some leeway in administering policy decisions on military awards, has ruled that Cody and the four other scouts are nonetheless deserving of the honor. . . . Buffalo Bill, known to his contemporaries as a Pony Express rider, Indian scout and buffalo hunter, received the honor for valor after leading a cavalry charge against a group of Sioux. He killed two, recovered several horses, and pursued the retreating Indians. Although his name was stricken from the Medal of Honor roll in February, 1917, one month after he died, the medal itself was never recalled and remains in the Buffalo Bill Historical Center here in Cody, a town named for Buffalo Bill."

120   Rough Riders: The largest circus billboard ever produced, in 1899, carried the banner headline "THE GLORIOUS DRAMA OF CIVILIZATION, BUFFALO BILL'S WILD WEST AND CONGRESS OF ROUGH RIDERS OF THE WORLD." It was longer than four average-sized billboards. Baraboo reassembled eighty-eight sheets in 1983 for a *National Geographic* photographer. W. W. Cole was runner-up with a 100-sheet poster in the 1800s: Robert L. Parkinson to author, Sept. 19, 1989.

"Conditions were bad": Hamid, *Circus; as told to his son*, p. 18.

"more than anywhere else": Ibid., p. 9.

133   "PRIVATE . . . Would you like to publish for the holidays": Autographed letter in the collection of Leonidas Westervelt, published in Werner, *Barnum*, p. 347. The book that resulted was apparently *Autobiography of Matthew Scott, Jumbo's Keeper; also Jumbo's biography, by the same author*, attributed to Matthew Scott and published in 1885.

139   "If Barnum had not": Werner, *Barnum*, p. 360.

        Lalla Rookh means "Tulip Cheek": Thomas Moore, *Lalla Rookh: An Oriental Romance* (Philadelphia, 1842), p. 5.

        Marilyn Monroe's guest appearance in 1955: Duane "Uncle Soapy" Thorpe, veteran Ringling clown, to author, 1976.

145   "John Ringling knows more": Fred E. Sterling, quoted in Louis La Coss, "The Lieutenant Governor of Illinois Spends His Vacations Traveling with A CIRCUS," *St. Louis Globe-Democrat Magazine*, Aug. 4, 1929, p. 1. This article gives a good example of the personal way the Ringlings ran their circus. Sterling, born in Dixon, Ill., in 1869, was city editor of a Rockford newspaper when they met him and later became three-time lieutenant governor of Illinois. In 1899, an advance man for Ringling Bros. came to Rockford and plastered the town with advertisements. Immediately, the advance man for an older circus came and covered over the Ringling advertisements with his own. One of the era's frequent "circus wars" ensued, often breaking into violence. Sterling thought the aggressor was the other circus, and said so in an editorial. The Ringlings never forgot the gesture. That same summer they invited the city editor to spend his vacation traveling with their circus. He accepted and went, and the invitation was repeated annually from 1899 through 1928. "It sure has spoiled me for ordinary travel," he told La Coss. "The Ringling car is a little palace on wheels. It has every comfort that the modern home can command, even to a brass bed and a grand piano. The Ringlings are—rather they were until all passed along except John—the most delightful hosts."

152   The Forty-Horse Hitch Then: See Jake Posey, *The Last of the Forty Horse Drivers*; see also Fox and Kelley, *The Great Circus Street Parade in Pictures*.

153   The Forty-Horse Hitch Now: See Louis A. Goth, "The Parade That's Making Milwaukee Famous," *Reader's Digest*, June 1989, pp. 154–60. "When Bob Parkinson, parade director, gives the signal to move out," the four-mile march of almost 700 horses, many circus performers past and present, and "around 70 priceless historic wagons from the Circus World Museum in Baraboo" included, in 1989, the Two Hemispheres bandwagon pulled, for the first time since 1903, by a forty-horse hitch.

154   " 'When I get through my work' ": Slivers Oakley quoted in Sherwood, *Here We Go Again*, p. 79.

161   "The horses make the loveliest pattern of dreams": Hemingway quoted in RBB&B 1953 Program.

172   "pretty of face": *New York Clipper*, quoted in Durant and Durant, *Pictorial History*, p. 188.

173   "Clowns, elephants, pretty ladies": John Ringling, "We Divided the Job—But Stuck Together," *American*, Sept. 1919; reprinted in its entirety in Fox, *A Ticket to the Circus*, pp. 39–46. Quote occurs on p. 43.

        "when the greater circuses": Thomas Wolfe, "The Circus at Dawn," in *Only the Dead Know Brooklyn* (New York, 1947), p. 32.

180   "garbed in vestments": Taylor, *Center Ring*, p. 229.

181 "Slowly the star": Bradna and Spence, *The Big Top*, p. 148.
"She had a grand piano" and "She was a storm center": Jenny Rooney, quoted in Taylor, *Center Ring*, pp. 238–39.
"Leitzel was a little bit of a thing": Bradna and Spence, *The Big Top*, p. 180.

185 "a beautiful little rag doll": Taylor, *Center Ring*, p. 13.

193 "Fifty years ago": Dexter Fellows in *This Way to the Big Show*, p. 216.

194 "To tell the truth": Walt Disney, "The Marceline I Knew," *Marceline News*, Sept. 2, 1938, p. 1.
Swan Bandwagon saved by Disney: Fox and Kelley, *The Great Circus Parade in Pictures*, p. 113; also see pp. 20–21.
On the Moellers: Fox, *A Ticket to the Circus*, pp. 174–75.
"Listen!": Fellows and Freeman, *This Way to the Big Show*, p. 231.

195 "He had come": F. Scott Fitzgerald, *The Great Gatsby* (New York, 1925), p. 218.

201 RBB&B railroad cars: RBB&B 1989–90 Program.

203 "Personally, I believe": Clyde Beatty was quoted to me in 1973 by Bill Ballantine, who prints a long interview with Beatty in *Wild Tigers and Tame Fleas*.

215 Hunt Bros. Circus: See Charles T. Hunt, Sr., as told to John C. Cloutman, *The Story of Mr. Circus* (Rochester, N.H., 1954).
Kelly was increasingly melancholy: See my "Unforgettable Emmett Kelly."

216 Clyde Beatty with lion and chair: "Clyde Beatty & Captive," *Time* cover story, March 29, 1937; see also "Forty Years in the Center Ring."
"beauty of face and form": *Billboard*, quoted in Bob Taber, "The Hodgini Family," *White Tops*, May–June 1961, p. 20. For tabloid coverage, see "End of the Circus Romance," *American Weekly*, Jan. 14, 1945. Her story reminds me of the circus definition given by Emmett Kelly in *Clown*: "A circus is a bright, spangled girl with a date in a town a hundred miles away tomorrow morning" (p. 257).

217 On Alfred Court: See his *My Life with the Big Cats*.
"fighting act": Ballantine, *Wild Tigers and Tame Fleas*, p. 116.

219 "shot through space": Poster reproduced in Fox and Parkinson, *The Circus in America*, p. 257.
"They had to fire them": Fellini, *Fellini on Fellini*, p. 87.

225 "The Largest Gorilla Ever Exhibited": Poster reproduced in Fox and Parkinson, *The Circus in America*, p. 262. "The Terror Is Coming": Bob Parkinson, historian of Circus World Museum, remembers this billboard as the genesis of his passion for the circus (Robert L. Parkinson to author, Baraboo, Wis., 1983).

232 The Cole Bros. and Clyde Beatty Combined Circus was photographed at the old Hippodrome on Sixth Avenue between Forty-third and Forty-fourth streets in New York City early in 1937.
"We'll do the same thing with circus wagons!": Fox and Parkinson, *The Circus in America*, p. 186; see also "Telescoping Tableaux" in Fox and Kelley, *The Great Circus Street Parade in Pictures*, pp. 28–35.
"Friday, I tasted life": See Mabel Todd Loomis, *Letters of Emily Dickinson*, letter to her sister, circa 1857, pp. 142–43, quoted in Burke, *Outrageous Good Fortune*, p. 178.

235   An escaped tiger: Kelly, *Clown*, pp. 257–58.

"Two car-building firms were responsible": Parkinson and Fox, *The Circus Moves by Rail*, p. 97.

238   "Incautiously, she turned her back": North and Hatch, *The Circus Kings*, p. 273.

241   A Gag Is Born: Kelly, *Clown*, p. 125.

244   "Stravinsky asked, 'How old?'": 1971 souvenir program of Balanchine's New York City Ballet, quoted in Rennert, *100 Years of Circus Posters*, p. 12.

The photograph of Balanchine and Stravinsky with three-dimensional models of Hyacinth Hippo by T. Hee and Walt Disney is in John Culhane, *Walt Disney's Fantasia* (New York, 1983), p. 168.

"They would have done": Ringling clown Prince Paul Alpert to author, 1974.

"Stravinsky cranked out": Taylor, *Center Ring*, pp. 43–44.

250   "We must forget the fire": Emmett Kelly quoted in "Fire Destroys the Big Top," *Life*, July 17, 1944.

251   "Prior to the advent": May, *From Rome to Ringling*, p. 199. For background on the Cristiani family, see Hubler, *The Cristianis*; for the Davenports, Loyal-Repenskys, and Hannefords, see Bradna and Spence, *The Big Top*, particularly pp. 77–79, 309–311; for the Hodgini family, see Bob Taber, "The Hodgini Family," *White Tops*, May–June 1961.

252   Roustabouts: The section "Canvas City," in Fox, *A Ticket to the Circus*, pp. 89–107, deals in evocative words and pictures with the erecting of the big tents, including a description of the operation from the 1895 Ringling Bros. and Barnum & Bailey route book.

"There was no further fear": Bradna and Spence, *The Big Top*, p. 263.

257   "Trunk up!": Buckles Woodcock to author, Venice, Fla., Dec. 1977.

268   "In your dreams": Ernest Hemingway, "The Circus," RBB&B 1953 Program, p. 7. In addition to Hemingway, this program contains an ineffable example of advertising prose adapted for the circus audience: "I dreamed I went to the Circus in my Maidenform bra / I'm the Circe of the circus . . . the gal in the gallery with the gala Maidenform figure! Clowns jump for joy in the center ring—and the applause is all for my curves . . . circled so spectacularly by circular-stitched Chansonette!" (p. 61).

269   On Hubert Castle: O'Brien, *Circus: Cinders to Sawdust*, pp. 135–36. Castle was a star of the 1940 season of Cole Bros. Circus with Clyde Beatty, in which two great clowns, Otto Griebling and Freddie Freeman, put on the boxing match in which Griebling was forced to fight both Freeman and the referee.

Burt Lancaster: See Taylor, *Center Ring*, p. 181.

271   "The long mount is the kick-line": Kenneth Feld to author, Dec. 1985.

278   "The tented circus": North quoted in "Goodbye to the Gallant and Gay," *Newsweek*, July 30, 1956.

"A magical era has passed": "Big Top Bows Out Forever," *Life*, July 30, 1956.

"definite possibility for the future": Kenneth Feld to author, Dec. 31, 1988.

281   First camel seen by Americans: Vail, *Random Notes*, p. 8.

Two camels, a male and female: Ibid., p. 9.

283   "A Star of the Circus": Glenn Collins, *New York Times*, Feb. 7, 1989.

293   "To get inside the head": John Culhane, "Gunther Gebel-Williams," *Reader's Digest*, Nov. 1989, p. 95.

294   "Only the Big Top Died": My interview with Naylor, in *Rockford* (Ill.) *Register-Republic*, Aug. 7, 1956.

295   Gebel-Williams with Dickie the giraffe: "Barnum & Bailey's initial season together . . . headlined a pair of full-grown African giraffes, harnessed to a float which they towed around the hippodrome track" (Greg Parkinson, "Expect the Unexpected," RBB&B 1985 Program). But giraffes proved fragile, and though seen in menageries, they rarely performed in American circuses after that first three-ring show in 1881—until Gunther presented his son riding Dickie around the hippodome track.

"I must be very careful": Gebel-Williams, quoted in Culhane, "The Lord of the Ring," p. 61.

303   The Quadruple: When I saw my first quad at Madison Square Garden the achievement of the Vazquez brothers reminded me of Alfred North Whitehead's definition of style: "the direct attainment of a foreseen end, simply and without waste."

321   "master of jimcrackery": Ballantine, *Clown Alley*, p. 264.

323   "At first I thought he was joking": Sherwood, *Here We Are Again*, quoted in Fenner and Fenner, *The Circus, Lure and Legend*, pp. 77–78.

328   "A clown who": Bradna and Spence, *The Big Top*, p. 315.

341   "$180 a week": Clown College reunion in *Life*, Nov. 1987.

351   "Seventeen years ago": Pacino quoted in Glenn Plaskin, "And Now—on the High Wire," *New York Daily News*, Sept. 12, 1989.

356   "Several generations of my own family": Helen Wallenda to author, 1983.

"After carrying her on his shoulders": O'Brien, *Circus: Cinders to Sawdust*, pp. 136–37.

"For Ez-dur Zeels": in Ballantine, *Clown Alley*, p. 79.

361   "It is some years now": From the introduction to *Memoirs of Joseph Grimaldi*, ed. by Charles Dickens (1838).

Origin of "clown alley": Ballantine, *Clown Alley*, p. i.

369   King Tusk: Kenneth Feld presented King Tusk by first introducing ever larger elephants into the ring to show by contrast how stupendous, gigantic, colossal King Tusk really was. Then enter the King, wearing, said the RBB&B 1987 Program, "a glorious, gilded robe, weighing 1200 pounds and requiring twelve attendants." Before Barnum introduced Jumbo to the circus a century before, presentations so elaborate were virtually unknown.

"Doc" Van Alstine, who joined Yankee Robinson's Mighty Robinson Circus in about 1880, said in an interview in 1939 that "There just ain't no comparison between the circus of today and the circus of the past. The circus in this day and age seems really to be the stupendous, gigantic, colossal exhibition the advance billing and the 'barkers,' 'spielers,' and 'grinders' claim for it. The circus your grandfather went to see as a boy was nothing more than a variety, or vaudeville, show under canvas. Pretty near all the acts they done in the circus could have been put on in even the ordinary theaters of the time, but the kids of today ain't so wide-eyed and amazed at what they see at a circus as they was a quarter of a century ago. So many marvelous things goes on all the time in this day and age that kids probably expect more from a circus now than it's humanly possible to give." (Ann Banks, *First-Person America* [New York, 1981], pp. 203–4.)

379 "The People's Republic had never": Kenneth Feld quoted in "Shanghai Acrobatic Troupe."

380 On Tahar: Seeing Tahar's act inspired me to compose a variation upon the old poem about Isaac Van Amburgh sticking his head in a lion's mouth, to wit:

> He sticks his head in an alligator's mouth
> And leaves it there awhile,
> And when he takes it out again, Tahar won't even smile;
> For he heard you commit an unpardonable gaffe:
> You called it a crocodile.

"One elephant lays down": Buckles Woodcock to author, 1983.

381 "Steve Martin, who knows all about being funny": D. E. Haupt, "The Sight Fantastic," *Life*, Oct. 1988, p. 98.

382 "the Nureyev of show business": Edward Hoagland, "Here Comes the Circus," *Life*, April 23, 1971, p. 66; quoted in John Culhane, "Gunther Gebel-Williams," *Reader's Digest*, Nov. 1989.

BIBLIOGRAPHY

On the specific subject of the circus, more than 1,250 books exist in English. My starting place, of course, was the four volumes of R. Toole-Stott's *Circus and Allied Arts: A World Bibliography*. My smaller bibliography deals with those books pertaining to the American circus (with very few exceptions) that are historical and factual, plus a selection of magazine and newspaper articles and some pamphlets and brochures with the same virtues. In addition, I have listed the novels *Chad Hanna*, *Toby Tyler*, and *Cat Man*, the classics of circus fiction that give a real feel for the circus world, and Mark Twain's *The Adventures of Huckleberry Finn*, which has the best description ever of the effect of a good circus on a good imagination.

BOOKS

Alden, W. L. *Among the Freaks*. Longmans, Green, 1896.

Allen, Edward, and F. Beverly Kelley. *Fun by the Ton*. New York: Hastings House, 1941. A book on elephants by the man who had the Cole Bros. and Clyde Beatty herd in 1937.

American Heritage Magazine. *Great Days of the Circus*. New York: American Heritage Publishing, 1962.

Anderson, Marian. *My Lord, What a Morning*. New York: Viking, 1956. The great African-American contralto remembers the Barnum & Bailey circuses of her childhood.

Atherton, Lewis. *Main Street on the Middle Border*. Bloomington: Indiana University Press, 1954. "Of all attractions, the circus held first place," says Atherton in the circus section (p. 135) of this social history of the midwestern small town from the 1860s to the 1950s.

Bailey, Olga. *Mollie Bailey*. Dallas: Harben-Spotts, 1943.

Baily, Waldron. *The Autobiography of Waldron Baily*. New York: Exposition Press, n.d. The life of the novelist and politician from North Carolina, with an account of the "Grand Showman's Ball" of 1849.

Baker, Carlos. *Ernest Hemingway: A Life Story*. New York: Charles Scribner's Sons, 1969.

Ballantine, Bill. *Wild Tigers and Tame Fleas*. New York: Rinehart, 1958.

———. *Clown Alley*. Boston: Little, Brown, 1982.

Banks, Ann, ed. *First-Person America*. New York: Vintage Books, 1981. Oral histories as gathered and transcribed in the 1930s by the WPA Writers' Project include A. C. Sherbert's 1939 interview with "Doc" Van Alstine, who spent almost sixty years with circuses, from the Mighty Robinson Circus about 1880 to later shows where he was "boss canvasman." Illustrated with a photograph of a circus billboard taken by artist Ben Shahn.

Banks, G. L. *Blondin, His Life and Performances*. Routledge, Warne & Routledge, 1862.

Barnum, Phineas Taylor. *Struggles and Triumphs: or, Forty Years' Recollections of P. T. Barnum Written by P. T. Barnum*. Buffalo, N.Y.: The Courier Co., 1877.

———. *Animal Stories*. Akron, Ohio: Saalfield Publishing, 1926.

———. *Barnum's Own Story*. Edited by Waldo R. Browne. New York: Viking, 1927.

Baumann, Charly, with Leonard A. Stevens. *Tiger Tiger: My Twenty-five Years with the Big Cats*. Chicago: Playboy Press, 1976.

Beatty, Clyde. *The Big Cage*. New York: Century, 1933.

———, and Edward Anthony. *Facing the Big Cats*. Garden City, N.Y.: Doubleday, 1965. Much of *The Big Cage* is incorporated in this version, but it contains some new material, such as Beatty's memories of the well-known wild animal trainer Louis Roth.

Bergson, Henri, and George Meredith. *Comedy*. New York: Doubleday, 1956.

Bishop, George. *The World of Clowns*. Los Angeles: Brooke House Publishers, 1976.

Böll, Heinrich. *The Clown*. New York: McGraw-Hill, 1971.

Boorstin, Daniel J. *The Image: or, What Happened to the American Dream*. New York: Atheneum, 1962.

———, and Brooks Mather Kelley with Ruth Frankel Boorstin. *A History of the United States*. Lexington, Mass.: Ginn, 1981.

Botkin, B. A., ed. *The Pocket Treasury of American Folklore*. New York: Pocket Books, 1950.

Bouissac, Paul. *Circus and Culture: A Semiotic Approach*. Bloomington: Indiana University Press, 1976.

Bradna, Fred, and Hartzell Spence. *The Big Top: My Forty Years with the Greatest Show on Earth*. New York: Simon and Schuster, 1952.

Bramble, Mark. *Barnum*. Garden City, N.Y.: Nelson Doubleday, 1980. Includes the lyrics by Michael Stewart.

Brown, Dee. *Bury My Heart at Wounded Knee*. New York: Holt, Rinehart & Winston, 1971. Reprint: New York: Bantam Books, 1972. An Indian history of the American West, well documented on Buffalo Bill and Sitting Bull.

Brown, Maria Ward. *The Life of Dan Rice*. Long Branch, N.J.: published by the author, 1901. Ms. Brown was Rice's cousin and Rice is the direct source.

Brown, William R. *Imagemaker: Will Rogers and the American Dream*. Columbia: University of Missouri Press, 1970.

Brownlow, Kevin. *The War, the West, and the Wilderness*. New York: Alfred A. Knopf, 1979.

Burgess, Hovey. *Circus Techniques*. New York: Drama Book Specialists, 1976. The best explanation of the broad range of circus skills by the master teacher of circus techniques at New York University. He also taught the arts of juggling, stilt walking, and unicycle riding at the Ringling Bros. and Barnum & Bailey Clown College.

Burke, Billie, with Cameron Shipp. *With a Feather on My Nose*. New York: Appleton-Century-Crofts, 1949. Autobiography of Billie Burke, now best known for playing Glinda, the Good Witch, in the 1939 film *The Wizard of Oz*. She was the daughter of the singing circus clown Billy Burke, who was born in Knox County, Ohio, in 1844. She sketches her father's career in chap. 1, "The Clown's Daughter."

Burke, Billy. *Billy Burke's Barnum and Great London Circus Songster*. New York, 1882. A song book such as singing clowns were permitted to sell at the circus. Burke "was said to have been one of the last clowns to retain the songbook sale privileges" (Towsen, *Clowns*, p. 127).

Burke, Michael. *Outrageous Good Fortune*. Boston: Little, Brown, 1984. Burke was general manager of Ringling Bros. and Barnum & Bailey Circus during its last years as a tent show.

Campbell, Joseph, with Bill Moyers. *The Power of Myth*. New York: Doubleday, 1988. Campbell tells Moyers (p. 11), "I fell in love with American Indians because Buffalo Bill used to come every year to Madison Square Garden . . ."

Carey, Gary. *Katharine Hepburn: A Hollywood Yankee*. New York: St. Martin's, 1983.

Chaplin, Charlie. *My Autobiography*. New York: Simon & Schuster, 1964. Contains personal reminiscences of the great circus clown Marceline.

Chindahl, George. *History of the Circus in America*. Caldwell, Id.: Caxton, 1959. The only comprehensive histories of the circus in America are May (1932), Chindahl (1959), and Fox and Parkinson (1969)—and only Chindahl is fully documented. As an appendix, he includes a partial list of American circuses and menageries circa 1771 through 1956.

Church, Charles A. *Past and Present of the City of Rockford and Winnebago County, Illinois*. Chicago: S. J. Clarke Publishing Co., 1905. Contains a biographical sketch of Fred E. Sterling, friend of the five Ringling brothers. In the Rockford (Illinois) College Library.

Churchill, Winston S. *A History of the English-Speaking Peoples*. Volume I: *The Birth of Britain*. New York: Dodd, Mead, 1956.

Cody, Louisa F., and Courtney Ryley Cooper. *Memories of Buffalo Bill*. New York: Appleton, 1919.

Cody, William F. *The Life of Hon. Wm. F. Cody, Known as Buffalo Bill; An Autobiography*. 1879.

Collier, Edmund. *The Story of Annie Oakley*. New York: Grosset & Dunlap, 1956.

Collings, Ellsworth. *101 Ranch*. Norman: University of Oklahoma Press, 1938.

Conklin, George, with Harvey W. Root. *Ways of the Circus; being the Memoirs and Adventures of George Conklin, Tamer of Lions*. New York: Harper & Bros., 1921.

Cooke, Charles. *Big Show*. New York: Harper & Bros., 1938.

Cooper, Courtney Ryley. *Under the Big Top*. Boston: Little, Brown, 1923.

———. *Lions 'n Tigers 'n' Everything*. Boston: Little, Brown, 1924.

———. *With the Circus*. Boston: Little, Brown, 1924.

———. *Annie Oakley, Woman at Arms*. New York: Duffield & Brothers, 1927.

———. *Circus Day*. New York: Farrar & Rinehart, 1931.

Cooper, Frank C. *The Stirring Lives of Buffalo Bill and Pawnee Bill*. New York: S. L. Parsons, 1912.

Coplan, Maxwell Frederick, and F. Beverly Kelley. *Pink Lemonade*. New York: McGraw-Hill, 1945.

Coup, William Cameron. *Sawdust and Spangles*. Chicago: Herbert S. Stone, 1901.

Croft-Cooke, Rupert, ed. *The Circus Book, with a note on the tenting show by W. S. Meadmore.* London: Sampson Low, Marston, 1947.

———, and W. S. Meadmore. *Buffalo Bill: The Legend, the Man of Action, the Showman.* London: Sampson Low, Marston, 1952.

———, and Peter Cotes. *Circus: A World History.* New York: Macmillan, 1976.

Court, Alfred. *My Life with the Big Cats.* New York: Simon and Schuster, 1955.

Culhane, John. *Special Effects in the Movies.* New York: Ballantine, 1981. Describes stunts and special effects for the circus films *The Greatest Show on Earth* (1952) and *Trapeze* (1956).

———. *Walt Disney's Fantasia.* New York: Harry N. Abrams, 1983. Gives Disney's comments on comedy, which derived in part from his observation of clowns in the circus, vaudeville, and silent films.

Decastro, Jacob. *The Memoirs of J. Decastro, Comedian.* London, 1824.

Dickens, Charles. *American Notes.* 1842.

———, ed. *Memoirs of Joseph Grimaldi.* 1838.

Dingess, R. S. "Memoirs." Unpublished manuscript in Harry Hertzberg Circus Collection, San Antonio Public Library. Dingess was general agent for the *Floating Palace* in 1858.

Disher, Maurice Willson. *Clowns and Pantomimes.* London: Constable, 1925.

———. *Greatest Show on Earth (As Performed for Over a Century at Astley's—afterwards Sanger's— Royal Amphitheatre of Arts, Westminster Bridge Road).* 1937. Reprint: New York: Benjamin Blom, 1969.

Dressler, Albert, ed. *California's Pioneer Circus.* San Francisco: H. S. Crocker, 1926. History of Rowe's California Circus, which opened in a San Francisco theater on Oct. 29, 1849, during the gold rush.

Ducharte, Pierre Louis. *The Italian Comedy.* New York: John Day, 1929. Links the Italian comedy of the sixteenth century to such twentiety-century circus clowns as the Fratellini and Grock.

Durang, John. *The Memoir of John Durang, American Actor 1785–1816.* Edited by Alan S. Downer. Pittsburgh, Pa.: University of Pittsburgh Press, 1966. Lost for many years, this is an extremely important memoir of the early days of Ricketts's circus, and an invaluable source of information about the American circus in its first four decades. Never previously published in its entirety.

Durant, John, and Alice Durant. *Pictorial History of the American Circus.* New York: A. S. Barnes, 1957. Essentially a picture book–history of the circus in America with informative captions; but invaluable for the eleven-page annotated list of circuses compiled by Tom Parkinson, former circus editor of *Billboard*, in 1957.

Edmonds, Walter D. *Chad Hanna.* Boston: Little, Brown, 1940; Bantam Pathfinder edition, 1963. This novel of circus life in America in the 1830s contains wonderful descriptions of a somersault on the back of a running horse (pp. 173–74 in Bantam edition); a cage wagon (p. 159); and the act known as "The Taylor Rides to Brentford" (p. 309).

Edwards, W. F. L. *Story of Jumbo.* New York: Sutherland Press, 1935.

Emery, Sarah Anna. *Reminiscences of a Nonagenarian.* William H. Huse, 1879.

Fellini, Federico. *I Clowns.* Bologna, Italy: a cura di Rento Renti, Capelli Editore, 1970. The screenplay for Fellini's documentary on the circus clown, made for Italian television then released theatrically in 1971.

———. *Fellini on Fellini.* New York: Delacorte Press/Seymour Lawrence, 1974. Fellini superbly defines the difference between whiteface and *auguste* clowns on pp. 134–35.

Fellows, Dexter, and Andrew Freeman. *This Way to the Big Show*. Garden City, N.Y.: Halcyon House, 1938.

Fenner, Mildred Sandison, and Wolcott Fenner, comps. and eds. *The Circus, Lure and Legend*. Englewood Cliffs, N.J.: Prentice-Hall, 1970.

Ferguson, O. J. *Biographical Sketch of I. A. Van Amburgh*. Booth & Co., 1865.

Ferguson, Otis. *The Otis Ferguson Reader*. Edited by Dorothy Chamberlain and Robert Wilson. Highland, Ill.: December Press, 1982. Contains "The Circus on the Road" from *New Republic*, 8 July 1940.

Field, Rachel. *A Circus Garland*. In Fenner and Fenner, *The Circus, Lure and Legend*, p. 174. Her circus poems.

Fitzgerald, F. Scott. *The Great Gatsby*. New York: Charles Scribner's Sons, 1925.

Fowler, Gene. *Timber Line: A Story of Bonfils and Tammen*. New York: Covici, 1933. Harry Tammen, a barkeeper in Denver, met Fred Bonfils of Kansas City, who had been running a "policy shop," or local lottery. They formed a partnership, bought the *Denver Post*, amassed fame and fortune, started the Floto Dog and Pony Show in 1902, and ran the Sells Floto and Sells Floto–Buffalo Bill Circus.

————, and Bess Meredyth. *Mighty Barnum: A Screen Play*. New York: Corvici-Friede, 1934. Illustrated with scenes from the 1934 film starring former circus elephant man Wallace Beery as P. T. Barnum.

Fowlie, Wallace. *Pantomime*. Chicago: Henry Regnery, 1951.

Fox, Charles Philip. *Circus Trains*. Milwaukee: Kalmbach Publishing, 1947.

————. *Circus Parades*. New York: Century House, 1953.

————. *A Ticket to the Circus*. Seattle: Superior Publishing, 1959.

————. *Pictorial History of Performing Horses*. Seattle: Superior Publishing, 1960.

————, ed. *American Circus Posters*. New York: Dover Publications, 1978. Contains "Twisting Double Somersault, A Feat Never Attempted by the Most Intrepid Aerialists," a 1904 "Greatest Show on Earth" poster for the Clarkonians apparently doing a version of the double-double.

————, and F. Beverly Kelley. *The Great Circus Street Parade in Pictures*. New York: Dover Publications, 1978.

————, and Tom Parkinson. *The Circus in America*. Waukesha, Wis.: Country Beautiful, 1969.

Fried, Frederick. *Artists in Wood*. New York: Clarkson N. Potter, 1970. Chapter 5 is "Circus Wagons—Builders and Carvers."

Frost, Thomas. *Circus Life and Circus Celebrities*. Detroit: Singing Tree Press, 1970. Originally published in 1875.

Garland, Hamlin. *Boy Life on the Prairie*. New York: Harper's, 1907.

————. *A Son of the Middle Border*. New York: Macmillan, 1920.

Garraty, John A., and Jerome L. Sternstein, eds. *Encyclopedia of American Biography*. New York: Harper & Row, 1974.

Gassner, John, ed. *Best American Plays, Third Series—1945–1951*. New York: Crown, 1952. Contains *The Iceman Cometh*, by Eugene O'Neill.

Gelb, Barbara, and Arthur Gelb. *O'Neill*. New York: Harper & Row, 1962. Reprint: New York: Dell, 1964. The Gelbs tell the story of O'Neill's relationship with Bill Clarke, billed as Volo the Volitant, the circus daredevil who was his model for the character of Ed Mosher in *The*

Iceman Cometh (Dell pp. 297–98) and quote O'Neill as saying that "The idea for Emperor Jones came from [another] old circus man I knew," Jack Croak (Dell p. 438).

Gillette, Don Carle. *He Made Lincoln Laugh: The Story of Dan Rice.* New York: Exposition Press, 1967.

Glenroy, John H. *Ins and Outs of Circus Life.* M. M. Wing & Co., 1885.

Gollmar, R. H. *My Father Owned a Circus.* Caldwell, Id.: Caxton Printers, 1965.

Greenwood, Isaac J. *The Circus; Its Origins and Growth Prior to 1835.* New York: Dunlap Society, 1898.

Hagenbeck, Karl. *Von Tieren und Menschen* [*Of Beasts and Men*]. Berlin: "Vita" Deutsches, 1908. Karl (or Carl) Hagenbeck, 1844–1913, animal dealer and founder of the Stellingen Zoo at Hamburg, Germany, revolutionized the presentation of wild animal acts in circuses by developing new and humane methods of training and sustaining animals in captivity. Charly Baumann and Gunther Gebel-Williams have further developed these methods in America.

Hamid, George Abou. *Circus; as told to his son George A. Hamid Jr.* New York: Sterling Publishing, 1950.

Harlow, Alvin F. *The Ringlings: Wizards of the Circus.* New York: Julian Messner, 1952.

Harmon, Jim. *The Great Radio Comedians.* Garden City, N.Y.: Doubleday, 1970.

Harris, Neil. *Humbug: The Art of P. T. Barnum.* Chicago: University of Chicago Press, 1973. Good documentation and footnotes.

Havighurst, Walter. *Annie Oakley of the Wild West.* Chicago: University of Chicago Press, 1954.

Hawthorne, Nathaniel. *Passages from the American Note-Books of Nathaniel Hawthorne.* Boston: Houghton, Mifflin, 1898. The entry for 4 September 1838 tells of Hawthorne's visit to an exhibition of animals where he saw a man who was probably Isaac Van Amburgh put his head in a lion's mouth.

Henderson, J. Y. *Circus Doctor.* Boston: Little, Brown, 1966.

Heymann, C. David. *A Woman Called Jackie.* New York: Carol Communications, 1989.

Hoagland, Edward. *Cat Man.* New York: Houghton-Mifflin, 1956. The first book by this contemporary master of the essay was a fine circus novel.

———. *Walking the Dead Diamond River.* New York: Random House, 1973.

———. *The Tugman's Passage.* New York: Random House, 1982. Contains an appreciation of Emmett Kelly and Otto Griebling on pp. 177–78.

Holst, Linda W. *Center Ring Circus Cuisine.* Lenexa, Kans.: Cookbook Publishers, 1979. Contains reminiscences of the circus cookhouse as well as the favorite recipes of circus folk from veterinarian J. Y. Henderson to author Holst, showgirl and wife of RBB&B's production coordinator Tim Holst.

Howe, Edgar Watson. *Plain People.* New York: Dodd, Mead, 1929. In this autobiography, Ed Howe (1853–1937), the influential editor, novelist, and essayist, lists (on pp. 44–45) a performance in 1864 of Miles Orton's circus at Bethany, Mo., as first among the few wonderful things that had happened to him in his life.

Hubler, Richard. *The Cristianis.* Boston: Little, Brown, 1966.

Hunt, Charles T., Sr., as told to John C. Cloutman. *The Story of Mr. Circus.* Rochester, N.H.: Record Press, 1954. Annals of the author's circus.

Isenberg, Arthur V. *My Town and the Big Top.* Published by the author, 1954. An account of many of the circuses and menageries that showed in Johnson City, Tenn., from Dan Rice's

Circus and Robinson and Lake's Circus and Menagerie just after the Civil War to the 1950s. Copy in the Somers Historical Society.

Johnson, Allen, and Dumas Malone, eds. *Dictionary of American Biography*. 3 vols. New York: Charles Scribner's Sons, 1958. Volume 1 contains the biographical sketch of P. T. Barnum by Frederic Logan Paxson; Volume 2, W. F. Cody by W. J. Ghent; Volume 3, Dan Rice by George Harvey Genzmer.

Keaton, Buster. *My Wonderful World of Slapstick*. Garden City, N.Y.: Doubleday, 1960.

Kelly, Emmett, with F. Beverly Kelley. *Clown*. New York: Prentice-Hall, 1954.

Kilmer, Joyce. *The Circus and Other Essays and Fugitive Pieces*. New York: George H. Doran, 1921. Eyewitness account of Zip, the What-is-it? that "most venerable of freaks," and other circus wonders of the time by the author of "Trees," who was killed in World War I.

Koestler, Arthur. *The Act of Creation*. New York: Dell, 1975. This study of the conscious and unconscious in science and art contains perceptive comments on clowns.

Krementz, Jill. *A Very Young Circus Flyer*. New York: Alfred A. Knopf, 1979. Nine-year-old Tato Farfan trains and performs with the Flying Farfans in words and pictures.

Kronenberger, Louis. *Company Manners: A Cultural Inquiry into American Life*. New York: Bobbs-Merrill, 1954.

Kunzog, John C. *The One-Horse Show: The Life and Times of Dan Rice, Circus Jester and Philanthropist (A Chronicle of Early Circus Days)*. Jamestown, N.Y.: published by the author, 1962.

———. *Tanbark and Tinsel*. Jamestown, N.Y.: published by the author, 1970.

Kurtz, O. H., comp. *Official Route Book of Ringling Brothers' World's Greatest Railroad Shows, Season of 1892*. Buffalo: The Courier Co., 1892. Kurtz was a juggler on the show.

Kurz, Rudolph Friederich. *Journal of Rudolph Friederich Kurz: An Account of His Experiences Among Fur Traders and American Indians on the Mississippi and the Upper Missouri Rivers During the Years 1846 to 1852*. Edited by J. N. B. Hewitt. Washington: U.S. Government Printing Office, 1937. See pp. 47–48.

Logan, Sheridan A. *Old Saint Jo: Gateway to the West, 1799–1932*. St. Joseph, Mo.: John Sublett Logan Foundation, 1979.

Lord of the Rings: Gunther Gebel-Williams. New York: Tenth Avenue Editions, 1988.

Manchester, William. *The Glory and the Dream: A Narrative History of America, 1932–1972*. Boston: Little, Brown, 1973.

May, Earl Chapin. *The Circus from Rome to Ringling*. New York: Duffield & Green, 1932. Reprint: New York: Dover Publications, 1963, with a new introduction by Leonard V. Farley, Librarian, Hertzberg Circus Collection, San Antonio Public Library, surveying American circus history from 1932 to 1963.

Mayo, Bernard. *Jefferson Himself: The Personal Narrative of a Many-Sided American*. Charlottesville, Va.: University of Virginia Press, 1970.

McWhirter, Norris, and Ross McWhirter. *Guinness Book of World Records*. New York: Bantam Books, 1975, et seq.

Merk, Frederick. *History of the Westward Movement*. New York: Alfred A. Knopf, 1978.

Meyer, Charles R. *How to Be a Clown*. New York: Ringling Bros. and Barnum & Bailey Books, 1977.

———. *How to Be a Juggler*. New York: Ringling Bros. and Barnum & Bailey Books, 1977.

———. *How to Be an Acrobat*. New York: Ringling Bros. and Barnum & Bailey Books, 1978.

———. *How to Be a Magician*. New York: Ringling Bros. and Barnum & Bailey Books, 1978.

Each of these four books contains practical instructions in circus skills in sixty-four pages.

Miller, Henry. *The Smile at the Foot of the Ladder*. New York: New Directions, 1948. In an epilogue, the novelist tells about his conviction that "I had in me all there was to be known about clowns and circuses" (p. 45).

Mix, Olive Stokes. *The Fabulous Tom Mix*. Englewood Cliffs, N.J.: Prentice-Hall, 1957.

Mix, Paul. *The Life and Legend of Tom Mix*. New York: A. S. Barnes, 1972.

Moore, Thomas. *Lalla Rookh: An Oriental Romance*. Philadelphia: John Locken, 1842. The poem that inspired the first beauty contest, Adam Forepaugh's $10,000 search for "the handsomest woman in America," won (though it was fixed) by Louise Montague, who led Forepaugh's street pageant, "Lalla Rookh's Departure for Delhi," in 1880 and 1881.

Nash, Ogden. *Verses from 1929 On*. Boston: Little, Brown, 1936. Contains his circus poems.

Nelson, C. Hal, ed. *Sinnissippi Saga: A History of Rockford and Winnebago County, Illinois*. Winnebago County Illinois Sesquicentennial Committee. Mendota, Ill.: Wayside Press, 1968. In the Rockford (Illinois) College Library.

Niklaus, Thelma. *Harlequin*. New York: George Braziller, 1956. Links the four-hundred-year history of the clown Harlequin with the kind of clown Joseph Grimaldi played, and concludes: "Even when Clown disappeared from pantomime, the Joey clown of the Circus ring kept Grimaldi's memory alive" (p. 166).

North, Henry Ringling, and Alden Hatch. *The Circus Kings*. Garden City, N.Y.: Doubleday, 1960. The story of the Ringling family, by a nephew of the Ringling brothers who in 1989 was still a vice president of Ringling Bros. and Barnum & Bailey Circus.

O'Brien, Esse Forrester. *Circus: Cinders to Sawdust*. San Antonio: Naylor, 1959.

Odell, George C. D. *Annals of the New York Stage*. 15 vols. New York: Columbia University Press, 1927–1949. This monumental and invaluable work, carefully indexed, includes a brief mention of all menageries and exhibitions having circus characteristics that appeared in Manhattan and environs from the beginning through September 1948, based on local newspaper mention. Available for circus research at the Somers Historical Society in the Elephant Hotel, Somers, New York.

Otis, James. *Toby Tyler*. New York: Harper Bros., 1880. (See also the Walt Disney film *Toby Tyler, or Ten Weeks with a Circus* [1960], for a clear visualization of learning circus riding with the use of a mechanic.)

Parkinson, Robert L., and Antony Dacres Hippisley Coxe. "Circus." *The New Encyclopedia Britannica, Macropaedia*. 15th ed. Vol. 4. Chicago: Encyclopedia Britannica, 1974. Parkinson, chief librarian and historian of Circus World Museum, and Coxe, author of *A Seat at the Circus*, collaborated on this article.

Parkinson, Tom, and Charles Philip Fox. *The Circus Moves by Rail*. Boulder, Colo.: Pruett Publishing, 1978.

Payne, Robert. *Charlie Chaplin* (originally titled *The Great God Pan*). New York: Ace Books, 1952.

Peet, Bill. *Bill Peet: An Autobiography*. Boston: Houghton-Mifflin, 1989. A writer-illustrator on such Disney film classics as *Dumbo* tells how the circus trains and Big Top circuses of his boyhood years in Indiana farm country led also to his popular children's book *Chester the Worldly Pig*.

Petit, Philippe. *On the High Wire*. New York: Random House, 1985. Foreword by Marcel Marceau.

Plowden, Gene. *Those Amazing Ringlings and Their Circus*. Introduction by Roland Butler. New York: Bonanza Books, 1967. Roland Butler, general press representative of Ringling Bros. and Barnum & Bailey Combined Circus for more than thirty years ending in June 1954, said in the foreword he wrote shortly before his death on October 20, 1961, that Plowden's book was "the first completely authentic history of the Ringlings and their circus ever put on paper." It does not have an index or notes, but Plowden, a reporter for both the United Press and the Associated Press, knew John Ringling from 1927 until his death.

Pollock, Thomas Clark. *The Philadelphia Theatre in the Eighteenth Century*. Philadelphia: University of Pennsylvania Press, 1933. Contains detailed, documented history of Ricketts's and Lailson's circuses in Philadelphia.

Posey, Jake. *Last of the Forty Horse Drivers*. New York: Vantage Press, 1959.

Powledge, Fred. *Mud Show: A Circus Season*. New York: Harcourt Brace Jovanovich, 1975. The author followed the Hoxie Bros. Circus for its full 1974 season.

Priestly, J. B. *Charles Dickens and His World*. New York: Charles Scribner's Sons, 1961. Chronology (pp. 130–31) tells of Dickens's two visits to the United States, in 1842 and 1867–68.

Quiller-Couch, Arthur. *The Oxford Book of English Verse*. New York: Oxford University Press, 1940.

Rennert, Jack. *100 Years of Circus Posters*. New York: Darien House, 1974. Valuable not only for its many fine reproductions of circus posters, particularly those of the Strobridge Lithographic Co. of Cincinnati, Ohio, but also for its documented notes by a man who has devoted most of his life to the preservation, propagation, and creation of posters.

Ringling, Alf. T. *Life Story of the Ringling Brothers*. Chicago: R. R. Donnelley & Sons, 1900. Copy at the Somers Historical Society in Somers, New York.

Ringling Bros. and Barnum & Bailey Combined Shows, Inc. *Lord of the Rings: Gunther Gebel-Williams*. Introduction by Kenneth Feld, Ringling Bros. and Barnum & Bailey president and producer. New York: Tenth Avenue Editions, 1988.

Robeson, Dave. *Al G. Barnes, Master Showman*. Caldwell, Id.: Caxton Printers, 1935. Based on conversations with the circus proprietor in his last year.

———. *Louis Roth: Forty Years with Jungle Killers*. Caldwell, Id.: Caxton Printers, 1941. Describes Roth's experiences as a trainer of wild animals.

Robinson, Gil. *Old Wagon Show Days*. Cincinnati: Brockwell Publishers, 1925. Based on the author's recollections and family traditions concerning the circus of his father, John Robinson, including the arrival of Old Bet in America, which he says "occurred in 1805, three years after the birth of my father" (p. 32). This book also contains invaluable lists of traveling circuses from 1861 to 1889, and of performers, managers, bosses, agents, and others who traveled with John Robinson's shows from 1857 to 1893.

Root, Harvey W. *The Ways of the Circus; being the Memoirs and Adventures of George Conklin, Tamer of Lions*. New York: Harper & Brothers, 1921.

Rosa, Joseph G. *They Called Him Wild Bill: The Life and Adventures of James Butler Hickok*. Norman: University of Oklahoma Press, 1964.

Rowe, J. A. *California's Pioneer Circus*. San Francisco: H. S. Crocker Co., 1926.

Russell, Don. *The Lives and Legends of Buffalo Bill: A Study in Heroics*. Norman: University of Oklahoma Press, 1960.

———. *The Wild West: A History of Wild West Shows*. Fort Worth: Amon Carter Museum, 1970.

Sandburg, Carl. *Abraham Lincoln: The Prairie Years*. 2 vols. New York: Harcourt, Brace, 1926.

———. *Abraham Lincoln: The War Years*. 4 vols. New York: Harcourt, Brace, 1939.

———. *Always the Young Strangers*. New York: Harcourt, Brace, 1953. Has a wonderful evocation of circus freak shows.

Sanders, Toby. *How to Be a Compleat Clown*. New York: Stein and Day, 1978. A practical handbook on the art of clowning by the former producing clown for the Circus Kirk and for the Lions' All-Star Circus.

Saroyan, William. *My Name Is Aram*. New York: Harcourt, Brace and World, 1938. Has an evocative description of "any time a circus came to town" (pp. 133–45).

Saxon, A. H. *Enter Foot and Horse: A History of Hippodrama in England and France*. New Haven, 1968.

———. *The Life and Art of Andrew Ducrow & The Romantic Age of the English Circus*. Hamden, Conn.: Archon Books, 1978.

Scharf, J. Thomas. *History of Westchester County*. 2 vols. 1886. The chapter on Somers, New York, and its early circus history was written by Charles E. Culver, a descendant of early residents of the town. Culver says that Hackaliah Bailey was "the originator of the menagerie business in this country. In fact, it may be stated that Somerstown was the birthplace of this branch of the 'show' business, and Hackaliah Bailey was its 'father.' " (p. 480).

Scott, Matthew. *Autobiography of Matthew Scott, Jumbo's Keeper; also Jumbo's biography, by the same author*. Trows Printing & Booking Co., 1885.

Sell, H. B., and Victor Weybright. *Buffalo Bill and the Wild West*. New York: Oxford University Press, 1955.

Senelick, Lawrence. *A Cavalcade of Clowns*. San Francisco: Bellerophon Books, 1977.

Sherwood, Robert. *Here We Are Again: Recollections of an Old Circus Clown*. Indianapolis: Bobbs-Merrill, 1926.

———. *Hold Yer Hosses! The Elephants Are Coming*. New York: Macmillan, 1932.

Simon, Peter Angelo. *Big Apple Circus*. New York: Penguin, 1978.

Sokan, Robert. *A Descriptive and Bibliographic Catalog of the Circus and Related Arts Collection of Illinois State University, Normal, Illinois*. Bloomington, Ill.: Scarlet Ibis Press, 1975.

Snyder, Clifford L. *Somers Remembered: A History of Somers, New York*. Somers: Somers Historical Society, 1976. Quotes documents on the early days of the circus.

Stark, Mabel, and Gertrude Orr. *Hold That Tiger*. Caldwell, Id.: Caxton Printers, 1940. Biography of the wild animal trainer and description of her training methods.

Stone, Fred. *Rolling Stone*. New York: Whittlesey House/McGraw-Hill, 1945. Stone was a clown with Seiber and Barry's circus in the wild west (p. 53) and a friend of Annie Oakley (pp. 148–50).

Swortzell, Lowell. *Here Come the Clowns*. New York: Viking, 1978. Overview history of clowning.

Tarkington, Booth. *The Gentleman from Indiana*. New York: Grosset & Dunlap, 1902. Contains a magnificent description of a circus street parade.

Taylor, Robert Lewis. *Center Ring: The People of the Circus*. Garden City, N.Y.: Doubleday, 1956. An entertaining account of Ringling Bros. and Barnum & Bailey Circus life under John Ringling North, based on the series of articles Taylor wrote for *The New Yorker*.

Thayer, Stuart. *Annals of the American Circus, 1793–1829*. Manchester, Mich: Rymack Printing Co., 1976. An outstanding example of thorough and painstaking research into circus history in old newspaper files.

Thompson, W. C. *On the Road with a Circus.* New York: Goldmann, 1903. Based on the author's experiences with the Forepaugh-Sells show, about 1900.

Todd, Mabel Loomis, ed. *Letters of Emily Dickinson.* New York: Grosset & Dunlap, 1962. Contains Dickinson's letter to her sister, circa 1857, telling her feelings when "a circus passed the house . . ." (pp. 142–43).

Toll, Robert C. *Blacking Up: The Minstrel Show in Nineteenth-Century America.* New York: Oxford University Press, 1974.

———. *On with the Show: The First Century of Show Business in America.* New York: Oxford University Press, 1976.

Toole-Stott, R. *Circus and Allied Arts: A World Bibliography.* 4 vols. Derby, Eng.: Harpur and Sons, 1958–1971.

Towsen, John H. *Clowns.* New York: Hawthorn Books, 1976. A comprehensive and well-documented survey of the clown throughout the world, written by a graduate of Ringling Bros. and Barnum & Bailey's Clown College.

Trollope, Frances. *Domestic Manners of the Americans.* Edited by Donald Smalley. New York: Alfred A. Knopf, 1949.

Turnour, Jules. *The Autobiography of a Clown.* As told to Isaac F. Marcosson. New York: Dodd, Mead, 1910.

Twain, Mark [Samuel L. Clemens]. *The Adventures of Huckleberry Finn.* New York: Harper & Bros., 1882. Reprint: New York: Modern Library, 1985.

Tyron, John. *The Old Clown's History.* New York: Torrey Bros., 1872.

Vail, R. W. G. *Random Notes on the History of the American Circus.* Worcester, Mass.: American Antiquarian Society, 1934. Reprinted from the *Proceedings* of the American Antiquarian Society for April 1933.

Verney, Peter. *Here Comes the Circus.* New York: Paddington Press, 1978.

Wallace, Irving. *The Fabulous Showman: The Life and Times of P. T. Barnum.* New York: Alfred A. Knopf, 1959. Reprint: New York: New American Library, 1962.

Wallett, William F. *The Public Life of W. F. Wallett, the Queen's Jester.* London: Bemrose & Sons, 1870.

Walsh, Richard John, and Milton S. Salsbury. *Making of Buffalo Bill: A Study in Heroics.* Indianapolis: Bobbs-Merrill, 1928.

Ware, James A. *Gargantua the Great.* New York: William Morrow, 1959.

Webber, Malcolm. *Medicine Show.* Caldwell, Id.: Caxton Printers, 1941.

Wells, Helen Frances. *Barnum: Showman of America.* New York: David McKay, 1957.

Werner, Morris Robert. *Barnum.* New York: Harcourt, Brace, 1923.

Westervelt, Leonidas. *The Circus in Literature.* Privately printed, 1931. A brief sketch but well documented.

Wetmore, Helen Cody, and Zane Grey. *Last of the Great Scouts.* 1899. Buffalo Bill's sister remembers him.

White, E. B. *The Points of My Compass.* New York: Harper & Row, 1956. Contains "The Ring of Time," a superb essay on a circus rider, which originally appeared in *The New Yorker.*

Williams, Edgar I., and Frances Billingsley. *The Elephant Hotel: Its Architecture and History.* Somers, N.Y.: Somers Historical Society, 1962. Introduction by Otto E. Koegel, Somers town historian. "Somers Town House" tells how Hackaliah Bailey of Somers built it in 1820–25. Contains early circus history.

Willis, Patricia C., ed. *The Complete Prose of Marianne Moore*. New York: Viking, 1986. Includes the poet's review, in *Dance Index*, 5 (June 1946), p. 145, of the 1942 RBB&B, in which Balanchine "taught the elephants their routine" to Stravinsky's "Circus Polka." Moore calls "the spiral of the elephant's trunk repeating the spirals of the dancing . . . a moment of magnificence."

Willson, Dixie. *Where the World Folds Up at Night*. New York: Appleton, 1932.

Wilson, Arthur H. *A History of the Philadelphia Theatre, 1835 to 1855*. Philadelphia: University of Pennsylvania Press, 1935.

Wirth, George. *Round the World with a Circus*. Port Melbourne, Victoria, Australia: Troedel & Cooper, 1925.

Wittke, Carl. *Tambo and Bones: A History of the American Minstrel Stage*. Durham, N.C.: Duke University Press, 1930.

Wolfe, Thomas. *Only the Dead Know Brooklyn*. New York: Signet/New American Library, 1947. Contains "Circus at Dawn" (p. 32).

Wood, Ed. J. *Giants and Dwarfs*. Richard Bentley, 1868.

Woodward, Ian. *Clowns*. London: Ladybird Books, 1976. An overview of the character of the clown since 2270 B.C.

Xenophon. *The Art of Horsemanship*. Boston: Little, Brown, 1893. Written about 320 B.C., it lays the foundation of modern animal training by observing: "Horses are taught, not by harshness, but by gentleness."

Zora, Lucia. *Sawdust and Solitude*. Boston: Little, Brown, 1928.

MAGAZINE AND NEWSPAPER ARTICLES, CIRCUS PROGRAMS, PAMPHLETS, AND BROCHURES

"AB's 1974 Survey of Carnivals & Circuses." *Amusement Business*, 1974.

Allen, Sidney P. "Ringling 1970 Financial Report." *San Francisco Chronicle*, 28 Aug. 1970.

"Animal Conservation." RBB&B 1989 Program. RBB&B's policy for wildlife preservation includes breeding the rare Asian elephant. The circus's tigers are born and raised in captivity, "ensuring that no animal is taken from its natural environment."

Ardman, H. A. "Phineas T. Barnum's Charming Beast; Jumbo the Elephant." *Natural History*, Feb. 1973.

Ballantine, Bill. "Circus: the Second Hundred Years." *Holiday*, April 1970, pp. 50–51. On RBB&B's second century.

"Big Cat with Big Cats: Animal Trainer Gunther Gebel-Williams." *Time*, 24 May 1971, p. 67.

"Big Top Bows Out Forever." *Life*, 30 July 1956.

"Big Top Quietly Steals Away." *Business Week*, 21 July 1956. With editorial comment.

"Big Top's Royal Family." *Cosmopolitan*, Aug. 1955. Profile of the Cristianis.

Blackstone, Sarah. "Buffalo Bill's Wild West Show: Images a Hundred Years Later." *Bandwagon*, Nov.–Dec. 1983. A version of this paper was read at the 1983 Circus Historical Society Convention at Akron, Ohio.

Blassingame, Wyatt. "Let's Meet the Clowns." *Family Circle*, Aug. 1953, p. 91.

Blyte, Paul. "Class Clown Reunion." *Palm Beach* (Fla.) *Post*, 18 Oct. 1987, p. F1.

Boeth, Richard. "Fall of the Great Wallenda." *Newsweek*, 3 April 1978, pp. 36–38.

Bonventre, Peter. "Queen of the Rings." *Newsweek*, 31 July 1978, p. 73. Profiles Dolly Jacobs, aerialist daughter of veteran Ringling clown Lou Jacobs and model turned aerialist Jean Rockwell Jacobs, and sister of circus acrobat LuAnn Jacobs.

Bowen, Elbert R. "The Circus in Early Rural Missouri." *Bandwagon*, Sept.–Oct. 1966, pp. 12–17.

Braathen, Sverre O. "The Sheet Anchor Failed." *Bandwagon*, May–June 1972, pp. 27–32. The Great Depression.

Bradbury, Joseph T. "Gollmar Brothers' Circus: Season of 1922." *Bandwagon*, Jan.–Feb. 1965.

———. "The Adkins and Terrell Cole Bros. Circus Seasons, 1935 through 1940." *Bandwagon*, May–June 1965 through Nov.–Dec. 1967. Thirteen profusely illustrated installments.

———. "The Cole Bros. Winter Quarters at Rochester, Indiana." *Bandwagon*, May–June 1972, pp. 18–26.

Braden, Frank. "Snootier Than '21'," RBB&B 1953 Program. "World's largest traveling restaurant . . . feeds 1,400 people three times per day"—by a Ringling publicist.

"Bread from Circuses: Ringling Bros. and Barnum & Bailey Going Public." *Time*, 21 Feb. 1969, p. 75.

Bridges, H. "The Big Apple Circus." *Gourmet*, Dec. 1986, p. 48.

Brown, Carlton. "Have Midget, Will Travel." *Cavalier*, Sept. 1958. Barnum and Tom Thumb.

Bruce, J. "Great American Elephant Hunt: Carson and Barnes Circus Elephants Lost in the Hugo Lake Reservoir, Oklahoma." *Sports Illustrated*, 4 Aug. 1975.

Bryan, J. III. "Big Shot of the Big Top." *Saturday Evening Post*, 24 Aug. 1940. Profile of John Ringling North.

———. "Wife in Fame Only: Toto, the Female Animal as a Mate for Gargantua." *Colliers*, 3 May 1941.

"Buckles Woodcock." RBB&B 1978 Program. Profile of the elephant trainer and his family.

Buckvar, Felice. "Circus Date Marked." *New York Times*, 20 Jan. 1984. "Somers, which calls itself 'The Birthplace of the American Circus,' is now marking the 150th anniversary of an agreement setting up a cooperative of menagerie owners."

"Buffalo Bill's Medal Restored." *New York Times*, 9 July 1989, p. 23.

Busch, R. "Jill Freedman: Circus Days." *Popular Photography*, June 1976.

Butler, Roland. "Monsters to Mistin." RBB&B 1953 Program. A publicist's view of how John Ringling North produced the 1953 edition of The Greatest Show on Earth. Unfortunately for North, Mr. Mistin, Jr., five-year-old xylophone virtuoso from Belgium, did not become a star.

Byrne, J. A. "You Can't Let the Lions Go Hungry." *Forbes*, 24 May 1982. Profile of Clyde Beatty–Cole Bros. Circus owner D. Holwadel.

"Carrillo Brothers, The" RBB&B 1989 Program. Pedro Carrillo, his young son, Pedro Jr., and Luis Posso perform "on a tightly-wound 5/8-inch steel strand suspended 40 feet above the hard arena floor."

"Cat Man—Clyde Beatty." *Newsweek*, 18 Feb. 1963.

"Cats & Kinkers: Ringling's Labor Troubles." *Saturday Evening Post*, 25 March 1939.

"China: The Shanghai Acrobatic Troupe." Foreword by Kenneth J. Feld, president and producer, Ringling Bros. and Barnum & Bailey Circus, 1987. Brochure.

Cianci, Laura. "Old Time Circus Wagons Roll Again: Rockford's Paul Ingrassia Helps Revive Milwaukee's Parade Tradition." *Rockford* (Ill.) *Register-Star*, n.d. (1980s).

"Circus, The," *Fortune*, July 1947. Describes tearing down, moving, and resetting RBB&B.

"Circus Flora Enchants Audiences with a Precious Pachyderm and That One Ring of Authenticity." *People Weekly*, 7 July 1986, pp. 126–27.

"Circus Lingo." RBB&B 1974 Program. Circus definitions from "Aerial Ballet" to "Spec" (or Spectacle) from "spectacular": "Traditional parade pageant of the circus which includes most of the personnel and animals, and embroiders some imaginative or historical theme."

"Circus Plays a Sad Last Act: Bankrupt King Brothers." *Life*, 16 July 1956, pp. 30–31.

"Circus Queen: Head of Hanneford Family Still Works in Ring at Age of 76." *Life*, 8 July 1946.

Circus Report, The. America's Favorite Circus Weekly. Compiled and edited by Don Marcks. El Cerrito, Calif., 1979. A circus newsletter.

"Circus Star's Wife Dies of Pistol Wounds / Codona's Body to Be Buried Near Lillian Leitzel's Ashes / Killed in 1931." *Rockford* (Ill.) *Morning Star*, 1 Aug. 1937. The July 31 Associated Press story from Long Beach, Calif.

Cirque du Soleil. Official Program, Tour 1985. Foreword by Rene Levesque, prime minister of Quebec.

———. Official Program, Tour 1986. Foreword by Guy Laliberté, president and general manager.

"Cirque du Soleil." *Seventeen*, Oct. 1988, p. 68.

"Clyde Beatty & Captive." *Time*, 29 March 1937. Cover story on the wild animal trainer.

"Clyde Beatty Here July 17." *Rockford* (Ill.) *Morning Star*, 8 July 1937. Publicist's interview with Beatty at the top of his career.

Codona, Alfredo, as told to Courtney Ryley Cooper. "Split Seconds." *Saturday Evening Post*, 6 Dec. 1930.

Coe, Richard L. "Irvin Feld's Eye for Talent." *Washington Post*, 10 Sept. 1984, p. B3. The theater critic emeritus for the *Washington Post* writes an appreciation of the careers of Irvin Feld and his brother and partner, Israel Feld.

"Col. Cody is Praised by Col. Roosevelt." *New York Times*, 11 Feb. 1917.

Collins, Glenn. "A Quadruple for the Flying Miguel Vazquez." *New York Times*, 11 July 1982, p. 1.

———. "Well-Flung Pies a Smash at School: 20th Anniversary Reunion at Clown College, Venice, Fla." *New York Times*, 15 Oct. 1987, p. C1.

———. "Ringling Brothers Celebrates the Classic Clowning Moments." *New York Times*, 23 March 1988. The firehouse gag from 1924, the clown car gag from 1940, and the soap suds gag from 1949 all revived for the 1988 edition of RBB&B.

———. "A Star of the Circus Is Turning in His Whip." *New York Times*, 7 Feb. 1989. Gunther Gebel-Williams begins two-year farewell tour.

———. "A Showplace for a Showman." *New York Times*, 6 June 1989, p. C15. "With appropriate fanfare, a new Barnum Museum" in Bridgeport, Conn. For the ribbon-cutting, the mayor was laid on top of the ribbon and sawed in half.

Couderc, Pierre. "Risley." Installment No. 6, "Truth or Fiction, Legend or Fact: Important Trivia." *Bandwagon*, Jan.–Feb. 1965.

———. Installment No. 9, "Truth or Fiction, Legend or Fact: Important Trivia." *Bandwagon*, July–Aug. 1965. Contains documentation from clippings found in the traveling trunk of Nellie Jordan that Lena Jordan accomplished the first triple somersault from the flying trapeze to the hands of the catcher, in Sydney, Australia, in 1897.

Culhane, Hind Rassam. "Across the Generations." *Cross Currents*, vol. 31, no. 2 (Summer 1981). Psychological importance of grandparents and grandchildren sharing such events as visits to the circus.

Culhane, Isabel. "Behind the Painted Smiles Clown College Is No Laughing Matter." *North End Times* (Rockford, Ill.), June 1988.

———. "Genial, Affable, Kind and Courteous: Meet Lt. Gov. Sterling from Rockford's Greater North End." *North End Times* (Rockford, Ill.), July 1988. Tells of Fred Sterling's twenty-nine vacations with John Ringling aboard Ringling's private railroad car, between 1899 and 1929.

Culhane, John. "Only Big Top Died—Circus Coming Back." *Rockford* (Ill.) *Register-Republic*, 7 Aug. 1956. Interview with William B. Naylor, circus press agent from the Sells-Floto Circus (1921) to Polack Bros. Shrine Circus (1950–1956).

———. "Rockford Has Heart." *Rockford* (Ill.) *Register-Republic*, 7 Aug. 1959. My daily "Off the Beat" column, devoted to the story of Eddie Arvida, Clyde Bros. circus aerialist. Arvida fell on opening day of the annual Shrine Circus in Rockford in 1958, was helped by Dr. Burt Canfield and night nurse Martha Larson to accept the fact that he would never fly again, and rejoined the circus in 1959 in the Clyde Bros. clown alley of producing clown Jack LaPearl.

———. "Take Me to the Garden." *New York Times Magazine*, 11 Feb. 1973. A history of Madison Square Garden.

———. "The Lord of the Ring." *New York Times Magazine*, 13 May 1973. Profile of wild animal trainer Gunther Gebel-Williams.

———. "School for Clowns." *New York Times Magazine*, 30 Dec. 1973. History of the Ringling Bros. and Barnum & Bailey Clown College and circus clowning in America.

———. "Clown for a Day . . . You Gotta Be Kidding." *Signature*, July 1974. The author clowns with The Greatest Show on Earth in Madison Square Garden and takes a pie in the face from Ron Severeni and "Prince Paul" Alpert.

———. "Defying Death and Taming Fear at the Circus." *Argosy*, April 1975.

———. "Star-Spangled History of the Circus." *Argosy*, April 1975.

———. "The Culhane Motif-Index and Thesaurus of Gags." *New York Times Magazine*, 7 March 1976. A system for classifying and connecting those humorous bits known as gags. Used by the author to classify the gags he participates in as a guest clown with various circuses.

———. Review of *Tiger Tiger: My 25 Years with the Big Cats*, by Charly Baumann with Leonard A. Stevens. *New York Times Book Review*, 14 March 1976, p. 26.

———. "Superstars, Superprofits, Superfeats." *Holiday*, March 1976, pp. 44–47.

———. "Comeback of the Circus in America." *Reader's Digest*, March 1976, pp. 96–100. Slightly altered condensation of my *Holiday* (March 1976) article.

———. "Dreaming the Impossible Dream: Irvin Feld." *106th Edition Souvenir Program & Magazine*, Ringling Bros. and Barnum & Bailey Combined Shows, 1976.

———. "Trapeze—the Quest for the 'Impossible' Quadruple Somersault." *New York Times Magazine*, 19 March 1978. A history of circus aerialists and of their greatest challenge.

———. "Final Tribute: A Delicate Balance." *New Times*, 17 April 1978, p. 92. The life and death of wire walker Karl Wallenda. In the week following Wallenda's death on March 22, 1978, I also wrote appreciations of his career published in the *Baltimore Sun*, the *Miami Herald*, and the *New York Times* Syndicate.

———. "The Stebbing Circus: All in the Family." *GEO*, Aug. 1979. The author travels through the American South with the Stebbing Royal European Circus, a small, one-ring mud show (one that travels by truck).

———. "Unforgettable Emmett Kelly." *Reader's Digest*, Dec. 1979. The author's recollections of meeting Emmett Kelly and seeing him perform.

———. "Lords of the Rings: Irvin and Kenneth Feld Are Making The Greatest Show on Earth Even Better." *Signature*, March 1981.

———. "Barnum to Ringling to Feld." *113th Edition Souvenir Program & Magazine*, Ringling Bros. and Barnum & Bailey Combined Shows, 1983.

———. "The Feld Approach." *113th Edition Souvenir Program & Magazine*, Ringling Bros. and Barnum & Bailey Combined Shows, 1983.

———. "How Well Do You Know the Big Top?" *Reader's Digest*, Aug. 1984, pp. 176–77.

———. "Marian Ferrer's Clay Circus." *White Tops*, Nov.–Dec. 1986. Artist makes sculptures of people and scenes from circus history.

———. "The One-Ring Circus Revival." *Signature*, April 1987. The Pickle Family Circus, the Big Apple Circus, Circus Flora, Cirque du Soleil.

———. "World's Greatest Showman." *Reader's Digest*, Nov. 1989, pp. 90–95. On Gunther Gebel-Williams's farewell tour.

"Death of Buffalo Bill." Career and editorial: *New York Times*, 11 Jan. 1917, pp. 14:2, 15:3. Body lies in state in Denver and funeral: *New York Times*, 15 Jan., p. 9:4.

"Death of Fred Bradna." *White Tops*, March–Apr. 1955.

deFrances, Richard. "James M. June & Co.'s American and European Amphitheatre, New York State Summer Tour." *Bulletin of the North Salem Historical Society*, Winter 1988. An article on June (1809–1862), the North Salem, N.Y., pioneer circus and menagerie organizer, by the North Salem town historian.

De Mille, Cecil B. "Soul of the Circus." RBB&B 1950 Program.

———. "The Greatest Show on Earth." RBB&B 1951 Program.

De Roos, Robert. "The Magic Worlds of Walt Disney." *National Geographic*, Aug. 1963. Tells of aerialist Tiny Kline.

Disney, Walt. "The Marceline I Knew." *Marceline* (Mo.) *News*, 2 Sept. 1938. Disney describes the importance to him of "seeing my first circus parade."

Dobbs, Katy. "Muppet Magazine Visits The Greatest Show on Earth." *Muppet Magazine*, Fall 1983. Interview with Mark Oliver Gebel.

"Don Foote Designs the Greatest Wardrobe on Earth." RBB&B 1982 Program. Sketch of the late designer of the costumes, props, and scenery for RBB&B from 1969 into the 1980s.

Dooley, Meg. "In the Middle of the Magic." *Columbia*, Oct. 1984. Paul Binder's Big Apple Circus.

Dunning, Jennifer. "Stage: Spoleto's Circus (Circus Floral)." *New York Times*, 4 June 1986, p. C24.

———. "A Show by the Pickle Family, Starring Clowning." *New York Times*, 24 July 1989.

"Edwin Hanneford, 75, Is Dead; Noted Bareback-Riding Circus Clown." *New York Times*, 11 Dec. 1967.

"Emmett Kelly Dies." *New York Times*, 29 March 1979, p. 34.

"Emmett Kelly's Woes Make Millions Laugh." *Life*, 21 July 1947.

"End of the Circus Romance." *American Weekly*, 14 Jan. 1945. Account of Harriett Hodgini's marriage to F. Harold Van Orman, hotel owner and former lieutenant governor of Indiana.

"End of the Trail for Clyde Beatty's Circus." *Time*, 28 May 1956, p. 28.

"Famous Artist Dies in Fall from High Wire." *New York Times*, 23 March 1978.

Fein, Esther B. "For Big Apple Aerialist, a Lifetime in the Circus." *New York Times*, 27 Dec. 1985, p. C28. Profile of Dolly Jacobs, performing on rings with the Big Apple Circus.

"Feld Brothers, The." *Business Week*, 13 April 1968. On the purchase of Ringling Bros. and Barnum & Bailey Circus by Irvin Feld, Israel Feld, and Roy M. Hofheinz of Houston, Tex.

Fetterman, J. "On the Road with an Old-Time Circus: Hoxie Bros. Gigantic 3-Ring Circus." *National Geographic*, March 1972, pp. 410–34.

"Fire Destroys the Big Top." *Life*, 17 July 1944.

Folkart, Burt A. "John Ringling North, 81; Ran 'The Greatest Show on Earth,' " *Boston Globe*, 7 June 1985. Obituary by *Los Angeles Times* writer says that North "was credited by the entertainment publication *Variety* in 1951 with 'furthering the evolution from old concepts of a circus to that of Billy Rose,' who is considered a master showman. . . . After the circus was sold, he became an Irish citizen and lived alternately in Switzerland and Belgium."

"Forty Years in the Center Ring." *Bandwagon*, July–Aug. 1965.

Fox, Charles Philip. "Circus Trains." *Trains*, July 1946. The author was director of the circus museum in Baraboo, Wis., for twelve years.

———. "The Circus in America: A 200-Year Tradition." RBB&B 1975 Program. Fox's profusely illustrated article reproduces, in color, Raymond & Company's poster used to advertise their 1847 menagerie; it is reputed to be the first circus poster printed in color.

———. "Here Come the Elephants." *107th Edition Souvenir Program & Magazine*, Ringling Bros. and Barnum & Bailey Combined Shows, 1977.

Frankel, Max. "Soviet Clowns Gravely Discuss How to Be the Life of the Party." *New York Times*, Nov. 26, 1959, p. 39.

"Frosty Little: Celebrated Captain of Caprice." RBB&B 1986 Program. In 1981, whiteface Glen "Frosty" Little was appointed to supervise all clowns and clowning on both RBB&B units.

Gallagher, Jim. "Flyin' High: The Magic of Miguel Vazquez." *Chicago Tribune Magazine*, 5 Dec. 1982.

"Gargantua the Great, Star of New Ringling Circus." *Newsweek*, 11 April 1938. Cover story.

Gill, Brendan. "Theatre." *New Yorker*, 28 Dec. 1981. Article on the Big Apple Circus by a theater critic.

"Goodbye to the Gallant and Gay." *Newsweek*, 30 July 1956, p. 28. RBB&B folds its Big Top.

Goth, Louis A. "The Parade That's Making Milwaukee Famous." *Reader's Digest*, June 1989. From the Circus World Museum's first Great Circus Parade, organized by C. P. "Chappie" Fox in 1963 as the museum's first director, to the 1988 parade, with Robert L. Parkinson, historian of the museum, as parade director.

Grace, John P. "The Ringling Bros. Circus, 1884–1918." *White Tops*, July–Aug. 1933.

"Greatest Show on Earth: Ringling Bros. and Barnum & Bailey Circus Sold." *Time*, 24 Nov. 1967, p. 98.

"Greatest Show on Earth Strikes Its Tent: Ringling Bros." *U.S. News & World Report*, 27 July 1956, p. 22.

"Greatest Showman on Earth." *Time*, 4 May 1970. Emergence of Irvin Feld as circus showman.

Griffith, Helen. "Circus More Alive Than Ever." *Sarasota* (Fla.) *Herald-Tribune*, 27 March 1976.

Toby Ballantine, son of RBB&B Clown College dean Bill Ballantine, and boss clown with Gatti-Charles American Continental Circus, trains little black-and-white pig to join his act, in the manner of Felix Adler.

Gussow, Mel. "Highlights and a Few Sidelights from the Circus." *New York Times*, 1 April 1983, p. C1. *Times* reviewer notes debut of Mark Oliver Gebel.

Haley, J. L. "Colossus of His Kind." *American Heritage*, Aug. 1973. On Jumbo.

Hall, Elizabeth. "Lord of the Ring: Charisma, Control, and Tradition." *Psychology Today*, Oct. 1983. Conversation on animal behavior with Gunther Gebel-Williams.

Hall, William B. III. "Tanbark Tropics." *White Tops*, Nov.–Dec. 1986.

"Happy: Oscar Winner John Avildsen Clowns under the Big Top." *People Weekly*, 9 May 1977, p. 103. John Culhane and the Academy Award–winning director of *Rocky* are guest clowns with The Greatest Show on Earth, along with Culhane's sons Michael and T.H.

Haupt, D. E. "The Sight Fantastic." *Life*, Oct. 1988, pp. 98–102. Canada's Cirque du Soleil tours the United States.

Hecht, Ben. "Rendezvous of Love." *Reader's Digest*, Sept. 1945. Hecht covered the reopening of the Hagenbeck-Wallace Circus in Beloit, Wis., after its 1918 train wreck, for the old *Chicago Daily News*. He reveals here, twenty-seven years later, that the lion tamer's husband, who was nearly killed taking over her act, was actually trying to commit suicide because he had shot his wife to death as she lay trapped, doomed and suffering, in the wreckage.

Hemingway, Ernest. "The Circus." *Ringling Bros. and Barnum & Bailey Circus Magazine & Program*, 1953 edition.

———. "My Pal Gargantua the Gorilla." *Ken*, 28 July 1938.

Hentoff, Nat. "Hooked on Trapeze: Look Dad, No Hands!" *Wall Street Journal*, 16 Sept. 1986. The American jazz authority writes about his daughter's double trapeze act, Hentoff and Hoyer (Jessica Hentoff–Kathie Hoyer), which featured a heel-to-heel feat.

"High Wire Act Big Thriller." *Rockford* (Ill.) *Morning Star*, 6 Aug. 1937. Description of the Wallenda high-wire act with RBB&B in 1937, with picture of Helen Wallenda.

"History of Circus Cycling, A." *108th Edition Souvenir Program & Magazine*, Ringling Bros. and Barnum & Bailey Combined Shows, 1978. Sketches careers of Volo the Volitant and the Great Ancillotti, as well as the Elliotts, the Stirk Family, the 8 Kaufman Girls, the King Charles Troupe, and others.

Hoagland, Edward. "Soul of the Tiger." *Esquire*, July 1971.

———. "Here Comes the Circus." *Life*, 23 April 1971, pp. 66–70A.

———. "Mud Show." *New York Times Book Review*, 9 Nov. 1975. An essay about books on the circus and a review of Fred Powledge's *A Circus Season*.

Hubbard, Elizabeth Thaxter. "Life Was Lovely." *Harvard Magazine*, Nov.–Dec. 1988. e.e. cummings's childhood playmate reveals the poet's circus ambitions.

"I Can't Hold On Anymore: Accident of the Great Wallenda Troupe." *Newsweek*, 12 Feb. 1962.

James, Theodore, Jr. "Giant Wedding of the Little People." *White Tops*, Jan.–Feb. 1975, pp. 9–12. Reprinted from *Smithsonian*, Sept. 1973, and adapted from Theodore James, Jr., *Fifth Avenue* (New York: Walker & Co., 1972).

Jando, Dominique. "Roots: The Art of Classical Circus in America." The Big Apple Circus 1985 Program. The associate artistic director of the Big Apple Circus writes an essay on early

American circus history, illustrated with a reproduction of Gilbert Stuart's painting of John Bill Ricketts from the National Gallery of Art, Washington, D.C.

———. "The Chinese Acrobatic Theatre." The Big Apple Circus 1988 Program. An essay to accompany the appearances of the Nanjing Acrobatic Troupe and Yang Xiao Di as the Monkey King in the 1988 edition of the circus.

Jaynes, Gregory. "In Oklahoma: A Big Top Moves Out." *Time*, 12 May 1986, pp. 20–21.

"John Ringling Dies of Pneumonia at 70 / Organizer of Great Circus Business Succumbs to Illness at Home Here. / Last of the Brothers. / Father's Harness Sale Started Them on Career That Led to 'Greatest Show on Earth'." *New York Times*, 2 Dec. 1936, p. 27.

Johnson, W. "World's Greatest Trapeze Performer: Tito Gaona." *Sports Illustrated*, 8 April 1974; condensed in *Reader's Digest* as "Daring Young Man on the Flying Trapeze," Nov. 1974.

"Jumbo." *Bandwagon*, Jan.–Feb. 1983. Cover story includes the disposition of Jumbo's remains.

"Karl Wallenda, Famous Aerialist, Dies in Fall from High-wire, San Juan, Puerto Rico." *New York Times*, 23 March 1978, p. II:8. Memorial service: *New York Times*, 27 March, p. V:6, and 28 March, p. 40.

Kelley, Francis Beverly. "The Land of Sawdust and Spangles." *National Geographic*, Oct. 1931.

———. "The Wonder City That Moves by Night." *National Geographic*, March 1948.

Keneas, A. "Colossal Centennial: Ringling Bros. and Barnum & Bailey." *Newsweek*, 6 April 1970, p. 98.

"Kenneth Feld's World." RBB&B 1989 Program. Tells of "the inauguration of the new 'Special International Edition' of Ringling Bros. and Barnum & Bailey Circus in Japan. This marks the first time in more than 32 years that the show has gone back to its roots and appeared under the Big Top."

"King Charles Troupe, The." RBB&B 1976, 1978, and 1986 programs. Profiles of the black unicycling basketballers.

Kirkpatrick, Curry. "The Greatest Showman on Earth." *Sports Illustrated*, 26 Sept. 1977, p. 84. Profile of Gunther Gebel-Williams.

Kobler, John. "Close-up: John Ringling North." *Life*, 8 Aug. 1948.

———. "Zacchinis." *Life*, 26 April 1948.

Knecht, Jannie, and Karl Kae. "How the C.F.A. Was Organized." *White Tops*, March–April 1951. Articles on the Circus Fans Association of America.

La Coss, Louis. "The Lieutenant Governor of Illinois Spends His Vacations Traveling with A CIRCUS." *St. Louis Globe-Democrat Magazine*, 4 Aug. 1929, p. 1. "Fred E. Sterling, newspaper publisher of Rockford, Ill., formed a friendship with the Ringling Brothers thirty years ago and, every year since, except last year, he has been their guest for a short time, with the result that today he is a devout follower of the big top."

Lader, Lawrence. "The Cristianis." *Coronet*, Sept. 1947.

Langdon, D. "Irvin Feld Has Made a Fading Circus the Greatest Show on Earth Again." *People*, 12 May 1980, p. 50.

LaPointe, Joe. "Stadiums Enter Era of Luxury." *New York Times*, 25 Sept. 1989, p. C1. Boom in construction and renovation of arenas has implications for the future of the circus in America.

LaTour, Octavie. "The Limit of Human Daring." *New York World*, 8 April 1905.

"Mammal-of-the-Year." *Time*, 29 Dec. 1941. Disney's Dumbo.

"Man Who Saved the Circus." *New York Times*, 11 Sept. 1984. Editorial on the death of Irvin Feld.

Marchionni, Carmel Camise. "Circus: Film Documents the Staging of a Circus." *Herald-Statesman* (Yonkers, N.Y.), 1 March 1983, p. B1. Walt Disney Productions' documentary on the 113th edition of Ringling Bros. and Barnum & Bailey Circus, coproduced by John Culhane of Westchester, to be the first presentation of the new national pay-TV Disney channel.

Matre, Van. "Agnes Lake & Emma Lake." *Circus Banner Line*, 1 Oct. 1978. Matre, editor and publisher of "World's Only Once a Month Circus Publication," profiles the woman proprietor of Lake's Hippo-Olympiad & Mammoth Circus and her bareback-rider daughter, Emma.

————. "Barnum & Bailey Abroad." *Circus Banner Line*, 1 Dec. 1978, pp. 2–41. Matre re-creates the Barnum & Bailey European tour, 1897–1902, using "Mrs. Bailey's scrapbook on the tour, pictures, a diary, routebooks and letters," plus "a newspaper collection I had received as a gift from the late [Barnum & Bailey publicist] Roland Butler."

McDonald, Don. "Life's a 3-Ring Circus for the Daring." *New York Post*, 1 April 1983. Profile of the Bauer family, whose sway-pole act was a highlight of the 1983 RBB&B show.

McEvoy, J. P. "The Siamese Twins." *Kiwanis Magazine*, Sept. 1943.

McNeil, Donald G., Jr. "High-Wire Walker Finds New Challenges to Span." *New York Times*, 13 Aug. 1979. Phillipe Petit talks about RBB&B and Big Apple circuses.

McQuiston, John T. "Michael Burke, Ex-Executive with the Yankees, Dies at 70." *New York Times*, 7 Feb. 1987, p. 10. Burke was general manager of RBB&B during its last years as a tent show.

Murphy, T. E. "Day the Clowns Cried." *Reader's Digest*, June 1953. The RBB&B fire in Hartford.

"139 Die, More Than 225 Hurt in Circus Fire / Five Arrested on Manslaughter Charges / Panic and Blaze Trap Hundreds / Flames of Death Sweep Across Big Top Filled with Circus Crowd." *Hartford* (Conn.) *Courant*, 7 July 1944, p. 1. The subhead continued: "Relatives Seek Their Dead at State Armory; Hospitals Crowded; Cages Block Exit for Many as Flames Sweep over Big Top in 10 Minutes . . . Wide Inquiry Started; Inquest Set for Tuesday."

"Otto Griebling Dies." *Bandwagon*, May–June 1972, p. 3.

"Patience, Affection, Attention, and Meat: Work of Circus Trainer Gunther Gebel-Williams." *New Yorker*, 21 April 1975, pp. 30–32.

Parkinson, Greg. "Celestial Daredevils on the Lofty Silver Strand: A History of Big Top Wire-Walking." *109th Edition Souvenir Program & Magazine*, Ringling Bros. and Barnum & Bailey Combined Shows, 1979.

————. "The Wild West: Pageantry of the Plains." *112th Edition Souvenir Program & Magazine*, Ringling Bros. and Barnum & Bailey Combined Shows, 1982. Buffalo Bill's and other Wild West shows.

————. "Attaining the Impossible: They Said It Couldn't Be Done." *114th Edition Souvenir Program & Magazine*, Ringling Bros. and Barnum & Bailey Combined Shows, 1984.

————. "Expect the Unexpected." *115th Edition Souvenir Program & Magazine*, Ringling Bros. and Barnum & Bailey Combined Shows, 1985. An essay putting the Living Unicorn in historic perspective as a circus attraction.

————. "Circus—an International World of Excitement." *116th Edition Souvenir Program & Magazine*, Ringling Bros. and Barnum & Bailey Combined Shows, 1986. Greg Parkinson, now executive director of Circus World Museum, the nation's major repository for circus history, tells how "the history of the circus has been written in nearly every corner of the world."

Petit, Philippe. "Two Towers, I Walk." *Reader's Digest*, April 1975.

Pfening, Fred D., Jr. "Tractors and Trucks on Circuses." *Bandwagon*, Jan.–Feb. 1965.

———. "Forty Years in the Center Ring." *Bandwagon*, July–Aug. 1965. Obituary of Clyde Beatty.

———. "Masters of the Steel Arena." *Bandwagon*, May–June 1972.

Pfening, Fred D. III. "The Circus Year in Review." *Bandwagon*, Jan.–Feb. 1984. At this time, Fred D. Pfening, Jr., was editor of *Bandwagon*, Fred D. Pfening III was managing editor, and Joseph T. Bradbury was associate editor of the invaluable bimonthly journal of the Circus Historical Society.

"Philippe Petit, Aerialist Famous for His High Wire Walk Between Towers of World Trade Center, Interviewed on His Upcoming Plans." *New York Times*, 13 Aug. 1979, p. II:1.

"Philippe Petit Le Funambule." *Bicentennial Edition Souvenir Program & Magazine*, Ringling Bros. and Barnum & Bailey Combined Shows, 1975.

"Pinito del Oro: Queen of the Circus Trapeze." *Vogue*, 15 May 1956.

Plaskin, Glenn. "And Now—on the High Wire." *New York Daily News*, 12 Sept. 1989.

Poarch, L. Wilson, Jr. "Fan-Fare." *Southern Sawdust*, Summer 1978. This issue of a "quarterly circus publication for troupers, fans, collectors and all who love the circus," edited by Poarch, features the Flying Cavarettas, then appearing at the Circus-Circus Hotel-Casino in Las Vegas.

Prideaux, Tom. "Theatrical Thoughts on a Dog Act: The Circus Canines, Presented by the Stevenson Family." *Life*, 7 July 1969.

Pruyn, William. "The Sounds of the Circus." RBB&B 1974 Program. Pruyn, music director of the Ringling Bros. and Barnum & Bailey Circus, joined the circus band in the 1940s as a "windjammer"—a trumpeter under the baton of Merle Evans, who had been RBB&B bandleader since 1919.

"Psst. The Prince of Humbug Lives!" *U.S. News and World Report*, 19 June 1989. Reopening of the redesigned P. T. Barnum Museum in Bridgeport, Conn.

Recio, M. E. "Ladies and Gentlemen, Presenting—Kenneth Feld." *Business Week*, 8 June 1987.

"Richard Barstow." RBB&B 1975 Program. Barstow staged and directed every edition of Ringling Bros. and Barnum & Bailey Circus for over twenty-five years, until 1978—as well as Judy Garland's Palace Theatre engagements and her musical numbers in the film *A Star Is Born*.

"Rietta Wallenda and Enrico Bogino, Part of Great Wallendas Aerialist Act, Are Performing at Bertrand Island Amusement Park in New Jersey." *New York Times*, 20 Aug. 1979, p. 5:1. The Wallendas return to the high wire after Karl's violent death.

Ringling Bros. and Barnum & Bailey Circus Presents How to Make Your Own Clown Face. RBB&B, 1974. "All Circus Clown Faces Come from Only Three Basic Types: Whiteface, Auguste, Character. Every Clown Face in the World Is a Variation of One of These Three." Illustrated, eight-page pamphlet.

"Ringling Bros.–Barnum & Bailey Gives Last Performance Under Tents, Pittsburgh; High Costs, Labor Trouble, Weather, Traffic and TV Seen Causes; J R North Calls Tented Circus Outdated; 2 Other Tent Shows That Folded Recently Noted." *New York Times*, 17 July 1956, p. 1.

Ringling, John. "We Divided the Job—But Stuck Together." *American*, Sept. 1919. Reprinted in its entirety in Charles Philip Fox, *A Ticket to the Circus* (Seattle: Superior Publishing, 1959), pp. 39–46.

"Ringling Revenues Zooming." *Amusement Business*, 15 Aug. 1970.

"Ringling's Egress." *Newsweek*, 27 Nov. 1967, p. 81. RBB&B sold by North to Feld.

"Ringling Wrangling: 3 Sets of Heirs Squabbling for Control of the Circus." *Fortune*, July 1947.

"Royal Hanneford Circus." *Circus Report*, 26 March 1979, p. 15. Compiled and edited by Don Marcks. El Cerrito, Calif. A reliable circus source telling who is performing where.

Ryan, Jack. "Notes on a Daring Decade . . ." RBB&B 1980 Program. Ryan was a member of Ringling's national public relations staff from 1968 through 1973, and served during that period as editor of the RBB&B program.

Sanders, Francis E. "Carson & Barnes Circus." *White Tops*, Nov.–Dec. 1986, p. 32.

"Satin." RBB&B 1983 Program. Profile of Denise Aubrey and Pamela Hernandez, former Ringling showgirls who created "the first black aerial act in the 113-year history of the Greatest Show on Earth," called "Satin."

Saxon, Wolfgang. "John Ringling North, Leader of Family Circus for 30 Years." *New York Times*, 7 June 1985. Obituary quotes North's 1956 statement, "The tented circus as it now exists is in my opinion a thing of the past."

Schick, Joseph S. "Early Showboat and Circus in the Upper Valley." *Mid-America*, Oct. 1950. Documented account of Spalding & Rogers's *Floating Palace*, the *James Raymond*, and the *Banjo*, with references to other circuses.

Schickel, Richard. "Gebel-Williams Burning Bright." *Harper's*, Aug. 1971.

Scripps, J. B. T. "Gargantua, World's Most Successful Animal, Lives for One Purpose Only: Murder." *Life*, 26 Feb. 1940. Later condensed in *Reader's Digest*, May 1940.

"Shanghai Acrobatic Troupe." Ringling Bros. and Barnum & Bailey Combined Shows. Washington, D.C.: 1986. Informational brochure.

"Shanghai Acrobatic Troupe dazzles audiences at Ringling Brothers and Barnum & Bailey Circus performances in New York City; Ringling pres. Kenneth Feld describes rigorous training and his long struggle to win Chinese Government permission for US tour." *New York Times*, 2 April 1986, sec. III, p. 19.

Shepard, Richard F. Review of King Charles Troupe. *New York Times*, 4 April 1984.

———. "Stage: Ringling Brothers and Barnum & Bailey." *New York Times*, 26 March 1986, p. C14. Reviewer says "The circus is continuing its renaissance of clowns . . . you had better unplug the headphones, turn off the VCR and see it yourself. You may think you remember it, but each time the something old seems to be somehow something new."

Sigurdsson, Haraldur, and Steven Carey. "The Far Reach of Tambora." *Natural History*, June 1988. When I read Dr. Bentley's diary in Vail, *Random Notes on the History of the American Circus*—"the poor elephant was destroyed in Maine because he took money from those who could not afford to spend it"—I connected the eruption of a volcano in Indonesia with the execution of Old Bet, America's second elephant.

"Sit Down, Poppy, Sit Down!" *Time*, 3 April 1978, p. 27. The death of Karl Wallenda.

Starrett, Vincent. "Blondin—Prince of Manila." *Saturday Evening Post*, 26 Oct. 1929.

Sterling, Janet. "The Shoe That Danced Around the World." *White Tops*, Spring 1941. Bird Millman.

"Story of Ballyhoo, The." RBB&B 1979 Program. Profile of Allen J. Bloom, senior vice president of marketing and sales for The Greatest Show on Earth, who has been associated with the Felds for forty years.

"Strange Case of the Circus Arsonist: Youth Who Started Hartford Fire." *Life*, 17 July 1950.

Sturtevant, C. G. "The Metamorphosis of the Flying Act." *Billboard*, 8 Dec. 1928.

————. "The Flying Act and Its Technique." *White Tops*, May 1932.

————. "The Circus in Philadelphia." *White Tops*, Nov.–Dec. 1949. "In 1774 the Act of Congress forbade any amusement performances, and it was not until the year 1780 that there was an exhibition of slack wire walking by one Templman . . . Center Square was on the South side of Market Street, between Schuykill, Seventh, and Eighth Streets. Here August 15th, 1785 was erected the first circus which was built in Philadelphia. One Pool, an American equestrian, was the adventurer . . ." (p. 3).

————. "The Circus in America During the Civil War." *White Tops*, Christmas 1950.

Taber, Bob. "The Hodgini Family." *White Tops*, May–June 1961.

"There's a Customer Born Every Minute." *U.S. News & World Report*, 20 Feb. 1989, p. 15. Gunther Gebel-Williams begins his two-year farewell tour.

Thomas, Bill. "King of the Big Top." *Washingtonian*, Dec. 1986. Subtitled: "Kenneth Feld Inherited the Greatest Show on Earth from His Brilliant Father."

"Tom Mix Circus to Give Two Shows Here Today." *Rockford* (Ill.) *Morning Star*, 23 July 1938. Tom Mix and horse Tony in person. Among the sixty clowns were Bumpsy Anthony and Jack Knapp.

"Trunk Line." *New York Daily News*, 18 May 1971, p. 1. RBB&B animals walk through the Lincoln Tunnel from New Jersey to Manhattan in time for New York circus opening.

"Unus." RBB&B 1948 Program. In the center ring, alone, he seemed to do a handstand on his forefinger.

"Victoria Unus." RBB&B 1976 Program. The daughter of the Great Unus "slips her hand and wrist through a rope loop which is attached to a swivel and ring, and throws herself over and around in a series of swing-overs, or one-arm planges," à la Lillian Leitzel, while audiences counted each flip aloud.

Weil, Martin. "American Impresario Irvin Feld Dies; Was Owner of Ringling Bros. Circus." *Washington Post*, 7 Sept. 1984, p. C5.

Wilde, J. "In New York: Mortar and the Cathedral." *Time*, 25 May 1981, pp. 6–7. Philippe Petit, "the soaring seraph of acrobats," walks a high wire to celebrate the resumption of construction of New York City's Cathedral of St. John the Divine.

Williams, Gary. "Circus Goes 'Glitter' in New Show." *Sarasota* (Fla.) *Journal*, 3 Jan. 1975, p. 1. Review of circus debut of Philippe Petit and U.S. debut of the Carrillo Brothers.

MISCELLANEOUS

Circus in Art, The. Sarasota, Fla.: John and Mable Ringling Museum of Art, 1977. Catalogue of exhibit held at the museum 20 Jan. to 6 March, 1977.

Circus World Collection of Important Circus Artifacts and Carousel Carvings, The, Encompassing the Collections of Charles Philip Fox, Robert Clarke and William Donahue. Tuxedo Park, N.Y.: Guernsey's, 1985. Catalogue for auction held at Seventh Regiment Armory, New York City, Feb. 16–17, 1985.

Circus World Museum Annual Program Report. Baraboo, Wis.: Circus World Museum, 1982.

Circus World Museum Library, the Circus Research Center of the World: A Guide to Its Holdings and Services. Baraboo, Wis.: Circus World Museum, 1973. Robert L. Parkinson, chief librarian and historian of the Circus World Museum Library, describes the holdings in the repository and archive on a thirty-three-acre complex in Baraboo, part of which was the original winter quarters of the Ringling Bros. Circus from 1884 through 1918.

"Gunther Gebel-Williams." *CBS News Nightwatch*, 19 April 1988. 27 minutes.

My Father, the Circus King. NBC-TV special, 15 April 1981. Mark Oliver Gebel tells the story of his father, Gunther Gebel-Williams. 58 minutes.

115th Edition of Ringling Bros. and Barnum & Bailey Circus, The. Family Home Entertainment, 1987. Videocassette of the 1985 show with Gunther Gebel-Williams and the Living Unicorn.

Petition to the Postmaster General of the United States in support of the claim of Somers, New York as the Birthplace of the American Circus and that in issuing the proposed United States stamp Commemorative of the American Circus, Somers, New York, should not be ignored as the place of 'First Day of Issue,' " Somers, N.Y., 1966. On 2 Jan. 1966 the U.S. Postal Service announced "A five-cent stamp, 'American Circus May 2, 1966 Delavan, Wisconsin, 53115,' a town that many circus buffs regard as the cradle of the American Circus. During 1847–1894 twenty-six circuses winter quartered in Delavan." This petition provides documentation for Somers's prior claim, including this statement by Otto E. Koegel, attorney for petitioners and town historian: "Somers, New York was where William Delavan signed the articles of Association of [the] Zoological Institute in 1835. One hundred and twenty-eight individuals and firms signed these articles, subscribing to $329,325 of the Association. They included practically all the important menagerie and circus people of the country, including names that every student of circus history would instantly recognize as pioneers, such as Titus, Angevine, Crane, June, Lent, Baily, Howe, Waring, Ballard, and, of lesser importance, Delavan. . . . Even Matthew Buckley was a signer of the Articles in Somers in 1835. He is now euphemistically referred to as the 'Grandfather of the Delavan Circus Colony.' As to the others in the Delavan claim, only two or three of them were born when the Somers, New York neighborhood was cradling the American circus." Despite the protest and documentation, the Postmaster General dedicated the stamp at Delavan.

Ringling Bros. and Barnum & Bailey Clown College Media Guide. Washington, D.C.: RBB&B Media Center, 1982. A fifty-five-page guide to the Clown College, including faculty and student rosters, a brief history of clowning, bibliography, and a biography of Master Clown Lou Jacobs.

Rotondo, Bonnie McCandless. "John Culhane Will Speak on 'Westchester: Cradle of the American Circus.'" Press release, Hammond Museum, North Salem, N.Y., July 1988. "Culhane will solve the 'murder' of [the elephant] Old Bet, which was mysteriously linked to the eruption of the volcano Tambora in Indonesia in 1815." The talk accompanied the exhibition "North Salem, New York, 1788–1988," which included a gallery featuring the nineteenth-century activities in North Salem of American circus pioneers James June and G. F. Bailey.

Woodcock, William H. Letters to Col. C. G. Sturtevant, 8 Jan. 1941 and circa March 1941. Unpublished letters on circus history by the great elephant trainer, photocopied and given to the author by Woodcock's elephant trainer son, Bill "Buckles" Woodcock.

Index

Page numbers in italic refer to illustration captions.

INDEX

INDEX

INDEX